THE AMERICAN COLONIES

IN THE

SEVENTEENTH CENTURY

THE AMERICAN COLONIES

IN THE

SEVENTEENTH CENTURY

BY

HERBERT L. OSGOOD, Ph.D.

PROFESSOR OF HISTORY IN COLUMBIA UNIVERSITY

VOLUME I

THE CHARTERED COLONIES. BEGINNINGS OF
SELF–GOVERNMENT

GLOUCESTER, MASS.

PETER SMITH

1957

PREFACE

THIS work has a double purpose. It is intended to exhibit in outline the early development of English colonization on its political and administrative side. At the same time it is a study of the origin of English-American political institutions. Because of this double object attention has been almost exclusively devoted to the continental colonies. Had the commercial and economic aspects of colonization been the subject of the work, the picture must needs have been painted on a larger canvas.

The two volumes which are now published are concerned wholly with the American side of the subject. But they do not tell the whole of the story, even so far as it relates to the seventeenth century. Another volume will follow, the subject of which will be the beginnings of imperial administration and control. In that volume the British side of the problem will be discussed. The entire work, while serving as an introduction to American institutional history, will at the same time, it is hoped, illustrate the principles of British colonization, so far as those were revealed in the early relations between the home government and its colonies on the North American continent.

The author is fully aware that the attempt to analyze and compare the institutions of fifteen colonies, and to trace their political history, even in part, during a period of half a century or more, is a work of some complexity. In his effort to do this he has limited himself, in nearly all instances, to the seventeenth century and to the material which was accessible for that period of time. This it was necessary to do in order to show what the governmental system was before the transition from the chartered colonies to the system of royal provinces occurred.

iii

As a result of pursuing this course the author, in the case of some colonies, has found himself hampered by the fragmentariness of accessible material.   But that is a condition which confronts every student of origins.   Notwithstanding this defect, it is believed that sufficient evidence has been brought together to reveal the essential features of American institutions as they were at the beginning.   That evidence, as it has been classified in this work, will, it is hoped, furnish a background from which the later colonial period and the Revolution will become more intelligible.   If the critic seeks other explanations of defects, they will probably be found to result from the personal equation — for every book must have an author — and from the fact that this is a pioneer work in the domain of early American institutional history.

The inquiries, of which this work is a result, were undertaken, years ago, at the suggestion of Professor John W. Burgess.   Special thanks are also due to Professor Franklin H. Giddings, who has read the work in manuscript, and to Dr. W. Roy Smith, of Bryn Mawr College, who has assisted in reading the proofs.   The index has been prepared by Dr. Newton D. Mereness, of Cornell University.

COLUMBIA UNIVERSITY,
    March, 1904.

CONTENTS

INTRODUCTION

PAGE

The purpose and character of the work xxv
 An institutional history of the British-American colonies in the
  seventeenth century xxv
 Suggestions as to classification of colonial government . . . xxvii
 Main subdivisions of the work xxvii

PART FIRST

THE PROPRIETARY PROVINCE IN ITS EARLIEST FORM

CHAPTER I

CHARTERS OF DISCOVERY. EXPERIMENTS OF GILBERT AND RALEIGH

Share of private enterprise in originating the chartered colonies . . 3
 The charters of discovery 4
 Charters of the Cabots and other early explorers 4
 Revival of interest in colonization in age of Elizabeth due to con-
  flict with Spain 5
 Charter and voyages of Gilbert. Northwest passage, 1578, 1582 . 6
 Earliest sketch of large proprietary grants 9
 The Southampton adventurers with Gilbert 9
 Charter of Raleigh, 1584. Earliest suggestion of province of
  Virginia 14
 Lane and Grenville on the outward voyage 16
 Governor Lane and the colonists at Roanoke 18
 Settlement, officials, Indian relations, food supply. First abandon-
  ment of Roanoke 18
 Second voyage of Grenville 20
 Renewal of efforts by Raleigh. Governor and assistants of city of
  Raleigh 20
 Governor White and second attempt to settle at Roanoke . . 21
 Activity of White's council 21
 White returns to England. Disappearance of the colonists and
  final abandonment of Roanoke, 1590 22

v

CHAPTER II

Virginia as a Proprietary Province. Experiments under the Charter of 1606

PAGE

Discovery continued in form of private enterprises under James I . 23

Voyages of Gosnold, Weymouth, and others. Ferdinando Gorges becomes interested 24

Suggestions also of initiative and control by the government . . 24

An early written argument in favor of state-aided colonization . 25

Outline of charter of 1606. More precise definition of Virginia . . 26

Private or proprietary element. Provisions relating to the patentees. Two joint companies 26

Royal element. Provision relating to king's council for Virginia and to local councils 27

Mixed and therefore transitional character of the system . . 29

The problem which confronted the patentees of 1606. Agricultural colonies 29

Two colonies planted, at Sagadahoc and Jamestown. Their patrons . 32

An "instruction by way of advice" 32

The settlements at Sagadahoc and Jamestown were of the proprietary and plantation type 34

Natural and social aspects of settlements at Sagadahoc and Jamestown 34

Their location described and compared 35

The forts and the buildings which they contained 36

Time of landing and the consequences which followed . . . 38

How the labor force was first employed 39

Beginning of trade with the Indians, especially at Jamestown. John Smith as an Indian trader 39

The "supplies." Their economic and political functions . . 41

Sickness and the death rate 43

Government at Sagadahoc and Jamestown. An experiment in conciliar government 44

Dissensions at Jamestown; aggravated by sickness and by loose administrative methods. President Wingfield deposed. Gradual elimination of councillors till one autocratic president — Smith — is left 45

This process checked, but not defeated, by visits of Newport . . 49

Attitude of Smith toward colonists and patentees 52

CHAPTER III

Virginia as a Proprietary Province. Administration of Sir Thomas Smith

Defects in system of 1606 lead the London patentees to apply for new charter. Enterprise greatly enlarged 56

Royal charters of 1609 and 1612 57

Patentees fully incorporated. The general court of the company . 57

Disappearance of the royal council for Virginia 57

PAGE

Triumph of the proprietary element 58
The treasurer and the quarter courts. Sir Thomas Smith, treasurer . 60
Transition in Virginia from system of 1606 to that of 1609 . . . 61
The third supply and its disaster 64
Close of Smith's presidency in Virginia 65
The "starving time" of 1609–1610. Indian war 67
Appointment of first governor of Virginia — Lord Delaware . . 68
Arrival of Gates and Delaware at Jamestown. Rescue of the
colony 68
System of rigid discipline instituted under Governor Dale . . . 69
Origin and provisions of the "Lawes Divine and Martiall" . . 69
Dale's ideal of colonial life 69
Peace with the Indians. Indian trade 72
Considerable influx of settlers. Gradual decline of death rate . 73
Expansion of settlement begins under Dale 73
Founding of Henrico and neighboring settlements 74
Private gardens to settlers 75
Earliest suggestion of a system of head rights 76
Yeardley in 1617 slightly extends private grants 77
Reaction under Argall 77
Waste of resources of the company 77
Progress of colony retarded 79

CHAPTER IV

Virginia as a Proprietary Province. Administrations of Sandys and the Earl of Southampton

Change in administration of company. Sir Edwin Sandys elected
treasurer in place of Sir Thomas Smith 80
Attempt to settle Smith's accounts 81
Earl of Warwick favors the change, but soon returns to alliance with
Smith 81
Sandys and Southampton pursue liberalized policy toward Virginia . 81
Great activity in despatching colonists, cattle, and supplies to
Virginia 81
Attempt to diversify industry in the colony 82
System of reserves for company, college, and ministers . . . 83
Grant of private plantations. Their place in the beginnings of
local government in Virginia 84
Disappearance of joint trading system 89
Plantations, corporations, hundreds, boroughs, cities . . . 90
Distinction between towns and province appears 91
Grant of a House of Burgesses to Virginia 92
The Assembly of 1619 92
Action of the company on the by-laws of the assembly . . . 94
The assemblies of 1621 and 1624. The instruction of 1621 . 96
Steps taken to perfect the organization of provincial and local
government in Virginia 96

CHAPTER V

THE NEW ENGLAND COUNCIL

	PAGE
Fishing voyages of the Plymouth patentees till 1620	98
Origin of Charter of 1620	98
Opposition by London company to its grant	99
Opposition carried into parliament in 1621	100
Gorges examined in reference to the monopolistic features of the grant	100
Provisions of Charter of 1620. Organization of the New England council	102
The council unsuccessful from the first	103
To encourage its work Gorges publishes his *Briefe Relation*, 1622	103
Gorges's plan of a proprietary province	103
Early negotiations between the Leyden Congregation of Separatists and the London company	105
The Wincob patent	105
The Separatists negotiate with Thomas Weston for assistance	106
Lack of agreement between Weston, the adventurer, and the Leyden Congregation	107
The articles of agreement not signed	109
The *Mayflower* sails without instructions, though loaded with supplies by the joint action of adventurers and colonists	109
Founding of colony and town of Plymouth within the grant to the New England council	109
The town located and laid out	109
System of joint labor with separate homesteads	110
The town as seen by De Rasieres in 1627	110
Sickness during the first winter	111
Journeys of discovery and opening of relations with the Indians	112
The "supplies" at Plymouth. The *Fortune*, the *Anne*, the *Little James*	112
Arrival of the "perticulers" in 1623	113
Differences between the colonists and the adventurers	114
Weston's colony at Wessagussett	114
The New England council grants a patent to John Pierce and associates in 1621	115
Grant of a second patent to John Pierce as sole proprietor in 1622	116
Pierce forced to assign his second patent to associates	116
In 1627 the colonists buy out the claims of the adventurers to the land	117
Land and cattle divided. System of individual property introduced	117
The "undertakers," however, manage the trade of the colony in joint stock till 1642	118
The proprietary element in the organization of Plymouth disappears	118
Efforts of New England council to uphold its monopoly and found a colony	119

PAGE

The royal proclamation of 1622 119
Grant to Robert Gorges and his appointment as Lieutenant-General
of New England 119
Efforts to procure subscriptions and awaken interest within the
council 120
Drawing of lots for shares, June, 1623 121
Robert Gorges spends winter of 1623–1624 in New England . . 121
Relations between Robert Gorges and Weston 122
Return of Gorges to England and collapse of plan to found a great
province 122
New England council limits its efforts to the granting of territory along
its northern coasts 122
John Mason shares prominently with Gorges in these grants . . 123
Partial list of the grants 123
Grants made according to two models, one for public and another
for private plantations 126
The Laconia company 127
The indenture of 1628 to the Massachusetts patentees . . . 128
The Dorchester fishing adventure at Cape Ann 128
Expansion of Dorchester adventurers into Massachusetts patentees 130
Formation of the Massachusetts company and the royal charter of 1629 131
Internal organization of the company 131
Massachusetts founded as a proprietary province 132
Instructions to its officials at Salem 132
Policy of the colony at Salem as to land and government . . 135

PART SECOND

THE CORPORATE COLONIES OF NEW ENGLAND

CHAPTER I

THE TRANSFER OF GOVERNMENT INTO MASSACHUSETTS.
THE GENERAL COURT

Distinction between the early proprietary provinces and the corporate
colonies 141
The London company chosen as a model by the Massachusetts
patentees 142
But the form of the colony was radically changed by the removal
of the Massachusetts company to New England . . . 142
The removal 144
Occasion of the removal 144
Steps preliminary to removal 145
Final action of the general court 146
Adjustment of business relations in England 147

PAGE

Effects of the removal on the land system and system of trade of
the colony 149
Its effect on the character of the freemen.   Winthrop's "Modell" 152
The early development of the general court in Massachusetts . . 153
Its chartered powers reaffirmed 154
The freeman's oath 155
Addition of the deputies 155
Opposition to the exclusive claims of the magistrates continued . 157
General court divided into two houses, 1644 157
Legislative equality of deputies with magistrates affirmed in 1636 . 158
Form and procedure of the two houses 158
Both houses elective 158
The court of election 158
Cases of disputed elections in towns 159
Employment of committees 159
Initiation of measures through petitions 160
Position of governor in general court 161
Controversies between the two houses 163
These due to connection between civil and ecclesiastical power in
colony 163
Position of magistrates as quorum in general court . . . 164
Question of the negative voice, 1634–1636 164
Question of the negative voice, 1642–1644.   Case of Sherman vs.
Keayne 165
Contention of magistrates and clergy prevails 166

CHAPTER II

THE EXECUTIVE AND JUDICIAL SYSTEM IN MASSACHUSETTS

Massachusetts was governed by an executive board 167
Its members were closely united 167
They were steadily reëlected for annual terms . . . 167
Because of nature of board's function and dearth of records, it is
difficult to follow its history 168
Position of the governor in relation to the assistants . . . 169
Early history and powers of the board of assistants . . . 170
General court of October, 1630, gives them the right to legislate
and elect officers 171
Court of May, 1631, withdraws powers to elect governor and
deputy, but does not forbid them to legislate . . . 171
At a meeting of the board in 1631 Winthrop explains the nature of
the Massachusetts government 172
Controversies between Winthrop and Dudley in 1632 . . . 173
In 1634 the general court assumes full legislative power . . 176
In 1637, under influence of the clergy, the magistrates assume an
attitude of greater dignity and severity toward offenders . 177

PAGE

Discussion of life tenure for magistrates. Experiment with a council
  for life, 1636. Its failure 178
Controversy over executive discretion, 1635–1644 180
  Leads to further exposition of the nature of Massachusetts govern-
    ment 181
  Views of the magistrates and clergy prevail 182
Assumption of judicial powers by the government of Massachusetts . 182
  Judicial functions of the general court 183
    Opinion of Winthrop and the elders in 1644 in relation to this . 184
  The assistants were the stated judicial court of the colony . . 184
    Variety of cases which early came before them 185
    No idea of separation of powers 185
    Quarterly sessions at Boston begin in 1636 186
    Procedure before this tribunal. Character of the administration
      of justice in general 186
  The local courts of Massachusetts 190
    The county courts and their jurisdiction 190
    The courts for the trial of small causes 191
  Controversy over the judicial discretion of the magistrates, 1636–
    1645 193
    Deputies attempt to limit it, but Winthrop and the elders main-
      tain that only maximum and minimum penalties shall be
      prescribed by law 193
    Subject brought up again by the "Hingham Case" . . . 195
    Winthrop's trial 197
    View of magistrates and elders prevails. The "little speech" . 199

CHAPTER III

RELATIONS BETWEEN CHURCH AND COMMONWEALTH IN MASSACHUSETTS

The importance of religious motive in determining the form and policy
  of government in Massachusetts 200
Calvin's view of the nature of government and of the relations be-
  tween church and state 201
This was substantially adopted by the Puritans 203
Attitude of the Massachusetts leaders toward the Established Church
  when they left England 203
  The utterance of Rev. Francis Higginson 203
  The affair of the Browns at Salem 204
  The founding of the church at Salem 204
  The "Humble Request" 205
But by force of circumstances, as well as by choice, the Puritans of
  New England became Separatists 206
  Their churches were based on covenant 206
  English orders were practically ignored 206

PAGE

Though professions of loyalty to the Mother Church were for a
time continued, communion with her soon ceased   .   .   . 207
Position of the clergy in Massachusetts .   .   .   .   .   . 2??
They were the only learned and professional class .   .   . 208
They were the expounders and defenders of the church-state system 209
Their view of the relation between church and state   .   . 210
The relations between church and commonwealth as fixed by law   . 212
The religious test, 1631, 1664. Its effect   212
The consent of the magistrates required in founding of churches . 213
All inhabitants taxed for support of the clergy   .   .   . 213
Conditions under which churches must be founded were prescribed
by law   213
Relations of the general court to councils and synods   .   . 213
Declarations of the Cambridge Platform of Discipline .   .   . 214
Sabbath legislation 215
Legislation concerning heresy 215
Attendance at church made compulsory 216
No one could preach in the colony who was disapproved by the
magistrates or general court   216
Preaching of the truth to be directly encouraged and enforced by
government   217
The clergy support the magistrates in the capacity of an extra-legal
board of referees   217
No room for religious dissent in Massachusetts   .   .   . 218
The closest possible union of church and commonwealth   .   . 218
The conditions which led to this 221

CHAPTER IV

The Working of the Massachusetts System as illustrated by the Controversies with Roger Williams and the Antinomians

The controversy with Roger Williams   224
The high estimate placed by the Puritans on their charter .   . 224
The attack of Williams on their claim to land, which was derived
through the charter 225
Williams proclaims himself a Separatist and a believer in religious
freedom   226
First effort of the magistrates to prevent the Salem church from
calling Williams as its teacher 226
Williams on his return from Plymouth assumes a submissive attitude 226
After he resumed preaching at Salem Williams begins again to
attack land titles derived from the charter and to proclaim his
Separatist views   227
Admonition begins 227
Williams protests against oaths   228

PAGE

He is summoned before the magistrates, but at the same time is
called to pastorate of Salem church 228
This action of Salem church condemned by magistrates and clergy 229
Character of the questions involved and the order of their im-
portance 229
General court rejects petition of Salem for land on Marblehead
Neck 231
Williams and his church appeal to churches of the colony against
the members of the general court 231
Williams's followers detached from him 232
Town of Salem forced into submission 232
Williams tried and banished 233
The merits of the case 234
The Antinomian controversy 236
The leaders of the two parties to that controversy 236
Mrs. Hutchinson's conventicles 236
The Antinomian doctrine 237
Attitude of the body of the clergy toward this 237
Attitude of the Boston church toward it. Rev. John Wilson . 238
The proposal to call Rev. John Wheelwright to the pulpit of the
Boston church 238
Attitude of Governor Vane toward the controversy . . . 238
The ministers labor with him, with Mrs. Hutchinson, and with
Cotton 239
Wheelwright's Fast Day sermon 241
Attack on the Antinomians begun 242
Trial of Wheelwright. He was found guilty of sedition and
contempt 242
Court of election at Newtown, May, 1637. Defeat of the Antino-
mians. Election of Winthrop as governor 244
Vane returns to England 246
The synod at Newtown, September, 1637. Cotton falls into line.
Formal condemnation of Antinomian doctrines . . . 246
General court made more intensely conservative by another elec-
tion. Meets in November 247
Exclusion of members from Boston because of its previous petitions 247
Wheelwright sentenced to banishment 248
Punishment of Coggshall and Aspinwall 249
Trial of Mrs. Hutchinson. She is sentenced to banishment . . 250
Proceedings against other supporters of the Antinomian cause in
Boston and elsewhere 253
The Boston church, now purged of its heretics, excommunicates
Mrs. Hutchinson 253
Effect of the triumph of Puritan orthodoxy 254

CHAPTER V

THE WORKING OF THE MASSACHUSETTS SYSTEM AS ILLUSTRATED
BY THE CONTROVERSIES WITH THE PRESBYTERIANS, THE BAP-
TISTS, AND THE QUAKERS

                                                                      PAGE
The controversy with the Presbyterians 256
    The triumph of the Presbyterians in England in 1646 reacts upon
        Massachusetts 256
    Dr. Child and his associates petition general court for larger in-
        dulgence. This a protest of the unenfranchised against the
        divergence of Massachusetts law from that of England . . 257
    Reply of the general court. Defence of its policy 260
    The petitioners declare their intention to appeal to England . . 261
    This draws from the magistrates and clergy a denial of the right of
        appeal and of the binding force of English law within the colony 261
    The petition is sent to England in spite of strenuous efforts on part
        of the magistrates to prevent it 263
    No result, however, follows 264
The controversy with the Baptists 264
    Puritan feeling toward Baptists colored by their horror of the
        excesses of Münster 264
    The essential Puritanism of the Baptists 264
    The two points upon which they differed from the Puritans . . 264
    Early proceedings against Baptists. Act of 1644 . . . 265
    The case of John Clarke and Obadiah Holmes 266
    The Baptists secure a foothold in Massachusetts after the Restoration 269
The struggle with the Quakers 269
    The religious characteristics of Quakers were intensely offensive to
        Puritans 269
    The Puritans charged the Quakers with wrongfully forcing their
        way into the colonies 272
    There was no law which required Massachusetts to receive the
        Quakers or forbade their exclusion 274
    Their advent seemed like the inroad of wild animals or of a con-
        tagious disease 277
The measures adopted to meet the successive arrivals of Quakers . . 277
    Mary Fisher and Anne Austin 277
    Quaker books to be seized ; Quakers to be imprisoned till they could
        be sent out of the colony, 1656 278
    Act of October, 1656. Whipping of Quakers begins. Imprison-
        ment and banishment continued 278
    Cases of Anne Burden, Mary Clarke, Christopher Holder, John
        Copeland, and others 279
    Sympathy shown for Quakers. Quakerism begins to spread in
        Massachusetts 280
    Harris, Leddra, Brend, and Norton 280
    Quaker meetings forbidden, May, 1658 282
    Death threatened against those who returned after banishment,
        October, 1658 282

PAGE

Severity in the treatment of Quakers constantly increases . . 283

Execution of Robinson and Stevenson, 1659 283

Execution of Mary Dyer and Leddra, 1660, 1661 284

Adoption of a milder policy 285

This due in part to intervention of the king 285

Increase of Quaker activity 286

Continuance of repressive measures until attention was diverted from the Quakers by Philip's war and controversy with the home government 287

Relations between the other New England colonies and the Quakers . 287

CHAPTER VI

PLYMOUTH AS A CORPORATE COLONY

Reasons for the appearance and the disappearance of a proprietary element in this colony 290

The organs of government within Plymouth 290

The general court originated in the Mayflower compact . . . 290

Early duties of governor, assistant, and captain 291

Informal character of government at the beginning . . . 292

General assumption of powers 295

Differentiation of the town from the colony 297

Evolution of counties 298

Plymouth conforms in all respects to the model of the corporate colony 299

CHAPTER VII

CONNECTICUT AS A CORPORATE COLONY

The colony of the River Towns 301

Reasons for the removal from Massachusetts 301

Government established under authority from Massachusetts . . 303

Town and colony government develop at the same time . . . 305

Discretion of the magistrates limited from the first in the River Towns 305

The Fundamental Orders of 1639 309

The essential identity between them and earlier legislation in Massachusetts and Plymouth 309

Development of the general court and of the executive . . . 312

Relations between church and civil power 314

The River Towns a genuine corporate and Puritan colony . . 316

The Warwick patent and colony at Saybrook 319

Purchase of Saybrook by River Towns 320

The founding of New Haven colony 321

Beginnings of town and colony government 322

The religious test 322

PAGE

The "combination" of 1643. Development of colony government
    completed 324
The Connecticut charter of 1662   327
    Its provisions relating to government   328
    Its provisions relating to boundary 329
    Controversy between Connecticut and New Haven   .   .   . 329
    Final submission of New Haven   331
    The enlarged Connecticut   331

CHAPTER VIII

RHODE ISLAND AS A CORPORATE COLONY

Rhode Island was formed by the union of towns 332
The relation of Roger Williams to its founding   332
    The founding of Providence   334
      Location of the town site   334
      The "Providence purchase" and the "Pawtuxet purchase"   . 335
      The plantation covenant   336
      Issue of the "initial deed" 337
      Agreement of October 8, 1638   338
      Efforts of Harris and associates to enlarge bounds of the town
        and develop a board of proprietors 338
      Plan of 1640 for arbitration 340
      Gorton at Providence 340
    The settlement of Portsmouth and Newport   341
      The original plantation covenant 341
      The settlement at Pocasset 342
      Removal to Newport, and its town compact   .   .   . 343
      Removal from Pocasset to Portsmouth and another plantation
        covenant 344
      Union of Portsmouth and Newport into the colony of Rhode
        Island   345
    The settlement of Warwick   345
      Character and early history of Samuel Gorton   .   .   . 345
      Gorton at Plymouth and Newport   347
      Gorton and his associates purchase Shawomet   .   .   . 348
      William Arnold and associates of Pawtuxet put themselves under
        protection of Massachusetts   348
      Conflict between the Gortonists and Massachusetts   .   . 350
      The Gortonists, after release from imprisonment in Massachu-
        setts, appeal to England and induce Narragansetts to put them-
        selves under English protection   351
Peril from outside compels the Narragansett settlements to unite .   . 352
    Williams procures charter of 1644 354
    Massachusetts attempts to secure a patent for the entire country
      about Narragansett bay   354
    Terms of the charter of 1644   354

PAGE

Institution of government under the charter of 1644 355
　Court of election of May, 1647, at Portsmouth 355
　Charter accepted by this body 356
　Rhode Island takes the lead in organizing government . . . 357
　The general court of commissioners 358
　Position of the towns in reference to the colony government . . 358
　Colony officials and court of trials 359
　Employment of committees by the general court 361
William Coddington attempts to separate the island from the mainland
　towns 362
　They remain separate from November, 1651, till May, 1654 . . 363
　The colony further disturbed by the Dutch war 364
　Failure of Coddington's scheme 364
　Government under the charter of 1644 reëstablished . . . 364
Boundary disputes relating to the Narragansett country . . . 365
　The Shawomet grant 367
　The settlement of Richard Smith 367
　The Pettiquamscutt Purchase 367
　The encroachments of Massachusetts through the Atherton company 367
　The Westerly Purchase. Conflict between its settlers and those of
　　Massachusetts at Southertown 368
　Pretensions of Massachusetts excluded by grant of Connecticut
　　charter, 1662 369
Issue of the Royal Charter of 1664 to Rhode Island 369
　The Pawcatuck river designated as the western boundary of the
　　colony 369
　Complete religious liberty guarantied by this charter . . . 370

CHAPTER IX

The Northward Expansion of Massachusetts

The settlements on the Piscataqua 371
　Their condition after the collapse of the early plans of Gorges and
　　Mason 371
　The Anglican settlement at Strawberry Bank 371
　The settlement at Hilton's Point. Patent of 1630 372
　This patent located north of Little bay 372
　Bristol merchants become interested in it 373
　The Piscataqua grant to Laconia company 373
　Thomas Wiggin induces Lord Say and Sele and other Puritan
　　noblemen to buy Hilton's Point from the Bristol merchants . 373
　Hilton's Point becomes the Puritan settlement of Dover . . 374
　Plantation covenant of Dover, 1640 374
　Conflicts at Dover between Puritans and Anglicans . . . 374
　Exeter, another Puritan town, founded by Rev. John Wheelwright
　　and associates 375
　Settlement of Hampton 376

PAGE

Extension of the sway of Massachusetts over the Piscataqua towns . 376
    The northern boundary of Massachusetts 376
    Arguments in favor of annexing the Piscataqua towns . . 377
    The Squamscot patent and the submission of Dover, 1641 . . 378
    Exeter submits in 1643 380
    Jurisdiction of Massachusetts fully extended over the Piscataqua
      towns 380
    Subsequent protests of Mason's agents 381
The Maine settlements 382
    Government under Gorges maintained at Saco and York . . 383
    Trelawny's settlement on Richmond's island 383
    Cleeve and Tucker secure grants on the adjacent mainland . . 383
    Trelawny's agent, Winter, disputes the claim of Cleeve and Tucker
      to a part of their grant 384
    Case is heard before court of Governor Thomas Gorges at Saco . 386
    Cleeve induces the Puritan, Alexander Rigby, to buy the Lygonia
      patent. Its extent 386
    Cleeve appointed governor of Lygonia 386
    Controversy over jurisdiction between Cleeve and the representa-
      tives of Gorges at Saco 387
    Appeal to Massachusetts, 1646. No decision 387
    Rigby's patent confirmed by Commissioners of Plantations . . 387
    Gorges' control now restricted to settlements between Kennebunk
      and Piscataqua 388
    Those towns submit to Massachusetts, 1653 389
    The settlements under Cleeve submit in 1658 389
    Massachusetts extends its county system over all the northern
      settlements and grants them representation in the general
      court 390

CHAPTER X

INTERCOLONIAL RELATIONS. THE NEW ENGLAND CONFEDERACY

Relations among New England colonies which demanded joint action . 392
    Murder of Hocking on the Kennebec river 392
    Controversy between settlers on the Connecticut . . . 393
    Controversy over northern boundary of Plymouth . . . 394
    Dispute over Springfield 394
    Relations with Dutch, French, and Indians 395
    Common feeling among New Englanders 397
The formation of the confederacy 397
    Early suggestion from Massachusetts and Connecticut . . 397
    The drafting of the articles in 1643 399
    Provisions of the articles 399
    It was a union between unequals 402
Questions of interpretation 403
    Right to interpret rested finally with general courts . . 403
    Controversy of 1653. Decided by Massachusetts . . . 404

PAGE

Relations with the Dutch 406
The commissioners correspond with Kieft:
About the Dutch at Good Hope 406
About the seizure of Westerhouse's ship 406
About duties at Manhattan 406
Peter Stuyvesant and the Treaty of Hartford, 1650 . . . 406
Relations with the French 409
D'Aunay on the Penobscot and La Tour in Acadia . . . 410
Friendly dealings between Massachusetts and La Tour . . . 411
D'Aunay claims to represent the French government . . . 411
Filibustering expedition of Gibbons and Hawkins against D'Aunay 411
Warnerton of Piscataqua attacks D'Aunay 412
Strong protest in Massachusetts against aiding La Tour . . 412
D'Aunay proves rightfulness of his claims 414
La Tour is abandoned and peace concluded with D'Aunay . 414
The affair before the commissioners 414
Relations with the Indians 414
Commissioners labor to keep the peace among the Indians and
between the Indians and the English 414
Feud between Mohegans and Narragansetts 415
Treaty of 1645. Efforts to secure its execution . . . 415
The commissioners and the controversy relating to Springfield . 416
Attitude of Massachusetts in that controversy 417
Labors of the commissioners in the interest of schools, the churches,
and missionary work 419
They recommend contributions for Harvard College . . 420
They aid the churches in maintaining the purity of the faith . . . 420
They urge strong measures against the Quakers . . . 421
They encourage missionary work among the Indians . . 422
Their connection with the Society for the Propagation of the Gospel
in New England 422

CHAPTER XI

THE LAND SYSTEM IN THE CORPORATE COLONIES OF NEW ENGLAND

The system of group settlement 424
How it originated in New England 425
The groups were democratically organized 425
The towns, which they settled, were manors with the monarchical
element left out 426
Territorial administration in Massachusetts 427
No land office or system of rents 428
Superintendence of founding of towns by colony government . 429
Instances of this from the history of various Massachusetts towns . 429
Boundaries, common fields, admission of freemen, town herds, to
an extent regulated by legislation 433

PAGE

The land system of the other corporate colonies 434

    In all important particulars it was the same as that of Massa-
        chusetts 434

    In all colonies of this type the management of land was left chiefly
        to the towns 436

Comparison of the territorial arrangement of New England towns . 436

    The lay-out of towns. Varied topography of towns . . . 436

    Many of the oldest towns founded by spontaneous act of their
        settlers 438

    Laying out of village plot and assignment of home lots . . . 438

    Allotments of arable land and meadow 439

    The lay-out of towns illustrated in the case of Salem and of many
        other typical New England towns 440

    Result of this was that the estate of each individual consisted of a
        number of small tracts scattered over the town plot . . 449

    Tendency to consolidation of tracts 451

Common fields and fences 451

    Their regulation illustrated from the records of Salem and of many
        other towns 451

Common herds and herdsmen 454

    Similarly illustrated 455

Rule of proportionality in the allotment of land 456

    Use of town rate for the purpose 457

    Equalization of allotments 458

Boards of commoners or proprietors 461

    Origin of these boards 461

    Proprietors of special tracts 462

    Original identity of proprietors with town-meeting 462

    This fact illustrated in case of Plymouth and many other towns . 462

    But there were always residents who were not proprietors . 464

    This body kept increasing, while the proprietors remained fixed . 465

    This led in many towns to struggles between non-commoners
        and commoners 466

CHAPTER XII

THE FINANCIAL SYSTEM OF THE CORPORATE COLONIES

Taxable property and taxes in the corporate colonies 468

    Payment of taxes in kind 469

Direct taxes 470

    A development from assessments on stockholders 470

    The " rate " 470

    The rate was a general property tax 471

    Upon what it was levied 471

    With the rate was combined a poll tax and sometimes a form of
        income tax 472

PAGE

Levies on incomes appear in Massachusetts, Connecticut, and New
Haven 472
Levy of the country rate by quotas on towns 472
In Massachusetts, Connecticut, and New Haven it became a penny
in the pound 473
In this form it became approximately a fixed sum 473
Multiples and fractions of rates 474
The poll tax changed accordingly 474
System of assessing and collecting rates 474
County rates 476
Indirect taxes 477
Export duties of slight importance except in Plymouth . . . 477
A tonnage or powder duty was levied in Massachusetts . . . 477
Import duties by far the most important 477
Levied on liquors and general merchandise 478
Excise on retailing of liquors 478
Levies on mackerel fishery and on drift whales at Cape Cod . . 478
Indirect taxes in Connecticut and Rhode Island 479
Administration of the customs 480
The collector in Massachusetts and his duties 480
Customs officers in Connecticut 481
Expenditures 481
Chief object of expenditure was defence 481
This involved payment for soldiers, officers, forts, and supplies . 481
Heavy expenditures in connection with Philip's war . . . 482
Pension system in Massachusetts and Plymouth 483
Development of a system of salaries for officials 483
Gratuities and special grants for public service 483
Entries relating to gratuities and salaries in Plymouth . . . 487
Payment of colonial agents 488
Support of ministry, churches, and schools 489
Miscellaneous expenditures 490
Appropriations and payments from the public chest 491
Degree to which appropriation acts were specific 491
Development of the office of colony treasurer 491
Accounting by the treasurers 493
Legislative committees of audit 493
Office of auditor general in Massachusetts, 1645–1657 . . . 494
Act for auditing accounts in Rhode Island, 1670 494

CHAPTER XIII

The System of Defence in the New England Colonies

General conditions affecting defence 496
Provisions of the Massachusetts charter 496
Assumption of similar powers by the other colonies . . . 496
The militant spirit of the Puritans 497

PAGE

Subordination of the military to the civil power 497
Lack of genuine military training and experience among the
    colonists 498
The militia system 499
    Based on the assize of arms 499
    Regulations for keeping of arms, armor, and ammunition . . 499
    The pike retained till Philip's war 501
    The matchlock and firelock muskets 501
    Trained bands or militia companies of the towns . . . 502
    The clerk of the band 503
    Troopers and their equipment 504
    Trainings, their frequency 505
    Classes which were liable to trainings and exempt from trainings . 506
    Regimental trainings for horse and foot 507
    Regulations for trainings in each of the respective colonies . . 507
    Constables' watches in the towns 509
    Regulations for giving alarms 509
    Regimenting of the militia in Massachusetts 510
    The council of war 511
    The sergeant-major and shire lieutenant 512
    The sergeant-major general 512
    The surveyor-general of arms 513
    No permanently organized commissariat 514
    During the seventeenth century in no corporate colony except
        Massachusetts was the militia regimented . . . 515
Forts, stockades, and garrison houses 516
    The distribution of forts among the towns 516
    The " barricado " in Boston 517
    Early history of the defences on Castle island . . . 518
    Garrison houses 520
    Their increase and distribution during Philip's war . . 520
    Stockades vs. garrison houses 521
Military administration 521
    Regulated by acts of the general court 521
    Controlled by the governor, assistants, and special councils and
        commissions 521
    Special councils of war 522
        In Massachusetts 522
        In Plymouth 523
        In Connecticut 524
    Method of filling military offices 524
    Permanence of tenure 526

CHAPTER XIV

INDIAN RELATIONS, PHILIP'S WAR

PAGE

Indian relations in general 527
    Indian policy had to be worked out immediately and on the spot . 527
    Origin and location of Indian tribes 527
    Method of extinguishing Indian titles to land 529
    Regulations of trade with the Indians 530
        Trade in arms, ammunition, and liquors 530
    Watchfulness in relation to feuds and danger of Indian attacks . 532
Development of a protectorate over the Indians 533
    A result in part of the Pequot war and of the alliance of Uncas
        with the English 533
    Formation of a Pequot reservation in Connecticut 536
    The Golden Hill reservation 536
    In Massachusetts a similar development was caused by the mis-
        sionary work of Eliot 536
    Reservations of praying Indians in Massachusetts 537
    Similar reservations in Plymouth 539
    Missionary efforts in Connecticut 539
Conditions which occasioned Philip's war 540
    Effect of the advance of English settlements 540
    Early dealings between Philip and Plymouth 540
    Massachusetts and the other colonies interpose 541
    Philip fights to avoid a protectorate 542
    This is a war between whites and unassisted natives . . . 542
The New England frontier 543
Numerical strength of the Indians 543
Conditions under which joint action of the colonies was possible . . 544
Character of military operations 545
First phase of the war 546
    Local conflict near Mount Hope 546
    Armed negotiation with the Narragansetts 548
Second phase of the war 549
    Flight of Philip from Pocasset 549
    Uprising of the Nipmucks of central Massachusetts . . . 550
    Encounter near Brookfield 550
    Extension of the war to the Connecticut valley 551
    Connecticut drawn into the conflict 551
    Relations between authorities at Hartford and the Massachusetts
        valley towns 551
    Encounters at Northfield and Deerfield 554
    Policy of expeditions vs. garrisons 554
    Attack on Springfield. Retirement of Pynchon from command . 556
    Appleton succeeds. His policy of defence 556
    Relations between Appleton and the Connecticut authorities . . 558
    Operations in eastern Massachusetts 560

  PAGE

Third phase of the war : uprising of Narragansetts 560
    The joint expedition of December, 1675 560
    The "swamp fight" 562
    Active alliance between Narragansetts and Nipmucks . . . 564
    The "hungry march" of January, 1676 565
    Desolating attacks on many towns of central Massachusetts . . 566
    Continued operations in the Connecticut valley, Turner's Falls . 566
    Capture and death of Canonchet 567
    Measures of defence in Plymouth colony 568
    Operations in central Massachusetts 569
    Raids through the Narragansett country 570
    Collapse of Indian resources. Death of Philip 571
Fourth phase of the war 572
    Early attacks on the northeastern settlements 572
    Narragansetts and Nipmucks join northern Indians, summer of 1676 573
    Stratagem of Major Waldron 573
    Prolongation of hostilities till Treaty of Casco, 1678. Peace . . 574
The war greatly strengthened English control over the Indians . . 574
    Plymouth law of 1682 574
    Treatment of the praying Indians by Massachusetts during the war 575
    The praying Indians after the war 576
    Connecticut extends policy of reservations after the war . . 576

INTRODUCTION

It is the purpose of the author of the work, of which these volumes form a part, to trace the growth of the British-American colonies as institutions of government and as parts of a great colonial system. The beginnings of that system, in one of its phases, will be passed in review.

In order properly to accomplish this task a discriminating use must be made of much known material. The political and social sciences have now reached such development that it is impossible to present in a single view all known aspects of any period of history. A choice must be made between those which are distinctly political and those that are social, and upon the one or the other the emphasis must be laid. This should be done not in a narrow or exclusive spirit, but with a due regard to the fact that political events and forms of government are very largely the product of social causes, while institutions in their turn are the avenues through which social forces act. In this work attention will be specially directed to forms of government and to the forces and events from which their development has sprung. Material of a social or economic nature will be utilized not directly for its own sake, but for a light which it may throw on political growth. In other words, an attempt will be made to interpret early American history in the terms of public law. The treatment of material will be subordinated to that end.

In this fact will be found a leading justification for the existence of the book itself. General histories of the period we have, and additions to their number are not infrequently made. Constitutional histories of the United States have been written, but no one has hitherto undertaken to produce an institutional history of the American colonies.

To all serious students, however, it must be clear that without research in that direction the period can never be
properly understood. A correct view of forms of colonial
government, of the relations between the church and the
civil power in the colonies, of the legal relations between
the colonies and the mother country, and of other, but
similar, questions, is absolutely fundamental. The time
has come when we must know in some connected way how
the Atlantic, so to speak, was institutionally bridged ; in
other words, we must know under what forms English institutions were reproduced on the American continent, and
how, if at all, they were modified by the influence of kindred European peoples who settled near or among the
English colonists. Their slow unfolding and change must
be traced and an effort must be made to ascertain how far
this was due to internal causes, and to what degree it was
produced by pressure from the home government. The
origin of American institutions is not to be found wholly
in those documents and principles which originated in the
second half of the eighteenth century, but as well in certain
earlier forms which had undergone steady development for
a century and a half before the date of independence. These
forms in their growth illustrate and reveal at the same time
one of the most important phases of British colonization.

This fact suggests a further distinction which must be
observed in the treatment of the subject. Colonization, at
least in modern times, means the reproduction of dependencies. In the study of the process of colonization attention must be fixed not only upon the colony or dependency
itself, but on the relations which it bears to the parent
community or state whence it sprang. The nature of colonies themselves, and of the historical process which gives
rise to them, suggests the two main divisions of the subject.
The earlier writers on the period, with one or two exceptions, have concerned themselves almost wholly with the
colonies, and have failed to give a clear or continuous account of their relations with the home government. No
systematic attempt has been made to ascertain what the
constitutional law and practice of the old British colonial

empire was, or to set it forth in its historical development.
In no book can a satisfactory description be found of the
organs of the British government which were employed in
colonial administration, or of the functions which they performed. The principles of British policy have never been
adequately discussed. In a word, the history of British
colonial administration, so far as it affected the American
colonies, has yet to be written ; one might almost say that
the materials for it have yet to be collected. But it is evident that the neglect of this side of our development during
the seventeenth and eighteenth centuries is a defect almost
as serious as would be the omission of federal relations in
United States history. One side of the story is left untold
or is referred to as something foreign and inimical to the
colonies. In fact, it is the very essence of the colonial relation, and without it the meaning of the period is to a large
extent lost. An attempt will be made in this work to bring
out into something like their proper relief both the colonies
with their institutions and policies, and the system of imperial control which was exercised over them.

The main outline of the subject, the key to the history of
the period as a whole, is furnished by the thought just expressed — the colonies as they were in themselves and in
their relation to the sovereign power from which their existence sprang. The student of colonial institutions is concerned with only those two subjects ; they are all-inclusive.
Under the one or the other will fall every other minor topic
which he will find it necessary to discuss. He will classify
the colonies not according to their location or to their social
characteristics, but according to the forms of government
which existed within them. This he will find to be determined by the form of their executives and by the constitutional relations which existed between the executives and
the legislatures, as the legislature developed in each colony.
The main divisions of his subject will be suggested by the
relations in which the colonies stood to the home government. The tendencies of historical development during the
period he will find in the changes which came about in
those relations and also in the internal organization of the

colonies themselves. From this point of view the unfolding
relations between sovereignty and liberty will be duly
illustrated.

Institutionally considered, the history of the American
colonies falls into two phases or periods. The two phases
appear in the system of chartered colonies and the system
of royal provinces, with the transition from one to the other.
This comprises all there is in the constitutional history of
that period. The meaning of the period, its unity and di-
versity, the character of the colonies as special jurisdictions,
as well as their relations with the sovereign imperial power,
will become sufficiently clear if these subjects are properly
treated. The fundamental trend of events during the period
will also become evident.

By the chartered colonies is meant the corporate colonies
of New England and the proprietary provinces. The term
"chartered" signifies nothing as to the internal organization
of the dependencies to which it is applied, but relates only
to the method of their origin. They all originated in
grants from the English crown, the privileges being conveyed through royal charters. Permissions to undertake
voyages of discovery were issued in this form. All the
colonies were founded under grants of this nature, and their
development embodied the results contributed by private
and local enterprise to the general movement. Their founders and settlers bore the risks, hardships, and losses which
were incident to the beginnings of colonization. Their
efforts, under authority from the English government, gave
rise to a group of colonies which possessed variety of internal
organization and enjoyed a large degree of independence.
They were emphatically special jurisdictions, and their
founders and inhabitants exhibited all the love for corporate
liberty which characterizes the history of such jurisdictions.
The corporate colonies of New England were practically
commonwealths and developed with scarcely any recognition
of the sovereignty of England. Their ecclesiastical polity
differed from that of England. Their land system and the
relations between their executives and legislatures were
peculiar to themselves. They founded a confederation with-

out the consent of the home government, taking advantage
of the civil troubles in England for the purpose.

Of the proprietary provinces, the earliest were founded by trading companies resident in England, and at the outset joint management of land and trade were prominent characteristics of their policy. This, however, soon passed away and left a body of free tenants. The later proprietary provinces were founded by individuals or boards of proprietors, through whom political rights passed to the inhabitants. In some of these provinces the proprietors and their appointees retained at the beginning large powers in their own hands, and only gradually did these come to be shared by the people through their representatives in the lower house of the legislature. In others the proprietors at the beginning admitted the representatives of the colonists to a large, or even the largest, share of power. Thus varieties of a common type appear prominently in this class of provinces; institutions shade off into one another.

Before the close of the seventeenth century, however, all the colonies of this type had suffered temporary eclipse, and nearly all of them had disappeared. Royal provinces had taken their place. This was the most important and significant transition in American history previous to the colonial revolt. It was effected in part by causes operative in the colonies themselves and in part by pressure from the home government. Internal changes were chiefly active in the proprietary provinces, and least so in the corporate colonies. The latter attained at the outset an organization which suited their needs and temper. Under it for nearly half a century they enjoyed *de facto* self-government, and they were under no temptation to change it for anything different. In the proprietary provinces the conditions were by no means stable. The inefficient administration of many of the proprietors, the narrow pseudo-dynastic policy of others, the confusion which sometimes resulted from doubt as to the governmental or territorial rights of proprietors, not infrequently led the colonists to prefer government by the crown. Against not a few phases of proprietary government, when at its best, the people were always protesting, with the result that gradually

the powers of the proprietor were limited, and that thereby
the institutions and political life of the province were broadened and strengthened.

But the most important cause of the disappearance of
the chartered colonies, whether they were corporations or
provinces, was pressure from the home government. The
treatment of this subject leads necessarily to the discussion
of the powers and functions of the British government so
far as they were exercised in colonial administration, the
policy which the imperial government adopted toward its
dependencies, and the relation which it bore to the chartered
colonies in particular. From the point of view of administrative organization the fact of chief importance connected
with the system of chartered colonies is this, that under that
system no provision was made for an imperial executive resident in the colonies. For this reason, when the home government adopted a comprehensive policy for the colonies, it
found itself hampered in the execution of it by the lack of
officials of its own who were resident in America, the place
where, as things then were, much of the most important
administrative work must be done. In many ways the
chartered colonies obstructed, by a course of passive resistance, the enforcement of the policy which the home government thought it wise to support. When viewed from the
imperialist standpoint, looseness and inefficiency seemed to
characterize much that was done by the chartered colonies.
Their tendencies toward an independent course, it was
thought, should be checked. Greater regard for general
interests, it was held, should be secured in the spheres of
commercial relations, imperial defence, and the administration of justice, while in New England the pride and exclusiveness of the Puritans should be curbed to such an extent
that a foothold might be obtained for representatives of the
English Church.

Of the fact that, toward the close of the seventeenth
century, this was the view of substantially all Englishmen
who were largely concerned in colonial administration, there
can be no doubt. Whether it was a statesmanlike view of
the case, this is not the place to inquire. It is sufficient for

present purposes to know that, under the circumstances, it
was a natural conclusion of the administrative mind. Its adoption, moreover, was the signal for an attack on the chartered colonies individually and as a system. Such an attack had begun as early as 1624, when Virginia became a royal province, and would have continued, had it not been for the temporary overthrow of the Stuarts. Toward the close of the reign of Charles II it was resumed and was persisted in for a generation. In combination with other causes which were operative exclusively within the colonies themselves or among their proprietors, it temporarily substituted royal provinces for all, and permanently for all except four, of the chartered colonies. The four that remained — Rhode Island, Connecticut, Pennsylvania, and Maryland, together with Georgia, which was settled in 1732 and continued for twenty years as a proprietary province — it subjected in part to the system of administrative routine which developed in England during the early years of the eighteenth century. Thus the transition from the system of chartered colonies to that of royal provinces was effected.

From the beginning of the eighteenth century until the war for independence the royal province was altogether the prevailing form of colonial government. It differed from the proprietary province in the fact that the king was its proprietor, while a royal executive and judicial system existed within it. Its existence was closely bound up with the system of colonial administration in general. The relation between the crown and its legislature and officials was immediate. It was not a special jurisdiction in the extreme sense which attached to that term when it was applied to the chartered colonies. In short, the advent of the royal provinces as a system was an important step toward imperial unity, and at the same time toward uniformity in the internal organization of the colonies themselves. For these reasons the royal provinces cannot be discussed apart from the system of imperial control, as is the case with the chartered colonies; but the two are parts or aspects of the same whole. As the nature of the royal province has not until recently been understood, and as, until lately, no systematic attention has been paid to the period of our history when it was the leading form of colonial government, the treatment of that subject must be almost entirely original.   But it is in some respects the more important phase of our colonial development, and a knowledge of the precedents which were slowly established within the royal provinces is indispensable to an understanding of the Revolution.   The constitutional questions which were at issue during that crisis originated largely within the royal provinces and concerned their structure and workings.   Amid the action and reaction of provincial assemblies and executives, the executives being guided by the acts of parliament and the royal commissions and instructions to which they were subject, and all feeling more or less keenly the pressure of the long commercial and military struggle with France, the colonies and mother country slowly approached the point when claims and policies, which from the outset had been divergent, clashed, and it was found impossible to harmonize them.

American colonial history, especially when studied from the institutional standpoint, is not limited or narrow in its bearings.   Its outlook is broad, and the issues with which it is connected affect deeply the history of the world at large.   Viewed in one connection, it is the record of the beginnings of English-American institutions.   Looked at from another point of view, it fills an important place in the history of British colonization.   It leads outward in two directions, toward the history of the greatest of federal republics, and toward the later and freer development of the greatest of commercial empires.   If the colonial and the imperial forces which were operating can be fully traced and clearly revealed, the significance of the period in its twofold connection will be made apparent.

PART FIRST

THE PROPRIETARY PROVINCE IN ITS
EARLIEST FORM

CHAPTER I

CHARTERS OF DISCOVERY. EXPERIMENTS OF GILBERT AND RALEIGH

COLONIZATION, like many other social activities, has owed its origin and development to the coöperation of private enterprise with governmental patronage and control. The forms which colonial systems assume depend largely on the way in which these two elements are combined. Among all nations private initiative has been especially prominent in the early stages of colonization. As a rule discoverers have been self-developed, and have turned to government to secure recognition and support for the adventures which they have undertaken or were ready to undertake. The discoverer is always potentially the colonizer, and the relations of the two toward the civil power are likely to be much the same. The impulse toward migration has usually originated with individuals, groups, or classes that for some reason or other have sought a change of environment, going in many cases even so far as to choose removal into distant and almost unknown climes. Especially is this true of such movements in their earliest stages, and particularly as they appear among the English. Monarchs and finance ministers have as a rule been slow to commit the government to the active support of enterprises so uncertain as the founding of colonies in distant and newly discovered continents. They have been ready to legalize such schemes, to grant charters and incorporate, to convey large tracts of land, rights of trade and powers of government, also to appoint officials and issue instructions; but from directly undertaking the work of planting colonies, with the financial risks it involved, they have usually held aloof. This they have preferred to see individuals and corporations undertake.

3

To these causes the system of corporate and proprietary colonies in British North America owes its origin. The individuals and corporations that actually founded these colonies and bore the risks and losses involved therein were the proprietors and planters. Without their initiative the colonies never could have been settled ; and conversely, the first form of colony which necessarily came into existence was the proprietorship. Viewing the subject technically and from the standpoint of the colonizing power, the proprietors and planters were its agents, acting under authority derived from it, for the purpose of establishing a colonial system.

In applying to the government, as they did, for legal authority and recognition, the early discoverers and colonizers committed themselves to the adoption for their dependencies of such forms of local organization as were characteristic of the parent state, or such as the crown lawyers and officers might accept or choose. Upon these forms the relation of both colonies and their founders with the parent state came largely to depend. When under the Tudors the earliest charters of discovery were granted, the fief was chosen as the model of the grants. For a time after the accession of the Stuarts the trading corporation was selected for the same purpose. The fief, however, was by no means abandoned, but was utilized under the form of the county palatine in the grants to Lord Baltimore, Sir Ferdinando Gorges, and other proprietors who received their patents subsequent to the Restoration. Thus the fief suggested the form under which most of the proprietary grants were made, though trading corporations which continued resident in England also founded a type of proprietary colony which is of great interest and importance.

The charter which was issued in 1497 to John Cabot and his three sons provided that they should subdue and possess the territories they discovered as the " vassals and lieutenants " of the king.[1] The " rule, title, and jurisdiction " over these lands were to remain in the king, while the grantees should enjoy the monopoly of trade with their provinces, subject to the payment of one-fifth of their total gains to the

[1] Hakluyt, Collection of Voyages, III. 26.

crown. When it is also noted that Cabot, his heirs, and
assigns, were required to make Bristol the terminus of their
voyages, it will be seen that this charter contained in germ
several of the most important features of the later colonial
system. The second patent, granted to Cabot the following
year,[1] simply gave him the right to visit the lands which in
the name of the king he had recently discovered, taking with
him as many as six English ships.

By the charter[2] of 1501, issued to Richard Warde, Thomas
Ashehurst, and others, the grantees were empowered to occupy the territories they should discover as vassals of the
crown, holding their lands by fealty without payment, and
enjoying rights of government and exclusive rights of trade.
In this document, as well as in that issued the next year[3] to
several of the same patentees, the main features of the original grant to Cabot reappear, elaborated and stated in greater
detail.

After an interval of eighty years, and with the impulse
toward maritime development which accompanied the struggle with the Catholic powers of the Continent, the work of
discovery was resumed, and it now led, after a short delay,
to experiments in colonization. The movement at this time
centred among the Elizabethan soldiers and seamen, leaders
who were founding plantations in Ireland and who were
invading Spanish and Portuguese dominions in every quarter
of the globe. Walsingham and Leicester were the official
leaders of the war party, and Drake proved himself to be the
genius of the movement as it was when viewed in its purely
maritime aspects. Humphrey Gilbert and Walter Raleigh
were interested in many Irish enterprises, and when they
came to undertake discovery and settlement across the sea,
may very well have followed precedents which they had
learned in Ireland. In the eyes of these men the Spanish
power was not only the arch enemy of Protestantism, and so
of the queen, but it was the sentinel which, under authority
derived partly from occupation but more from the papal bull,
stood guard over the vast stretches of the newly discovered

---

[1] Biddle, Life of Sebastian Cabot, 75.   [2] *Ibid.* 306.
[3] Rymer, Fœdera, XIII. 37.

continents and sought to monopolize their united wealth and trade. It was the dream of power and wealth for England and for themselves which nerved those men to seize the treasure fleets, to invade the Spanish Main, and to attempt the occupation of the hundreds of miles of coast which Spain was unable to colonize. In conception the plan was military and commercial,—military in order that it might become commercial,—and colonization was its final and more permanent phase.

Humphrey and Adrian Gilbert—and to an extent their half-brother Raleigh was associated with them—were specially interested in the discovery of a northwest passage to Cathay and the East Indies. They held that America was the fabled island of Atlantis, and that around its northern end was the most convenient route to the east. Humphrey Gilbert wrote a "discourse" in support of this theory and defended it before the queen and council against the arguments urged by Anthony Jenkinson on behalf of the Merchant Adventurers and in favor of the northeast passage.[1] The voyages of Frobisher and Davis were the outcome of Gilbert's idea, and when, in 1578, having been knighted, he procured a patent from the queen, it was with a view to further exploration and possible colonization within unoccupied regions in comparatively northern latitudes.

In the patent[2] to Sir Humphrey Gilbert the concessions made through earlier grants reappear, but in greater detail and in forms and phraseology which were to characterize the charters of the seventeenth and eighteenth centuries. The lands which it was expected that the patentee would discover were to be held by homage as a royal fief, but all services should be discharged by the payment of one-fifth of the gold and silver ore to be found in the soil. This commutation transformed the tenure practically into one of

[1] Hakluyt, III. 32.

[2] *Ibid.* 174. See petition to queen for this, signed by Gilbert, Sir George Peckham, Mr. Carlile, Sir Richard Grenville, and others; also a letter to the Earl of Lincoln, Lord High Admiral of England, urging him to support the petition. Colonial Papers, 1675–1676, Addenda. Colonial Papers, 1574–1660, 1.

socage,[1] even though the oath of homage continued to be taken. Permission was given to Gilbert, during a period of six years and under license from the lord high treasurer and the privy council, to transport subjects from England and establish one or more colonies within the regions which he should discover. The colonists should remain under allegiance to the crown, but be subject to subordinate rights of government administered by the patentee, these to be in general agreement with the laws and polity of England and not inconsistent with the form of religion professed by the English Church. When a place of settlement should be determined upon, the authority of the proprietor, his right to grant land and his exclusive rights of trade, should extend over a territory encompassing the settlement on all sides to a distance of two hundred leagues. No limit was set to the number of such provinces which Sir Humphrey Gilbert might establish.

Gilbert from the first turned his eyes toward Newfoundland and the coasts which for more than a century had been visited by fishermen from the leading states of western Europe. He proposed to take the northern route across the Atlantic, the course over which Cabot had sailed and the one which would bring him most directly to the American coast. Large preparations were at once made for a voyage. In these preparations Gilbert had the support not only of Sir George Peckham, Sir Richard Grenville, and many other knights and inhabitants,[2] chiefly of the south and west of England, but of Walsingham himself, "the pillar unto whom I leant." By September, 1578, eleven vessels, with five hundred men, all provisioned for a year, were gathered at Dartmouth. Among them were George and William Carew, Henry and Francis Knollys, and, greatest of all, Gilbert's half-brother, Walter Raleigh.

---

[1] Pollock and Maitland, History of English Law, I. 286.

[2] The names of many who contributed toward the voyage are given in Colonial Papers, 1675–1676, Addenda, 16. Sir George Peckham and Sir Thomas Gerrard, the latter of whom appears subsequently among Gilbert's supporters, were Catholics, and, like the Earl of Arundel at the beginning of the reign of James I, were interested in plans for the settlement of Catholic recusants in America. Baxter, Gorges, I. 65 ; Holinshed, Chronicle, III. 1369.

Like all bodies of men who at that time went on expeditions to the west, they were piratically inclined. Many
wild spirits among them sought only plunder, and they
apparently insisted that Gilbert should choose the southern
route, because it offered the best chance of seizing Spanish
territory or Spanish treasure ships. The government, however, was unwilling that Spain should be openly attacked,
and somewhat later brought pressure directly to bear to
prevent this. Dissensions broke out among Gilbert's force,
and Henry Knollys, with four vessels and 160 men, withdrew.
Gilbert soon after set sail with seven vessels and 389 men,
and chose the route to the southwest. This brought him
into Spanish waters, where he met with some disaster. Of
this the only positive knowledge that we have is, that one
of the ships, of which Miles Morgan[1] was captain, was lost.
Gilbert wrote later that he returned with great loss from his
first expedition, because he would not himself do, or suffer
any one of his company to do, anything contrary to the
pledges which he had given to the queen and Walsingham ;[2]
if he had not preferred credit to gain, he need not have
returned so poor as he did.

The voyage was now abandoned, and Gilbert, with a part
of his vessels, was for a time occupied again with Irish
affairs. The losses consequent on the failure of his expedition seriously embarrassed him, so that in 1581 he
complained to Walsingham of " daily arrests, executions and
outlawries," and declared that he was forced to pledge his
wife's clothing in order to secure his creditors. He petitioned for the recovery of £2000 due him from the government in Ireland.

But by the summer of 1582 the courage of Gilbert had so
far revived that he was actively preparing for another voyage, which it was his intention to conduct in person. Four
out of the six years within which according to his patent he
must found a colony or forfeit his grant had already passed,
and it was necessary to act with promptness. Fortunately
his old friend had not lost confidence in him, and many

---

[1] Dasent, Acts of the Privy Council, 1578–1580, 109, 142–146.
[2] Colonial Papers, 1675–1676, Addenda, p. 18.

others came to his assistance, though the queen expressed CHAP.
the wish that he might stay at home, and reminded him of   I.
his reputation for ill luck at sea. Fortunately an important series of documents has been preserved[1] which reveal
in outline the nature and extent of the support which
Gilbert secured for this the last enterprise of his life, and
the form of the provinces which, as a result, he intended to
establish across sea. Because of the light which they throw
upon this and later schemes of colonization, it is necessary
to refer to their contents.

Like all other recipients of proprietary grants, Gilbert
sought contributions toward the expense of his enterprise
by offering in return trade privileges and grants of land
along the coasts and within the vast unoccupied territories
which he had obtained the exclusive privilege of visiting.
We infer that a number of small contributions had been
secured in this way for the first voyage. Now the same was
attempted on a larger scale. To this end an association of
merchants and their apprentices living in and about Southampton was formed, to be known, until incorporated under
some other name, as the Merchant Adventurers with Sir
Humphrey Gilbert.[2] Southampton was to be the staple for
all their trade with the prospective provinces in America,
the merchants themselves paying half customs, and their
apprentices the full rates. Every adventurer who contributed £5 should be entitled, in addition to the return
thereupon, to one thousand acres of land. Those who went
in person, and without goods, should enjoy freedom of trade
and the benefit of a single or double share of land according
to their rank. Those who on the first voyage should both
contribute and go in person should receive a double share of

[1] Colonial Papers, Addenda, 8 *et seq.* The papers relating to Gilbert
are now in print in full in Slafter's Sir Humphrey Gylberte, Pubs. of Prince
Society, vol. 17.

[2] Besides various organizations of merchant adventurers which had been
in existence in England for nearly two centuries, Gilbert might suggest as a
precedent for this the fact that in 1565 by act of parliament a corporation
was established for the discovery of new trades, *i.c.* for the encouragement
of colonization. Of this body Gilbert was a member. 8 Eliz. c. 17. Doyle,
English in America, Southern Colonies, 57.

land.   Land was to be subject to a perpetual quitrent of ten shillings per thousand acres.   Sir Humphrey, his wife, and all his blood relatives were to be forever free of the said territories and to enjoy all privileges without fines, while other adventurers, presumably when in the colonies, were to be free both in persons and goods from torture, martial law, arbitrary arrests, and attachments in all forms.   A possible suggestion of Sir Humphrey's opposition to the theory of the northeast passage may be seen in his requirement that none of the merchants of the Muscovy company or their issue should be admitted to the new society.   The same prohibition was to apply to residents of Southampton who had not contributed toward Gilbert's previous voyage, or who should not aid him in the present one.   On the other hand, those who had been adventurers with him in 1578 and who had continued with him until the expedition had returned to Kinsale in Ireland, were thereby to be entitled to full shares in the present enterprise.   All who became colonists must give bond to obey the articles of agreement and the queen's commission, and to conform as near as possible to the rules and policy of the society and of the proprietor.   The officials of the society were to be a governor, eight assistants, a treasurer, agent, and secretary.   General courts of the company were to meet twice every year. These bodies were given power to elect the assistants.   The other officers were in the first instance to be appointed by the proprietor, but in his absence Secretary Walsingham was to appoint in each case from a list of three nominated by the society.   New adventurers might be admitted to the society on the payment of certain dues, with the reservation of a part of these to the proprietor, his heirs, and assigns.   Thus as a means of securing funds the preliminary steps for the organization of a trading company were taken which might traffic and colonize within the vast domain that Sir Humphrey had received, but no rights of government appear to have been expressly conferred on the company.

Four other agreements were also drawn and enrolled by which Sir Humphrey sought to reward his most valued friends by empowering them to discover, settle, and establish subordinate proprietorships within his domain. The first of these empowered Sir Thomas Gerrard and Sir George Peckham to occupy 1,500,000 acres, together with two adjoining islands, at some point between the Cape of Florida and Cape Breton; by the second Sir George Peckham was granted 500,000 acres, near the former tract; while by a third he and his son were authorized to take possession of the region supposed to comprise all of Narragansett bay and the islands within it, together with 1,500,000 acres adjoining thereto. The fourth enrolment provided for a grant of 3,000,000 acres to Sir Philip Sidney, which he immediately transferred to Peckham. All these were to be held by socage, subject to the payment of a quitrent to the chief proprietor, and with the enjoyment of rights of trade and the usual nominal jurisdictions.

Finally, before he sailed, Sir Humphrey made an assignment — to take effect in case of his death or other serious mishap — of all his estate, right, and authority under the patent of 1578 to Sir John Gilbert, Sir George Peckham, and William Archer. This document reveals the fact that he had planned for the reservation of certain seigniories or lordships, fifty English miles square, for his widow and sons; also for a grant of twenty miles square in fee simple for each of his daughters; these all to be subject to rent and the obligation of military service, and to carry with them rights of jurisdiction. The assigns were also empowered to grant the land not otherwise provided for in small lots in fee farm or leasehold, reserving the best places for towns, commons, forts, the support of the poor, and the support of captains and governors. Provision was made for the transportation and settlement of tenants and servants, as well as small freeholders, and for the reproduction in the province of the ordinary features of tenant right. Servants and tenants might be sent over by the state or by adventurers. The province was to be divided into parishes, with a system of tithes and glebes. The existence of a bishop, or even of an archbishop, within the province was also suggested. The obligations of the assize of arms were to be enforced, while general assessments should be levied for purposes of defence.

This money should be used with the consent of the chief
governor and of the majority of a body of thirteen councillors
chosen by the people. The produce of the customs, chief
rents, royalties, and jurisdictions were reserved to the heirs
male and the widow of the chief proprietor. The assignees
should jointly exercise the appointing and other administrative powers.

The writings of Sir Humphrey Gilbert concerning the
northwest passage, his persistent urging of his views, the
great sacrifices which he repeatedly and willingly bore in
order to realize them, had already proved him to be an ideal-
ist in the sphere of discovery. A powerful imagination and
strong will, together with the lofty ambition born of these,
must indeed characterize all leaders in such hazardous enterprises. From the plans which have just been outlined it
appears that before his mind floated also the vision of a great
proprietary dominion in America which, with its landed
gentry, freeholders, tenants, counties, boroughs, should reproduce the chief features of English political and industrial
society. He had thought this scheme out even to its details a
generation before an English colonist was to be permanently
settled on the American coasts, and while as yet they had
scarcely been visited by an English vessel. Sir Humphrey
Gilbert appears then as the precursor of Sir Ferdinando
Gorges, Sir William Alexander, the Calverts, the Earl of
Shaftesbury, and John Locke, as the first in the series of
colonizers from among the British nobility and gentry who
desired to see the aristocratic system in state and church,
with which they were familiar in England, reproduced in the
new world.

But how small in this case were the results actually
reached, when compared with the plans that were formulated!
After having sold much of his estate, with the aid of Raleigh
five ships were fitted out, the largest of two hundred tons'
burden, and the smallest of ten tons' burden.[1] According to
the custom of the time one was termed the admiral, another
the vice-admiral, a third the rear-admiral. Two hundred
and sixty men, many of whom were lawless adventurers, were

[1] Hakluyt, III. 189. Relation of Edward Haies.

enlisted for the voyage.   Among the men were a variety of
artisans, miners, and workers in metals.   Small wares were
taken for the Indian trade.   In June, 1583, under the
authority of a special commission from the crown, the fleet
sailed, Gilbert leading it in person with the title of general.
Raleigh's ship, the largest of all and holding the place of
vice-admiral, soon turned back, and only the four other
vessels pursued the voyage to the end.   About the close of
July they entered the harbor of Saint John's, Newfoundland,
where the royal commission was shown to the fishermen of
various nationalities who were in the port, and afterwards
read and interpreted for the benefit of the foreigners who
were present.[1]   By virtue of this, and in accordance with
ancient custom, possession of the soil within a radius of two
hundred leagues was taken in the name of the queen and of
her grantees by the transfer of the rod and turf.   Proclamation was then made by Gilbert that the soil would henceforth
be held of the queen and of himself, and that ordinances
would be issued for the government of those who should
inhabit the province or trade within it.   Three such were at
once proclaimed, to the effect that the religion of the Church
of England would be maintained ; that any assault upon the
sovereign rights of the crown over the territory would be
adjudged high treason and punished as such ; that, if any
one should utter words to the dishonor of the queen, he
should lose his ears, and his ship and goods should be confis-
cated.   Obedience was promised by the general voice and
consent of those who were present, both foreigners and Englishmen.   After the assembly had dispersed, the arms of
England were set up, and several parcels of land adjacent to
the shore, both in the harbor of Saint John's and elsewhere,
were granted to the fishermen to be used in the prosecution
of their business.   These were held subject to rent and service.

With this Sir Humphrey Gilbert's positive work in connection with the settlement of North America came to an
end.   Many of his colonists escaped from his control, and
fled into the woods, or became freebooters.   Others, on

[1] Hakluyt, III. 192.

their own request, were taken back to England. With
those who remained, after revictualling from the stock of
provisions already available in Newfoundland, Gilbert pursued his voyage of discovery toward the southwest. Buf-
feted by storms of increasing violence and visited by a series
of disasters, after little more than a month had passed he
was forced to turn his course homeward. But on the way
the tiny craft in which he insisted upon sailing was lost, and
with it Gilbert himself perished. We are told that he had
already formed a project for sending out two fleets the next
year, and that he hoped for large assistance from the queen.
But his assigns took no steps to execute this plan, though
Peckham did publish one of the best pamphlets[1] of the time
on the prospects and advantages of colonization in America.
Captain J. Carlile,[2] a son-in-law of Walsingham, also urged
the Muscovy company, because of obstacles which hindered
the success of the Russian trade, to turn its efforts toward
America, and a committee considered the proposal. In 1584
Adrian Gilbert, with certain associates, procured a patent
incorporating them for five years under the name of the
Colleagues of the Fellowship for the Discovery of the Northwest Passage. Their objects were similar to those set forth
in the patent of 1578, though they sought to obtain them under
the form of a corporation. But these projects came to
naught, and it was reserved for Walter Raleigh to take up
the work where his relative and associate had left it and
carry it on a stage farther toward success.

The royal charter[3] which Raleigh procured, March 25,
1584, was an almost exact reproduction of that issued to
Gilbert six years before. The period prescribed as that
within which a colony must be established was the same,
and the territory over which rights of trade and government
should extend was to have the same radius as that specified
in Gilbert's charter. Raleigh drew his support from much

---

[1] Hakluyt, III. 208.

[2] *Ibid.* 228.

[3] *Ibid.* 297 ; Hazard, State Papers, I. 33 ; Tarbox, Sir Walter Raleigh and
His Colony in America (Prince Soc.), 95. Printed also in many other
places.

the same class as did Gilbert, Sir Richard Grenville, Ralph
Lane, Thomas Cavendish representing well the spirit of
Elizabethan seamen. Still, merchants appear to have borne
a larger share in the later than in the earlier enterprise, and
it was conducted in a more practical spirit, with less of
dreamy idealism than had characterized Gilbert. Raleigh
chose the southern route and sought warmer climes than did
his predecessor. Two captains, Amidas and Barlow, were
sent out in advance to select a site for the colony. Each of
the expeditions which followed delayed for a longer or
shorter time in the West Indies, thus coming directly and
in a somewhat hostile manner into contact with the Spanish
power. The place selected for the colony was adjacent to
Florida as then understood in American geography. The
province of Virginia, as it now comes dimly into view, had
it approximated at all closely to the extent suggested in the
charter, would have overlapped the Spanish possessions on
the south and extended almost to the frozen regions of the
north. The spot, however, which was actually settled and
held at intervals for about three years, was Roanoke island,
within the sounds of North Carolina, while the explorations
of the colonists extended from somewhat beyond Cape Look-
out on the south to the region of Norfolk, Virginia, on the
north — more than 200 miles — and inland to a distance
somewhat less than 150 miles. About eighteen of the
modern counties within the coast district[1] of North Carolina are supposed to have been visited by them.

At Roanoke within this vast province of Virginia two
colonies were established, one under Ralph Lane, and later
a second under Captain John White. We desire in this
connection to consider these only so far as they illustrate
the history of the proprietary province in its rudimentary
form. No commissions or instructions from Raleigh, the
proprietor, have been preserved, but we know that such in
some form must have been issued by him. Tudor officialism[2]

[1] Hawks, History of North Carolina, I. 108, 111.
[2] Proof of these statements and of those which follow will be found in the
relations of Lane and White in the third volume of Hakluyt's Voyages, and
in the letters of Lane printed in Archæologia Americana, IV.

with its pretentious titles was present even in this small settlement. We hear of a provost marshal or "high marshal,"
of a treasurer and vice-treasurer, of a master of the victuals,
and a keeper of the store. Philip Amidas, who had been
one of the captains on the previous voyage, held under Lane
the post of "admiral of the country," and was a sort of
deputy-governor. Ralph Lane himself was governor, and
was specially intrusted with the duty of founding the colony and administering its affairs. John White bore a similar relation toward the second colony.

Sir Richard Grenville held the office of general in the
first expedition and exercised its functions, whatever they
were, at Roanoke for about two months. His departure for
England at the end of that time brought to a close his connection with the first colony, though not with its patrons in
England. Grenville's title directs attention prominently to
the military side of the enterprise. In a writing which
probably emanated from him, Lane is referred to as his
"deputy." Lane himself states that he occupied the "second place" under Grenville.[1] The inference is that, when
the two were serving together, Grenville was the chief and
Lane the subordinate. Of course Lane would be unwilling
to acknowledge that he was a subordinate, and we must
doubt if Raleigh had clearly defined the relations between
the two leaders in his commissions. We know, indeed, that
Lane and Grenville quarrelled on the way over, and it is
possible that it was concerning questions of jurisdiction, or
of policy and jurisdiction combined. Lane wrote back to
Walsingham charging Grenville with tyrannical conduct,
continued through the entire outward voyage, and refers to
a "book" dedicated to Raleigh in which this is set down in
detail. He also cites the testimony of Thomas Cavendish,
Edward Gorges, and John Clarke, captain of the flyboat,
in support of the complaints. It is stated that Grenville
even threatened to have Lane executed. On the general's

[1] Hakluyt, III. 323 ; Arch. Am. IV. 27. Major thinks that Grenville
was simply commander of the expedition. Strachey, Hist. of Travaile into
Virginia (Hakluyt Soc.), 144. Doyle, 78, states that Grenville "was to
establish the settlement and leave it under the charge of Ralph Lane."

arrival in England it was supposed that he, in turn, would submit to Walsingham and Raleigh charges against several of the prominent men of the colony. "For mine own part," writes Lane, " I have had so much experience of his government as I am humbly to desire your honor, and the rest of my honorablest friends, to give me their favors to be freed from that place where Sir R. Grenville is to carry any authority in chief." Have we here an instance of such strife as was later caused and continued between the governors and intendants in the French province of Canada, as the result of locating the military and civil power in different hands? Lane, in his subsequent dealings with the Indians and his management of the affairs of the colony, proved that he had some of the spirit later shown by Captain John Smith. Grenville possessed the fierce, indomitable nature which later won for him imperishable renown as the commander of the *Revenge*, which indeed characterized all the Elizabethan seamen who distinguished themselves by assaults on Spain. It is not difficult, then, to imagine how, under the circumstances, two such natures, though ardent supporters of the same cause, might become involved in an almost deadly feud. But after Grenville's return to England we hear no more of the strife. When he and Lane met again, it was as co-workers in the preparations for the defence of England against the Armada.[1]

Some of the chief men of the first colony, we are told, acted as "assistants for counsel and good directions in the voyage," but that they did so by appointment from the proprietor is not stated and is scarcely probable. Cavendish, Arundel, Stukeley, and others are mentioned in this connection. Prior to the time when the question, whether or not they should leave Roanoke and return home with Drake, was under discussion, the consultations to which reference is made are such as were always held by bodies of men who are exploring the wilderness, seeking mines or places for settlement, holding interviews with the Indians or preparing for defence against them, building a fort or procuring means of subsistence. After Grenville left, and indeed as soon

[1] Arch. Am. IV. 332.

as the voyage ended and the work of founding the colony began in earnest, Lane's function as governor grew steadily in importance. So far as we know, perfect harmony existed between him and the body of the colonists.

One hundred and seven colonists, all men, came over on the first expedition. Their names have been preserved, and among them fourteen appear with the title of master. Of these, Thomas Hariot had received the degree of bachelor of arts from Oxford, and became the missionary and scientific chronicler of the colony. We hear of several other "gentlemen," some of whose names have already been mentioned ; but we do not know that they all remained in the colony throughout the year of its existence.

A small fort and probably some rude dwellings were built by the first settlers on Roanoke island. These formed the nucleus of the colony. From this as a centre, and partly under suggestions from the Indians, explorations were made by water and land, toward the south, west, and north. These revealed the fruitfulness of the country, and also, because of poor harbors and shifting sand bars, the unsuitableness of the location for a permanent colony. Through reports of the Indians, Lane soon heard of the region about Chesapeake bay, and that it would be more suitable for colonization. A trend in that direction was at once started which would probably have soon resulted in the transfer of the colony thither, or the founding of a new one, had Raleigh's experiment proved permanently successful.

Lane, profiting by the relations which Amidas and Barlow had established with the natives, made skilful use of their help, not only to increase his knowledge of the country, but in supplying the colony with fish, maize, and fruits. Like all colonizers of his generation, who were imitating Spain while they were fighting her, Lane considered the two chief objects of his enterprise to be the discovery of a gold mine and of a route to the South Sea. Indian tales stimulated his search for these, especially up the course of the Moratoc or Roanoke river, and the journeyings in turn extended relations with the Indians. Suspicions concerning the purposes of the newcomers developed in the minds of

the natives, which were increased by Lane's activity and
address. A combination was soon formed among them to
cut off the colonists' supply of food. This had immediately
a twofold result: it involved the English in their first conflict with the Indians, in which the superiority of European
warfare was shown, and Pemisapan, the leader of the hostile
natives, was slain ; on the other hand, it necessitated a certain dispersion of the colonists to points within the circle of
their explorations where they could more easily supply
themselves with food. As the famine grew severe, Captain
Stafford with twenty men was sent to the admiral's station
at Croatan, eleven men were sent to Hatteras to live there
with the provost marshal, and every week from sixteen to
twenty of the rest of the company were despatched to the
mainland opposite Roanoke to live upon the oysters and
other food procurable there. Hariot [1] stated that Raleigh
had granted land in estates of five hundred acres or more to
those who had come over in person. But we do not learn
that these grants were laid out or improved. The soil, however, was jointly cultivated to an extent, and we are told
that in the spring of 1586 " they sowed, planted, and set
such things as were necessary for their relief in so plentiful
a manner as might have sufficed them two years without any
further labor," and that by the close of June their corn
would have been ready to harvest.[2] Hariot's relation also
shows that they had gained an unusually comprehensive view
of the resources of the country, and knew that they were
abundant.

But the colony was not yet self-supporting, the supply
which they expected from England had not arrived, they
were also exposed to the danger of Indian attacks and of
destruction by the Spaniards. In the mind of Lane, we may
surmise, lay also the conviction that colonization at Roanoke
would always be carried on under great difficulties, and that
the experiment had better be tried again on the Chesapeake.
He may also well have dreaded further dealings with Grenville, should the general return. Therefore, when in June,
1586, about a year after the settlement of the colony, Drake

[1] Hakluyt, III. 323, 340.   [2] *Ibid.* 323.

appeared off the coast homeward bound from the West Indies, the temptation to accompany him was strong. This, however, does not seem at first to have been suggested. Drake offered to leave with the colonists provisions, arms, a bark of seventy tons, various smaller craft, all manned and furnished with two of his best captains. Lane at first simply requested that Drake would take home a number of the colonists who were weak and unfit for service. But in a great storm which followed, the bark intended for the colony was driven out to sea and did not return. Drake then offered a ship of 170 tons, but this was too large to pass the inlet, and therefore would be of little use to the settlement. Thereupon the captains and gentlemen among the colonists urged Lane to ask that they all might be taken back to England. The request was at once granted, and Roanoke was abandoned. In the hurry of embarkation the sailors, in disgust at being delayed so long on that stormy coast, threw overboard the books and records of the colonists, and thus perished writings which would probably have thrown light on the internal history of the experiment.

That the resolve of Governor Lane and his associates to abandon Roanoke was a hasty one is evidenced by the fact that within a month after the colonists had left, three vessels — two under the command of Grenville — arrived with supplies and additional settlers. Finding no one, Grenville left fifteen men, provisioned for two years, and returned to England. These, as later events showed, perished at the hands of the Indians.

Raleigh, profiting by experience, now addressed himself more systematically [1] than before to the founding of a colony. Imitating presumably the example of Sir Humphrey Gilbert and others, he associated with himself nineteen London merchants as adventurers, who were to contribute toward the expense of the enterprise and share its profits. Prominent among these was Thomas Smith, afterward treasurer of the London company. [2] The names of nine others appear both

---

[1] See indenture in Hazard, I. 42 ; Hawks, I. 194. Tarbox for some reason omits this document.

[2] Hawks, I. 195.

in this connection and among the adventurers of the Virginia colony which was later founded at Jamestown. With them were also joined thirteen gentlemen of London who proposed to settle in the colony, and who were made governor and assistants of the city of Raleigh, which it was hoped would be built and become the capital of the province. At their head was John White, who by the charter of incorporation was made governor. All who became members of the corporation should enjoy freedom of trade with any colony which Raleigh should thereafter found in America, and be exempt from all rents and subsidies, as well as from all duties and customs. Thus the office of general was dropped, the strength of the mercantile element in the undertaking was increased, and a borough government was expressly provided for the colony. Raleigh retained for himself the title of " chief governor of Virginia."

A body of about one hundred and fifty colonists was brought together, among whom were several women — another indication of greater wisdom in the founding of the enterprise. Instructions were also issued by the proprietor that Roanoke should be definitely abandoned and a new settlement made in the Chesapeake region. But this part of Raleigh's plan was thwarted by Simon Ferdinando, presumably a Spaniard, but who was one of the assistants and was master of the largest vessel on the outward voyage. When they had reached Roanoke, in July, 1587, and were searching for the men whom Grenville had left, Ferdinando and the sailors insisted that a landing should be made there at once, and White was overruled. They found the houses which the first colony had built on the island still standing, but the new colony succeeded to the feud with the Indians and reopened the struggle with the natural difficulties of the place.

Had Grenville or Lane been governor, with such powers as they enjoyed over the first colony, we may imagine that the proprietor's instructions would have been obeyed. But White seems to have been a more pliable man, somewhat easily turned from his course by the assistants and other colonists. The real executive of the second colony seems to have been a council rather than the governor, and they

shared quite fully the desires, and even whims, of the body
of the colonists.   Proof of this soon appeared.   Controversies, we are told, arose between the governor and assistants
over the question of choosing two of the latter to return to
England as factors of the company ; only one among the
assistants wished to go.   Thereupon both planters and assistants began with one voice to urge the governor to go.
This, of course, was a step which was likely to prove the ruin
of the colony, for it needed above all a strong executive head
to carry it through the perils of the approaching winter.
White urged many and strong reasons against the idea,
among which occurs the interesting suggestion that his presence was especially necessary because they intended to remove the seat of the colony fifty miles inland.   But to the
unanimous and persistent entreaties White at last yielded
and sailed for home.   With this event, whether it was the
cause of the catastrophe or a mere incident, the colony vanishes from sight.   Of those who persuaded him to go not one
survived to tell the story of their fate.   A strong, even a
despotic, leader might possibly have saved them ; but, as it
was, they all fell victims either to the ocean or to a savage
foe.

When White reached England he found the nation exert-
ing all its strength in the preparations for defence against
the Armada.   Not until 1590 could White procure three
ships in which to return to America.   Long delays occurred
during the voyage, and when he arrived at Roanoke and
searched the neighboring coast, no living trace of the colonists could be found.   Twelve years passed, and in 1602
Raleigh sent out another vessel under Samuel Mace,[1] a captain of his own appointment, who made a last attempt to
find the lost colonists.   But it was in vain.

[1] Purchas, Pilgrimes, IV. 1653.

CHAPTER II

THE voyages of discovery, the commercial enterprises, the single experiment in colonization of the reign of Elizabeth, were the results of private enterprise. Individuals, associations, or companies furnished the means, the state giving the requisite authority and verbal encouragement or guidance. Its financial resources, especially when administered with the caution that characterized Cecil and the queen, were husbanded for purposes of more direct and pressing utility. From the standpoint of the government discovery and colonization were as yet remote interests. Attention was being directed to them through the conflict with Spain, but the pressing need was the maintenance of English national independence, of that system of relations in church and state which it was hoped had been definitively established when Elizabeth came to the throne. During the early stages of the war with Spain, even naval operations had been left to a considerable extent to individual initiative — a survival of mediæval conditions, when the state and its resources were relatively weak. It was therefore scarcely to be expected that a different policy would be pursued in the domain of colonization. If it should ever be adopted, it must be under the pressure of commercial or political rivalry, and after transmarine interests of magnitude and generally recognized value had developed.

Still, however, with the accession of the Stuarts to the throne an experiment was tried which suggested, not the assumption by the exchequer of responsibility for the expense of colonization, for its losses or gains, but a much more systematic control over it than had ever characterized

23

Elizabethan policy. Though some of the features of this, and some of its consequences, will best be understood when presented in another connection, yet it must be discussed at this point in order that its place in the development of the forms of colonial government may be seen. I refer to the system inaugurated under the charter of 1606, which resulted in the permanent colonization of Virginia. In this the private or proprietary element appears in the form of a body of patentees, much like the Southampton Associates of Sir Humphrey Gilbert, or the freemen of the city of Raleigh, but they are brought for practically all purposes under the control of a special royal council. The following events brought together the patentees, and committed them to the enterprise.

During the three or four years before this charter was issued, several private voyages of discovery were sent to the coast of Northern Virginia, later New England. These were commanded by Bartholomew Gosnold, Martin Pring, George Weymouth. Henry Challons was also despatched on a similar errand, but he fell into the hands of the Spaniards and suffered a long imprisonment. Besides the aid given by certain Bristol, and possibly London, merchants, these voyages were made chiefly under the patronage of the Earl of Southampton, Baron Arundel of Wardour, Sir John Popham, Chief Justice of King's Bench, and Sir Ferdinando Gorges. Toward their success Richard Hakluyt had contributed the help of his enthusiasm, and his wide knowledge of geography and of the history of discovery and colonization. The voyages were made partly with and partly without the consent of Raleigh, whose rights[1] prior to his attainder had not been expressly extinguished, though they might have been held to have lapsed. The result of these voyages was to reveal more clearly the nature of the American coast north of the fortieth degree of latitude, the value of the fisheries and fur trade available there, the resources of the region in timber and other naval stores. Certain natives who were carried to England by Weymouth

[1] Hazard, Historical Collections, I. 42 ; Palfrey, History of New England, I. 81 n.

also greatly interested Gorges. These causes aroused anew
the interest of influential private parties in American colonization, and brought together the London and Plymouth
patentees of 1606. The moving spirits in this enterprise at
the outset are supposed to have been Chief Justice Popham
and Sir Ferdinando Gorges, though their names do not
appear among those of the petitioners for the charter. But
of these petitioners, all except Richard Hakluyt had seen
service either by land or sea in the recent war with Spain.
One was a son of Sir Humphrey Gilbert, and another a
brother of Sir John Popham. Still another, Sir George
Somers, had repeatedly served under Raleigh. Thus a close
connection existed between this group and the earlier generation of seamen and discoverers.

At about the time when the charter of 1606 was issued, a
paper[1] was prepared setting forth reasons for raising a public
fund to be used in aid of discovery and colonization. After
referring to some of the advantages, chiefly commercial, which
colonies would bring to England, the writer affirms that it
were better if the state would directly support their establishment, than if it secured this by granting private monopolies.   A prestige would thus be given to colonization
which otherwise it could never attain.   Contributions
toward it would come in much more freely from the nation
at large, and foreign nations would be less likely to threaten
or otherwise injure the colonies.   The author therefore
proposed that commissioners should be appointed under an
act of parliament, who should collect money for the purpose,
drawing it so far as possible from the superfluous expenditures of the nation.   Privileges and license to transport
colonists should be procured from the king, and his honor
should be pledged to assist and protect the project.   Parliament was not at this juncture to share in the work of colonization, and when its period of activity did come it assumed
a form quite different from the one here suggested.   But
the paper expresses a desire for governmental backing which

---

[1] Brown, Genesis of the United States, 37 ; First Republic, 5. This with
some show of reason he attributes to Edward Haies, who accompanied Gilbert on his last voyage and wrote the relation concerning it.

was an advance on anything that Elizabeth had offered, and which, in a certain form, James I was quite ready to grant.

It is supposed that Sir John Popham prepared the first draft of the charter of 1606, and Sir Edward Coke was attorney-general when it passed the seals. The recipients of the grants were two groups of adventurers, or would-be settlers, one resident at London and the other at Plymouth. To the activities of these men which preceded the issue of the charter reference has already been made. The usual words of incorporation do not appear in the charter, but instead only the expressions " first colony," " second colony," "adventurers," " associates." In the first set of instructions issued by the king concerning this enterprise — and the only set preserved — it is said that the king had " given license " to sundry of his "loving subjects" and " to their associates," " to deduce and conduct two several colonies or plantations of settlers to America." To these patentees, as in the charters issued to Gilbert and Raleigh, permission was granted to establish settlements within a specified territory. The choice of a place for a colony was to secure to the grantees possession of a tract one hundred miles square, so located that the settlement should lie in the middle of the eastern or coast line of the tract. As there were two groups of patentees and presumably at least two colonies would be established, and as a middle region three degrees broad was left open for joint settlement, the further provision became necessary that the colonies should be located at least one hundred miles apart. But this bestowment of land was not made in such way that the patentees could grant it out to settlers. In the eighteenth and nineteenth clauses of the charter it was provided that such grants should be made by the king through letters patent under the great seal, and to those persons in whose behalf a petition should be presented by the council of the colony in which they were resident, or with which they were connected.

The right to transport settlers and their supplies into the colonies, with the power to defend them, was given to the patentees, and by implication also the right to trade with them, though the latter was not bestowed in monopolistic form. Subjects other than adventurers or planters could trade with the colonists on the payment of a duty of two and one-half per cent, and foreigners on the payment of five per cent, on imports and exports, the revenue during the first twenty-one· years to go to the colonies and afterward to the king. In the instructions it was prescribed that for five years trade should be carried on jointly, or in two or three stocks, and that all products of the colonies and all commodities from England should pass through magazines or storehouses, of which in the colonies a cape-merchant should have charge. Each body of patentees was authorized during the period of five years to select three from its own number to serve as factors in England, receiving commodities from the colonies, sending out goods, and guarding the interests of the adventurers. Though the existence in the colonies of individual property in land was not forbidden, the joint system of trade was almost inconsistent with its development, and we know that it did not develop till several years later.

Such were the functions of the patentees in the scheme of 1606. They were proprietary, that is, industrial and commercial, in their character. This group of men furnished the capital for the enterprise, procured settlers, had immediate charge of trade, and expected a profit as the result of their efforts. These are the functions which in all cases, though with varying degrees of effectiveness, proprietors have performed. The colonies which they founded were plantations, worked by servants and laborers under various forms of contract, and managed by overseers or factors. The functions of these proprietors were similar to those of Gilbert, Raleigh, and their associates, and to the work performed by many other individuals and groups that were to follow. Such bodies of men were the prime movers in the initial stage of colonization. They embodied the power of private initiative, and, impelled by desire for gain, the spirit of adventure, or religious zeal, they started a movement toward colonization which was gradually to become national.

But in the system of 1606 was another element, the royal or governmental, which must now be described. Powers of government were not directly bestowed on the grantees. Instead, provision was made for three councils, one resident in England and one in each of the two colonies. The first was called the Royal Council for Virginia. Its members were appointed by the crown. The charter provided that they should be thirteen in number, but the first instructions reveal the fact that there were fourteen.[1] They were, however, selected partly from the patentees for the first colony and partly from those of the second. Experience soon revealed the fact that it was very difficult to bring enough of these together to do business, and for that reason, by an ordinance issued in March, 1607, the number was increased, at the request of the patentees themselves, to about forty.[2] In both these documents, also, it was stated that the king might increase or change the membership at will. The council was then his creature, though the members actually appointed were patentees. Each of the other two councils consisted of thirteen members, appointed by the royal council under instructions from the king, but endowed with power to choose their own president and fill vacancies among their own number.[3] They likewise, being planters, were either patentees or closely connected therewith.

Through these bodies, and by means of instructions given to them, the king governed the colonies. Each council had a seal, which was the seal not of the patentees, but " of the king for his council." To the royal council was given control " of and for all matters that shall or may concern the government," not only within the colonies, but throughout the territory between the thirty-fourth and forty-fifth parallels. To the local councils was given power to regulate the internal affairs of the colonies in pursuance of such instructions as should be issued to them under the sign manual and privy seal of the king. The oath which was formulated for the president of the local council contained a promise of fidelity not to the patentees, but to the king.[4] By his first set of instructions the king prescribed what judicial powers[5] the local council should exercise and how they should be

---

[1] Brown, Genesis, 66.　　[2] Ibid. 93.　　[3] Ibid. 67.
[4] Ibid. 78.　　　　　　[5] Ibid. 68 et seq.

exercised, decreed what punishments should be inflicted
for the more serious offences, and authorized the president
to reprieve, but not to pardon. By the same authority,
as we have seen, the entire industrial and commercial system
of the colonies was prescribed. Even directions as to the
place and method of settlement were issued by the royal
council.

We have thus under the charter and instructions of 1606
a mixed form of organization. On the one side it was private or proprietary ; on the other side it was public or royal.
It was neither wholly the one nor wholly the other. The
assumption of strict royal control — presumably as a condition of the grant — prevented the system from being
wholly proprietary ; the need which the king had of the
resources of the patentees made their function indispensable. While founding a royal colony he made use of the
patentees, and of no others, as his agents or appointees for
the work. They thus not only managed the trade of the
colonies, but governed them, though they performed the
latter function as the immediate representatives of the king.
If we call Virginia under this charter a royal province, we
must remember that it had peculiar features, unlike the
royal provinces of later times and such as were characteristic
of the earliest stage of colonization. It was, in other words,
a rudimentary or transitional form of organization, which
was destined to give way to others that were more self-
consistent.

The problem which now confronted the patentees of 1606
was briefly this : with the limited capital at their disposal
they must procure a sufficient number of colonists for their
purpose, convey them in the small sailing craft of the time
across the ocean, establish them in chosen sites on the western shore of the Atlantic, and maintain and protect them
there until they should become self-supporting. As precedents to guide them in this task they had the experience
of various European nations, especially Spain and Portugal,
so far as it had then gone ; the history of the plantations
which had been established or were in process of establishment in Ireland ; and the recent experiment of Raleigh in

trans-oceanic colonization. It is to be noted that very much
of the experience upon which they could draw for examples
had been gained by purely commercial companies, which
had limited their efforts to the founding of trading factories
in the East. The dreams of the discoverers concerning the
wealth of the Indies and the routes which might lead to it
also influenced their minds at the outset, as did, even to a
larger extent, the success of the Spanish in working the
Mexican and Peruvian mines.

These precedents had an influence in determining the
selection of colonists, the form of the colonies planted, and
the objects toward which in the early years the efforts of the
colonists were directed. To Spain, to mines and possible
routes to the South Sea, we find abundant reference both in
the instructions of the early patentees and in the writings of
the first generation of colonizers. The impulse to exploration among the early settlers and their patrons was due
largely to the example of Spain and to the hypothesis of
Verrazano concerning the location of the Western Sea.
But these explorations failed to reveal a second Potosi, while
from any mountain top which they could reach it was impossible to discern the shores of that ocean concerning which
the natives and the early navigators told such alluring tales.
The Alleghanies presented an obstacle to discovery and cut
off access to the interior of the continent. Aversion to life
among the Indians had a similar confining effect. Hence
mining and discovery on an ambitious scale soon faded out
of English-American colonization, and left colonies of the
agricultural type, with commercial, political, and social interests which grew up in connection therewith.

The form assumed by these colonies was the resultant of
the combined action of the patentees or proprietors who
were resident in England, and of the settlers who took up
their residence in America. The proprietors planned the
enterprises, selected the colonists, appointed and instructed
the officials and factors who had immediate charge of the
work of settlement, furnished the vessels which transported
the settlers across the ocean and which carried supplies and
products of the colonies to and fro for an indefinite period

thereafter. The proprietors were the investors in these enterprises, and, under the more or less rigid supervision of the crown, their administrators ; resources and administrative direction, in the full sense of the term, though to varying degrees, came from them. Being at the outset merchants, or knights and noblemen who were acting under the commercial impulse, they were guided, as we have said, to an extent by the experience of older commercial companies. But in the main we must suppose that their plans involved an immediate adaptation of means to ends. They attempted to give such form to their colonies, and to support them in such way, as seemed best adapted to the conditions as they found them. Perhaps the influence of earlier experience is seen more clearly in the organization assumed by the patentees themselves, than in any of the colonies which they founded.

The colonists, with their resident officials, furnished the labor power and superintending skill which constituted the essence of the colony itself. They faced the perils of the outward voyage, and the still greater risk of famine, disease, and death in the new settlements. Their labor cleared the forests, built the towns, cultivated the fields, and established all the relations through which the food supply of the colony was procured. Such returns, in agricultural products, lumber, furs, dyestuffs, ores, fish, as the proprietors might hope to receive from their investment, came directly from the efforts of the colonists. The knowledge of the new country by which the proprietors must be guided in the development of their policy came from the labors and observations of the colonists. Though they were under direction from home, yet the colonists must in the main provide for their own defence, develop relations with the natives, give spirit and extension to the institutions of government which had been mapped out for them by the proprietors. In such close interaction between proprietors and planters as has just been indicated, appears the essential nature of colonization under the earliest proprietary form. Then economic interests were of prime importance, and the connection between the colony and its proprietors was especially close. Later, the colony became economically more independent, and developed a more than rudimentary political organism. With these changes the proprietary province in its later form appears, and exists under conditions of greater freedom and with characteristics different from those of the mere plantation. Reference to these general facts will, it is believed, contribute to a clearer understanding of the nature of the earliest English colonies.

By the patentees of 1606 two colonies were planted, one at Jamestown in South Virginia and the other at Sagadahoc in North Virginia ; the former by the London group of adventurers, the latter by the Plymouth group. Sir Thomas Gates, Sir George Somers, Richard Hakluyt, Bartholomew Gosnold, and a little later Sir Thomas Smith, were the leading patrons of the first colony, while Chief Justice Popham and Sir Ferdinando Gorges most actively promoted the interests of the second. The great majority of the patentees — who were at the same time councillors of both colonies — belonged to the English knighthood, the names of only a few merchants appearing among them. They belonged distinctively to the English official and military class, though many of them were deeply interested in discovery, trade, and colonization, and were members of companies which were engaged in such enterprises in Europe and the East. One of their number, Richard Hakluyt, was a systematic student of geography and colonization, and could bring to their attention such useful precedents as history afforded.

An "instruction by way of advice," thought to have been prepared by Hakluyt, under the direction of the royal council,[1] was given to the first body of colonists that was sent out, for their guidance in selecting a place of settlement. With the resolve perhaps that the errors of Raleigh's colonists should not be repeated, Newport and his followers were directed to settle on the bank of some navigable river. That they might be the better protected against possible attack by the Spanish, they should establish their colony

[1] Neill, History of the Virginia Company, 8; Brown, Genesis of the United States, 79.

some distance inland, but should have a small outpost near the sea to warn the main settlement of approaching danger. With a view to the possible discovery of a route to the South Sea — a prominent object of pursuit now as in the time of Gilbert — a river should be selected whose source was far inland, and if they chanced upon several rivers with branches, let them choose the one which "bendeth most toward the northwest, for that way you shall soonest find the other sea." The importance of selecting a healthy location for the settlement was enforced, and directions given respecting the opening of trade and other relations with the natives. That the colonists were regarded as a unit under centralized control, and that they should be manipulated so as best to secure the objects of the managers, is shown by the advice concerning the method of settlement. They were told that, after their food and munitions had been landed, it would be well to divide the colonists into three groups, one to build and fortify the town, attention being first paid to the storehouse ; the second to clear and prepare ground for planting ; the third to explore the river above the settlement. Dispersion of the colonists was not contemplated. The establishment of a single fortified post which should serve as a centre for exploration, for the discovery of mines, for trade with the Indians, and the exploiting of the resources of the country for the support of the colonists and the benefit of the adventurers, is the type of colonization suggested by the "advice." Captain Newport, the commander of the expedition, would soon return to England for additional supplies and colonists ; he would carry with him specimens of the products of the colony, and as full information as it was possible to secure respecting the country and its resources. He would thus act as an intermediary between the colony and those who supported and governed it ; but no one was to be allowed to return without a passport, and nothing should be written which might discourage others. "The way to prosper and achieve good success is to make yourselves all of one mind for the good of your country and your own." Of the issue of similar instructions to those who settled in North Virginia we have no record, but it is not improbable that such were issued, as they proceeded from the council which had jurisdiction over both colonies, and since also the type of colony formed at Sagadahoc was the same, so far as the nature of the country would admit, as that established at Jamestown.

Of the methods used by the adventurers at the outset to procure colonists we have no information, but the lists given by Smith for the Jamestown settlement show that from one-third to one-half bore the designation of gentlemen, while the rest were artisans and laborers. During the early years no women were employed and only a few boys. An effort was made to have each of the important trades represented in the colony, but agriculture became by the force of circumstances so predominant and inclusive as an occupation, that it absorbed the services of gentlemen as well as laborers. Among the gentlemen were doubtless some of decayed fortune and doubtful reputations, but the positively criminal element in this emigration was probably small. The laborers came largely from the yeomanry of England, the agricultural tenants and laborers who, owing to persistently low wages or displacement by war or other cause, had become so reduced in circumstances as to look upon removal to a new and distant continent as likely to result in gain.

The colonies which were founded at Sagadahoc and Jamestown were both plantations, owned, officered, and managed by the proprietors or company.[1] The colonists were servants of the company. They were freely transported to Virginia in its vessels, and there worked for the company under prescribed regulations. They were fed and housed out of the products of the total labor of the colony, supplemented by cargoes of provisions received from home. When, if ever, the colony became able to furnish a surplus product, — lumber, furs, tobacco, — it was sent home in the vessels of the company and sold for the benefit of the adventurers. A profit, supposedly large, was also made by the adventurers and officers of their vessels on European goods taken to the colony and sold. These, as well as supplies of provisions

---

[1] See a suggestive article by L. D. Scisco on The Plantation Type of Colony in Am. Hist. Rev. VIII. 260.

from England, were regularly stored in a magazine or storehouse, under the charge of a cape-merchant, whence they
were delivered to the colonists. The magazine, and the
wharf where the supplies from England were loaded and
whence the products of the colony were shipped, were the
economic centres of the settlement. The ships which
brought out colonists and transported cargoes back and
forth, were most important connecting links between the
colony and its proprietors. Until the colony became self-
supporting, its very existence depended on the prompt arrival
of supplies. At Jamestown, under the first charter, they
measured time by the intervals between "supplies"; later
the periods in the history of the colony were measured by
governorships. At this early period the duties of the
colonial officials were more economic than political. They
had to attend to a hundred petty details of colony house-
keeping, and these overshadowed in number and importance
the political, military, or judicial functions which they had
to perform. They were more truly overseers and factors
than governors, councillors, and judges in the later meaning
of those terms. The captains who commanded the vessels
which brought supplies, by virtue of this function, and independent of any office which they might hold, exerted a great
influence over the fortunes of the colony.

Much light will be thrown on the nature of these settlements by studying the form in which they were made. As
we have seen, in selecting a site, reference was had to necessities of defence, healthfulness, and accessibility to navigable water. Jamestown was located on a peninsula which
extended into the James river from its northern bank, and
where the adjacent channel was broad and so deep that ships
could be moored to trees on the shore. As it was more than
thirty miles from the mouth of the river, it was thought to
be sufficiently protected against Spanish attack, while it was
accessible to the interior of the country which the colonists
wished to explore and with which they desired to open relations of various kinds. The result proved that healthfulness
was, perhaps, not sufficiently considered in the selection of
the site, while there was no cleared land in the vicinity, and

much exhausting labor in felling trees was at once imposed on the settlers.

A location was selected at Sagadahoc which, so far as the region admitted or necessitated, was similar to that chosen for Jamestown. A sandy and rocky peninsula on the western bank of the Kennebec river near its mouth was selected for the purpose. In the channel opposite, or in an inlet adjacent to the peninsula, vessels could be anchored or moored. The situation was healthful, and the labor of clearing not so great as on the James river. The remoteness of the Spaniard from latitude forty-three and one-half degrees made it unnecessary to settle far inland, and the Frenchman, who was establishing himself at Port Royal and other points to the eastward, had not then developed activity as a colonist sufficient to make his presence seem dangerous.

On both rivers the first work of the colonists after landing and clearing sufficient ground was the building of a fort. These were rectangular or triangular palisaded enclosures, so situated that one or more sides were adjacent to the water. Of the one at Sagadahoc, named Saint George, a contemporary plan [1] has been preserved, which shows that walls surrounded the entire settlement. Within it were located about nine dwellings, besides a chapel, a storehouse, munition house, court of guard, kitchen, buttery, bakehouse, smithery, and cooperage. That all of these were actually built cannot be affirmed, but they were planned, while provision was made that the leading officials should have separate dwellings. At the angles of the fort small cannon were placed. Outside the walls space was cleared for gardens and cultivated fields. This drawing throws a more vivid light on the character of this settlement than any other source of information we have concerning it. It suggests a communal group like a trading factory in the East Indies.

Of the fort at Jamestown no plan or drawing of date earlier than 1620 has been preserved.[2] But from contemporary descriptions we know in general the form and character of the settlement. "The fifteenth day of June" (1607),

---

[1] Brown, Genesis of the United States, 190 *et seq.*; Publications of the Gorges Society, Thayer, Sagadahoc Colony, 167 *et seq.*

[2] Tyler, Cradle of the Republic, frontispiece.

writes George Percy, " we [1] had built and finished our fort, which was triangle wise, having three bulwarks at every corner like a half-moon, and four or five pieces of artillery mounted in them." Smith states that when autumn came no houses for the settlers had been built, their cabins were " worse than naught," and the tents, under which many had probably lived, were rotten.[2]   But we know that by January, 1608, several buildings had been erected within the fort, among which were a storehouse [3] for provision and ammunition, a chapel, and dwellings for at least a part of the colonists. On the arrival of Newport with the first supply from England, early in January, a fire broke out which consumed a part of the palisade and all the buildings in the fort with the exception of three.   Clothing and provisions were destroyed, and the minister, Mr. Hunt, lost his library.   But with the assistance of Newport and his men the damage was soon repaired and the houses and chapel were rebuilt in somewhat improved fashion and arrangement.

William Strachey has left a description [4] of Jamestown fort as it was when Gates and Somers, and later Lord Delaware, arrived in 1610, and we may be certain that it pictures the settlement substantially as it was during all the early years of its existence.   The fort was triangular in shape, one side of the triangle being parallel and adjacent to the river.   It was surrounded with a palisade of planks and strong posts of oak, walnut, and other woods, all driven four feet into the ground.   The palisade extended along the river bank 140 yards, accommodating itself thus to the nature of the ground, while the palisade on each of the other sides of the triangle was only one hundred yards in length.[5]   At every one of the three angles a bulwark,

[1] Brown, Genesis, 165.

[2] True Relation, Arber, Works of Captain John Smith, 9.

[3] Letter of Francis Perkins, Brown, Genesis, 175 ; Smith, Advertisements for the Unexperienced, in Arber, 957 ; Wingfield in Arch. Am. IV. 96 ; Smith, True Relation, and Map, in Arber.

[4] A True Repertory, etc., in Purchas, Pilgrimes, IV. 1752 ; Tyler, The Cradle of the Republic, 25, 69.

[5] This means that the palisade adjacent to the river extended some distance beyond one or both of the southern angles of the fort.

or watch-tower, was built, in each of which one or two small cannon were mounted. Within the palisade and along each of its three sides was "a settled street of houses,"[1] or more properly "cabins covered with clapboard and thatched with reeds or covered with bark." In the middle of the enclosure was a market-place, storehouse, *corps de garde*, and chapel. At each of the bulwarks was a gate defended by a demi-culverin, but the principal gate was the one which opened toward the river, through which passed to and fro the chief traffic of the settlement. During the administration of Smith a well had been dug in the fort, but the water from it proved to be brackish and unwholesome. From these statements and descriptions the substantial identity of the fort at Jamestown with that at Sagadahoc is evident.

The first settlers landed at Jamestown in May, 1607, while the landing at Sagadahoc was not effected till near the close of August. The result of this was that the northern colony could raise nothing for its subsistence during the first winter and had to depend wholly on the supplies they brought with them, additional supplies from England, and such food as they could procure by hunting, fishing, and trading with the Indians. The number of colonists who came out on the first vessels was about 120, substantially the same numerically as those who accompanied Newport on his first voyage. But a great mistake had been made in the timing of the voyage to Sagadahoc, and this probably contributed as much toward the failure of that enterprise as any other cause. Apparently by the middle of December it had become evident that the full number of colonists could not find subsistence till the following summer. Hence at that time all except forty-five of the colonists returned to England, accompanied by complaints of the severity of the climate. This was the beginning of

---

[1] It is stated in Smith's Generall Historie (Arber, 486) that when Smith left the colony in October, 1609, Jamestown was strongly palisaded and contained some fifty or sixty houses. It is not probable that all of these could have been located within the fort proper, not at least if, as Strachey says, it covered only half an acre of ground.

the end.   Those who remained seem to have been adequately
supplied with food, and there was not much sickness ; but
the suspension of their activities during the long, cold winter
proved too much for the weakened resolution of the forty-
five who remained.   It is probable that during the next
spring one or more small tracts were planted, but Sagadahoc
was abandoned before it became in any true sense an agricultural settlement.   A pinnace was built, and with it a few
voyages of discovery were made up the river and along the
coast to the east and west.   Traffic on a small scale was
opened with the Indians, and in the main friendly relations
seem to have been established with them.   But beyond this
the Sagadahoc colonists did nothing to make themselves self-
supporting.

Acting under the "advice" from the royal council, the
officers at Jamestown at the very outset set a part of the
labor force of the community at work sowing wheat on
the area of four acres or less, from which the trees used
in the construction of the fort had just been removed.[1]
The seed for this had been brought from Europe.   Seeds
of fruits and vegetables, brought also from Europe, were
planted in this limited area, the colony garden.   A part of
the sustenance of the colony for the first year was secured
in this way.   The second year, more land having been
cleared, the experiment with English wheat was tried a
second time, but without conspicuous success.   In 1609,
while John Smith was at the head of affairs, the lesson of
cultivating maize was learned from the Indians, forty acres
were planted with it, and in this way the food-producing
capacity of the colony was greatly increased.[2]   The supply
of fish and game in the fall was very large.   The soil was
found to be exceedingly fertile.   But still the colony had
not become self-supporting or free from the danger of
famine.   Moreover, while taking these preliminary steps,
more than one serious crisis was passed, when the colony
seemed on the verge of destruction.

These small efforts had therefore to be supplemented by

---

[1] Bruce, Economic History of Virginia, 194.
[2] *Ibid.* 195 *et seq.;* Smith, Works, 154.

trade with the Indians. They, in that climate and from
soil of such fertility as that of Virginia, were able to harvest
considerable quantities of maize.[1] The Accomac Indians
produced enough to supply their needs for the entire twelvemonth. Though this was not the case with those who lived
on the mainland, yet the authorities agree in the statement
that the voyages made to the Indian settlements during the
fall and early winter found them well supplied with corn,
from which purchases were readily made by the English.
The trade thus opened served a threefold purpose; it
brought to Jamestown supplies of food without which its
continued existence would have been impossible, it opened
up friendly relations with the natives, and it facilitated and
encouraged discovery. The chief service rendered by John
Smith to the colony is to be found in the fact that when,
on the death of Studley, he became cape-merchant, he
instituted trading expeditions for the purpose of procuring
corn, and continued them at intervals during the two
winters he was in the colony. His first expedition for this
purpose was to Kecoughtan (Hampton), near the mouth of
the river. Upon this he says he " was sent." [2] Later, in the
autumn and early winter, Smith made his three famous
journeys up the Chickahominy. On the first two of these
he was moderately successful and found the natives eager
to trade. The third brought him intimately into connection with Indian life, for as a captive he was taken
through a large extent of country and brought even to
the residence of the Powhatan himself. From a later
expedition, to the York River with Captain Newport, he
returned with 250 bushels of corn, and this exploit was
repeated on two or three other occasions. In the spring of
1608 a quantity of corn is said to have been extorted[3] from
the Nansemond Indians as a condition of peace. In the
early winter of 1609 another notable trading expedition was
made to the residence of the Powhatan and of Opechancanough on the York river. By means of all of these the

[1] Bruce, 157 et seq.
[2] True Relation, in Arber, 9.
[3] Generall Historie of Virginia, Arber, 432.

store of food at the fort was increased, while Smith's energy
as a leader and his skill in dealing with the natives was
clearly revealed.

To the importance of the supplies periodically received
from England as an additional source whence the colonists
at Sagadahoc, as well as Jamestown, procured sustenance,
reference has already been made. The name was applied, at
least in Jamestown, not only to the commodities brought,
but to the vessels bringing them. Using the term in the
latter sense, only one supply, properly speaking, was sent
to Sagadahoc. It consisted of two vessels despatched by
the adventurers in the spring of 1608, followed the next
summer by a third vessel. These were loaded with commodities, sent out with a view to insure the permanence of
the colony; but these same vessels on their return voyage
carried back the entire body of colonists to England.

At Jamestown under the first charter two such supplies
arrived, while in the summer of 1609 came a third, being
part of the large fleet sent out immediately after the issue
of the second charter. The commander of all three, while
at sea, was Captain Christopher Newport, and his authority
there was supreme. The first supply consisted of two vessels, the *John and Francis* and the *Phœnix*. Of these the
former arrived at Jamestown about the middle of January,
1608, while the latter, having wintered in the West Indies,
did not reach port till the close of the following April. Newport remained with his vessel at Jamestown till April 20,
when, thinking his consort lost, he sailed for England.
Captain Nelson, with the *Phœnix*, remained at Jamestown
till June 12, when he began his return voyage. The second
supply consisted of only one ship, in which Newport arrived
early in October, 1608. He now remained in the colony two
months, when he returned to England. Nothing more was
received or heard from the mother country till seven storm-
beaten vessels came straggling in during the latter half of
the summer of 1609.[1]

The vessels were small, more likely to be under than over

[1] Works of Smith, Arber's edition, 161, 479; Letter of Gabriel Archer,
in Brown, Genesis, 328 *et seq.*

one hundred tons burden. Their voyages were few and long; the vessels might be injured or destroyed by storms, captured by pirates or by the Spaniards; disease usually prevailed to an extent on board, yellow fever if they delayed long in the tropics. Besides the officers and crew, they carried, for their size, a considerable number of colonists. Their outward cargoes consisted of a variety of supplies for the colony. Medicines, spirits, beer, clothing, household furniture and utensils, tools, arms and ammunition, seeds, domestic animals, were brought to the colony in these vessels. And in addition a variety of articles of food were brought, such as meal, bread, butter, cheese, salted meat and fish, pease, preserved fruits. These, if they arrived in good condition, added not only to the amount, but especially to the variety, of colonial fare.

But we often hear not only that they were injured on shipboard, but that they were partly or wholly destroyed while in the storehouse at Jamestown awaiting consumption. The officers and crew of the vessels had also to be supported out of the total resources of the colony during their long sojourns at Jamestown. Of this feature of the system Smith and his writers loudly and repeatedly complain. They also declare that the mariners seriously interfered with the course of Indian trade by ruthlessly bartering the tools, arms, and other possessions of the colonists for whatever the savages had which awakened their fancy or cupidity.[1] It is stated that during the fourteen weeks when the vessel which brought the second supply lay at Jamestown, nearly all the beef, pork, oil, aqua vitæ, fish, butter, cheese, beer, and other similar articles of food which had been brought over for the colonists, were consumed. Smith's indictment is repeated for a later time by Strachey, and the truth of it is admitted by the company itself.[2] Strachey charges the mariners with greatly cheapening the value of English commodities by their reckless trading with the natives.[3] Goods which were to be sold in the colony seem also to have been con-

---

[1] Arber, 95, 103, 128, and corresponding passages in the Generall Historie.
[2] True Repertory, etc., Purchas, Pilgrimes, IV. 1751.
[3] A True Declaration of Virginia, 17; Force, Tracts, III.

signed to masters and pursers of the vessels, and they refused to part with them except at enormous profits. The most which in the long run the system of supplies, with the magazine, could do for the colony was to furnish it to an extent with salted provisions, spirits, and certain foreign luxuries. The staple articles of food the colonists must produce from the soil, or procure by hunting, fishing, or traffic with the natives.

The supply, however, was more than merely a phase of the economic life of the colony. It served as the means of communication between the colony on the one side and the proprietors and home government on the other. Its commander performed in a rude way a function analogous to that of the later colonial agents. Not only did his ships carry letters, pamphlets, instructions, and other communications to and from the colony, but he himself laid before the authorities at home his view of the situation and needs of the plantation. He doubtless communicated in a similar way to the colonists the views and plans of the patentees. Newport at least performed to its full extent the function as an intermediary, and might well do it, for he was a member of the plantation council. Later commanders lacked the official prestige of Newport.

The early colonists at Jamestown, as elsewhere, had to struggle not only against famine, but against disease. Smith states, as we have seen, that, when the first autumn came, suitable shelter had not been provided by the settlers. For such neglect, which the warmth of the climate and natural inertia permitted, the settlement paid dearly in the death of nearly forty of its members and the paralysis of effort through the sickness of the rest. At one time during this first visitation there were but six healthy men in the fort. Gosnold, the most trusted member of the council, died, and nearly all the other councillors were seriously ill. Industry almost ceased, and the leaders were driven to Indian trade as the only escape from certain destitution. Heat, the miasma of the swamps, the general unsanitary conditions of the settlement, poor and insufficient food, combined in their effect on the untrained bodies of the colonists to produce this result. It is only the first of a hundred such phenomena which have appeared not only in the early settlements, but in the military camps of the colonial wars, and in those of later conflicts down even to our own times. The death-rate among the first generation of Europeans who attempted to settle America was enormous, and it required a high birth-rate and frequent reënforcements from home to counterbalance the loss. Nearly all of those who came to Southern Virginia during the first two years of its existence as a colony perished in the process of becoming acclimated. The liabilities to sickness and death in the earliest settlements were among the greatest obstacles to colonization. They occasioned great losses to proprietors, and furnished, as in this case, a strong temptation to the abandonment of colonies during the early years of their existence. But after a few colonies had been founded, which became subsidiary food centres, and a degree of experience had thus been gained, suffering in this form greatly decreased, and does not constitute a prominent feature in the history of the later colonies.

Life in the compact settlements and under the trying circumstances which have been described, soon tested the wisdom of the plan which the crown and patentees had devised for the government of the colonies, and proved it to be ill adapted to the purpose. The executive power was lodged in the council ; the president was its creature, and of himself had no special independence or authority. Dissensions naturally soon broke out in the council, and these contributed materially to the defeat of the enterprise. Of such dissensions we hear something in Sagadahoc. In the case of both colonies the crown had ordered that the instructions designating who the councillors were should not be opened till the vessels arrived at their destination. Thus the possibility of such conflicts as that which may have occurred between Sir Richard Grenville and Ralph Lane was avoided. On the arrival at Sagadahoc it was found that six — or possibly eight — out of the thirteen required by the charter had been designated as councillors. They elected George Popham, brother of the chief patron, and himself already an old man,

to be president. A long list of subordinate officials were
also appointed, among whom Tudor military titles appear
with great prominence. The list included an admiral,
vice-admiral, marshal, master of the ordnance, sergeant
major, captain of the fort, corporal, secretary, chaplain,
and searcher. These offices were distributed chiefly among
the councillors.

We hear later that the president was charged with weak-
ness and lack of proper self-assertion. Raleigh Gilbert also
became impressed [1] with the idea that the colony lay within
the territories formerly granted to his father, and, thinking
that the charter of 1574 had not lapsed, sought to raise a
faction in England and the colony in support of his claims
under it. Sir Ferdinando Gorges presently learned of this,
and in his irritation suggested to Robert Cecil, the secretary
of state, that the king should take the colony into his own
hands. But intervention by the government did not come.
In the course of the winter George Popham died, and Gilbert was chosen as his successor. When, the next season,
the vessels brought from England the news of the death
of Chief Justice Popham and of Sir John Gilbert,
elder brother of Raleigh Gilbert, the president thought it
necessary that he should return home. No one was left who
was willing to take his place. This then became an added
reason for the abandonment of the colony.

But in the history of Jamestown and under the severer
tests which its fortunes imposed, we can clearly trace the
progress of dissensions in the council and the elimination of
one member after another until a practical autocracy was
the result. While the first expedition under Newport was
at sea, rumors of an intended mutiny were circulated, and
John Smith, for alleged concealment of this, or other connection with it, was kept in restraint for some four months,
not being fully released till some six weeks after the colonists arrived in Virginia. Smith declared that in this he
suffered gross injustice. But Wingfield apparently believed
to an extent in the complicity of Smith, for he was later
fined two hundred pounds for saying that Smith "did con-

[1] Baxter, Gorges, III. 158 *et seq.*

ceal an intended mutiny."[1]   In this affair, whatever it was, the seed of further dissension was sown.

On the arrival of the colonists in Virginia the seals were broken, and it was found that the members of the council were Bartholomew Gosnold, Edward Maria Wingfield, Christopher Newport, John Smith, John Ratcliffe,[2] John Martin, and George Kendall. Smith was not admitted to his place on the board till his release from detention. Wingfield was chosen president for the first year. Of the pretentious list of official titles which appears at Sagadahoc we hear almost nothing.[3]

We soon learn that Kendall was removed from the council and imprisoned, "for that it did manifestly appeare he did practice to sowe discord between the president and councell."[4]   But serious troubles began during the first period of sickness in the colony. President Wingfield was not a man of great energy. He did not join the exploring expeditions, or try very actively to open trade with the Indians. Toward some of the serious problems which the colonists were facing he maintained a passive attitude, remaining quietly at Jamestown and administering affairs there. Though a man of scrupulous honor, he was not fitted for the rough task of piloting the colony through to a condition of economic stability, and he probably knew it. We can hardly imagine him disciplining the indolent colonists as Smith did at a later time, and to skill in dealing with the natives he seems to have made no pretension. Free and easy administrative methods, characteristic of the time and of colonial life everywhere, were also tolerated. The cape-merchant[5] received merchandise from the vessels in gross, and delivered it in such instalments as the president desired without preparing itemized lists. " I likewise," says Wingfield, "as occation moved me, spent them (*i.e.* commodities) in trade or by guift amongst the Indians. So likewise did Captain Newport take

---

[1] Wingfield's Discourse; Smith, True Relation, Map, and Generall Historie.

[2] His real name is said to have been Sicklemore.

[3] Arber, 105, 408.

[4] Wingfield's Discourse, Arch. Am. IV. 80.

[5] *Ibid.* 86.

of them, when he went up to discover the King's river, what he thought good, without any noate of his hand mentioning the certainty; and disposed of them as was fitt for him. Of these likewise I could make no accompt; only I was well assured I had never bestowed the valewe of three penny whitles to my own use, nor to the private use of any other; for I never carryed any favorite over with me, or intertayned any there."

But, as the period of sickness progressed, Wingfield felt compelled to keep a strict watch over the limited stores of spirits, oil, vinegar, and similar articles. He refused some informal applications from councillors for such articles, but declared that he would not do so if warrants were duly presented, or if the council voted for an increase of allowances to all members alike; but this it would not do. The president's sudden demand for vouchers provoked charges that he was keeping the supplies for his own use. Because of the administrative looseness which had prevailed, the written proofs were lacking, and it was difficult for him to do more than assert his innocence.

As soon as Wingfield felt that he was being criticised, he offered to resign. Presently, however, it appeared that Ratcliffe, Martin, and Smith, influenced by Gabriel Archer, who was not a member of the council, had formed a plan to depose the president. This plan they executed very informally and without resistance on the part of Wingfield, electing Ratcliffe in his place. At an equally informal hearing, which took place the next day, Archer was appointed recorder, and in that capacity read a list of charges against Wingfield, and the others presented certain personal complaints against him. Except in the case of Smith, these referred to the alleged niggardliness of Wingfield in dispensing the common store, while he lived in plenty himself. The charges, so far as they implied wrong on his part, Wingfield stoutly[1] denies. Smith said that the president charged him with falsehood and twitted him of his humble origin. During the hearing Wingfield declared that he would appeal to the king, and was detained as a prisoner in

[1] Wingfield's Discourse, Arch. Am. IV. 88.

the pinnace till Newport on his second voyage took him back
to England.

Owing to the death of Gosnold, the absence of Newport,
the removal of Kendall, and the suspension of Wingfield, the
number of the council in Virginia was now reduced to three,
Ratcliffe as president, Smith, and Martin. For some time
no effort was made to fill the vacancies. Wingfield was
tried under two suits for damages, found guilty, and heavily
fined. "Then Mr. Recorder did very learnedly comfort me,
that, if I had wrong, I might bring my writ of error in
London; whereat I smiled."[1]   Further light was soon
thrown on the functions of the president, as well as on the
bitterness of faction, by the statement that Ratcliffe beat
James Read, that Smith and Read struck him in turn.[2]
For this, by a jury, Read was found guilty and condemned
to be hanged. But just before he was to be turned off, he
accused Kendall privately before the president of a mutiny,
"and so escaped himself." Kendall, whose mutiny seems to
have taken the form of an attempt to abandon the colony
and return to England,[3] was found guilty and shot. In all
these events Archer doubtless bore a prominent part, as he
was now apparently the chief authority among the colonists
on legal and political forms.

As one member after another of the council was eliminated
and the power to fill vacancies was left dormant, Smith
begins to appear in the foreground. To him now came the
opportunity to show the talent which he thought till this
time had been unjustly obscured. On the most famous of
his journeys up the Chickahominy, two of his companions
were slain. Four weeks elapsed before he was able to

[1] Wingfield's Discourse, Arch. Am. IV. 89.

[2] Wingfield, though without special confirmation from other sources, states
that it was common for the president, councillors, and other officers to beat
men at their pleasure. " One lyeth sick till death, another walketh lame,
the third crieth out of all his boanes ; which myseryes they do take upon
their consciences to come to them by this their almes of beating. Were this
whipping, lawing, beating and hanging in Virginia knowne in England, I
fear it would drive many well-affected mynds from this honorable action of
Virginia."   Ibid. 90.

[3] Arber, 13, 97.

return to Jamestown. In the meantime Ratcliffe, on his own responsibility and contrary both to the king's instructions and to the agreement previously reached by the councillors, had admitted Archer to the council.[1] The new councillor, with far more than Puritan rigor, had Smith indicted for murder on the ground that he was responsible for the death of his two followers who had been slain by the Indians, and the Levitical law required that "he that[2] killeth a man, he shall be put to death." "He had his trial," says Wingfield, "the same day of his return, and, I believe, his hanging the same or the next day, so speedy is our law there. But it pleased God to send Captain Newport unto us the same evening, to our unspeakable comfort; whose arrival saved Mr. Smith's life and mine, because he took me out of the pinnace" (where because of exposure Wingfield's health was suffering) "and gave me leave to lie in the town." Such occurrences as these make the reader wonder whether this settlement should be regarded as a military camp or a tropical plantation, and of what avail in remote Virginia was the guaranty in the charter that subjects dwelling in the colony should enjoy all the rights and immunities which were possessed by those living within the realm. Individual property did not as yet exist at Jamestown, and life was subject to the whim of one or two councillors.

Yet Gabriel Archer, who, though a judge, was calmly ignoring the precedents of English criminal law, was at the same time talking about calling a "parliament" in the little village of Jamestown. Wingfield states that, by the arrival of Newport, "was prevented a parliament, which the new councillor, Mr. Recorder, intended there to summon." We may suppose that his innovating zeal was quenched when he found the membership of the council suddenly increased and himself excluded on the ground of irregular appointment.[3]

[1] Arch. Am. IV. 83, 93; True Relation, in Arber, 22; Brown, Genesis, I. 67.

[2] Both Wingfield and the writers of Smith's Generall Historie state that Archer based his charge on the Levitical law, and the passage referred to, Lev. xxiv. 17-21, is supposed to contain the provision on which the indictment was based. Arch. Am. IV. 95.

[3] True Relation, Arber, 23.

Newport, on his arrival with the first supply, again took his seat as councillor. He brought with him Matthew Scrivener, who had received appointment as councillor in England. Smith and Wingfield were released and took their seats. The advice of Wingfield may be supposed to have again carried some weight. So long as Newport remained, the revival of government according to the charter and instructions was assured.

Newport, on his return to England, took Wingfield and Archer with him. Martin returned on the *Phœnix*. Ratcliffe was left as president, with Smith and Scrivener as the only two councillors. After further explorations up the James river had been abandoned, Smith made his first voyage along the shores of Chesapeake bay. While he was absent, if we are to believe the account of Smith's friends, Ratcliffe was guilty of wastefulness and extravagance. On Smith's return, in July, in response, it is said, to a general demand, the second president was deposed, and, if we are right in our interpretation, Scrivener was made president by Smith[1] for the unexpired term. On Smith's return, in September, from his second voyage up the Chesapeake, Scrivener gave way to him, and the hero of Werowocomoco became president of Virginia. He was not president in the original sense, as provided in the charter and instructions, but autocrat of the colony. Of opposition on the part of the other two councillors there was practically none. Conciliar government had again practically disappeared.

But in less than three weeks it was revived again by the arrival of Newport with the second supply. As in the previous January, so now, the autocratic power of the president, or of the president and one or two councillors, was broken by the arrival of additional councillors[2] and instructions from England. The control of the proprietors and crown over the remote settlement was thus periodically reasserted, while during the intervals between it drifted along under exclusively local influences. The arrival of Newport with the first supply saved Smith's life; his arrival with the

---

[1] The Map, Arber, 115, 121 ; Generall Historie, Arber, 420, 433.
[2] Arber, 122.

second supply curtailed Smith's power.   This, it is believed, should be borne carefully in mind by those who would explain aright the criticisms, in the later writings which go under Smith's name, of those who planned and brought the second supply.   Little or no criticism of Newport's course prior to this time appears, while what he now attempted to do was in many respects only a continuation of what Smith himself had undertaken.   The statement in the Generall Historie[1] that, "although Smith was President, yet after the arrival of the second supply, the Major part of the Councell had the authoritie and ruled it as they listed," throws much light on what followed.

Judging from events, one must infer that Newport's second return from the colony had occasioned a forward movement on the part of the patentees in England.   Seventy new colonists, among whom were three women, were procured ; two councillors, captains Richard Waldo and Peter Wynne, were appointed, while Francis West, brother of Lord Delaware, now came to the colony for the first time.[2] A refiner of metals appears.   Eight Hollanders and Poles, skilful in the production of naval stores, were sent out to instruct the colonists in that form of production.   Under orders also from England the Powhatan was to be crowned by Newport, and the James river explored for some distance above the falls.   It is stated in Smith's writings that Newport had been instructed to find the South Sea, a mine of gold, or Raleigh's lost colonists.   If the instruction had been given in this form, it was certainly somewhat absurd ; but still it included two of the objects which from the first had been prominently before the minds of the proprietors, and in the work of exploration Smith had certainly always been willing to share.   He had twice taken a considerable body of men to explore the shores of the Chesapeake, when the demand for their aid in procuring a food supply for the colony was as great as it was after Newport's second return. But if we are to trust his later compilations, he now opposed such projects, and insisted that all measures which did not lead directly to the procuring of a food supply

[1] Arber, 435.   [2] Generall Historie, Arber, 438.

should be avoided. The colony he thought not sufficiently far advanced to engage in the production of naval stores. He properly regarded the coronation of the Indian chief as an idle show. It is no doubt true that the presence of seventy more mouths to fill in the colony, and that on the approach of winter, increased the seriousness of the food problem. Neither mines, nor western seas, nor lost colonists were found, though the march of four days above the falls was in itself a commendable achievement. Newport, as a matter of course, could take back to England only specimens of pitch,[1] tar, glass, and potash made in the colony, and with them a cargo of clapboard and wainscot. The results were small, but the policy was certainly not mistaken, even though the Dutchmen did later barter away a few firearms to the natives.

If the document which we possess is a correct copy, Smith sent to the royal council by Newport's returning vessel a letter[2] the equal of which for rude frankness and imperious self-conceit it would be difficult to find in the whole body of American correspondence. In reply to alleged criticisms by the council of factional strife in the colony and of a project of Ratcliffe to divide the country, and to a command that they obey Newport and defray the cost of his voyage by the return cargo or "remain as banished men," Smith sharply criticised almost every phase of the council's policy, and in effect told them that they knew nothing of the conditions in the colony except from the information which he by his writings and map had conveyed to them. He heavily discounted the value of Newport's cargo to the colonists, complained of the amount consumed by his mariners, declared that the colony was not prepared to produce naval stores, and roundly asserted that he was opposed to obeying Newport's instructions, though he was overruled in the matter by the council. The implication of this letter is that, if knowledge, experience, and practical insight entitle one to leadership in an enterprise, Smith, rather than the members of the royal council, had the right to instruct. With that idea in mind, he entreated them, in the oft-quoted passage,

[1] Generall Historie, Arber, 443.   [2] *Ibid.* 442.

to send thirty artisans, fishermen, and farmers, rather than a thousand inexperienced and unseasoned men, of whom there were far too many at Jamestown.

This was excellent advice, and, like many other passages in Smith's writings, it shows that he was by instinct a good colonizer. And yet, though a few months later the publications of the company were filled with the same sentiment, it is by no means necessary to suppose that the patentees were indebted to Smith for the idea. How much weight his representations may have had with them it is quite impossible to affirm. The judicious critic, however, will not be inclined to overestimate [1] it.

In the course of the winter of 1609 the three councillors who were left, on Newport's departure, as Smith's associates, died. Scrivener and Waldo were drowned in the James river, while we are informed only of the fact, and not of the circumstances, of Captain Wynne's death. [2] Thus Smith was again left as the sole magistrate and overseer in the colony, and so continued till May, 1609. Taking advantage of this fact, in a speech to the settlers he told them that laziness would no longer be tolerated as in the days when the council held authority. "Seeing nowe the authoritie resteth wholly in my selfe, you must obay this for a law, that he that will not worke shall not eat, except by sicknesse he be disabled." [3] The letters patent should be read to them each week, that they might know the president's power extended even to life and death; and now that "there are no more councils to

---

[1] In speaking of events and views which for their authority rest wholly on the Map and the Generall Historie, which were compiled by Smith or were issued under his name after he left Virginia, it is necessary to speak hypothetically. The sufficient reason for this is to be found in the partisan tone which runs through all those publications. A comparison of them with the True Relation and with the other sources which have survived, reveals exaggerations and a tendency to exalt the merits of Smith, which decidedly weaken their authority as historic documents. In most cases it is impossible to affirm that their statements are false ; still, so highly colored are many of them, that, without further evidence, it is impossible to accept them without question. It is fortunate that we are left solely to the guidance of these authorities only for a few months of Virginia history.

[2] Map, in Arber, 143, 157 ; also mentioned in Generall Historie.

[3] *Ibid.* 149, 466.

protect you, nor curb my endeavors," let every offender "assuredly expect his due punishment." These statements would indicate that Smith was ready to imitate the summary measures which had nearly cost him his own life, and that he was not going to allow the settlers even the benefit of jury trial, a right which was granted to them by the royal instructions. But his threatened severity does not seem to have banished indolence or faction from the settlement, for later the president, in his famous speech to the drones,[1] had to declare that every one who gathered not every day as much as he himself did, should be banished from the fort and sent across the river, there to support himself or starve. Notwithstanding these severe orders, it is stated that only about one-fourth of the settlers were vigorous workers. By them the Indian trade was continued and the settlement defended against the attacks of the hostile savages who lived in its immediate vicinity. Within the space of three months three or four lasts of pitch, tar, and potash were made, and a trial of glass produced ; also a well was dug in the fort, twenty dwellings were built, the church was newly covered, a blockhouse was built on the Neck for protection against the Indians, and thirty or forty acres of ground were planted. The domestic animals in the colony were also rapidly multiplying. But as the supply of grain brought from England was eaten by the rats, the settlers had to rely almost wholly on the country for supplies. Many were sent down the river for oysters and fish, and others, under West, to the region of the Falls. Some also were billeted among the savages. Thus under the vigorous rule of Smith, in which he himself set the example of activity, the colony survived the winter in fair condition. But it was still confined to Jamestown and its immediate vicinity, was not self-supporting or beyond the possibility of ultimate failure.[2] Internal dissensions and sloth had not been removed and could not be, so long as the system of joint management was maintained. Friendly relations with the Indians had not been securely

[1] Arber, 156, 473.

[2] A True and Sincere Declaration. Statements from report of Argall, Brown, Genesis, 344.

established.   Government through a council had broken
down, and autocratic administration had proved under the
circumstances inadequate to meet the needs of the colony.
What it needed was a larger investment in the enterprise, a
larger population, with such components as would make the
formation of homes possible, the multiplication of settlements in more healthful localities, the development of a free
tenantry, or better a yeomanry of freeholders.   As the result
of the reports brought back by Newport on his last voyage,
steps were being taken in England which were gradually to
make these changes possible.

CHAPTER III

VIRGINIA AS A PROPRIETARY PROVINCE. THE ADMINISTRATION OF SIR THOMAS SMITH

PART
I.

WE know from an authoritative source[1] that the decisive reason which led the patentees to apply for a new charter was the defects which experience revealed in the form of government created by the charter of 1606. Whether the appointment of the councils by the crown was found to be an important source of difficulty, we are not informed; but we are told that in this connection a chief object of desire on the part of the patentees was to send out a large supply of colonists under " one able and absolute governor." " The equality of governors " in the colony, it was further declared, and " some outrages and follies committed by them," " had a little shaken so tender a body." To the patentees, as to all others who were concerned, it was evident that the attempt to govern the colony through a resident council had proved a failure. The opposite system was now to be tried.

A second cause of evil was thought to be the length of the outward voyages by the way of the West Indies, and the consequent exposure of the passengers to disease and to attacks by the Spaniard. As a means of remedying this evil Captain Argall was sent out with a single vessel and with orders to choose the most direct route. By following a course midway between the southern and northern routes he reached Virginia in about nine weeks, and, by fishing in the waters there, not only relieved the needs of the colonists, but revealed anew the resources of the colony, especially in sturgeon. In this way one of the difficulties seemed to be solved. Already decisive steps had also been taken which

[1] A True and Sincere Declaration, Brown, Genesis, I. 342.

56

it was believed would remove the evils of the government.
Closely connected with the reform that was desired lay the
need of increasing the scope of the enterprise.   In order to
accomplish that result the number of patentees must be
enlarged, and with this the volume of contributions.   A
condition necessary to the securing of this end was the full
incorporation of the patentees and the express bestowment
upon them of the land of the colony and of rights of
government.

The change was effected through the royal charters of
1609 and 1612.   By the former the process of incorporating
the London patentees as a joint stock company, after the
manner of some of the older trading companies, was completed.   The corporate name of " The Treasurer and Company of Adventurers and Planters of the City of London for
the First Colony in Virginia," was given to them, and they
were thenceforth to have a seal.   The authority to transport
emigrants and carry on trade, which had been enjoyed by
the former patentees, was conferred on these.   But in addition they received a territory four hundred miles broad and
extending through the North American continent, with
power to grant the same to adventurers and settlers.   The
new company also received the organization necessary for
the exercise of such powers.   This consisted of a "general
court" of all the members, various subordinate courts and
committees ; a treasurer and deputy treasurer, with power
to create other offices ; and a council.   The council was the
successor of the royal council of 1606, and retained the name
of " Our Council for the said Company of Adventurers and
Planters in Virginia."   Upon it governmental powers were
bestowed, and from some of the words in the charter of 1609
one might infer that the king, through this body, intended
still to retain the government of the colony in his own hands.
But provision was also made in that charter that vacancies
in the council should be filled by the company, and by the
charter of 1612 power was expressly given to the company
to elect the council.   The effect of this was to make it a
permanent administrative body within the company, wholly
subject to its control like any other standing committee.   By

virtue of this change the patentees came to have the power of directly governing the colony, though of course, like all other corporations, they were subject to the sovereign control of crown and parliament.

The London patentees, in the form of an incorporated body, now became in the full sense of the term the proprietor of their colony. The company existed for fifteen years, and during that period it continued to perform the duties of proprietor; for that length of time the colony on the James river was a proprietary province with a commercial company as its overlord. For a brief time under the charter of 1612 the Bermuda Islands were united with Virginia as a part of the company's province; but soon a distinct corporation was organized for their government, though its members were drawn very largely from the London company.

This body was empowered to increase its membership at will. This it did by selling shares, or bills of adventure, which were transferable and represented a contribution to the common stock of £12, 10s. each.[1] Adventurers were those who invested their money in shares of this value, instead of removing to the colony as planters. Planters invested their labor, and that of their families and servants, and were entitled to shares therefor. It was agreed by the company that for the period of seven years after the issue of the new patent, that is from 1609 to 1616, the system of corporate management maintained by the former patentees should be continued in the colony. There should be no landholding or trading by individuals, but the company should, as formerly, provide all necessities and receive all products. In the meantime, such dividends as the business would warrant should be declared for the benefit of the adventurers, and the planters would be guaranteed their support.[2] At the end of the seven years the division of the

---

[1] A blank bill of adventure, entitling the holder to land in Virginia, is printed on page 471 of the Genesis of the United States. Another is printed in Va. Mag. of Hist. II. 186. The establishment of the joint stock is described in *Nova Britannia*, a pamphlet which is supposed to have been written by Alderman Robert Johnson, who was deputy treasurer of the company. It was issued in 1610. Force, Tracts, I.

[2] Brown, First Republic, 104.

lands in the colony among the adventurers and planters in proportion to their several investments, as indicated on the register of the corporation, should begin.   Thus, except the sending of women and children as well as men to the colony, no immediate departure from the plantation system established under the charter of 1606, was contemplated.   The colony was to continue for a series of years unchanged, though it was hoped that much larger investments would be made in it.   In other words, as a direct result of the charter of 1609, the planters gained no liberties, though the corporation gained many such.

Both before and after the issue of the charter of 1609 the enterprise was systematically advertised.   Letters, broadsides, and pamphlets were issued explaining the plans of the managers, and setting forth the prospective wealth and attractions of the colony.   The Plymouth[1] adventurers, with the understanding that their efforts for the time were at a standstill, were invited to coöperate.   It was declared that the only type of colonist desired was the husbandman or artisan, reared in the Protestant faith, and honest in his past life.   By the labor of these an abundance of commodities, like naval stores, would be produced, for the supply of which England was now dependent on foreign countries. Special appeals were made to the city of London and its trading companies, as well as to others.

The result of these efforts[2] was that, when the charter passed the great seal, the number of incorporators had been so increased as to include 56 city companies of London, and 659 individuals.   Of the latter 21 were peers, 96 were knights, 11 were members of the learned professions, 53 were captains, 58 were gentlemen, 110 were merchants, 282 were citizens and others not classified.   Of these about 230 subscribed for three shares or more each (£37, 10s.); 229 subscribed for less than that number.   About 200 seem to have paid in nothing.   But, as it was, the active adventurers represented the nobility, clergy, and merchants, while the planters were being drawn to a large extent from the lower classes.   A company considerable both in social weight and

---

[1] Brown, Genesis, 238.   [2] Ibid. 228.

numbers was thus brought together. Sir Thomas Smith, a prince among London merchants, an assignee of Raleigh and a charter member of several other large companies, was chosen treasurer and was reëlected to that office for nearly ten years in succession. Sir Edwin Sandys, who drafted the charter of 1609, and was rising to leadership among the opposition in the House of Commons, gradually became more influential in the management of the company. When, however, reverses came, as they not infrequently did, members fell off and it became more than usually difficult to collect subscriptions. In 1611 some returned without license from the colony, who spread damaging reports about it, and stringent provision for their restraint was introduced into the charter of 1612. To such straits also was the company then reduced for funds, that the privilege of holding lotteries was granted to it by that charter. It is stated [1] that at times during the administration of Sir Thomas Smith it was difficult to secure an attendance of twenty at the quarter courts, though, subsequent to 1619, when the office of treasurer was held by Sandys and the Earl of Southampton, two hundred were often in attendance. The membership of the company during the last four years of its existence is also said to have reached one thousand, while we have a list,[2] approaching respectably near that number, of those who joined when Smith was treasurer. At all times within this body was a group of varying size — noblemen, merchants, officials — who were constant in attendance, spent their time and energies for the company and colony, and enjoyed the honors and responsibilities which came therefrom. Among them were some of the most distinguished men in England, and when assembled they formed a dignified body.

The records of the company prior to 1619 — the period of the administration of Sir Thomas Smith — have been lost or destroyed, and a connected account of its proceedings during that time cannot be given. For the period from 1619 to 1624 — that of the Sandys-Southampton régime — very

[1] Recs. of the Co. II. 150, 158.   [2] Force, Tracts, III.

full minutes [1] of the general court and of some of the subordinate courts have been preserved.   The Orders and Constitutions,[2] compiled in 1619, are also accessible, and contain
statements of the powers and duties of the officials and committees of the company, rules of procedure followed in its
courts in the granting of land, in trade, and some other
matters.   From the Orders and Constitutions we learn that
in the company's chest, under the care of the secretary, were
kept a variety of account books, record and minute books,
and original papers, all of which, save the minutes just
referred to, have now been lost.   But the reference to these,
together with the records which have been preserved, reveals
the fact that this chartered company, at least during the
later years of its existence, did far more business annually,
and did it with greater care than any other proprietor, or
proprietary body — save the crown — which ever had to do
with an American colony.   But before this can be reviewed
in greater detail, the changes which took place in the colony
while Smith was treasurer of the corporation must be noted.

The patentees under the charter of 1606 had sent to Virginia not far from three hundred colonists.   Of these probably less than one hundred survived till midsummer, 1609.[3]
The new company despatched in the spring of that year nine
vessels, carrying about five hundred planters.   With them
went Sir Thomas Gates, as "sole and absolute governor,"
accompanied by Sir George Somers as admiral, and Captain
Newport as vice-admiral.[4]   The instructions to Gates have
recently been discovered, and their fulness and suggestiveness,
added to the fact that they were the earliest set of instructions
to a governor which we now possess, justify more than a
passing reference.   Moreover, notwithstanding the disaster
which overtook Gates, these instructions were put into force,

[1] Extracts from these have been printed in vols. 7 and 8 of the Collections
of the Virginia Historical Society.

[2] Printed in Force, Tracts, III.

[3] Brown, First Republic, 71, 97.

[4] The instructions to Gates, as well as those to Lord Delaware, are among
the Ashmolean Manuscripts in the Bodleian Library at Oxford.   They have
recently been brought to light by Miss S. M. Kingsbury, and to her I am
indebted for permission to use them.

the most important among them being given to Lord Delaware for his guidance.   They contained in outline the entire
scheme of policy which was followed by Delaware, Gates, and
Dale, that by which the fortunes of the colony were guided
until the time came for the introduction of individual property.
We can now clearly see that the policy of the years 1610 to
1617 was formulated in the councils of the company while
the new charter was being procured and while the company
was adding to its resources and energies.   The instructions
were issued by his Majesty's council for Virginia.   In them
Gates was told to avoid the old course by way of Dominica,
lest he might fall into the hands of the Spaniard ; but he
was not instructed to altogether avoid the southern route.
Provision was made that, when upon his arrival in Virginia
it became necessary to reorganize the government, Gates
should select as his councillors Somers, — who was to be
admiral of the province, — Smith, Ratcliffe, and the other
leading officials who were already in the colony ; they were
named as councillors in the instructions.   But their advice
should not be binding upon the governor, nor should they
have the right to negative his decisions.   He, on the other
hand, might suspend any of them from office and report the
fact to the royal council.   Over other officers for whom provision had not been made by the royal council, the governor
was to possess the full power of appointment and removal.
"Whomsoever you consult of any business of importance wee
advise you to consider and deliberate all things patiently &
willingly and to heare every man his oppinion and objeccion,
but the resultants out of them or your own Determinacon,
what you intend to Doe, not to imparte to any whatsoever,
but to such onely as shall execute it, and to them also under
the sealles of your comaundement and but at the instant of
their partinge from you for the execucon of your will."
Thus completely did the authority of a provincial governor
differ from that which had originally been held by the president under the previous charter.   Another instance of the
extent of his discretion is furnished by the instruction that,
in order to prevent false and unfavorable reports concerning the plantation reaching England, the governor should

inform himself, so far as possible, as to the substance of all letters and messages which were sent home, and transmit his knowledge to the royal council.

In the instruction relating to the administration of justice the rule was laid down which, as we shall see, was to guide the judges throughout the colonies in very much of their work. In cases of mutiny and rebellion the governor was authorized to proceed by martial law, but "in all matters of Civill Justice you shall finde it properest and usefullest for your government to proceede rather as a Chancellor than as a Judge, rather uppon the naturall right and equity than uppon the niceness and lettre of the lawe, which perplexeth in this tender body rather than dispatcheth all Causes; so that a summary and arbitrary way of Justice discreetly mingled with those gravities and fourmes of magistracy as shall in your discrecon seeme aptest for you and that place, will be of most use both for expedicon and for example."

Detailed instructions were given to the effect that the chief seat of the colony should be removed from Jamestown to some point above the Falls, a point which an European enemy could not easily reach even by land, but one whence access could be had to a food supply through the main river or its branches. Further exploration and even settlement of the region toward Roanoke was urged. The colony should be allowed to expand. The cultivation of trade with the Indians, yet not so as to seem dependent on them, was enforced. Traffic with them must be carefully regulated. Great stress was also laid on the necessity of civilizing and christianizing them, the council even going so far as to recommend the seizure of their medicine men or priests, in order that by this means superstitious rites might be destroyed. Worship according to the forms of the established church was to be carefully maintained, and constant attendance at church was to be required of all the colonists.

Specific regulations were also made as to trade and manual labor within the colony, the substance of which will appear when we come to speak of the system that was enforced by Dale. The plantation system was to be continued with great rigor, the colonists working in gangs under officials as overseers, eating at common tables and living in common barracks. So detailed are these instructions and so many points in the later history of colonization are anticipated by them, that one is almost forced to the conclusion that Sandys was their author or that he at least had a hand in their preparation.

Unfortunately Gates and his expedition followed the route over which Newport had so often sailed by way of the Canaries and West Indies. Not only did a considerable amount of sickness among the passengers result from this, but the fleet itself was dispersed by a great storm which it encountered off the Bahama Islands. The vessel carrying Gates, Somers, and Newport was wrecked on the Bermudas, and some nine months passed before its officers and passengers reached Jamestown. Seven of the vessels of the fleet, however, weathered the storm, and with two hundred colonists or more arrived at their destination before the close of the summer of 1609.[1] The supplies which the new arrivals might have contributed to the comfort of the colonists had been greatly injured by the storm, and much that was fit to land was, as usual, wasted. By these events the plans of the company were thrown into confusion and the colony was plunged anew into distresses which came near terminating its existence.

By the charter provision was made that on the arrival in Virginia of the new governor, or other principal officer appointed by the council, and notice by him given, all authority under the president and council which was derived from the charter of 1606 should cease. But in this case the governor failed to appear, or any one who was commissioned to exercise authority. Those who did come were Smith's rivals and enemies. For a time some confusion existed, but it was finally decided[2] that Captain Francis West should succeed Smith on the close of the latter's term — which occurred about the 20th of September. In the meantime, however, Smith sent Martin and George Percy with sixty

---

[1] The pinnace *Virginia*, Captain Davis, master, did not arrive till October; Arber, 170.

[2] Letter of Gabriel Archer, Brown, Genesis, 331.

people to settle near the mouth of the Nansemond river,
but owing to conflicts with the Indians this enterprise
finally had to be abandoned. West, with one hundred men,
was sent about the same time to settle near the Falls. That
settlement was likewise attacked by the Indians. Smith
himself went thither,[1] and a controversy at once arose between him and West and the latter's company about the
selection of a site for the settlement. In the midst of this
Smith returned to Jamestown, and on the way was acciden-
tally wounded. But notwithstanding this he was tempted to
prolong his tenure of office beyond its legal term. He was
thereupon deposed by Archer, Martin, and Ratcliffe, who
considered themselves entitled to act under their original
authority as councillors. West, who had been designated
as Smith's successor, being now at the Falls, Percy[2] was
elected to act as president until legal authority under the
existing charter should arrive. Smith was sent home under
charges on one of the vessels of Gates's fleet, all except two
of which returned in the fall of 1609.

When these vessels reached England, the full extent of the
misfortune which had visited the first effort of the new patentees became known. It was also seen that the colony was
left in a precarious condition. Some who had returned with
the vessels began also to spread evil reports concerning the
colony and the management of its affairs. This caused discouragement among the adventurers, and many now ceased
any longer to support the enterprise. But the group among
the patentees, whose hearts were wholly in the work, devoted
themselves all the more to its prosecution. The *True and
Sincere Declaration* was issued to show what the situation
was, how it had come about, and that there was no ground
for discouragement. In a broadside the appeal was renewed
for assistance, and for an additional supply of artisans and
farmers as colonists. Sir Thomas West, Lord Delaware, a
slow and formal man, selected because of his rank, was
appointed governor, and preparations were at once made to
send him out at the head of a relief expedition.

[1] Map and Generall Historie, Arber, 162, 481 ; First Republic, 94.
[2] Genesis, 334.

Delaware's commission [1] proceeded from the treasurer and company through the council for Virginia. By it he was made "governor, commander, and captain general both by land and sea over the said colony and all other colonies planted or to be planted in Virginia." He was to be admiral of the fleet which should carry him to Virginia. Within the colony and on the passage thither he was authorized to execute martial law and to act as judge in civil and criminal cases as provided in the charter and instructions from the council, or, in defect of such instructions, under ordinances issued with the advice of the council in the colony. He was given full power to appoint and remove all officers in the colony (including councillors), save those who had commissions from the council of the company. These he might suspend. He was also empowered to reward meritorious services by increasing bills of adventure for land. Full authority over matters of defence was also given him, while additional powers and instructions were to be granted when necessary. In April, 1610, the new governor, with three vessels and about one hundred and fifty colonists, sailed from England, and under the guidance of Captain Argall reached the mouth of the James river at the middle of June. The appointment of Delaware had been made and his expedition sent out under the supposition that Gates and his associates at the Bermudas had all perished and that the establishment of government anew in the colony would now be necessary. But of their mistake in this particular, as well as of the disastrous condition of affairs at Jamestown, they were made aware on their arrival.

It appears that soon after Smith's departure the previous fall, Percy, because of illness, surrendered all but nominal power into the hands of Ratcliffe, Archer, and Martin. The strenuous methods of Smith were at once abandoned, and affairs were systematically mismanaged, a fact which goes far to justify Smith's criticisms of these men. As winter approached, the natives became more hostile. This was an attitude which, with their knowledge of the straits to which the colonists were soon reduced, they would naturally assume,

[1] Brown, Genesis, 376.

but to which they may possibly have been urged by Spanish influence from the south.[1] At any rate, they forced West to abandon his settlement at the Falls. Throughout the winter they refused to trade with the English, and so far as possible carried on active hostilities against them. In December Ratcliffe, while attempting to trade with them, was lured into an ambush and killed. Anarchy and sloth seem to have prevailed, existing resources were not husbanded, even the domestic animals were killed for food. A period of famine and disease began which was almost as destructive as that of the summer of 1607. During the winter one hundred and fifty, out of a total of little more than two hundred, died, among those who perished being Captain Archer. Only about sixty were left in the colony.[2] The church was allowed to decay, and many of the houses, with much of the fortifications, were destroyed for fuel.

At the beginning of June Gates, and the one hundred and fifty colonists who were with him, arrived in craft which they had built in the Bermudas. They found[3] the palisades of the fort down, the ports open, the gates off their hinges, "the Indians as fast killing without as the famine and pestilence within." The blockhouse[4] alone afforded some protection to the survivors, yet this could probably not have shielded them much longer against the attacks of the Indians. Gates was not in a position to render much aid, for he brought only such supplies as might be necessary for his own colonists during a sea voyage. Indian trade could not be relied on, especially at that season and in the midst of an Indian war. To fishing they could not resort, because neither sufficient seine or nets could be found in the fort. Therefore, after repeatedly consulting with the former councillors, and finding that there was only food enough in store for sixteen days at the rate of two cakes daily for each colonist, it was

[1] First Republic, 112, etc.

[2] Ibid. 97, 129.

[3] The Council in Virginia to the Virginia Company, Brown, Genesis, 405; Strachey, True Repertory, Purchas, Pilgrimes, IV. 1749; A True Declaration of Virginia, Force, III.

[4] This was built in the spring of 1609 on the neck which connected the peninsula of Jamestown with the mainland.

resolved to abandon the settlement. Some even desired to burn what remained of the town, but this fatal step Gates prevented. He caused all the people to be embarked, and sent down the river with the purpose of carrying them to Newfoundland, whence they might obtain passage to England.

But fortunately Delaware was already at the mouth of the river, and when he learned of the situation was determined to save and reëstablish the colony. Through Captain Edward Brewster, who was sent by Delaware to meet Gates, the vessels were ordered to return to Jamestown. This they did, Delaware himself following a day or two later. Thus the most serious crisis in the history of Virginia, — far more serious in its nature than that which had resulted in Lane's return from Roanoke, — was passed, and a repetition of the experiment in colonization on the James river was insured. It was at this juncture that the system of management which was planned by the patentees under the charter of 1609 went really into operation.

As soon as Lord Delaware landed and the work of cleansing and repairing the town had been begun, he announced the names of those whom he had selected to be his councillors and to fill the other offices of the colony, and administered to them the oaths of allegiance and supremacy, with one of fidelity to the colony. Now for the first time at Jamestown appears the elaborate official system of a military type which was instituted at Sagadahoc. Of the six members [1] of the council, one held the special title of lieutenant general, another of admiral, and still others that of captain of fifty, master of ordnance, vice-admiral. Only one of the six bore the title of a civilian; that one being William Strachey, who was secretary and recorder. The other officials of the settlement were almost wholly military in character, as one was master of the battery works for steel and iron, another was sergeant-major of the fort, and five were captains of the companies into which the inhabitants were

---

[1] Strachey, True Repertory, Purchas, Pilgrimes, IV. 1754. Lord Delaware and Sir Ferdinando Gorges seem to have had somewhat the same ideas about the management of a colony.

organized for the purpose of defence.   Two of the settlers were clerks of the council and two were clerks of the store. Since it was known that the Spanish government was carefully watching the company, and, as we know, was already planning to discover the location of its colony, the erection of two forts at Hampton, near the mouth of the river, was a natural act of precaution.   A stockade or fort had been built the previous year [1] at Point Comfort.

The contemporary utterances of the company [2] show it to have been convinced that the failure of the experiment hitherto had been due, at least in part, to negligence and lack of discipline among the colonists.   It was therefore resolved that there should be no lack of rigor in the future. Up to this time the settlement had had no written laws.   A code [3] was now prepared for it, the enforcement of which was intrusted to Gates, afterwards to Delaware, and later to Dale.   It was a civil and martial code combined, the former part having been compiled by William Strachey, while the latter is said to have been borrowed from military regulations in force in the Netherlands, but greatly extended by Dale in 1611. [4]   Though the whole of this body of law was probably never enforced in the colony with rigor and in detail, yet it was in being there for nine years, [5] and the governors throughout that time can hardly have failed to use it for a variety of purposes.   No other extant authority reveals so clearly the type of plantation which it was the purpose of the company and officials to encourage in Virginia.   The stern and energetic spirit of Governor Dale can be seen in it

[1] The two forts at Hampton, however, had to be abandoned before the close of 1610, but Dale occupied them again on his arrival.   Brown, First Republic, 136, 149, 152.

[2] A True Declaration of Virginia, in Force, Tracts, III. ; the commission of Lord Delaware ; the Letters of the council in Virginia to the Virginia company, Brown, Genesis, 402 ; the speech of Delaware on his landing, as reported by Strachey and others.

[3] Lawes and Orders, Divine, Politique, and Martiall, for the Colony of Virginia ; Force, Tracts, III.

[4] The part which we can be reasonably sure that Dale added begins with the instructions of the marshal, on page 28 of the edition printed by Force. Dale may have revised the whole of the martial code.

[5] Brown, First Republic, 312.   See also pp. 154, 225.

quite as distinctly as elsewhere, and it contains some of his weightiest utterances.

According to this code, freedom of action within the colony was to be reduced to a minimum. The colony was to be regarded and treated as an absolute unit. The traditional forces of military discipline, severe penal enactments, and strict religious observance were brought to bear, to repress disorder and direct the productive energies of the settlement. In that age it was not strange that, under the civil enactments, more than twenty crimes were punishable with death, while many small offences were threatened with whipping. But it was also declared that the provisions of the martial code might also be applied to these offences, martial law in the last instance being supreme. Some of the provisions showed a correct understanding of evils which had previously existed, as those which prohibited unlicensed trading with the Indians, killing of cattle or poultry without license, destruction of growing crops, embezzlement by the cape-merchant or keeper of the store, the practice of extortion by captains or seamen in the sale of goods, stealing of the boats or vessels of the colony, escape from the colony without license from the governor. But these, like treason, were among the capital offences.

So also was persistent refusal to attend church. It was made the duty of the captain in each plantation, half an hour before service on Sundays, to shut the gates and place sentinels at them. After service began he should search all the houses and command all to repair to church, after which he should accompany his guards thither with their arms and lay the keys before the governor. Characteristic emphasis throughout the code was laid both on obedience to civil authority and on external religious observances. Under the first charter Anglican worship had been regularly celebrated in the settlement, the patentees having sent over a worthy clergyman with the first colonists. Others accompanied or soon followed Delaware. Mention is prominently made of the care shown by the governor in the repair of the chapel. The code required that prayers should be read there twice every day, that there should be preaching every Wednesday and twice on Sunday, with catechising, and that all these services should be attended by every settler on threat of heavy punishment for disobedience.   Every Sunday the Lord Governor attended church in state, "accompanied with all the councillors, captains, other officers, and all the gentlemen, and with a guard of fifty halberdiers in his Lordship's livery, fair red cloaks, on each side and behind him.   The Lord Governor sat in the choir, in a green velvet chair, with a velvet cushion before him on which he knelt, and the council, captains, and officers sat on each side of him, each in their place ; and when the Lord Governor returned home, he was waited on in the same manner to his house."   A mental comparison of the picture presented by these colonists on their way to church with the description given by De Rasieres a decade later of the procession he saw on a Sabbath morning at Plymouth will be found suggestive.

The instructions of Dale show it to have been the intention to order all activities of the colonists according to military routine.   The governor at Jamestown, as well as at each outlying plantation, was to perform the double duty of military commander and overseer.   The same was true of all the officers under him, and they all bore military titles. The ordinary colonist was plainly told that he was both soldier and husbandman, and the rigid discipline of the former calling was to dominate the latter.   A strict watch and system of training was to be maintained, and at appointed times the soldier was to lay down his gun in order to take up the spade or other tool.   The day [1] was so divided that the hours of labor in the morning continued from six to ten o'clock, and in the afternoon from two until four.   These periods began and closed with the beat of drum, and at their close all the settlers were marched to the church to hear prayers.   Under the supervision of officers all tools

[1] Arber, 502.   In the Lawes Divine and Martiall, 45, the hours are given somewhat differently.   The way in which the details of the code were departed from, while its spirit and the general force of its provisions were retained, is illustrated by a series of ordinances issued by Governor Argall in 1618.   Brown, First Republic, 278.

were taken day by day for use from the storehouse and
returned thither again. To the mind of Dale, who in his
energy and enthusiasm for colonization as state-building
resembled John Smith, the duties of the colonist and of the
soldier were but different aspects of the same function;
"which compriseth and involveth here as well all the industrious knowledges and practices of the husbandman and of
his spade, as of the soldier and of his sword." To train
husbandmen in Virginia who should have the regularity
and persistence of soldiers was the aim of the managers of
the system. Smith and Dale worked in much the same
lines. But, for the reason stated by Ralph Hamor,[1] the
ideal was unattainable : "When our people were fed out
of the common store, and labored jointly together, glad was
he who could slip from his labor, or slumber over his task he
cared not how, nay, the most honest among them would
hardly take so much true pains in a week, as now they
themselves will do in a day : neither cared they for the
increase, presuming that howsoever the harvest prospered,
the general store must maintain them. . . ."

The imperative need of food in the colony on the arrival
of Delaware was met by fishing and by special expeditions
in search of supplies. Argall, who started for the Bermudas
with Somers for the purpose, was driven northward, and off
the coast of northern Virginia procured a cargo of fish with
which he returned to Jamestown. To this source of supply
resort was annually made thereafter. During the following
years Argall engaged to a considerable extent in Indian
trade, and in exploration connected therewith. While on
one of these expeditions in the region of the Potomac in
1613 he captured Pocahontas, and by skilful use of this
advantage was able to procure peace, with return of captives
and booty, from the Powhatan. By two voyages, in addition to the capture of the Indian maiden, Argall is said
to have procured several hundred bushels of corn.[2] Somewhat later Dale concluded peace with the Chickahominies,
and thus the resources of the natives were again opened to
the English. The analogy between the work of Argall at

[1] Arber, 516.   [2] *Ibid.* 512, 536.

this juncture, and that of John Smith at an earlier date, is
perfectly clear. Both, in the capacity of successful Indian
traders, helped to make the colony self-supporting.

Throughout the years of which we are speaking sickness
prevailed, much as it had done prior to 1610. During the
first two years of its existence, the company sent a considerable number of emigrants to Virginia. Delaware brought
150 ;[1] Dale and Gates, in 1611, about 600. Not so many
were sent thereafter. The usual proportion of these newcomers fell sick and died. During the summer and fall after
Delaware's arrival about 150 died. The governor himself
suffered so much from the climate that he was forced to
leave the colony the following spring. In the spring of 1612
Dale writes that, of the 300 whom he brought the previous
year, not 60 were able to work ; but the incapacity of many
of these he attributes to their " crazed bodies." Only planters
who had survived in the colony for two or three summers
could be relied on. So great was the mortality that, in
April, 1616, out of a total of more than 1000 who were in
the colony in July, 1610, or had landed there since that date,
only 351 survived. The loss to the adventurers, as well as
to the planters, indicated by these figures, was very great.
After 1616 we hear at times of great mortality, but gradually the proportion of acclimated colonists increased;
women were brought over, and native births filled more and
more the gaps made by disease. The Indian massacre of
1622 proved as destructive to the labor power of the colony
as some of the earlier visitations of fever. But gradually,
and by the process indicated, the colony became adjusted
to its physical environment and reached a firm basis of
health. This, as much as anything else, liberated it from
its dependence on "supplies," an ' enabled it to be a colony
instead of a mere plantation.

An essential condition of the growth of Virginia, as of
every other social body, was its own internal expansion.
Partly because Governor Dale's ideal was what it has been
described to be, expansion in permanent and effective form
began with him. More or less ineffective attempts had been

[1] See figures in Brown, First Republic, 129, 149, 156, 171 et seq.

made before his arrival to found a settlement at the Falls and military posts near the mouth of the river. As soon as Dale appeared in the capacity of deputy governor, and in consequence of his determination that the colony should be made self-supporting by the increase of the cultivation of corn and other forms of husbandry, the country[1] was explored for the purpose of discovering an available site for a new settlement. The spot selected was the modern Farrar's island and the neighboring region, about forty miles above Jamestown. The site was chosen because of its fertility, the amount of open ground available, and the ease with which, because of the bends on the river, a considerable area could be surrounded with palings. There, on what was then a narrow peninsula on the north bank of the river, the town of Henrico was founded. This was done by enclosing seven acres of ground with a stockade protected by watch-towers, and building within this a storehouse, church, and three rows of houses for himself and men. The houses were built partly of brick made on the spot.[2] A building was also especially set apart as a hospital for the sick or wounded. Across the neck of the peninsula, and again two miles farther inland, palings were built by means of which a large area of cleared land was secured and laid off into fields for corn. Within this tract, it was claimed, enough grain could be produced to support the existing population of Virginia and all who were likely to arrive for three years to come. Certain Indian lands between the Appomattox and James rivers, and a short distance below Henrico, were seized and impaled, additional corn land thus being secured. On the south side of the river a range for hogs was also enclosed and made defensible. Still another tract between Farrar's island and the Appomattox was made into an enclosure for the domestic cattle, larger numbers of which were now being brought into the colony in vessels specially adapted for the purpose. Provision was made for the defence of each of the enclosures, and colonists were established within them.

[1] Bruce, Economic History of Virginia, 208.
[2] In this task Dale had the aid of from 300 to 350 men. Brown, First Republic, 156.

Thus a group of settlements was founded, less exposed to foreign attack and more healthfully located than Jamestown. These Dale intended to make the centre of the colony. Governor Gates, however, when in the colony, continued to reside at Jamestown and cared for its improvement. This insured its continuance as at least the centre of government, though by 1616 the upper settlements contained more than half of the inhabitants of the colony.[1]

While Dale was founding Henrico and its neighboring settlements, the period during which the common stock was to be maintained approached its close. But he did not wait for that time to come before taking the initial step toward the introduction of private holdings. Soon after Dale's arrival, perhaps in response to a petition already presented to Gates, he consulted the council respecting the advisability of allotting to each man a "private garden." Later, probably in 1614, a considerable number of allotments were made of three acres each, to be held under lease. Those who received them were called farmers, and paid an annual rent into the common store of two and one-half barrels of corn for each male worker. They were exempted from all labor for the community, save during one month in the year, and that not in seed-time or harvest.[2]

As a result of this change, when in 1616 John Rolfe wrote his *Relation*, the planters consisted of officers, laborers, and farmers. The officers had supervision over each of the other classes, in the sense that they cared for their protection from enemies, and saw that they performed the daily tasks to which they were bound. They also labored for their own support. The class of laborers included the agricultural servants and many, at least, of the artisans. The servants worked in the "common garden," that is for the company, eleven months in the year, all the results of their labor for that time going into the general store. The remaining month was their own. The artisans also tilled the ground for a part of their support. In Bermuda Hundred lived a group of servants who, probably in response to a petition of

---

[1] Rolfe's Relation, Virginia Historical Register, I. 109, 110.
[2] Hamor, Arber's edition of Smith, 516.

their own, were allowed for their own use, in addition to one month annually, one day in each week from the first of May until harvest. The farmers were the tenants created by Dale, who lived under the comparatively easy terms described above.[1]

In order further to encourage the development of tenant right, and the cultivation of commodities which were useful as food, Dale assured to every man with a family who came into the colony a house with four rooms, which he was permitted to occupy for at least a year without the payment of rent. Twelve acres fenced and adjacent to the house were assigned for cultivation. With this went tools, live stock, and provisions adequate to the support of the family during a twelvemonth. After that time the newcomer was expected to maintain himself.

When Dale finally returned to England in 1616, six settlements had been founded along the lower and middle course of the James river: Henrico, Bermuda Hundred, and West and Sherley Hundred, all in the vicinity of Farrar's island ; Jamestown, and Kicoughtan, the latter near the mouth of the river; Dale's Gift, near Cape Charles, the extremity of Accomac peninsula. In the entire colony was a population of only 381, including women and children. Of these about 200 were in the upper settlements founded by Dale, while the rest were distributed between Jamestown and the two lower settlements. The officers and laborers together numbered 205, and the farmers 81. Though the number was small, it consisted of those who had become acclimated and hence fitted to be the nucleus of a permanent colony. Though no plough was yet in use, the colonists possessed a large supply of goats, hogs, and poultry, 6 horses, and 144 domestic cattle. At Dale's Gift salt was made and fishing carried on. The production of tobacco had already begun, and thus Virginia was soon to possess a staple which she could export in large quantities. The price of tobacco at that time ranged very high, and under its influence the amount raised and sent to England rapidly increased. But special care was taken, now as always, to encourage the raising of articles of food ample in amount to support the inhabitants of the colony.

[1] Rolfe, Relation, Va. Hist. Reg. I. 107 ; Bruce, 214, 217.

When Governor Dale returned to England in 1616, the time for the expiration of the system of joint management as applied to land had nearly arrived. Early in that year the company had made preparations for the first division, which should include the land adjacent to the existing settlements in Virginia.[1] In 1617, while George Yeardley, who had coöperated with Dale in the founding of his settlements at and near Henrico, was deputy governor, the laborers who three years before had been granted special privileges at Bermuda Hundred were, it is supposed, made farmers or free rent-paying tenants.[2] Not far from the same time a few grants of land in fee simple were made to other colonists.

But Yeardley was soon superseded by Samuel Argall, who now returned to Virginia as deputy governor and as the protégé of Sir Robert Rich, afterwards Earl of Warwick.[3] During the two years of his administration, 1617–1619, no private grants were made. By this it is not meant that the company's land was cultivated with diligence, or the commercial system utilized for the benefit of adventurers and planters. Instead, both the lands and trade of the company were recklessly exploited for the benefit of the governor and his friends. The "ancient colony men," who were entitled to their freedom, and the laborers from the common garden, were kept at work as the governor directed, and largely for his personal advantage. The stores of grain accumulated from the rents at Charles City, as well as the public cattle, were appropriated for his use. A stock of hides belonging to the company and estimated to be worth £400 he withheld from sale, and thus caused it considerable loss. At the same time he allowed ship captains and private traders to export the sassafras and tobacco produced in the colony, thus bringing the operations of the magazine almost to a standstill. The Indian trade he was also charged with appropriating to himself.

Sir Edwin Sandys described the effects of Argall's ad-

---

[1] Brown, Genesis, 777 ; A Brief Declaration.
[2] Calendar of State Papers, Colonial, 1574–1660, 68 ; Bruce, 221.
[3] Recs. of Va. Co. I. 22, 80 ; II. 29–45, 195, 200 *et seq.*

ministration of the company's garden as follows : " The
Deputy Governor, on his arrival at that place, which
was in or about May 1617, hath left and delivered to him
by his predecessor a portion of public land called the
Company's garden, which yielded unto them in one year
about £300 profit.   Fifty-four servants employed in that
same garden and in salt-works set up for the service of the
colony ; tenants, eighty-one yielded a yearly rent-corn
and services, which rent-corn, together with the tribute-
corn from the barbarians, amounted to above twelve hundred of our bushels by the year ; kine, eighty ; goats,
eighty-eight.   About two years after — viz., Easter, 1619 —
at the coming away of the said Deputy Governor, his whole
estate of the public was gone and consumed, there being not
left at that time to the Company either the land aforesaid or
any tenant, servant, rent or tribute corn, cow or salt-work,
and but six goats only, without one penny yielded to the
Company for their so great loss in way of account or restitution to this very day." [1]

When Captain Edward Brewster ventured [2] to withdraw
some of Lord Delaware's tenants and servants from the work
to which the governor had set them, Argall, taking advantage of the martial code, had him tried and condemned to
death.   But on the application of the members of the court
and of the clergymen who were present, Brewster was
allowed to return to England on condition that he would
never revisit the colony, or say anything to its disparage-
ment or that of Governor Argall.

As soon as the company was informed of the extent to
which Argall was violating its instructions and plundering
the colony, Lord Delaware, who was on the way to assume
the duties of his office in person, was ordered to send Argall
home, and to seize what of his plunder he could.[3]   But the
governor died on the outward voyage.   Sir George Yeardley
was then appointed governor and instructed to proceed
against Argall.   But the latter was brought away from
Virginia in one of Sir Robert Rich's vessels, and after some
delay returned to England.   There he found that Brewster

---

[1] Recs. of Va. Co. I. 65.   [2] *Ibid.* II. 41.   [3] *Ibid.* II. 35.

had appealed to the company against him.[1]   Based on this
and other information, charges against him were formulated
by the company, to some of which he attempted to reply.
By a quarter court his proceedings against Brewster were
pronounced unjust and illegal.   But on the other points no
definite result was ever reached.   It is not improbable that
this was due to the influence of Warwick.   The case of
Argall helped to arouse bitter feelings within the company,
but itself was partially obscured by the larger controversies
to the origin of which it contributed.   The significance of
his administration appears in the fact that it delayed the
process of economic transition in the colony for two years.

[1] Recs. of Va. Co. I. 6.

CHAPTER IV

VIRGINIA AS A PROPRIETARY PROVINCE. THE ADMINIS-
TRATIONS OF SANDYS AND THE EARL OF SOUTHAMPTON

PART
I.
The Argall incident contributed toward an important change in the administration of the company. It strength-ened the resolve of Lord Rich to remove the merchants — Smith, Johnson, and their friends — from its control. This for the time was favorable to the prospects of Sir Edwin Sandys, who by his ability had risen to be the leader among those in the company who favored a liberal policy toward the plantation. With him were associated the Earl of South-ampton, Lord Cavendish, who was also at the head of the Somers Islands company, John and Nicholas Ferrar, and many other prominent and able men. Sandys and his asso-ciates were also closely identified with the so-called "country party," the opposition in parliament. There they worked against the corrupt policy of favorites, undue Spanish influence, monopolies and impositions, and strove to counter-balance in all ways the large power of the crown. This fact brought them into opposition to Sir Thomas Smith and Alderman Johnson, who at this time identified themselves to an extent at least with the court. Sir Thomas Smith, who was already well advanced in years, accepted the office of a commissioner of the navy. He had already served for ten years in succession as treasurer of the London company. These facts, together with his many other interests, caused him to decline reëlection for the year 1619, and to desire that his accounts might be audited and fully adjusted before he died. His wish was gratified by the company, the friends of Rich and Sandys coöperating toward the result. Sandys was elected treasurer, with John Ferrar as deputy in the place of Alderman Johnson. The auditors were set to work

on Smith's accounts, but they found them so defective and
intricate[1] as to make it impossible to disentangle them.   As
late as 1623 Smith was urging their settlement, but it was
then declared to be an impossibility, and no proof is extant
that they ever were cleared up.   Though apparently the
transfer of control from Smith to Sandys was made with
ease, it laid the foundation for prolonged strife.   The attitude of Sandys toward Argall, combined, it is probable, with
many other causes, soon broke the temporary union with the
Rich or Warwick faction, and formed a natural alliance[2] of
the latter with Smith and Johnson.   As time passed their
union with the court became more intimate, and all important measures of the company came to be affected not only
by the struggle between these factions, but by English politics as well.   The complications, however, to which this led
belong to another division of the subject.   It remains at
this point to trace the policy of the Sandys-Southampton
party in so far as it immediately affected the colony.

In general it may be said that it involved no radical departure from that followed by the company during the later
years of Dale's administration and after the recall of Argall.
It emphasized the best tendencies of that policy, expanding
and improving upon it in various ways, and introducing
more vigor and system than apparently had characterized
the earlier methods of the company.   The records show that
Sir Edwin Sandys was an almost ideal administrator, and
not a little of his wisdom appears in the fact that he fully
recognized the merit of Gates and Dale.[3]   Sandys at the
outset devoted himself to the task of reclaiming " the public " or company's land from the exhausted condition in
which Argall had left it.   This he considered the root or
body of the tree, and private plantations the branches.[4]   In
pursuing his object he sought in all directions for tenants
with whom to people it.   He advertised for laborers and

---

[1] Recs. of Va. Co. II. 84, 220.

[2] Brown, First Republic, 356, 522; Neill, History of the Virginia Company, 120.

[3] Recs. of Va. Co. I. 21.

[4] *Ibid.* 20 *et seq.*, 64 *et seq.*

artisans.   He applied to the mayor of London for one hundred apprentices, twelve years of age and over.   The king threw his plans into some confusion by insisting that he should find homes in Virginia for an hundred dissolute persons from the capital.   After considerable delay and negotiation provision was made for a part or all of them.   Domestic cattle and supplies of all kinds were bought and shipped. The settlement of private plantations, as well as the improvement of the public land, was also encouraged.   During 1619 the company sent out eight ships, ranging from seventy tons burden to one thousand tons, and carrying 871 colonists. Three hundred were sent the same year by private adventurers.   Though about three hundred died that year in Virginia, the energy of the company far more than made good this loss.   Of those sent to the colony the great majority were servants, lists of whose names, with the contracts into which they entered with their masters, were kept . by the company.   They received free transportation to Virginia, were furnished with food for one year, also with apparel, cattle, tools, and weapons.   The tenants on the public lands were expected to return to the company one-half of their annual product, and to remain in its employment for seven years.   After that time the tenant could renew the contract, or receive an estate in fee simple as a dividend.

In connection also with the encouragement of emigration a strong effort was made to diversify the industry of Virginia.   Of those who were sent out in 1619, one hundred and fifty were ordered to devote themselves to the production of iron, others were instructed to build saw-mills, " divers skilful vigneroons " were sent to develop and cultivate vineyards ; directions were given for the sowing of hemp and flax and for the cultivation of the silk-grass of the region, which made good cordage ; the production of silk was also encouraged, while the Poles already in the colony were sent back to the work of making pitch and tar, potash and soap ashes.   The production of grain was everywhere encouraged. This policy was continued as long as the company existed, and the prosecution of it was the chief task of the treasurer and his associates.   They continued to be managers of a productive enterprise. Virginia was still the company's plantation, and, in spite of all that could be done, the returns from it came chiefly in the form of tobacco.

But the introduction of free tenancy and the development of private plantations in addition to the company's land was all the time changing the nature of the colony and preparing the way for its transition from the plantation to the provincial type. This change had begun with Dale, and was continued under Yeardley in 1619. Yeardley's instructions mark an epoch in the history of the transition. As Dale acted under the authority of Sir Thomas Smith and his associates, and since Yeardley's instructions were prepared before Smith and Johnson left office, due credit should be given to them for a share in the work. The system of joint management of land and trade was never intended to be more than temporary, an arrangement devised to meet the needs of the colony in its earliest stage, and when the conditions were ripe for its abandonment, Sir Thomas Smith put no obstacles in the way. It was by virtue of instructions given to Yeardley not long before Smith left office, that the system of reserves from the unoccupied domain for various public purposes was instituted.[1] One thousand acres were reserved for the maintenance of the ministers of the gospel, three thousand for the support of the governor, ten thousand for the endowment of a college, twelve thousand for the use of the company itself. The first three reserves were located on the north side of the river, between Henrico and the Falls, while the company's reserve was divided into four apportionments of three thousand acres each, one of which was located near each of the four settlements along the river. As other offices were created by the company, additional reserves were made for them. It was for the peopling and improvement of these reserves that Sandys and his successors labored.

The reserve for the college was, for example, a prominent object of Sandys' care. One of his first acts after assuming office[2] was to procure an order from the company for the expenditure of some £1500 for the settling and improve-

[1] Va. Mag. of Hist. II. 154 *et seq.*; Recs. of Va. Co. I. 22.
[2] Recs. of Va. Co. I. 6 *et seq.*

ment of this land. His plan was to send fifty tenants to it,
who should be entitled to one-half the product of their labor,
while the other half should go for the maintenance of tutors
and scholars. Among the tenants should be a number of
artisans. A ship should be hired by the company partly for
their transportation, which, on its return voyage, for a freight
of four pence per pound, would bring back all the company's
tobacco. A special committee was appointed to take charge
of this business, while, pursuant to orders from the king,
application was made to the bishop to have collections taken
in the dioceses of the kingdom for the support of the college.[1] Some gifts were received for this purpose. Later,[2]
George Thorpe was appointed superintendent of the college
land.

Another form of grant which appeared at this time and
played an important part in the development of Virginia till
after the dissolution of the company[3] was the sub-patent
issued to private societies. The earliest of these were issued
in 1618, when several gentlemen of the company in order to
strengthen the colony united into societies and offered to
establish plantations at their own cost. By combining their
shares, or purchasing additional ones, the associations thus
formed entitled themselves to very large grants of land in
Virginia, and to a corresponding increase of those on later
divisions. It was the intention of the company that the
grantees should settle and improve the tracts in person, or
send tenants and servants for the purpose. In some cases,
but not in all, this was done. As the policy tended to
absorb rapidly the available land and also to destroy the
unity of the province, it was viewed with some distrust by
the company. The first private plantation thus granted was
Southampton or Smith's Hundred, consisting of two hundred
thousand acres, and located near the mouth of the Chickahominy river. Within this some three hundred tenants were
settled. Shortly after other grants were made to " Argall
and his associates," " Hamor and his associates," " Martin

---

[1] *Ibid.* 12, 29.

[2] *Ibid.* 54, 58.

[3] *Ibid.* 64 ; Brown, First Republic, 256.

and his associates." Of these the last, known as Martin's
Plantation or Hundred, and the only one of the three to be
developed, was situated at Martin's Brandon, on the south
side of the James river. The grantee was Captain John
Martin, who had been connected with the fortunes of the
colony from the outset. The grant contained eighty thousand acres. In 1619, through Sir John Wolstenholme, application was made to the company[1] that Martin's Hundred, in
consideration of losses which it had recently sustained, might
receive a share of land in Virginia for every £12, 10s. which it
had spent. This, it was said, would encourage the association
to send out fifty more men. But for various reasons Sandys
opposed the request, and no record appears of its being
granted.

Before the close of 1619 we learn of the existence of Captain Lawne's plantation and Captain Warde's plantation.[2]
In 1620 four additional patents were granted to similar associations,[3] among them being one to Captain John Bargrave,
one to Captain John Ward, and one to John Berkeley
Esq., and their associates. Entries of other, though in most
cases smaller, grants appear at intervals thereafter[4] till the
close of the company's existence.

The grantees were permitted, till the government of the
colony should be systematized, to issue orders for the regulation of their servants and business, provided they were not
repugnant to the laws of England.[5] Care was, however,
exercised lest members should be added to the societies
without the consent of the company, and lest the managers
of the private plantations should run a too independent
course in trade or promote faction in the colony.[6] They
occupied a position within the colony analogous to that of
manors, and bore a similar relation to the development of its
local institutions. When the first assembly met, John Martin

[1] Recs. of Va. Co. I. 13.
[2] Neill, The Virginia Company, 140; Brown, First Republic, 291.
[3] Recs. of Va. Co. I. 62.
[4] *Ibid.* I. 152; II. 212, 225.
[5] *Ibid.* I. 39.
[6] Yeardley's Instructions, Va. Mag. of Hist. II. 160; Brown, First Republic, 258, 267.

claimed all the privileges of a manorial lord in England, but he was forced to submit to the general regulations of the company. In 1622, on the occasion of his petitioning with others for concessions in the so-called "king's forest," he was sharply reproved by the company [1] for having made his territory a receptacle for bankrupts, vagabonds, and other disorderly persons who, with other enormities, had occasioned public complaint. Testimony to this effect, and to the effect that Martin had resisted the officers of the colony, was received at the time. Two months later Martin petitioned again that his patent might be amended and those provisions removed which were injurious to the colony or which transcended the powers that should be conveyed by such a grant. He was advised to surrender his patent and take out a new one. This he at first refused to do, but later consented and delivered it up in open court to be cancelled. Order was then given that a new one should be made out before the next quarter court, and it was duly issued.[2] This was in accordance with a regulation upon which the company had always acted, and which had recently been reduced to writing,[3] that none but the company in quarter court could grant land, the functions of the governor in the premises being wholly ministerial. The grantee or chief officer of a private plantation or hundred was known as its commander, and these grants appear to have had a semi-military organization. This they seem to have retained till about the time of the dissolution of the company. During that time, as the result of settlement, they became not merely grants, but localities or local units. In consequence of that, soon after Virginia became a royal province, they were merged on the one side among the large estates and on the other among the institutions of local government which were slowly unfolding in Virginia.

The issue of patents for large private plantations, or manors, was only one step in the transition from the joint stock system, as applied to land, to individual ownership. Another and more important one was the successive divi-

---

[1] Recs. of Va. Co. I. 187, II. 14.
[2] *Ibid.* II. 252.   [3] *Ibid.* II. 6.

sions of the unoccupied land of the province among the settlers and adventurers. The former had contributed by their persons, the latter by their purses, and with the beginning of Yeardley's term as governor they began to receive their dividends in the form of land. The regulation of the company provided that, for each share of £12, 10s., or its equivalent, one hundred acres of land should be granted on the first division. On the second division a tract of equal size should be bestowed, provided the first grant had been sufficiently peopled. The system of head rights was also introduced, by virtue of which for every person who, before midsummer, 1625, should be transported into the colony and remain there three years, the planter or adventurer at whose expense he came should receive fifty acres on the first division and fifty more on the second division. The system of head rights played a prominent part in the settlement of Virginia, and of the other provinces as well, for generations to come, and by it the supply of the colonies with a due proportion of servants was insured. As an additional inducement to private settlers it was ordered that those who received their bills of adventure before midsummer, 1625, should be free from the payment of quitrents. Those issued later than this date were subject to that obligation. As the result of successive divisions and the multiplication of private grants, large and small, the unoccupied land of the province gradually became the property of individual freeholders. Those who possessed the smaller estates worked them themselves with the aid of a few laborers or servants. The larger grantees employed many servants, — or later, slaves, — and in some cases leased their estates partly or wholly to tenants.[1]

So long as the company continued to exist, its reserves and those of its officials and beneficiaries, with their troops of servants and tenants, constituted an important feature of the land system of the province. But the Indian massacre of 1622 blasted the project for a college, while on the dissolution of the company its lands were divided and became absorbed into the general land system of the province. By

[1] Bruce, 412 *et seq.*

that time also the province had reached a permanent, self-supporting basis. It was no longer dependent on "supplies" in the earlier and technical sense of the word. General indolence, of which John Smith and Dale complained, disappeared with the advent of the system of individual estates. The province also outgrew unusual visitations of disease and famine. The development of energy which accompanies competition, applied mainly in this instance to the production of tobacco, furnished the inhabitants of the province with such European goods as they needed. The necessary agricultural products they themselves raised or in later times imported from neighboring colonies. Viewed from the institutional standpoint, the significant fact is that the province had now come to possess, so far as the whites were concerned, a system of tolerably free labor, and on this system of freeholders and free tenants the political structure of Virginia was erected.

But the disappearance of the system of joint land ownership was not followed by the immediate abandonment of common trade,[1] though a change was made in its management. Until the time of which we are speaking, the business of furnishing supplies for the colony and marketing its products had been carried on at a heavy loss. Since the company had controlled the magazine, this loss had fallen upon the entire body of stockholders. Owing to the exhaustion of funds thus produced, in 1616 a private association was formed among the adventurers for the purpose of carrying on this trade. It was known as the Society of Particular Adventurers for Traffic with the People of Virginia in Joint Stock. Through this the business of the magazine was managed until 1620. Subscribers to it held separate meetings, while its affairs were regularly administered by a director and committee of five councillors. Its accounts were passed upon by the auditors of the company. The cape-merchant acted as the factor of the associates in the colony. Ships were sent out at intervals, which were

---

[1] Bruce, *op. cit.* II. 279 *et seq.* ; Brown, First Republic, 258 *et seq.;* Orders and Constitutions, 23 ; Recs. of Va. Co. I ; Colls. of N. Y. Hist. Soc., Second Series, III. 343.

loaded with miscellaneous commodities intended for sale at
fixed prices to the colonists.   The ships brought back tobacco and sassafras, bought also at fixed rates.   They thus
performed the functions of the earlier supplies, and it was
intended that the monopoly of trade should be secured as
fully to the magazine in the one case as in the other.   During Argall's administration, however, this was impossible
for the reason that, in violation of orders, he allowed the
masters and seamen of vessels, as well as the settlers, to
traffic freely in the products of the colony, thus destroying
the market for the imports brought over by the "magazine."
Adventurers in the private plantations also enjoyed the
right of marketing their products and procuring their own
supplies from England.   It was also possible through official
influence for a private trader now and then to secure admission to Virginia.   According also to a law of the first
assembly, if the supplies in the magazine did not include
some desired article which was recognized as a necessity of
life, it might be purchased from any one who offered it for
sale.   Because of these limitations of the monopoly, the cape-
merchant suggested that the system of fixed prices be abolished and he be permitted to barter goods for tobacco on
such terms as he could make.   But his suggestion was not
approved.   He was therefore limited in his sales to a profit
of twenty-five per cent on the original cost of the goods, and
in his purchases was required to pay 3s. per pound for the
highest grade of tobacco and 18d. for the lowest.   In order
to insure the honesty of the cape-merchant, he was required
to prepare two vouchers for each transaction, one of which
was deposited with the governor.[1]   Between 1620 and the
dissolution of the company the magazine was kept supplied
by a succession of particular associations united in temporary
joint stock, the adventurers throughout struggling not only
against the attempted competition of outsiders, but against
the declining price of tobacco.   With the establishment of
Virginia as a royal province the system of joint trading
through a magazine entirely disappeared, and private in-

[1] Colls. of N. Y. Hist. Soc., Second Series, III. 349 ; Proceedings of First
Assembly of Virginia.

itiative, regulated by English and provincial law, took its place.

The multiplication of settlements by the company, the founding of private plantations, and the general abandonment of joint management of the land, opened the way for the development within the province of an administrative organization and a political system. Political conditions and forces begin thus to take their place beside those of an essentially commercial and economic character. To this phase of the transition of the years 1618 and 1619 it is now necessary to turn our attention.

The development of local institutions in Virginia was the immediate result of the settlement of Henrico and its adjacent posts and of the establishment of the private plantations. The former were in origin agricultural settlements and military outposts ; the latter were of the same nature, but were private jurisdictions and hence germinal manors. So far as the settlements, both public and private, had churches and were the residences of clergymen, they were, on the ecclesiastical side, germinal parishes. Soon after the founding of Henrico and its neighboring settlements, they begin to be variously designated as corporations, cities, boroughs, hundreds. Bermuda, — later Charles City, — Henrico, and Jamestown were known as cities, and reference is made to certain of their inhabitants as members of the corporation. The private settlements, as well as some of the public, were known as hundreds, or plantations, or by some strictly local designation, as Martin's Brandon, Argall's Gift. During the administration of Argall, or a little later, extensive districts adjacent to Henrico, Charles City, James City, and Kecoughtan — the four original settlements along the river — were joined with them under the general designations of "corporations." [1] The Corporation of Henrico included all settlements on both sides of the James river from Farrar's island westward ; that of Charles City all from Farrar's island to the mouth of the Chickahominy river ; that of James City from the mouth of the Chickahominy possibly to Elizabeth river or its neighborhood ; that of Kecoughtan,

[1] Brown, First Republic, 313.

from the bounds of the James City corporation to the bay. Within these were included all the towns, hundreds, and plantations, whether public or private, within the colony. The corporation of Henrico was only one borough, though it contained the district settlements of Henrico, Coxendale, and Arrahattock. The corporation of Charles City contained five boroughs : that consisting of the old plantations of Bermuda Hundred, Sherley Hundred, and Charles City, and in addition Smith's Hundred, Flowerdieu Hundred, Martin's Brandon, Captain Warde's Plantation. The corporation of James City contained four boroughs : James City, Argall's Gift, Martin's Hundred, Captain Lawne's Plantation. The corporation of Kecoughtan was then only one borough. With the growth of local subdivisions the distinction between the town, or original settlement, and the province appears with great clearness. Jamestown was once town and colony combined. It can now no longer be mistaken for the colony, and appears simply as the chief town, the residence of the governor, the place where the council meets, the port to and from which trade chiefly proceeds.

It was not necessary that the administrative development of the colony should have proceeded farther at that time. For an indefinite period its affairs might have been administered through a governor and council. It was possible to guarantee the private rights of the free planters through such administrative and judicial powers as might have been bestowed upon those officials. More than this the planters could not legally claim, and even on this basis a system much less rigid than that of the *Lawes Divine and Martiall* could have been developed. But the Sandys-Southampton party, which in 1618 secured control of the company, was in strong sympathy with the parliamentary opposition in England. It also wished, as soon as possible, to remove from both company and colony the effects of the misgovernment of Argall. As a condition of further growth, it favored the total abandonment of the monopolistic policy of Sir Thomas Smith and the merchants, with the plantation type of colony that accompanied it. It favored the establishment under due restrictions of private plantations, the encouragement of

emigration to the colony on a larger scale, the granting of
land under easy conditions, the largest possible freedom
of trade. It desired to elicit to the fullest extent the co-
operation of the colonists with the company in this work.
In order to Secure this it was resolved in 1618 by the general
court of the company that there should be an equal and
uniform government in the colony, consisting of " two
supreme councils."[1] One of these was the governor and
council, chosen and appointed by the company in England.
The other should be the general assembly, which should consist of the council of state and two burgesses chosen by the
planters from each "town, hundred, or other particular
plantation" in Virginia. An instruction to this effect was
sent out with Governor Yeardley, which resulted in the
meeting of the first Virginia assembly at the close of
July, 1619.

The burgesses,[2] or elected members of this body, were
twenty-two in number, returned from the eleven boroughs,
hundreds, or plantations, to which reference has already been
made. By this means the union of the localities as parts of
one colony government was assured. The representatives
met with the governor and council in a joint assembly, presided over by the secretary of the colony, John Pory, who
was chosen speaker. The place of meeting was the church
at Jamestown, the governor and council occupying the choir,
as they did during service, and the burgesses the body of the
church. The speaker sat in front of the governor, and thus
was accessible to both components of the assembly. Burgesses were admitted on showing their credentials and taking the oath of supremacy. Some hesitation was shown
about admitting the two representatives from Captain
Warde's Plantation, because he had founded a settlement
without authority from the company. But in view of his
past services to the colony in fishing and trading and on
his promise to procure legal authority for his settlement
before the next assembly, he and his associates were admitted.

A more extended controversy occurred over the seating of

[1] Brown, First Republic, 309.
[2] Colls. of N. Y. Hist. Soc., Second Series, III. 335 *et seq.*

the burgesses from Martin's Brandon.   The patent which
Captain John Martin had procured from the company for
this plantation exempted him from all services for the colony
save in war against a foreign or domestic enemy, and guaranteed to him rights as ample as those enjoyed upon any of
the manors in England.   Martin was also accused of trading
with the Indians without license.   The burgesses from Martin's Brandon were ordered to return till such time as Captain Martin should appear before the assembly.   When he
came he promised to abandon independent trading, and gave
security for good conduct toward the Indians ; but he refused to consent to any change in his patent.   Therefore his
burgesses were excluded, and the assembly petitioned the
company that it would examine Martin's patent, and if it
found any of its provisions inconsistent with the due uniformity and equality of laws, that they might be corrected.

After the burgesses had been duly seated, the business of
the session was taken up.   The attitude taken by the assembly revealed a suggestive combination of initiative with
subordination.   As classified by the speaker, the business
consisted in a consideration of the instructions which had
been issued to the governors since the orders brought over
by Yeardley and called the "great charter," for the purpose
of ascertaining what provisions of these "might conveniently
putt on the habite of laws " ; what laws might be passed on
the initiative of the assembly itself ; what petitions might
properly be sent to the company in England.   The speaker
in his report of the proceedings was careful to state that
their object in examining the " charter " and instructions was
not " to correct or controll anything therein contained ; but
onely in case we should finde aught not perfectly squaring
with the State of this Colony, or any law which did presse
or binde too hard, that we might by waye of humble petition seek to have it redressed."   Two committees were appointed to examine the orders sent by Yeardley, while the
governor and the rest of the assembly examined the earlier
instructions.

The consideration of Yeardley's orders resulted in the
following petitions to the company : That the grants of land

made to the ancient planters be confirmed, so that they might not be disturbed by any grants now or later to be made to others; that colonists be sent to occupy the company's land belonging to the "four incorporations," and tenants for the ministers' glebes situated therein; that the ancient planters, both those who had come at their own cost and at that of the company, might receive their second, third, and later divisions of land in as large and free manner as any other planters; that a sub-treasurer might be appointed to reside in the colony and collect the company's rents there in kind, so that the inconveniences of payment in England might be obviated; that workmen might be sent to erect a college, and that the name Kecoughtan might be changed. The assembly then proceeded to enact into laws a number of the company's instructions relating to the morals and religion of the colonists, the civilizing of the Indians, the encouragement of grape, silk, and hemp culture, contracts with tenants and servants, and the maintenance of the magazine. To these were added a number of enactments initiated by the members of the assembly itself, regulating dealings with the Indians, religious observances, trade and morals within the colony. This, together with the trial of a civil suit involving the claim of Argall to certain payments, and a criminal suit in which Henry Spelman was charged with using to Opechancanough words calculated to degrade Governor Yeardley in the eyes of the Indian chief, comprises all the business done by the assembly. Admitting fully the right of the company to disallow the acts, the assembly requested that they might be regarded as in force till report of their rejection should come from England, and also that in due time the assembly might be authorized to disallow orders of the company's court, as it was empowered to reject acts of assembly. Thus early something like legislative equality with the court of the company in England was sought.

Several entries appear in the records of the company during the spring and summer of 1620, which reveal the fact that the acts of the general assembly had arrived and were **under consideration.** As was to be expected, Sir Edwin

Sandys carefully perused them, and "found them in their greatest part to be very well and judiciously carried and performed." On April 8 he moved that a committee be appointed "to draw them into a head and to ripen the business," that it might be submitted to a quarter court, with which body exclusively lay the power of approval or rejection. The committee was appointed, and at a later date, because they found their task "intricate and full of labor," received an extension of time. Their report should have come before the quarter court of midsummer, 1620, but no reference to it appears in the journal of that session. Nor has any reference been noted to the subject thereafter in the records, and it cannot, therefore, be positively affirmed that the acts of this first legislature ever received the approval of the company.[1]

When, in July, 1624, Sir Francis Wyatt, who had been appointed as Yeardley's successor, was about to depart for Virginia[2] an instruction with provisions concerning an assembly similar to those issued to Yeardley was given to him. This body was given free power to treat, consult, and conclude concerning the public weal of the province on "all emergent occasions," and also to enact such general laws and orders for its government as from time to time should appear necessary. In addition the promise was held out that, after the government of the province had become well framed and established, no orders of the court of the company should bind the colony unless ratified by its general assemblies. The time for the issue of this concession never came, but had it come Virginia would have enjoyed greater liberty than was ever promised by the crown or by any other English proprietor. It would have stood from the outset on the basis which was ultimately claimed by the colonies in 1776, and would have been forever freed from the binding force of instructions. But it remained only a benevolent promise, and is to be classed, with the many assertions of full legislative competence made by colonial assemblies, as suggestive claims rather than sober statements of fact. The instruction to Wyatt, which gave to the

[1] Hening, Statutes of Virginia, I. 122 n.
[2] Stith, History of Virginia, Appendix, IV ; Hening, I. 110.

governor the casting vote in council and judicial tribunal and the negative voice in assembly, which required the observance in administrative and judicial concerns of the forms of English law, and which were largely concerned with affairs of land and trade, expressed much more clearly the spirit of the British colonial system than did the promise which implied a contractual relation between colony and proprietor. The transition of a community within a decade from a state of subjection, such as that portrayed in the writings of Smith, or in the *Lawes Divine and Martiall*, to a condition such as that suggested by the promise of the company, would awaken surprise in any age of the world, and most of all, perhaps, in the seventeenth century.

Near the close of 1621 the second assembly in the history of Virginia was held. Its acts have not been preserved, but from the hints which have come down concerning them we know that they related only to immediate needs of the province, and especially to the introduction of the silk culture and that of other staple commodities in which the company was interested. In March, 1624, the last assembly of proprietary Virginia met. A list of what are probably brief outlines of thirty-five acts and orders which it passed has been preserved.[1] Several of these related to the fostering within the province of religious worship according to the forms of the English Church, and to the organization of the plantations and other local settlements into parishes. Provision was also made for monthly courts at Charles City and Elizabeth City for the punishment of petty offences and the trial of suits which did not involve more than one hundred pounds of tobacco. These courts should consist of the commanders of the localities where they met, and of such others as the governor and council should commission as judges, the commanders to be the quorum, and sentences to be given by majority vote. The right of appeal to the governor and council was reserved. By this law the foundation of local government in Virginia was laid. Provision was made for a capitation tax of ten pounds of tobacco to meet the general expenses of the province. But at the same

[1] Hening, I. 121.

time the general assembly affirmed its control over the taxing power by forbidding any taxes to be laid on land or commodities in the province except by its authority, and by requiring that they should be levied and employed as it should direct.

CHAPTER V

THE NEW ENGLAND COUNCIL

PART
I.

WE come now to consider an organization of a type somewhat different from the London company, though closely
connected with it in origin and history. After the failure
of the experiment at Sagadahoc, the Plymouth patentees
limited their efforts to fishing voyages and to the detailed
exploration of the coast of northern Virginia. The number
of the patentees was small and their resources were limited.
They slumbered on while the London merchants procured
two new charters, by which the extent of their domain was
made more definite, and under the authority of which they
successfully founded a colony on the James river.

Finally, in 1620, moved partly, as Gorges suggests, by
emulation, the survivors among the Plymouth patentees
petitioned the king for a new charter.[1] By this time
northern Virginia had been christened New England, and
the patentees by adopting the name as the designation of
their province established its connection forever with the
coast region north of the fortieth, and later of the forty-first,
degree. They now asked for the region, the vast extent of
which they could not comprehend, lying between the fortieth
and forty-eighth degrees and extending from sea to sea, and
it was granted to them. But before the charter passed the
great seal, a protest against the grant was raised by the
patrons of the southern colony, which delayed its issue for
a time and involved questions of some moment.[2]

Under the charter of 1606 the two groups of patentees
were not prohibited from enjoying privileges, such as those
of fishing, within each other's limits. There is evidence

[1] Gorges, Briefe Relation, Baxter, Gorges, I. 217.
[2] N. Y. Col. Docs. III. 2, 3.

98

that, from the time when Argall, in 1610, relieved the neces- CHAP.
sities of Jamestown with a cargo of fish which he had caught, V.
it may be near Cape Cod, fishing expeditions had been sent
from the southern colony to the New England coast. That
coast had also been for years a favorite resort of English
fishermen. The expeditions of Argall against the French
at Port Royal are familiar examples of operations by one
company within the limits of the other. When, in December, 1619, in the court of the London company, John Del-
bridge applied for permission to fish at Cape Cod,[1] Sir
Ferdinando Gorges, who was also a member and was present, objected on the ground that the petitioner should have
applied to the patentees of the northern colony. Sir Edwin
Sandys, then treasurer, declared in reply not only that the
sea was free to both companies, but that it was clear from
the letters patent that each might fish along the coasts of
the other. Gorges affirmed his belief that the rights of
each were exclusive, and offered to submit the point to
the council of both companies. This was agreed to, and the
council, the majority of whom in attendance may quite
probably have been members of the London company, supported the view of Sandys. License was thereupon given
to the society of Smith's Hundred "to go a-fishing." But
certain of the patentees of the northern colony were not
satisfied, and insisted upon considering the question further.
It seems to have been referred to the Duke of Lenox and
the Earl of Arundel, who failed to reach a decision satisfactory to either party.

In the midst of this discussion Gorges and his associates
petitioned for the new charter, and proposed the introduction into it of a clause securing to them the monopoly of
trade and fishing along their entire coast. This the London
patentees claimed to be an infringement of their chartered
rights. It was also a violation of the principle held by
some of them, that the sea was as free as air. It was
therefore voted to petition the king. The petition drew
from the privy council an order[2] that the two companies
should fish along each other's coasts, though only to the

[1] Recs. of Va. Co. I. 27.   [2] N. Y. Col. Docs. III. 4.

extent which was necessary for the support of their respective colonies, or of those bound thither. The king also declared that, if anything injurious to the southern colony had been introduced into the patent, it had been surreptitiously done, and it was ordered that the affixing of the seal, or at least the delivery of the patent, should be postponed.[1]

An understanding was now reached to the effect that the charters of both companies should be amended, and the officers of the London company set about the drafting of a new patent of their own. This it was proposed to lay before parliament for its confirmation, that thereby the colony might be strengthened. During the early months of 1621, Sandys was busy with his task. One of the changes which he proposed was the substitution of governor for treasurer as the title of the chief executive of the company. When, however, the draft was shown to Attorney-General Coventry, he expressed the opinion that the change in the name of the corporation which this necessitated would require the surrender of the existing charters. At any rate, he must have a special warrant from the king before he could insert the new clauses. A petition was accordingly sent to the king for this purpose. But before a reply to the petition was received, the struggle between the two companies was carried into the House of Commons.

In the House the Virginia interest was strong, and during the session of 1621 Gorges was three times summoned[2] before the Commons on the charge that, under the color of planting a colony, he and his associates were establishing a monopoly, which was a "grievance of the commonwealth." Personally and through counsel he defended himself against the charge, showing both adroitness and vigor. When asked to produce the patent before the House, he replied that, for aught he knew, it was still in the crown office of the chancery, where it had been left in order that certain faults in it might be amended, and thence the House might procure it at its pleasure. He denied that it was intended to convert the profits derived from fishing on the New Eng-

[1] Recs. of Va. Co. I. 27, 33, 49, 52, 90, 93, 97.
[2] Gorges, Briefe Narration, Baxter, II. 35 *et seq.*

land coast to private uses, but affirmed that instead they were to be used for the establishment of a plantation, the importance of which to the entire kingdom Gorges was not slow to emphasize before the members of the House. The benefits sought, he said, were no more than those enjoyed by many lords of manors in their counties, and were not inconsistent with the laws. At a later hearing, supplementing the arguments of his counsel from his own abundant knowledge, he described the disorders committed by the fishermen along the coast, and called attention to the danger that, because of these, the whole region, with its fishing interests, would fall into the possession of the French, Spanish, or Dutch. In his defence Gorges had the sympathy and support of the Smith faction within the London company, some of whom were members of the Commons. He had also secured as the New England patentees a large part of the nobles who were most influential at court, — Buckingham, Lenox, Salisbury, Arundel, Pembroke, Hamilton, and others. Upon their influence he relied, while the Sandys party in the London company was becoming more obnoxious to the king because of its political connections and the disputes which arose over the tobacco question. A bill for freer liberty of fishing and fishing voyages was introduced into the Commons, and of this Sandys was the chief promoter. It was debated at length, but before any decisive step could be taken, Sandys and Southampton were arrested, June, 1621. This put an end to proceedings against the charter in parliament.

An order in council[1] was issued, on June 18, providing that the New England charter should be delivered to the patentees, but with the additional specifications that colonists from Virginia should have the freedom of the shore for the purpose of drying their nets, taking and saving their fish, and at reasonable rates they should have the wood necessary for their use. This concession, however, was not introduced into the charter itself. As no further reference to the proposed new Virginia patent appears, the conclusion must be that it was suppressed. Thus, through influence at

[1] N. Y. Col. Docs. III. 4.

court and after a struggle of nearly two years, Gorges had secured his grant, without the omission of the obnoxious clause.

The charter provided for a new company under the title of the "Council established at Plymouth in the County of Devon for the Planting, Ruling, and Governing of New England in America." The strongest words of incorporation were used, and the territory between the fortieth and forty-eighth degrees of north latitude, and extending through the continent, was bestowed, with power to grant it out to settlers. The customary rights of settlement and trade were given, though in a somewhat detailed and monopolistic form. Powers of government were also bestowed, and in much the same language as was used in the London charter of 1609. The right was given to constitute officers, as well those in England as those employed in the colony, and to issue instructions for the guidance of magistrates in New England. An official oath was to be formulated and administered to those in the plantation service, and also a judicial oath to be used in the examination of persons touching the plantation or its business.

But the New England council is interesting in the present connection chiefly because of its name and its organization. In name it was the same as the Royal Council for Virginia. In number of members the two were not unlike. The members of both were required to take an oath of office before the lord chancellor, the lord high treasurer, or the lord chamberlain. In both cases they were the grantees of governmental powers. But in the London system of 1609 the council, though originally distinct, became merely a part of the corporation, losing thereby its separate existence. In the New England system the council was the corporation, and thus was the grantee of all powers. The two were closely joined as they were under the London charter; but in this case the corporation was merged in the council, the latter holding the chief place and giving character to the system. This council, then, like the council in the London company, was the body to which the king addressed his instructions, if he had any to give. Its relation to the king and the privy council was direct. Its relation to the colonists was also direct, and it did not share the work of administration with the corporation, for it was the corporation.

The last distinction to be noted between the New England council and the London company is this : the council was a closed body, limited to forty members. These, with a few exceptions, were members of the nobility and knighthood, and were connected with the court party. Some were also members of the London company. Vacancies were to be filled by coöptation. It never could become, then, a large and dignified body like that which met at Sir Thomas Smith's and John Ferrar's.

After the grant of the charter had been assured, the patentees agreed to contribute £100 each toward starting the enterprise,[1] and an appeal was issued to the towns and cities of the west urging the formation of joint stocks for trade and colonization under the license and protection of the council. But the reports concerning the monopolistic character of the grant, which were spread broadcast as a result of the debates in parliament, prejudiced many against the company. Subscriptions did not come in. The people of the west generally took little interest in the scheme, and it languished from the outset.

To meet the crisis, in 1622, the council issued, from the pen of Gorges, *The Briefe Relation of the Discovery and Plantation of New England*, in which the history of the efforts of the Plymouth patentees was reviewed from the beginning, the existing perplexities of the council and the reasons for them were set forth, the advantages offered by New England for trade and settlement were described, and a scheme of government propounded. This plan was clearly provincial and monarchical in character, in certain features suggestive of the schemes of Sir Humphrey Gilbert, and in others of the official system at Sagadahoc. The writer begins with the statement, " As there is no Commonwealth that can stand without Government, so the best governments have ever had their beginnings from one supreme head, who both disposed of the administration of Justice, and execution

---

[1] Briefe Relation, Baxter, I. 223.

of publike affairs, either according to laws established or by
the advice, or counsell of the most eminent, discreetest, and
best able in their kinde."

After a brief description of the administrative organization of England, he continues, " This foundation being so
certaine, there is no reason for us to vary from it, and therefore we have resolved to build our Edifices upon it, and to
frame the same after the platform already layd, and from
whence we take our denomination." Then follows the
sketch of a governmental system which is English and feudal in every point.[1]

Authority in all cases was to proceed from above down-
wards. The council proposed to commit the general management to a governor, who should be advised by as many of
the patentees as should be resident in the province, assisted
by the resident officials. These were to be the treasurer,
marshal, admiral, master of ordnance, and such others as the
patentees should think fit. They were to be guided by the
authority given them by the president and council. Two-
thirds of the province should be assigned to the patentees
as counties, to be settled by themselves and their friends.
The remaining one-third should be reserved as a source of
revenue, through grants and rents, for general purposes.
The entire province should be divided into counties, baro-
nies, hundreds, manors, incorporated towns, and other local
subdivisions with which Englishmen were familiar, and representatives from these should meet under authority from
the patentees, as a provincial legislature. In this body the
clergy, as well as the laity, should be represented. No sign
of a communal land or trade system appears in this plan, but
instead the council was careful to state, partly as a defence
against the charge of monopoly, that particular adventurers
would be left to the management of their own estates and
officials. " We covet not," said they, " to engross anything
at all unto ourselves ; " but they would fain arouse more of
the nation to share in the settlement of their vast domain.
It was a plan fairly representative of the views of an English
courtier, churchman, and territorial lord respecting what a

[1] Briefe Relation, Baxter, I. 234 *et seq.*

colony in America should be. It was an improvement upon CHAP.
the plantation system of Virginia, and foreshadowed what V.
the later proprietary provinces became, but it contained too
many monarchical features to be wholly practical. An effort
was at once made to organize the province on this model,
but, in order to understand its result, reference must first be
made to certain other significant events.

Among those who, toward 1620, began to consider the
project of founding a private plantation in Virginia was the
congregation of Separatists at Leyden which was ministered
to by John Robinson. With the religious side of their enterprise we have in this connection nothing to do, except to
state that it was a subject of negotiation with the London
company and the king as early as 1617. Sandys' secretary,
Naunton, Sir John Wolstenholme, and others were desirous
that they should settle in Virginia and that the king should
officially guarantee to them liberty of worship. The most,
however, that James could be induced to do was to connive at
their removal, and refrain from molesting them, provided they
kept the peace. While engaged in these negotiations the
Separatists were further perplexed by news of the disaster
which had attended the voyage of Francis Blackwell to Virginia. Blackwell was a seceder from the non-conformist
church at Amsterdam, and had come with a group of followers to London for the purpose of embarking for the
colony. While there, and in attendance upon a conventicle,
he was arrested, and, to obtain his freedom, recanted. With
one vessel, carrying approximately two hundred colonists,
"flocked together like herrings," he then sailed for Virginia. During the voyage, disease carried off about 130
of the passengers, including Blackwell himself and the
captain of the vessel. The desire of the Leyden Separatists, however, to preserve their nationality and faith triumphed over the fears naturally aroused by reports like
these, and in June, 1619, a patent for a private plantation
was secured.[1] It was granted by the London company in
the name of John Wincob, a clergyman, who was introduced

[1] Bradford, History of Plymouth Plantation, 4 Mass. Hist. Colls. III. 41;
Neill, Va. Co. 128; Recs. of Va. Co. I. 69.

by the Earl of Lincoln, as one intending, with associates, to settle in Virginia. The document was sent to Leyden, and with it propositions which were then under debate between the congregation and such merchants and others as would adventure with them and contribute toward the shipping and other necessary expenses. These were prayerfully considered, and it was resolved that part of the congregation should go and that part, with the pastor, should abide for a time in Leyden ; but that, as soon as circumstances permitted, they should all again be united in America. As the result proved, however, Wincob remained in England, and no use was made of his patent.

Among other patents which, in February, 1620, were granted to private adventurers by the London company, was one to John Pierce and associates.[1] One of the associates was Thomas Weston, a merchant and clothworker of London, who had known of the plans of the Leyden congregation. He now visited them, advised them to reject certain propositions recently made by the Dutch, and made them offers of assistance, with the fairness of which they were much impressed. Articles of agreement were prepared, which, after approval by Weston, were sent to England by John Carver, who, together with Robert Cushman, was appointed agent of the congregation and instructed to receive funds and make provision for the voyage.

About this time the New England council was procuring its charter. Weston informed the Leyden people of the fact and, because fishing seemed likely to yield a more immediate profit than the raising of such commodities as could be produced south of the fortieth parallel, he began to urge them to settle within its domain. This caused considerable uncertainty and distraction, but finally it was resolved to choose a northerly location, though no move was made to procure a patent from the New England council. Indeed that would then have been impossible, for the charter had not yet been

---

[1] Smith is authority for the statement (Works, 783) that the group of adventurers who were interested in the Leyden enterprise numbered about seventy, some merchants, some handicraftsmen, and that they subscribed all together about £7000.

delivered to the council. But the chief cause of anxiety to
the leaders of the enterprise arose from the articles of agreement on which the adventurers insisted as the condition
upon which alone they would advance funds. The congregation could not act independently, because it had not sufficient resources for the establishment of a colony. Therefore
it must not only conform to the general regulations of the
company concerning the founding of private plantations, but
it must submit to terms from its special adventurers, which
seemed irksome, but which the merchants thought necessary
as guarantees of profit. As the prime object of the Leyden
people was to secure religious freedom, and the sole interest of the adventurers in the scheme was profit, it was
evident from the outset that there would be much friction.
The women and children of the Separatists were also to
be taken with them, and their family organization carefully
preserved. So limited were their means, that servants appear
in very small numbers among them. From these considerations it appears that the character of the colonists would in
this case exert a profound, if not a controlling, influence
over the enterprise. They would not be to such an extent clay in the hands of the potter, as even the men and
women with whom companies and proprietors usually in
that century had to deal. But the fact that at the start
the Pilgrims had to accommodate themselves to the joint
stock system inaugurated in American colonization by the
London company, explains much in the early history of
Plymouth, and serves as an important connecting link
between the development of Virginia and that of New
England.

After his return to England, and because he thought more
subscriptions would by this means be secured, Weston
insisted that certain changes should be made in the articles
of agreement. To save time and, as they thought, further
the enterprise, the agents accepted the changes without
writing for special authority from Leyden. Cushman took
the lead in this course of action, thus exposing himself to
criticism. To the criticisms he replied in terms which were
to an extent justifiable, but which also revealed impatience

and a failure duly to appreciate the motives and scruples of those whom he was trying to serve.

Following with some strictness the traditions of the London company, the articles upon which Weston laid stress provided that for a period of seven years the plantation should be managed as a joint stock. Single shares should be valued at £10, and every planter or colonist, sixteen years old and upward, should be rated at that amount. An additional contribution of money or supplies to the value of £10 should entitle one to a double share when the division of land and other property should come. Every youth between ten and sixteen years of age should be considered the equivalent of a half share. For every child under ten years, fifty acres of unimproved land should be allowed in the division. For late comers and those who should die before the end of the seven-year period, shares should be allowed proportioned to the length of time they were in the colony. The business of the plantation should be fishing, agriculture, and the making of such commodities as would be most useful to the colony.[1] The change introduced by the adventurers, to which the Leyden people objected, was the omission of clauses which in the earlier agreement had secured to the planters the right to separate houses[2] and home lots for themselves and families, and the

---

[1] Bradford, 46–57. The language of the agreement, so far as it related to the point in question, was this: "The persons transported & ye adventurers shall continue their joynt stock & partnership togeather, ye space of 7. years (excepte some unexpected impediments doe cause ye whole company to agree otherwise) during which time, all profits & benefits that are got by trade, traffick, trucking, working, fishing, or any other means of any person or persons, remains still in ye common stock until ye division. That at their coming ther, they choose out such a number of fit persons, as may furnish their ships and boats for fishing on ye sea ; employing the rest in their several faculties upon ye land ; as building houses, tilling, and planting ye ground, & making such commodities as shall be most useful for ye colony. That at ye end of ye 7. years, Ye capitall and profits, *viz.*, the houses, lands, goods and chattels, be equally divided betwixt ye adventurers, and planters ; wch done, everyman shall be free from other of them of any debt or detrimente concerning this adventure. . . . That all such persons as are of this colony are to have their meate, drink, apparel, and all provisions out of ye common stock and goods of ye said collonie."

[2] On the slight loss that was likely to come to the adventurers from such a

right to two days in the week in which to work for themselves. Upon the restoration of these clauses they now insisted, and refused to sign the agreement in its existing form. When the *Speedwell* reached Southampton, Weston came down expecting that the articles would be signed, but his urgency availed nothing against the resolve of the planters, and the instructions of those who had remained behind. At this he was offended, and told them as he departed, "that they must look to stand on their own legs." Cushman was so irritated and discouraged by the difficulties he encountered in collecting supplies at London, to be shipped from Southampton, and in vain efforts to adjust relations between adventurers and planters, that he abandoned the expedition after it had started. The anxieties of the voyagers were increased by all of these complications, and by the necessity they were under of selling some of their supplies in order to pay a debt for which they found that the agents had made no provision. From this time forth Weston was an enemy of the Plymouth settlers, while both planters and adventurers had begun to suffer from incompatibility of temper. So great was their divergence in character and ideal as to ultimately destroy the partnership, and change New Plymouth from a proprietary plantation, conceived on the Virginia model, into a corporate colony of the later New England type.

The vessel which carried the Pilgrims to America was hired and loaded with supplies through the joint action of the adventurers and colonists. So far as we know, she sailed without definite instructions as to a landing place. In the region where the landing was effected, the colonists were squatters, destitute of legal rights of settlement. Left for the time wholly to themselves, as the result of three journeys of exploration along Cape Cod they selected Plymouth as the site of their settlement. It was chosen because it combined the advantages of cleared land, running water,

concession, see Robinson's letter to Carver, Bradford, 49. Cushman, in replying to objections, insisted that temporary dwellings should be built at first, so that, if need be, they might be abandoned. This, with coöperation in general, would best be served through the community system.

a good harbor for vessels of light draught.[1] A good supply
of food also seemed immediately accessible in the adjacent
waters and forests.

The first step taken toward the building of a town was the
erection by joint labor of the common house. This, located
a little back from the shore and near the town brook, at first
sheltered the colonists and later became their storehouse or
magazine. Another common structure was the platform on
the hill, where the artillery was planted. The town itself was
laid out in the form of two streets, the principal one running
back from the shore to Fort Hill, and another crossing it at
right angles. Along the first of these streets were located
the dwellings of the settlers. As the agreement had not been
signed in England, the colonists were free to found separate
homesteads, and immediately did so. " We divided by lot[2]
the plot of ground whereon to build our town, after the proportion formerly allotted. We agreed that every man should
build his own house, thinking by that course men would make
more haste than working in common." The allotment, previously made, was for nineteen families, it being provided
that the single men should join with some family. The
larger lots were assigned to the larger families, to each
person in the proportion of $8\frac{1}{4}$ feet front and $49\frac{1}{2}$ feet in
depth. Some twelve houses[3] were built at the outset.

At the beginning Plymouth was not impaled. Owing
to the recent destruction of the natives in the region by a
pestilence this seemed unnecessary. But after about a year
had passed, owing to rumors of a hostile spirit among the
Narragansetts, " they agreed," says Bradford, " to inclose
their dwellings with a good strong pale, and make flankers
in convenient places, with gates to shute, which were every
night locked, and a watch kept, and when neede required
there was also warding in ye daytime."

When Secretary De Rasieres visited the settlement in 1627,
he found the houses " constructed of hewn planks, with gar-

---

[1] Young, Chronicles of the Pilgrims, 162 *et seq*. On page 167 it is stated,
" After our landing and viewing of the places, so well as we could."

[2] *Ibid*. 173 ; Plymouth Colony Recs. VII. 1.

[3] Goodwin, Pilgrim Republic, 106.

dens also enclosed behind and at the sides with hewn planks, so that their houses and courtyards are arranged in very good order, with a stockade against a sudden attack; at the ends of the streets are three wooden gates. In the centre, on the cross street, stands the governor's house, before which is a square enclosure upon which four patereros are mounted, so as to flank along the streets." [1]

The common house was used at the beginning as a chapel, but later, when the platform, or fort, on the hill was enlarged, a room built underneath it was used for the purpose. De Rasieres spent Sunday at Plymouth, and described what he saw. "They assembled by beat of drum, each with his musket or firelock, in front of the captain's door; they have their cloaks on, and place themselves in order, three abreast, and are led by a sergeant with beat of drum. Behind comes the governor in a long robe; beside him, on the right hand, comes the preacher with his cloak on, and on the left hand the captain with his side-arms and cloak on, and with a small cane in his hand; and so they march in good order, and each sets his arms down near him. Thus they are constantly on their guard, night and day."

At Jamestown the summer and early autumn brought sickness and death; at Plymouth the winter occasioned the greatest difficulties of this kind. During the first winter, of the 102 colonists who came over in the *Mayflower*, almost one-half died from the effects of the voyage, and of the exposure which followed [2] it. Scurvy and other diseases prevailed, so that in March not more than six or seven well persons remained in the settlement. The living were scarce able to bury the dead. But with the advance of spring the mortality ceased and the sick recovered. During the summer they did not lack for wholesome food, and when the second winter came round, the survivors had become so far acclimated and were so well housed, that a second visitation of disease was avoided. To the comparative healthfulness of the climate, and the dryness, not to say the poverty, of the soil, the survival of the colony was due. Had the climate of New England been so unlike that of old England as was that

---

[1] Colls. of N.Y. Hist. Soc. First Series, II. 351, 352.   [2] Young, 198.

of Virginia, the Plymouth enterprise must have perished in the cradle. The resources of the Pilgrims and of their patrons would have been exhausted by a second experience like that of the first winter. From the nature of the case the number of planters who could be sent to such a colony was limited, while its financial support was beyond comparison weaker than that provided by the London company. But at Plymouth there was no thought of abandoning the settlement, and little or none of the sloth against which Smith and Dale had so long to contend in Virginia. Bradford could proudly refer to those who died the first winter as honest and industrious men, whose lives " cannot be valued at any price."

Adjacent to the settlement were the common fields of the colony. These were cultivated by the common labor of the planters. The Indian Tisquantum taught them how to plant corn, and they fertilized it with alewives caught by a weir in the town brook. This became the chief product of their husbandry and an important object of trade with the natives. As the agreement, with all the provisions introduced by the adventurers, was signed by the planters in 1621,[1] it is certain that no private labor was permitted save that which was expended on the dwellings and the plots of ground adjacent to them. The entire product, both of husbandry and trade, went into the common store and was used for the support of the colony and in the form of returns to the adventurers. Various trading expeditions were made along the Cape and the shores of Massachusetts bay for the purpose of obtaining corn and beaver, and of opening friendly relations with the Indians whom the pestilence had left scattered through the region. These journeys at first could not be long, because the only craft possessed by the colonists was a shallop; and the returns from them to the adventurers were very slight.

The colony was furnished with European commodities and received additions to its numbers through the system of "supplies." The *Fortune*[2] landed in November, 1621, with about thirty-five colonists, but without additional food

---

[1] Bradford, 108.　　　　　[2] *Ibid.* 105 ; Young, 234.

supplies. It brought Cushman as an agent of the adventurers, and a letter from Weston complaining sharply of the
failure of the colonists to sign the agreement. It was doubtless this and the influence of Cushman which procured their
signatures and enabled him to take back a copy with him.
A cargo of clapboard, with two hogsheads of beaver and
otter skins, was returned on the vessel. She had also
to be revictualled by the colonists. Cushman, on reaching
England again, acted for a time as the agent of the colony,[1]
but on the return of the next ship his place was taken by
Edward Winslow, a leading planter, who was followed by
Miles Standish, and later by Isaac Allerton.

Owing in part to disasters at sea, it was not until the
summer of 1623 that the colony was visited by another supply ship which was intended directly for its relief. The
ship *Anne* and the pinnace *Little James*, which came at that
time, brought ninety-six emigrants, and food for their sustenance till they themselves could raise a crop. The pinnace remained in the colony, and the *Anne* returned with a
cargo of clapboard and furs. The following year the first
domestic cattle were brought into the settlement. In this
way, throughout the early period of the colony's existence,
connection between it and its sources of supply in Europe
was maintained, but unlike Virginia almost no governmental
control was exercised by this means.

On the *Anne*, in 1623, the adventurers sent over the body
of colonists known as the " perticulers." Instructions were
sent with them to the effect that they should be given
separate allotments of land, but should remain under the
government of the colony. Had they been allowed to take
up land at a considerable distance from Plymouth, something like the Virginia plantation might have come into
existence within this colony; but to avoid dispersion they
were allotted habitations within the town. They were
excluded from trade, while, in consideration of their exemption from common labor, they were taxed for the support
of the governor and other officials. They were also required
to share in the common defence and in " such other imploy-

[1] Goodwin, 243.

ments as tend to ye perpetuall good of ye colony." In the
spring of 1623, however, before the "perticulers" arrived, a
general desire for the abandonment of the system of common
labor and for allotments of land was manifested by the
settlers. In a well-known passage the historian of the
colony relates how the community system was found to
breed confusion and discontent. The strong and able men
repined because they must spend their time for others, while
in the division of food and clothing they received no more
than the weak and inefficient. The aged and graver were
ranked in labor and reward with the younger and meaner.
Above all, that men's wives should be compelled to do service for other men, as dressing their meat, washing their
clothes, and the like, was deemed a kind of slavery, and
many husbands could not well brook it. In short, they considered the system to be contrary to "those relations that
God hath set amongst men," and their experience of it to
prove the vanity of the ancient philosophers, who, like Plato,
insisted "that the taking away of property . . . would
make them happy and flourishing." After discussion, therefore, the governor consented that for the year 1623 every
one should plant corn for himself. The plan proved a success, and a system of barter was established. The next year
an acre of land near the town was granted in perpetuity to
every person.[1] In this way, when the septennial period was
little more than half over, a serious inroad was made on the
joint land system.

Moreover, as time passed, the relations between the
planters and the adventurers became less satisfactory.
Weston, notwithstanding a recent assertion of unending
fidelity, abandoned the partnership, and to the surprise and
great discomfort of the Plymouth colonists, attempted to
found an independent settlement[2] at Wessagussett, on the
southern side of what was later Boston harbor. This he did
under a patent from the New England council, though all
trace of the document has now been lost. The colonists

---

[1] Bradford, 134, 167 ; Recs. XII. 4.

[2] The details of his movements will be found in Adams, Three Episodes
of Massachusetts History, I.

which he sent over were vagabonds and adventurers, picked
up from the streets of London. They were neither properly
furnished with supplies, nor informed concerning the coasts
where they were to settle. Trade and fishing was their
errand, and speedy returns were the desire of their employers.
But recklessness and the pressure of hunger in due time
involved them in difficulties with the Indians, and at the
close of the first winter, 1622–1623, the settlement was
abandoned. Throughout its brief existence it was dependent
on Plymouth for support and protection, though planted
with no friendly purpose.

The adventurers who, after the retirement of Weston, remained in partnership with the planters at Plymouth did not
agree among themselves.[1] Severe losses were suffered and
debts were incurred. The planters desired that the Leyden
congregation should be brought over at the common expense,
but the adventurers were opposed to doing this. From a
commercial standpoint the enterprise was not a success ; and
the complaints of the adventurers naturally irritated the
planters, who were stoutly contending against great difficulties. Many who were sent over as colonists were in character not acceptable to the planters, and it would have been
strange had they been so. Recriminations early became
mutual,[2] and so divergent were their respective interests and
policies that events tended inevitably toward a dissolution
of the partnership. By that means alone could the colony
attain the freedom to pursue the natural course of its
development.

But meantime events had occurred, resulting from their
choice of a location for the colony north of the fortieth parallel, which made the planters tenants of the New England
council. As soon as it became known where the colony
was situated, John Pierce procured a deed of grant from
the council. It was dated[3] June 1, 1621, and was issued
to Pierce and his associates, who were the adventurers and
planters.

This, Thomas Weston wrote, was better than their former

[1] Bradford, 158 *et seq.*   [2] *Ibid.* 109 *et seq.*
[3] *Ibid.* 107, 138 ; 4 Mass. Hist. Colls. II. 156.

charter, " and with less limitation." [1]   However that may
have been, it contained simply a grant of land, in amount
proportional to the number of permanent settlers, with liberty to trade with the neighboring Indians, to hunt and fish
in any places not inhabited by the English, and to import
goods and products into England or elsewhere, subject to
English duties.   No attempt was made to bound the grant
or to specify its location otherwise than by the statement
that the land taken up should not lie within ten miles of any
other English settlement, unless the two were on opposite
sides of some large navigable river.   Provision was made
for the payment to the council of a quitrent of two shillings
per hundred acres.   The patentees were temporarily granted
the power to issue such ordinances as were necessary " for
their better government," and to put them into execution
through elected officers.   They were also promised that, if
after seven years the request was presented, the grantees
should be incorporated with some fit name and receive additional powers of government; but how this could be legally
effected without a royal charter does not appear.   Before a
year had passed Pierce obtained for himself in joint interest
with his associates another patent; but on the same day,
April 20, 1622, he surrendered it and secured in its place a
" deed pole," which was drawn on behalf of Pierce himself,
his associates, heirs, and assigns.[2]   By this step, surreptitiously taken, Pierce apparently intended to transform his
trusteeship into a proprietorship.   Bradford states, "he mente
to keep it to him selfe and alow them what he pleased, to
hold of him as tenants, and sue to his courts as chiefe Lord."
" But ye Lord marvelously crost him," for in the ship *Para-
gon* he was twice wrecked, and his losses were so heavy that
he had to assign to the adventurers the patent he last procured.[3]   As assigns of Pierce the associates enjoyed, till
1629, all the rights to which he had been entitled.

But from the proprietary relations, loose though they might

---

[1] Young, Chronicles, 234 n.

[2] Bradford, 138, 139 n.; Records of New England Council, in Proceedings
of American Antiquarian Society, April, 1867, 91 *et seq.*

[3] Bradford, 139; Goodwin, Pilgrim Republic, 236.

be, and from the more onerous communal system, the planters
desired to free themselves. As soon as the colony had attained sufficient resources and economic independence to
make it possible, negotiations with a view to separation
were begun. Early in 1627 Isaac Allerton, who had been
appointed agent by the planters, brought from England an
offer of the adventurers to sell all their claims to the land and
other property connected with the colony for £1800.[1] The
offer was accepted by the planters, and eight of the chief
among them bound themselves on behalf of the whole body
to pay the debt. These eight were known as "the undertakers." The period during which the joint land system
was to be maintained had expired; and since the settlers
were so strongly opposed to it, it naturally disappeared after
the partnership had been dissolved. As soon as it had been
decided to accept the proposal of the adventurers, "ye company " was called together, and it was determined to receive
among the active and responsible sharers in the enterprise all
heads of families and all young men who were "able to
governe themselves with meete discretion, and their affairs
so as to be helpfull to ye common-welth."[2] Then it was
resolved to divide the tillable land near the town among the
heads of families and the able young men.[3] This was done
by lot, the poorer land and the meadow remote from the
town being left common. At the same time the common
stock of domestic animals was divided. In 1633, owing to
the increased demand for hay caused by the exportation of
corn and cattle, the meadow was also divided.[4] Thus joint
landholding as a system disappeared in the town and colony
of Plymouth. There was another side to the transaction in
the spring of 1627. Not only was the offer of the adventurers
accepted and the arable divided, but the eight colonists who
had undertaken to pay the £1800 associated with themselves
all the heads of families and single young men just mentioned, in joint responsibility for the payment not only of

[1] Bradford, 203, 210, 212, 214, 226, 373 n.
[2] Ibid. 214.
[3] Ibid. 216 ; Recs. XII. 13 ; Hazard, Hist. Colls. I. 180, 181.
[4] Recs. I. 14.

the debt due the adventurers, but also of the other debts
of the colony, then amounting to £600.[1] In order to procure the resources needed for this, it was resolved to carry
on the trade of the colony for six years on a joint stock basis,
the colonists as a whole forming the company. Each single
man was offered one share, and each head of a family as
many shares as there were persons in his family, with the
possibility that some would ultimately be disposed of to
meritorious servants. Those who took these shares were
known later as the "purchasers or old-comers."[2] With
them were associated four of the old adventurers, who
retained an interest in the trade of the colony. Isaac Allerton was employed as the agent of the "purchasers," at the
head of whom, in the capacity both of managers and of
responsible members of the company, stood "the undertakers." The last half of Bradford's history is filled with
the details of the trading operations of "the undertakers,"
and of the independent course which was run by Allerton.
It was by them that the patents for land on the Kennebec river
were obtained, and two trading posts established, one at Fort
Popham and the other on the site of the modern Augusta.[3]
That enterprise occasioned the planting of the post on
Penobscot bay, and the independent undertaking of Allerton
at Machias.[4] In 1633 the trading post on the Connecticut
was established. Of these posts the only one which continued long and was governed as a dependency of the
colony was that on the Kennebec. Business relations between "the undertakers" and the four English partners
continued until 1642,[5] when a final settlement was effected,
though the last of the debts of the colony arising from its
trading operations were not paid until four years later.

Before Plymouth, by the process just traced, emerged from
its original state as a proprietary plantation and became a
corporate colony, the New England council had attempted

[1] Bradford, 215, 226.

[2] *Ibid.* 372 n.; 1 Mass. Hist. Colls. III. 60.

[3] Williamson, History of Maine, I. 237, 252; Goodwin, Pilgrim Republic,
322.

[4] Bradford, 255 *et seq.*; Goodwin, 333 *et seq.*

[5] Bradford, 379, 400 *et seq.*; Goodwin, 411.

to establish a government within its vast domains. The
issue of Gorges's *Briefe Relation*, to which reference has
already been made, was a step preparatory to this. The
extant records [1] of the council, a part of which cover certain
months of 1622 and 1623, show that it was then striving
to secure the payment of the subscriptions of £100 each
which had been promised by the patentees, to regulate
fishing along its coasts, to encourage private voyages and
colonizing enterprise, and to build a ship of its own. In
November, 1622, a royal proclamation [2] was issued at the
request of the council, forbidding all persons to trade with
the natives or visit the coast between the fortieth and forty-
eighth parallels without its license, on penalty of forfeiture of
vessel and cargo. The license fee for fishermen, agreed upon
by the council, was " five fishes out of every hundred." Certain men might be left at the fishing stations while the vessels
were marketing their cargoes, with supplies sufficient to
enable them to continue the business. [3] Both the proclamation and the regulations of the council for enforcing it should
be posted on the mainmast of every ship engaged in the
fishing industry along the New England coast. In the new
charter which it was proposed to secure, the monopoly of
the sea was, if possible, to be continued, [4] while socage tenure
was to be abandoned and a military tenure substituted, with
the power to create titles of honor and precedency.

As another and a most important step toward enforcing
its monopoly, the council commissioned Robert Gorges,
second son of Sir Ferdinando, as lieutenant-general of New
England, [5] and a grant of land was made to him extending
about ten miles along the coast and thirty miles inland. [6]
Captain Francis West was appointed admiral for one voyage
with Captain Thomas Squibb as his assistant. West was
sent out in advance of Gorges. It was partly in order to

[1] Proceedings of Am. Antiq. Soc., 1867.
[2] Hazard, Hist. Colls. I. 151.
[3] Records of Council, 67, 70, 73.
[4] *Ibid.* 63, 67.
[5] Baxter, Gorges, 11, 49 *et seq.*
[6] It comprised the territory between the mouth of the Charles river and
Nahant, and extended inland to the vicinity of Concord.

fit out the lieutenant-general, that repeated and stringent orders were issued from the council for the payment of arrearages by patentees. But there were few favorable responses. Even threats to strike the names of patentees from the lists failed to move the courtiers who had given their names to the enterprise at the outset chiefly because their political influence was needed in its behalf. A loan of £100,000 was offered by certain merchants, but this had to be " respited in regard of the difficulty of finding security." The vessel which was building for the transportation of Robert Gorges had to be mortgaged in order to procure money with which to pay for her equipment. Owing to neglect in the payment for shares, the membership of the council was not full. Of the forty required by the charter scarcely more than twenty had paid up. Rarely did more than half a dozen members attend its meetings, and the only two who were regularly present were Sir Ferdinando Gorges and Dr. Barnabee Gooch. Though the council was located at Plymouth, its meetings were held at some place in London. The meetings were not called general courts, and were not such, for this corporation had no generality. There were no ordinary courts. The only executive offices mentioned were a president, whose title was later changed to that of governor, a treasurer, clerk, and auditors, though committees were occasionally appointed to facilitate business. Inasmuch as membership and attendance never approximated to the proportions suggested by the charter, the council was much like a board of proprietors — like that body which later founded the two Carolinas. Gorges always directed its policy, and for a time was its official, as well as its real, head. During the discussion of a new patent in 1622, it was even proposed to change the grant into a proprietorship. " Not to make a corporation," it was said, " but to take the land to us and our heirs." When, ten years later, the question of a new patent came up again, it was agreed that a copy of the charter for Maryland, recently granted to Lord Baltimore, should be given to Sir Henry Spelman for his use in preparing the draft.[1] The

[1] Records of Council, 68, 90, 111.

grants made by the council were in the nature of feudal
principalities.

A reason prominently urged by the adventurers in explanation of the failure to pay in their shares, was this, that
they did not know what they were to receive for their
money. To meet this difficulty, it was resolved by the
council to allot its domains among the patentees, and to
mark out the allotments on a map so that they could be
clearly seen. A drawing of the lots took place at Greenwich in the presence of the king, on a Sunday in June,
1623. But though the territories to be disposed of were
large enough to make respectable kingdoms of the mediæval type, only eleven out of the twenty patentees took
interest enough to be present. Twenty lots of two shares
each were drawn, so that by a series of assignments of
the extra shares, forty adventurers — if so many should
pay up — might receive grants. Of the region between
the Saint Croix and Buzzards bay, as shown in Sir William
Alexander's map — which was used for the purpose — the
Earl of Arundel and Sir Ferdinando Gorges drew the
easternmost shares. The Mount Desert region was drawn
by Sir Robert Mansell, and that of Casco bay by the Earl
of Holdernesse. A part of what later became southern
New Hampshire fell to Buckingham, and Cape Ann to the
Earl of Warwick. Boston harbor and its adjacent territory
went to Lord Gorges, and Cape Cod to Dr. Gooch. Twenty
shares in all were marked on the map.

Within a few weeks after this division of New England
on paper, Robert Gorges sailed for America to assume the
governor generalship over the entire domain of the council.
A council was appointed to assist him, consisting of the
admiral, Captain Francis West, Christopher Levett, and the
governor of Plymouth *ex officio*. He received a commission giving authority in civil and criminal matters. He
was also accompanied by two clergymen of the English
Church, and by a small number of mechanics, farmers, and
traders.[1] But these were not enough to found a colony,
while they were absurdly inadequate to the task of enforcing

[1] Adams, Three Episodes, I. 142.

submission among the scattered settlers and of regulating the doings of the fishermen who had their rendezvous at points on the eastern coast. Gorges landed in New England early in the autumn and remained over winter in the settlement which had recently been abandoned by Weston's men. In the spring he returned to England in disgust. Thomas Weston was at the time a fugitive in New England, having fled from home under a charge of fraudulently exporting to the continent a quantity of ordnance and munitions which he had procured under the false pretence that they were for use in his American colony. During Gorges' sojourn in New England, with the aid of Governor Bradford of Plymouth he had charged Weston with his offence and had brought him into submission. But beyond this Gorges accomplished nothing. The few settlers whom he left behind abandoned Wessagussett and sought more favorable locations about Massachusetts bay, where they were found by the Puritans on their arrival four or five years later. Young Gorges himself died not long after his return to England, leaving the territorial claim which had arisen from his unimproved grant to his brother, from whom it passed to John Oldham and Sir William Brereton.[1] This, with a few scattering farms, was all that survived of the attempt of the New England council to enforce its monopoly over trade and fishing, and to found a great proprietary province in which the Anglican ritual should be the only form of worship legally recognized.[2] New Plymouth was thus enabled to pursue its course practically unhindered. The fisheries remained open to Englishmen, notwithstanding the monopolistic clause in the charter of 1620.

Since the plans of Sir Ferdinando Gorges to increase the resources of the council did not succeed, and since no steps were taken by those adventurers who had received allotments

[1] Massachusetts and its Early History, Lowell Institute Lectures, 154.

[2] Captain Henry Josselyn is authority for the statement that, in 1631, Captain Walter Neal of the Laconia company was appointed governor of that part of New England between Massachusetts and the Saint Croix river, but of real assertion of control by him we hear nothing. Jenness, New Hampshire Documents, 75.

in 1623 to improve them or even to take out patents for them, all that could be done by the council was to grant its domain in parcels to such as would undertake to found private or subordinate public plantations. It was too weak to directly colonize or govern. Substantially all that remains of its history, except its final dissolution, is to be found in the catalogue of its grants; and in the making of them it ignored the allotment of 1623. Of the grants the largest number were made in favor of Sir Ferdinando Gorges and John Mason, with their heirs and associates. They were issued at dates extending through almost the entire life of the council. Mason, however, did not become a member of the council until 1632, and his activity in that body was closed by his death in 1635. The Earl of Warwick was then president, but he soon ceased to attend the meetings. Repeated efforts were made, though in vain, to procure from him the seal of the company. It was then proposed that the number of the council should be filled; that all patents should be called for, perused, and confirmed, if the council saw fit; that a surveyor should be sent over to set the bounds of every grant that had been made, and that other steps should be taken to uphold the monopoly of the council, and to regulate affairs within its domain. But no effective measures were taken to execute these plans.

The earliest grant to Mason was the territory, named Mariana, which lay between the Naumkeag or Salem river and the Merrimac, and which extended inland to the head of the first-mentioned stream. This patent was issued March 9, 1622. On August 10, 1622, to Gorges and Mason jointly was granted the region between the Merrimac and Kennebec rivers, and extending sixty miles inland. This was to be known as the Province of Maine. On December 30, 1622, the grant to Robert Gorges, already referred to, was made. On November 7, 1629, that part of the region already conveyed to Gorges and Mason jointly which lay between the Merrimac and Piscataqua rivers, was granted to John Mason. It was his intention to call this New Hampshire, from the county in England where he had long resided.

On November 17, 1629, the so-called Laconia grant was issued. This purported to convey to Gorges, Mason, and associates the territory bordering Lake Champlain — called in the grant, " the river and lake or rivers and lakes of the Iroquois," — and extending ten miles south and east therefrom, and thence westward halfway to Lake Ontario and northward to the river Saint Lawrence. The patentees were also authorized to select a tract of one thousand acres on the sea-coast, where they should find one unoccupied. The peculiar location of this grant originated from the supposition that the Piscataqua river had its source in Lake Champlain, and that the fur trade could be prosecuted along its course with the nations of the Great Lakes and Saint Lawrence, the central trading post of the company being located on a thousand-acre tract near the mouth of the Piscataqua. The fact that two mountain chains and a river valley intervened between the two sections of this grant was of itself enough to defeat its purpose. On November 3, 1631, the Laconia patentees received from the council, under the name of the Pescataway Grant, a tract including the Isles of Shoals and territory on both sides of the Piscataqua river, extending on the northern bank a distance of thirty miles inland. On April 22, 1635, the share of Mason in the final division of the domain of the New England council was confirmed to him, and the confirmation was entered on the minutes of the council. This comprised the territory between the Salem and Piscataqua rivers and extending sixty miles inland, also the southern half of the Isles of Shoals, and a tract of ten thousand acres lying just east of the mouth of the Kennebec river, to be known as Masonia. To the royal charters, granted, and alleged to have been granted, to Gorges and Mason, reference will be made in another connection.

To the four patents which were granted between 1621 and 1630 to trustees and associates connected with the colony of Plymouth reference has already been made. In the same connection mention should also be made of the indenture of March 19, 1628, to the Massachusetts company. This included the territory between lines drawn three miles north of the Merrimac and three miles south of the Charles river, and extending through to the South Sea.

Other miscellaneous grants were : two at the mouth of the Saco river, which developed into the towns of Saco and Biddeford, Maine ; the Muscongus Grant, later known as the Waldo Patent, comprising a territory thirty miles square, extending back from the seaboard between the Penobscot and Muscongus rivers ; the Lygonia, or Plough Patent, extending along the coast of Maine from Cape Porpoise to Sagadahoc and forty miles inland ; the Black Point Grant of fifteen hundred acres in Scarborough, Maine, to Thomas Cammock ; a grant of fifteen hundred acres to Richard Bradshaw, located above the head of the Pejepscot river ; to Trelawney and Goodyear, Richmond's Island and a tract extending from the Black Point Patent to Casco bay or river ; to Robert Aldworth and Giles Eldridge, a large tract of land near Pemaquid, increasing in extent with the number of colonists that might settle there ; a grant of six thousand acres and one island at Little Harbor, near the mouth of the Piscataqua river, to David Thomson[1] and others ; Hilton's Point on the Piscataqua river, to Edward Hilton ; and possibly the so-called Swamscot Patent, covering a tract south of the lower course of the Piscataqua river in New Hampshire. Various other smaller grants were also made.

Only a few of these concessions were perfected, and of only a small number of them was seisin taken. Owing to the ignorance and carelessness of the parties concerned, not only were their bounds in many cases so stipulated as to overlap, but in some cases later grants superseded earlier and unperfected ones. About the mouth of the Piscataqua river was a network of grants, the bounds of which it is not easy to disentangle.

The most important case of an earlier grant being superseded by a later one was that of the patent to Robert Gorges. He had taken possession of it, and settlers brought over by him had been established within it ; yet, about four years later, by means not clearly known but declared by the

[1] Deane, Proceedings of Mass. Hist. Soc. XIV. 358 *et seq.*

Gorges family to have been surreptitious, the Massachusetts company obtained from the council a grant which included all of the Robert Gorges patent and extended far beyond it on three sides. This grant also superseded the Mariana patent of 1622, within which, however, it is scarcely probable that Mason had planted any colonists.

The grants were made according to two models, one for private and another for public plantations. As specified in the regulation of the council of December 1, 1631,[1] the tenants or freeholders of the private plantations should receive a quantity of land, allotted and bounded by the commissioner of survey. The conditions of grant should be such as the council should order, including the stipulation not to alienate without leave, and within five years to settle upon the grant a certain number of people with their cattle and other possessions. Gorges and his associates cherished the plan of developing not only private plantations, but fully organized sub-fiefs, with institutions of government, all subordinate to a governor-generalship of New England. The larger grants should carry with them authority to call an assembly, make by-laws, and appoint magistrates subordinate to the general government of the entire province of New England. A provision was introduced into the patent of Robert Gorges for appeals from all judgments rendered in his grant to "the Court of parliament" hereafter to be in New England, while he was to supply fourteen armed men to the governor-general when ordered so to do. The Mariana, Maine, and New Hampshire grants are examples of the second class, for they expressly mentioned powers of government. Concessions of that sort, however, were invalid from the first, for the council had received no authority from the king to bestow such powers. Before rights of this nature could be legally exercised, confirmation by the king was necessary.

The smaller grants, or private plantations, correspond to those established in Virginia by the London company, and were in plan fundamentally like Plymouth in early days. The indenture to David Thomson provided for a partnership

[1] Records of New England Council, 99.

between him and three merchants named in the document, and required that for five years their land and trade should be organized as a joint stock. Thomson should go in person to Piscataqua, taking with him men and supplies furnished by the merchants; buildings should be erected, and trading, fishing, and farming begun as a joint enterprise. If Thomson, however, should not bear his share of the expense, which was three-fourths of the whole, the merchants might employ ships and fish independently. At convenient intervals, beginning with the close of a five-year period, sections of the land should be divided in the proportion of three-fourths to Thomson and one-fourth to his partners, while the profits should also be divided in the same ratio. It was a small enterprise; not more than ten persons were probably concerned in it. The only woman known to have been in the settlement was the wife of Thomson himself. But it was a typical example of a large group of settlements of that class in early New England. The partnership was dissolved at the close of the five-year period,[1] and Thomson removed to an island in Boston harbor.

The Laconia company was a private association formed for trading and fishing. By joint contributions it furnished and sent over in 1630 the bark *Warwick*, of eighty tons' burden. She brought a governor of the settlement and a factor. They took possession, and later the company became the owner of the house which Thomson had built and left standing at Odiorne's Point; perhaps also of a part of his plantation. A larger residence, called "the great house," and later " Mason Hall," was built at Strawberry Bank, near the original settlement, by an "artificer" named Chadbourne, who was sent over as an employee of the company. We hear also of Thomas Eyre, one of the company, acting as clerk and accountant, that is, superintendent or manager of the business in England. Besides the plantation at Strawberry Bank, another plantation was formed on the Newichwannock river, where the town of South Berwick, Maine, is now located. At the latter place one or more saw-mills were erected, and lumbering was carried on in

[1] Jenness, Notes on the First Planting of New Hampshire, 10.

connection with these. Land was cleared at both places and farm products were raised for the subsistence of the employees of the company. Stock-raising was also developed to an extent. Potash was manufactured. Fishing was carried on along the neighboring coasts, especially off the Isles of Shoals. But at both plantations the beaver trade was the most important form of industry.[1] Ships plied between the settlement and Europe, bringing supplies and carrying products to market. An ill-timed voyage of the *Lyon's Whelp*, under Captain John Gibbs, in 1632, resulted in heavy loss to the company. The returns from the plantations were not sufficient to cover this. The route for trade to Lake Champlain was, of course, not discovered, though explorations to the west were attempted. In the summer of 1633 Walter Neale, the governor, returned to England to report, and a few months later the partnership was dissolved. The land and other property of the patentees was divided. As a result of this Gorges and Mason separated; the interests of the one being confined to the north, and those of the other to the south, of the Piscataqua river.

Operations similar to those just described were conducted at Richmond's island and in the other settlements along the Maine coast. But extended reference to some of these will more appropriately be made under another head.

The last of the plantations of the proprietary type to be described in this connection is the one founded by the Massachusetts company at Salem. This has been reserved till the close, not because it was the latest to be established or because its form at the outset differed materially from that of the other public plantations to which reference has been made, but because of the historic importance which attaches to it. That importance, however, it attained not as a proprietary plantation, but by reason of its development into a corporate colony. Its history appropriately concludes the treatment of the proprietorship in its earliest form, and opens the way for the consideration of the corporate colony.

The story of the development of the Massachusetts com-

[1] Details are given in the correspondence printed by Tuttle in his Captain John Mason; Publications of the Prince Society.

pany out of an association of adventurers living in the
neighborhood of Dorchester, England, who in 1623 founded
a fishing-station at Cape Ann, has been many times told.
But it has not been brought into proper connection with
other related phenomena.   The enterprise of the Dorchester
fishermen was similar to those started by many others
along the New England coast, those of Plymouth included.[1]
But in addition to fishing the Dorchester adventurers sent
over enough spare men to build rude dwellings, plant corn,
and secure other provisions in quantity sufficient to keep
them through the winter.   During the fishing season they
coöperated with the crews in securing the catch.   Fresh food
was also supplied by them to the crews.   Thus it was hoped
that a colony would be planted, by means of which the
fishing and trading enterprise would be strengthened.
Finding the Plymouth people already fishing and trading at
Cape Ann under an indenture from Lord Sheffield, the Dorchester men duly secured their permit for the settlement,
and Roger Conant was appointed manager or governor.
Mr. Lyford is said to have been invited to be the minister of
the colony, and John Oldham to trade for them with the
Indians.   The last two, however, had been expelled from
Plymouth.   But, as was frequently the case, the departure of the ships which were sent by the associates from
England was not well timed.   They arrived too late for the
fishing season on the New England coast.   In two cases this
mistake was caused by delays resulting from defective repairs
of the vessels.   One of the failures was more than made good by
a successful catch off Newfoundland, but the profits expected
from this were in turn lost as a result of the outbreak of war
between England and Spain in 1625, and the inability of the
adventurers to successfully market their cargo in France.
It was also found that fishermen did not make good husbandmen, and hence that the attempt to found a colony did not
succeed.   These causes combined to involve these adventurers in debt, and to lead them in 1626 to abandon the

[1] The Planter's Plea, by Rev. John White, Force, Tracts, II ; Hubbard,
History of New England, 2 Mass. Hist. Colls. V. 102 ; Thornton, The Landing
at Cape Ann.

enterprise. But fortunately a few of the settlers, among them Roger Conant, were left behind at Cape Ann to care for the cattle through the approaching winter. Some also of the adventurers were unwilling to abandon the enterprise, and conferred with friends in London respecting its prosecution. The lead in this negotiation, if not in the earlier stages of the work, was taken by the Rev. John White, of Dorchester, a clergyman of the established church, but with a strong leaning toward Puritanism and a wide acquaintance among those who held that type of opinion. He congratulated himself much on winning the support of his parishioner John Endicott for the enterprise. Meantime Conant and his friends, dissatisfied with the location at Cape Ann, removed to Naumkeag, a short distance to the west. One of their number was sent to England for supplies.

In March, 1628, the adventurers secured a patent from the New England council for the territory within the bounds already stated. With this land governmental powers in the full and proper sense of the term were not and could not be bestowed. Neither were the grantees [1] incorporated, but the grant was made expressly to them, " their heirs and assigns." They were made tenants, like any body of proprietors, though, according to the provision of this indenture, they held not of the New England council, but of the crown. Apparently, then, the council, in obedience to the statute *Quia Emptores*, resigned all its rights of soil and jurisdiction, and left the patentees face to face with the king. [2] Indeed, it may be

[1] The names of the grantees were Sir Henry Roswell, Sir John Young, Thomas Southcott, John Humfrey, John Endicott, and Symon Whitcombe. Of these Humfrey, son-in-law of the Earl of Lincoln, was the only one known to have been connected with the earlier fishing enterprise.

[2] That this grant was not wholly regular is indicated by the fact that within its bounds was included the territory which the New England council had granted to Robert Gorges in 1622. Years after, Sir Ferdinando Gorges wrote in his *Briefe Narration* that, when the Earl of Warwick requested his consent to the issue of the patent to Sir Henry Roswell and his associates, he gave it " so far forth as it might not be prejudiciall " to the interests of his son, Robert Gorges. But apparently those interests were in no way regarded. Baxter, Gorges, II. 51, 59.

The Massachusetts company, however, had been advised that the grant of Robert Gorges was void in law. Recs. I. 389.

supposed that at the time the grantees considered this indenture only as a means of extinguishing the territorial rights of the council, preliminary to the securing of a charter from the crown. A year later the patentees took advantage of their right to associate others with themselves. A number of east-of-England men, among them Sir Richard Saltonstall, Matthew Cradock, Isaac Johnson, George Howard, Increase Nowell, Richard Bellingham, Samuel Vassall, Theophilus Eaton, and William Pynchon, became interested in the enterprise. These men, whether conversant with the London company or not, were at least in political sympathy with Sir Edwin Sandys and his party in that corporation. The result of the impulse which they gave was the procuring of a royal charter in March, 1629, confirming the grant of territory already made and adding thereto full corporate and governmental rights.

It should be noticed that the company of Massachusetts Bay in New England, which was created by this grant, was modelled after the London company organized twenty years before. Provision was made in the charter for a general court, which should meet four times a year during the law terms, and the Easter session of which should be called the court of election. Provision was also made for a governor, deputy governor, and board of eighteen assistants, all of whom should be chosen by the general court. They had powers corresponding to those of the treasurer, his deputy, and the council in the London company. In the Massachusetts board of assistants we find no suggestion whatever of a royal council, showing that the old combination of 1606 had been entirely outgrown, and that the way had been cleared for the exercise of royal control directly through the privy council or a board of commissioners closely affiliated therewith. The governor, deputy, and assistants were also empowered to meet monthly in a court [1] which in function corresponded with the ordinary court of the London company. In one respect, however, the assistants of the Massachusetts company had a position different from that of the council in

[1] For the doings of such courts of assistants, while the company was resident in England, see Mass. Col. Recs. I. 42–44.

the London corporation under the charter of 1612; six of
them, with the governor or deputy governor, constituted a
quorum of the general court, and therefore, according to the
common law, must be present whenever business was transacted. Thus the Massachusetts assistants had in the legislative body a distinct place, which did not belong to the
Virginia council. All the customary powers were to be
exercised by the general court, either directly or through the
machinery thus provided. Less elaboration was necessary
than in the case of the London company, because the membership [1] of the corporation was by no means as large, and much
less business was done. Still we find that the Massachusetts
men had their auditors, secretary, treasurer, and special
committees. Finally, to the general court of the Massachusetts company, as to that of its progenitor, the power to
increase the membership of the body was given. The word
" freemen " also made its appearance in the Massachusetts
charter as the designation of the members, whereas in the
earlier patents for colonization the terms " associates " and
" adventurers" had been commonly used.

During that period of the history of the Massachusetts
patentees, under the indenture of 1628 and the charter of
1629, with which we are now concerned, they, like the London company, were the joint proprietors of a plantation, the
same in external type as those which have already been
described. As soon as the indenture was procured, John
Endicott was appointed governor of the plantation and was
sent out with a small body of colonists. He superseded
Conant, and permanently established the settlement at
Naumkeag, which was now called Salem. Meantime Matthew Cradock was appointed governor of the company in
England. From a letter of his to Endicott, which contains
a number of instructions, we learn that one ship had been
bought and two others had been hired by the company.
These, with possibly a third, would soon sail for the colony,

[1] The total membership of the Massachusetts company was 110, and these
included no livery companies and no individuals above the rank of knight.
See S. F. Haven, Introduction to the Records of the Massachusetts Company,
Archaeologia Americana, III. 134 *et seq.*

carrying between two hundred and three hundred persons respectively, and one hundred head of cattle. Endicott was desired to provide shelter for these new arrivals, and to send the vessels promptly back laden with fish or lumber, with sassafras, sarsaparilla root, sumach, silk-grass, and "aught else that may be useful for dyeing or in physic." He was also desired to keep a watchful eye on the company's servants that they might not only lead moral lives, but make a favorable impression on the natives. The massacre in Virginia had certainly made a strong impression, for Endicott was warned to learn, by the mistakes of that colony, not to be too confident of the fidelity of the savages. The coming change in the objects of the colonizing scheme was, however, indicated not merely by the statement that the company intended to send over two ministers, but by the emphasis which was laid on this as the "work of the Lord." One would scarce expect to find such an expression as that in the letters or records of the London company, but it frequently occurs from the outset in the communications of the Massachusetts patentees.

The records of the company open with a variety of entries relating to the outfit of the vessels just referred to, which sailed for the colony in the spring of 1629. Seeds, roots, provisions, cooking utensils, clothing and arms for one hundred men were to be sent. The question of procuring various artisans for the plantations, as an ironmaster, an engineer and surveyor, an armorer, a carpenter, a fisherman, was considered. Plans were discussed for the production of salt. The contract with Thomas Graves, who undertook to serve the company in the discovery of mines, care of forts, surveying of land, building of dams and sluiceways, and manufacturing, has been preserved. It provided that, if he remained only a year, the cost of his transportation to and from the colony and his support, clothing excepted, while there should be borne by the company, and that he should be paid £5 per month while in New England. If he remained three years, his family should be brought into the colony at the expense of the company, a house should be built, and one hundred acres of land assigned for his use, and his wages should be £50 per year.[1] Contracts were also made with a surgeon, physician, and three ministers. The Revs. Francis Higginson, Samuel Skelton, and Francis Bright undertook "to do their true endeavor . . . as well in preaching, catechising, as also in teaching, or causing to be taught the company's servants and their children, as also the savages and their children." They with their families were sent on the company's ships ; land and houses were provided, and they received a yearly stipend.

Provision was made that Conant and his men, who were known as the "old planters," should continue to enjoy their lands, be admitted as planters, and have a share in the common stock. But the raising of tobacco, to which they had committed themselves, was not encouraged by the company and soon was actually prohibited. The reason for this was not only the declining price of the commodity in the European market, but objections to its use. Its sale or use by any servants in the colony, except in limited quantities as a drug, was prohibited. A considerable number of servants were employed by the company, and directions for their management occupy a prominent place in the instructions to Endicott. They were to be distributed into families under competent religious overseers who should keep registers of the work they did. Strict supervision should be kept over their conduct, and corporal punishment or confinement in the house of correction inflicted when necessary. Drones should not be tolerated. "Our desire is to use lenity all that may be, but in case of necessity not to neglect the other, knowing that correction is for the fool's back." Swearing and disorders of all kinds, among the free planters as well as the servants, were to be promptly punished.

From the instructions of the company it may be seen that fishing was still prosecuted as a common enterprise, for references occur to the sending of supplies to the fishermen, to the building of a storehouse where their tools and implements might be kept, and to the freighting of vessels with fish for their homeward voyages. Supplies for the building of small vessels were sent to Salem. The manufacture of salt

---

[1] Mass. Recs. I. 32.

was of importance to the colony chiefly because of its usefulness in this industry. But with the transfer of the settlement to Salem and the increase in the number of colonists, agriculture attained predominant importance. It was a principle with this company, as with the London patentees, that Indian claims should be extinguished by some form of purchase, and this ever continued to be their rule of action. For a time after the grant of the royal charter, John Oldham, one of the assignees under the Robert Gorges patent, gave the company much annoyance by his insistence that he should have the management of the common stock, and with others should have the right of free trade with the Indians. Free trade with the natives was not allowed to any of the planters, while Oldham's self-will and his connection with the Gorges interest convinced the Massachusetts company that he was "a man altogether unfit for us to deal with." Therefore he was left to his own course, and Endicott was warned to settle the agreement with the "old planters," and to beware how he meddled with Oldham. In order to checkmate any move which the Gorges interest might make, planters were soon despatched southward, and possession was taken of the region which later became Charlestown.

The system of joint land-holding was not instituted at Salem. The planters were under no contract which required it, and in the summer of 1629 an instruction[1] was sent to Endicott to allot to the adventurers in the proportion of two acres for each sum of £50, or fraction or multiple thereof, which was invested in the enterprise. The grantees were given the liberty to build and improve where they pleased, except that a tract should be reserved for a town. A town lot one-half acre in extent should also be granted to each adventurer who desired it. Planters who had also purchased shares in the common stock should receive fifty acres for each person in their families, while persons other than adventurers who brought families at their own expense into the colony should receive fifty acres for the master of the family and such additional allotments as, "according to their

[1] Mass. Recs. I. 43.

charge and quality," might be provided through special agreement with the company or by the magistrates in the colony. Those who brought or at their own charge sent servants into the colony should receive fifty acres for each of them. No mention is made in the records of the requirement of a quitrent on any of the grants to adventurers, but those who were not such must annually render some suit or service. In case planters should come in groups and desire to settle together, their wish in that respect should be gratified. Provision was made in the scheme for private plantations, and Matthew Cradock, the governor of the company, was a large investor in one of these. Reference is frequently made to the despatch of servants, supplies, cattle, material for ship-building and fishing on his account. On some vessels he sent nearly as much as went on the company's [1] account. As we have already noticed, the company also had its plantations, which were cultivated by servants and managed by the governor under instructions from England. It thus appears that, before it had been in existence a year, the colony at Salem reached the stage of development which was inaugurated in Virginia by Governor Dale.

Finally, by action of the company, at the close of April, 1629, John Endicott was elected governor of the colony for the ensuing year, and provision was made for a council of thirteen to assist him in its government. Of these seven, including the three ministers, were chosen by the company, while it was ordered that the old planters might choose two more, and the governor and council itself complete the number by appointment. The governor and council should also select a deputy governor, while a secretary and such other officers as were deemed necessary for the government of the colony should be designated by them. Having taken oaths of office, they should meet, the governor or deputy governor always being present, and, guided by instructions, should exercise within the colony the powers of government which the company had received from the crown. The term of office for all magistrates should be one year.

[1] Mass. Recs. I. 402.

Thus the structure of Massachusetts as a proprietary province, in which the company so managed its estate as to secure a profit therefrom, was completed.   That a special religious element, akin to that of Plymouth and manifest in no other plantation, was already beginning to show itself at Salem, will be seen in a later chapter.

PART SECOND

THE CORPORATE COLONIES OF NEW ENGLAND

CHAPTER I

THE TRANSFER OF GOVERNMENT INTO MASSACHUSETTS.
THE GENERAL COURT

AT the beginning and for the purpose of comparison, it is necessary again to call attention to two leading characteristics of the colonies which have thus far been described. In the first place, they were founded and managed chiefly for profit, and thus assumed the form of plantations. Though at the outset mines were sought, that soon became a subsidiary object, and agriculture, trade, and fishing commanded the chief attention. The management of the land, the administration of the stock employed in trade and fishing, suggest the topics of greatest interest and importance in the study of colonies of this type. The reason for this is that the colonies here referred to were passing through the early stages of settlement, and that while in this condition they were under the control of parties who had undertaken to develop them as an investment.

In the second place, these colonies were managed by proprietors, trading companies, and land companies, that were resident in England. From them came financial support, food, tools, cattle, and other supplies in considerable variety, without which the plantations could not have secured their start. Officials, authority to do and restrain, direction as to the course and form which the colony should take, all came from the same source. That too was a distant source, where misapprehension and indifference were likely to prevail. Because of their remoteness from one another the company and colony were essentially distinct. The colonists in no sense enjoyed rights of self-government. They were to a large extent indented servants, and were subject to the

141

rigid control of their overseers. Whether free or unfree tenants, they were under an authority of three grades : that of their magistrates, of the proprietors, and of the king, for the monarch himself might possibly interfere to change the policy of the company, or the terms of its charter, or to remove it out of the way altogether.   The experience of the London company, as well as that of many others which were trading and colonizing elsewhere than on the American continent, showed that the possibility of this was always present.   The risk of loss and disaster in such enterprises was also great, and events of this nature might terminate the existence of the company.   Such considerations as these will help to explain the revolutionary step taken by the Massachusetts patentees, the character and results of which must now be described.

It is important to notice in this connection that the model chosen for imitation by the Massachusetts patentees was the London company.   That was an open, not a closed, body ; the significance of that expression being that its membership could be indefinitely increased.   If, as was not improbable, the Massachusetts patentees had thought beforehand of expanding their corporation into a colony, they could not have taken the New England council as their model.   There was no need of adopting or devising a third form of corporation, had that been possible, for the London system gave them what they wanted.   It was chosen and readjusted by those who within a few months came into control of the corporation, so as to give form to a colony which was not only independent of proprietors, but, so far as possible, of the home government itself.   The readjustment was effected by the transfer of the governing body of the corporation — its governor and assistants — into the colony which it was creating.   This removal was a fact of the greatest importance, not only in the history of New England, but in the development of modern social and governmental forms, and as such it is worthy of detailed study.

That a transaction of this kind was considered possible by some of the patentees when the royal charter of 1629 was procured, is indicated, though not fully established, by con-

temporary evidence. Thomas Dudley[1] states that as early CHAP.
as 1627 the project of planting the gospel in New England $\underbrace{\qquad}_{}$ I.
was under discussion among the Puritans of Lincolnshire,
and that, by letters and messages, they imparted their views
to " some in London and the west country." The proposition was considered, and by means of it a connection was
established between the Puritans of the east counties and
those who had been interested in the fishing enterprise at
Cape Ann. At length, "with often negotiation," the business was so ripened, that the royal charter was procured.
John Winthrop, at a much later date though in most direct
and authoritative terms,[2] stated that it was intended " to keep
the chief government in the hands of the company residing
in England," as had been provided in the charters of Virginia and the Bermudas. This part of the statement is
confirmed by the docket attached to the " King's bill," in
which the provisions of the patent were outlined. It
mentions the existence in the document of " clauses for the
election of governors and officers here in England," and
states that such privileges were bestowed as " are usuallie
allowed to corporations in England." [3]

But in the charter as it passed the great seal are no words
which necessitate the residence of the corporation in England. Winthrop, in the passage just cited, explains this
omission of the usual clause necessitating residence in England, by the statement that " with much difficulty we got it
abscinded." So effectually were legal obstacles to removal
eliminated from the charter, that chief justices Rainsford
and North, in an opinion which they delivered in the reign
of Charles II, interpreting the words " in New England "
which occur in the corporate name, declared that the company was created a corporation on the place. And yet,
for a year after the issue of the charter the corporation was actually resident in England and there transacted

---

[1] Letter to the Countess of Lincoln, Young, Chronicles of Massachusetts,
309.

[2] Winthrop, Life and Letters of John Winthrop, II. 443.

[3] Deane, Forms used in issuing Letters-patent, Proceedings of the Mass.
Hist. Soc., 1869–1870, 173.

its business. During that time conditions were ripening
which led to removal, though not till five months after the
issue of the charter was the project mentioned in the general
court.   The history of the company, therefore, shows that it
became established in New England as the result rather of
removal than of original creation.

The Puritans of New England, at least that group among
them which became interested in the Massachusetts colony,
regarded the prospect before the reformed churches in
Europe in 1629 as gloomy in the extreme. The victories
of the imperial forces in the Thirty Years' War and the
defeat of the Huguenot party in France seemed to involve
the permanent triumph of the reactionist cause.   In England
Charles I had dissolved his third parliament in anger and
had entered upon a régime of personal government, a leading feature of which was an ecclesiastical policy that met
with the full approval of the bishops of the Anglo-Catholic
party.   In a little more. than two months after the dissolution of parliament John Winthrop wrote to his wife, "I am
veryly persuaded God will bring some heavye Affliction upon
this land and that speedylye." To him times seemed growing
worse and worse. All the other churches had been smitten,
and had been made to drink the cup of tribulation even unto
death.   England had seen this, but had not turned from its
evil ways, and "therefore he is turninge the Cuppe towards
us also, & because we are the last, our portion must be to
drink the verye dreges which remaine."

Soon after this Winthrop lost his position [1] as attorney before the court of wards, and was able to return to his home
in Suffolk for a period of greater leisure. Not far from this
time a paper was prepared entitled, "Reasons to be considered for justifieinge the undertakeres of the intended Plantation in New England," of which there is strong evidence
that Winthrop was the author.[2] In this the evil conditions
existing in England, including the alleged social and moral
decline of the common people which occupies so prominent
a place in the writings of those interested in colonization,
are described, and removal to a new continent is urged as a

[1] Winthrop, Life and Letters, I, 296, 298, 301.   [2] *Ibid.* 309.

way of escape which has the divine approval. " The whole
earth is the Lords garden and He hath given it to the sonnes
of men with a general Commission, Gen. i. 28, 'increace and
multiplie and replenish the earth and subdue it.' Why
then should we stand here striving for places of habitation,
. . . & in the mean time suffer a whole continent, as fruit-
ful & convenient for the use of man, to lie waste without
any improvement ? " The ill success of Virginia should
not deter those who are interested in the undertaking, for
the projectors of that colony committed the fundamental
error of pursuing an object that was " casual and not religious," of using " unfit instruments " — a multitude of rude
persons, the scum of the land — and of not establishing " a
right form of government." The Massachusetts patentees
in their letters to Endicott had laid great stress on the con-
version and education of the Indians, but the authors of
this paper speak of the enterprise as the founding of a
" church," of " a particular church," which is the " work
of God," to be used for the increase of religious faith and
the removal of " the scandal of worldly and sinister respects
which is cast upon the adventurers." These expressions
indicate a desire to make religious objects and motives controlling within the Massachusetts company. The several
versions of this paper which have been preserved, as well as
references to it, show that it was circulated among the
Massachusetts patentees and their friends.

The earliest reference to the matter in the general court
of the company was made on July 28,[1] when the governor,
Mr. Cradock, read a certain proposal to the effect that, for
the advancement of the plantation and the encouragement of
" persons of worth and quality " to remove themselves and
families thither, the government of the plantation should be
transferred to those that shall inhabit there, and " not to continue the same in subordination to the Company here, as it now
is." After some debate, and a resolve that the members
present should seriously consider the question in private,
noting the reasons for and against it and report the same at
the next general court, the company adjourned for a month.

[1] Mass. Col. Recs. I. 49.

Near the close of that interval Winthrop by invitation met a number of the patentees at Cambridge, and a common agreement[1] was reached and reduced to writing. It was to the effect that the signers, with their families and with such supplies as they could conveniently carry, would be ready to embark for New England by the first of the following March. But the condition of their going must be that, by order of the company, the government and patent should be removed into the colony, there to permanently remain. Among the signers of this, besides Winthrop, were Saltonstall, Dudley, Johnson, Humphrey, Nowell, and Pynchon.

At the next meeting of the general court,[2] which occurred on August 28, two days after the agreement was signed at Cambridge, preparations were made for a debate on the question of removal. The debate was held on the 29th, and at its close, by a practically unanimous vote, it was agreed to transfer the patent and government to New England. Among the members of a committee appointed at the meeting of September 19 the name of John Winthrop appears, though the first general court which he attended was that of the 15th of October. At the time when Winthrop joined the company one of its committees[3] was taking the advice of counsel as to the legality of the course they had resolved upon. It was also considering the proper time for the removal, how the affairs of the company should be arranged so that its interests in England might be properly safeguarded, and to whom as governor and magistrates the fortunes of the company should be intrusted during the crisis of its removal. To the last of these questions an answer was given on October 20 by the election[4] of Winthrop as governor of the company and colony. Humphrey was chosen deputy governor, and the full number of eighteen assistants was elected, among the list of whom appear the names of nearly all who signed the agreement at Cambridge.

Later, when the time of departure actually came, those of the assistants who decided to remain in England resigned their places, and, so far as possible, the vacancies were filled

---

[1] Young, Chronicles of Massachusetts, 281.   [3] Ibid. 52.
[2] Mass. Col. Recs. I. 50.   [4] Ibid. 59.

from among those who were ready to embark.   Under the
circumstances, however, it was not possible to fill all the
eighteen places required by the charter.   John Humphrey,
having resolved to stay behind in England, resigned his
office of deputy governor, and Thomas Dudley was chosen
in his place.   This was the only business done at the last
court of assistants which met in England, the session being
held on board the ship *Arbella*, one of the company's vessels,
March 23 (O.S.), 1629-30.   The first session of the court
in New England was held at Charlestown, August 23, 1630,
somewhat more than two months after the landing at Salem
of Winthrop and his immediate companions.   Seventeen
vessels in all came over that year under the auspices of the
Massachusetts company, bringing about a thousand colonists
with their supplies.   Although only a part of the patentees
ever emigrated, no further sessions of the general court were
held in England.   It met for the first time in Massachusetts, October 19, 1630.[1]   The removal of the company's
charter into Massachusetts was a matter of slight importance ; the significant fact was that the governor, the
deputy governor, and assistants, with enough of the patentees to constitute a general court, came over.   The governing body of the company was thus removed into the colony.
But before referring to the changes which took place in its
organization and in the motives which underlay its later
action, we must note how the business affairs of the company were settled.

When the removal into New England was decided upon,
the company was in debt to the amount of £2500, while
£1500 were needed for immediate disbursement.[2]   It was
suggested that the need of the hour might be met in one
of three ways.   Apparently on the supposition that the
business side of the enterprise was to be continued and was
to remain, as formerly, under the management of the company, it was proposed that the adventurers should double
their subscriptions.   On the other hand, with the view that
the company should at once go out of business, it was proposed that all its assets, save land, should be sold, and the

[1] Mass. Col. Recs. I. 79.   [2] *Ibid.* 62, 63.

subscribers to the joint stock be paid the proportions which should accrue to them from the sale.

The third proposition was a compromise between the other two, and suggested the creation of a temporary trusteeship. It was the one adopted. At a meeting of the company, held November 30, 1629, a board of ten, called undertakers and made up equally of planters and adventurers, was chosen to take charge for seven years of the joint stock. They were to assume both the assets and liabilities of the company, and were guaranteed five per cent net profit on the business done. They were to receive half the profits of the fur trade with the colony ; and were assured a monopoly of salt-making, of the transportation of passengers and goods to and from the colony, and of furnishing the colonial magazine at fixed rates.[1] They were also to receive subscriptions to the common stock from such as might choose to invest, and on such terms as they, as managers, might determine. A treasurer was chosen to receive, care for, and disburse all funds, and Governor Winthrop was made the head of the board. The undertakers provided vessels for the transportation of those who went with Winthrop, and possibly for a time thereafter ; but to their subsequent activity, along this or any other line mentioned in the contract, we find almost no reference in the printed authorities. The settlement of the Dutch on the Connecticut and the Hudson, the preoccupation of the Kennebec by Plymouth and of the Piscataqua by John Mason and his associates, prevented Massachusetts from absorbing a large part of the fur trade of New England. Such trade of this nature as there was appears to have been carried on by individuals or associations under conditions prescribed by the general court ; [2] but of connection of the undertakers with it no evidence has been found.

[1] Mass. Col. Recs. I. 62 et seq.

[2] Ibid. I. 88, 93, 96, 179, 208, 322 ; II. 44, 83, 86, 110, 138 ; III. 152. In the Body of Liberties of 1641 there was no provision concerning Indian trade ; but in the Laws and Liberties of 1649, as issued in 1660, appear acts for its regulation. One of these declares that " the trade of furrs with the Indians in this Jurisdiction doth properly belong to this Common-wealth, and not unto particular persons." See Whitmore's edition of the Colonial Laws of Massachusetts (1889), 161, 242. The votes of the general court concerning

The meagre references in the *Records* and other contemporary authorities to the salt industry show that it was not of sufficient importance to demand much regulation,[1] and not the slightest trace of its being carried on by the undertakers appears. The part played by the magazine in the trade system of Massachusetts must also have been slight, for neither in the writings of Winthrop nor in the minutes of the company have we any account of its existence in the colony subsequent to 1630.[2] In fact, immediately after Winthrop's arrival in Massachusetts, he was forced to send back to Bristol by John Pierce and Isaac Allerton of Plymouth for a supply of provisions.[3] Early the following summer Allerton arrived in the *White Angel* with livestock and provisions for both Massachusetts and Plymouth.[4]

Private trading appears soon to have become the rule in the Bay colony. Of the undertakers who were expected to take up their residence in New England, Isaac Johnson soon died, while John Revell returned to England.[5] This left Winthrop and Dudley in Massachusetts as the only survivors of the board from whom active participation in its work might be expected. But in Winthrop's correspondence, as preserved, the only references to business transactions with the undertakers in England concern payment for the ships which brought over the emigrants of 1630.[6] With Samuel Aldersey, who, as treasurer of the company when Winthrop left England, was to care for the moneys of the "joint stock"[7] and pay them out upon warrants under the bonds

this trade, and the licenses it granted for its prosecution, show how this principle was applied in practice.

[1] Mass. Col. Recs. I. 331; II. 229. These references show that, while permission to experiment with new processes of manufacture was obtained from the general court, freedom to produce this commodity was enjoyed by all the inhabitants of the colony.

[2] Of the existence of a magazine previous to that time there is abundant evidence. Recs. I. 393, etc.

[3] Winthrop, History of New England, Savage's Edition, 1853, I. 448. This will also be referred to as Winthrop's Journal.

[4] *Ibid.* I. 69.

[5] Young, Chronicles of Massachusetts, 315, 317, 336 ; Winthrop, I. 451.

[6] Winthrop, 448 *et seq*.

[7] Mass. Col. Recs. I. 65.

of the undertakers, or any three of them, he apparently
did not correspond at all.[1] In his *Letter to the Countess of
Lincoln* Thomas Dudley said[2] that the loss of the livestock
which had died on the outward voyage, the failure to send a
supply of the same from Ireland, and the delay in building,
"weakened our estates, especially the estates of the undertakers, who were 3 or £4000 engaged in the joint stock,
which was now not above so many hundreds." Still, in
1634, a committee, most if not all of whom were patentees
resident in England, was appointed to choose from among
themselves one to be treasurer for a year " for this plantation " and to grant a full discharge to the existing treasurer;
and in 1638 George Harwood, the treasurer, was requested
to present his account. These entries indicate that commercial relations of some sort were for a number of years
kept up with adventurers resident in England, but not
with the undertakers as such. The hints which have been
preserved concerning such relations do not seriously modify
the conclusion that by the close of 1630 the joint stock or
purely commercial element in the Massachusetts enterprise
had practically disappeared. It was decided that henceforth
that company should not directly engage in trade, but should
confine itself to regulating it. With the removal of the
patentees into the colony, they began to devote themselves to
the work of settlement and government. Trade continued
and expanded, but it was in private hands, subject to the
legislative and administrative control of the colonial government.

An analogous change was wrought in the land system of
the colony at the time of the transfer of the government to
Massachusetts. After Winthrop's arrival, as will be shown
in detail in a later chapter, the corporation acted no longer
in the capacity of a land company, it no longer sought to
obtain a profit from its domain. Instead, the township system developed, as was occurring under similar conditions
in Plymouth. This means that, owing to the circum-

---

[1] During the first year of Winthrop's residence in Massachusetts his son
John was his business correspondent in England.

[2] Young, Chronicles, 321.

stances attending the migration and settlement, the colonists established themselves in detached groups about Massachusetts bay. Sickness, which Winthrop on his arrival found prevailing at Salem, caused him to seek a place of settlement elsewhere. The lack of food caused by the sickness and by the arrival of so many new colonists forced the liberation of 180 servants, and so broke up completely the system of cultivating the company's land by means of them. Owing to the outbreak of sickness among the newcomers, it became necessary to abandon the project, characteristic of colonization thus far, of building a fortified town some distance inland. The variety of the coast, with the rivers which flow into Massachusetts bay, offered several attractive places for settlement, at one of which Cradock's plantation was established. Therefore Winthrop and his associates yielded at once to the natural course of events, and seven different settlements immediately sprang into existence about the bay.[1]

The removal of the seat of the colonial government from Salem to Charlestown caused Salem to appear distinctly as a town. Charlestown had enjoyed a separate existence for a brief time before it became the temporary residence of the governor and other magistrates. As the result of a second removal, Boston became both a town and the permanent place of residence of the colonial authorities. These and the other early settlements were established without express authorization from the general court, but soon the court began to name them[2] and to provide for fixing their boundaries. Constables were also appointed,[3] and other provision was made for the exercise within them of local powers, subject to control by the colonial government.[4] For our purpose the important point is that the towns as communities became the chief grantees of the company's land. After the town had been established and its limits fixed, those of its inhabitants who were the direct objects of the grant became the proprietors of the land within its bounds, and either held and managed it as common or disposed of it to individuals. The colony as such made no effort to secure a

[1] Young, Chronicles, 313.
[2] Recs. I. 75, 94, 127.
[3] Ibid. I. 76, 79.
[4] Ibid. I. 167, 172.

territorial revenue; it did not establish a land office or a system of quitrents. Thus one of the most characteristic features of the provincial system was lacking. In the towns, even when the commons were divided or when grants were occasionally made to individuals, the land was not often sold or leased. Rent only occasionally appeared, and in no sense did it form a characteristic element of the system. At the same time all titles derived their validity from some prior grant of the general court.

We have now seen what was the policy of the corporation of Massachusetts bay concerning trade and land. In form, at least, the corporation was created to be a land and trading company. But it was not the intention of its founders that it should chiefly pursue those lines of enterprise. In fact, after the removal of the corporation into Massachusetts, a form of organization was assumed which was incompatible with the direct cultivation of land and prosecution of trade. This may be regarded as the negative result of the process we are describing.

The transition from the colonial or trading corporation to the corporate colony will appear most clearly when we notice the change which it wrought in the character of the freemen. But in order to understand the ideal from which that sprang, reference should first be made to Winthrop's *Modell of Christian Charity*,[1] a sort of sermon, or meditation on Christian love, which he wrote during the voyage from England. The suggestive part of the discourse is the application of its thought to the problem before the colonists of Massachusetts. In the view of the writer, the work upon which they had entered was one of peculiar importance. Instead of undertaking to found a colony for profit or in order that thereby the power and dominions of the English crown might be increased, they, by mutual consent and with the special approval of true Christian churches, were seeking a place where they could live together under "a due form of government both civil and ecclesiastical." Not only must they do that to which they were accustomed when they lived in England, but more. They must not only profess, but live,

[1] 3 Colls. of Mass. Hist. Soc. VII. 33.

Christianity. They must learn to bear one another's bur-dens, and be united by such strong social bonds that "the care of the public" would "oversway all private respects." The object of the enterprise, in short, was "the comfort and increase of the body of Christ, whereof we are all members." "Thus stands the cause between God and us. We are en-tered into a covenant with Him for this work. We have taken out a commission. The Lord hath given us leave to draw our own articles. We have professed to enterprise these and those accounts, upon these and those ends. We have hereupon besought Him of favor and blessing. Now if the Lord shall please to hear us, and bring us in peace to the place we desire, then hath He ratified this covenant and sealed our commission, and will effect a strict performance of the articles contained in it : but if we shall neglect the observation of these articles which are the ends we have pro-pounded, and, dissembling with our God, shall fall to em-brace this present world and prosecute our carnal intentions, seeking great things for ourselves and our posterity, the Lord will surely break out in wrath against us ; be revenged of such a sinful people, and make us know the price of the breach of such a covenant."

This was the thought, clearly grasped by the leaders, and by many of their less prominent associates, which from the outset had strongly influenced the Massachusetts enterprise, and which now suddenly transformed it and gave rise to a colony of a peculiar religious and political type.

For some months after the arrival of Winthrop and his followers, the magistrates constituted nearly all the members of the corporation who were present in Massachusetts.[1] But at the general court, held October 19 of that year, more than one hundred persons, several of them old planters, applied for admission as freemen.[2] Had these been simply adven-turers, offering to purchase shares in a commercial enterprise or to move into a dependent colony and take up land there, they would have been welcomed. Instead, we find the Massachusetts authorities hesitating. They seem to be cast-ing about for means to save their enterprise from being

---

[1] Palfrey, History of New England, I. 323 n.   [2] Col. Recs. I. 79.

swamped. They apparently desired to ascertain the political qualifications of the would be freemen, and not their capacity to become good farmers or to pay for the stock for which they subscribed; and, as things were, their fitness politically had to be determined largely by moral and religious considerations. The magistrates first and naturally sought to perpetuate their power by procuring the assent of the settlers to an order giving to the assistants not only the right of choosing the governor and deputy governor, but, with them, of making laws and appointing the officers to execute them. To the freemen was left simply the power to elect the assistants.[1] This was clearly a violation of the patent,[2] and was so acknowledged at the next session of the general court. At that time, May, 1631, John Winthrop was reëlected governor "by the general consent of the Court, according to the meaning of the patent"; and by the same body Thomas Dudley was chosen deputy governor. If we seek for an explanation of this sudden return to the form prescribed in the charter, and the abandonment of the narrow oligarchical system of the previous year, we shall probably find it in the religious test which was established by the court at this session : —

" To the end the body of the commons may be preserved of honest & good men, it was likewise ordered and agreed that for time to come no man shall be admitted to the freedome of this body polliticke but such as are members of some of the churches within the lymitts of the[3] same." With this condition established it was safe to admit freemen[4] and

[1] Mass. Col. Recs. I. 79.

[2] On April 30, 1629, the general court in England created, as we have seen, a subordinate government for the colony, consisting of a governor and council, and authorized them to pass all necessary orders for the control of the plantation and its inhabitants, sending copies of all such orders from time to time to the company in London. Recs. I. 38. But this act could not serve as a precedent for the order of October 19, 1630, because the two referred to different institutions of government. The attempt to substitute the governor and assistants as a legislative body for the general court was distinctly inconsistent with the charter.

[3] Mass. Col. Recs. I. 87. Notice in this connection that the freemen are coming to be called "commons" and "people."

[4] The list of those admitted as freemen in 1631 is in Recs. I. 366.

to intrust to them the election of all the magistrates, together
with legislative power. The difficulty which had threatened
the enterprise the year before was thus overcome, the first
hard question was solved. By this act more than by any
other, except the transfer of government, was effected the
transition from the colonial corporation to the Puritan commonwealth. It was done by attaching to the position of
freeman a wholly new qualification, and as the result of the
change he became no longer an adventurer, but an active
citizen.

In May, 1632, it was voted that the governor, deputy governor, and assistants should be chosen in the court of election,
and that the governor should always be selected from among
the assistants.[1] In May, 1634, the powers of the general court
as contained in the charter were reaffirmed. It was then
declared that it alone had power to admit freemen, to make
laws, to elect and appoint officers, to raise money and grant
lands. The freeman's oath of fidelity to the government, as
established, was enacted by this court. It took the place of
an earlier freeman's oath which apparently has not been
preserved. If by the reference is meant an oath administered to members of the corporation while resident in England, the nature of the two was wholly different. The oath
of 1634 provided for submission and loyalty to the "government . . . of this commonweale," and had reference to
nothing but political obligations.

The merging of the corporation in the colony, taken in
connection with the early dispersion of settlements and increase of the number of freemen, necessitated the development of the deputies, the element representing the localities
in the general court. This was a change not contemplated
in the charter, and it resulted in the creation of a colonial
legislature by a process quite different from that followed
in Virginia and the later proprietary provinces. It was
created in Massachusetts not under authority of an instruction from the company or proprietor in England, but by the
expansion of the general court of an open corporation when
removed into the colony itself.

[1] Mass. Col. Recs. I. 95.

Governor Winthrop told certain representatives who appeared before him in 1634, "When the patent was granted, the number of freemen was supposed to be (as in like corporations) so few, as they might well join in making laws ; but now they were grown to so great a body, as it was not possible for them to make or execute laws, but they must choose others for that purpose."[1]

As is well known, the deputies appeared as the immediate result of a protest against the narrow oligarchy established by the magistrates in 1630, and the levy of taxes by them alone. The protest of Watertown, though it was followed by submission, occasioned some important results. In the first place, it drew from Governor Winthrop the declaration that, "this government was rather in the nature of a parliament" than of a mayor and aldermen, as the objectors had thought.[2] This is the earliest authoritative statement from a leader in the enterprise of a change which it was believed had been wrought by the transfer of government to Massachusetts. Expressed in modern scientific terms, it meant that by the change in the qualification of freemen the corporation had been raised from the domain of private law into that of public law. It was regarded as no longer in the proper sense of the word a corporation, but a commonwealth. As a result of this development, the assistants, who, as Winthrop claimed, were representatives of the freemen, had become possessed, like members of parliament, of full discretionary power to legislate and to levy taxes ; while the freemen could exercise political control over them through elections and the presentation of grievances.

It is also probable that the protest from Watertown contributed to the legislation of May 9, 1632, which restored to the general court the right of electing the governor and deputy governor. It certainly caused the issue of an order by that court that two from every plantation should be appointed "to conferre with the Court about raiseing of a

[1] Winthrop, I. 153.

[2] *Ibid.* I. 84. Of course, as has been shown, the type of corporation from which the corporate colony developed was not the municipality, but the trading company.

publique stocke."[1] The language of Winthrop concerning
this event, and the fact that this was a court of election, leads
to the inference that the conferrees were chosen then and there
by the freemen who were present from the respective towns.[2]
Winthrop says they were chosen "to be at the next court to
advise with the governor and assistants about the raising of
a public stock."[3] There is no proof, however, that the conferrees ever met. They are not mentioned again in the
Records, and Winthrop makes no further reference to them.
There is, furthermore, no record of the levy of another tax
till March 4, 1633, and that was voted by the assistants.[4]

The movement, however, though stifled for the time, was
secretly spreading. Shortly before the meeting of the May
court of 1634, representatives from each town met to consider matters which were to be brought before that body.[5]
They desired to see the patent. The reply of the governor
to them shows that they also urged the establishment of a
representative system. He put them off with the proposal
that a committee of deputies from the towns should yearly
be appointed to revise the laws and present grievances to the
assistants, but not to make new laws. This was by no
means satisfactory, and by the next court it was ordered[6]
that thereafter the freemen of each town might choose two
or three representatives to prepare business for the general
court and to act therein with full authority on their behalf
in the making of laws, granting of lands, and doing of whatever else the freemen might do, elections only excepted.
From and after this time, the general court of Massachusetts
consisted of the assistants and the deputies. They sat
together in one house till 1644, though in March, 1636, as a

---

[1] Mass. Col. Recs. I. 95.

[2] Winthrop, I. 91.

[3] Winthrop's language implies that the court of assistants is here meant.
This interpretation is also necessitated by all the circumstances of the case.
The only regular session of the general court at that time in Massachusetts
was the court of election, and that did not meet again until May, 1633. During the intervening twelvemonth, the general court did not meet at all.

[4] Recs. I. 103.

[5] Winthrop, I. 152, 153.

[6] Recs. I. 118.

result of the controversy over the settlement of the river towns of Connecticut, the legislative equality of the two branches was declared.[1] Thus within a period of fourteen years from the transfer of the government the Massachusetts legislature had assumed its final form.

It always bore, however, not only in name but in character, the marks of its origin. As in the corporation, so in the colony, the general court was the source of power. Says the act of 1634, repeatedly confirmed in later years, "It is hereby declared that the General Court . . . is the Chief Civil power of this Commonwealth, which onely hath power to raise taxes upon the whole Country, & dispose of lands, . . . and may act in all affairs of this Commonwealth according to such power, both in matters of Counsel, making of Lawes & matters of judicature, by impeaching & sentencing any person, or persons according to law, & by receiving & hearing any complaints orderly presented against any person[2] or Court."

Like the general court of the corporation, it was wholly an elected body. The governor and assistants were elected just as truly as were the deputies, and for the same terms. From this point of view the only difference between the assistants and deputies was that the former received their mandate from the freemen as a collective body in the court of election while the deputies received theirs from the freemen organized into towns. Over the former the governor presided, while the latter chose a speaker for a single session or a shorter period;[3] under the law of 1636 there were two regular sessions annually, in May and October. The one

---

[1] Recs. I. 170 ; II. 58.

[2] Colonial Laws (1889), 142.

[3] In October, 1647, Joseph Hill was elected speaker " for this week." The speaker was sometimes called moderator. Savage, in his edition of Winthrop, II. 63, gives a list of the speakers under the first charter. The House made its rules, and the speaker simply aided in enforcing them, and had a casting vote when there was a tie. In 1674 two "comptrollers of ye house" were chosen to see that no one spoke more than once till all who desired had spoken. This order seems to have been in force in 1646. Each house had a clerk, elected for a year. Other officers of the deputies, as doorkeeper and steward, were chosen for a single session or less. Col. Recs. III. 115, 19, 4, 78.

was devoted to the business of election and legislation, the
other to legislation. Before either, as will subsequently
appear, important cases might be brought for trial. The
court of election differed from that of legislation in that it
was a joint session of the outgoing magistrates, together
with the new deputies and such freemen as chose to attend
in person, and it appears to have been presided over by the
outgoing governor.

Regularly two deputies were returned from each town.[1]
Cases of disputed election begin to appear in 1635. In that
year five commissioners were appointed by the court to investigate the election of the deputies from Ipswich. It was
decided that two of them had been irregularly chosen, and
they were dismissed. At the same session, however, it was
enacted that the deputies should have authority to hear and
determine differences that might arise about the election of
their own members.[2] But it would seem from the language
of later entries that the court confirmed the action of the
deputies in such cases. In May, 1642, a writ for a new
election was ordered to be sent to Salem, on the ground
that the court was doubtful about the choice of one of the
deputies from that town.[3] In 1654, because of uncertainty
as to its numbers and membership, the court ordered that
constables, on penalty of fine, should thereafter return the
names of persons chosen as deputies by their respective
towns, and whether they were chosen for one session or two
sessions.[4] Occasionally constables had been fined by the
court for neglecting to do this.[5] If non-freemen voted
for deputies, or if freemen voted for one who was unsound
in belief, was unfaithful to the government, or who was
under bond to keep the peace, they themselves were liable
to penalties.[6]

As was the practice among the trading companies of England, both houses made frequent use of committees.[7] This

---

[1] Col. Recs. I. 254.   [3] *Ibid.* II. 2.   [5] *Ibid.* I. 220.

[2] *Ibid.* 142.   [4] *Ibid.* IV[1]. 203.   [6] *Ibid.* 221 ; IV[1]. 206.

[7] In 1644 the elders, in replying to certain queries concerning the relations
of the magistrates and the general court, made this statement respecting the
power of the court to appoint committees. "The General Court hath power

was especially true after 1637. But comparatively few of these were in the proper sense of the word legislative committees. Of this character were committees appointed in March, 1638, October, 1666, and May, 1669, to examine petitions before the court and report what should be done with them ; and many that were appointed during the controversy with the home government subsequent to 1660. But by far the larger number of the committees mentioned in the records were composed in part of individuals who were not members of the general court and were properly executive committees. They were created to supplement the general executive work of the magistrates.

Petitions in large numbers and on a variety of subjects were presented before the general court, and in many cases they occasioned legislation. One of the earliest, as well as one of the most famous, was the Boston petition and remonstrance of March, 1637,[1] against the action of the court in the case of Rev. John Wheelwright. This was signed by more than sixty persons, and resulted in the expulsion of many of its signers from the colony. The Boston petition was probably the result of an effort to settle matters out of court, though in any case, if the committee chose, matters thus broached might be brought before the court. The petition of the inhabitants of Springfield, in 1641, concerning their relation with the river towns of Connecticut was read in open court[2] and referred to a committee. On their report it was further considered, with the result that the control of Massachusetts over Springfield was fully asserted. In 1646, and perhaps earlier, the court had passed an order that no peti-

by patent in such particular cases to choose any officers & commissioners, either Assistants or freemen, exempting all others, to give them commission to set forth their power and places ; which yet wee understand with the distinction, viz., that if the affaires committed to such officers & commissioners be of general concernment, we conceive the freemen, according to patent, are to choose them, the General Court to set forth their powers and places ; but if the affaires committed to such officers or commissioners be of meerly particular concernment, then we conceive the General Court may both choose and set forth their power and places." Col. Recs. II. 92.

[1] *Ibid.* I. 205 ; Winthrop's Journal, I. 293.

[2] Mass. Recs. I. 320.

tions should be received after the first three days of the session, but this was repealed in the November session of that year.[1] In 1654, however, such was the inconvenience arising from the presentation of petitions late in the session, that it was ordered that none be received after the first four days of a court of election, or after the first week of the other sessions.[2]

By the middle of the century petitions had become numerous and varied, as a reference to the journals will show.[3] For some years subsequent to 1650 the entries in the journals fall roughly into the classes of laws, petitions, and miscellaneous orders.[4] Petitions were presented for the bestowment of office, for license to keep ordinaries or to sell liquor, for permission to carry on the business of salt-making, for grant of lands, for permission to buy or sell lands, for confirmation of sales, for the bounding of towns, for the probate of wills, the payment of dues, the redress of wrongs of all kinds, remission of fines and other penalties. An examination of the entries reveals the fact that a large majority of the petitions had reference to matters of a private nature, and called for action of an administrative or judicial character. This statement is further confirmed by a detailed order of May, 1680,[5] respecting the fees payable on reception of petitions. Because the members were put to expense and much time was spent every session in considering petitions, it was ordered that the fees collected on the reception of them be divided among the members according to the same rule which was observed when cases were heard in open court. As this would reduce the emoluments which the secretary of the colony had been receiving from this source, it was provided that one-fourth of his salary should be paid in money from the treasury. Only occasionally do petitions with a distinct political purpose appear.

The governor occupied toward the general court substan-

---

[1] Mass. Recs. III. 82.   [2] *Ibid.* IV[1]. 183.
[3] A good example is furnished by the entries for the May session of 1649. Col. Recs. II. 273.
[4] *Ibid.* IV[1]. 30 *et seq.*   [5] *Ibid.* V. 268.

tially the same position which he held toward the court of the corporation in England. He possessed no veto power. As in the charter, so now, the number of sessions of the general court which must be annually held was specified.[1] After 1639 the court of election met without special summons. Though the governor called the court together on extraordinary occasions[2] and presided over its deliberations, he was not empowered to adjourn or dissolve the court without its consent. On these, as on other questions, he simply declared the will of the majority of that body.[3] His assent to legislation was not required. Therefore, in Massachusetts, the governor could not be considered a branch of the legislature; in no sense was he its constituting officer.[4] He was simply its president, as he had been of the court of the corporation in England, and had the casting vote when there was a tie.[5] When the court was divided into two houses, he presided over that of the assistants. It was in his magisterial power, then, rather than in his connection with the legislature, that the governor of Massachusetts found his strength. During his term, as will appear later and more in detail, he was the permanent administrative head of the colony, and presided over its highest judicial court. Through the exercise of these functions he, with the men who surrounded him, could restrain and conserve, but the onward flow of legislation the governor could modify only through personal and official influence. His position, therefore, was in every way analogous to that occupied by Sir Edwin Sandys in the London company, while in important respects it differed from that of the proprietary or royal governors. His position was stronger than theirs in one respect — he was an elected officer, and thus might be

[1] Col. Recs. I. 118, 170.

[2] Colonial Laws (ed. of 1889), 142.

[3] Body of Liberties, clause 69.

[4] In the General Laws as revised and issued in 1658 the general court is said to consist of the magistrates and deputies. No distinction is there made between the governor and the other magistrates. Colonial Laws (1889), 141.

[5] Laws of 1641, Colonial Laws, 143. The governor also had the casting vote in the court of assistants. Body of Liberties, clause 71.

supposed to carry with him the support of his constituents. His means of controlling legislation were much less direct than theirs, though, as events proved, they may have been quite as effective. The position of the governor in Massachusetts is but typical of the system of which he formed a part. It was a system in which tenure by election predominated, a characteristic which resulted from the merging of the corporation in the colony and which made all the easier the transition to the commonwealth.

Though both the house of magistrates and the house of deputies in the Massachusetts general court were elective, and that for the same terms ; though both were elected by the same body of freemen, and Massachusetts society from which they proceeded was not sharply divided into classes, yet persistent conflicts arose between the two branches of the legislature and continued until, after the Restoration, both were forced to combine in passive resistance to the crown. The explanation of this is to be found in the connection between the civil and the ecclesiastical power in the colony. In order to secure that, and to maintain it when secured, magistrates and elders combined in close alliance, and thus became strong enough usually to control elections and the general court. This, with other causes, insured the retention of the same individuals in the magistracy for long periods. The magistrates were men of ability, who, because of their adherence to the ideal which Winthrop set forth in his *Modell of Christian Charity*, soon came to have strong administrative traditions. They were not believers in equality, and least of all did they cherish anarchical tendencies. These they repressed in order that, as Puritans, they might attain the ideal to which they had committed themselves. Hence the element of leadership and the aristocratic temper from which it originates, were strong among the magistrates and clergy of Massachusetts. It led them to form a clique, and against its predominance and exclusiveness a party in the deputies kept up a prolonged conflict. This struggle forms one of the main features of Massachusetts political life during the first twenty years of the colony's existence. It took the form of an attack on the

CHAP.
I.

legislative independence and equality of the magistrates —
the so-called negative voice — and on their administrative discretion.   With only the former are we here concerned.

It has already been noticed that the charter of 1629,
unlike those which were granted to the London company,
provided for a quorum of assistants whose presence was
necessary for the transaction of business.   Its language was,
" We do . . . give and grant . . . that the governor or
. . . the deputy governor and such of the assistants and
freemen of the said company as shall be present, or the
greater number of them so assembled, whereof the governor,
or deputy governor, and six of the assistants, at least to be
seven, shall have full power," etc.   According to the common law, this quorum must be present when business was
being transacted in the general court, and this fact gave to
the assistants in the Massachusetts legislature a distinct
place which the council in Virginia could not claim by the
words of their royal charter, though they could claim it
under orders of the company.

When, in 1634, the inhabitants of Newtown asked for leave
to remove to the banks of the Connecticut, the majority of
the assistants opposed the proposition and the majority of
the deputies favored it.   " Upon this," [1] says Winthrop, " grew
a great difference between the governor and assistants and
the deputies.   They would not yield the assistants a negative voice, and the others (considering how dangerous it
might be to the commonwealth, if they should not keep that
strength to balance the greater number of the deputies)
thought it safe to stand upon it."   What the deputies evidently wanted at that time was, that the general court
should sit and vote as a single democratically organized
assembly ; and in that case the numerical superiority of the
deputies would enable them to carry the day.   A fast was
kept, and John Cotton preached.   He argued that society
consisted of magistracy, ministry, and people ; the first
standing for authority, the second for purity, the third for
liberty.   Each of these, he said, had a negative on the others,

[1] Journal, I. 168.

and the ultimate decision must be reached by the agreement of the whole. This argument closed the mouths of the opposition, and the attack on the negative voice of the magistrates was for the time abandoned. As we have seen, the legislative equality of the two branches of the court was soon affirmed.

But in 1642 the controversy was resumed. At this time an element of sectionalism also appears, for Salem and the adjacent towns were jealous because the colony was governed so exclusively by a group of magistrates and clergy who lived in, or near, Boston. An incident resulting in part from this feeling was the severe criticism of Winthrop's management of relations with the rival French claimants of territory to the eastward, D'Aunay and La Tour. But the specific occasion of the renewal of the controversy over the negative voice was the famous suit of Mrs. Sherman, a poor widow, against Robert Keayne, a well-to-do Boston shopkeeper, for the recovery of a lost sow.[1] Popular prejudice against Keayne, and in favor of the widow, was strong, and it was increased by the fact that a few years before Keayne had been punished because he charged exorbitant prices for his goods. There was no evidence, however, to show that he was guilty of the charge brought against him by the widow Sherman, and the assistants, as a result of a jury trial, declared him innocent. But the case was appealed to the general court, and there the majority of the magistrates voted for Keayne, while the majority of the deputies favored Mrs. Sherman. This brought up again the question of the negative voice. Winthrop wrote a defence of it,[2] basing his argument on the doctrine of the quorum as he found it in English precedents. By virtue of it he claimed that the negative voice of the magistrates was original and fundamental, and that they had the authority to assent to or reject all propositions which were brought before the general court. Not only, he argued, was the presence of the quorum of assistants necessary to a legal session of the general court, but they, as a distinct body, must legislate in it. Saltonstall in a pamphlet attacked

[1] Winthrop, II. 83, 143 ; Recs. II. 40.
[2] Winthrop, Life and Letters of John Winthrop, II. 428.

the executive as embodied in the standing council, and in this
Bellingham supported him.   This led to prolonged discussions in the court and among the elders, the latter in all
cases defending institutions as they were.   So warm did the
discussion become, that, when the session of May, 1643, was
about to adjourn, an order was passed that every member
should take pains to inform himself about the negative voice,
and any one might soberly discuss it orally or in writing.
But Mrs. Sherman and her supporters finding it impossible
to convict Keayne, the interest in the constitutional aspects
of the subject subsided.   In 1644 the question was forever
laid to rest by the legal separation[1] of the legislature into
two coequal houses.   Thus the contention of the magistrates prevailed.

[1] Recs. II. 58.

CHAPTER II

THE EXECUTIVE AND JUDICIAL SYSTEMS IN MASSACHUSETTS

In Massachusetts, as in the other corporate colonies, the executive power was lodged in the governor and board of assistants. Not only was this a multiple executive or board, but all its members were chosen by the freemen in court of election for the term of one year. For a long period subsequent to the removal of the board into the colony its membership was not kept full. Instead of eighteen members required by the charter, only nine, or even less, were elected. At the outset this was due in part to the lack of suitable candidates for the office, but the continuance of the policy is to be explained by the necessity of reducing the size of the executive board in the interest of its efficiency. Its functions in the colony were quite different from what they were while the company was resident in England, and it was necessary that unity and promptness of action should be secured. These qualities were greatly enhanced by the close alliance of the members among themselves and with the clergy. By means of this also the independence of the executive was in a large measure secured, which otherwise, owing to its tenure by election and its brief term of office, it might have lacked. The same spirit of solidarity kept the leaders among the assistants in office year after year, and thus secured great permanence of tenure.

Massachusetts, notwithstanding its seemingly democratic form, was really governed by a very few men. This fact will clearly appear when we consider how continuously the leading members of the board of assistants held office. Bradstreet held office as an assistant without interruption from 1632 until 1679, and then he was elected governor. That office he retained until government under the first charter

was dissolved.   Between 1630 and 1648 — the date of his
death — Winthrop was governor for twelve years, and was
either deputy governor or assistant the rest of the time.
In one or another of these capacities Dudley served continuously during the entire period of his life in Massachusetts.   During every year but one between 1649 and 1664
John Endicott was governor.   Previous to 1649 he had
served three years as deputy governor and several years as
an assistant.   Bellingham served continuously as governor
from 1665 to 1672.   Leverett was reëlected to the office
every year from 1673 to 1678.   During the last-mentioned
period Symonds served continuously as deputy governor,
while Danforth was the colleague of Bradstreet from 1679
to 1686.   Besides the men already mentioned one might
at any time be almost certain to find among the assistants
during the first generation Nowell, Humphrey, John Winthrop, Jr., and Pynchon.   Gookin, Dennison, Willard,
Atherton, and Stoughton occupy equally prominent places
subsequent to 1650.   Doubtless this record could be paralleled from the history of all the other corporate colonies.
Rhode Island was no exception to the rule.   An appointed
executive could not have been more permanent, or its
traditions more abiding, than was the case with the elected
assistants of the corporate colonies.

Like the council of the province, the board of assistants
also constituted one of the houses of the legislature, and
was the highest judicial court in the colony.   Thus, by
means of it, the executive, legislature, and judiciary were
closely bound up together, as in the English system of
government, though in a way very different.   The idea
that a separation of powers was possible or desirable had
not occurred to the founders of government in the American
colonies.

Owing to these facts and to the dearth of records, it is
not easy to disentangle the work of the executive from the
web of Massachusetts history.   The assistants kept no
journal.   In the journal of the general court, after the first
few years, only occasional references to their action appear.
If we were left wholly to the records, the task would have to

be abandoned as hopeless. But for dates prior to the close of 1648 many and most valuable references to the work of the executive are made in Winthrop's *History of New England*, which is familiarly known as his *Journal*. It was written by one who bore a leading part in all of its deliberations during that period, and is a storehouse of material for the early history of the board of assistants and its relations with the clergy. For the period which it covers, it supplies in part the lack of a journal of the assistants. After Winthrop's death we are left in the dark, and can only infer the acts of the executive from hints and from its known relation to the general court.

The president of the board was the governor, and yet, though elected, he was not an assistant. Still, with the rest, when attention was directed chiefly to their judicial functions, he might be called a magistrate. The governor presumably called special meetings of the board, though often on the advice of one or more of the assistants, and bore a leading part in the conduct of business in regular, as well as special, meetings. His functions, however, were more continuous than those of the other members, so that they might be termed his associates, though they in no sense derived their official status from him. When it was physically possible, the governor was constantly ready at his post as an executive officer. Abundant evidence appears in the pages of Winthrop of the manifoldness of his duties, especially in the earlier years of the colony, and of their continuity. As the chief executive the burden of responsibility rested mainly upon him. It was therefore necessary that he should reside at the seat of government. In the early days he superintended the work of settlement. Then and at all times, during intervals between meetings of the board of assistants, the governor had conducted the correspondence of the colony, held or ordered inquiries, received messengers from various parts of the colony, from the Indians, from neighboring English or foreign colonies; or perhaps had arrested and detained offenders, or put them under bonds. This he may have done alone, with the coöperation of the deputy governor and one or more of the assistants, or with them after advising with some of the elders. In a variety of ways business came into his hands, and when the assistants met, the governor may be supposed to have brought forward more business than any associate, more perhaps than all the associates together.   But the governor had no status apart from the board and the legislature, of which he was president, and therefore was bound by the action of the board.   It acted as a unit, and did not simply give advice which the governor could accept, ignore, or reject.   The governmental centre of the colony became its capital, not so much because the governor lived there, but because it was the place where the general court usually met and where the judicial and executive sessions of the assistants were held.   Boston was fixed upon as the most convenient place for "meetings."

Unlike the province, the system of government in the corporate colony was one in which the weight of the governor among the assistants, as elsewhere, depended much on his personality, on the extent to which he was in harmony with the views of the entire body of magistrates and elders, or could control them.   A political, *de facto*, leadership was the only one possible.   For nearly twenty years, at the beginning of the colony's history, John Winthrop fulfilled these requirements to a high degree and both as governor and assistant enjoyed a corresponding influence.   The only man who ever seriously posed as his rival was Thomas Dudley.   For a time the rivalry was sharp between them, but Dudley showed himself to be the inferior man, and before the first decade had passed fell back into an inferior place.

The assistants who first ordered affairs in Massachusetts were elected in England and derived their office from the general court.   After its removal to the colony the board was chosen in the peculiarly organized court of election. During the first three or four years the assistants, as an executive, bore a relatively more important part in the affairs of the colony than at any subsequent time.   This was due to the fact that, because of the small number of freemen, and the simplicity of all relations, there was little about which to legislate.   The functions of the general court were

for a time partially suspended.   The assistants thus were
largely without a rival.   The initial work of colonization,
requiring as it did single specific acts in a continuous series,
was preëminently administrative in character.   In this respect, notwithstanding the difference in their organization,
the similarity between the New England colonies and the
provinces is clear.   In the course of the four months which
followed Winthrop's landing, the assistants met four times,
and a variety of administrative business was done.   Provision[1] was made for the support of the ministers and military
captains, a house was ordered to be built for Mr. Gager, the
surgeon, and other provision was made for his support ; a
beadle was appointed to attend upon the governor and be
ready to execute his commands ; the time of holding courts
was determined ; the first of a long list of orders fixing wages
of carpenters and other workmen was issued ; the process of
naming towns, of electing and swearing in their constables,
was begun ; the admission of settlers into the colony without a permit from the governor and assistants was forbidden; trade with the Indians without permission was also
forbidden ; a tax was levied, the arrest of Thomas Morton
was ordered, and judicial business was done.

The general court of October 19, 1630, sat but a single
day, and the most it did was to give legislative power, and
the right to elect officers, to the assistants, thus centring
all power within the colony in the hands of the executive.
During the months which followed, before the spring court
of election, the magistrates were free to strike out new
courses, untrammelled by precedents drawn from England
or from earlier doings at Salem.   But they pursued the ordinary routine,[1] offering a reward for the killing of wolves,
providing for a ferry to Charlestown, sending several
would-be colonists back to England as unfit for Massachusetts, warning Salem against Roger Williams, forbidding
the use of money in Indian trade, considering whether or
not Newtown should be fortified.

Though the general court of May, 1631, took from the
assistants the power of choosing the governor and deputy

---

[1] Recs. I. 73 et seq.   [2] Ibid. I. 81 et seq.

governor, it did not forbid them to legislate.[1] During the year which passed before the next session of the general court, we have record of eleven meetings. Then, as in later years, meetings were held less frequently in winter than during the other seasons. Measures which were now adopted by the assistants, but which at a later time might well have passed the general court, provided that the bounds of New-town and Charlestown should be run by commissioners, that all islands in the colony should be appropriated for public use, should be under the control of the governor and assist-ants, and be leased by them to relieve public charges ; that an island in the harbor should be granted to Winthrop as the " governor's garden"; that corn should pass for all debts at the usual price, unless money or beaver were especially mentioned ; that none should leave the colony without permission or carry money or beaver to England without leave of the governor. A few police regulations were issued, servants were frequently whipped for leaving their masters and for other offences. Sir Christopher Gar-dener,[2] who had appeared in the colony as an agent of Gorges, was arrested, but finally was allowed to retire to the eastern settlements, whence he later returned to England. Every assistant was empowered to issue warrants, summonses, and attachments, and the acts of the board were declared authen-tic, if they passed under the secretary's hand.

Upon three meetings of the board held this year the state-ments of Winthrop throw much light.[3] On the first occasion the pastor and elder of the church at Watertown, and others of the inhabitants of that town, came in response to sum-mons to answer for their conduct touching the levy by the assistants of a rate for fortifying Newtown. An assembly of the people at Watertown had been called, before which the pastor, elder, and others had declared that it was not safe to pay money in that way, for there was danger that they would bring themselves and posterity into bondage. As the result of a long discussion with the assistants, the offenders from Watertown were convinced that they had erroneously

---

[1] Mass. Col. Recs. I. 87.   [2] Winthrop, I. 65, 68; Mass. Col. Recs. I. 83.
[3] Winthrop, I. 84, 87, 98.

taken the government of the colony, as then organized, to CHAP.
rank no higher than an English municipality. When it was II.
explained to them that the assistants were annually elected,
and that once a year, before the general court, all grievances
could be presented, they declared themselves satisfied, and
when their submission had been publicly made it was accepted. In this discussion, as we have seen, the claim was
boldly advanced that the colony, though a corporation, ranked
higher than a municipality, and that its legislature and executive combined partook of the nature of a parliament.

At a private meeting of the board on May-day,[1] 1632, two
months and more after the debate with the Watertown
people, the relations between Winthrop and Dudley came
under consideration. Dudley, contrary to usage in such
cases, had suddenly resigned his office as deputy governor.
Two questions were raised touching this act : why he did
it, and whether it was a valid act. Concerning the second
question the opinion was unanimous, that only the power
which placed the deputy in his office could remove him from
it. In reply to the first question, Dudley stated that he had
resigned in order to get an opportunity to speak his mind
freely. Then in sharp words he told how the governor had
criticised him because he had sold to some poor members of
the congregation seven and one-half bushels of corn on condition that they should deliver ten to him after harvest.
This the governor had declared " oppressing usury, and
within compass of the statute." But Dudley insisted that
it was lawful, and hot words arose about it, which Winthrop
says he " took notice of," but " bore them with more patience than he had done on a like occasion at another time."
Dudley also stated that the governor had reproved him for
expending so much on wainscoting and other adornments
for his house ; it was not only a bad example, but the
expense had better be saved for meeting the public charge.
To this Dudley had replied that he had simply nailed clapboard to the wall of his house in the form of wainscot to
make it warmer, and that the cost had been little. " These
and other speeches passed before dinner."

---

[1] Winthrop, I. 87 *et seq.*

After dinner " Mr. Ludlow grew into a passion." The
occasion of this was a statement by Winthrop, that he had
heard that the freemen had intended at the next general court
to resume to themselves the election of the governor, and
that the assistants should be chosen once every year. Ludlow then exclaimed that for a time every year there would
be no government but an interim wherein every man might
do what he pleased. The other assistants showed that he was
wrong, but he refused to admit it, and protested that he
would return to England. Some other affairs having been
attended to, the meeting broke up without a reconciliation
between the governor and deputy. But the day before the
general court met, all differences were smoothed over. The
court adjudged Dudley's resignation a nullity, and he accepted the office for another term.

But relations between Winthrop and Dudley did not
long continue harmonious.[1] The latter, on the expectation
that Newtown was to be the chief town of the colony, had
settled there, and the governor and others had also promised
to erect their houses at that place.   But, in violation of
contract, as Dudley alleged, Winthrop, after having partly
completed a house at Newtown, had suddenly torn it down
and removed to Boston.   Winthrop's explanation of this
was, that the rest of the assistants would not build at Newtown, and that some of his neighbors at Boston, having been
dissuaded by the deputy himself from removing to Newtown,
had petitioned him (the governor) not to recede from a
promise he had made them when they sat down with him
at Boston to the effect that he would not remove thence
unless they went with him.

In order, if possible, to end the dispute, a meeting was
arranged between the governor, deputy, and four of the
ministers, the earliest conspicuous instance of its kind.
After prayer, and the statement of the case by the two
parties, the ministers retired for an hour, and returning
delivered the opinion that the governor was at fault in
removing back to Boston so suddenly, but if the deputy had
dissuaded Boston men from removing to Newtown, it would

[1] Winthrop, I. 98 *et seq.*

excuse the governor *a tanto* but not *a toto*. The governor, therefore, in deference to the judgment of so many wise and godly friends, " acknowledged himself faulty."

Dudley then launched into the second and more important article of his indictment, involving the position of the governor within the board of assistants, and the discretionary power which he possessed. On the admission of Winthrop that he was bound by the patent, Dudley affirmed that, except his precedency and power to call courts, the governor had no more authority than any assistant. Winthrop claimed that he had more, " for the patent," he declared, " making him a governor, gave him whatsoever power belonged to a governor by common law or the statutes." Upon his asking Dudley to state wherein he had exceeded his authority, the latter flew into a passion, and high words passed between the two. But the mediators soon calmed them, and then Dudley cited seven instances in which he thought Winthrop had acted with too great independence. The governor was able to produce law or precedent which clearly justified his conduct in three of the cases ; in one other he was able to show that he acted in coöperation with several of the assistants, in another he stated that he was disposing of his own property. The secretary, if any one, was responsible for another alleged delinquency. In only one case, that of encouragement given to the inhabitants of Watertown to erect a weir on Charles river, did Winthrop admit that he had acted with large discretion, but in this instance he had only expressed his desire that the people would act, promising to use all his influence with the next court to procure an order in their favor.[1] In his journal Winthrop states that he answered these charges, not because he was under obligation to do so, but to convince his colleagues that he was not trying " to gain absolute power and bring all the assistants under his subjection." The improbability of this assumption should have been evident, he says, from the fact that he himself had drawn articles limiting the authority of his office, and they had been approved and

---

[1] The general court of May, 1632, confirmed the action of Watertown in building the weir. Col. Recs. I. 96.

established by the court. These he had not transgressed. Winthrop's defence apparently seemed so clear that the elders found no call for mediation, and so the meeting broke up. Thereafter, we are told, the governor and deputy "kept peace and good correspondency together in love and friendship."

Until May, 1634, the board continued to be the chief organ of government in Massachusetts. Only one meeting of the general court, the court of election, was held annually, and it did little business except electing officers. It laid no commands of importance on the assistants. They continued to grant lands, establish the boundaries of towns, specify what lands should be common, vote rates, fix the rate of wages, and do every variety of colony business. The committee of two which the general court [1] of May, 1632, ordered to be chosen from every plantation to confer about a public stock, apparently conferred, if at all, with the assistants. One of the most important acts of the board was the preparation by it, in 1634, of the resident's oath,[2] and the issue of the order that it should be taken by every resident within the jurisdiction above the age of twenty years. But with the organization of a representative system by the admission of deputies to the general court in 1634, that body assumed again its former place as the chief organ of the system. It then declared, as has been already stated, that it alone had the authority to admit freemen, to make laws, to elect officers, raise money, grant and confirm lands. Two annual sessions of the general court, and sometimes more, are thenceforward regularly held. Orders of an administrative nature, as well as laws, emanated from it. The board of assistants from that time became a purely administrative and judicial body. The work of legislation done by them, they now did as members of the general court. The records of their doings outside the legislature soon fail us, but the few that remain [3] show us that they continued to swear in

[1] Winthrop, I. 91.

[2] Mass. Col. Recs. I. 115. The term "resident" in this connection has a technical meaning. It implies a householder or sojourner who was not a freeman.

[3] *Ibid.* I. 121 *et seq.*

constables and magistrates, to regulate the conduct of servants and their contracts, and to bind over to keep the peace.
But from Winthrop we learn that the volume of administrative work, to say nothing of the judicial business, which
they continued to do was large. That, except in the winter,
the meetings continued to be held monthly or oftener is
certain. Many orders issued by the general court were
executed by the assistants. In the pages of Winthrop we
see the assistants providing for the defence at Castle island,
taking action about the defacement of the flag at Salem,
deliberating about a treaty with the Pequot Indians, concerning themselves repeatedly and intimately with the case
of Roger Williams, consulting the ministers as to the course
which should be pursued if a general governor should be
sent from England, sending an expedition to Block island to
avenge the death of John Oldham, treating with the Narragansett Indians, corresponding with the neighboring colonies
about coöperation against the Pequots, causing the preparation of a defence of the policy of the colony toward the
Antinomians, and so on through the entire period. The
continuous executive work of the colony was done as fully
by the governor and assistants in corporate colonies, though
they held by an elective tenure, as it was by the king and
council in England.

Early in 1635, when the colony was facing serious peril,
the question of the degree of mildness or severity which it
was proper for the assistants to manifest in the treatment of
offenders arose. The policy of Winthrop, in accord with his
habitual temper, had been comparatively mild ; that followed
by Dudley, who had recently closed a term as governor, had
been characteristically severe. Still the two men continued
to act as friends. But the Rev. Hugh Peters and Henry
Vane, newcomers in the colony, thought they saw factions
developing about the two magistrates, and hence had a conference summoned,[1] much like that of 1632. It was attended
by Haynes and Bellingham, who were then the governor
and deputy governor, by Winthrop and Dudley, Vane and
Peters, and by three of the older ministers of the colony.

[1] Winthrop, I. 211 *et seq.*

As Dudley and Winthrop professed mutual friendship and ignorance of any occasion for the conference, it devolved on Haynes to specify certain cases in which he thought Winthrop had "dealt too remissly in point of justice." Winthrop admitted some fault, but declared it to be his judgment that, because of the ignorance of the people respecting new laws, and the labors and hardships they had to endure, "in the infancy of plantations justice should be administered with more lenity than in a settled state." But if it was made clear to him that he was in error, he would adopt a stricter course. The question was then referred to the ministers for an opinion, and the next morning, in contradiction of Winthrop's opinion, they unanimously reported that in plantations strict discipline in military affairs and in the punishment of criminals was more needful than in a settled state, because it tended "to the honor and safety of the gospel." That military discipline in any of the colonies was likely to be excessive is not probable ; but their criminal law and procedure might conceivably have been more humane. However, the experience and worldly wisdom of the best of all their governors was ignored by the elders, and the colony was committed to a policy of rigor. Such was the power of the clergy, that Winthrop acknowledged himself convinced and promised to follow a stricter course hereafter. A set of articles was prepared by the conference with the purpose of strengthening harmony and coöperation among the magistrates. The last of these provided that acts of contempt toward the court or any of the magistrates should be specially noted and punished, and that the magistrates "should appear more solemnly in public, with attendance, apparel, and open notice of their entrance into court."

In 1635 and 1636 the aristocratic tendencies in Massachusetts were strengthened by reports that certain Puritan noblemen from England — Lord Say and Sele, Lord Brook, and others — were intending to remove thither. The correspondence [1] which resulted from this revealed the fact that the order of magistracy and the rank of gentleman [2] were

---

[1] Hutchinson, History of Massachusetts, I. Appendixes II and III.

[2] In the Body of Liberties, sect. 43, it was enacted that no true gentleman,

considered very nearly synonymous by the Massachusetts leaders, though they were not quite ready to admit that office and rank should be hereditary. That democracy was not ordained of God and that their system was not democratic, they expressly affirmed. But they were not ready to give up annual elections, though they insisted that the bestowment of office through them be limited by a strict regard for fitness. That, as we have seen, resulted in a permanency of official tenure which carried with it a suggestion of the hereditary quality. John Cotton, in a sermon preached before the general court in 1634, expressed the view that an office was analogous to a freehold.[1] Both he and others found sanction in the Bible for the belief that the higher magistrates should hold for life.[2] This opinion seems to have prevailed especially among the clergy.

On the advice of the elders who held this view, and as a concession to Lord Say and Sele and his friends, the general court, in the session of March, 1636, ordered[3] that at the next election, and from time to time thereafter, a certain number of magistrates should be chosen for life, and be removed only for crime, inefficiency, or other weighty cause. These were to constitute a standing council, of which the governor should always be president. It should have such power as the general court saw fit to bestow upon it. The following May Winthrop and Dudley were chosen members.[4] A year later Endicott was added. Vane, like his successors, was president during the year of his office as governor. No other members were ever chosen. No duties seem to have been imposed on this body, except that of issuing commissions to military officers during the Pequot War, and of preparing for defence against a possible interference of the home government in 1636. It soon became apparent that there was no place for the standing council in the Massachusetts system; it was always unpopular and therefore never developed.

or none equal to a gentleman, should be punished with whipping, unless his crime was very shameful and his course of life vicious and profligate.

[1] Winthrop, I. 157.

[2] *Ibid.* 220 ; Hutchinson, I. Appendixes II and III ; Winthrop, I. 363.

[3] Mass. Col. Recs. I. 167.

[4] *Ibid.* I. 174, 195 ; Winthrop, I. 220.

In 1637 [1] a statement by one of the elders that, according to the practice of Israel and the best governments of Europe, a governor ought to hold for life, elicited from the deputies a proposal that no councillor, chosen for life, should have authority as a magistrate unless he was also chosen at the annual elections to one of the places of magistracy established by the patent. Governor Winthrop, rightly interpreting this as an attack on the standing council, refused to put it to vote until the magistrates had considered it. This they did, and proposed instead a declaration,[2] that the intent of the order creating the standing council was that its members should be chosen from those who had been magistrates, and that no new order of magistracy should be created. An order was therefore now passed that no one of these councillors perform any act of magistracy, unless he were annually chosen according to the patent. Thus the prejudice which the council was occasioning was appeased. But at the same time the order was an acknowledgment of the utter uselessness of the council, and with the death of Winthrop it vanishes from sight. No further attempt was made in the corporate colonies to coquet with hereditary orders or terms of office for life.

In a previous connection it was stated that, when the negative voice of the magistrates was under discussion, their administrative discretion was also an object of criticism. It played a part, too, in the controversy between Winthrop and Dudley. The discretion of the assistants, especially as an executive body, was without express limitations. Provisions of such a nature found no place in royal charters, and legislation developed too slowly during the early years of the colony to put any effective checks on their discretion. It was exercised freely in the interest of the church-state, and upon it hinged much of the discussion of the executive power in the early history of Massachusetts. In 1635 the deputies complained [3] of the possible danger to the state arising from the fact that, owing to positive laws, the magistrates might proceed according to their discretion. This led to the appointment of the first commission to frame a

---

[1] Winthrop, I. 363.   [2] Mass. Col. Recs. I. 264.   [3] Winthrop, I. 191.

body of laws "in resemblance to a Magna Charta." That
act, after many delays and the appointment of many other
committees, resulted in the draft and issue of the Body of
Liberties of 1641. But its provisions limited the judicial,
more than the administrative, discretion of the board, and
therefore failed to quiet the complaint.

In 1644 objection was made to the assistants — who are
now sometimes referred to as the council — acting as a council for the administration [1] of the affairs of the colony during
the recesses of the general court. This involved a denial of
the permanent executive power of the assistants. The opposition was in part sectional, as was that directed against the
negative voice, and the members from Essex county carried
through the deputies a bill empowering seven of the magistrates and three of the deputies, together with Rev. Nathaniel Ward, of Ipswich, to order all the affairs of the colony
during the approaching vacancy of the general court. This
was a proposition to transfer to a committee of the general
court powers which had been exercised by the assistants
since the founding of the colony, and which were an outgrowth of the powers they possessed while the company was
resident in England. The magistrates returned the bill with
the answer that they thought it tended to subvert the government and the liberty of the freemen by taking from them
the right of election ; also that by it four of the magistrates
would be put out of office. They finally asserted that the
assistants already had by charter the power of a permanent
council, and should not accept it by commission.

The discussion suggests an important difference between
the view of the assistants and that of the opposition concerning the relations in which the charter stood to the government of the colony. The argument of the assistants implied
that in such a case an appeal to the charter was final; that
the general court was limited by it ; that the assistants had
powers of government before the colony had written laws or
general courts had been held ; that the office of governor
presupposed the power to govern, though positive laws were
lacking; that the general court could direct the exercise of

[1] Winthrop, II. 204, 250 ; Col. Recs. II. 90.

power by the magistrates, but not deprive them of it.   The deputies held that the general court was supreme within the colony, and that it was useless to appeal from its acts to the charter ; the assistants had no power out of court save that which was given them by the general court.   The deputies stood upon the platform of legislative absolutism.

The scheme for the time was defeated by the refusal of the magistrates who were designated in the bill to serve on the commission.   At the next session, however, not only the question of administrative discretion, but that of the place of the assistants as an executive board in the colony government, came up again, and the elders were called on for their opinion.   In well-reasoned and moderate statements they sustained the position of the board of assistants as a part of the system of government in the corporate colony.[1]   Governor Winthrop also wrote a vindication of Massachusetts against the charge that it had an arbitrary government.   He based his argument, so far as it was political in character, on the fact of the election of officials by the freemen, and on representation of the freemen in the general court.   These utterances were decisive, and the position of the assistants as an executive board was never again questioned.

But it was in their judicial even more than in their executive capacity that the discretionary power of the magistrates was assailed.   This leads us to a consideration of the judicial system of colonial Massachusetts,[2] a subject which will not

---

[1] Mass. Col. Recs. II. 90, 93 ; Winthrop, II. 251, 256 ; Winthrop, Life and Letters, II. 440.

[2] The time has not yet come when a thorough comparative study can be made of the judicial institutions of the American colonies.   The sources, at best, for the seventeenth century are fragmentary.   They are also not easily accessible.   A knowledge of contemporary judicial institutions and legal procedure in England, such as is scarcely yet possessed by any one, is a requisite for the undertaking.   But when the conditions shall be ripe for the study, a rich harvest awaits the legal historian who shall attempt thoroughly to investigate the history of the introduction of English law into the American colonies.   In the Suffolk court files, and doubtless also in the records of the county courts of eastern Massachusetts, a mass of valuable material remains yet unexplored.   A most praiseworthy step toward making this accessible has been taken in the publication of the Records of the Court of Assistants, 1673–1692.

only complete our view of the activity of the assistants, but CHAP.
exhibit another and important function of the colony govern-   II.
ment as a whole.

The development of Massachusetts after it became a corporate colony furnishes a striking example of the rapid and
spontaneous unfolding of institutions from an original germ.
It suggests familiar flowering processes in the physical
world. The company, as it was in England, was a simple
organism, with power to direct or oversee the growth of a
colony, but without authority or instrumentalities for making or executing laws, administering justice, collecting or
expending a revenue, carrying on war, or developing the institutions of education and religion. Those functions must be
performed in the colony itself and by the forces and authorities there. Had the company continued to reside in England, it would have superintended the growth and exercise
of these functions, but would have directly performed none
of them. As the immediate consequence of its removal into
the colony, however, the company began to assume all these
powers and to exercise them directly. By losing itself in
the colony it became a fully developed political organism.
Starting with the general court, or at the beginning with
the assistants as a substitute for it, the company developed
all the organs which were necessary for the government of
the jurisdiction. In the full and direct assumption of governmental powers by the company itself appears the essence
of the corporate system.[1]

From the outset the general court transacted some judicial business, and by law judicial functions were attributed
to it. But after 1634, when it became specifically the legislature of the colony, the trial of ordinary suits before it was
discouraged. Two special features of its work, as time went

[1] Winthrop states that one of the reasons why the magistrates hesitated
to have a written code of laws prepared was their feeling that, though it
would be a violation of the charter to make laws which were repugnant
to those of England, "to raise up laws by practice and custom" would be no
transgression of it. If the civil marriage were expressly legalized, such a
law would be repugnant to English statutes; "but to bring it to a custom
by practice for the magistrates to perform it, is no law made repugnant, etc."
Winthrop, I. 388.

on, were the hearing of suits in chancery and the trial of such admiralty cases as arose. Original cases of a judicial nature were brought before it by petition. Though many such were presented and the cases were heard, yet it was those of chief importance, especially such as had a political bearing, with which the general court was mainly concerned. In 1642 the first attempt was made by law [1] to distinguish between the sphere of the general court and that of the assistants, and this was occasioned by the large amount of time consumed in hearing civil cases which properly belonged to the inferior courts. Hence it was ordered that such cases should first be heard in the lower courts, and only when justice could not be there obtained should the general court [2] be applied to for relief. The records, however, show that much judicial business continued to be done in the general court.

When, in 1644, the question was put to the elders, as referees, whether the general court had judicial authority, they could not [3] find that it was granted by charter, though they did find that that body could remove a delinquent official. When also a law of the colony provided for appeals, or the reserve of special cases for the general court, then it might hear them. Of these they specially mentioned cases of banishment, loss of life or limb, cases which were weighty or difficult or without express law.[4] In such cases only could the freemen exercise judicial power. Winthrop, in his paper on the negative voice, argued that the deputies, as such, had no judicial powers, but by association with the magistrates in the general court they obtained the right to share the exercise of all the powers which the magistrates could employ in that court. When they were in judicial session the two houses sat together, and the deputies were put under a special oath. Cases were decided then by majority vote of the whole court.

From the beginning the assistants heard and decided most of the suits which arose in the colony. As the institutions

---

[1] Mass. Col. Recs. II. 16.

[2] A case of appeal from the assistants to the general court was that of Saltonstall and D. Yale *vs.* Abraham Shurt, 1648. *Ibid.* II. 231.

[3] Mass. Col. Recs. II. 93.   [4] Winthrop, II. 255.

of the colony grew and became differentiated, they clearly
appear as its highest regular judicial court.   The close union
of executive and judicial functions in their hands is illustrated by the fact that, for a decade and probably longer after
the founding of Massachusetts, the records of the assistants
as a council and as a court were kept indiscriminately in the
same book.   A similar union of administrative and judicial
powers in the same hands appears at the beginning in all the
other colonies, and gives evidence of the rudimentary and
undeveloped character of their institutions.   It suggests the
union of justice and administration in primitive communities, where the activity of government was directed largely
toward the keeping of the peace.   The earliest cases which
were tried by the assistants had distinctly this object, to
decisively establish the supremacy of the founders of Massachusetts over recalcitrants who appeared or were found
within its borders.   Thomas Morton, Philip Ratcliff, Henry
Lyn, Thomas Dexter, were offenders of this order, and they
were dealt with by a process as summary as the Star Chamber
would have used in similar cases.   The freedom of action, or,
in other words, the discretionary power of the magistrates,
was increased by the fact that they fell back on the Mosaic
law for principles and precedents, when those which they
were able to draw from English sources failed them.   The
same tendency to the administration of a summary type of
frontier justice was also strengthened by the fact that few,
even of the magistrates, were trained lawyers, while it was
necessary that controversies should be settled with the least
possible cost.   Winthrop, Bellingham, and Humphrey were
the only magistrates under the first charter who are known
to have been lawyers, though possibly Pelham and Bradstreet
may be added to the list.[1]

In the early days, before their powers were at all defined,
a variety of cases came before them, as " felony," man-
slaughter, theft, assault, suits for civil damages, debts,
various offences of servants and apprentices, drunkenness,
and other public disorders ; while coroner's inquests were

[1] Washburn, Judicial History of Massachusetts, 50 ; Savage, Winthrop,
II. 44.

instituted and wills proven. For several years practically
all the judicial business in the colony was done by the
assistants, and they acted as a police court for Boston.
Though this was an exercise of power which in England
would have been impossible, its continuance resulted in their
becoming the chief judicial court of the colony.

In 1636 it was enacted that the assistants should hold
four judicial sessions annually at Boston, which were
known as the great quarter courts.[1] Three years later, in
1639, the number[2] of regular sessions was reduced to two,
the one in the spring and the other in the fall. They were
occupied with actions on appeal from inferior courts,
divorce, and criminal cases extending to life, member, and
banishment. These sessions were attended by the governor, deputy governor, and " the rest of the magistrates."
In the case of a tie, the governor had the casting vote.
The magistrate[3] who sat in the court from which an appeal
was taken could not vote on the appealed case when it was before the court of assistants. Special sessions might be called
by the governor for the trial of capital cases. Because of
the increase of business it was also enacted that those members of the court who lived near Boston should hold four[4]
special sessions yearly to hear civil suits, provided they did
not involve more than £20, and criminal cases which did
not involve life, member, or banishment. In spite of the
enactment of 1639, the custom of holding four sessions
annually must have been continued, for, in 1649, we find an
order[5] to the effect that the number of quarter courts, which
had regularly been four, should be reduced to two each year.

As the right of appeal to the court of assistants was
unlimited, its jurisdiction was very broad,[6] the intention
apparently being to remove the necessity of the general court
acting in any but public business. The court of assistants
was currently held to possess a jurisdiction as broad as
that of the three great English common law courts, while it
also granted letters of administration. When the lower

---

[1] Mass. Col. Recs. I. 169.
[2] Laws, ed. of 1889, 143.
[3] Ibid. 122.
[4] Mass. Col. Recs. I. 276.
[5] Ibid. II. 286.
[6] Washburn, Judicial History of Massachusetts, 30.

courts were instituted, the assistants ceased to hear so many
petty cases, or to act so much in the capacity of a local
police court as they did in the earlier years of the colony.

Much the same use was made of the jury, both in civil
and criminal cases, as in the courts of England. Regularly
the jurors found the fact, and the court declared the law,
"or they may direct the jury to find according to the law."[1]
In the form of writs and in all matters of procedure, brevity
and promptness were sought. In appeal cases the rule was
that no additional evidence should be taken, but that the
evidence which was presented from the lower court should
be exclusively relied on. Proceedings before the court seem
to have been mostly in writing. Because of the obstructions to travel and the need which people were under to
attend constantly to their domestic concerns, it was difficult
to bring them to court to testify. For this reason depositions were in many cases taken and sworn to in the homes
of witnesses, and were read in court. When parties could
appear, they testified orally, questions probably being asked
by the court, and the substance of the testimony was taken
down in writing. Attorneys or counsel, in the modern sense
of those terms, there were few or none. A lawyer here or
there, or a friend who was experienced in business, might
assist in drawing papers, but it is not certain, even then,
that they would appear or speak in court, as on behalf of a
client. The general prejudice among the colonists against
lawyers as a class, and the desire to keep down the cost of
litigation, prevented the employment of attorneys. Suitors
therefore had to manage their cases as best they could. In
many instances they consulted magistrates privately, in
advance, and tried thus to secure the favorable opinion of
one or more of those who were to be their judges. So
general did this custom become,[2] that a law was passed
providing that magistrates should not vote in the decision
of civil cases in which their relatives or tenants were concerned, or in which they had given advice. The evidence
taken in written form was given to the jury, and upon that

[1] Mass. Col. Recs. II. 21.
[2] Winthrop, II. 42–44; Washburn, *op. cit.* 51; Mass. Col. Recs. II. 39.

their verdicts were rendered.   The verdicts were brief, and were often delivered sealed to the magistrates.

The records which have survived indicate that the administration of justice was regular and systematic, that great respect for the order and dignity of the magistrates in and out of court was enforced, while on the other hand civil rights, on ordinary occasions, were duly guarantied.   The magistrates maintained a somewhat patriarchal attitude, and in the justice which they administered there was a large element of equity.   Their religious opinions naturally led them to seek, when possible, the reform of the criminal, as well as the satisfaction of the ends of justice.   The impression gained from the records is that, on the whole, the declarations contained in the first clauses of the Body of Liberties,[1] guarantying the resident against arbitrary judicial action, were made good in practice.   The spirit of justice was there, although by no means all its modern safeguards, such as elaborate judicial formalities and rules of evidence, the activity of attorneys, and the presumption that the accused is innocent until he is proven guilty.

This means that offenders against whom popular prejudice ran high, who placed themselves in antagonism to the cherished plans or views of the magistrates and freemen, could not expect mild treatment, or even justice, from the tribunals which then existed.   The same was true in England, and, indeed, among all civilized people at that time.   Under such conditions the jury trial, even if it was permitted, afforded little protection.   The control of the bench and of government attorneys, where there were such, over the admission and interpretation of evidence was almost unlimited, and before them the accused stood helpless.   In Massachusetts the magistrates were both judges and attorneys, and if they chose to exercise their power to crush an offender, he had no protection against them.   These statements apply to such trials as those of the Antinomians and Quakers; with qualification also to the trials of the unfortunates who were accused of witchcraft.   The accounts which have come from Quaker sources concerning the trials of their co-reli-

[1] Colonial Laws, ed. of 1889, 33.

gionists in Massachusetts show that, on some occasions, the magistrates there could act and talk as brutally as did the most notorious among the judges of the same period in England.

The trial of Mrs. Hutchinson, which was at the same time a legislative hearing in a case of the highest political importance, was characterized by great informality and great partiality. The jury was not employed. The magistrates and clergy, who were the prosecutors, furnished, with a few exceptions, all the witnesses, and were at the same time the most influential of the judges. Nearly all the testimony was given by and for them. Except in the case of two of the clergy, it was not given under oath, and no attempt was made to sift it or test its worth. Mrs. Hutchinson had no counsel and she questioned witnesses very little. The governor presided and, with an occasional interruption, conducted the examination of Mrs. Hutchinson. It was essentially a colloquy between her and the court, interrupted at times by statements from others and by her speech respecting her revelations. Throughout the trial the court made no effort to conceal its prejudice against the accused, and the spirit which it exhibited would have well become an attorney for the government. The same is true of the trial of Wheelwright and of all accused persons who were considered to be foes of the Puritan system of religion and morals. Trials in the proper sense of the word they were not, but relentless inquisitions used by the government for the purpose of crushing opposition. By means of them, offences which differed in form from any that could well have been committed in England were punished by heavy penalties, while scant regard was paid to the rules of English procedure. In these proceedings, as in all others before the Massachusetts courts prior to 1660, no mention was made of the king or of his authority. But, as has already been suggested, the spirit shown in these famous cases was the exception rather than the rule. If sweeping conclusions were drawn from these cases, numerous though they were, the facts of history would be seriously misrepresented. The administration of justice in the Puritan colonies proceeded in an even and steady course, according to precedents which were a free adaptation from English practice, and in general with a due regard to the rights of all concerned. Only for brief periods and in a special class of cases was it diverted from this channel by the influence of passion.

But the activities of the assistants as judges were not confined to their functions in the central court of the colony. They were felt far and wide in the lower courts and in the system of local justice. In 1636 it was ordered that a court should be held quarterly at Ipswich, Salem, Newtown, and Boston. In 1639 [1] the decisive step toward the formation of counties was taken by the establishment of county courts. Four counties were thus formed, — Suffolk, Middlesex, Essex, and Norfolk. It was provided that courts in these jurisdictions should be held by the magistrates who lived in the respective counties, or by any other magistrate who could attend them, or by such as the general court should appoint for the purpose, together with such persons of worth as the general court should designate from time to time on nomination by the freemen of the towns to be joined as associates in commission with the assistants. In each county there should be in all five magistrates and associates, and the presence of three of them — one being a magistrate — should be required as the necessary quorum for holding a court. In 1650 an act was passed which provided that at the time when votes were cast for town magistrates, associates should be elected by ballot in the towns of their respective counties. They were then to be presented before the court of election for its confirmation. [2] The county courts were given power to hear and determine both civil and criminal cases. Their jurisdiction extended to cases of divorce, to civil suits which did not involve more than £10, and to criminal cases which did not extend to life, member, or banishment. Like the court of assistants, they might employ jury trial. The courts should appoint clerks and other necessary officers. Their criminal jurisdiction was

[1] Mass. Recs. I. 169 ; Laws (1889), 143.
[2] *Ibid.* III. 211 ; V. 31. See many instances of confirmation by the general court.

analogous to that of quarter sessions in England, and in that
capacity they performed a great variety of functions.   They
appointed commissioners to hear small causes, trustees of
public legacies, persons to lay out highways, a master of
the house of correction, searchers of money, and viewers
of fish.   They confirmed the nomination of military officers,
apportioned charges for the repair of bridges; they licensed
innkeepers, and packers of sturgeon, and punished violation
of licenses; they ordered the removal of obstructions on
highways, punished idle persons, punished excess of apparel,
compelled restitution of overcharge by merchants, determined
rates of wages in case of dispute, provided for the poor; they
admitted freemen who were church members, fixed ministers'
allowances, saw that they were paid, inquired into the publication of heretical doctrines, punished heretics and pro-
faners of the Sabbath, saw that Indians were civilized and
received religious instruction, did all varieties of probate
business, punished those who carried on unlicensed trade
with the Indians.   Full provision was made for appeal to
the court of assistants.

In 1638, to avoid the cost necessitated by bringing small
causes before the assistants, it was enacted that any magistrate, in the town where he dwelt, might hear and determine
at his discretion all causes wherein the debt or damage
involved did not exceed twenty shillings, and that in towns
where no magistrate lived the general court should from time
to time commission three men for the purpose.   Later, the
county courts appointed these on request or approval, and
their jurisdiction was extended to cases involving forty shillings.   When one of the commissioners was a party to a
case, the selectmen might act as judges; they might also try
offences against by-laws of towns, when the penalty did not
exceed twenty shillings.   The jurisdiction of commissioners
of small causes was confined to their own towns, but, when
the parties lived in two different towns, the plaintiff had the
right to choose the town in which the trial should be held.
The commissioners could not enforce any judgment by imprisonment, and when a party refused to give satisfaction and
had no property in the town, they could only remit the case

to the county court for execution. The criminal jurisdiction of the commissioners was confined to the issue of search warrants and warrants for the arrest of offenders, when no court or magistrates were at hand to issue such orders. By an act of 1663 these commissioners were authorized to take testimony of witnesses in civil and criminal cases, and to exercise the authority formerly given to associates of the county courts in administering oaths and taking the acknowledgment of deeds and of surrender of right of dowry made out of court.

In every town there was also "a clerk of the writs," who was chosen by the town and approved by the county courts. He was authorized " to grant summons and attachments in civil actions" and "summons for witnesses," "to grant replevins and to take bonds with sufficient security to the party to prosecute the suit." Appeals lay from all lesser magistrates and commissioners to the county courts.

Until 1685 the general court had exercised original chancery jurisdiction, but its business had become so great that it was necessary to create another court to relieve it of a part of its business. An act was then passed [1] which provided that the magistrates of each county court should be authorized to act as a court of chancery. On the exhibition to them of an information " concerning matters of apparent equity," they were to grant summons and examine the parties to the suit and their witnesses under oath, and issue decrees according to the rule of equity, *secundum aequum et bonum*. Appeals might be granted to the court of assistants, and the magistrates who had heard the case might then state the reasons of their judgment, but were not permitted to vote on the case in the assistants' court. The judgment of the assistants was final, unless on appeal the general court saw fit to order a rehearing before the magistrates of the county court, with liberty of appeal as before. In arduous and difficult cases the general court itself might admit a hearing at its own bar. It therefore appears that the establishment of a court of chancery merely involved an extension of the powers of the county court.

[1] Mass. Recs. V. 477.

An order [1] of 1636, passed when the subject of preparing written laws was broached, described the system under which the magistrates had acted and were still to act in many affairs as long as the colony charter remained in force. They were to hear and to determine cases according to law, but, where there was no law, "then as near the law of God as they can." In administering criminal justice, as well as in all other relations, that was the rule by which they professed to be guided. This gave rise to an attack on their discretion as judges which was even more persistent than that which was directed against them in their administrative capacity. The objection was raised that, in imposing sentences, as well as in arresting, detaining, or otherwise proceeding with accused persons, the magistrates acted arbitrarily, under a discretion which was practically unlimited. Partiality, cruelty, all forms of injustice might result from such absolute power. Therefore the deputies, with Saltonstall and Bellingham among the magistrates, demanded that specific penalties for crime should be prescribed in the laws. This was a part of the special effort they made, culminating in 1644, to reduce the discretion of the executive to a minimum. It was the same effort which their contemporaries were making in England, which was also made in American provinces, and which recurs under every system of government. But, though justified, from the nature of the case it could be only partially successful, and its success came far more through the gradual development of the written law of the colony than as the result of special agitation. Some progress had been made when in the first section of the Body of Liberties, echoing the spirit of section 39 of Magna Carta, it was declared, "No man's honor or good name shall be stained, no man's person shall be arrested, restrained, banished, dismembered, nor any ways punished, no man shall be deprived of his wife or children, no man's goods or estate shall be taken away from him, nor anyway indammaged under color of law or countenance of authority, unless it be by virtue or equity of some express law of the country warranting the same, established by a general court and sufficiently published."

[1] Mass. Col. Recs. I. 174.

But even this enactment carried with it the exception that in defect of a law covering a particular case, the law of God should be followed. Specific guaranties, and especially a rational procedure in trials, were needed, if this declaration was to avail much as a protection against injustice.

The elders, when the whole subject was referred to them,[1] fell back for their authority upon the Old Testament, holding that specific penalties ought to be prescribed for capital crimes, but enlarging on the necessity of leaving an opportunity for the judge to exercise his discretion in determining the punishment of lighter crimes and offences. They very reasonably advocated in general the specification of maximum and minimum penalties in the statutes. Winthrop argued the question out in characteristic fashion in his tract on *Arbitrary Government*.[2] In this he referred briefly to the fact that in English law judges and juries were allowed great freedom in awarding damages in cases of slander, trespass, battery, breach of covenant, and the like. But nearly his whole prolonged argument hinged upon the Mosaic legislation, and the discretion employed by the Deity and his agents in inflicting penalties upon offenders among the ancient Hebrews. "By these it appears that the officers of this body politic have a rule to walk by in all their administrations, which rule is the word of God, and such conclusions and deductions as are, or shall be, regularly drawn from thence." From the fact that God in his law specified few penalties, except for capital crimes, Winthrop inferred that he intended human lawgivers to do the same. According to Winthrop it was not the divine method to lay down many and definite precedents, but to leave it to the judges to adjust penalties to offences, that being the only way in which substantial justice could be done. In this way the judge could mingle admonition with the sentence, and thus fulfil another divine ordinance, warranted by Scripture, as appeared in Solomon's admonition to Adonijah, and that of Nehemiah to those who broke the Sabbath.[3] Judges were

---

[1] Mass. Col. Recs. II. 93.   [2] Life and Letters, IV. 445 *et seq.*

[3] " The words of the wise are as goads, and as nails fastened by the Masters of Assemblies, . . . by these, my son, be admonished," Eccl. xii. 11, 12. " A

gods upon earth, and it was their duty to hold forth the wisdom and mercy of God, as well as his justice. If they would keep an open mind in the hour of pronouncing judgment, they would be taught what sentence to declare, and would thus imitate most closely the divine method in dispensing justice. If fixed rules and penalties were prescribed, said Winthrop, it would be by men naturally as fallible as the judges, and those who at the same time look at the subject in the abstract, without the experience and the divine calling which comes to men on the bench. Still he admitted that for the security of men's estates against heavy fines, it would be well to have a general law like Magna Carta, and certain restrictions as to the inflicting of capital punishment. It would also be well if each court were kept by not more than three or five magistrates, and the others were left free for greater attention to the review of cases on appeal or petition. These were the only changes he could suggest, while he strongly contended that, since they had the rule of God's word to go by, the administration of justice in Massachusetts could not be arbitrary.

Winthrop, as the exponent of Puritan orthodoxy, was to have one more encounter with the opponents of judicial and administrative discretion. This had its origin in the somewhat famous case of the Government *vs.* Peter Hobart and others of the town of Hingham. The controversy arose in 1645, near the close of Winthrop's career, and was occasioned by the course which he as deputy governor pursued in committing and binding over parties for trial.[1] As had long been the custom among the towns, Anthony Emes, who for some years had been lieutenant of the militia company of Hingham, was chosen captain by his fellow-townsmen, in the spring of 1645, and his name was presented to the standing council for confirmation. But because of some slight offence taken against him by certain inhabitants of the town, before he was confirmed, one Bozoun Allen was elected in his place and presented to the magistrates. The

reproof entereth more into a wise man than an hundred stripes into a fool," Prov. xvii. 10.

[1] Winthrop, II. 271 *et seq.*

magistrates refused to confirm Allen, and charged all to keep the peace and every militia officer his place till the general court met, to which the case should be referred. But when the next training-day came, Allen's friends refused to train under Emes. Emes referred them to the order of the magistrates, but it was scorned. One declared that it was signed by only three or four of the assistants, others that they had the right to choose their own officers, and demanded what the magistrates had to do with the case. Then, amid tumult, the majority of the company chose Allen. He accepted and took command. About two-thirds of the company followed him.

The scene was then transferred to the church. Of this Peter Hobart was pastor, and three of his brothers were active supporters of Allen. Emes was called to answer before the church to the charge that, on training-day, he had denied that any one in authority had commanded him to lay down his office. He denied the charge, and testimony about it was conflicting. Hobart, the pastor, took up actively against Emes, and urged that he be excommunicated.

When the magistrates heard of these disturbances, three of them, with Winthrop, met at Boston and summoned before them the three Hobarts and two others. This so offended the clergyman, who was of robust temper, that he appeared with his brothers. Such high words followed between him and the magistrates that he was threatened with arrest. The accused were then bound over to appear at the next court of assistants. Later, five others were sent for because of untruths they had uttered about the magistrates at the church meeting. The five met the deputy alone, and demanded the cause of their summons, as well as the names of their accusers. For the former he referred them to Secretary Rawson, while as to the latter, he said that a judge at his discretion might refuse to disclose the names of accusers until the day of trial. They then refused to give bail, and two of them were committed.

The court of election met before the date of the next court of assistants, and about ninety of the inhabitants of

Hingham, with the minister's name at the head,[1] petitioned   CHAP.
it that the case might be heard by the general court.   The   II.
statement was made in the document that the principles
of English liberty had been violated by the imprisonment
of persons for criticising the government.   The deputies
at once expressed their readiness to hear the case, and
asked the concurrence of the magistrates.   At this the
magistrates were offended, because the lower house had not
first conferred privately with them and formally ascertained
the names of the accused and the nature of the charge
against them.   On the demand of the deputies the petitioners then singled out the deputy governor, and undertook to act as his prosecutors.   It being Winthrop's desire
that the case should have a public hearing, for the effect it
might have on the issue so long mooted between the magistrates and deputies, the assistants agreed.   In the presence
of the elders and "a great assembly of people," the vener-
able deputy governor took his place within the bar and sat
uncovered, as might any criminal, while his trial proceeded.[2]

Now began, under the scanty semblance of judicial forms,
one of the most prolonged and ardent party struggles in
the history of colonial Massachusetts.   The trial was but
the prelude to it.   In that Winthrop was easily able to
show that his conduct had been in harmony not only with
law and practice in England, but with usage in Massachusetts.   He had acted upon credible information of "mutinous
practice," and "slighting of authority" at Hingham.   He
declared that he knew no law of God or man which required
him to make known to a party his accusers — who were the
witnesses for the prosecution — before the case came to a
hearing.   Though it might be thought that at some point he
had erred in judgment, — which he was scarcely ready to
admit, — nothing criminal could be laid to his charge.   Still,
however, two of the magistrates, — presumably Saltonstall
and Bellingham, — together with the majority of the deputies, thought the magistrates had too much power, and

---

[1] The petition is in Child's New Englands Jonas cast up at London, Force.
Tracts, IV.

[2] Winthrop, II. 275 *et seq.*

that the liberties of the freemen were in danger. The remainder of the magistrates and nearly one-half of the deputies were of the opposite opinion, and thought, if the excessive "slighting" of authority, which was in vogue, was not checked, the government would degenerate into a democracy. So ardent were feelings on this point that sometimes, during the trial, proceedings were tumultuous.

When the time came for a verdict, the deputies wrangled for a whole day without reaching a decision. They then sent to the magistrates for their views. The magistrates, after deliberation, agreed upon four points : that the petition was false and scandalous, that all concerned in it were offenders, though in different degrees ; that those who had been bound over, with those who were committed and with all the petitioners, should be censured ; that the deputy governor should be fully acquitted. Over these points the deputies spent "divers days," consulting the magistrates two or three times during the interval. They agreed with the assistants concerning the petition, but would not agree to a censure or to the full acquittal of Winthrop. The magistrates refused to yield. Thus a deadlock ensued between the houses which was prolonged for nearly three months, the trial beginning in the middle of May and an agreement not being reached till the fifth of August. During the interval, the legislature took a recess of one week. The deputies were finally brought to terms by the conviction that, if the case was not otherwise disposed of, it would have to be referred to the elders as arbitrators. This they did not desire, for they knew that the clergy "were more careful to uphold the honor and power of the magistrates than themselves well liked of." To avoid this a committee of conference was arranged between the houses. By this the fines which should be imposed upon the Hingham offenders were agreed upon, and it was also resolved that Winthrop should be fully acquitted. The decision was accepted, and thus the long conflict over the discretion of the magistrates was ended. Winthrop took his seat again on the bench, with the full consciousness that he had been vindicated, and that the cause[1] for which he had stood so long had won its final triumph.

As a fitting conclusion of the whole matter, Winthrop, as soon as he had returned to the magistrate's bench, craved the indulgence of the assembly while he made a "little speech." With modesty and true eloquence, after admitting that magistrates might err in judgment and insisting that for that reason they should be held responsible chiefly for their fidelity, he gave a brief exposition of the relations between authority and liberty. It is one of the rare gems of Puritan literature, and contains the root idea of modern republicanism. After distinguishing between natural and civil liberty, and showing how the former was synonymous with anarchy, he explained that the latter revealed itself in the covenant between God and man, in the moral law, and in politic covenants and constitutions among men. This liberty, said he, "is the proper end and object of authority"; and, he added with almost Miltonic phrase, "is a liberty to that only which is good, just, and honest." "This liberty is maintained and exercised in a way of subjection to authority; it is the same kind of liberty wherewith Christ hath made us free." After gracefully illustrating it under the simile of marriage and of the subjection of the church to Christ, the deputy concluded with a practical lesson, that, if the people wished to enjoy the lawful liberties of which they had become possessed, they must quietly and cheerfully submit to the authority which was set over them. "So shall your liberties be preserved, in upholding the honor and power of authority amongst you."

[1] Winthrop, on pages 282–286 of his second volume, sums up the main points of the entire controversy.

CHAPTER III

PART
II.

THE chief features of the governmental system of Massachusetts, the typical representative of the corporate colony, have now been described. It was a complete and
well-rounded whole. It sufficed for all the purposes of the
colony without the interposition of any outside power whatsoever. The executive in its organization was as self-contained
as was the legislature. The structure itself, as well as the
process by which it was developed, suggest independence,
the resolve on the part of its architects to go their own way
in paths hitherto untrodden. The prime cause of this is to
be found, as already indicated, not in political or economic
forces, but in the religious motive. The founders of the Puritan commonwealth of New England were in a preëminent
sense self-conscious. It is true that they brought with them
to the new world law and institutions of government to which
they had been accustomed at home. In common with the
settlers of the other colonies, they were also subject to the
influence of frontier life and of comparative isolation upon a
remote continent. But in addition to that they were advo-
cates of a definite religious system, which they came to the
new world to put into practice. That this was their purpose
they never lost an opportunity to declare. So important did
this system seem to them that they made all interests, social
and political, contribute to its maintenance and advancement.
From it originated the motive which led them to transfer the
government of the colony into New England and to renounce
forever trade and land speculation as a corporate function.
Relations with the home government, intercourse with the
neighboring colonies, conduct toward immigrants, the

200

bestowment and withdrawal of citizenship, the political and social life of town and commonwealth, were ultimately determined by their bearing on the supreme question — the maintenance of the Puritan system of belief.   Said the general court in its first letter to Charles II : " This viz. our liberty to walke in the faith of the gospell with all good conscience according to the order of the gospell, . . . was the cause of our transporting ourselves, with our wives, our little ones and our substance, from that pleasant land over the Atlanticke Ocean into this vast and waste wilderness, choosing rather the pure Scripture worship, with a good conscience, in a poore, remote wilderness, amongst the heathens, than the pleasures of England with submission to the impositions of the then so disposed and so far prevayling hierarchie, which we could not do without an evill conscience." [1]

Calvin's *Institutes of the Christian Religion* was the chief religious and political text-book of the English Puritans. In the light of Calvin they interpreted the Bible, and from his standpoint they viewed the history of the early church. When circumstances made them a political party, the courses of policy which they followed were consistent with the principles and practice of the Genevan reformer.

From the Latin Fathers Calvin drew the doctrine of the sovereignty of God, and he followed it relentlessly to its conclusion.   The Bible, containing the law of God, was to be accepted as an authority from the utterances of which there was no appeal.   To the commands of Christ and the apostles, therein set forth, the strictest obedience must be given.[2]   At the same time full validity was claimed for precedents drawn from the Mosaic system.   Calvin would banish everything which thrust itself between the soul of the individual worshipper and God.   According to his conception the church was a community of believers, by which the commands of God were obeyed in the preaching of the word and the administering of the sacraments, and to which no persons

[1] Mass. Col. Recs. IV[1]. 450.

[2] Institutes, Book I. Chaps. 7, 8 ; Book IV. Chaps. 8, 9.   The doctrine is brought out with special force in Chapter 10 of the same book, where Calvin attacks the traditions of the Catholic church.

should find admission until their piety had been subjected to rigorous tests.[1] The life of each member was constantly exposed to the scrutiny and criticism of others. The strictest discipline, too, was enforced. All were compelled to prove, so far as by human evidence it was possible, that they were the elect of God.

The organization of such a church could hardly fail in theory to be democratic. Christ was regarded as the sovereign of the church, and under him the clergy was an official class, a ministry, whose authority came from the church itself.[2] To the church Christ committed the power of the keys. Its members, united by covenant, chose the ministry and inflicted excommunication. But the possession of these powers by the congregation must not lead to disorder or anarchy. Instead, freedom of thought and practice must be limited, and power necessary to effect this must be bestowed on the clergy. In this way a strong aristocratic tendency was introduced, which, if the progress of the system were resisted, might become predominant.

According to this system an organic connection existed between church and state. It was the duty of the church to create a perfect Christian society, and of the state to furnish the necessary external conditions. Though the sphere of the church was far higher and the issues toward which it labored were loftier and more permanent than those of the state, they could not be reached without the assistance of the civil power. Hence Calvin defended governments against the assaults of Antinomians, declaring that lawful magistrates were divinely commissioned, that their work was a part of the plan of Providence, and that to resist them was to attack the sovereignty of God. But on the other hand, since religion is the basis of public morality, the state needs the support of the church, for from the teachings of the latter comes the moral health without which successful government is impossible. In the name, then, of public order and for the security of property, Calvin would have the state punish idolatry, blasphemy, and a long series of offences against religion. Viewed from one standpoint, his doctrine

---

[1] Institutes, Book IV. Chap. 1.   [2] Ibid. IV. Chap. 12.

implied separation of church from state, yet over against this stood the necessity of their indissoluble union. Neither could survive without the support of the other. This idea seemed to open the way toward toleration, but it was speedily closed again by the necessity of suppressing all deviation from a strict moral and religious code. The church assumed supreme control over opinion. The tendency toward rationalism was checked by the demand that allegiance be sworn to the text of Scripture as interpreted by unchanging canons of criticism. Finally, the tendency toward democracy in ecclesiastical and civil government was counterbalanced by the necessity for the maintenance of order and authority. The more aristocratic phases of this system were reproduced by the Presbyterians of England and Scotland; the more democratic by Robert Brown and his followers, the Separatists. An intermediate position [1] came to be occupied by the Puritans of New England.

The settlers of Massachusetts left England just as the Puritans were becoming a political party. A Separatist church, as will be explained in a subsequent chapter, was already in existence in Plymouth. Higginson, Skelton, and Bright, the three ministers whom the company had sent to Salem, had been appointed members of the local council and were thus given a part in civil affairs.[2] It is well known that the Rev. John Davenport, already prominent among the young clergymen of London who inclined to nonconformity, was a member of the Massachusetts company and was consulted about questions respecting which his opinion would carry weight. The teaching of religion and good morals and their enforcement were recommended in the letters of the company to Endicott. These all are indications that the clergy were to bear a prominent part in the development of this colony, though suggesting little more than what occurred in the early history of Virginia.

According to the credible tradition reported by Cotton Mather,[3] Higginson, on leaving England, declared that they went, not as separatists from the church but only from its

---

[1] Dexter, Congregationalism as seen in its Literature, 463.
[2] Young, 14. [3] Magnalia, Book III.

corruptions, and that their purpose was "to practice the positive part of church reformation, and propagate the gospel in America." This was a proclamation of nonconformity, and the meaning of the phrase, "positive part of church reformation," it was left to events to reveal. Because of certain doings of the ministers on the outward voyage which they considered irregular, John and Samuel Brown, members of the council and men of standing among the colonists, after their arrival at Salem, gathered a company apart and had the Book of Common Prayer read to them. This establishes the fact that it was not used in the religious meetings at Salem. A spirited controversy followed between the Browns and the ministers, in which the latter had the support of Governor Endicott and the colonists. Finding that the speeches of the two brothers tended to "mutiny and faction," the governor told them that "New England was no place for such as they," and sent them home on the returning ship. Their case, together with the damages which they claimed to have suffered, was referred to committees of the company, but what decision was reached we are not told.[1]

With the organization of the church at Salem, in July and August, 1629, the nonconformity of the colonists, respecting which the Browns complained, blossomed out into practical Independency or Separatism. The congregation met on July 6, and, after listening to a prayer and sermon, chose Skelton as its pastor, and Higginson, who was already in orders, as its teacher. Higginson and three or four of the gravest men laid their hands on Skelton's head and prayed. Then Higginson was set apart for the work of the ministry in the same way by his colleague. Thereupon Higginson drew up a confession of faith and church covenant, "according to the Scripture," and copies of this were delivered to thirty persons. Invitation was also sent to Plymouth to send messengers, or, as they would now be called, delegates. On August 6 the congregation met again. The ministers prayed and preached, and thirty persons, by assenting to the covenant, associated themselves together as a church. Then the ministers were ordained by imposition of hands of some

[1] Mass. Col. Recs. I. 51–54, 60, 69, 407.

of the brethren selected by the church.   Governor Bradford
and others, coming by sea from Plymouth, were delayed by unfavorable winds, and hence did not arrive until the services had been in progress for some time; but they gave the Salem church the right hand of fellowship [1] and wished it all success in its beginnings.   We have the express testimony of Endicott to the fact that Dr. Fuller of Plymouth, who the previous spring had been ministering to the sick at Salem, had convinced him of the biblical authority for the Separatist or democratic model of church polity.   This fact, together with the natural influence of removal from England into a new continent whither the arm of the bishops could scarcely reach, accounts for the change which we see so quickly wrought in Salem.   The expulsion of the Browns proves that Endicott at least intended that the newly organized church should not be disturbed by any Anglican rival.

When Winthrop and his fellow-voyagers left England, more formal and elaborate expression was given to the affection with which the mother church was regarded by them.[2] "We desire," wrote they, "you would be pleased to take notice of the principals and body of our Company, as those who esteem it our honor to call the Church of England, from whence we rise, our dear mother: . . . ever acknowledging that such hope and part as we have obtained in the common salvation, we have received in her bosom and sucked it from her breasts."   A fervent desire for her welfare and enlargement was expressed, while her prayers were sought on behalf of the enterprise which the colonists had undertaken.   Of the sincerity of this utterance we have no reason to doubt, but in connection with it notice should be taken of the equally ardent conviction, expressed by Winthrop in his *Modell of Christian Charity*, that something of more than ordinary importance to the religious world was to result from the settlement of Massachusetts. White, the Puritan minister of Dorchester, said with some

---

[1] Bradford, 266 ; Morton's Memorial ; Felt, Ecclesiastical History of New England, I. 113 *et seq.*; Dexter, 415.

[2] The Humble Request, Young, 295.

truth, in the *Planter's Plea*, that under the new conditions in America both religious and political differences might arise.

Under the liberty which circumstances afforded, the Salem model was substantially followed in the founding of all the local churches planted about Massachusetts bay as the result of Winthrop's migration. Still it is true that among most of those bodies the spirit of Separatism was less strong than in Salem. Rev. George Phillips, who became pastor of the church at Watertown, expressly disclaimed the validity of his episcopal ordination. In the covenant which was adopted by the members of his church, all idolatry, superstition, human traditions, and inventions were renounced.[1] Election and imposition of hands were resorted to in filling the offices of the church at Charlestown, but the latter ceremony was accomplished, says Winthrop,[2] with the protestation that it was only a sign of election and not of an intent that the teacher, Mr. Wilson, should renounce his English orders. The same forms were resorted to in organizing the Boston church, though no mention is made of the protestation.[3] All followed the same general model. The description given by Thomas Lechford,[4] of the method of gathering churches which was followed about 1640, confirms what has been said.

He says that a convenient or competent number came together publicly and confessed their sins and professed their faith. Then they entered into a church covenant "to forsake the Devill and all his works, and the vanities of the sinfull world, and all their former lusts, and corruptions they have lived and walked in, and to cleave unto and obey the Lord Jesus Christ, as their only Priest and Prophet, and to walk together with that Church, in the unity of the faith, and brotherly love, and to submit themselves one unto another, in all the ordinances of Christ, to mutuall edification and comfort, to watch over and support one another." This was the essential step in the process; the adoption of the covenant — which was really a social compact — made them a visible church. After it had been adopted, officers were

[1] Felt, I. 138.
[2] Winthrop, I. 38.
[3] *Ibid.* I. 114.
[4] Plain Dealing, 12.

elected, and on a later day were ordained or installed in their places. In the *Platform of Church Discipline*,[1] which was adopted by the New England churches in 1649, a church is defined as "a company of people combined together for the worship of God." As it was the covenant which made the children of Israel "a church and people unto God," so among the Puritans it was through it alone that "members can have church-power over one another mutually."[2]

The principal officers of the local body were the pastor, teacher, and ruling elder. Of these the special work of the first named was practical exhortation to right living; that of the teacher was the inculcation of doctrine.[3] But these functions were often confounded or united in the hands of the same person. The ruling elder was always a layman, and though by no means to the exclusion of the pastor and teacher, he was still the regular administrative officer of the church. He summoned and dismissed the congregation,[4] coöperated in the admission and excommunication of members and in the ordination of officers, prepared business for the church meetings and presided over the same, watched the conduct of members, and admonished those who needed it; when called for, he visited the sick and guided the church "in all matters whatsoever pertaining to church administrations and actions."

The majority of the Massachusetts Puritans continued for a time to affirm, especially in their writings and on public occasions, that they still held communion with the Church of England. Thomas Dudley affirmed this, and, with others, strongly deprecated being called a Brownist.[5] One of the first acts of Roger Williams, which provoked sinister opinions concerning him, was his refusal to join with the church at Boston,[6] because its members would not publicly declare their repentance for having communed with the churches of England while they lived there.

[1] Mather, Magnalia, Book V.

[2] *Ibid.* Among the passages of Scripture cited are Gen. xvii. 7 ; Eph. ii. 12, 18 ; Ex. xix. 5, 8 ; Deut. xxix. 12, 13.

[3] Platform of Church Discipline, Chap. 6.

[4] *Ibid.* Chap. 7.

[5] Letter to the Countess of Lincoln, Young, 331.   [6] Winthrop, I. 63.

Frequently the elders, in explaining or defending their course to English critics, repeat the statement that they have separated only from the " corruptions " of the English Church, meaning its polity and ritual; but they could listen to the preaching of the gospel by its clergy. New England clergymen, when revisiting England, doubtless did this. It was stated, probably with truth, that those who believed in episcopacy as the only true system attended the churches of New England without molestation so long as they kept their opinions to themselves.[1] It was only occasionally insisted by a congregation that a candidate for its pulpit should renounce his orders.

But on the other hand, as time passed, actual communion with English churches ceased. From the first the New England Puritans had renounced two of the most essential parts of the Anglican system, episcopacy and the ritual. The connection which they maintained with the civil power was far different in form from that which existed in England. With the successful progress of the Civil War, it became unnecessary to keep up the pretence of communion from motives of policy. Soon after that date the New England church system was completed, and references to the English Church, except as a rival or hostile body, disappear. Thus all pretence of ecclesiastical connection with Anglicanism ceased, and New England became in that domain practically independent of the mother country.

The ministry was the only learned or professional class then in New England. They were men whose characters and attainments alone would have given them great influence in such communities; but the fact that they and the magistrates were fully agreed that the main object of the colony should be to uphold the Puritan faith and to form a society in harmony therewith greatly increased their power. Believing that their form of church government was of divine origin, they nurtured, expanded, and defended it in sermon and treatise. Cotton, Hooker, Richard Mather, Eliot, and Davenport led in the discussion, which lasted for a quarter of a century. All the ministers took some share in it. Care-

[1] Felt, I. 367, 381.

ful expositions of their polity as a whole were composed under the authority of the clergy and sent to England.   In these apologies and treatises the process of forming the individual church was described in the greatest detail.   The obligations arising from the covenant were analyzed with the greatest scholastic ingenuity.   The election of ministers and elders by the congregation, and the powers of each, were dwelt upon at equal length.   Finally, the theory of censure and excommunication, the punitive power of churches, was elaborated.   They never tired of repeating the idea of Robinson, that in the visible church there is an aristocratic and a democratic element, — namely, the officers and the congregation.   In the decision of any question both of these elements should have a voice, but the elders should have large discretionary powers for the discipline and guidance of the whole.   Thus a position was accorded them similar to that claimed by the magistrates in civil affairs.   Both church and commonwealth possessed a moderately aristocratic organization.   Soon also it was found that coöperation between the local congregations was necessary.   Plans for a federal union were discussed until, partly under the pressure of necessity, they took shape in the calling of occasional synods.   These were usually, if not always, attended by delegates from all the four Puritan colonies, and thus helped to perfect among them a network of ecclesiastical relations.

The founding of Harvard College, mainly for the training of ministers and common missionary operations, developed these relations.   The synods adopted a common creed and platform of discipline, and expressed the consensus of the churches upon important theological questions.   Though the influence of the clergy was great, this was in essence a federal-republican system of church government, the elements of which were derived both from the Mosaic and the apostolic systems.   Precedents were drawn freely from both, but, as will appear, the spirit shown in the administration of the system was more Jewish than Christian.[1]

[1] See the statements of the divines sent to England in 1637 and 1639; also the writings of John Cotton, especially his Way of the Churches of Christ in New England.   The works of Hooker and Davenport are also very full on

The theory of the New England clergy concerning the power of the magistrates and the relation between church and commonwealth was thoroughly Calvinistic. On theoretical as well as legal grounds, they and the magistrates were in agreement on these points. In the *Model of Church and Civil Power*,[1] written probably by Richard Mather and sent, with the approval of the other ministers, to the Salem church during the controversy with Roger Williams, they argue that the power of the magistrate, while conferred by the people, " is limited by the only perfect rule and word of God." "As all free men are only stewards of God, they may not give the magistrate power over these things as they please, but as God pleases." By the same rule, in their opinion, was the legislative power of the representatives of the people limited. It was necessary to go back of the simple will of the legislator to find the reason of laws. A right reason, or full justification of them, could be found only when they expressed the will of God. Here we have the idea of the Biblical Commonwealth, or democracy regulated and modified by the necessity of upholding a divinely ordered ecclesiastical system. That was what the clergy conceived the corporate colony to be ; it was what Winthrop also had in mind when he wrote his *Modell of Christian Charity*.

The corporate form of colonial government was brought into existence in order that this ideal might be realized. The legal precedents of such a state as a matter of course would not be drawn exclusively from England, but also from Geneva and the ancient polity of the Jews. It was held that such laws from the Mosaic code as were found useful were obligatory in New England and should be put in force.[2]

In the writings of the clergy, state and church are considered as distinct in the sense that they work for different

this subject. Hooker's Survey of the Summe of Church Discipline is the most elaborate and detailed of all the treatises.

[1] Quoted by Williams in his Bloody Tenent of Persecution.

[2] See John Eliot, The Christian Commonwealth, London, 1659. Also the Apologie of the Churches of New England . . . touching the Covenant (sent over in 1639, published in 1643). This tract is anonymous, but is expressly acknowledged by the clergy to be authentic.

objects and are controlled by different persons.   The end
of the state is to preserve "external and temporal peace,"
and that of the church to "maintain internal and spiritual
peace."   Both are to be guided by the rules of the word.
The church is to promote holiness, and thus is to be the
bulwark of the commonwealth.   The commonwealth in return is to give "free passage" to the gospel.   This it must
do by divinely ordered laws concerning religion.   It must
punish sedition, contempt of authority in the church, heresy,
blasphemy, slander, and similar offences, though in most
cases not until the offender had been "dealt with in a
church way."   The magistrates should also compel all to
hear the word, encourage people to join the church, and
disperse all irregular assemblies, because they "destroy the
peace of the churches" and dissolve the continuity of the
state.   They may also compel those who hear the word to
support its ministers, and establish and control schools for
furnishing the church with educated pastors.   It is their
duty also to reform the corrupted worship of God, and to
defend with the sword the pure worship.   Still they have no
authority to interfere in the election of church officers, to
perform any ecclesiastical functions, or to establish anything
but a pure form of worship.   Finally, all freemen should be
church members and magistrates should be chosen expressly
from them.

Such was the statement in theoretical form of what in Massachusetts was fully carried into practice.   To such an extent
was the distinction between church and commonwealth a
formal one, that under the stress of circumstances it might
be lost sight of and the two become practically identified.
If in Massachusetts the ecclesiastical did not so completely
overmaster the political as in Geneva, it was because the
resistance to the policy of the clergy was not so great.   As
it was, however, until about 1660 the theocratic element distinctly predominated.   Every public question had its religious bearing, and in many cases that aspect attracted the
chief attention.   The magistrates, with an occasional exception, were orthodox, and the ministers could usually count
upon a majority among the deputies.   The course of legisla-

tion and practice which resulted from this union of the civil and ecclesiastical powers will now be traced.

The religious test of 1631, to which extended reference has already been made, limited active citizenship in the colony to church members. In 1660 the general court declared that only those could be freemen who were in full communion with the churches.[1] The test continued in force in the form in which it was enacted until 1664.[2] Then, under pressure from the home government, an obscurely worded act was passed which modified it as follows : All Englishmen presenting certificates signed by a minister or ministers of the place where they lived that they were orthodox in religion and not vicious in life, and also certificates under the hands of the selectmen of the place, or a majority of them, that they were freeholders and were ratable at a single country rate to the sum of ten shillings, or that they were in full communion with some church, being also twenty-four years of age, householders and settled inhabitants, might apply to the general court for admission as freemen. The certificates required were of such a nature and came from such sources that the act made practically no change in the system. It in fact was not changed so long as the first charter existed. According to the court lists, the total number of freemen admitted up to 1674 was 2527.[3] This was probably about one in five of the adult male residents during that period. It thus appears that the test cut deeply and excluded from active citizenship the great majority of the men of the colony. A freeholder franchise probably would have been much less exclusive. The consideration of this fact brings into distinct relief the aristocratic tendency of the Puritan church-state system.

The suffrage in town meeting was not strictly confined to freemen. In 1635 it was enacted that only freemen should vote in those meetings on measures of necessity and authority, as the receiving of inhabitants, laying out of lands, and the like. This implied that non-freemen might vote on other questions.

[1] Col. Recs. IV¹. 420.   [2] *Ibid.* IV². 118.
[3] Ellis, Puritan Age in Massachusetts, 203.

It appears that in some cases church members, in order to avoid the burdens of office-holding, neglected to apply for admission as freemen. By acts of 1643 and 1647 it was provided that all who were pursuing that course should be dealt with by the churches and be made to fulfil their civil obligations.

A review of the laws which specify the support, direction, and control given by the civil power to the churches will illustrate anew the intimacy of relations between them. An incident of this was the union of the churches themselves into a compact body. In 1635 the elders were asked to prepare an order of discipline, and to consider how far the court might interfere to preserve the uniformity and peace of the churches. In 1636 the power of the magistrates over the institution of churches was first asserted. It was declared that the board would approve of no churches thereafter organized, unless the magistrates and elders of the majority of churches had been previously informed and approved thereof. No person who was not a member of a church thus approved should be admitted as a freeman. The passage of orders for the taxation of all inhabitants for the support of the clergy and worship began with the founding of the colony and was regularly continued.

In the Body of Liberties, which was an enactment by the civil power, the conditions under which churches might be formed were comprehensively stated. It was therein provided that all people of God in the colony, who were orthodox in judgment and not scandalous in life, might gather themselves into a church estate, "provided they do it in a Christian way, with due observation of the rules of Christ revealed in his word." Every congregation was also to have liberty to use the ordinances of God according to the rules of Scripture ; and to elect and ordain its officers, provided they were "able, pious, and orthodox." It will be noted that on every side the freedom of the church was limited by the necessity of conforming to the word of God.

In the act of 1646,[1] calling the second synod that was held in Massachusetts, the general court expressed itself at some

[1] Col. Recs. II. 154.

length on the relations between the civil and ecclesiastical power. It asserted the right to sanction the correct form of government and discipline, when these were established by the churches. It also made no question of its right " to assemble the churches or their messengers upon occasion of counsell, or anything which may concern the practice of the churches." Still, because all church members were not clear on this point, the court, instead of commanding them to assemble, expressed the desire that they would meet at the time and place and for the purpose stated in the act. It also expressed its sorrow at the departure of the churches from uniformity of belief and practice respecting the baptism of infants whose parents were not church members, and in reference to other points. For this reason it desired the clergy to continue the sessions of the synod until a uniform plan of government and discipline had been adopted. When completed, this should be transmitted, through the governor or deputy governor, to the general court, that it might give the system its approval if found agreeable to the word of God. The synod met at Cambridge and completed its labors in 1647.[1] They were embodied in the Cambridge Platform of Discipline, to which reference has already been made. In October, 1649,[2] the general court commended this document to the churches of the commonwealth for their consideration, and desired a return from them at the next session. Owing to the delay of some of the churches and the presentation of objections by some, final action[3] was not taken till October, 1651. Then the court expressly approved of the Book of Discipline, " that for the substance thereof it is that wee have practised and doe believe."

In the Cambridge Platform the clergy claimed[4] the support of the civil power as fully as ever the Jewish priesthood did. It was declared that the magistrate should "improve his civil authority for the observing of the duties commanded ". in both tables of the law. The object of his activity was not only to secure peace, righteousness, and honesty in society, but godliness as well. Like the judges and kings

---

[1] Mather, Magnalia, Book V.
[2] Col. Recs. II. 285.
[3] *Ibid*. IV[1]. 157.
[4] Platform, Chap. 17.

of the Hebrews, several of whom were cited as examples,
the magistrates were to put forth their authority in matters
of religion. Idolatry, blasphemy, schism, heresy, the venting of corrupt and pernicious opinions, open contempt of the
word preached, profanation of the Lord's day, disturbance of
the public worship, and similar offences were to be punished
by civil authority. These provisions leave no sphere of
church activity free from the possibility of interference by
the civil power.

Naturally, then, Sabbath legislation and legislation against
blasphemy, drunkenness, games, showy apparel, and all forms
of immorality appear prominently in the Massachusetts
statute book. In the Body of Liberties blasphemy and the
worship of any but the true God appear in the catalogue of
capital crimes. By an act of 1646[1] blasphemy was again
expressly made a capital offence. In 1653 playing in the
streets, uncivilly walking in the streets or fields, travelling
from town to town, going on shipboard, frequenting taverns
and other places to drink, or misspending the time in other
ways on Sunday were forbidden on the penalty of fine or
whipping. In 1658 similar penalties were attached to
these offences[2] if committed on Saturday nights or on
Sundays after dark. But the evil against which these laws
were directed continued, especially drinking in taverns on
Saturday and Sunday nights, and repeatedly orders were
issued against it.[3]

In 1646 appears the first act against heresy.[4] In the preamble to this law the distinction between violating the conscience and suppressing notorious impiety, universally in
vogue at the time among Anglicans as well as Puritans, is
suggested, and thus an attempt is made to remove it from the
category of persecuting acts. Whether the distinction was
a valid one or not may be inferred from the list of heretical
opinions given in the act itself. They were the denial of
the immortality of the soul, of the resurrection of the body,

[1] Col. Recs. II. 176.
[2] *Ibid.* IV[1]. 150, 200 ; Laws, 1887, 189 *et seq.*
[3] Col. Recs. IV[1]. 347 ; IV[2]. 395, 562 ; V. 133, 155, 239, 243.
[4] *Ibid.* II. 177 ; Laws, 1889, 154 ; Laws, 1887, 58.

of sin, of atonement through the death of Christ, of the morality of the fourth commandment, of the baptism of infants, of the ordinance of magistracy or of the magistrates' authority to punish breaches of the first Table. Those who held these opinions and tried to induce others to adopt them should be banished. In 1651·the titles of the books of the Old and New Testaments were recited, and the denial that these were the infallible word of God was declared to be punishable with a fine of £50 and whipping with not more than forty strokes. Particular forms of heresy, as Antinomianism, Anabaptism, and Quakerism, were denounced and punished as they appeared in the colony. In 1647[1] an act was passed, as severe as any on the English statute book, for the punishment of Catholic priests who might be found in the colony. In the mode of treatment prescribed for them it foreshadows the later legislation against Quakers.

The laws also prove not only that the proclamation of false doctrine was forbidden, but that the preaching of the truth was encouraged and commanded. Attendance at church was compulsory, and by the act of 1646 a fine of five shillings was imposed for every absence. Disturbance and interruption of public services, contemptuous behavior toward the word or its messengers, were forbidden[2] by various acts and penalties. The system of providing for the regular public support of the ministry was extended in 1654 by a law requiring each town to provide a house for the minister's use. At the same time the county courts were ordered, when informed that a town was delinquent in the support of its minister, to issue a warrant to the selectmen to levy a special rate for the purpose. The general court declared in this act that it was its intention to secure an honorable allowance for the ministry. In 1658 the general court declared that it was the duty of the Christian magistrate " to take care that the people be fed with wholesome and sound doctrine." Therefore it ordered that no one should regularly preach or be ordained as a teaching elder, with whose doctrine or practice any two churches, or the council of state, or general court, declared

---

[1] Mass. Recs. II. 193.   [2] Laws, 1887, 144 *et seq.*

their dissatisfaction. In 1660 the general court,[1] in further
pursuance of its duty to secure an able and faithful ministry,
required that the county courts should carefully execute its
orders about the maintenance of the ministry, the purging
of towns from ministers of vicious life or heterodox beliefs,
and procuring faithful laborers in their places ; that rates
for the support of the clergy be regularly levied ; and that
the aid of the grand juries be invoked for these ends. In
the performance of this function the general court sometimes took counsel with individual churches, as with a
Boston church[2] in 1652. In 1656 the general court advised
that a council be called to heal divisions in the church at
Ipswich.[3] In 1657 the court interfered to settle a controversy between the churches of Salisbury[4] and Haverhill.
The same course was pursued in the case of the church at
Wells[5] in 1660 and in several other instances. The great
controversies, in which the colony as a whole became
involved, also furnished striking examples of the same
thing.

The civil power not only supported the churches in these
manifold ways, but it claimed and received great help in
return. The moral support given by the clergy to the government was continuous, save when the civil power in the
hands of Vane sought to discredit the great body of the
ministers. In times of crisis the clergy were always in
the forefront, rousing all to support the government.
As their reliance for the suppression of heresy and schism
was on the secular arm, so they did all they could to
strengthen it. Special providences without limit were cited
as encouragements to action or warnings against dangers
and mistakes.

As we have had occasion repeatedly to notice, when cases
of importance came before the magistrates or the general
court, the advice of the clergy was sought and almost
invariably followed. The clergy in an extra-legal capacity
acted as a board of referees on important questions of
legislation, judicature, and practical policy. With the

---

[1] Col. Recs. IV[1]. 417.   [2] Ibid. 113, 177, 210, 212.
[3] Ibid. 225, 310.   [4] Ibid. 309.   [5] Ibid. 426, 434.

exception of Winthrop, they were the chief expounders of the public law and policy of Massachusetts, and their utterances are among the most valuable and authoritative we have. They were consulted about relations with the Indians and with the mother country. Their advice was sought on the question of the distribution of power between the magistrates and the deputies. They prepared elaborate statements respecting the form of the Massachusetts government and the relations of its several parts. To clergymen was assigned the task of preparing the first draft of laws for the colony. Sermons, whether delivered before the general court or elsewhere, might at any time have a political bearing, and convey direct political instruction. Like the ecclesiastics of the middle age, the ministers of New England were statesmen and political leaders. No affair of government was indifferent to them. They helped to uphold the church and commonwealth against threats of attack by the home government, the efforts of Gorges and Mason, the complaints and agitations of schismatics. They coöperated in forming the New England Confederacy. They gave their active support to a system of common and higher education, and to the other social institutions which contributed to that self-denying and heroic, but cheerless, Puritan life. With the magistrates they acted as censors of the press, and when a book, pamphlet, or sermon appeared, — like some by Roger Williams, Pynchon, Saltonstall, John Eliot, — which advocated doctrines or policies about which there was doubt, it was referred to them for examination. Upon their report hung the decision whether it should be allowed to circulate or be suppressed. With the magistrates, they constituted for half a century the governing class of Massachusetts — the oligarchy which shaped its policy and growth. As at Geneva, the result was a narrow, forced, and one-sided development.

That in a community of this type persecution would be resorted to as a means of suppressing unwelcome opinions, goes without saying. That, moreover, the range of ignored or prohibited opinions was incomparably wider than the circle of tolerated beliefs, is a fact equally apparent. The

meagre output of the press in Puritan New England consisted almost wholly of books on religion.   The same is true
of the works relating to those colonies which were published
in England.   Literature, art, morals, save as they were
related to the accepted dogmatic system, were as closed
books.   Science as yet had no existence.   The only history
for which they cared was that of the Hebrews, of the early
church, and of some of the reforming sects.   Though the
divines, and possibly now and then a magistrate, could read
the language of Plato and Aristotle, philosophy had no place
even in their imaginations.   It is true that most of these
conditions the New Englanders shared with the people of
the other colonies, but the intensity of the mental activity of
the Puritan in certain lines makes the narrowness of his
horizon all the clearer.   It is fair that he should be in a
measure held responsible for defects which would not be
noticed in a merchant, an Indian trader, a planter, or an indented servant.   We wonder when a young man of university training and possessed of the general intelligence of
John Winthrop, Jr., writes to his father, after a tour on the
European continent,[1] "For myself, I have seen so much of
the vanity of the world, that I esteem no more of the diver-
sities of countries than so many inns, whereof the traveller
that hath lodged in the best, or in the worst, findeth no difference when he cometh to his journey's end."   Too much
contemplation of the world to come made many of the best
minds of that generation as insensible to the real glories of
the world that now is as any peasant could well be.

The only opinions likely to be expressed in New England which would meet with disapproval were those which
affected in some way the religious system of the colonies or
their political security.   They might relate to conduct or to
belief.   From the utterances of the Puritan leaders, and
particularly of John Cotton in his controversy with Roger
Williams, and of John Norton in the controversy with the
Quakers, we know what their theoretical views were concerning the way in which erroneous opinions should be dealt
with.   They were of such a nature that practically no room

[1] Life and Letters of Winthrop, I. 307.

PART
II.

was left for the expression of dissent.   The essentials of the faith and the foundations of the political system were in no case to be attacked.   The idea of essentials was very indefinite, and might be stretched by the Puritan to cover nearly the whole body of his faith.   The interests of public order might also be invoked to silence outspoken opposition to less important doctrines.   Individuals who were found to hold and express heretical views should be admonished by some persons in authority.   The process of admonishing, which was very characteristic of the Calvinistic system, was called in the speech of the time " dealing " with the offender, and was resorted to as soon as possible after symptoms of heresy made their appearance.   Dissentients, who had been sufficiently admonished and still remained unconvinced, were said to have become wedded to their errors, and were sources of evil against whom the community must be protected.   Their mouths must then be closed.   Thus the only opportunity really granted for the utterance of dissenting opinions was that during which the person who held them was subject to admonition.   According to Cotton, — and he was not alone in his opinion, — the punishment of the persistent heretic was not persecution.   The argument used to show this was that the presentation of the truth by admonition must convince the conscience of error ; but the corrupt will then interposed and caused the unbeliever to hold out stubbornly against the truth.   Consequently, if the magistrate took him in hand, it could not be said that he was persecuted, because that term is applied only to the constraining of the conscience.   Say rather that he was punished as a " culpable and damnable " person, a turbulent heretic and schismatic.[1]   According to this argument and to many of the utterances of the time, the free expression of novel or heretical opinions was closely

[1] John Norton, in his *Heart of New England Rent*, stated the doctrine in this form : Conscience, he said, was man's judgment answering to that of God.   It must then act according to principle.   Freedom of conscience was liberty from all human impediment, "in acting according to rule."   But liberty to believe and propagate error was not liberty of conscience, but liberty to blaspheme, to seduce others from the true God, to tell lies in the name of the Lord.   It was indeed liberty unto bondage, and restraint from it was restraint from bondage.

akin to sedition or rebellion, and the punishment of it was not persecution, but the infliction of the appropriate penalty for a crime. Heresy could hardly exist in the abstract, but as soon as uttered became concrete, and as such begat social evil and corrupted the state. Though the church might initiate proceedings, presently the magistrate must be called in to remove the offenders, as the Jews banished unclean persons from the congregation.

The mass of the inhabitants of Massachusetts, the agricultural laborers, farmers, small traders, those who, because they were not members of the churches, appear simply as residents, did not differ materially in character or ambitions from the settlers in the other colonies. A large proportion also of the church members may be supposed to have been easy-going, commonplace people, seeking no outlet for their energies except that which their own occupations or neighborhoods afforded. Politically these were either altogether or largely without significance. They were the hull and ballast of the colony craft, not in any sense the steering or propelling apparatus. If freemen, they served in the militia during war, voted for deputies to the general court, or might share in sending a proxy to the court of election. When the colony was profoundly moved by some controversy or menaced by some peril, they contributed to the volume of opinion which gathered and in a way to the expression or action which might follow. But with these things their influence over affairs of the jurisdiction ended. In the local and family records of the time the activity of the ordinary freemen can be traced in faint and broken lines ; but the non-freemen have left scarcely a memorial behind. Save in a few conspicuous instances, they are mutes, as much so as the slave population of an ancient city republic. That which was peculiar and significant in the Puritan colonies of New England was contributed by the active freemen, at whose head stood the magistrates and clergy. They sketched the plan of the colonies and filled it out in action. The fact that Massachusetts passed at a single bound from the status of a plantation to that of a corporate colony was due to their devising skill. In the towns they were as much the

leaders as in the commonwealth at large.   The reproduction
in New England of the Biblical commonwealth was their
work.   It was the jewel, the preservation of which enlisted
all their care and energy.   The faith and practice of the
churches was the feature of the system which they chiefly
esteemed.   The civil authority was developed and organized
mainly for the purpose of protecting the church.   The two
together then became the object of perpetual care.   The
regeneration of the world seemed to these men to depend on
the maintenance of this system; to their minds it held a
place in the scheme of redemption second in importance only
to the Jewish commonwealth and the apostolic church.   It
was a constant and chief object of divine care.   Its friends
might ever expect special divine favors, and its foes, or those
who were indifferent to it, equally marked evidences of the
displeasure of God.   They were a light set on a hill for the
illumination of the nations.

But the possibilities that this enterprise, on which the
leaders had so passionately set their hearts, might be ship-
wrecked or come to nothing, were numerous.   These arose
not from the mere fact that church and commonwealth were
closely joined in Massachusetts, or that the secular power
was pledged to support the spiritual by all means at its
command.   Such a relation, in the world as it then was, was
the rule rather than the exception.   But the difficulty lay in
the form under which the union was effected, and the circumstances attending its origin and perpetuation.   Whatever might be the assertions of the Puritan leaders, their
policy, considered as a whole, was a most pronounced
declaration of independence toward the English Church.
The removal of the colony government to New England
implied an equally strong determination to escape as far as
possible from the restraints of the English government.   The
scheme therefore had no friends among the ruling classes in
the mother country, or, one may say, in Europe at large.
But in this connection we are more concerned with the possible foes of the Puritans in their own household.   They
had been dissenters in England, and one form of dissent,
especially in those times, was likely to occasion the birth of

numerous other forms.   So novel was the Puritan experiment
that other dissenters might easily claim equality of rights
with it.   Even adherents of ancient faiths might appear to
be dangerous schismatics if transplanted into Massachusetts.
The Puritans could not fall back on antiquity as a justification for their exclusiveness ; and, being the rulers of a
mere colony, and weak at that, they must scrutinize every
appearance of evil and, if possible, smother it at the very
beginning.   The leaders must be equally alert to discover
attacks on the civil and ecclesiastical order, — for both were
vulnerable, — and crush them if possible.   Assaults on the
one might easily imperil the other, and hence clergy and
magistrates must coöperate in defence of both.   The admission of persons into the colony who might betray its
interests, the silencing or removal of declared critics and
enemies, their conduct and whereabouts after discipline, the
possibility of their corresponding with the enemies of the
colonies in England, or of their founding rival colonies near
by, all these and many other things must be the objects of
constant attention on the part of the Puritan oligarchy, if
its experiment was to escape ruin.   Necessarily then Massachusetts, and to a less extent the other Puritan colonies,
were under a sort of perpetual state of siege.   To say
nothing of external foes, group after group of malcontents
sprang into existence within its own borders, or forced their
way in from outside, from whose malign influence the leaders
considered it necessary that the colony should be purged.
Our inquiry, in its next stage, will be directed toward the
controversies which, originating in the way that has been
suggested, agitated Massachusetts during the first thirty
years of its existence.   A detailed history of them will not
be attempted, for many such are accessible elsewhere.
Neither will they be studied exclusively for their own sake,
but an effort will be made to use them as illustrations of the
working of the Puritan state-church system.

CHAPTER IV

THE WORKING OF THE MASSACHUSETTS SYSTEM AS ILLUS-
TRATED BY THE CONTROVERSIES WITH ROGER WILLIAMS
AND THE ANTINOMIANS

PART
II.
As the church and commonwealth in Massachusetts, if not
one, were at least indissoluble, an attack on the foundations of the civil power might easily arouse the churches
and have wide-reaching effects on ecclesiastical policy.
This, it is believed, is the real lesson of the Roger Williams
episode.

Next to the Bible the Massachusetts Puritans esteemed
and valued their charter. It guarantied to them the possession of their lands as against all adverse claims which might
originate with Gorges, Mason, or others of the New England
council; it was the basis of their civil order, and by skilful
use of its provisions they had been able to give such form
as they desired to their institutions of government; from
their reliance on it, as time advanced, proceeded not a little
of the imperiousness shown by Massachusetts in its dealings
with neighbors who had no charters; the last twenty years
of the existence of the Puritan oligarchy was spent in defending this instrument, and when it was cancelled the
Biblical commonwealth became simply a memory and an
influence. None save Connecticut was in sentiment so
emphatically a chartered colony as was Massachusetts.
This fact, in the case of both, was intimately connected with
the Puritan's love for covenanted relations, for ascertained,
limited, and guarantied rights, as well as his need of such
protection as was available against the crown. These guaranties, it will be noted, he wished for himself, but viewed
with indifference any proposal to extend their benefits to

his opponents. He believed in liberty for the elect, for
" men that fear God," not in human rights as such.[1]

A central fact in the career of Roger Williams as an inhabitant of Massachusetts was his attack on the claim to
their lands which the colonists derived from the crown
through their charter. Much of Williams's life as a colonist
was spent among the Indians. Some of the noblest aspects
of his character appear in his relations with them. His usefulness to his contemporaries arose quite as much from his
knowledge of Indian life and his ability to maintain friendly
relations with the savages as from any other source. His
first prolonged residence among them occurred in and about
1632, when he was an inhabitant of Plymouth colony.
Then he began to gain that familiarity with their tongue
which afterwards enabled him to write his *Key into the
Language of America*. Though Williams was unacquainted
with any but the Puritan type of culture, he was an
humanitarian ; he respected man as man. He also knew
little of the law, and perhaps had never seen a copy of a
royal charter. While in Plymouth Williams prepared in
manuscript a small book or tract,[2] which he addressed to
the governor and council of that colony and in which he
denied that title to land could be derived from the king's
grant, and asserted that it must be secured by compounding
with the natives. To rely upon a title derived from the
crown was to commit usurpation. That there was an element
of truth in Williams's contention, the entire history of the
dealings of English colonists with the natives proves. They
everywhere, and especially in New England, sought to extinguish Indian claims by a form of purchase. This admitted them peacefully to joint occupancy with the natives,
the Europeans taking immediate and exclusive possession
of certain tracts for agricultural purposes, while the Indians
continued to enjoy hunting and fishing privileges within
the rest. But ownership of the soil it was impossible for

---

[1] Williams, writing in later life to Major Mason of Connecticut, said,
"Yourselves pretend liberty of conscience, but alas ! it is but self, the great
god self, only to yourselves." Pubs. of Narragansett Club, VI. 346.

[2] Winthrop, I. 145.

the Indian to grant, for he had never had more than possession. Guaranties of possession against other Englishmen
or Europeans he could not give. According to a general
principle of law, guaranties of this kind, together with
ownership of the soil, must be derived from the crown, and
were transferred by means of a charter. This Williams
denied.

During his first residence in Massachusetts, Williams had
attracted unfavorable notice [1] by his pronounced separatism
and his avowal of the belief that the secular power had
no right to punish breaches of the first table of the law.[2]
Therefore, when, on the death of Higginson, the Salem
church called Williams to be its teacher, the magistrates
interposed and asked them to delay till a conference could
be held about it. If this was an official act of the board of
assistants, it was not justified by any existing law of which
we have knowledge, and it is to be regarded as one of the
earliest assertions of the authority of the civil power to
warn and restrain the individual churches in the interest of
uniformity. Williams was not installed, and soon removed
to Plymouth, where he resided for some two years. At
the end of that time he returned to Salem, where he preached
as an assistant of Mr. Skelton, though at first without admission to any office in the church. Thus another proof was
afforded of the separatist tendency in the Salem church.

It was after his return, but before his appointment as
Skelton's successor, that Williams's "treatise" [3] on the charter
was considered by the magistrates at Boston. The advice of
"some of the most judicious ministers," — Cotton and Wilson, — was taken, and they "much condemned Mr. Williams's
error and presumption." It was ordered that he should be
"convented at the next court to be censured." But in the
meantime Governor Winthrop wrote to Endicott, who had
been absent from the meeting of the assistants, to let him

[1] Winthrop, I. 63.

[2] Strictly interpreted, this phrase would mean that he had denied the right
of the civil government to punish idolatry, blasphemy, perjury, and Sabbath
breaking (Palfrey, I. 407), which were at that time very generally regarded
as penal offences in Protestant countries.

[3] Winthrop, I. 145–147.

know what had been done, asking him also to induce
Williams, if possible, to retract his utterances. To all concerned, including Endicott, Winthrop, and the court, Williams
now returned very submissive answers, stating that he had
no intention of publishing his opinions, and professing loyalty
to the government. Cotton and Wilson also reported that,
on further considering the book, they did not find its sentiments so evil as they at first thought. They also agreed that,
if Mr. Williams would retract and take the oath of allegiance
to the king, it should be passed over. We have no record of
his doing either of these things, and from what we know of
Williams and of the attitude of the magistrates generally
toward the oath of allegiance, the inference is a probable
one that neither of the conditions was exacted.

The impression is strengthened by the fact that, about
a year later, information reached the magistrates[1] that
Williams was again "teaching publicly against the king's
patent, and our great sin in claiming right thereby to this
country." He was also denouncing the churches of England
as anti-Christian. Winthrop states that in doing this he
had "broken his promise"; but if the breach of an oath
had been involved, the annalist would probably have so
stated it. Williams was summoned to appear at the next
court. But before the time for that came, Mr. Cotton[2]
requested the magistrates to forbear civil prosecution
against him till he could be dealt with in a church way, and
thus convicted of his offence as a sin. This was a method
of procedure in such cases of which Cotton made much in
his writings, and he now had a good opportunity to apply
it. At the same time he seems to have had some insight
into Williams's real nature, for he surmised that "his violent
course did rather spring from scruple of conscience than
from a seditious principle." But, as we have seen, it was
also Cotton's belief, that if scruples of conscience did not
vanish under admonition, they became transformed into
turbulent heresy and schism, which withal was close akin to

[1] Winthrop, I. 180.
[2] Cotton's Reply to Mr. Williams, his Examination, Narragansett Club
Edition, 38.

sedition. Just this change seems to have been wrought in the case of Mr. Williams. The gentle offices of admonition did not avail to turn him from his opinion, as they did in the case of Mr. Eliot and of others. Instead, they left him more stubborn and persistent than ever. Indeed, upon the Calvinistic system of admonition as a whole a judgment must be passed similar to that of Lord Burghley concerning Whitgift's Articles ; it was " rather a device to seek for offenders than to reform any." When combined with the action of the civil power, it made a machine as well contrived for the manufacture of heretics as any the world has ever seen.

But another element was added to the problem before it came to the final issue. In April, 1634, the residents' oath, to which reference has already been made, was enacted and its enforcement began. This was resorted to as an additional protection for the government in view of the influx of inhabitants and of the perils which threatened the colony from England and elsewhere. Williams was a resident, having never been admitted to the number of freemen, and hence was directly affected by the new enactment. The fact that he was not a freeman, of course, magnified his offences in the eyes of the magistrates and clergy. He naturally seemed to them like an outsider, who had come into their midst simply to make trouble. And certainly no one among the non-freemen of Massachusetts ever made himself heard so effectively as did Roger Williams.

Conscientious scruples now moved him to protest and preach publicly against the oath. His argument was that oath-taking was an act of worship.[1] Therefore a magistrate[2] ought not to tender an oath to an unregenerate man, for he thereby had " communion with a wicked man in the worship of God," and caused him "to take the name of God in vain." In April, 1635, the assistants sent for him on this count, and heard and " confuted " him in the presence of "all the ministers." At first Endicott supported Williams, but later he "gave place to the truth." Williams, however, again refused to be convinced. Therefore he was summoned to appear before

---

[1] Hireling Ministry none of Christ's.   [2] Winthrop, I. 188.

the general court. But his popularity in Salem at this time is evidenced by his call, on the death of Mr. Skelton, to the office of teacher of that church.[1] At a session of the general court, which occurred in the summer of 1635, a series[2] of charges was presented against Williams, among which his theory concerning land titles does not appear. This would indicate that during the past few months his public utterances of an offensive nature had been confined to the question of the oath and to the right of the civil power to punish violations of the first four commandments. He was charged with teaching that the magistrate ought not to punish breaches of the first table, unless the public peace was disturbed, and that he ought not to tender an oath to an unregenerate man. Two other charges were also presented, but they were simply corollaries of the second proposition. Notice was also taken of the fact that, while Mr. Williams was under admonition, the Salem church had called him to be its teacher. After a full debate, in which the ministers, at their own desire, took part, his opinions were unanimously adjudged to be erroneous and dangerous, and the action of the Salem church in calling him to office at that time as " a great contempt of authority." At the special request of the court the ministers also declared that he who obstinately maintained opinions whereby a church might apostatize or run into heresy without a possibility of interference by the civil power should be removed ; and the other churches ought to request the magistrates so to act. It was finally resolved to give the Salem church till the next session of the general court to consider these things, and then, if it did not give satisfaction, it might expect the sentence.

From the list of charges preferred against Williams at this time it is evident that he had again been preaching about the first table of the law, a subject to which only one earlier reference appears, and that in 1631. Positive proof is therefore lacking that it played a large part in the controversy till, in 1635, its last stage was reached. Previous to this time the attack on land titles and on the oath seem to have occupied the chief attention. Substantially all the contem-

[1] Dexter, As to Roger Williams, 36.   [2] Winthrop, I. 193.

porary testimony [1] we have is to the effect that these were
the chief questions at issue.   But this testimony is possibly
to an extent biassed, because of the desire of the Puritan
leaders who gave it to prove that the banishment of Williams from Massachusetts was an act of civil justice, and
not in any sense persecution.   So meagre are the statements
which have come down to us concerning Williams's opinions
at this time, on the relations between the civil and ecclesiastical power, that it is impossible to know exactly what
stage they had reached.   In the case of most men at that
time the natural inference would be that experience was
gradually bringing him to the point where he would be
ready to affirm the total separation of the two powers.   As
he divulged novel opinions, one after another, he found his
way blocked by the Massachusetts authorities, and himself
subjected to the comfortable process of being "dealt with."
Such a discussion as that which probably occurred in the
general court would, in the case of an ardent tempera-
ment like his, help to commit him to sweeping views on the
subject.   As such inquiries were beautifully contrived for
the purpose of making heretics, it is quite possible to suppose that Williams then uttered for almost the first time in
public the views which stood first in the list of charges
against him.   But even in that case it is necessary to remember his admission that the magistrate might interfere
when the civil peace was endangered.

On the other hand it should be borne in mind that Williams was dominated more by feeling than by reason ; we
instinctively speak of him as a "prophet."   Such men leap
at conclusions, see things as wholes rather than piecemeal.
Moreover, his solution of the difficulty, as he finally reached
it, was simple, one that could be quickly grasped as soon as
it occurred to the mind.   For the world, as it then was,
Williams's doctrine of the separation of church from state
was not so much the solution of a problem as the denial of
its existence.   It was an attempt to cut the knot rather than
to untie it.   Hence it is possible to suppose that his theory
was already formulated, and that, had the occasion arisen

[1] Cited by Palfrey, I. 416 n.

as early as 1631 for him to share in the founding of a commonwealth, he would have pursued the same course in the matter which was later followed at Providence.   Still it is difficult to believe that, had Williams thus early reached definite views on the subject of "soul liberty," they would have played so small a part in his controversy with Massachusetts.

However this may be, the question of the first table of the law was almost as much civil as ecclesiastical, and, the crisis of the dispute having been reached, we can see how the Massachusetts system responded to such an impact.   Four years earlier it had been necessary for the magistrates to deal[1] with an elder of Watertown, because he expressed the opinion that the Roman Catholic church was a true church ; but relations in that case were quickly harmonized.   Now a much more difficult case was in hand.   Mr. Williams had raised three serious questions, and his church supported him.   The magistrates and clergy stood in united opposition to them.   According to the Brownist theory of the autonomous local church, the Salem body should have been left to go its way.   But this was not to be thought of ; if for no other reason, because secular issues were involved, and the town could be coerced if the church could not.

Before the general court at the very session when Williams was convented, the town of Salem petitioned for a grant of land on Marblehead[2] neck which it claimed as rightfully its own.   "But, because they had chosen Mr. Williams their teacher, while he stood under question of authority, and so offered contempt to the magistrates," their petition was refused till proper submission was made.   Thereupon the Salem church took up the matter, and set the ecclesiastical machinery in motion for the purpose of punishing the magistrates and deputies, because in their civil capacity they had done an unfair act.   Williams, with the approval of the church, wrote sharp letters of admonition to all the churches of the colony, to which the members of the general court belonged, urging that they be reproved for their conduct as a "heinous sin."   This at once spread

[1] Winthrop, I. 70, 81.   [2] *Ibid.* 195.

the debate throughout the colony. It was an appeal to the whole body of the freemen, in their ecclesiastical capacity, against the general court. It was the first serious act of opposition with which the leaders had found it necessary to deal.

Steps were at once taken by individual magistrates and elders to win over from Williams the members of his own church. In this they succeeded, and the majority resolved to abandon him rather than to abandon the other churches. When Williams learned this, he wrote a letter to his church[1] declaring that he had severed connection with the churches of the bay, and would cease to commune with his brethren in Salem if they did not break off communion with the rest. But this made no difference, and he was left with a few followers who attended private services in his house. He even refused to pray with his own wife because she continued to attend the public assembly.

The town of Salem was brought into line by an order of the next general court that their deputies should be sent home to obtain satisfaction for the letters that had been sent, or the arguments of those who would undertake to defend them, with their names subscribed thereto.[2] Endicott, who had already been suspended from office because he had mutilated the colors, but who was present in the court, protested against this course in such strong language that he was committed for contempt; but later, on acknowledging his fault, he was set free. A more stringent order, however, was adopted concerning the town, to the effect that the majority of its freemen must disclaim[3] the letters recently sent to the churches before their deputies could be seated. The practical effect of that was to exclude the representatives of Salem from the court during the September session.

It now remained to inflict the final penalty on Mr. Williams, who, though left almost alone, abated not a tittle of his resolution. The case came up during the session at Newtown, from active participation in which the Salem deputies had been excluded. All the ministers in the bay were

[1] Winthrop, I. 198.   [2] *Ibid.* 195; Recs. I. 156.   [3] *Ibid.* 158.

invited to be present.[1] In addition to the opinions for
which Williams was already held responsible, he was now
charged with the letters to the churches complaining of
injustice and oppression on the part of the magistrates, and
with his letter to his own church urging it to renounce
communion with all the other churches because they were
full of anti-Christian pollution.   Both of these letters he
justified, and maintained all his opinions.   He was then asked
whether, after taking a month for reflection, he would come
and argue the matter before them.   This offer he declined,
and " chose to dispute presently."   Thomas Hooker of
Newtown, who till his removal to Connecticut occupied
the leading place among Massachusetts divines, was then
appointed to debate with Williams.   Of their discussion we
know nothing except a reference to a minor point, which is
preserved in one of the later controversial writings of Mr.
Cotton.[2]   A large part of a single sitting was devoted to
this colloquy, but without result.   Mr. Hooker " could not
reduce him from any of his errors."   The next morning the
governor, John Haynes, summed[3] up the charges, giving
the first place, if correctly reported, to Williams's views concerning land titles, the second to those concerning the oath,
the third to his opinion that it was not lawful to hear any
of the ministers of the parish assemblies in England, the last
to his theory that the power of the civil magistrate extends
only to the bodies, goods, and outward state of men.   Then
the sentence of banishment[4] was pronounced against him,
its words implying that it was justified by the fact that the
accused had proclaimed new and dangerous opinions against
the authority of magistrates, had written letters of defama-
tion concerning both magistrates and churches, and that
he continued to defend his course of action.   For these
reasons he was ordered to depart out of the jurisdiction
within six weeks ; if he neglected so to do, the governor and

[1] Winthrop, I. 204 ; Dexter, 56.

[2] Reply to Mr. Williams, his Examination, Narragansett Club Edition,
52.

[3] Williams, Mr. Cotton's Letter Examined, Narragansett Club Edition, 40.

[4] Col. Recs. I. 160.

two of the magistrates might send him out, not to return any more without license from the court.

When the date set for his departure came, he was reported to be ill. It was therefore resolved by the magistrates that he might have respite till spring. But about the beginning of winter report came that he was still uttering the opinions for which he was censured, and that he was holding meetings at his house for the purpose. He had won the adherence of about twenty persons, who would coöperate with him in the founding of a plantation in Narragansett bay, from which it was feared that the infection would spread into Massachusetts. That Winthrop, however, at that time did not fear infection from that quarter is shown by the fact,[1] related by Williams forty years afterwards, that Winthrop privately wrote him to steer his course thither, for the place was free from English claims or patents. When the messenger sent by the magistrates reached Salem, in January, 1636, for the purpose of arresting him, Williams had fled, and his connection with Massachusetts as a resident had ended.

At the meeting of the general court the following March, " it was proved . . . that Marble Neck belongs to Salem."[2] Deputies from that town also took their seats. These events, together with the removal of the chief malcontents to Narragansett bay, permitted affairs to again resume their orderly course in that town. But an element of radicalism survived there, which, together with sectional feeling, repeatedly arrayed Salem with other northern towns against the magistrates and elders. Winthrop states[3] that after Williams's departure the spirit of Separatism there was so strong that the Salem church asked if it were not better for them to be dismissed to form an independent church. But this of course the magistrates and elders would not for a moment consider.

In estimating the early career of Roger Williams it may be said that his one valuable idea — that of religious freedom — was the logical outgrowth of Protestantism. It was one of the tendencies which were rooted in Calvinism itself. Not only was it a fundamental tenet of Robert Browne, but

[1] Letter to Major Mason, Pubs. of Narr. Club, VI. 335 ; 1 Mass. Hist. Col. II. 276.   [2] Col. Recs. I. 165.   [3] Journal, I. 221.

it lay at the basis of true Independency.   The Puritans of Massachusetts were in theory Independents, and had they remained true to the principle upon which their movement began, they must have welcomed the doctrine with which the name of Roger Williams is identified.   But, largely under the pressure of political necessity, the Massachusetts leaders had from the beginning committed themselves to a limited or presbyterianized Independency.   In order to secure unity and strength they had sacrificed freedom.   Williams could truly claim that he was the one consistent and logical Independent, and that those who condemned him were the innovators.   But that as a practical contention could avail nothing.   Though the decision of the leaders had scarcely antedated his protest against it, and was even being formed while their controversy with him was in progress, it was held with such tenacity and was so far in harmony with their spirit and situation as to render it impossible for any one to make headway against it single-handed.

It is true that Williams did not stand quite alone in his opposition to the magistrates and clergy, but his following was small and was confined to a single locality.   He was also one of the poorest of political managers, in truth almost destitute of skill in such matters.   Two of the three indictments which he urged against the Massachusetts polity were flimsy and unjustifiable.   By putting these forward at the outset he won for himself the reputation of an overscrupulous busybody and agitator.   Had it not been for what he afterwards suffered and accomplished and for the influence which the views that he shared with other prophets of his time have had upon later generations, his place in history would be among that class, and among its most ineffective representatives.   Like all pronounced individualists, he had friends, but few followers.   His friends were won by his sincerity, frankness, and attractive personality.   But throughout his career few of his friends stood ready to follow his lead in affairs of large practical moment.   It must be admitted that in the main he received as considerate treatment from Massachusetts authorities as was possible under the conditions which then existed.

No sooner had the magistrates and elders of Massachusetts rid themselves of Williams than they became involved in another controversy [1] and one of far greater seriousness and importance. This had its origin in the domain of theological metaphysics, but worked itself out as a political issue of the first magnitude, originating party catchwords and dividing the colony into two bitterly contending factions.

The parties to this struggle were the so-called Antinomians, who had secured control of the Boston church, and the great body of the clergy and other freemen of the colony. The leaders of the Antinomians were Mistress Anne Hutchinson, her brother-in-law, the Rev. John Wheelwright, and Governor Vane ; while Mr. Cotton was for a time more or less identified with that group. The leaders of the conservatives were Governor Winthrop and Mr. Wilson, the pastor of the Boston church, and they had the assistance of all the magistrates and elders outside the chief town of the colony. Boston was in the beginning the centre of this strife, as Salem had been of that which concerned Roger Williams. Though considerably larger than Salem, it was still only a village of some two thousand inhabitants.

The trouble began with the holding of conventicles, or private meetings, chiefly at the house of Mrs. Hutchinson, a woman of marked ability who had come to the colony from England in 1634 as a follower and admirer of Mr. Cotton. She, with her husband, had been admitted to membership in the Boston church. Some time after, as a result of the wide acquaintance which she gained among the women of the village, she began to hold meetings, attended exclusively by them, at which she repeated the substance of recent sermons for the benefit of those who had been unable to attend church. She presently began to add comments and interpretations of her own. These were of a mystical and inspirationist character, which made the talks all the

---

[1] For a most detailed and satisfactory account of this controversy, see Adams, Three Episodes of Massachusetts History. The original sources, except what is contained in Winthrop's Journal, are in Adams's Antinomianism in Massachusetts Bay and Bell's John Wheelwright, both of which are among the publications of the Prince Society.

more attractive to many of her listeners. The numbers in attendance largely increased, including some of the ministers and magistrates, and even Governor Vane himself. Mrs. Hutchinson thus quickly rose to be an important public figure, and that in a community, one of whose cardinal tenets was that women should keep silence in the public assembly.

Mrs. Hutchinson's likes and dislikes, together with her ambition, soon betrayed her into statements which set the colony aflame. For herself, Mr. Cotton, and Mr. Wheelwright — after his arrival in the colony — she began to claim a superior enlightenment of the spirit, a peculiar indwelling of the Holy Ghost which raised them above the level of ordinary preachers of the word. In her opinion, and according to the theological phraseology then in vogue, this brought them under the "covenant of grace." All the other ministers of the colony were classed as preachers of a "covenant of works," meaning thereby, that they lacked the inspiration, or inner light, given by the indwelling of the Holy Ghost, and were thus legalists, having to depend on the careful observance of a rigid moral and religious code. They could not rise into the true freedom of the gospel, and hence could not interpret the Bible and its mysteries aright. Their lips were not sealed.

Mr. Wilson, the pastor of the Boston church, whom Mrs. Hutchinson intensely disliked, and the clergymen of the colony with whom he was classed as a mere legalist, naturally resented the imputation. The Bible was their text-book. They considered themselves divinely appointed interpreters. They had been trained in what seemed to them to be the only true system of interpretation. To have this thrust one side, and another which, in their opinion, savored of all the extravagances of Münster put in its place, was more than could be borne. If the position of the clergy and their criteria of interpretation were discredited, the entire fabric of the church-state would collapse. Pique, self-interest, professional pride, combined to strengthen the resisting power of the clergy. The result was that the conflict was soon carried over into the domain of secular politics and was there fought out with the utmost bitterness.

Mrs. Hutchinson early gained the adherence of all the Boston church, except Mr. Wilson, the pastor, Mr. Winthrop, the deputy governor, and a few others. Soon after Wheelwright's arrival in the colony a blow was struck at Wilson by a proposal that the newcomer should be appointed assistant teacher. Before the time for a final vote on this arrived, a conference of the ministers[1] of the colony was held for the purpose of discussing the new views and restoring harmony, if possible, in the Boston church. Both Cotton and Wheelwright appeared and made it clear that their views on the theological questions in debate were more moderate than some to which Mrs. Hutchinson had given utterance. Nothing, however, was accomplished toward the restoration of harmony.

On the following Sunday the proposal respecting the appointment of Wheelwright came before the Boston church for final action. Winthrop then stood up alone and opposed it.[2] The unanswerable argument which he urged was, that the church was already well supplied with able ministers. In addition to that he deprecated the calling of one " whose spirit they knew not," and one who seemed to "dissent in judgment." On his referring to two doctrinal points on which Wheelwright seemed to show the Antinomian heresy, some discussion occurred in which Vane, Cotton, and Wheelwright took part. At its close Winthrop, while admitting that Wheelwright was an able and godly man, yet "seeing he was apt to raise doubtful disputations," he could not consent to his election. Upon this the church gave way, and Wheelwright was soon after settled over a chapel instituted as a branch of the Boston church at Mount Wollaston.

When it became known that Vane's opinions were in full harmony with those expressed by Mrs. Hutchinson, his popularity through the colony at large began to diminish. That of Winthrop, whom the Hutchinson excitement and the charge of too great lenity had thrown into the background, began correspondingly to revive. This so nettled the young governor that he began to talk of resigning and going

[1] Winthrop, I. 240.   [2] *Ibid.* 241.

home.   On one occasion, with a strange outburst of tears in
the presence of the board of assistants,[1] he stated that the
reason he desired release from office was that he was charged
with being responsible for all the dissensions which had
arisen in the colony.   The majority of the assistants would
not have been unwilling to see him resign, and arrangements
were made to hold a special court of election.   But the
Boston church could not afford to lose his influence.   Therefore, on their interposition he remained.

Vane's hesitating course occasioned him new troubles,
because in connection with the proposed special court of
election a conference between the ministers and magistrates
was arranged, and that without the governor's knowledge.
It was held in December, 1636.   In that conference,[2] Hugh
Peters, who had come over with Vane and was now the successor of Williams at Salem, took the governor roundly to
task because he seemed to be opposed to such conferences, because he had occasioned much strife, and had assumed the per-
emptory airs characteristic of young and inexperienced men.
This tirade the young governor, who was present, vainly endeavored to check.   After it closed Mr. Wilson "made a
very sad speech" on the alienations and divisions among the
brethren, which would lead to complete separation if not
remedied.   The cause of these troubles he found in the
novel opinions which had lately appeared among them.
With this view all the magistrates, except the governor
and two others, agreed, and all the ministers but two.   But
the tone of the speech was so harsh as to seriously offend
Mr. Cotton and the members of the Boston church.

Mrs. Hutchinson was also called before the ministers at the
same time and place.   Led by Peters[3] they questioned her for
the purpose of ascertaining why it was that she asserted that
they taught a covenant of works.   After some hesitation,
she boldly reaffirmed her charge, and gave as the reason that
they were not sealed, and were no more able ministers of the
gospel than were the disciples before the resurrection of
Christ.   She even cited individuals among those present in

[1] Winthrop, I. 247.   [2] *Ibid.* 249.
[3] Antinomianism in Massachusetts Bay, 246.

illustration of the point she wished to make, while the distinction she drew between Cotton and all the rest was so marked as to draw from him a protest. The conference broke up without contributing in any way toward the restoration of harmony.

On the other hand Wilson's speech had greatly increased the bitterness of feeling in the Boston church, and this expressed itself in an effort to formally censure the pastor.[1] Though Wilson and others affirmed that no rule of conduct had been broken, yet he was called to answer before a public meeting of the church. Then Vane "pressed it violently against him," and so did all the congregation except Winthrop and one or two more. Cotton, the teacher, acted with the majority, though with much greater moderation, and restrained them from immediate censure on the ground that the church was not unanimous.

A debate in writing was now opened by Winthrop with Cotton, in which the deputy governor "laid before him divers failings [as he supposed] and some reasons to justify Mr. Wilson, and dealt very plainly with him." Mr. Cotton "made a very loving and gentle answer," but justified his course with "divers arguments." The general discussion also engendered at this time opinions more radical than any previously uttered :[2] as that faith is no cause of justification, a man being justified before he believes ; that the covenant of works was held forth in the ten commandments or in the letter of Scripture, while the covenant of grace was in the spirit and was known only to believers as the consequence of immediate revelation.

As this seemed to be downright inspirationism and was accepted by all the Boston church except four or five, the clergy undertook to labor directly with Cotton. They drew up sixteen points, and asked him to declare his judgment concerning them. This he did, clearing some doubts, but in other cases giving no satisfaction. The ministers then replied to his answers, showing their dissent and the grounds thereof. The ministers now publicly declared their sentiments in their own pulpits, and the discussion[3] became gen-

---

[1] Winthrop, I. 250.   [2] *Ibid.* I. 252.   [3] *Ibid.* 254 *et seq.*

eral throughout the colony. The strife had now reached such dimensions that, near the close of January, 1637, a general fast was kept.

The fast day proved to be a turning-point in the struggle. Mr. Wheelwright on this occasion attended the afternoon services in the Boston church. After Mr. Cotton had finished, he was asked " to exercise as a private brother," and preached his famous fast-day sermon.[1] Whatever may have been his reason for so doing, he took as his subject the thought which was uppermost in all minds, the covenant of grace and the covenant of works. Adopting, according to familiar Scripture usage, the figure of a battle, he spoke of the adherents of the covenant of grace as confronted by the necessity of spiritual combat, if they would not have Christ taken from them. They must put on the whole armor of God, have their swords ready, show themselves valiant, lay hold upon their enemies, kill them with the word of the Lord. But he was careful throughout to specify that he meant a spiritual not a physical combat, carried on not with carnal weapons, but with spiritual. Except for the occasion on which it was delivered, it was an ordinary, a somewhat dull, and to an extent an incomprehensible Puritan sermon. But Wilson was forced to listen to it in his own pulpit; it was by implication an arraignment of his party. It contained expressions which, if taken out of their context and sufficiently twisted by interpretation, could be made to look like seditious utterances, as if the sermon was an incitement to civil war. Before the sermon was delivered, so grave had seemed the situation that the clergy had resolved to discontinue[2] lectures for three weeks about the first of March, that they might meet then with the general court and " bring things to some issue." As the ministers were called to advise the court on that occasion, it was decided to inquire into the proceedings of the Boston church against Mr. Wilson and into Wheelwright's sermon.

On all the questions the majority of the court showed itself, from the ministerial standpoint, to be sound. One Stephen Greensmith, for saying[3] that all the ministers ex-

[1] Bell, John Wheelwright; Winthrop, I. 256.   [2] Ibid. 253.   [3] Ibid. 256.

cept Cotton, Wheelwright, and Hooker taught a covenant of
works, was fined £40, and ordered to acknowledge his fault
in every church. The proceedings of the Boston church
against Mr. Wilson, as well as his "sad speech" which was
the occasion of it, were fully discussed. The speech was
declared to have been "a seasonable advice," and to have
carried "no charge or accusation." This was a pointed rebuke for Vane. Though probably for political reasons none
of the members who had accused Wilson were at this time
punished, the elders were specially consulted. They,[1] with
the apparent approval of all, proclaimed and defended two
principles: that no member of the court — including thereby
those who were advising it — should, without its license, be
publicly questioned by a church for any speech made in the
court; and that on the appearance among church members
of errors or heresies which were clearly dangerous to the
state, the court should act without waiting for the church.
The first of these was intended to meet such cases as those
of Mr. Wilson, while the second would give the court the
initiative against a church, like that of Boston, the majority
of whose members were serious offenders.

These preliminaries having been disposed of, it was resolved to begin, in the person of Wheelwright, the attack on
the leaders of the Antinomians. His fast-day sermon was
utilized for the purpose. He was summoned before the general court and notes taken at the time of the delivery of his
discourse were produced. He was asked if he admitted their
correctness. In reply he submitted his own manuscript, and
was dismissed.[2] Before he was summoned again the next
day, a petition, signed by nearly all[3] the members of the
Boston church, was presented. It requested that judicial
hearings might be conducted publicly, and that they as freemen be permitted to be present; also that cases of conscience
might first be dealt with before the church. Though the
propriety of this act was beyond question, it was denounced
by the court as unjustifiable and presumptuous, and the
petition was rejected with the reply that judicial sessions of

[1] Winthrop, I. 255.   [2] Antinomianism in Massachusetts Bay, 193 *et seq.*
[3] Winthrop, 256.

the court were always public, though those held for consultation and in preparation for trials were private.

The examination of Wheelwright was then begun in private. When called in he asked for his accusers, and was told that, his sermon having been acknowledged by himself and being then in court, it might proceed *ex officio*. This at once suggested Star Chamber and High Commission proceedings, as a result of which they had been driven out of England, and loud protest was raised on this account by some members of the court who were friendly to the accused. To this the reply was made that the term *ex officio* was proper, since it signified only the authority and duty of the court in such cases, and it was not proposed to examine the accused by oath or to imprison him. A question was then asked which Wheelwright declined to answer, and which his friends denounced as intended to insnare him. Upon his then refusing to answer any more questions, the secret session broke up, and the subsequent hearings were held in public.

In the afternoon of the same day, in the presence of the ministers and of a general assembly of the people, the examination of Wheelwright was resumed. It consisted in the reading of various passages from his sermon, and his justification of the same. He declared that he meant any whose manner and spirit were such as he had described under the term "covenant of works." In thoroughly characteristic fashion, as arbiters though under the guise of witnesses, the ministers were then asked if they taught and practised what had been described as the covenant of works. The next morning all except Cotton returned an affirmative answer.

This has been rightly considered as equivalent to a verdict; but the judgment of the court had still to be formally registered. Hence it went again into secret session, and the opposing factions under the lead of Winthrop and Vane struggled over the issue for two days. At last two of the magistrates were won over to the side of the ministers [1] and the party of the clergy and magistrates triumphed. Wheelwright was voted guilty of sedition and contempt. Against the judgment as pronounced Vane protested, but the court

---

[1] Coddington to Fretwell, Felt, II. 611.

refused to enter his protest on its journal. A second petition [1] was also presented by sixty members of the church of
Boston, in which, in moderate and respectful language, they
denied that the accused had uttered seditious doctrine or had
been guilty of a seditious act. In justification of this statement they called attention to the fact that the peace had not
been disturbed as the result of his sermon. This was received without objection and entered upon the records of the
court. Though the conservatives had won, the struggle had
been so obstinate that the sentence of Wheelwright was deferred till the next general court. The question, whether or
not he should in the meantime be silenced, then came up,
and, in the interest of conciliation, it was decided to com-
mend his case to the Boston church.[2]

But a clear indication that the conflict was in its earlier
stages appeared when it was moved that the next court,
which was the court of election, should meet at Newtown.
The reason for this was, that it might be free from the influence of the Antinomians who so fully controlled opinion in
Boston. As means of communication then were, a removal
only so far as that would be sufficient to accomplish the purpose which the conservatives intended, and it was from them
that the proposal came. Though it had already become customary for the general court to meet in Boston, it was not
bound by law to that place, and now, as a century and a
half later, its temporary removal for political reasons to an
outlying town was proposed. But Vane, seeing its object,
as presiding officer refused to put the motion. Winthrop, as
deputy governor, might have done it, but because he was an
inhabitant of Boston, and for other reasons, he hesitated unless the court expressly commanded him to do so. Thereupon Endicott rose, put the motion, and declared it carried.

In connection with the meeting of this court of election,
which was held May, 1637, at Newtown, the political bearings of the controversy became evident on a large scale.
Party lines were clearly drawn throughout the province.
Winthrop and Vane were, in the political field, the recog-

[1] Antinomianism in Massachusetts Bay, 133; Winthrop, I. 481–483.
[2] Winthrop, I. 258.

nized leaders of the two forces, and they were the candidates for the governorship. The court [1] met out of doors, and its attention was first directed to the Boston petition, which had been presented to the last court after its adverse vote against Winthrop. It was now brought again into requisition as a means of placing the Boston version of the issue directly before the freemen. But as the first business of this court was the election of magistrates, this was properly regarded as irregular. But Vane, as presiding officer, insisted that the petition should be read ; Winthrop declared that it was out of order and that the hearing of petitions should be postponed till after election. In this he had the support of many others, and a heated debate ensued. Fierce speeches were uttered, angry words passed to and fro, and "some laid hands on others." In the midst of the turmoil, Mr. Wilson climbed the trunk of the large oak which overshadowed the place of meeting, and exhorted the freemen to look to their charter and proceed to election. This appeal evoked cries of "Election ! Election !" Winthrop then put the question himself, and a large majority were for election. Vane, however, still held out, and yielded only when Winthrop told him that if he would not go on, they would proceed without him.

In the election which followed, the Antinomians were totally defeated. Winthrop was chosen governor and Dudley deputy governor, while Endicott was rewarded for the evidence he had given of the abandonment of his radicalism by appointment as a member of the standing council. All supporters of the Boston heresy were also left off the board of magistracy. The reply of Boston to this act was prompt and emphatic. It had postponed the election of its deputies till after the meeting of the court. As soon as its result was learned it chose Vane, Coddington, and Hough, its defeated candidates for the magistracy, as its representatives among the deputies. This the general court considered an affront, and on the pretext that two of the freemen of Boston had not been notified, declared the election there to be invalid and issued a new warrant. To this the town responded by

[1] Winthrop, I. 261 *et seq.*

returning the same deputies a second time. The court, "not finding how they might reject them," had to accept the inevitable, and they were admitted to their seats.

So strong was party feeling that, on Winthrop's election, the sergeants who had attended Vane to the court, being Boston men, laid down their halberds and went home. Winthrop was forced to make use of his own servants as attendants thereafter. The levy for the expedition against the Pequot Indians was just being called out, and not a church member in Boston would serve, for the reason that their pastor, Mr. Wilson, had been selected by lot as chaplain and he was under a covenant of works. In social relations Vane became totally estranged from Winthrop, and so remained till he finally returned to England the following August. The order passed by the spring court of 1637 forbidding strangers to be harbored in the colony a longer period than three weeks without the consent of the magistrates and threatening towns with special penalties for its violation, still further irritated the Boston people, for they then expected arrivals from England which would strengthen their party, and the conservative magistrates now forbade their admission.

All the churches of the colony, save one, were now united. The civil government was entirely in the control of their members. It was possible to keep out all unwelcome intruders. The Pequot war was quickly brought to a successful end. These events prepared the way for the complete crushing out of the Antinomian heresy and the expulsion of its persistent adherents from Massachusetts. The first step which led directly to this result was the meeting of the synod [1] at Newtown in September. This was the first assembly of its kind in America, and its object was to establish criteria of orthodoxy on the disputed points and brand all divergent opinions as heretical. This would compel all to identify themselves fully with the majority or incur the necessary penalties. The departure of Vane had removed one of the most serious obstacles to success in the application of pressure. Its effect upon the position of Cotton soon

[1] Winthrop, I. 284 *et seq.*; Antinomianism in Massachusetts Bay, 95 *et seq.*

became apparent, for he was now left practically alone among the leaders, and found it daily more difficult to maintain his independent position.   Special efforts were made before the synod met to bring Cotton, Wilson, and Wheelwright to an understanding, and these bore some encouraging fruit in the case of the Boston teacher.   The overwhelming conservative majority in the synod, and the fact that it early found eighty-two of the opinions of Mrs. Hutchinson and her sympathizers to be erroneous or blasphemous, confirmed him in this tendency to harmony.   Cotton had not the spirit of a martyr, and while the Boston members retired from the synod and Wheelwright consistently maintained his attitude, Cotton declared that he had seen a light, and thus in good time saved himself and family from the pains of banishment.   At the last session it was resolved that such meetings as those which Mrs. Hutchinson had held in Boston were "disorderly and without rule."   As Mrs. Hutchinson, Mr. Wheelwright, and the Boston church had withstood the efforts at conciliation which it was supposed had proceeded from the synod, they were now regarded as legitimate subjects of discipline under the charge of being refractory. The great practical service of the synod was, that it made Cotton ready to join in the work of discipline.

Notwithstanding the circumstances under which the general court of May, 1637, had been elected, it had showed little disposition to proceed earnestly against the Antinomians. Hence, though it was elected for a year, after the synod broke up it was suddenly [1] dissolved, and another court was elected.   Of its thirty-three members, twenty-one were new men.   Coddington, Aspinwall, and Coggshall, however, were returned from Boston.   The new court met early in November, prepared to execute the policy of purge already resolved upon.   "Finding upon consultation," [2] writes Winthrop, "that two so opposite parties could not contain in the same body, without apparent hazard of ruin to the whole, we agreed to send away some of the principal."   A "fair opportunity" was presented by the remonstrance or petition which had been presented the previous March by the members of the

[1] Mass. Recs. I. 205.   [2] Winthrop, I. 292.

Boston church, the discussion about which had occasioned such tumult at the May court. Though the modern eye can detect nothing seditious in it, yet it was now condemned as such. Aspinwall,[1] one of its signers, was not allowed to take the seat to which he was elected. Coggshall, though not a signer, because he expressed his approval of it, was also dismissed, and Boston was ordered to choose two others. Coddington, the remaining deputy, then moved that the censure on Wheelwright, and also the order respecting the admission of inhabitants into the colony, be rescinded; but this was without result. The Boston freemen at first resolved to send back the rejected deputies, but Cotton persuaded them not to do so. William Colburn and John Oliver were chosen in their places. The latter, however, was found to have signed the petition, and he was therefore not allowed to take his seat. No one was elected in his place.

Wheelwright was then called for sentence,[2] Winthrop presiding and acting as spokesman for the court. He was asked to acknowledge his offence or submit to judgment. He replied that he had not been guilty of sedition or contempt. Then, by the characteristic turn of argument to which reference has already been made, he was told that it was not his doctrine which was condemned, but its effect on the community. By laying the clergy and churches under a covenant of works, a party of opposition was created, things were "turned upside down amongst us"; the evil had spread to families, then to public affairs, and thus was breeding sedition. The political results, it was alleged, appeared in the attitude of Boston toward the Pequot war, while the same spirit was shown in the levy of town rates, the assignment of town lots, and in other business. The court claimed to have acted with patience, and to have sought to turn Wheelwright from his opinions, but in vain. Wheelwright, on the other hand, insisted that the seditious words in his sermon should be pointed out. The court replied that it was not necessary to do this; sedition was there by implication, in that he had tried to bring "the people of God" into discredit by laying

---

[1] Antinomianism in Massachusetts Bay, 136 *et seq.*   [2] *Ibid.* 140 *et seq.*

them under a covenant of works.   He was then sentenced to disfranchisement and to banishment, and, unless he gave security to depart before the end of the following March, he should be taken into custody.   Wheelwright then declared that he would appeal to the king.   He was told in reply to this that " an appeal did not lie in this case, for the king having given us authority by his grant under his great seal of England to hear and determine all causes without any reservation, we are not to admit of any such appeal . . .; and if an appeal should lie in one case, it might be challenged in all, and then there would be no use of government amongst us."   Wheelwright then abandoned his claim to an appeal, and, refusing to give security, was taken into custody.   The next day he offered to give security, but would not agree to refrain from preaching in the meantime.   Therefore the court declared that, if he did not depart within fourteen days, he must remain as a prisoner in the house of one of the magistrates until the court should dispose of him. Though it was now early winter, within that limit of time he turned his steps northward, and with the friends who followed him the next spring he founded Exeter, New Hampshire.

The cases of Coggshall and Aspinwall were then taken up for final action, and on the ground that the petition which they had signed was seditious and that in connection with the earlier proceedings of the court against them they had used seditious language, the former was disfranchised and banished.   To Aspinwall the court expressed its opinion of his share in the Boston petition to the effect that for him, being a member of a civil body, " to stop the course of justice in countenancing seditious persons and practices against the face of authority, this made him a seditious person."   Aspinwall replied by citing a petition of Mephibosheth to David and one from Esther to Ahasuerus as precedents, but these did not avail.   He then fell back on the right of the English subject to petition.   The court replied that the document referred to was not a petition, but a seditious libel.   When sentence was about to be pronounced, Aspinwall desired a Scripture precedent for banishment.   The case of Hagar and Ishmael was cited, and with this, though he was inclined to cavil, he had to be satisfied.

After other similar cases had been disposed of the trial[1] of Mrs. Hutchinson, or more properly the legislative hearing in her case, was begun. Questions relating to the procedure followed in this case have been discussed elsewhere ; here it is necessary to call attention to the controversial points on which the case turned. The charge against Mrs. Hutchinson was not sedition, — though every offence might easily end in that, — but " traducing the ministers." With this were closely connected the offences of holding largely attended public meetings, and giving aid and sympathy to those who had signed the Boston petition. When at the beginning of the trial the accused was confronted with some of these charges, she asked what rule or law she had broken. The reply was, the fifth commandment, as the command to honor father and mother includes magistrates, " the fathers of the commonwealth." Mrs. Hutchinson, taking up this forced analogy, asked if a child might not entertain and honor one who feared the Lord, even though its parent would not allow it. This she might have done in supporting Wheelwright and the petition. The court replied that this was not to the purpose. " We cannot stand to dispute cases with you now."

Winthrop then took up the subject of the weekly meetings, and asked if Mrs. Hutchinson could justify them. She replied that there were such before she came, but she did not attend them, and to save herself from the reputation of being proud she began holding her own meetings. On her citing Titus ii. 3–5, in which the apostle charged the aged women to teach the young women the rules of good conduct, Winthrop met this by the quotation of the favorite text, 1 Cor. xiv. 34–35, which commands women to keep silent in the churches, and denounced her meetings as prejudicial to the commonwealth. Mrs. Hutchinson contended that they were private prophesyings, like those of the Bereans and of Aquila and Priscilla, and the court that they were public, without valid precedent, and dangerous.

---

[1] Two reports of this trial exist. See Antinomianism in Massachusetts Bay, 164 *et seq.*, 235 *et seq.*

The court next took up Mrs. Hutchinson's charges against the ministers, which were the real source of feelings of hatred toward her.   The discussion of this hinged on the report given by Peters, Welde, Eliot, and the other ministers who were present, of the statements she had made during the conference a year before at Cotton's house, where she had declared " that there was a wide difference between Master Cotton's ministry and theirs, and that they could not hold forth a covenant of free grace because they had not the seal of the spirit, and that they were not able ministers of the New Testament."   The ministers were questioned concerning what at that time was said.   All of them agreed that the alleged statements were made in direct and harsh form.

At the opening of the session of the next day Mrs. Hutchinson stated that since going to her home she had read certain of the notes which had been taken at the time of the conference, and found "things not to be as hath been alleged." Because of that she demanded that the ministers, who were testifying in their own cause, should be sworn.[1]   This occasioned much discussion in the court, as it was considered by the leaders to be unnecessary and, in a way, a reflection on the sacred character of the clergy.   The governor ruled that, as this was not a jury case, the court was at liberty to grant or reject the demand.   The argument, suggested by Mrs. Hutchinson, that an oath was the end of all strife had much weight, when it was seen that many in the court would not be satisfied without it.   Before, however, the oath was administered it was resolved to hear what Mrs. Hutchinson's witnesses had to say.   Mr. Coggshall, the first to be called, declared that he was present at the conference and that she " did not say all that which they lay against her." But Peters's rebuke, " How dare you look into the court to say such a word ? " reduced him at once to silence.   Mr. Leverett affirmed that she had said that they did not preach a covenant of grace so clearly as did Mr. Cotton.   The Boston teacher himself was the third witness for the accused, and on their being called had taken his seat beside her.

[1] See Antinomianism in Massachusetts Bay, 256.

Now in an eloquent and diplomatic speech — decidedly superior in spirit to anything else which was said during the
trial — Mr. Cotton formulated the alleged utterances of Mrs.
Hutchinson at the conference[1] in such mild and negative
fashion as to leave little of which the court could complain.

But at this point Mrs. Hutchinson betrayed her own cause
by indiscreet words. Almost as soon as Cotton had finished,
she launched out upon an account of the rise in her, during
her residence in England, of the notion that she was a subject of immediate revelations. After Cotton had removed
to New England and Wheelwright had been silenced, she
came to Massachusetts under a revelation from God that she
should hear the true gospel preached there, but should suffer
persecution. This was confirmed to her by the words of the
prophets which this day they saw fulfilled. But she should
be delivered from their hands, as Daniel was, and a curse
would follow her accusers and their posterity for the course
they had pursued against her. These were just the ideas
to which Mrs. Hutchinson's enemies had been saying that
her belief led, and in which lay their peril. Her utterances
therefore furnished the evidence they were looking for. Special providences they believed in and utilized by the whole-
sale, but they stopped short at that point. Miracles and revelations, with characteristic halfway logic, they excluded. Mr.
Cotton was asked what he believed to be the character of
Mrs. Hutchinson's revelations. His first answer was non-com-
mittal. On being asked again, he turned to Mrs. Hutchinson
and inquired if she expected deliverance from the power of
the court by a great miracle, one that was beyond the power
of nature. She finally answered that she did not expect deliverance from the power of the court, but from the " calamity
of it."

The idea of the majority, as expressed by Winthrop, now
was that by a special providence Mrs. Hutchinson's own
words had condemned her. She had admitted that she had
acted under pretended direct revelations, and not according
to any rule of Scripture. Before she left England it had
been revealed to her that the ministers of New England

[1] See Antinomianism in Massachusetts Bay, 172, 265.

were "anti-Christian." Such beliefs could not stand with
the peace of any state. They savored of the extravagances
of Münster. Therefore, after two of the ministers had testified under oath and on behalf of the whole body to the truth
of what they had said concerning Mrs. Hutchinson's utterances in the conference, with only two opposing votes she
was found guilty.[1] The governor then sentenced her to
banishment as "a woman not fit for our society," she to be
detained as a prisoner till the court should send her away.

Captain John Underhill, the famous Boston soldier, was
then removed from office and disfranchised because he had
signed the obnoxious petition. On November 20, the general court[2] decreed that, because of their share in the dangerous errors of Mr. Wheelwright and Mrs. Hutchinson, and
the fear arising therefrom that upon some revelation they
might suddenly attack those who differed from them,
fifty-eight persons in Boston should be disarmed, five in
Salem, three in Newbury, five in Roxbury, two in Ipswich,
two in Charlestown. Still, in its endeavor to make it appear
that this act was liberal and tolerant and that it proceeded
wholly from care for the public peace, the court declared
that it did not intend to restrict the freedom of petition, or
the use, when private means failed, of any lawful public
means for the reform of the court or any member of the
same. Winthrop, also, in defending himself against the
charges of many of the Boston church who desired to call
him to account, declared that he had acted throughout for
the public good, and thus had fulfilled the obligations of his
official oath.

Mrs. Hutchinson, after being detained in a private house
at Roxbury during the winter and subjected at intervals to
arguments and questionings by the ministers, was brought
to trial before the Boston church in March, 1638. The
abandonment by Mr. Cotton of his Antinomian opinions and
the purging to which the Boston church had been subjected
had by this time reclaimed that body from its errors. The
entire clergy of the colony also interested itself in this trial,
and thus brought to bear upon the Boston congregation a

[1] See Antinomianism in Massachusetts Bay, 283.   [2] Col. Recs. I. 211.

force of orthodox opinion which was irresistible. In this trial the clergy were the managers and chief spokesmen, and by a form of procedure which was similar to that employed by the magistrates before the general court, they secured the conviction of Mrs. Hutchinson and her solemn excommunication. Mr. Wilson had the satisfaction of pronouncing the sentence which separated her forever from fellowship with the churches of Massachusetts.[1] Thus the arch-heretic was cast out, and when, five years later, she and several members of her family were slain by the Indians at the residence which they had finally chosen within the limits of New Netherland, the Puritans regarded the event as a special manifestation of divine justice.

By the attitude which they assumed toward the so-called Antinomian opinions the magistrates and clergy of Massachusetts definitely committed themselves to a close alliance for the purpose of upholding a system of strict orthodoxy. Tendencies which were operative when the religious test was enacted and when Roger Williams was banished, now came fully to prevail. Pressure was brought to bear from the churches united in a synod, from the clergy and magistrates in frequent conference, and from the general court as the highest expression of power in the colony, to keep local congregations and individuals alike in harmony with the doctrines and practices of the majority. From this union and resolve proceeded the body of legislation on ecclesiastical and moral subjects which has already been outlined. All parties must expressly or tacitly accept this, must yield it at least outward obedience, or leave the colony. Protest, whether by speech or action, was rigorously suppressed, and the secular power was resorted to for the purpose without hesitation. The life and thought of this colony and of other colonies, so far as its influence could be made to control them, was cast in one narrow Puritan mould, and was not allowed to escape from it. So little was there of enlightenment in New England outside the circle of ideas which the clergy imparted or controlled, that it was possible to maintain

[1] The report of the church trial is printed in Mr. Adams's volume on Antinomianism; also in 2 Proceedings Mass. Hist. Soc. IV.

strict conformity for sixty years, and a type of thought CHAP. IV. which was essentially Puritan for nearly one hundred and fifty years longer. This, with the rigorous administration and political system which accompanied it, was the result of the appearance of the first learned class within the American colonies, and of its alliance with the secular authorities. But, though we consider Puritan New England to have been narrow and intolerant, we should remember that the intellectual activity which made even that possible did not exist in the other colonies till the middle of the eighteenth century.

CHAPTER V

THE WORKING OF THE MASSACHUSETTS SYSTEM AS ILLUS-
TRATED BY THE CONTROVERSIES WITH THE PRESBYTE-
RIANS, THE BAPTISTS, AND THE QUAKERS

PART
II.

THE maintenance of religious tests and their employment
for the purpose of favoring one confession and partially or
wholly excluding all others from political influence, was in
the seventeenth century a prominent characteristic of the
policies of nearly all European states. The policy which in
this respect was pursued by Massachusetts, and by the other
distinctively Puritan colónies, was quite in harmony with the
spirit of the times. The only point at which, according to
the accepted views of the time, it was fairly open to attack,
was this : it was adopted by a colony, or a group of colonies,
and the sect which in their case it favored was not the one to
which similar favors were extended in the mother country.
Instead, it was a sect which the home government had
endeavored to suppress, but which of late had risen in
revolt and was prominently concerned in events which might
overthrow the English kingship. With the Independents,
whose church polity was in substantial agreement with that
which was upheld by the religious test in the Puritan colonies of New England, the Presbyterians of both England
and Scotland had been associated in the struggle against
Charles I. Minor points of church polity, and jealousies
growing out of national and political rivalry, separated these
two sects, rather than any differences of theological belief.
The Presbyterians were even less tolerant than the Independents, and were strongly in favor of a religious establishment. Still their rivalry became intense, and in 1646
the Presbyterians seemed likely to win in the diplomatic

256

game which they were playing with the king, and thus to
be able to dictate their policy to England.

These events led certain Presbyterian sympathizers and
other discontented residents of Massachusetts to present a
petition before the court of election in Boston.[1] The leaders
among them were Dr. Robert Child,[2] a physician who had
studied at Padua, but who lived in the colony without
practising his profession ; Samuel Maverick, who had lived
in New England since the time of Robert Gorges, but had
held aloof from its churches and leaders ; Thomas Fowle, a
merchant, who, though a church member, had not procured
admission as a freeman ; and John Dand, who was formerly
a grocer of London. They also had the support of Major
John Child, a brother of the first named, and of William
Vassall of Plymouth, who had been one of the first assistants of the Massachusetts company and was a brother
of Samuel Vassall, the influential Presbyterian leader in
England. William Vassall himself was a man of energy
and for some time had been laboring among the discontented
in both Plymouth and Massachusetts to secure larger indulgence[3] for all law-abiding Protestant dissenters, and greater
conformity with English law in the administration of government. The petitioners declared that a settled government
according to the laws of England did not seem to them to
have been established there ; they were not sure of the comfortable enjoyment of their lives, liberties, and estates as
freeborn English subjects. They lived in fear of illegal
commitments, unjust fines, taxes, and impressments, undue
oaths subject to exposition according to the will of those
who imposed them and not according to the " due and un-
bowed rule of law." Though the class of men whom the
petitioners represented were good and loyal subjects and
friends of parliament, though they had shared all burdens in

[1] Hutchinson Collection, Pubs. of Prince Society, I. 214 *et seq. ;* Winthrop,
II. 319, 340, 346 *et seq.*

[2] Child, New Englands Jonas cast up at London, in Force, Tracts, IV. ;
also in 2 Mass. Hist. Coll. IV ; Winslow, New Englands Salamander, in
3 Mass. Hist. Coll. II.

[3] Hutchinson Collection, I. 172–174.

the colony, yet they were debarred from civil employments and could not even vote for civil or military officers.[1]

The reason for this was that they were not church members. And yet they were in sympathy with the latest and best reformation in both England and Scotland. They therefore asked that the conditions of church membership be so broadened that members of the Church of England, who were not scandalous in their lives, might be admitted to full fellowship in the congregations. Further than this, they insisted that, upon the taking of the oath of allegiance, without the imposition of any oaths[2] or covenants which were not warranted by the patent, they might be admitted to the liberties to which all free Englishmen were accustomed both at home and in the plantations. They asked that none be banished from the colony unless they violated known laws of England. They objected also to the law of 1637 which required the assent of two magistrates as the condition of settlement by a newcomer in any town in the colony. This they said "hath procured a kind of banishment to some who might have been serviceable to this place, as they have been to the state of England."

It is probable that the men who drew this petition had suffered little in their families or estates from the conditions of which they complained. Their purely religious disabilities could have been removed by restoring in part the parish system of England and Scotland in the way later urged by the supporters of the so-called halfway covenant. Of the demand for that, this petition was an early intimation. It is not unlikely that the petitioners sought supremacy for their own party rather than full admission to the Massachusetts churches. It is certain that political change was what they chiefly sought, and that, if they were genuine Presbyterians, and could have reached political control, they would have favored a religious establishment with the proscription

---

[1] This the petitioners afterwards admitted to be an exaggeration, inasmuch as some non-freemen did vote in town affairs, and among the forms of business in which they shared was the election of local militia officers.

[2] To the oath of fidelity the petitioners objected without reason, for such an oath was required in all the chartered colonies.

of many forms of dissent. Their petition also contained
exaggerations and gave undue prominence to some matters
of inferior importance.   But notwithstanding these facts, it
touched the most vulnerable point in the Massachusetts
system, the religious test, and therefore was rightly regarded
by the magistrates and clergy as a serious attack.

The petition was a protest of the unenfranchised against
the policy which, without express warrant in the charter or
in English law, excluded them from equal privileges in
church and commonwealth.   A colony franchise which was
limited by a freehold qualification could provoke no criticism, because the qualification was of the same kind as that
which existed in the mother country.   But a religious qualification pure and simple, one, too, the object of which was to
commit the control of a colony to a body of dissenters which
until recently had enjoyed no special recognition at home,
naturally occasioned comment.   The justification for that
comment was increased by the prominence which was given
to the Mosaic Law and the practice of Israel as a source of
precedents.   It might be within the authority of the Massachusetts company to establish such a qualification and follow
such a course, but it was an unusual, an exceptional, thing to
do.   It involved a radical departure from general usage, one
which sharply distinguished the colonies that adopted it
from other colonies and from all the leading states of Europe
as well.   It gave to them a certain Utopian character.   For
this reason intelligent non-freemen, men of respectable social
position, in such a colony might properly feel that they were
cut loose from the moorings of English law and policy and
were subjects of a new régime.   The main purpose sought
by this government was distinct from those objects toward
which English effort had been directed.   Its laws might not
be generally or directly repugnant to those of England, but
some of the most important among them would look strange
in an English statute book.   The course of argument by
which policies were frequently approved or condemned would
sound still more strange to English ears.   The non-freeman,
moreover, however large the amount of property which he
might possess in the colony, could in no appreciable manner

influence its political life. He was embarked in a craft over whose steering apparatus he had no control. So far as he was concerned the discretion of the colony government was absolute. It might tax him as it chose, he was without representation ; while before its tribunals, civil or ecclesiastical, his cause was likely to receive a prejudiced hearing.

The guaranties which protected the freeman against governmental oppression were insufficient ; for the simple inhabitant they were almost non-existent. Winthrop's arguments on arbitrary government did not fully reach his case, and were scarcely intended to do so. It was through the petition of Child and his associates that these thoughts found almost their only expression in Puritan Massachusetts.

As complete religious freedom, or the separation of church from commonwealth, was not claimed, but instead attention was called to a divergence of the law and polity of Massachusetts from that of England, an appeal to the home government was at once suggested by the petitioners as a means of redress. It was from that quarter alone that the assumed independence of the colony could be threatened. For this reason a committee of the general court was appointed to answer the petition, and preparation was made to meet, through an agent, any charges which might be presented in England. Winthrop, Dudley, and Bellingham were the principal members of the committee. After emphasizing the frugal and honest manner in which the government of Massachusetts was conducted — a fact which the petitioners admitted at the outset — the committee in its reply undertook to compare at length the provisions of the Body of Liberties with those of Magna Carta and the principles of the common law, for the purpose of showing that they were in fundamental agreement, and that civil liberty was as well guarantied by the one as by the other. The comparison, though far from being exhaustive, showed, as a matter of course, a very satisfactory agreement, so far as the letter of the law concerning property, family relations, and the administration of justice went. But it failed to meet the chief point raised by the petitioners, for the reason that the law of the colony excluded the adherents of the leading religious confessions in

England from political rights in the colony. That condition of things was too unnatural to continue permanent. So long as it continued, if the dissenters in Massachusetts, emboldened by the favors they were enjoying in England, should attempt to worship by themselves they would at once be exposed to prosecution. If they petitioned against this, their petitions were more than likely to be treated as constructive sedition. Upon this charge they would speedily be brought before the magistrates or the general court and banished from the colony. The scenes enacted in the trials of the Antinomians would be repeated. There was no room for religious freedom and, as things then were, little room for schemes of religious comprehension, in Massachusetts. In its attitude toward non-freemen or others who were promoting such schemes the Massachusetts government was intolerant and arbitrary. Its judges and juries were prejudiced, and its judicial procedure offered no protection for the accused. When Winthrop undertook to defend the colony government against the charge of arbitrariness, he had in mind only its structure and the application of its power for the purposes of protecting such civil rights as non-freemen were generally believed to possess. Religious freedom was not among these, and almost any means were considered to be lawful which were found necessary for the suppression of dissent.

The knowledge that the petitioners intended to appeal to parliament or to the commissioners of plantations, drew from the Massachusetts authorities some very suggestive statements concerning the relations in which they understood the colony to stand toward the home government.[1] Both magistrates and clergy gave their opinions before the general court. All the magistrates agreed that the charter was the foundation of the government, but they divided on the extent of subordination which it required to the home government. Some thought that parliament might repeal the laws and reverse the judgments of Massachusetts, and therefore that a petition should be sent for an enlargement of power. Others were of opinion that, though the obligations of allegiance were due, yet Massachusetts was given authority by

[1] Winthrop, II. 340, 344.

the charter to establish all the necessary organs of government and to use them for administrative purposes. They did not need the help of a general governor or other superior power to complete their government. Allegiance did not involve subjection in matters of government, but was a relation growing out of tenure of land and a dependence upon the parent state for protection, advice, and counsel, and a continuance of the advantages of naturalization for the colonists and their posterity. In other words, it involved privileges without corresponding duties.

In a later conference with the petitioners the magistrates declared, "Our allegiance binds us not to the laws of England any longer than while we live in England, for the laws of the parliament of England reach no further, nor do the king's writs under the great seal go any further."[1] Corporations that were resident in England were bound by the laws of that kingdom, but those which were resident elsewhere were not so bound. Again emphasis was laid upon the claim that plantations, though bodies corporate, were higher in rank than ordinary corporations. Among the Greeks and Romans colonies like these had been esteemed " other than towns, yea than many cities, for they have been the foundations of great commonwealths." For this reason the petitioners were warned not to despise the day of small things. To those who held these views a petition for another charter seemed unnecessary and unwise. The time, moreover, was inopportune, since they could hope to procure only such a document as the Narragansett settlements had received, a charter granted by ordinance of parliament without the royal assent, and likely to contain a reserve of full parliamentary supremacy.

The clergy expressed substantially the same views, adding that the colony answered complaints in England only in way of justification, not of appeal or petition. Such full and ample powers of government had been conferred by the charter, that "no appeals or other ways of interrupting our proceedings do lie against us." The course of

[1] Winthrop, II. 352, 354.

passive resistance, which was later followed, was outlined
in the statement that, if parliament should oppose the
colony, " we must wait upon Providence for the preservation of our just liberties."

When, after prolonged conferences and arguments, it was
seen that Dr. Child and his associates were resolved to
appeal to parliament, they were heavily fined. This, however, did not deter them, and Child began as rapidly as
possible to collect signatures among the non-freemen and
the discontented. Preparations were also made for his
departure. The magistrates now, by a procedure which
reminds one very much of Star Chamber, had him arrested,
and searched his trunk and study and the study of Mr.
Dand, another petitioner, for incriminating evidence. In
Dand's study two petitions were found, addressed to the
commissioners of plantations. In one of these, signed by
the seven leaders of the movement, it was urged[1] that
Presbyterian churches might be established in Massachusetts, that the laws of England might be introduced, that
freeholders should enjoy the same privileges there as in
England, that the oath of allegiance should be administered
to all the colonists there, that a general governor or commissioners should be appointed to execute these measures.
The other petition was signed by about twenty-five non-
free-men, mostly young men of the artisan or servant class or
temporary residents. A paper was also found containing
queries about the validity of the charter, how it might
be revoked, whether certain speeches which had been made
in the pulpit and the court were not high treason, and
whether the general court could prevent the organization
of Presbyterian churches.

Though there was no proof that the movement which
found expression in these papers was widespread, the magistrates considered that they now had positive evidence of a
plot against the government of the colony. Five of the
leading offenders were therefore arrested and again heavily
fined. Those who were unable or unwilling to pay were
imprisoned. The petition, however, was carried to Eng-

[1] Winthrop, II. 357.

land[1] by William Vassall and Thomas Fowle. But when they arrived there, in 1647, the activity of the army had brought the Independents into the ascendant, and nothing could be accomplished. Had they seriously attempted it, Edward Winslow was present with instructions from Massachusetts to oppose the hearing of appeals from the colony.

To the Puritan mind, whether in England or in New England, the name Anabaptist was synonymous with anarchy in its most revolting forms. It suggested the excesses of John of Leyden and his followers at Münster in the sixteenth century, which culminated in a system of polygamy, sanction for which was found in alleged divine revelations. Extravagant enthusiasm, however, and not insistence on the rebaptism of adults, was the characteristic of the radical reformers in Germany who first bore the name Anabaptist. The later Baptists of England and America had nothing in common with the early fanatics of Germany, though they were forced throughout the struggles of the period to bear the stigma of their names. The Baptists were Calvinists in theology and independents in church polity, differing from the Puritans of Massachusetts and the adjacent colonies only in their denial of the validity of infant baptism and their insistence upon religious toleration. The name of Roger Williams was identified with the early history of the sect, and, though working within the limits of Calvinistic theology, it helped to disseminate and make effective his doctrine of soul liberty. In church polity they adhered to the simple democratic ideal of the group of autonomous local congregations united under some voluntary compact. Union with the civil power and coercion of the local body by secular authority they avoided. Their strict allegiance to the letter of Scripture also led them to reject the doctrine and practice of infant baptism, a feature of church polity by which the New England Puritan set great store.

It thus appears that the views which the Baptists really held, if publicly preached, were such as to make them sufficiently obnoxious to the magistrates and elders of Mas-

[1] Child, New Englands Jonas; Winthrop, II. 362 *et seq.*

sachusetts, even if none of the stigma of Anabaptism had
attached to their name.   But the Baptists who were known
to the New Englander congregated chiefly in Rhode Island.
At Newport, in 1640 or 1644, the first Baptist church in
America was organized.[1]   To the mind of an adherent of
the dominant Puritan sect the Narragansett Plantations
seemed a faint reflection of Münster, not that any thought
the sexual excesses of the German enthusiasts were repeated
there, but that it was the home of all strange and extreme
opinions which by any chance found their way into New
England.   The Massachusetts Puritan of the first generation never lost his feeling of supercilious contempt for the
colony which was founded by men whom he had cast out.
He was always quick to note manifestations of anarchy or
disturbance among them, and slow to mark their social
progress.   It was the "back door" through which many
of the sectaries who troubled Massachusetts found their
entrance.[2]   Not only did Williams and some of his followers
become Baptists, but some of the Antinomian exiles as well.
Winthrop,[3] referring perhaps to the organization of the first
Baptist church at Newport, wrote, "They also gathered a
church in a very disordered way ; for they took some excommunicated persons, and others who were members of the
church of Boston and not dismissed."

After Massachusetts had been in existence as a colony for
about a decade, Baptist opinions began to appear here and
there among its inhabitants.   In 1642 Lady Deborah Moody
of Lynn and two others were presented before the quarter
court at Salem for holding that "the baptizing of infants is
noe ordinance of God."[4]   Lady Moody was also admonished
by the church at Salem; but persisting in her belief, to avoid
further trouble, she removed to New Netherland, where, with
those who accompanied her, she founded the town of Graves-
end, Long Island.   Early in 1644, and again in 1645, the
case of William Witter, also of Lynn, was before the court

[1] Backus, Hist. of the Baptists, ed. of 1871, I. 125.
[2] Mass. Col. Recs. IV[1]. 385.
[3] Journal, I. 357.
[4] Lewis and Newhall, History of Lynn, 204, 231; Winthrop, II. 148.

at Salem. He was charged with holding Baptist opinions
and speaking disrespectfully of authority. Though he was at
length summoned before the assistants at Boston, final action
seems not to have been taken in his case. In November,
1651, however, he was again presented at the Salem court
"for neglecting discourses and being rebaptized."

In July, 1644, a poor and worthless man, named Painter,[1]
who refused to suffer his wife to have their child baptized,
was whipped. No law had then been enacted for the punishment of such an offence, and Winthrop states that it was
inflicted, "not for his opinion, but for his reproaching the
Lord's ordinance, and for his bold and evil behaviour both
at home and in the Court."

But, owing to the increase within the colony of Baptist
opinions,[2] the magistrates and elders were already considering a measure for their restraint. This was passed in
November, 1644.[3] In the preamble of this act not only is
the rising sect charged with being successors of the Anabaptists of Münster, but they are made to deny the lawful-
ness of magistracy and of making war, both of these being
opinions which they never held. The act provided that, if
any within the colony should openly condemn or oppose the
baptizing of infants, or secretly attempt to seduce others
from the use of that ordinance, or obstinately deny the
ordinance of magistracy or the right of the magistrate to
make war or to punish outward breaches of the first table
of the law, on conviction such persons should be banished.

In 1651 the Massachusetts authorities, acting partly under
this law and in part under the general laws for the maintenance of the established faith,[4] punished three of the fore-
most Baptists in the colonies. They were Mr. John Clarke,
founder of the Baptist church at Newport ; Obadiah Holmes,
who had formed a Baptist society at Rehoboth in Plymouth
colony, and John Crandall, who had previously been a deputy
to the general assembly from Newport. They were in no sense
fanatics, though they were persistent in the assertion of their

---

[1] Winthrop, II. 213.   [2] *Ibid.* 212.   [3] Mass. Col. Recs. II. 85.
[4] Clarke's Ill Newes from New England, 4 Mass. Hist. Coll. II ; Backus,
History of the Baptists, I. 173 *et seq.*

views. Holmes had previously been a resident of Salem.
Clarke had arrived in Massachusetts from England in the
midst of the Antinomian excitement, and because of the
dissensions had gone elsewhere, finally settling upon Rhode
Island. He was from the first a leading man of the colony,
and somewhat later than the date of which we are speaking
was to render it the most important services in England.
His writings, as well as his career, show him to have been
an energetic, clear-headed, and practical man.

These men, visiting Massachusetts on business, were entertained over Sunday at the house of William Witter, in Lynn.
In the forenoon of the Sabbath Clarke discoursed on the subject of temptation to the family and a few friends who came
to the house. In the midst of his talk two constables appeared, and, upon an order from a Salem magistrate, arrested
Clarke and his two companions. In the afternoon they
were taken to church, although Clarke declared in advance
that when there he should testify freely in opposition to the
accepted faith. When he and his friends entered the church,
they at first uncovered by way of greeting, but immediately
put on their hats again, and Clarke began reading. The
constable then snatched the hats from their heads. After
the sermon was over Clarke began to speak, but before he
had proceeded far he was silenced, and at the close of the
service all three were taken back to the place of detention,
which was the village inn. The next day, however, Clarke
found an opportunity to administer the sacrament at Witter's
house. A week later the three offenders were brought to
trial before the magistrates at Boston.

Endicott was now governor, and for a decade to come was
to enjoy a leadership in Massachusetts affairs from which the
superiority of Winthrop, among other causes, had hitherto
excluded him. He was a much harsher and more violent
man than Winthrop, and evidences of this fact were abundant both in his earlier and later career. He presided at the
court when Clarke and his friends were brought before it.
The usual heated colloquy was held between the judge and
the accused. " The governor," says Clarke, "upbraided us
with the name of Anabaptist; To whom I answered, I disown

the name.   I am neither an Anabaptist, nor a Pedobaptist, nor a Catabaptist !   He told me in haste I was all." After a further colloquy in much the same spirit, a trial in which, according to Clarke's statement, neither accuser, witness, nor jury, was produced, Clarke was sentenced to pay a fine of £20, Holmes of £30, Crandall of £5, or to be "well whipped." Clarke demanded to be shown the law under which the sentence was pronounced ; and well he might, for the only penalty mentioned in the law against Anabaptists was banishment. The governor then, says the narrator, " stepped up and told us we had denied infant baptism, and, being somewhat transported, broke forth and told me I had deserved death, and said he would not have such trash brought into their jurisdiction." The accused were then sent back to prison. As Endicott, notwithstanding his passion, had given a hint that a public discussion might be held, Clarke tried to get permission to debate the points of his belief with some of the ministers, but failed. While this matter was under discussion, some friends paid Clarke's fine, and he returned to Rhode Island. Crandall chose the same course. But Holmes resolved to testify to the truth of his belief under the lash, and has left a remarkable account of the extent to which his religious enthusiasm assuaged the pain, and enabled him to bear with ease what would otherwise have been a sharp infliction. Two of the spectators ventured to express admiration for Holmes's courage, but they were at once arrested and fined.

Clarke at once went to England, where he published an account of his experience, and that of his friends, in Massachusetts, with an address to parliament and the council of state. But the cause of Massachusetts was strongly supported in England by Hopkins[1] and Winslow, the latter of whom now stood high in the councils of the government. Owing, however, to the attitude of Cromwell toward Anabaptists and others with whom they were popularly associated, there was not at this period any prospect that the English government would interfere to check the strenuous measures of Massachusetts. The Baptists, however, persisted. Henry

[1] Hutchinson Collection, I. 303.

Dunster, the second president of Harvard College, accepted
their views, and, because of his avowal of them, was compelled to resign his position. Soon after the Restoration a Baptist society was organized in Boston and public services began. Against this the authorities struggled for a number of years, but at last they were compelled to acquiesce, and the existence of the society was thereafter silently tolerated.

Antinomian, Presbyterian, and Baptist had been forced to yield before the Massachusetts government when its power was fully exerted against them. The first-named party had for a short time seriously menaced the peace and unity of the jurisdiction, but it had been completely vanquished and its leaders cast out. The efforts of the Presbyterians and Baptists were of minor importance, except as they foreshadowed later changes, and they received no organized support. The controversy with Roger Williams was little more than a debate with an individual. These events gave clear evidence of the strength of the union between clergy and magistrates and of the difficulty of forming other combinations. Whether church or commonwealth was attacked, the full resources of both were readily brought to its defence.

With the advent of the Quakers, however, appeared an enemy of different character, one whose attack was more determined and perplexing. The earlier enemies of the Puritan system had shared to a greater extent than did the Quakers in its spirit, and in the purposes which were sought through it. Their social standing was in general higher than that of the Quakers, and they proceeded more from the body of New England people. Quakerism was an ultra-democratic phase of Protestantism, and the early adherents of the sect were decidedly plebeian in origin. Their views reflected well the character of the social classes whence they came. Though retaining the common ethical system of Protestantism, they sought to wholly dispense with its clerical and sacramental features. Many of the externals of religion — the sacraments, a paid and specially trained clergy, consecrated churches, the Sabbath as a specially sacred "Lord's day," formal prayer, and the usual forms of church service

— they discarded. With these went also the oath, war, and spiritual coercion in all forms. In the place of the Scripture as learnedly interpreted, and of the impressive externals of worship, the Quakers substituted the inner light which proceeded from the direct inspiration of the Holy Ghost. By this they claimed to be directly guided in all affairs of life ; the following of this was to them the essence of all religion.

It thus appears that the Quakers cherished all the beliefs and practices which had made Roger Williams and the Antinomians offensive to the Puritans, and many more of a similar nature. The rejection of oaths and the insistence on soul liberty were only two among a long list of articles in their belief which were unacceptable in Massachusetts. If the Antinomians had talked much about the indwelling of the Holy Spirit, about its light and inspiration, and about the superiority of grace to works, the Quakers far exceeded them in all this. When, moreover, Quakers first made their appearance in New England and legislation against them began, their beliefs were in the formative and controversial stage. The time had not yet come when Barclay could begin to systematize them, and bring them into the best possible harmony with accepted Protestant doctrine. Fox, Burroughs, Howgil, Nayler, and certain others had for a decade been travelling to and fro through the British Isles in uncouth garb, violating many accepted social customs, using a new form of personal address, and glorying in their eccentricities. Not a few women had enlisted among their followers and were imitating their example. One female convert journeyed as an apostle of the truth as far as the court of the Grand Turk. They had preached in the fields, in the streets, in private houses, wherever and whenever it was possible to hold conventicles. As occasion offered, these self-constituted preachers had appeared in the churches, and, with or without invitation, had proclaimed a gospel which they declared was purer than any to which the hireling who occupied the living and the pulpit could give utterance. With a towering self-conceit, born largely of simplicity and of ignorance concerning the difficulty which attends efforts at sweeping change in ancient and complex societies, they denounced the clergy, their preaching, and the ordinances which they administered, as useless or inadequate human institutions and inventions.

We are told that George Fox,[1] on one typical occasion, stood up in a steeple-house yard and told his hearers that he came not to hold up their idol temples, nor their priests, nor their tithes, nor their Jewish and heathenish ceremonies ; that the ground on which their temples stood was no more holy than any other piece of ground ; that all preaching and hearing ought to be free, as to time and place, as it was in the age of the apostles, and that the Lord God of heaven and earth had sent him to preach freely, and to draw the people away from the temples made with hands, where God dwelleth not. They ought to leave all their superstitious ceremonies, traditions, and doctrines of men, and not regard teachers of the word who took tithes and great wages, preaching for hire and divining for money. These, according to their own confession, — for they said they had never heard God's voice, — God and Christ had never sent. The people, therefore, should turn their backs on these preachers, and come to the spirit and grace of God in themselves, to the light of Jesus in their own hearts ; that so they might come to know Christ their free teacher, who would bring them salvation and open to them the Scriptures.

This teaching, though it sprang from the same root as Protestantism itself, was offensive both in manner and substance to the Puritan consciousness. By relegating the text of Scripture, authoritatively interpreted, to a second place, and appealing directly to the spirit or light which dwells in the soul of every man, even though it might have been kindled there by divine grace, seemed to the genuine Puritan a reversal of the true order of things. To him the word of God, and a church and civil order carefully and logically deduced therefrom, were the sum and substance of the truth. The Quaker found the truth, not in the letter of Scripture, in Sunday observance, or in preaching and church ordinances, but in a direct and immediate inspiration. This, he claimed, raised him to a higher level than the Puritan,

[1] Sewel, History of the Quakers, I. 79.

PART
II.

and made many of the latter's beliefs and observances as needless as was the ritualism of Anglican or Catholic. This position, moreover, at the first was somewhat proudly and defiantly maintained, in a spirit and manner which generally characterized the numerous sects that sprang into existence in the seventeenth century. From Quaker speech and bearing customary forms of respect toward dignities were excluded. No more pronounced assertion of social equality than this has been made. To the Puritan this seemed to be libertinism, anarchy, an attack on the foundations of social order. The restraints which he had so carefully devised as a means not only of holding the colony together, but that they might facilitate the transition from a mediæval to a modern Protestant society, seemed to him to be thrown aside. It seemed to be an effort to substitute ignorance for learning, license for liberty, and chaos for order. There was one word in his vocabulary which to the Puritan expressed the essence of Quakerism, and that was blasphemy. Into that biblical expression he concentrated his hatred of the Quaker dress, of his forms of expression, of his bearing toward magistrates and the clergy, of his contempt for the externals of religion, of his insistence upon individual liberty, and his resolve to follow the inner light; in short, of what was regarded as his irreverence and essential impiety. Blasphemy, moreover, stood in the Puritan code near the head of the list of capital crimes. Those who carried themselves toward magistrates and others in authority as did the Quakers, should, in his opinion, be visited with the punishment of Shimei.[1]

Another charge which held a prominent place in the indictment preferred by Massachusetts against the Quakers was this: that without permission they had entered the colony, had thrown it into agitation, and, as it were, had attempted to take possession of it by force. The right of themselves as grantees of the soil, the colonists compared to that of the individual to his house and private estate.[1] As he might forcibly expel intruders who came without legal authority,

---

[1] 2 Sam. xvi. 9 and xix. 21; 1 Kings ii. 8, 9, 44, 46.
[2] Mass. Col. Recs. IV[1]. 388.

so they might exclude or drive out Quakers who, coming from England, the Barbadoes, or Rhode Island, were found entering or wandering through the colony. They had left homes and in many cases dependent families to wander from place to place, pursuing their supposed divine mission. It is not surprising that they were regarded as vagabonds and so treated. Pushing the analogy to the extreme point, the general court agreed that, if private persons might rightfully shed the blood or take the lives of such invaders, the Quakers would have none to blame but themselves, if the guardians of the commonwealth should insist that their lives be forfeited as the penalty of their rash intrusion. And if this argument were not sufficient to justify the infliction of the death penalty, the magistrates and elders held still in reserve the necessity of protection against wild animals and contagious diseases.

In thus describing the attitude which was assumed by the Puritan toward the Quaker, and the arguments by which he supported it, no effort is made to justify or condemn the one party or the other. The sole object has been to show how the case appeared to minds of men in the seventeenth century whose intelligence was above the average, though their sympathies may not have been broader than those of most of their contemporaries. Both parties, as is customary in such cases, exaggerated their own excellencies and the faults of their opponents. The Quakers were not libertines, though some of them behaved as if they were such. Through their insistence upon the right of private judgment, their passive but determined opposition to war and to oppression in all forms, the preference they everywhere showed for simple and quiet modes of life, they contributed toward the humanitarian trend of the eighteenth century. But these things the Puritan could neither see nor appreciate. Had he seen or welcomed them, he would not have been a genuine Puritan ; such a feat would have proven that the individual who performed it was free from some of the essential limitations of Puritanism. Even Roger Williams was unable to perceive the excellencies which lay concealed under the harsh exterior of the early Quakers. That men with the views and temper of the Massachusetts leaders would make no effort to discover them goes without saying. To imply that they might have reacted against the impact of Quakerism otherwise than they did, is to becloud the subject and to apply to the events criteria which lay outside the mental horizon of the Puritan. Under the limitations which were inherent in their views concerning the mission they were to fulfil in the world, they could not have met the stubborn aggressiveness of the Quakers with measures essentially different from those which they employed. If Roger Williams or the Antinomians or the Baptists, after being banished because they refused to yield to admonition and conform, had repeatedly returned and sought to win converts, they would have been visited with the penalties from which the Quakers suffered. The infliction of the death penalty did not awaken the feelings in the seventeenth century which it occasions in the nineteenth and twentieth centuries. The list of capital crimes was then far larger than now, and the courts threw the burden of proof on the accused rather than on the government. When the general court explained the motives by which Massachusetts had been guided in its treatment of Quakers, it did not seek to apologize. It felt no need of apology ; it had simply acted naturally. The conduct of the other Puritan colonies was fundamentally the same as their own, the fact that they refrained from executing the death penalty being a matter of degree only, due perhaps to their lack of charters and to the fact that they were not molested so much as was Massachusetts.

Some modern writers have contended that Massachusetts, and therefore the other colonies as well, had no right to exclude Quakers from her borders ; but, however desirable it might be that she should not have that right, it is difficult to find the law that would deny it to her. No colony was required by charter to receive all who might come or be sent across its borders. We know that since 1637 one of her statutes had forbidden the harboring of strangers for more than three weeks within any town without the approval of the magistrates. That was still in force. It had not been submitted to the home government for its approval or disapproval; but Massachusetts was not required by her charter to do this, and none of her acts prior to 1690 were so submitted. They were, however, all valid laws in Massachusetts, and we know of no English enactment which would have made an exception of the so-called alien act of 1637, or of the acts which were specifically directed against Quakers or other sectaries. In Massachusetts itself there was no guaranty, either for freeholder, resident, or newcomer, against a law once passed and promulgated. Such was the neglect at the time of legal security for intellectual or religious dissent.

No English statute required that all subjects of the crown should be admitted into the colonies, and it is very doubtful if any principle of the common law deducible from Magna Carta required it. We know that the colonies generally exerted influence to prevent undesirable settlers from being forced upon them. All proprietors and others who had control over the despatch of emigrants exercised some choice and selection; they sought persons with desirable qualities and encouraged them to go; they avoided or discouraged the undesirable. This would imply the recognition of a certain right of that character. For aught we know it was as lawful for Massachusetts to exclude persons for religious reasons, as for Virginia to exclude them because they had been criminals or vagabonds. That matter had not been regulated by the English government, and hence remained under the control of the colonies. That the home government in the seventeenth century would never have forced any except a penal colony to receive Quakers is practically certain. In view of these considerations, and to those who are familiar with its religious system and with the efforts that were put forth to uphold it, the attitude which the Massachusetts authorities assumed toward the Quakers should occasion no surprise. To the adherents of the English Church, whether at home or abroad, the Quaker in the seventeenth century was an object of intense aversion. Among the Dutch he was far from welcome. To Catholics, had they been in power, he would have been equally offensive. To the Puritan, in whatever country or colony he might be, Quaker doctrines seemed to imperil not only the church and civil power, but the very foundations of morality as well.

The magistrates of Rhode Island wrote that "their doctrines tend to very absolute cutting downe and overturninge relations and civill government among men, if generally received." That Roger Williams's denunciation of them was unmeasured is well known, and it found abundant utterance in his disputation with the friends of George Fox.[1] The general court of Plymouth declared that their doctrine and practices tended "to the Subversion of the foundamentalls of the Christian Religion, Church order and the Civill peace of the Government, as appears by the Testimonies given in sundry depositions and otherwise."[2] The commissioners of the United Colonies, moved certainly in part by the strenuous feelings which prevailed in Massachusetts and New Haven, expressed Puritan sentiments in characteristic form in the preamble to their resolution[3] of September, 1658, "Whereas there is an accursed and pernisious sect of heretiques lately Risen up in the world whoe are commonly called Quakers whoe take upon them to bee ymediately sent of God and Infallably assisted; whoe doe speak and write blasphemos thinges dispising Government and the order of God in Church and Commonwealth, speaking evill of dignities, Reproaching and Reviling Magistrates and the ministers of the Gospell, seeking to turne the people from the faith and to gaine proselites to theire pernisious wayes; and whereas . . . they . . . arogantly and presumptuously doe presse into severall of the Jurisdictions and there vent theire pernisious and divellish opinions, which being permitted tends mannifestly to the Desturbance of our peace; the withdrawing of the harts of the people from their subjection to Government and soe in Issue to cause Devision and Ruein if not timely prevented . . . ." These views were reëchoed in the laws[4] of the several colonies which were enacted in pursuance of this resolution.

The Rev. John Norton, in his *Heart of New England Rent*,

[1] R. I. Recs. I. 377.   [3] *Ibid.* X. 212.
[2] Plymouth Recs. XI. 100.   [4] New Haven Col. Recs. II. 238.

which was prepared at the request of the general court of Massachusetts and therefore contains an authoritative argument on the subject, traced Quakerism to an origin among the "libertines and enthusiasts" of the early Reformation, who in turn reproduced some of the most dangerous tendencies that appeared in the early church. The Quakers, according to his view, were imitators rather than innovators, and the model which they copied was the Anabaptism of Münster. Norton's history was in this case as good as most which passed under that name in his time, though a modern would consider it worthless. But it was greedily accepted as truth, and it was confidently believed that the excesses of Münster would be reproduced in New England if the Quakers were allowed to gain a foothold there. Norton argued that their doctrines would undermine belief in the Trinity, in Christ as the Saviour, in the authority of Scripture, in the ordinances, in the ministry, in Christian magistrates,[1] and in civil order. To his mind, as to the minds of many others, Quakers seemed to be as dangerous as Jesuits, and it was inferred that laws which had been passed to rid the country of the latter might well be applied to the former. The conclusions set forth by Norton in his book were repeated in the declaration issued by the general court after the execution of Robinson and Stevenson.[2] In the declaration a characteristic turn was given to the argument, to the effect that, as one would protect his family from persons infected with the plague, or other contagious, noisome, or mortal diseases, and from those, too, who, while in that condition, should try to force their way into private dwellings, so the fathers of the commonwealth should protect it against the moral contagion which must result from the teachings of the Quakers. "And if sheepe and lambes," they continued with a change of figure, "cannot be preserved from the dainger of woolves, but the woolves will breake in amongst them, it is easy to see what the shepherd or keeper of the sheepe may lawfully doe in such a case."

In 1656 Quakers began to visit New England. In July of that year Mary Fisher and Anne Austin came to Boston

---

[1] Heart of New England Rent, 2 *et seq.*   [2] Mass. Col. Recs. IV[1]. 385.

in a vessel from Barbadoes. No sooner had they arrived than the council,[1] under the authority of the laws against heretics which were already in existence, ordered that their books should be seized, and that the women themselves should be kept in close imprisonment until the shipmaster who had brought them could remove them from the colony. The captain was put under heavy bonds to do this speedily. The Quakeresses were then brought on shore, the pamphlets found in their possession which set forth and defended the principles of their sect were burned, and after they had been lodged in prison, the accused were strictly examined to see if they might not be witches. After an imprisonment of about five weeks, during which time the window of their prison was kept boarded up so that no one should communicate with them, and they were denied writing materials and light, they were shipped for Barbadoes. A few days before their release eight more Quakers arrived from London, and they were treated in a similar manner, with the exception that the Rev. John Norton[2] held conferences with them in prison for two days, chiefly over the question whether the Scriptures were the only rule and guide of life, or were subordinate to the quickenings of the inner light. Endicott was governor, and Bellingham was deputy governor. The three men with whom the Quakers thus early came in contact were distinctly the leaders in the measures of opposition to the new sect which were adopted by the colony.

The commissioners of the United Colonies immediately adopted a resolution in favor of the expulsion of Quakers and Ranters, while the general court of Massachusetts, at its meeting in October, passed the first act directed specifically against them.[3] This forbade the master of any ship, under a penalty of £100 or imprisonment, to knowingly land Quakers in the colony. If under oath he could prove that he had brought them in by mistake, he must give bond to

---

[1] Besse, Sufferings of the Quakers, II. 177; Ellis, Puritan Age in Massachusetts, 436; Bishop, New England Judged by the Spirit of the Lord, 3 *et seq.*

[2] Norton had just been installed as the successor of John Cotton in the office of teacher of the church in Boston.

[3] Mass. Col. Recs. IV[1]. 277.

carry them back to the place whence he brought them.
All Quakers who came within the jurisdiction were forth-
with to be committed to the house of correction, whipped,
and set to hard labor. Penalties were also affixed to the
importation and sale of Quaker books, and to the defence
of their opinions. Those who should revile magistrates or
ministers, " as is usuall with the Quakers," should be punished with whipping or fine. Nicholas Upshall, a respected
citizen of Boston, sixty years of age, had expressed sympathy
with Mary Fisher and Anne Austin, and had given the
jailer five shillings a week for being allowed to bring food to
them. When the law just outlined was being proclaimed
through the town, Upshall uttered a protest against it,[1] for
which he was fined, imprisoned, and banished. He was the
first among the inhabitants of Massachusetts who openly
declared his sympathy with Quakers.

Anne Burden and Mary Dyer were the first[2] to appear
after the passage of this law. The former was a widow,
who had returned to Massachusetts to collect certain debts
which were due to her husband. The latter, who as a young
woman had been associated with Mrs. Hutchinson, was on
her way to join her husband in Rhode Island. Both were
imprisoned and sent out of the colony. Mary Clark, " being
a Mother of Children and having a Husband in England,"
came to Massachusetts under the inspiration of the Lord to
deliver his message unto them. She received twenty stripes
and was sent away. Christopher Holder and John Copeland,
being two of the eight who had previously been sent out of
the colony, now reappeared.[3] Holder tried to speak in the
Salem meeting-house after the close of the sermon, whereupon the two were arrested with great show of violence and
sent to Boston. There they each received thirty stripes.
Samuel Shattuck, a resident of Salem, because of the sympathy which he showed for the sufferers, was imprisoned
and afterwards whipped and banished. Lawrence and
Cassandra Southwick, an aged couple and members of the
church at Salem, were imprisoned because they had entertained Holder and Copeland. Richard Dowdney, who came

[1] Bishop, 39.   [2] *Ibid.* 47.   [3] *Ibid.* 50.

with a message from England, was arrested in Dedham, taken to Boston, and whipped with thirty stripes. His books were taken from him, and he was sent out of the country with the threat that, if he should return, he would lose his ears.

By this time sympathy with the Quakers was showing itself among the inhabitants of Salem and at other points. Because of the fact that at Salem they began to absent themselves from church and met for worship at their houses or in the woods, William Hathorne, the resident magistrate,[1] proceeded under the law of 1646 to fine them five shillings a week for absence from church. This occasioned more imprisonments, in which the Southwicks and others suffered. Fines were imposed on the accused; they, like all others, were compelled to pay for their support in prison. They were withdrawn for months at a time from their farms or shops, and their property was distrained for the payment of fines or for their support as prisoners. In this way not a few families were ruined or seriously crippled by the persecution.

Sarah Gibbens and Dorothy Waugh, who had already been once sent out of the colony, because of their reappearance and attempt to speak in the meeting-house at Boston, were whipped and nearly starved in prison. Thomas Harris, coming through Rhode Island to Boston, warned the people after sermon of "the Dreadful Terrible Day of the Lord which was coming upon that Town and Country," for which he was haled to prison, severely whipped, and kept five days without bread. He would have starved had not sympathizers fed him at night through the window. William Brend and William Leddra, "being moved of the Lord," came to Salem. After a conference which they had with "a priest at Newbury," they, with a number of sympathizers, were arrested and taken to Boston. Both Leddra and Brend were whipped, and the latter, because he refused to work in the prison, was nearly killed by the cruelties of the jailer.[2] This outrage awoke such response in the community that the jailer would have been prosecuted had it not been for the intervention of

[1] Bishop, 71, 74, 81.   [2] *Ibid.* 65.

Norton. Jailers were then instructed to whip Quakers who were in their custody twice a week if they refused to work, adding five stripes each time.

Humphrey Norton proved himself to be one of the boldest of the early witnesses. He stood up before "priest Norton" in his church at Boston and declared that, because of his sin, the sacrifice which he was offering was an abomination unto the Lord. For this he and his companion were hurried to prison under the charge of blasphemy. The prisoners insisted on appealing to England, but that was refused with derision. Then they were twice whipped, nearly starved in prison, and sent out of the colony. Norton was later branded in New Haven as a heretic.

The arrests were often accompanied by popular outrage and assault. The hearings were in all cases summary and most informal. Much invective was used to the prisoners by the judges and other officials who had them in charge, and by many of the accused equally sharp and denunciatory language was uttered in return. In the prisons hard labor was enforced; the coarsest food, and that in very small quantities, was provided, and weekly payments for lodging were enforced by the jailers. Imprisonments were prolonged, in many cases for months after scourging had been inflicted. Access of friends or relatives to the imprisoned was, so far as possible, prevented, and we presently find the general court ordering that a fence be built around the jail and house of correction [1] in Boston to debar persons from conversing with the prisoners. But the activity of the authorities was followed by a steady increase of the evil which they were trying to suppress. New offenders kept appearing, some coming direct from England, but more through the West Indies and Rhode Island. Some landed at New Amsterdam and traversed the New England colonies from that centre. Many who had been punished soon returned under alleged divine guidance, that they might testify and suffer again. The number of sympathizers with them, especially among the lower class of the people, tended to increase. The Quakers, native and foreign, gloried in their violations of custom and

[1] Mass. Col. Recs. IV[1]. 390.

rules of conduct, especially by wearing the hat in the meeting-houses and before the courts.   This, with their persistent
interruptions of public services, contributed as much as did
their doctrines to provoke persecution.   As months passed,
it became evident to the authorities that severer repressive
measures must be resorted to.   Many who had suffered
punishment and some who had been sent out of the colony,
returned and defied the authorities anew.   The Puritans of
Massachusetts could not understand the policy followed by
Rhode Island, a course of action which was well described in
1657 both by its magistrates and its general assembly in reply
to a letter from the Commissioners of the United Colonies.
They said they had found that, where the Quakers were
opposed by argument and not by force, they gained few converts, and did not like to come.   They wished to be persecuted, because thereby they won more adherents.   They
began to loathe Rhode Island, because there they were not
opposed and won few converts.   The general assembly took
its stand upon the principle of freedom of conscience, and
maintained it, even though Massachusetts threatened to
prohibit trade with her in order that the Puritan faith might
be preserved intact.[1]

In May, 1658,[2] Quaker meetings were forbidden, and those
who were found attending them were required to pay for every
such offence ten shillings, while every one who spoke at such
meeting should pay five pounds.   If the offenders had already
suffered punishment for venting Quaker opinions, they should
be imprisoned at hard labor until they gave bond, with two
acceptable sureties, that they would keep silent or leave the
jurisdiction.   In October of the same year, acting on the
advice of the Commissioners of the United Colonies, who had
recently met at Boston and whose resolution on this subject we
may suppose emanated largely from the Massachusetts members, the general court passed the act[3] denouncing banishment
against convicted Quakers on pain of death if they should
again return.   The petition which brought the subject of
the penalty in this form before the general court was signed
by twenty-five inhabitants of Boston, among them being

[1] R. I. Col. Recs. I. 377, 378, 398.   [2] Mass. Col. Recs. IV[1]. 321.   [1] *Ibid.* 345.

Wilson and Norton, the pastor and teacher of the Boston church.[1] Though individuals had in repeated instances been threatened by Massachusetts with this penalty, and though it was the common form of enactment against Catholic priests, Bishop[2] is authority for the statement that the act passed the deputies by a majority of only one, it being brought to vote when one of the opposition members was absent because of sickness. The magistrates also, supported by the clergy, are said to have originally excluded from the measure all provision for trials by jury. After the bill passed, the twelve who voted against it desired to enter their protest. The magistrates, seeing that the opposition was so strong, consented that a clause should be introduced permitting trial by " a special jury." The accused, however, in the absence of a magistrate, might be arrested without warrant. To John Norton the court at the same time committed the duty of preparing an authoritative declaration concerning the evils of Quaker tenets and practices. This was approved and published the next year,[3] as was also Norton's *Heart of New England Rent*.

The magistrates and clergy were fully prepared for the execution of this act, and their opponents soon showed themselves ready to squarely meet the issue. Six Quakers, among them Southwick and his wife, were banished by the October court and did not return.[4] The son and daughter of Southwick, because they could not pay their fines and would not work, were ordered to be sold as servants to any of the English in Virginia or Barbadoes who would contract for them. But no captain could be found who would transport them, and therefore they were allowed to remain. Meantime the law was preparing its own victims, though a year passed before they were ready. In the interval seven returned, after they had been banished with the sentence of death impending over them if they came back. But they all agreed finally to go away rather than meet death.

William Robinson, sometime in 1659, while walking with Christopher Holder from Newport, in Rhode Island, to the

---

[1] Palfrey, II. 470, 471.
[2] Bishop, *op. cit.* 101, 102.
[3] Mass. Col. Recs. IV[1]. 385.
[4] *Ibid.* 349, 366.

house of his friend,[1] Daniel Gold, felt constrained by the power of God to go to Boston and there to lay down his life for the accomplishment of the divine will. Marmaduke Stevenson, who in response to what he believed to be a divine call to be a prophet to the nations had left the plough and a dependent family in Yorkshire, and had journeyed to Barbadoes, now heard that Massachusetts had made a law " to put the Servants of the Living God to Death, if they returned after they were sentenced away." As he pondered this, the Lord seemed to say to him, " Thou knowest not but that thou mayest go thither." Acting under this impulse, he took ship for Rhode Island, and there joined Robinson on his journey into Massachusetts. About the same time Mary Dyer was moved of the Lord to visit Massachusetts again. The three were in due time banished on pain of death. Robinson and Stevenson went only to Piscataqua, and about a month later, shortly before the general court met, returned to Boston. Mary Dyer left the colony for a time, but afterwards returned. When arrested[2] and brought before the general court, they freely confessed the reason of their return. Upon them the death sentence was immediately passed. It was duly executed upon Robinson and Stevenson, while Mary Dyer was reprieved when at the place of execution, on condition that she leave the colony within forty-eight hours.[3] This offer she was persuaded to accept. She went to Rhode Island, but returned the following spring[4] to bear witness against the law of Massachusetts. Being again condemned to death, another reprieve was offered her at the gallows on the same condition as the former. This she declined, saying that she had come "in obedience to the will of the Lord" and "would abide faithful unto death."[5] In this spirit she died, June 1, 1660.

In October of that year the general court ordered that all who were in prison should receive their liberty if they would leave the colony.[6] Several availed themselves of this, but

---

[1] Bishop, *op. cit.* 114, 127–133.

[2] Mass. Col. Recs. IV[1]. 383 ; Bishop, 120.

[3] Mass. Col. Recs. IV[1]. 384 ; Bishop, 134.

[4] Mass. Col. Recs. IV[1]. 419.

[5] Mass. Col. Recs. IV[1]. 419 ; Sewel, History of the Quakers, I. 303.

[6] Mass. Col. Recs. IV[1]. 433.

William Leddra, who had been often and severely punished and banished with the threat of death if he should return, came back in November. He was imprisoned till March, 1661, and was then brought to trial. Though he claimed the right of appeal to the English courts, as did many other Quakers, he was condemned and executed.[1] During Leddra's trial Wenlock Christison, who had also been banished under penalty of death, appeared boldly in court.[2] When arrested and brought up for preliminary examination, he declared that he would neither change his religion nor seek to save his life. None had spoken with greater boldness than he. When on trial, he called down upon the court the wrath of God, denied its authority to pass such a law as that under which he was tried, and claimed the right to appeal to the home government for protection. The question, whether sentence of death should be executed, was laid before the court. As the Quakers did not appear at all daunted by whippings, imprisonments, or executions, and as the return of the king had made the problem of Massachusetts government more complex than it previously had been, it was seen that the time had come to hesitate. Some members of the general court refused to vote for the execution of Christison. The governor in a rage ordered that the names of the dissentients should be recorded. After the majority had voted yea, he pronounced sentence of death. But it was not executed. Instead, in May, 1661, a new law was passed providing that Quakers who came into the colony should first be whipped at the cart's tail from town to town till they reached the border, and then should be expelled. If they returned three times, they should be dealt with in the same way each time, or at the discretion of the court be branded. Should they return a fourth time, they might be put to death. Under this act Christison and twenty-seven others were released and expelled from the colony.

By Edward Burroughs and others in England the attention of the king was called to the treatment of the sect in

---

[1] Bishop, 323, 329. The account of his trial before the court of assistants is on page 315.

[2] *Ibid.* 334–340.

PART
II.

Massachusetts, and in September, 1661, a royal order[1] was sent commanding that Quakers who were under sentence of death, or who were imprisoned and were liable to other corporal punishment, should be sent to England for trial. This missive was brought and delivered to Governor Endicott by Samuel Shattuck, a banished Quaker from Salem. At once, upon advice of the elders, the general court resolved that the death penalty and corporal punishment should not again be executed upon Quakers until further order. In harmony with further advice from the elders, it was decided to send the prisoners-to England, and also to send a declaration to the king explaining the reasons for the conduct of the colony toward the Quakers. The despatch of Bradstreet and Norton as agents was decided on at the same time. It however appears that, though the prisoners were liberated and allowed to go to England if they chose, none were actually sent.[2]

The apparent intervention of the king in their behalf not unnaturally encouraged the Quakers to greater activity. This resulted in an increase of what the general court was not slow to term vagabondage throughout the colony. "Sundry persons,[3] as well inhabitants as forreigners," it was said, "wander from their familys, relations & dwelling places, from toune to toune, thereby drawing away children, servants & other persons, both younger & elder, from their lawfull callings and imployments, and hardening the hearts of one another against all subjection to the rules of God's holy word and the established lawes of this collony . . ." Against the offence of Quakerism under this description corporal punishment and imprisonment were again decreed. The court in the following October,[4] especially because of the large number of Quakers in the eastern parts, declared that the law of May, 1661, should again be in force, "provided that their whipping be but through three townes." As the fires of persecution were still raging hotly against the sect in England, the magistrates were justified in the assumption that they had little to fear from that quarter.

---

[1] Ellis, 479, 481 ; Mass. Col. Recs. IV². 34.   [3] Mass. Recs. IV². 43.
[2] Ellis, 487.   [4] *Ibid.* 59.

This fact became evident when the king's letter of June, CHAP.
1662, arrived,[1] in which he declared that he did not wish to V.
be understood as directing that any indulgence should be
granted to Quakers.   It was still the belief of the authorities
in England that Quaker principles were "inconsistent with
any kind of government," and since it was found necessary
to make sharp laws against them there, the king was content
if Massachusetts did the like.

This was decisive, and repressive measures continued to
be vigorously enforced.   In October, 1663,[2] an act was
passed disfranchising all, Quakers and others, who persistently absented themselves from church.   At intervals for
more than a decade whipping at the cart's tail and other
forms of punishment continued to be inflicted in all parts of
the colony.   Many women suffered cruel punishments.   Not
a few families were ruined by the prolonged imprisonment
of their members and by the seizure of their property for
the payment of fines and jailers' fees.   The enthusiasm of
the proscribed was not diminished by their sufferings.   In
some cases it rose to the height of frenzy.   It was during
this period that meetings were most seriously disturbed, and
that the worst outrages against public decency were committed.   It is reasonable to suppose that the extreme exhi-
bitions of zeal were to a large extent occasioned by the
persecution itself, and would have been avoided had the
milder course of the other Puritan colonies been pursued.
But with the deaths of the magistrates and elders who had
been zealous opponents of Quakerism at its first appearance,
with the Indian war and the struggle with the home government that followed, attention was gradually diverted and
officials as well as people became indifferent.   At the same
time the crudities of early propagandism somewhat abated
among the Quakers, and, as in England, by this gradual
process they won the toleration which they had sought.

With men of the type and strength of personality of
Roger Williams, with Antinomians and Baptists, the other
Puritan colonies had no experience of importance.   But
Quakers visited them all, or developed within their borders

[1] Mass. Recs. IV². 164.   [2] Ibid. 88.

in considerable numbers.   The policy which those colonies pursued toward them differed from that of Massachusetts only in the fact that it was less severe : the death penalty was not inflicted nor were ears cropped save in the Bay colony. Connecticut responded to the first suggestion from the Commissioners of the United Colonies, and forbade any town entertaining Quakers, Ranters, or Adamites for more than fourteen days, under penalty of £5 per week.[1]   Such heretics, if landed within the colony, were to be kept in prison and the master who brought them was bound to take them away at his next sailing under penalty of a fine of £20.   In 1657 and 1658 acts were passed for the banishment of heretics and the infliction of corporal punishment upon them.

New Haven prohibited any one settling in the colony without the consent of a magistrate.   In 1658 an elaborate act against Quakers and their writings was passed by this colony. Both were to be excluded from it on heavy penalties, though not involving death in any case.   Branding, hard labor, and banishment were the heaviest punishments.   Quakers, coming into the colony to do business, were allowed to go about for that purpose under guard, so that they might not disseminate their ideas.   New Haven also had a general law for punishing heresy when actively published, the penalties for which were fine, banishment, or such additional inflictions as the magistrates thought that the danger warranted.[2]

Plymouth was much disturbed by Quakers, especially by a group who lived in Sandwich.   In 1657 it was ordered that Quakers should not be entertained in the colony, on penalty of £5 or a whipping for every offence.   The following year provision was made by law for the arrest, imprisonment, and banishment of all Quakers ; also that no Quaker, or other person who refused to take the oath of fidelity, should become a freeman or have a voice in town affairs.   Freemen who became Quakers or defenders of them should be deprived of their political rights.   In 1658 it was enacted that a house of correction should be built for the reception of wandering Quakers and other vagrants.   Any

[1] Conn. Recs. I. 283, 303, 324.
[2] New Haven Col. Recs. II. 238-241, 590, 610.

one who brought a Quaker, or other notorious heretic, into
the colony, should upon order remove him or pay a fine
of twenty shillings for every week of delay thereafter.   All
Quaker literature which might be found was ordered to be
seized and brought to the magistrates.   It was made lawful
for any one to apprehend a Quaker and deliver him up to a
constable.   Public meetings could not be held[1] without permission.   Magistrates, like Thomas Prince, Thomas Hinck-
ley, and Josiah Winslow, very actively interested themselves
in imprisoning, whipping, and banishing heretics.

[1] Plymouth Col. Recs. XI. 100, 125, 127, 129, 130, 177, 205, 206.

CHAPTER VI

PLYMOUTH AS A CORPORATE COLONY

WHEN describing in a previous chapter the relations between the colonists of Plymouth and their English partners, attention was called to the fact that the former never willingly constituted a part of a proprietary system. To the limitations of that system they subjected themselves, because, unless they did so, it would have been impossible for them to procure the means with which to emigrate, or a measure of support while the colony was winning its way to economic independence. Because of the small number of the settlers, their poverty and the unfavorable conditions of the soil where they settled, the progress of the colony was slow. It was also a first experiment in Puritan colonization, and that without the advantages which come from the possession of a royal charter. In order to supplement agriculture by fishing and the Indian trade, subordinate plantations were started in the valleys of the Kennebec and Penobscot. These causes combined to prolong the somewhat loose and shifting relations with the partners till the close of the seven-year period, when they were dissolved. Joint trading continued for more than a decade longer. But with the dissolution of the original partnership, Plymouth settlers had come into control of both their land and trade. Politically dependent on the adventurers they had not been. Therefore the colony at that time appeared as a *de facto* corporation, — its essential character from the first, — and as such it may now be discussed. The marked difference between it and Virginia, or any genuine proprietary province, will appear at every step.

The internal development of the colony began with the famous compact signed in the cabin of the *Mayflower* while

she was riding at anchor in Provincetown harbor.[1] This
was the earliest of plantation covenants, and is memorable
solely for that reason. It was in substance reproduced on
many later occasions and in other places — by the river
towns of Connecticut,[2] at New Haven,[3] by the settlers at
Dover and Exeter[4] on the Piscataqua, at Providence, Portsmouth, and Newport[5] among the Narragansett settlements,
and by many other New England towns. A tacit assumption of authority equivalent to what these covenants implied
had to be made in all colonies where the exercise of the
higher powers of government was attempted without a direct
grant from the king. Finding themselves forced to settle
outside the jurisdiction of the company from which they had
received a patent, and threatened with revolt, the Pilgrims,
while acknowledging the authority of the king, solemnly
agreed to assume such power as was necessary for the fram-
ing of just and convenient ordinances, and the creating and
filling of offices ; and to such ordinances and officials they
promised obedience. So far as the act itself was concerned,
it might create a town or a colony. In this case it created
both, and the two did not become differentiated till more
than a decade later. Viewing the event from the standpoint
of the colony, the meeting in the cabin of the *Mayflower* was
in germ a general court, and the signers of the compact were
the earliest active citizens or freemen of Plymouth. They
were not made such by admission into any corporation, but
without legal authority they assumed the position and later
the name, and upon that assumption they proceeded to exercise political power in the colony.

Through their earlier negotiations these settlers must have
become somewhat familiar with the organization of the London company and its colonies, and from these it may be surmised that the title and office of governor were borrowed.

---

[1] Brigham, Laws of New Plymouth, 19.

[2] Conn. Col. Recs. I. 20.

[3] New Haven Col. Recs. I. 12–17.

[4] New Hampshire Provincial Papers, I. 125, 132 ; Jenness, Documents
Relating to New Hampshire, 36.

[5] R. I. Recs. I. 14, 52, 87.

The next office to be created was that of captain,[1] and this office, like all others in the little commonwealth, was elective, and that for an annual term. "Saturday, the 17th day,[2] in the morning," says Bradford and Winslow's *Relation*,[3] "we called a meeting for the establishing of military orders among ourselves ; and we chose Miles Standish our captain, and gave him authority of command in affairs." The sudden appearance of a number of savages gave them occasion at once to arm themselves and stand ready for conflict. Their "great ordinances" were now planted in "places most convenient." Twice again during the next four weeks the freemen met "to[4] conclude of laws and orders for ourselves, and to confirm those military orders that were formerly propounded, and twice broken off by the savages' coming." We also hear of another meeting on March 22 "about our public business," which, like its predecessors, was interrupted by the necessity of parleys with the Indians. The treaty with Massasoit, which resulted from these interviews, the annalist has preserved,[5] but the early orders to which reference is made have perished.

On the death of John Carver, the first governor, and the election of William Bradford as his successor in April, 1621, one assistant was chosen to aid him in the government.[6] Thenceforward elections were annually held. In 1624, at the request of Bradford himself, a request which was caused by the growth of business, the number of assistants was increased to five.[7] Later the board was again enlarged to seven, and at its meetings the governor was given simply a double vote. From that time his position, both in the board of assistants and in the general court, was the same as that which was later held by the governor of Massachusetts. As in Massachusetts, so within the colony of Plymouth, the general court was the actual source of political power.

In the early history of this settlement, as of other colonies, public and private functions were indistinguishably mingled. There was necessarily a return to primitive conditions, and

---

[1] Young, Chronicles of the Pilgrims, 180.   [2] Of February, 1621.
[3] Young, 180.   [4] *Ibid.* 189, 190.   [5] *Ibid.* 193.
[6] Bradford, ed. of 1856, 101, 110.   [7] *Ibid.* 156.

this fact was made more apparent by the joint management
of land and trade.   The governor and his assistant not only repressed disorder in the settlement, and led in negotiations with the Indians and in providing for defence, but they managed the common work, nursed the sick, fished, saw that the magazine was kept supplied, and acted as advisers and guides in all affairs.   The governor was also an elder in the church.   So long as relations with the adventurers were continued, these officials, though elected, acted as managers of a proprietary colony.   All official correspondence with the adventurers was conducted by the governor.   When agents were sent to England, as they frequently were, he doubtless had much influence in their selection.   When the ship *Fortune* had returned home in 1621,[1] the governor and assistant, having distributed the newcomers among families, took an account of provisions, and, when they found them insufficient, the colonists were put on half allowance.   When, on Christmas day of the same year, Governor Bradford returned from the fields and found some, who on a plea of conscience had been excused from work that day, playing games in the street, he " took away their impliments, and told them that was against his conscience that they should play & others worke."   If they observed Christmas from religious motives, let them stay indoors, "but there should be no gameing or revelling in the streets."   In these instances the governor acted as the overseer of an estate, much as the governor of Virginia might have done.   But by virtue of his elective tenure, he was not bound by instructions from the adventurers as a proprietary governor must be, while the religious and political motives of the colonists and their magistrates necessitated a unity and a freedom of choice which mere servants and planters could not possess.

Many decisions concerning public business must have been reached through informal consultations between the officials and other influential settlers.   When matters of special importance were to be decided, the whole company, consisting of *de facto* freemen, was called together.   It was by a vote of this body that the place of settlement was decided upon,[2]

[1] Bradford, 110.   [2] Young, 167, 170, 173.

and probably also the method of laying out the town. The ordinances which were first issued by this body were, as we have seen, on the subject of defence. Not until the close of 1623 do we find a record of the passage by the court of any order concerning judicial administration ;[1] but at that time trial by jury was introduced. When, earlier in that year, "the perticulers" arrived, "ye Gov', in ye name, and with ye consente of ye company," received them,[2] and the conditions on which they were allowed to settle were "agreed on between ye colony and them." Later, when these settlers began to arouse strife, the governor consulted "with ye ablest of ye generall body."[3] When, through the efforts of John Oldham, one of their number, aided by Lyford, the minister whom the adventurers had sent over, a dangerous opposition movement had been started, "ye Gov' called a courte and summoned ye whole company to appeare." Bradford having, by an act not uncommon then, but one which would now be branded as the grossest violation of honor, opened the letters which Lyford and Oldham were sending home, and found that they were filled with calumnious charges against the colony, now faced the offenders with them and compelled the minister to confess his offence with tears. They had tried, in the interest of the adventurers and of the English Church, to increase the number of the discontented, and by a combination of those with "the perticulers" and fresh recruits from England to seize control of the colony and manage it in their own interest. The dramatic proceedings of this court were varied by the reading of the letters which had been seized, by a furious appeal on the part of Oldham to those who previously had appeared to support him but who now sat unmoved, and by the examination of various parties by the magistrates. The session developed into an impromptu trial[4] of an offence amounting to treason against the colony, and ended in a vote for the expulsion of the accused. This sentence, after further offences by both, was executed.

The last among the early meetings of the general court to

---

[1] Brigham, Laws, 28.
[2] Bradford, 147.
[3] *Ibid.* 157.
[4] *Ibid.* 175 *et seq.*

which reference must be made was that called in 1627 to consider the division of the lands of the plantation. " Ye Gov' and counsell with other of their chiefe friends," had upon mature consideration resolved that a division of the lands was necessary. Thereupon " they caled ye company together, and conferred with them," with the result that a conclusion was reached which " gave all good contente." [1]

It was in the name of William Bradford, the governor of this democratic commonwealth, one of its founders and second to none among the leaders of the enterprise, that the patent of 1629 was granted. Associated with him in procuring the patent were Standish, Winslow, and the other prominent settlers. The powers of the grant, such as they were, therefore had to be exercised exclusively in the colony and by the settlers themselves. Before the patent was issued the political form which the colony was to assume had been determined, and the council made no effort through the grant to change it in any respect. Though legally Plymouth had to be regarded as a fief lying within the domain of the New England council, and after 1635 within the king's domain, it wholly lacked the feudal form of organization. Therefore, while Bradford continued to hold the patent as trustee, the colony followed the natural course of its development undisturbed. After 1632 the *Records* show that sessions of the council or court of assistants and of the general court were regularly held. The full power to legislate, to levy taxes, to organize a military force, to administer justice, and to inflict capital punishment [2] was assumed and exercised. Freemen were admitted by the general court; and in 1636 a freeman's oath was enacted which, except in its recognition of the sovereignty of England, was similar in purport to that of Massachusetts. As arable land near the town of Plymouth became insufficient longer to satisfy the demand, removals began. Land here and there on the common domain was taken up, though for reasons already stated dispersion began relatively much later than in Massachusetts. These settlements, at first called plantations, wards, or sides, gradually developed into

[1] Bradford, 214, 215; Brigham, Laws, 29.   [2] Bradford, 276.

towns, in spite of the opposition of the town of Plymouth and of the leaders who resided there. In January, 1634, the first constable was chosen in the general court for the settlement which later became known as Duxbury. A year later the evidence shows that there was such an officer at Scituate.[1] Annually thereafter constables for these settlements were elected or sworn in the general court.[2] In 1638 a constable appeared for Sandwich,[3] where a settlement had been made the previous year. In 1639 one appeared for Yarmouth, and in 1640 constables were "nominated" for Taunton and Barnstable.[4] In 1637, after it had been found impossible to locate a meeting-house which would be convenient for both its inhabitants and those of Plymouth, Duxbury was made a town, though its bounds were left to be fixed by the next court. Even earlier, in 1636, Scituate was called a town, and it was allowed to grant land and to make such orders as were found necessary, "provided they have, in case of justice, recourse unto Plymouth as before."[5] In 1638 it was enacted that all towns, allowed or to be allowed within the colony, should have the liberty to meet together and to issue such orders as were necessary for the herding of cattle and the doing of other needful things, provided they did not infringe any public acts.[6] They were then given the right to punish petty offences, and the next year were empowered to levy local rates. It was also enacted that the governor and assistants should, under the authority of the general court, appoint and set forth the bounds of townships, as they had formerly done.[7] Hence, as elsewhere in New England, and as was the case in the creation of the colony itself, the two things legally essential to the founding of a town were the grant of land and the grant of rights of local government, including the establishment of local offices. But that in Plymouth the control of the colony over the towns was more strict than elsewhere is indicated by the fact that their choice of selectmen, constables, and surveyors of the highways was subject to the approval of the general court of

[1] Plym. Recs. I. 21, 32. [4] *Ibid.* 116, 141. [6] Brigham, Laws, 64.
[2] *Ibid.* 36, 48, 80, etc. [5] *Ibid.* 44, 62. [7] *Ibid.* 68.
[3] *Ibid.* 57, 80.

election. This may perhaps have been due to the early opposition to the development of towns.[1]

In consequence of the multiplication of towns, Plymouth the town became differentiated from Plymouth the colony, and appeared as a distinct unit for purposes of local government. It was a slow process, the stages of which it is not easy to trace. Sometime between November, 1636, and the close of March, 1637, a separate record book for the town was opened;[2] but the entries were made by the clerk or secretary of the colony till 1685. Then, for the first time, a town clerk was chosen. In January, 1633, a constable had been chosen.[3] The earliest record of a town-meeting is dated the last day of March, 1637.[4] At a meeting held in July of the following year bounds for the town were provisionally agreed upon, but they were not fixed by the general court till 1640.[5] In February, 1650, the town chose selectmen and bestowed the usual powers upon them, though not till twelve years later did the general court empower the towns to elect such officers and itself define their authority. While by these steps its organization was being perfected, the leading inhabitants of Plymouth, among whom were some of the most prominent magistrates of the colony, viewed with jealousy the dispersion of the colonists and the founding of new towns. The traditions of the first decade were strong at the place of original settlement, and by the dispersion that town was losing prestige. To prevent this as far as possible, it was enacted in 1633 "that the chiefe government be tyed to the towne of Plymouth, and that the Governor for the time being be tyed there to keep his residence and dwelling; and there also to hold such Courts as concerne the whole."[6]

A necessary result of the dispersion of inhabitants and the formation of towns was the development of the representative system. In 1636 and 1637 committees from the outlying settlements had been appointed to join with the governor and assistants in preparing a revision of the laws, in dividing

[1] Plym. Recs. IV. 122, etc. ; Brigham, 257.
[2] Records of Town of Plymouth, I. Introduction.
[3] Col. Recs. I. 21.
[4] Town Recs. I. 3.
[5] Col. Recs. I. 164.
[6] Ibid. I. 16.

lands and in assessing a tax.[1] In June, 1639, "committees"
or deputies from the towns — five members from Plymouth
and two from each of the others — were added to the governor and assistants to form the general court.[2] After this the
freemen as such continued to attend only the annual court of
election, though to this, as in Massachusetts, they might send
proxies. The general court of Plymouth was never divided
into two houses, though apparently in 1649 such a proposition
was made, but defeated. A committee then reported, "yt
for the future, as formerly . . ., the Magestraits and Comit-
ties or Deputies bee Concidered together as one body."[3] In
Plymouth the religious test was never definitely established;
but after towns had come into existence the law required
that candidates for active citizenship should be approved by
the freemen of the towns where they lived and proposed
to the general court by the deputies of those towns.[4] Gradually the requirements concerning admission were made more
strict, till in 1671 a property qualification was required, and
also testimony from the neighbors of the applicant that he
was sober and peaceable in conversation and "orthodox in
the fundamentals of religion."[5]

The territory of Plymouth being small and relatively compact, the organization of counties did not become necessary
till almost the close of her separate existence. In 1685 the
colony was divided by its general court into three counties,
their boundaries being fixed and county courts established.
Thus the judicial system of the colony was completed. It
included selectmen's courts in the towns, with jurisdiction
over cases of debt, trespass, or damage not exceeding forty
shillings; and county courts held in each case by at least
three magistrates and associates, the latter being annually
chosen by the general court as special county magistrates to
coöperate with the resident assistants in transacting county
business. The latter, besides being the administrative body

[1] Recs. I. 43, 61, 67.
[2] *Ibid.* 126; Brigham, Laws, 63, 108.
[3] Plymouth Recs., Book of Laws, 55, 57.
[4] Act of 1656, Brigham, 100, 108.
[5] Brigham, 170, 258.

of the county, probated wills and had jurisdiction over civil and criminal cases, provided the penalties did not involve life, limb, or banishment. At the head of the judicial system was the court of magistrates or assistants, sitting in the later years of the colony three times annually at Plymouth, which heard appeals and could " call all the Inhabitants, Freemen, Planters, or others to accompt for the breach of any Laws or Orders established or for other misdemeanours . . ." It also exercised an equitable jurisdiction. In 1684 an admiralty court was established, consisting of not more than four of the assistants and such "substantiall persons " as the governor should commission under the seal of the colony.

The military and fiscal systems of the towns and of the colony were similar in all important respects to those of Massachusetts, and require no extended description here. The county, while it had its treasurer, who received money from the constables or town councils, had not been incorporated into the military system when the independent existence of the colony ceased. There seem to have been no county regiments. Their organization came after Plymouth was absorbed by Massachusetts.

Such in outline was the commonwealth which evolved from the compact signed in the *Mayflower*. It was consistently democratic, and possessed all the organs necessary for an independent existence. Though the king was recognized in its public acts and documents, so far as its political life was concerned it enjoyed an independence greater even than that of Massachusetts. Owing to its more moderate policy it did not provoke internal dissensions or multiply enemies in England. Therefore the quiet course of its existence was never seriously disturbed by foes from within or without.

The last step in the history of this commonwealth, so far as we need to follow it, was taken in 1641.[1] Then, with the approval of all parties concerned, William Bradford laid down his trusteeship and resigned the patent into the possession of the freemen of the colony assembled in general court. The surrender was accepted by the court ; and thencefor-

[1] Recs. II. 10 ; Bradford, 372–374.

ward the freemen, as the assigns of Bradford, were in name, as well as in fact, the grantees of such rights as were transferred by the patent.

"And ye said William Bradford doth, by ye free & full consente, .approbation, and agreemente of ye said old-planters, or purchasers, together with ye liking, approbation, and acceptation of ye other parte of ye said corporation, surrender into ye hands of ye whole courte, consisting of ye free-men of this corporation of New-Plimoth, all ye other right & title, power, authority, priviledges, immunities, & freedomes granted in ye said letters patents by ye said Honorable Counsell of New-England; reserveing his & their personall right of freemen, together with the said old plant-ers afforesaid, excepte ye said lands before excepted, declar-ing the freemen of this corporation, togeather with all such as shal be legally admitted into ye same, his associats."

When this transaction was completed, the freemen, like those in Massachusetts, were in every sense the actual possessors of political power.

CHAPTER VII

CONNECTICUT AS A CORPORATE COLONY

THE colony of Connecticut was formed by the union of the three River Towns — Hartford, Windsor, and Wethersfield — and of the plantations which they had established or annexed, with the jurisdiction of New Haven. It did not, then, develop from a single centre, as did Plymouth ; nor by the founding of a number of neighboring towns, all of which were from the outset coördinately related to a single colony government, as was the case in Massachusetts. Moreover, as these settlements, with the possible exception of Saybrook, were founded without the guaranty of charters of any sort, they had at first no express connection whatever with England.

They were not even under the nominal obligation imposed by the conditions of tenure within the manor of East Greenwich. In their case, during the early period of their existence, every vestige of such tenure, so far as it affected either external or internal relations, had vanished. These colonists left behind them in England no partners who could impose a system of common landholding or insist upon the maintenance of joint trading operations. It was not necessary for them to adjust any corporate business interests before leaving for the colonies which they intended to establish. The granting of shares of land to non-resident adventurers and the keeping of a colony magazine are not features in their early experience. In other words, these colonies did not develop from trading companies, and hence they do not exhibit any of the phenomena of transition which accompanied such a process.

Their settlers, as groups of emigrants animated by a more or less common purpose, came to Massachusetts, and thence —

301

some after a longer and some after a shorter sojourn —
sought a permanent home in the valley of the Connecticut.
In both stages of their migration they acted without the
sanction, and so far as possible without the knowledge, of
the English government. Hence, when finally settled, they
established a system in which political independence was
even more prominent than was commercial and territorial
isolation. Apart, then, from the theories which they held
concerning forms of civil and ecclesiastical government, we
must look for an explanation of the origin of their institutions to the example of Massachusetts. The River Towns, in
particular, were an offshoot from that colony ; and the influence which it had over their development has not always
been duly appreciated.

The families which settled Hartford, Windsor, and Wethersfield had been inhabitants of Massachusetts, some of
them since its foundation. They were, accordingly, familiar
with the system of government which existed there. The
motives which induced them to leave England were, in general, the same as those which animated the great body of
Massachusetts colonists ; they were Puritans to the core,
and were thus in sympathy with the general purposes of
the Massachusetts enterprise. But after a residence there
of a few years, they were induced by a combination of causes
to desire a removal still farther west. The majority of
those who joined in requesting from the general court permission to remove were probably influenced chiefly by the
reports concerning the richness and the accessibility of
the bottom lands of the Connecticut. Two or three of
the leaders in the enterprise may also have been moved by
feelings of jealousy and personal rivalry toward Governor
Winthrop and Mr. Cotton, though this assertion is based
upon rumor rather than upon positive evidence.

The later policy of the River Towns would lead to the
inference that one motive which induced them to remove
was their disapproval of the religious test, but no contemporary reference to this appears. That Watertown, which
was one of the towns that contributed largely to the emigration, was opposed to the assumption by the magistrates

of the power to legislate and to vote taxes, we are fully
aware. Thomas Hooker [1] also, in a letter which in 1638 he
wrote to Winthrop, objected to the almost unlimited discretion which it was then legally within the power of the
magistrates in Massachusetts to exercise in matters of judicature and administration. Hooker insisted that the judge
must have some rule to judge by, or government would
degenerate into tyranny and confusion — a condition under
which, said he, he would neither consent to live nor to leave
his posterity. As this became a prominent political question
in Massachusetts at the time when the Connecticut settlers
removed, the lack of a proper definition of the power of the
magistrates may have prejudiced the minds of some of their
number against the Bay colony. Light will be thrown on
the views of the Connecticut settlers concerning this question
by an examination of what they did to prevent the evils of unlimited executive power from developing in their own colony.
But, before this is undertaken, we must see by what steps
government was established on the banks of the Connecticut.

No body of men in the history of the world ever mastered
more thoroughly the art of forming and maintaining a compact political organization than did the magistrates and
elders of Massachusetts. Working under the form of a
corporation, they aimed to control not only the admission of
freemen, but that of inhabitants as well. Both the physical
and the spiritual activity of those who became residents of
the colony they sought so to regulate that the unity and
harmony of the whole should in no way be imperilled.
Moreover, all settlers in their midst whose views were in
tolerable agreement with their own they sought to retain.
The most notable exhibition of this policy was made when
the emigration to the Connecticut was proposed. The
question was under consideration for a year or more, and various efforts were made to divert the discontented from their
purpose. When finally it became necessary for the magistrates to yield, they did so on the condition that the new
settlements, though lying outside the bounds of Massachusetts, should continue under its government.

[1] Colls. of Conn. Hist. Soc. I. 11 ; Winthrop, Journal, II. 428.

In May, 1635, the general court granted permission to the inhabitants of Watertown and Roxbury to remove, "provided they continue still under this government." A month later similar permission was given to Dorchester.[1] In September it was enacted that constables chosen by towns on the Connecticut should be sworn in by some magistrate of Massachusetts. In March, 1636, before the more important migration from Newtown and Dorchester occurred, the general court created a commission of eight members, and empowered it to administer justice and regulate affairs in the Connecticut settlements for a period of one year.[2] Its executive control was to extend over trade, granting of lots, planting, building, military discipline, and defensive war. It was also empowered to summon the inhabitants as a court. Springfield lay within its jurisdiction, as well as the settlements further south. The members of this commission were men who had already gone to the Connecticut or were intending soon to go and therefore to become residents of the localities they were to govern. There is no evidence that after their appointment the parent colony sought to control their action by means of appeals or in any other way. Indeed they could not legally do so, for there was no proof that any of the proposed settlements, except Springfield, would lie within the Massachusetts bounds. Furthermore, careful provision was made in the commission for guarding such interests as the Warwick patentees might have in that region ; [3] and that surely could not have been done by annexing the River Towns to Massachusetts. Winthrop[4] states that Massachusetts never intended to make Connecticut subordinate to itself ; but in 1641, when replying to a petition from Springfield, the general court declared that there was in 1636 no intention of dismissing the Connecticut settlers from the jurisdiction of Massachusetts, but rather to reserve an interest on the river, and that so the Connecticut men understood it.[5]

---

[1] Mass. Col. Recs. I. 146, 148, 160.   [2] *Ibid.* 170.

[3] John Winthrop, Jr., who had been appointed governor by the Warwick patentees, was consulted in reference to the issue of this commission.

[4] Winthrop, Journal, I. 342.   [5] Mass. Recs. I. 321.

Judging from the way in which Massachusetts dealt with
the Narragansett settlements and with the settlements of
northeastern New England, one would infer that the chief
reason why she did not attempt to absorb the River Towns
was the fact that she lacked a favorable opportunity. Had
they not been peopled by orthodox Puritans and led by men
of the resolution and ability of Hooker and Haynes, and had
they not at once developed an independent life so vigorous
as to enable them to make headway against the Dutch and
the Indians, the possibilities of prolonged control implied in
the resolutions passed by Massachusetts at the time of their
removal might have been realized. As it was, however, the
three River Towns, lying outside Massachusetts bounds, never
by word or act acknowledged dependence upon her, thus
imitating in their relations with the parent colony the policy
which that colony systematically pursued toward the home
government.

Still, during the first year of their existence, the River
Towns were governed by commissioners who derived their
authority, such as it was, from the general court of Massachusetts. Their authority was not assumed; neither did it
proceed from election by the inhabitants of the towns themselves. What, now, did those commissioners accomplish
during the year of their existence? They swore in constables for the towns, though those officers had very likely
been elected by the localities they were to serve. They
ordered trainings, the keeping of a watch, and the enforcement of the assize of arms in each town. By their order
names were given to the towns, and under the authority of
the commissions town boundaries were fixed.[1] During that
year, then, the towns were not independent of each other
or of a power outside themselves.

On May 1, 1637, at the end of the official term of the
commissioners, a general court met at Hartford. As they
had power to call courts, it may be supposed that this one
was summoned by them. It consisted of six magistrates and
nine deputies elected by the towns,[2] those representing each
town being called its " committee." Hooker states that the

[1] Conn. Col. Recs. I. 1–9.   [2] *Ibid.* 9 *et seq.*

magistrates were elected by the committees, and by these their oath of office was administered.[1] This assembly was apparently organized in the same way as was the Massachusetts general court at that time. Its meeting was occasioned by the necessity not only of forming an independent government, but of raising men and supplies for the Pequot war. But the point with which we are immediately concerned is this : that the general court at once assumed a more complete control over the towns than the commissioners had exercised. During 1637 and 1638 it exercised over them the fullest degree of military control, culminating in the passage of a comprehensive militia act.[2] It also ordered a quota of men with supplies to be sent from the towns, to settle in the territory conquered from the Pequots and to hold it for the colony.[3] It levied taxes and chose a treasurer for the colony. It ordered the continuance of the judicial business which the commissioners had been transacting, by a resolve that a "perticular Courte" should be held at Hartford.[4] It regulated trade along the river and the relations between the Indians and the inhabitants of the towns. Therefore, substantially the same relations between the general court and the towns as those which existed in Massachusetts seem to have been continued in Connecticut. Connecticut was in no sense formed by a "consociation" of independent towns, for the simple reason that its towns were never independent. No imposing theory of federal union can be evolved from the early history of the River Towns without drawing very heavily on the imagination.

When, in the years 1638 and 1639, the River Towns undertook the task of organizing a government in a more formal and permanent fashion than before, they were negotiating with Massachusetts about an alliance or confederation.[5] The two colonies were jealous of one another. The River Towns charged Massachusetts with trying to prejudice would-be settlers from joining them, by exaggerating their poverty and their sufferings ; Massachusetts complained because the

---

[1] Conn. Hist. Colls. I. 13, 18.
[2] Recs. I. 9–16.
[3] *Ibid.* 10.
[4] *Ibid.* 12, 16.
[5] Winthrop, Journal, I. 283, 342.

Connecticut settlements claimed Springfield and would not
in all respects be bound by its Indian policy. The Connecticut towns feared that Massachusetts might still absorb them.
Hence, when in 1638 Massachusetts suggested a plan of
union, wherein power should be given the commissioners of
the respective colonies to settle finally all matters of difference between them, Connecticut objected. It would have
had the commissioners meet, with the understanding that, if
they could not agree, they should return to their several colonies for additional instructions and authority, and that they
should continue that process until an agreement could be
reached. Apparently it was fear of the superior influence of
Massachusetts that led the weaker colony to dread any union
with her, except under the loosest forms of confederation.

These differences and jealousies were canvassed at the
time in a correspondence between the leaders of the two
colonies, Hooker and Winthrop ; and these spokesmen were
naturally led to emphasize the divergence in their political
views. Winthrop "expostulated about the unwarrantable-
ness and unsafeness of referring matter of counsel or judicature to the body of the people, *quia* the best part is always
the least, and of that best part the wiser part is always the
lesser." In his *Journal*, also, he recorded the opinion that
the failure of Connecticut to show the desired spirit of harmony was due to the fact that she chose to office so many
men of no learning or judgment. This, he said, made it
necessary that the burden of public business should be assumed by one or more of her ministers, who, though men
of singular wisdom and godliness, showed the defects of
those who were acting outside their true sphere. Hooker
defended the course of Connecticut in reference to the proposed articles of confederation and all other matters as pru-
dent and just, while he expressed, in the terms already
stated,[1] his disbelief in unlimited magisterial discretion.

It seems that on the Connecticut the controverted points
in the plan of union were referred to the general court, or
possibly to a court of election ; while at Boston the magistrates preferred to conduct the entire negotiation. But

---

[1] Winthrop, Journal, I. 344 ; II. 428 ; Conn. Hist. Colls. I. 7 *et seq.*

when later the plan approached completion, the Massachusetts general court repeatedly took action by adding a number of deputies to the body of negotiators, by instructing
them as to one point and by approving the plan when perfected.[1] Thus, in the end, the procedure of Massachusetts
was not so different from that of Connecticut as one would
infer from the language of Winthrop and Hooker that it
might have been. This fact would indicate that, from the
fragments which remain of the correspondence between these
two men, possibly exaggerated inferences have been drawn
concerning the divergence between their opinions and the
difference between the systems and policies of government
which they contributed so much toward establishing.

Other evidence bearing on this point may, however, be
derived from the utterances of Hooker in connection with
the formal establishment of government in Connecticut.
From the very fragmentary notes that have been preserved
of the famous sermon which he preached before the general
court on May 31, 1638, one would infer that the thoughts
he chiefly sought to convey were these: that all public
officials should be elected, that their powers should be defined, and that both these things should be done by a body
of freemen as numerous and inclusive as would consist with
their acting " according to the blessed will and law of God." [2]
Here, again, Hooker must have expressed his distrust of the
Massachusetts system so long as the powers of its magistrates were undefined, while he also renounced the religious
test in the sharp and precise form which Massachusetts had
given to it. But Hooker was essentially a Puritan of the
Massachusetts type; he was not a believer in the separation
of church from state, or in manhood suffrage. In other
words, he was not a democrat in the modern sense of the
term, though much that has been written about him would
lead us to infer that he was. Hooker's democracy was a
compromise between the views of Winthrop and those of
Roger Williams. His scheme contemplated the application
of a moral test to those who desired to be admitted as free-

[1] Mass. Recs. II. 31, 35, 36, 38.
[2] Conn. Hist. Colls. I. 20.

men, and this test was to be applied either by those who were church members or by those who in their ethical views were in agreement with the church members. Not only does the later legislation of Connecticut show this to be true, but provision for it was made in Hooker's theory, by his insistence that political action should be guided by the will and law of God. The doctrine of the union of church and state is in the preamble of the Fundamental Orders, while the provision that the governor should be a member of some approved congregation shows the intention to maintain such union. Secularized democracy, an outgrowth of the dogma of equality and of voluntaryism in religion, would have been condemned by Hooker almost, if not quite, as vigorously as by Winthrop.

The Fundamental Orders, which were drawn up in 1638 and adopted early in 1639, embodied and set forth a scheme of government which was in harmony with Hooker's views and to the origin of which his influence in no small degree contributed. Connecticut historians and others have represented this as in form and contents radically new, and as suggestive of a theory and practice which was far in advance of anything previously attained. But if we compare the positive contents of the Fundamental Orders with the laws of Massachusetts and Plymouth, so far as they had been developed at the time, we shall find no important differences. The provision for a general court which should meet in two annual sessions, one of which should be attended by all the freemen for the purpose of electing the magistrates, was not original. The general court, when organized for legislation, was to consist, as in Massachusetts, of the magistrates and of representatives of the towns assembled in one house under the presidency of the governor. As in Massachusetts, the governor was empowered to summon the court for both regular and special sessions; while in both colonies the court punished disorder and the non-attendance of its members. The power of the freemen to call the general court was not specified in Massachusetts law; but in November, 1639, it was enacted that the court of election should meet at the time mentioned in the charter without

summons.[1] The ballot was used in the election of at least
a part of the magistrates in Massachusetts in 1634, but the
Fundamental Orders provided for its employment in the
choice of both magistrates and deputies.[2] The provision
for the nomination of magistrates was new, but it was introduced in Massachusetts in 1640.[3] The control of the general court over contested elections is brought out more
distinctly than in any Massachusetts law then existing; but
in 1635 an order had been passed by the general court at
Newtown empowering what we should now call a caucus of
the deputies, which met before the opening of the session,
to settle such disputes.[4] The specification of the legislative
powers of the general court is substantially the same as that
contained in Massachusetts law.[5] The method of raising
revenue by levies on the towns had been in vogue in Massachusetts from the first; and the quotas were fixed by the
general court, though in its early legislation we have no
record of its employing committees for the purpose.[6] The
oath of fidelity was administered in all the colonies. The
position and the power of the governor were exactly the same
in Massachusetts as in Connecticut, though they are more
precisely expressed in the Fundamental Orders than in the
early acts of Massachusetts. In Massachusetts, as in Connecticut, the general court was the tribunal before which
magistrates and other high offenders were brought to justice,
though this principle was more specifically stated in the
Fundamental Orders than in the laws of Massachusetts.[7]
The provision that no one should be governor for two terms
in succession [8] was, indeed, a new and significant departure
from Massachusetts policy; but in 1660 it was repealed.
Even in the omission of the religious test, the point in
which the document shows the widest departure from Mas-

[1] Mass. Recs. I. 277.

[2] Winthrop, Journal, I. 157 ; Fundamental Orders, Arts. 2 and 7.

[3] Mass. Recs. I. 293 ; Fundamental Orders, Art. 3.

[4] Mass. Recs. I. 142.

[5] *Ibid*. 117 ; Fundamental Orders, Art. 10.

[6] Mass. Recs. I. 77, etc. ; Fundamental Orders, Art. 10.

[7] Mass. Recs. II. 93 ; Fundamental Orders, Art. 10.

[8] Conn. Recs. I. 346, 347 ; Fundamental Orders, Art. 3.

sachusetts principles, Connecticut did not stand alone; for
Plymouth expressly established no such qualification for
citizenship. So it appears that, if we examine the Fundamental Orders in detail, we find in them no important departure from the system of government previously existing
in the two parent colonies of New England.

From the contemporary utterances of Hooker, indeed, one
would expect to find more specific limitations upon the discretion of the magistrates; but in fact the powers of governor and assistants were very loosely and imperfectly defined,
while no special attempt was made by supplementary legislation to specify the penalties which might be inflicted for
crime. We look in vain for the classification of the organs
and powers of government, and for the clear distinctions between them, which appear in modern written constitutions.
In fact, we find brought together in a single document what
in Massachusetts and Plymouth had been formulated in
a succession of statutes, and we find nothing more. Moreover, though the Fundamental Orders were evidently adopted
by a convention[1] of all the free planters held at Hartford,
January 14, 1639, and hence must rank formally as a fundamental law or written constitution, it should be remembered
that such a body would differ in no appreciable respect from
a court of election, and therefore would not bear the exceptional character which attaches to a modern American con-
stituent convention. Also, as the document contained no
provision for amendment, the general court assumed and
exercised the right to change it, as it would any statute,
in ordinary legislative session. As that right was unlimited
and its exercise unopposed, the Fundamental Orders did
not operate as a limitation on the powers of the general
court. So far as any authority within the colony was concerned, the supremacy of the general court was as complete
as that of the legislature of Massachusetts; and hence, until
the royal charter was granted, Connecticut lacked the steady-
ing influence which Massachusetts occasionally derived from
even the general and summary provisions of its patent.

[1] Trumbull, History of Connecticut, I. 110. See also Preamble of Fundamental Orders.

If marked originality is to be found anywhere in the Fundamental Orders, it must appear in the preamble. This is, in fact, the part of the document which has chiefly attracted the attention and awakened the imagination of historians. The frank declaration of independence which is there made, and the announcement of the fact that in the opinion of the framers an original compact was being formed, has given to this document most of its interest. The preamble has been dwelt on at greater length and with much greater enthusiasm than have the provisions of the constitution concerning government. It has been made to signify much more than the Mayflower compact, and its adoption has been regarded as the initial act in the development of American democracy. But really there is nothing in the preamble, or in the body of the Fundamental Orders, to indicate that, if the settlers of Connecticut had possessed a royal charter, they would have proceeded in a manner essentially different from that of the colonists of Massachusetts.

For Massachusetts the outline of a system of government, such as it became after the removal of the corporation, was given in its charter. Magistrates and a general court were in existence when the colony was founded. All that was needed there was that, through these organs and under the initiation of the executive, the work of government should be begun. Specific forms and details of government were assumed, but the right to establish government had not to be assumed. The Connecticut colonists, however, in the absence of legal authority, after the close of the year, during which the commissioners appointed by Massachusetts had administered their affairs, practically set up for themselves. The decisive step was taken at that time, although, owing probably to the pressure of the Pequot war, the formal declaration of the fact was postponed till the colony had justified its claim to separate existence by triumph in that conflict. Imitating the example of the churches, a plantation covenant was prefixed to the solemn announcement which they then made of the outline of their system of government. Wishing to recognize no outside authority, they declared that they associated themselves together as a

commonwealth — that they entered into combination among
themselves and with those who should later join them, and
on behalf of their posterity, to maintain both civil and ecclesiastical government.   But this was practically what had
been done by the Pilgrims in the *Mayflower;* it was precisely what was being done in several of the Narragansett
settlements; it was what New Haven did with almost painful
elaboration about five months later.   As the River Towns,
about two years before, had tacitly assumed the powers of
government which they now declared that they were assuming, and as the Fundamental Orders probably did not essentially change the system of government that already existed
on the Connecticut, one must infer that the course of history
would not have been much different from what it has been,
had the preamble of that document never been issued.   Declarations and covenants could not change the fact of the
case, — that Connecticut, while assuming the right to exercise authority, derived her governmental system by imitation
from Massachusetts and through that colony from the trading
companies of England.   The line of descent is clear and
unmistakable, while the process of inheritance was free and
natural.

From the adoption of the Fundamental Orders to the issue
of the royal charter, the development of the colony of the
River Towns was steady and normal.   According to the provision of the constitution (Art. 10), the general court alone
admitted freemen.   The qualifications required were admission as inhabitants by some town and the taking of the oath
of fidelity.   This oath, like that of Massachusetts, contained
an acknowledgment of submission to the government of
Connecticut, and a promise not to plot or share in any plot
against it, but promptly to reveal such schemes; to maintain the honor of the jurisdiction, and to vote conscientiously
for its best interests.[1]   In 1643 the general court reaffirmed
the provision of the Fundamental Orders, that only those
should be regarded as inhabitants of a town who had been
admitted as such by a majority of its voters.[2]   In 1646 it
was enacted that none who had been fined or whipped for

[1] Conn. Recs. I. 62.   [2] *Ibid.* 96.

any scandalous offence should be admitted to vote in town or commonwealth, or to serve on a jury till the general court should specially permit it.[1] The same court also enacted that the magistrates should administer the oath of fidelity to all males above sixteen years of age. When, in 1656, Quakers began to appear, it was ordered that those who desired admission as freemen by the general court should bring a certificate of peaceable and honest conversation signed by all or a majority of the deputies from their respective towns.[2] In 1662 candidates were required to bring a certificate to the above effect signed by a majority of the selectmen, instead of the deputies, of their town.[3] In 1659 a property qualification was introduced — the possession of a personal estate of £30.[4] Three years later the possession of real estate to the amount of £20 was required. When in 1665 the royal commissioners presented the requirement of the king, " that all men of competent estates and of civil conversation, though of different judgments, be admitted to be freemen," the general court replied that its " order for admission of freemen is consonant with that proposition." [5]

Still, there was a stringent moral requirement, which, when taken in connection with the character of the selectmen and of the members of the general court who enforced it, and with the care which they exercised over both churches and individuals, appears to have been semi-religious in its nature.[6] The ecclesiastical history of Connecticut shows that the body of freemen, from which the general court was elected, consisted of church members and of those who were in close sympathy with them. The regularity with which a

---

[1] Conn. Recs. I. 138, 139. The magistrates were permitted temporarily to readmit those who had been punished as specified in this act to the privileges of freemen on their presenting a certificate of good behavior.

[2] Ibid. 290.

[3] Ibid. 389.

[4] Ibid. 331, 389 ; II. 253.

[5] Ibid. I. 439.

[6] Trumbull, History of Connecticut, I. 287 et seq. ; Conn. Recs. I. 520, 523, etc. True and suggestive statements on these and other related subjects will be found in a paper by Henry Bronson on the " Early Government of Connecticut," Papers of New Haven Hist. Soc. III.

comparatively small number of men were reëlected to office — making the tenure of the magistrates, though they held elective offices, very permanent — is an indication of the same thing. It is a phenomenon which appears in Massachusetts as well, and helps to reveal the fact that the political conditions in those colonies were much the same.

The influence of the civil power over the churches in Connecticut was scarcely less than it was in Massachusetts. The code of 1650[1] contained a provision giving the civil government authority " to see the force, ordinances and rules of Christe bee observed in every church according to his word."

The power of interference thus asserted was almost unlimited, and it was used on many occasions and in many ways. The records show that the court interfered in conflicts within the churches over the settlement of ministers, over the authority of pastors to rule and overrule the brotherhood, over the right of admission to sacramental privileges. Councils were repeatedly called at its instance in the effort to settle these questions. The court on one occasion proposed to review a case of excommunication. It issued orders concerning the maintenance of ministers. The principles of the Cambridge Platform of Discipline were as fully accepted and enforced in Connecticut as they were in Massachusetts. The attitude of the Connecticut ministers toward Antinomianism and Quakerism was the same as that assumed by the clergy of Massachusetts.[2]

In the history of Connecticut, however, we have no clear evidence that the clergy and magistrates conferred so often or so fully over questions of policy as they did in Massachusetts. None of the clergy, save Hooker, undertook to expound principles of government, or especially to guide the

---

[1] Conn. Col. Recs. I. 524.

[2] *Ibid.* I. 106, 111, 356, 387, 412, 420, and the many references to the controversies in the churches of Hartford, Wethersfield, and Windsor. Leonard Bacon, The Relations of the Congregational Churches of Connecticut to Civil Government, Centennial Papers of the General Conference of Connecticut, 1877, 159 *et seq.*; Walker, History of the First Church in Hartford, 151 *et seq.*; Colls. Conn. Hist. Soc. 11, 53 *et seq.*; Stiles, Ancient Windsor, ed. of 1859, 166 *et seq.*; Trumbull, History of Connecticut, I. Chap. 8.

policy of the commonwealth. The clergy as a body was not called upon to explain the nature of the colony government. In other words, the caucus system was more fully developed in Massachusetts than in Connecticut. This was due to the fact that the conflicts with heresy were fought chiefly in the Bay colony, and upon these the magistrates and the great body of the clergy were a unit. The controversies of Connecticut were either confined to local congregations, or related to questions of less vital moment, upon which absolute unity of action was not necessary. They also arose later, after the fervor of Puritan zeal had somewhat abated, and when aggressive action was scarcely possible. The view which prevailed in the general court upon the chief question, that of the so-called halfway covenant, was decidedly moderate, an opinion such as laymen who were to an extent free from clerical influence would naturally adopt. The fact that the great body of the clergy was slow to accept these opinions, and that the court was unable, through councils or by other methods, to procure their general adoption, checked in a measure the influence of the government and its Presbyterianizing tendencies. But these are events which belong more to the second than to the first generation of New England Puritanism.

As we have seen, the development of the general court in Connecticut began at the point which it had reached in Massachusetts when the removal took place. For two years previous to that event deputies, or representatives of the towns, had sat in the general court of Massachusetts and no legislature met on the banks of the Connecticut without their presence. But deputies and magistrates continued to meet in one house until 1698,[1] a period of more than forty years after Massachusetts had possessed a legislature of two houses. After the issue of the Fundamental Orders little legislation appears concerning the organization or powers of the general court, and there was slight need of it. Prior to 1662 only a few minute changes in detail were made — such as the provision that a moderator should be chosen to preside in the absence of the governor and deputy governor,[2]

---

[1] Recs. IV. 267.   [2] Ibid. I. 256, 348, 365, etc.

and that in the absence of the same officials a majority of
the magistrates might call a session of the court.[1]

The business of the general court was very extensive.
Besides its two regular sessions, many extra sessions were
held.   In 1645 it met seven times; in 1658 it met twice in
March and once in May, in August and in October; in many
other years it met as often as in these.   As in the other corporate colonies, its work was legislative, administrative, and
judicial; while the character and volume of its product in
each of these lines were not materially different from that
which appears elsewhere in New England.   Its most important legislation — a subject which will receive further illustration in later chapters — had reference to towns, military
affairs, moral and ecclesiastical relations, the levy of rates,
Indian relations, crimes and their penalties.[2]   Not only did
the general court legislate comprehensively, as in October,
1639, for the establishment and regulation of towns,[3] but
by special orders it provided for the enforcement of this
legislation, and controlled the action of towns in many
ways.   As a result of these acts and of a series of land
grants, a town system similar to that of Massachusetts
and Plymouth was developed; and by means of this
system the territory of the colony was extended eastward
to include the Pequot country, southward to the mouth
of the river, and westward till it was met by the counter
claims of the Dutch.   By legislation beginning in 1637 a
militia system — with trainings and the assize of arms, foot-
soldiers, and troopers — was created, while the lower officers
who were elected by the towns were confirmed by the general court.   In the domain of finance, the elective office of
treasurer was strictly regulated; the accounts were yearly
audited by a committee of the general court; lists of taxables
and taxable property were annually returned to the general
court by the towns; and these lists served as a statistical
basis on which to levy the country rate.   The regular judicial business of the colony was transacted in the particular
court or court of magistrates.   Occasionally an appeal from

---

[1] Recs. IV. 256.   [2] See Records and Code of 1650, Recs. I. 509.
[3] Recs. I. 36.

this tribunal was heard by the general court.   The general
court also granted divorces and sometimes probated wills.
It held no state trials like those instituted by Massachusetts
against the parties who attacked her ecclesiastical system.
Though in both these colonies the judicial functions of the
general court were supplementary, the volume of business of
that nature done by the court of Massachusetts seems to have
been the greater.

The name "orders," which was often applied to the acts
of the general court, describes the major part of them more
accurately than the word "laws."   They were administrative
ordinances, occasioned by reports and petitions and adapted
to individual cases and particular events, rather than laws
intended to furnish permanent and general rules of action.
The issue of such orders constituted a large part of the business of each session, and the orders issued dealt with a great
variety of subjects.   Not only, for example, did the general
court legislate concerning the Indians, but it issued orders
for the settlement of disputes among them, and between them
and the English.   It concluded treaties with the Indians,
prosecuted and punished them for crime, corresponded with
the neighboring colonies about them, and executed the orders
of the Commissioners of the United Colonies in reference to
them.   The court acted in the same way in regard to the
relations with the Dutch.   By similar orders it provided for
the enforcement of its legislation concerning the internal
affairs of the colony and controlled the action of towns and
officials who were intrusted with the execution of its laws.
Through its power of choosing, commissioning, instructing,
removing, or otherwise disciplining officials, the general
court exercised continuous administrative influence, not only
over towns, but over all the business of the colony.   The
court also regularly appointed committees to execute its
orders.   These might consist exclusively, or only partially,
of members of the court.   In most, if not all, cases the governor and some of the assistants were placed upon such committees ; and deputies or others who were associated with
them were selected because they lived in the locality where
the business must be done, or because of their special knowl-

edge of the case.   When correspondence or negotiations were CHAP.
to be carried on, the governor and the magistrates were VII.
almost necessarily employed.   The similarity between this
and methods of government in the other corporate colonies
is already apparent.

The employment of committees, not only for legislative
but for distinctly executive purposes as well, is a prominent feature in the early practice of the legislatures of both
Massachusetts and Connecticut.   When compared with the
contemporary practice of parliament or of any other European legislature, it must appear as an important innovation.
It has already been explained as a continuation of the custom
of the trading companies of England, which frequently made
use of committees in the transaction of their business.   The
executive of the corporate colony, moreover, was elective in
origin and multiple in form : it was an executive board — an
annual committee, so to speak — of the freemen for certain
important purposes of government; and the bodies which
the general court created for more specific purposes were not
dissimilar.   So complete was the control of the general court
over the business of the corporate colony, that it was easy for
it not only to supplement but to assume the work of the
executive — a thing which, as the legislature of the province,
and of the kingdom in fact, was organized, the representative
branch could not always do without a struggle.   In the corporate colony, the executive was organically the agent of the
general court, and when the two were harmonious was actually
used as such; while in the province, the executive was the
rival and the competitor of the lower house.

The colony of the River Towns, having been founded without a royal charter, attained its ultimate limits by expansion
and by the absorption of two smaller colonies, neither of
which existed by virtue of rights superior to its own.   The
first colony to be absorbed was that founded at Saybrook.
The right of those who held the so-called Warwick patent[1]
to establish a settlement west of Narragansett bay can certainly not be affirmed.   No grant to the Earl of Warwick

[1] Trumbull, History of Connecticut, I. 27, 435 ; Johnston, Connecticut,
8 *et seq.* ; Conn. Recs. I. 568.

appears among the extant records of the New England council. To be sure, those records are not complete; but such a
grant was not brought to light in the seventeenth century,
though the Connecticut authorities were especially anxious
to establish claims to the territory in question.[1] Moreover,
in the extant patent of 1631 Warwick does not positively
assert title to land west of Narragansett bay, but simply
conveys such claims as he has. If it be compared with the
deeds of lease and release, by the grant of which the Duke
of York made Berkeley and Carteret proprietors of New
Jersey, the difference in the wording and implication will be
clear. Still, the patentees acted under the grant as if it were
genuine, and the conduct both of Massachusetts and of those
who settled the River Towns in 1636 implies the same belief.
This document is one of the indications that we do not yet
fully understand the relations which existed between the
Earl of Warwick and the New England council, on the one
hand, and the Puritans who were interested in New England
colonization, on the other.

Not until June, 1635, two months after the New England
council resigned its charter, did the Warwick patentees attempt to take possession of any part of the grant which they
claimed. Then John Winthrop, Jr., was appointed by them
governor for one year "of the river Connecticut with the
places adjoining thereunto," and was instructed to build a
fort and begin a settlement near the mouth of the river.[2]
These commands were executed by Winthrop, with the aid
of Lyon Gardiner, and thus a small proprietary colony was
established. In 1639 George Fenwick, one of the patentees,
settled there with his family, and the place was named Saybrook. A church was built; and possession was taken of a
tract of land lying on both sides of the river and extending
back about eight miles from its mouth. The River Towns
soon drew Fenwick into the closest possible relations with
themselves, by securing his appointment as one of the commissioners of the United Colonies and by contributing toward

[1] See the reply of Connecticut to New Haven's Case Stated, New Haven
Col. Recs. II. 533.
[2] Trumbull, I. 497.

the maintenance of the fort at Saybrook.[1] By this means
they secured his aid in thwarting the plans of Massachusetts
to obtain a part of the Pequot country, while they opened
the way for the purchase of Fenwick's plantation. This
they effected in December, 1644, Fenwick conveying the
fort and the lands over which he had jurisdiction, and promising that, if the territory lying between the Connecticut
and Narragansett bay and mentioned in the Warwick patent
came into his power, it should be transferred to Connecticut.
Fenwick was permitted to live at Saybrook for ten years
and to make use of certain buildings and land there. It
was finally agreed to pay him £180 annually during that
period, the payment to be made in good wheat, pease, rye,
or barley at fixed rates. The duty on the beaver trade
and the dues from Springfield, to which Fenwick was entitled, were also[2] continued. Fenwick soon returned to
England, where he died in 1659. As he left unfulfilled his
promise to secure for Connecticut jurisdiction over the territory mentioned in the Warwick patent, the colony tried to
recover from his agent and heirs a portion of the money
which had been paid. In 1660 it accepted a repayment of
£500 in lieu of all demands, and the dispute was closed.[3]
It thus appears that, prior to the grant of the royal charter,
Connecticut had not secured a valid title to the soil which
she had occupied, but she was in possession of the mouth
of the river and of a goodly stretch of shore along the
sound.

The jurisdiction of New Haven — the second colony to be
absorbed by that of the River Towns — was settled by Puritans of the strictest type, whose leaders, Eaton and Davenport, had been closely identified with the Massachusetts
enterprise in the early stage of its development. Their
motives and ideals were practically the same as those of
Winthrop and Cotton. Their migration, nevertheless, had
no official or corporate connection with that which resulted
in the settlement of Massachusetts: it pursued an indepen-

---

[1] Conn. Recs. I. 113 et seq., 170.
[2] Ibid. I. 268, 271, 568.
[3] Ibid. I. 575 and references.

dent course from its origin in England to its successful accomplishment on the shores of Long Island sound. The leaders of the enterprise, with a part of the settlers, landed at Boston, where they remained for a few months ; but they were not, and never intended to be, more than sojourners there, while they were looking for a permanent abiding-place. Though there was a certain commercial element in the enterprise, no relations continued with partners left behind in England which to any extent modified the development of this colony. It was even freer from influences of that nature than Massachusetts had been. Not only was New Haven from the outset independent of other colonies, but it assumed and enjoyed to an equal degree independence toward the mother country.

The process by which the inhabitants of New Haven assumed governmental powers has been too often described to call for elaborate treatment here. The date and text of their first plantation covenant have, indeed, been lost; but this loss is more than made good by the details which have been preserved concerning the doings of the " general meetinge " that was held in Newman's barn, June 4, 1639. This meeting took the decisive steps which led to the establishment of government in the plantation. The outcome was not essentially different from that which had been reached at Hartford the previous January, and elsewhere on other dates, some earlier, some later. But Puritanism of the *doctrinaire* type found more complete expression here than at any other time or place. All inherited political connections were tacitly renounced ; and by solemn and express agreement a new political body was formed, which was to consist only of the elect — of church members whose lives successfully bore the test of the most rigid scrutiny. After this condition of citizenship had been adopted as the cornerstone of the political edifice, the church was founded. The germ of this body was the famous " seven pillars," [1] or seven leading men of the settlement, selected by coöptation from a larger body of twelve which had been chosen by the "general

[1] " Wisdom hath builded her house, she hath hewn out her seven pillars." Prov. ix. 1.

meetinge." The "seven pillars" presumably added[1] to their own number those who were to be the original members of the church, and this body chose its pastor and other officials. The "seven," though not technically, were at the same time really, the only magistrates in the little settlement, and continued to be such till October 25, 1639. A freeman's oath with the customary provisions was drawn, and more than one hundred freemen signed the "foundamentall agreement . . . thatt church members onely shall be free burgesses."[2] This was apparently done, at least in part, while the "seven" held sway both in church and commonwealth.

On October 25, in the first public court of which there is record, the "seven" resigned such power or trust as they had received, and all who had been received into the fellowship of the church were admitted as members of the court.[3] Six who were members of other approved churches were also admitted to citizenship. After the freeman's oath had been administered, at least to some, and Davenport had preached from Hooker's text combined with Ex. xviii. 21, they chose a magistrate and four deputies or assistants, besides a secretary and a marshal or constable. It was also agreed that the term of office for all magistrates should be one year, and that the general court should meet in annual session the last week in October. Finally, with supreme self-confidence, they sought by a single resolution, not only to exclude English statute and common law from their settlement, but to forestall the necessity of important legislation on their own part. They resolved "thatt the worde of God shall be the onely rule to be attended unto in ordering the affayres of government in this plantation."

Like Plymouth, New Haven, as thus founded, was town and colony combined. In 1638 the land upon which the town was settled, together with a tract within which exist ten modern townships, was bought from the Indians. Outside this lay the territory upon which Guilford and

---

[1] As Trumbull, I. 285, expresses it, the church was "gathered to the seven pillars." The churches at Milford and Guilford were formed in the same way. Authority for these acts was also found in Prov. ix. 1.

[2] New Haven Recs. I. 17, 19.   [3] *Ibid.* 20, 21.

Milford were founded.   In 1640 land to the west of Fairfield was bought and the plantations of Stamford and
Greenwich were settled, though the latter did not finally
acknowledge itself a part of New Haven colony till 1656.[1]
In 1640, also, the purchase which became Southold on
Long Island was made.   In 1642 constables were chosen at
the New Haven court for Stamford and Southold.[2]   Milford
and Guilford were settled by families which, though they
shared in the common migration, were never more than
sojourners at New Haven.   The settlements which they
made were at the outset politically independent.[3]   Stamford and Branford were also settled largely by seceders from
the church and town of Wethersfield.   Hence it appears
that the degree of political and territorial unity which
existed in Plymouth did not obtain at the outset in the
colony of New Haven.   The plantations and towns in the
latter colony were not in all cases founded by the parent
settlement, and thus were not under its administrative control.   If, then, from these plantations one colony was to
emerge, and at the same time New⁻ Haven colony was to
become distinct from New Haven town, the change could
be effected only by a process of union or federation.   This
event occurred in 1643 and was brought about mainly by
the formation of the New England Confederacy, and the
necessity arising therefrom that New Haven should appear
in it as a unit comprising all the settlements which were
closely related to it.[4]

On July 6, 1643, Eaton and Gregson, who as delegates of
the town of New Haven and the plantations immediately
dependent upon it — "the jurisdiction," as it was beginning
to call itself — had met the commissioners from the other
colonies, reported the articles which they had agreed upon
as the constitution of the league.   These were approved,
July 6, by "a general court held att New Haven for the
plantations within this jurisdiction."   It was ordered that
all males in every plantation who were between the ages of

[1] Atwater, History of New Haven Colony, 413.   [2] Records, I. 70, 78.
[3] Smith, History of Guilford ; Lambert, History of New Haven Colony,
85 et seq.; Atwater, 155 et seq.   [4] Recs. I. 96 et seq.

sixteen and sixty should be numbered and armed, and that their arms and trained bands should be viewed. A tax was also imposed on the plantations to meet the expenses of " the combination," and it was ordered that the rules as to rating which had been in force at New Haven should be applied throughout the colony. It is important to note that at this court two members were admitted from Guilford. With their coöperation, then, these steps were taken preparatory to the organization of a colony government of the corporate type.

That organization was not completed till the following October. It was effected by transforming the outlying plantations of the jurisdiction, including Milford as well as Guilford, into towns with rights fully equal to the town of New Haven, it being expressly provided that New Haven should be the seat of government. A compromise was reached with Milford — which had admitted to the rights of freemen six inhabitants who were not church members — to the effect that no more such extensions of the franchise should be permitted, and that the six should perform no functions, outside of town affairs, except that of voting for deputies to the general court. Thus it was hoped that there would be no more violations of the "foundamentall order " concerning the suffrage. It was reaffirmed and placed at the head of the series of enactments which were passed by the October court of 1643, providing for the establishment of the new colony government. By this the continued existence of the town courts, with their magistrates, was guarantied. Provision was made for a " court of magistrates," to meet biennially at New Haven, with the powers of a tribunal of appeal and higher jurisdiction for the colony; and for a general court, consisting of the governor, deputy governor, and all the magistrates of the colony, together with two deputies from each town, all sitting together as one house. Provision was also made for two annual sessions, one of which, in October, should be the court of election. Upon this body the usual legislative powers, the right to administer oaths, and the functions of a highest court of appeal were bestowed.

If the document which contains these provisions be critically examined, and compared with the enactments which had preceded it in the other colonies, it will be found to come no nearer to the modern idea of a written constitution than do they. It was simply an important statute, passed by the general court and capable in all parts of amendment or repeal by the power which created it.   The religious test, though regarded as fundamental, might have been modified or repealed by the same process of legislation as was used or recommended in Massachusetts.   In the formation of New Haven colony, also, the federal element appears with greater prominence than in the case of Connecticut ; but it was the result of a union of parts whose origin was similar, whose influence was very unequal, and the period of whose separate existence had been very brief.

As a colony, New Haven enjoyed an uneventful existence for twenty years.   About 1653, when the settlements along the Connecticut were alarmed by rumors of attack by the Dutch and Indians, and those which lay furthest west thought themselves in imminent peril, agitation against the religious test was raised in Stamford and Southold.[1]   Complaints were also uttered that the colony did not adequately provide for the security of its outlying settlements, and some were bold enough to challenge the legality of the control which it exercised over them.   But the movement never assumed serious proportions, and subsided with the disappearance of danger.   Nothing else of political importance occurred to disturb the quiet of the colony.   Its institutions underwent slight development, though even under its peaceful conditions it was at once found necessary to forsake the Bible as a law book and to legislate much as other colonists did.   They even went so far as to bring their most important enactments together into a code, as did Massachusetts and Connecticut.   Its provisions, like the orders of court, conform to the ordinary New England type.

The Restoration found New Haven independent ; but it also found the colony of the River Towns in possession of the settlements along the river and thence eastward to the

[1] Recs. II. 48 *et seq.*

Narragansett country, together with Fairfield. The latter
plantation was so situated as to prevent the New Haven
colony from attaining territorial unity. The Restoration
also made the absence of legal guaranties of existence among
the colonies of southern New England painfully apparent.
Now that the king had returned, it behooved them all to
look to their title deeds, for the inquiries which Charles I
had been forced to abandon were likely to be resumed by
his son. The controversy which Connecticut had with the
Dutch over her western bounds, and that with Massachusetts
and the Narragansett plantations over those on the east,
early led her to take action toward procuring a royal charter.
Though her address to the king was not prepared till the
spring of 1661, a year before that the clause in the Fundamental Orders prohibiting the election of the same person as
governor oftener than once in two years was repealed. This
made it possible to reëlect John Winthrop for that year and
a number of succeeding years. In 1661 he was also made
agent to England, for the purpose of presenting the address
and procuring a charter. To that effect he was instructed,
and £500 were set aside for his use.[1] He was told to procure, if possible, a copy of the Warwick patent, or, if that
could not be done, to obtain a confirmation of it from the
heirs of the patentees, and to recover what had been paid
to Fenwick for the "jurisdiction right." In case a royal
charter should be granted, Winthrop was instructed to see
that it conformed as nearly as possible to the Massachusetts
patent. It was desired that the grant be made to several
patentees with their associates, with such as might be joined
with them, and their successors forever ; and that the freemen, or associates, should have the exclusive right to choose
officers for conducting the affairs of the colony. Eighteen
were designated as the number who, it was desired, should
be named in the patent.

Winthrop's success equalled, if it did not surpass, the
most sanguine expectations. He procured a royal charter,
dated April 23, 1662, which was more favorable to the
grantees than was the Massachusetts patent. It created the

[1] Conn. Recs. I. 346, 347, 361, 368, 369, 579, 582.

persons whose names — with a few exceptions — were in Winthrop's petition, together with their associates, a corporation on the place, under the name of the Governor and Company of Connecticut in New England in America. The usual corporate powers were expressly bestowed. The government actually existing, with the institutions which had grown up in the colony during the past twenty years, was recognized and guarantied. It was provided that there should be one governor, one deputy governor, and twelve assistants, — naming for the first year the patentees as incumbents of these offices, — to hold for an annual term, the elections of successors to be held at the May court of election. Provision was made for two annual meetings of the general court, or court of the corporation, which should consist of the governor, deputy governor, at least six of the assistants, and not exceeding two deputies from each town. The usual powers — those which it had been in the habit of exercising — were bestowed on the general court, and all that should be necessary to validate its acts was their issue under the seal of the colony. The king expressly reserved no control whatever over legislation or over the administration of justice within the colony.

The extreme liberality of these provisions shows that the charter which was granted must have been substantially the same as Winthrop's draft. As by it a corporation was created on the place, it was not necessary to refer in it to the administration of subordinate government in the colony. The provisions that were made for the government of the corporation itself were provisions also for the government of the colony, for the two were identical. This charter, then, was more perfectly adapted to the needs of Connecticut than was the charter of Massachusetts to the form and necessities of that colony. It was such a patent as the founders of Massachusetts would have welcomed, could they have frankly avowed their plans before they left England. The moderate religious policy of Connecticut, and the fact that no complaints against that colony were laid before the home government, now stood it in good stead. Massachusetts could scarcely have hoped to be able to exchange her charter for one like that of Connecticut.

The bounds of Connecticut were now unexpectedly extended through to the South Sea. New Haven was thus included within that colony; as she also would have been if the validity of the claims of Connecticut under the Warwick patent could have been established. This result was especially gratifying to the River Towns, in the minds of whose inhabitants the desire for territorial expansion was then especially strong. Also, in the controversy which was then agitating the New England churches, Connecticut favored the so-called halfway covenant, while New Haven adhered to the rigid practice of the first generation of Puritans. The strict adherence of New Haven to the religious test and her extreme independence would have operated strongly against her, had she attempted to secure guaranties in England for continued existence. These causes contributed to increase the difficulties which attended the efforts made by New Haven to save herself from annexation.

Before Winthrop left for England, Davenport secured from him a statement that the magistrates of Connecticut had agreed not to coerce their sister colony into a union.[1] Later, after the charter had been granted, he wrote from London that he had at the time assured the friends of New Haven that there was no intention of doing injury to her rights or interests, or of meddling with any town or plantation which was settled under her government;[2] and, had any other intention been declared, it would have increased the difficulty of procuring the charter without inserting in it a proportional number of New Haven names. Her membership in the New England Confederacy also gave New Haven a status among her sister colonies, though not in England; and her absorption by Connecticut would remove much of the little vitality which remained in the Union after the Restoration. When, therefore, in 1663, the delegates from New Haven appealed to the Commissioners of the United Colonies, they declared that the jurisdiction of that colony could not be violently invaded without a breach of the articles; and that, if any power had been exercised there without the authority of the colony, it should be recalled

[1] New Haven Recs. II. 521.   [2] Ibid. 523.

until the conditions were favorable to an orderly settlement.[1] But both the history of the Confederacy and its ultimate course in this case showed that, when the crisis should come, New Haven must be prepared to face her rival alone.[2] Pious wishes were all that the commissioners from Massachusetts and Plymouth could contribute for her support.

In this affair the general court and magistrates of Connecticut clearly exhibited the spirit of the bully, — the same spirit which at that time they and the other New-Englanders were showing toward their weaker neighbors, the Dutch. Of course their words and conduct were all in the interests of civilization, but they found expression in the imperative mood. Connecticut, prior to April, 1662, stood as naked and defenceless before the crown as did New Haven. Her charter she had secured without consulting the sister colony, whose political annihilation was involved in the issue of the document. As soon as the charter arrived at Hartford, still without consulting New Haven, she received the submission of the town of Southold and of the discontented faction in Stamford, Greenwich, and Guilford. Constables were appointed to act for Connecticut in Stamford and Guilford.[3] Then a committee was appointed to treat with New Haven. Connecticut, that is, first gave recognition and support to those in the colony of New Haven who, because of the religious test, or for any other reason, were discontented and ready to coöperate in its overthrow. After that had been done, and a long step had thus been taken toward the desired issue, resort was had to negotiation. The result was that bitter feelings were aroused, a riot at Guilford was encouraged, and the negotiations were disturbed and hindered by recriminations. The mild and peaceful methods which Winthrop recommended from England, after the first step had been taken, could not be tried. In the defence of her conduct Connecticut relied chiefly on the mere fact that she possessed a charter ;[4] and, considering the source whence they came, she made some most remarkable admissions concerning kings and the extent of royal authority.

---

[1] Plymouth Recs. X. 310.   [2] Ibid. 318.   [3] Conn. Recs. I. 388–390.
[4] Conn. Recs. I. 422 ; New Haven Recs. II. 535.

How long the controversy might have continued no one can tell. But early in 1664 came the news of approaching events which suddenly brought it to a close. New Netherland, with the Connecticut river as its eastern boundary, was to be granted to the Duke of York and Dutch rule overthrown. At the same time a royal commission was about to visit New England for the purpose of settling disputes and taking steps which would lead to the proper recognition of royal supremacy. To New Haven absorption by Connecticut was vastly preferable to submission to the Duke of York, with his unlimited proprietary power, and his province filled with an alien population. The necessity, also, that the Puritan colonies of New England should bury their differences and present a united front before the royal commissioners was instantly recognized. These considerations overcame at New Haven the irritation which had been provoked by the arbitrary conduct of Connecticut, and the weaker colony bowed gracefully to the inevitable. By legal steps, which it is not necessary here to particularize, her inhabitants were admitted to a full share in the benefits of the new charter and of government under it, while the annexation of her territory rounded off the Connecticut colony on the southwest, and completed the process of her expansion. The religious test in its original and precise form disappeared, and thus a serious occasion of controversy with England and a barrier to progress within Puritan society were removed. Davenport, who had led in its establishment and had always been its chief defender, removed to Boston, where in his declining years he might still enjoy the stricter Puritanism of the founders. The enlarged Connecticut, with a charter and a government which were suited to the genius of her people, continued on her peaceful way ; and, largely because of the close adaptation of government to society, earned for herself the name of the "land of steady habits." From the outset she had been a little more modern and progressive than Massachusetts and slightly more democratic ; and these qualities she continued to display throughout the colonial period.

CHAPTER VIII

RHODE ISLAND AS A CORPORATE COLONY

UNLIKE Massachusetts, Plymouth, and Connecticut, the colony of Rhode Island was formed by the union of plantations ; the town was distinctly the root whence the colony sprang. Between the spring of 1636 and that of 1639, the three germinal settlements were founded. These were Providence, at the head of Narragansett bay, Portsmouth, — earlier Pocasset, — and Newport on the island of Aquedneck, or Rhode Island. Later the town of Warwick, on the west side of Narragansett bay, was added. These towns existed for a time independent of each other and of all external control. In 1647, under the authority of a charter obtained from the revolutionary government in England, they combined into a colony. In order to understand the union thus formed, the organization and relations of the towns that formed it must first be briefly reviewed.

Roger Williams, when banished from Massachusetts, had no intention of founding a commonwealth, probably not a distinct plan of founding a town. In 1677 he wrote,[1] "It is not true that I was imployed by any, made covenant with any, was supplied by any, or desired any to come with me into these parts." His first thought seems to have been, that he would "do the natives good," but as events proved his work among them was to be that of an interpreter and mediator rather than that of a religious teacher like Eliot. Williams adds that, at their own request, he permitted a few individuals from Salem and elsewhere, who had fallen into disfavor in Massachusetts, to follow him. The fact that he was to have English companionship strengthened in Will-

[1] R. I. Tracts, No. 14, p. 53.

iams's mind the idea of religious freedom which was to give form to all his future plans. The sentiments from which it sprang had previously dominated his action. The idea itself had lain in his mind and had found expression, though not in specially clear or definite form. Henceforth its realization in institutions and its proclamation to the world were to be the chief work of his life.

The colony which Williams had a share in founding was destined, as he desired, to be a refuge for those who were oppressed for conscience sake. It exemplified more perfectly than any commonwealth that had existed, or that was to exist for more than a century, the idea of which Williams became a leading exponent. Within it the religious tests, the political activity of the clergy, the disciplining of individuals and churches, which fill so large a place in the history of the strictly Puritan colonies, found no place. Williams himself on two occasions rendered valuable service to the colony in England. Its peaceful relations with the Indians were due in large measure to the peculiar influence which he had among the savages. By his correspondence with Winthrop and others he labored to conciliate, while he maintained his own position and that of the colony of which he was a very prominent citizen. He shared largely in the founding of one of the Narragansett towns, and occasionally he held high office in the colony.

But Roger Williams had not the ambition or the organizing power which lead to the establishment of institutions on a firm basis. He was in no sense, like Winthrop, a judge or an administrator. He cared nothing for the details of executive work. He had not the patience or caution of the diplomatist. He was a persistent, somewhat irritable, but on the whole a genial and highly endowed individualist. It is possible to imagine him living such a life as did Blackstone, though with greater activity among the Indians.

Though Williams and the elder Winthrop were lifelong friends, they were men of very different types, and the shares which they had in the founding of the colonies with which their names are identified were as unlike as were the men themselves. In fact the beginnings of Rhode Island were not the result of conscious planning, as was the case with Plymouth, Massachusetts, and the colonies in the Connecticut valley. The contrast in this respect between it and the proprietary provinces is equally marked.

More than any other American colony, the settlement of Rhode Island was the result of unforeseen conditions, for which immediate provision had to be made. No man was its founder ; that appellation belongs to no single group of men. It was settled by bands of fugitives, who came from different quarters and at different times. Their movement was not the result of concerted action, though they removed thither to escape oppression in the strictly Puritan colonies or conditions there which to them had become intolerable. With the exception of a few who came from Salem, none were disciples of Roger Williams, nor did they go into exile in order to testify to the truth of his beliefs, or to their loyalty to him as a man. And yet common opposition to Massachusetts and the policy of which it was the leading representative, brought them into practical harmony with him. As time passed and the dangers which continued to surround them became evident, this was generalized into a principle, that of the exclusively secular community. It was declared first among the orders of Providence, later among those of the plantations on Aquedneck and in the legislation of the colony. But this action was occasioned by the relations that existed between the inhabitants of all those settlements and by the struggle in which they were all engaged, rather than by the personality or direct influence of Roger Williams.

Led by circumstances more than by definite choice and plan, Williams and his companions established themselves on the west side of the peninsula which separated the Mooshassuc from the mouth of the Blackstone river, and characteristically named the settlement Providence. The neck itself consisted of a ridge which furnished them with the upland that was immediately needed for the purposes of cultivation. To the west, the northwest, and the southwest lay the meadows adjacent to the banks of the Mooshassuc and the Wanasquatucket, two small fresh-water streams, the

currents of which united before they mingled with the CHAP.
"Great Salt River," — the name which the early settlers VIII.
gave to the northernmost arm of Narragansett bay.   To the
low ground along these streams the settlers must look for
their grass land and pasturage for their cattle.

As was to be expected, steps were early taken by Williams
to extinguish the claims of the Indians to the land of the
plantation.   His friendly relations with the Narragansett
chiefs of the region made this easy.   But like most of his
contemporaries among the colonists, Williams had little
acquaintance with English law, while he was personally
careless about details.   Two years passed after the so-called
"gift" was received from Canonicus and Miantonomi, before
a written record of it was obtained, not in the form of a
deed, but of a memorandum.   This was dated in March,
1638, and it not only confirmed the original purchase of the
lands and meadows on the Mooshassuc and Wanasquatucket,
but added "the grass and meadows" on the Pawtuxet, a
river which lay considerably farther to the southwest.
According to the language of this memorandum two tracts
had been conveyed, which were later known as the "Providence purchase" and the "Pawtuxet purchase."   The latter,
however, as later interpreted by Williams, was not intended [1]
to extend beyond the hill Neutaconkanut, which lay a considerable distance northeast of the middle course of the
Pawtuxet river.   But so indefinite was the language of the
memorandum, that it was susceptible of an interpretation
which would push the bounds twenty miles to the westward.

In 1639 Williams and Benedict Arnold also signed a
certificate in which it was stated that Miantonomi, one of the

[1] Williams wrote to Whipple, "The Sachems and I were hurried to those
short bounds by reason of the Indians then at Maushapog, Notakunkonet, and
Pawtucket, beyond whom the Sachems could not then goe. . . ."   "By ye
Sachems' grant to me of an abundant sufficiencie to myself and my Friends
. . . I never understood infinite and boundless matters, no nor 20 miles,
but what was of realty counted sufficient for any plantation or town in the
country."   R. I. Tract, No. 14, pp. 27, 30.   Williams also states that when the
grant was made, "that monstrous bound or business of up stream without
Limits was not thought of."   Ibid. 55.   See also the confirmation of 1661,
Staples, Annals of Providence, 30.

sachems concerned, had confirmed the previous grants, with the addition that the land " up streams without limits " might be used by the settlers for the pasturage of their cattle. This referred to the land on the Mooshassuc and Wanasquatucket, and was understood by Williams to concede to the English by "courtesy," joint use of the lands with the Indians. But the form of language was such as to make the western bounds of the plantation still more uncertain. By the wording of these documents the occasion was furnished for controversies which agitated [1] Providence at intervals for more than a generation.

By Williams and the half dozen men who accompanied him a town government was instituted early in 1636 and town meetings were held at intervals of a month or oftener. The only official, however, who is mentioned in the fragmentary records is an elected treasurer. That this government was based on a tacit, if not an express, plantation covenant, is clear. But some time in 1637,[2] on the arrival of a body of " second comers," a written covenant was adopted to the effect that they whose names were subscribed, desiring to inhabit in the town, subjected themselves " in active and passive obedience to all such orders and agreements as shall be made for public good of the body in an orderly way, by the major consent of the present inhabitants, masters of families incorporated together in a Towne fellowship, and others whom they shall admit unto them, only in civil things." The last clause expressed the

---

[1] The Memorandum and the certificate which was added to it, form the subject of 2 R. I. Tracts, No. 4, by Sidney S. Rider. In this he argues that the certificate and a part of the memorandum were forgeries. The documents in question are reproduced by Rider, and also by Hopkins in his monograph entitled The Home Lots of Providence. Later deeds bearing on the same transaction will be found in Early Records of Providence, IV. 70 ; V. 296, R. I. Col. Recs. I. 18–37, and in Staples, Annals of Providence, 26–33, 566–577. The chief references of Williams to the transactions and to the controversy which followed are in his Letter to Whipple and his Letter to the Commission of 1677, R. I. Hist. Tract, No. 14. Thorough discussions of the questions at issue will be found in Dorr, Proprietors of Providence and the Freeholders, Colls. R. I. Hist. Soc. IX, and in Richman, Rhode Island, I. 85, 152 ; II. 197.

[2] R. I. Col. Recs. I. 14.

resolve of the planters that the enjoyment of rights in the town should be in no way conditioned by church member- ship, and that any church which might be established should be a distinct and purely voluntary association. In order to become a townsman it was necessary only to sign the covenant and to prove the possession of such character and means as to justify the bestowment, on the payment of thirty shillings,[1] of the customary town lots.

These steps were taken before the certificate of confirma- tion was attached to the memorandum of the Indian grant, and before it was decided what the chief purpose of the settlement should be and how its land should be managed. Were the settlers to be tenants of Williams, or should a system of joint occupation, such as that which existed in other New England towns, be substituted? It is scarcely possible to imagine Roger Williams playing the part of a landed proprietor, or of individualists such as those who settled about Narragansett bay becoming tenants of him or of any other man. It was doubtless Williams's intention from the first to admit the settlers to a share in the purchase. But William Harris, one of those who had accompanied him from Salem, was unusually persistent in his demands that this should be done. Williams stated at a later time that Harris " wearied " him with his desires, and even pretended religion that he might the better secure[2] his object.

Harris, however, partially succeeded in his effort. Will- iams, in 1638, delivered the so-called " initial deed,"[3] of which not the original, but only a memorandum, exists. This stated that he, the sole purchaser of Providence, in consideration of the payment to him of £30 by the inhabit- ants of the place, conveyed to twelve of his " friends and neighbors . . . and such others as the major part of us shall admit into the same fellowship of vote with us," joint right with himself to enjoy and dispose of said lands. Again no attempt was made to state the bounds with accuracy, and in the first memorandum the names of the

[1] R. I. Col. Recs. I. 23.
[2] Williams to the Commissioners of 1677. R. I. Tract, No. 14, p. 55.
[3] R. I. Col. Recs. I. 19 ; Staples, 28, 31.

grantees or first proprietors were not written out in full. In a second memorandum, however, which was dated October 8, 1638, the full names were substituted for initials.[1] The effect of the document was to transfer the land to the thirteen — of whom Williams was one — as an association or quasi-corporation, to be held temporarily in trust by them for the rising town. This is clear not only from the language of the memorandum, but from the statement of Williams in the confirmation of the grant which was issued in 1661.[2]

On October 8, 1638, the date of the second issue of the memorandum of the "initial deed," an agreement[3] was reached between the thirteen proprietors for their joint occupation and ultimate division of the lands of the "Pawtuxet purchase"; but the boundary line between these lands and those of the "Providence purchase" was not specified. In this agreement, moreover, unlike the "initial deed," no reference is made to the admission of others than the "thirteen" to the fellowship. The implication of the language is that it was already a closed body, that no admissions to it were intended. If this was the intention of the document, it gives us the earliest suggestion of the purpose of Harris and of the leading spirits, with the exception of Williams, among his associates. That purpose became clear at a later time, both in reference to the lands of Providence and Pawtuxet. It was to secure control for these thirteen men, their heirs and assigns, of both the Providence and Pawtuxet purchase, to exclude all others from a share in their management and in the returns that might come from the sale or lease of those lands. Williams's purpose was to indefinitely enlarge the fellowship, and admit to its advantages many more of those who might flee to Providence as a refuge from persecution. The ideal of Harris was that of the narrow, exclusive town proprietorship, which should enjoy the power and wealth that might come from the settlement within the grant of an increasing body of non-commoners. The ideal of Williams was that of an expanding democratic community, which should pre-

---

[1] Staples, 33.   [2] *Ibid.* 31; Richman, I. 90; Dorr, 13 *et seq.*
[3] Staples, 34, 576; Rider, 46.

serve the consciousness of the humanitarian impulses of its founders. With reference to the Pawtuxet lands an agreement which implied the triumph of Harris's ideal had already been reached, while the obscure statements of the deeds relating to the boundaries of these lands later revealed to Harris the possibility of enlarging their area till they should include approximately three hundred thousand acres, — nearly all of the northern half of the colony of Rhode Island.

By confirmatory deeds which Harris and his party procured[1] in 1659 from the Narragansett sachems who had succeeded Canonicus and Miantonomi, the expression "up streams without limits" was interpreted as a grant for all purposes of settlement of the immense tract extending twenty miles westward from Fox's Hill on Providence neck. On March 26, 1660, the town of Providence ordered its southern line run, in accordance with these grants, twenty miles to the westward.[2] Viewed from the standpoint of Rhode Island interests in general, this was a politic move, because it was calculated to thwart the operations of Massachusetts and Connecticut in the same region. But it was a land-grabbing scheme, the purpose of which was to extend the bounds of Providence and Pawtuxet far beyond what had been contemplated at the time of the purchase. As such, and because Harris and his party had already succeeded in establishing the domination of the thirteen proprietors in Providence, Williams passionately opposed the plan. This he did, notwithstanding the fact that he was one of the thirteen, and he and his heirs were destined to share in the gain. In the end the plan was defeated.

From the conditions which have just been outlined developed one of the most protracted and bitter controversies between proprietors and non-commoners which ever agitated a New England town. As political managers Harris and Olney, the leaders of the proprietary party, were superior to Williams and their other opponents. They consolidated the board of proprietors, controlled the town meeting, and through that the granting of land and the admission of freemen. Providence, under their lead and that of their succes-

[1] R. I. Col. Recs. I. 35.   [2] Early Recs. of Providence, II. 125, 127.

sors, developed in general accordance with the New England model, but, in spite of the teachings of Williams, with special emphasis on the proprietary element.

In 1640, controversies about land being on the increase, a plan of settling differences by compulsory arbitration was adopted.[1] A board of five arbitrators or "disposers" was chosen by the town meeting, not only to settle disputes, but to dispose of town lands, fix their bounds, and act as an executive board for the town. This board was the equivalent of selectmen and town justices elsewhere, being ultimately responsible to the town meeting for their acts. That resort to compulsion in civil cases was contemplated as possible is evident from the provision that, if the parties to a controversy refused to choose arbitrators, the board could compel them to do so or select them itself and then "see their determination performed." This cumbersome machinery furnished a weak substitute for government in a plantation of squatters, that was rent by internal strife and was adjacent to two colonies which were ready to absorb it. Its efficiency was soon tested.

In little more than a year after the institution of the arbitrators Samuel Gorton, who had recently been expelled from Plymouth and from Aquedneck, settled within the limits of Providence. The one consistent feature in his stormy career was his refusal to submit to the authority of any government which had not a charter from the English government. The association of Providence he knew had no strict binding force in law. He also found many newcomers complaining because they had not been admitted to town privileges, to what they considered fair access to the common land, or who were dissatisfied with the administration of justice. The monopoly of the proprietors was probably the source of the difficulty. Finding it impossible after two applications to secure admission into town fellowship[2] Gorton joined with the disaffected, the unenfranchised, and the result soon was such tumult that Williams feared he would have to retire to "little Patience," and thirteen persons, including

[1] Col. Recs. 27 *et seq.*
[2] Arnold, History of Rhode Island, I. 174.

Harris and Benedict Arnold, but not Williams, appealed
to Massachusetts[1] for protection. Providence was apparently saved from serious complications not by its system
of arbitration, but by the opportune removal of Gorton
to Shawomet. This experience convinced the leaders that
it was time to seek more effective authority for government, and helped to open the way for procuring a colony
charter.

The island of Aquedneck was settled by William Coddington, John Clarke, William Hutchinson, and others, who had
removed or been banished from Massachusetts as a result
of the Antinomian controversy. With the help of Williams
and Henry Vane the land was bought from the Indians.[2]
In March, 1638, a plantation covenant was formed at Providence by eighteen original proprietors, together with Randall
Holden.[3] It ran as follows: " We whose names are underwritten do here solemnly, in the presence of Jehovah, incorporate ourselves into a bodie Politick, and, as he shall help,
will submit our persons, lives and estates unto our Lord
Jesus Christ, the King of Kings, and Lord of Lords, and to
all those perfect and most absolute lawes of his given in
his holy word of truth, to be guided and judged thereby —
Ex. xxiv. 3, 4 ; 2 Chron. xi. 3 ; 2 Kings, xi. 17."

A marked difference appears between this and the Providence compact. The one adopted by Coddington and his
associates is profoundly religious, even Mosaic in character.
Its language and the biblical quotations show that its authors
considered themselves to be in a way reproducing the covenant between Jehovah and the chosen people. Submission
is made, not to laws of their own making, but to those of
God. Nothing is said about submission in civil things only.
So far as the language of this covenant goes, one must infer
that those who framed it were men of the genuine Massachusetts type, and might have intended to form an association in which the civil and ecclesiastical power should be
united, — an Hebrew commonwealth. The impression is
strengthened when we find that William Coddington was

[1] Narr. Club, VI. 141 ; R. I. Hist. Colls. II. 191–193 ; Richman, I. 112.
[2] Col. Recs. I. 45.   [3] *Ibid.* I. 52.

elected their chief magistrate with the title of Judge, and that he covenanted to administer justice according to the laws of God, while the settlers agreed to honor him according to the same laws. At the same time, by the promise of the judge, recognition was given to the rights and privileges of the body politic, which later were to be "ratified according to God." We are brought back again into the modern era by the next entry, to the effect that William Aspinwall was chosen secretary and William Dyer clerk of the body.

Soon after the adoption of this covenant the settlers established themselves at Pocasset, near the northern end of the island. There, until April, 1639, they were a town and germinal colony in one. They were a body of associated *de facto* freemen, calling themselves sometimes a body politic, sometimes a society. Their assembly they called a "general meeting upon the public notice," or a "general meeting of the body." It was a town meeting, passing orders like that at Providence or elsewhere, about the laying out and sale of lots, care of the unimproved land, locating the meeting-house, repairing highways, building a mill, local police, and other similar affairs. It controlled its own membership under an order reserving to "the body" the right to receive inhabitants or freemen. But no express religious test was attached to membership, a feature of their plan which later opened the way for their union with Providence. Trained bands were established, trainings and the assize of arms were ordered, functions which, together with the independence of the settlement, suggest the colony more than the town.

Until January, 1639, the only officials referred to in the records of this plantation, besides those already mentioned, were two [1] treasurers and a marshal. Then three elders were elected, "to assist the Judge in the Execution of Justice and Judgment for the regulating and ordering of all offences and offenders, and for the drawing up and determining of all such Rules and Laws as shall be according to God, which may conduce to the good and welfare of the Commonweale,

[1] Col. Recs. I. 63 *et seq.*

. . ." Once every quarter the judge and elders should submit their acts and rules to "the body" for its review, and those which it disapproved should be repealed. It thus appears that it was the intention to allow the judge and his councillors or associates little discretion and to keep them under the close scrutiny of the community. Shortly after the issue of this order the officials were increased by the election of a constable and sergeant, the former to present cases of manifest breaches of the law, and the latter to keep the prison, and serve the judges like a modern sheriff.[1]

Within four months after the eldership was created, the elders—Easton, Coggshall, and Brenton—together with Coddington, the judge, and five others, removed to the southern end of the island, where they founded the plantation of Newport. There the leading settlers, among whom a relatively strong aristocratic spirit prevailed, signed a compact[2] in which they agreed to 'bear proportionable charges, and to abide by the decisions reached by the majority vote of judge and elders. The former was given a double voice. The wording of this document would indicate that greater discretion was to be allowed the magistrates than in the Pocasset settlement. The strong Mosaic element was also omitted from the Newport compact, but a later entry shows that the government was still to be administered according to the word of God. Soon provision was made for an annual meeting of the magistrates and "freemen," which should be called the "general court"[3] or assembly. The meeting of the magistrates appears as a "particular Court." The suggestion of the colony in this is striking.

The abandonment of Pocasset by its magistrates, though a majority of the incorporators and admitted members were left, necessitated a new covenant and the reëstablishment of government there. The covenant which was adopted at Pocasset on April 30, 1639, differed remarkably from the one of the year previous. "We . . . acknowledge ourselves the legall subjects of his Majestie King Charles, and in his name doe hereby binde ourzelves into a civill body politicke, unto his lawes according to matters of justice."[4] A possible

[1] Col. Recs. I. 65.   [2] *Ibid.* 87, 91.   [3] *Ibid.* 97, 98.   [4] *Ibid.* 70.

explanation of this change has been found[1] in the appearance among the signers of this compact of the names of Samuel Gorton, John Wickes, Sampson Shotton, and Robert Potter, men who were afterwards among the original purchasers of Shawomet or Warwick. Whether or not Gorton's influence was sufficient to produce the change, it is true that his view of the proper attitude of colonies toward the crown found recognition in the new Pocasset compact. Another indication of English influence was the earliest provision for jury trial which appears among the Narragansett plantations. The agreement was formed for only one year, and for that term officers were chosen. Thus we have on Aquedneck two small plantations, joint owners of the soil of the island, but otherwise independent of each other and of all other colonies ; the one acknowledging subjection to the king and the other recognizing no earthly superior.

But in November, 1639, the Newport settlers opened the way for the reunion of the two settlements by acknowledging King Charles as their sovereign, and voting to ask Mr. Vane to help procure a patent for the island. By this act theocracy on the island was abandoned and Newport practically announced its willingness to accept the secularized democratic system which was in vogue in the neighboring town. In March, 1640, ten of the leading inhabitants of Pocasset appeared at Newport and desired to be reunited with that body. Gorton and Mrs. Hutchinson, however, were opposed to the reunion, and Gorton and Wickes were not made freemen, but remained simply as inhabitants. The other friends of Gorton joined in the application[2] made at Newport. Their offer was accepted and the petitioners were received as " freemen of this Body." But by that act " the Bodye " became something more than Newport, with its land extending a few miles to the north. "The Body" came now to include all the inhabitants of the island. But they were differently organized from what they were when all lived together at Pocasset. Now there were two settlements or plantations, which by their union formed a colony.

[1] Brayton, Defence of Samuel Gorton, R. I. Tract, No. 17, p. 49.
[2] Col. Recs. I. 100 ; Brayton, op. cit. 53.

By virtue also of that union each plantation appears distinctly as a town, and is so called in the records. The name Pocasset was at the same time changed to Portsmouth.

The title of judge also disappears, and the chief magistrate of the colony receives the designation of governor. Provision was made for a deputy governor and four assistants,[1] also for two treasurers, a secretary, and a sergeant. A constable was chosen for each town. Five [2] men were selected to lay out the lands of Portsmouth and three to lay out those of Newport. A line was drawn between the two towns. It was ordered that each town [3] should transact its own special business, and that the magistrates of each should hold monthly courts for the trial of petty cases. All officials were elected. The governor and two assistants should be residents of one town, the deputy and the two remaining assistants should live in the other town. Provision was made for two annual sessions of the general court — that held in the spring being the court of election — and for a court of quarter sessions. An elaborate system of trainings was also established. These orders reveal the fact that the Massachusetts government was imitated in all save its religious test and its failure to expressly acknowledge submission to the crown. In 1641 [4] the government of this colony was solemnly declared to be democratic or popular, because the legislative power and the authority to choose officers to execute the laws resided in the freemen, or the majority of them, orderly assembled. By an order of September 19, 1642, the sale of lands on Aquedneck to outside jurisdictions or to Dutch settlers was forbidden. In 1644 the colony assumed the name Rhode Island, and with its simple democratic system and its two towns it continued to exist till 1647.

The origin and relations of Warwick, the fourth among the group of Narragansett towns, cannot be understood apart from the career of Samuel Gorton and the group of men who attached themselves to him. They exhibited more of the

---

[1] Col. Recs. I. 101 *et seq.*

[2] Later, because of the neglect of two, the duty was intrusted to the remaining three. *Ibid.* 109.

[3] *Ibid.* 106.   [4] *Ibid.* 112.

spirit of the English Levellers than did the settlers of Providence or Aquedneck. Gorton's mind and utterances were
saturated with the ideas and images of the Hebrew poets
and prophets. The imprecatory psalms and the Apocalypse
must have been frequent subjects of his perusal. From the
few mystical and confused writings which he has left it is
impossible to form a definite idea of his religious belief. But
it seems to have resembled in many of its features the inspirationism of Anne Hutchinson and her followers, and it was
at the time of the excitement over her preaching that Gorton
had arrived in New England. Baptists have also laid some
claim to kinship with him. He looked upon the Massachusetts churches as akin in spirit to the papal and other state-
church systems of Europe,[1] and therefore as wholly blind to
the true spiritual significance of Christ's kingdom. With a
tone of contempt worthy of the Antinomian prophetess, he
and his followers told the Massachusetts leaders that their
salvation was a shadow rather than a substance, that their
ordinances were vain,[2] and that the main object of their system
was to aggrandize the magistrates and clergy. They were
bringing forth nothing but fruit unto death ; true holiness
and the spiritual life in its real beauty lay not within their
" jurisdiction." The intolerance of the Puritans came in
for its due share of condemnation, as the strongest evidence
of their essentially worldly spirit. The use of the oath, to
which they so often resorted, was denounced as the assumption of a divine prerogative.

Gorton himself was a constant reader of the Bible, and often
acted as lay preacher, both in Old and New England. He
was ardent and contentious, always ready to champion the
cause of the weak and oppressed. He also firmly refused to
recognize the validity of any of the colonial governments which
were based simply on agreement, and insisted that the only
sufficient basis of authority was a grant from the English government. His opposition to the intolerance and priestcraft
of Massachusetts brought him into conflict with that colony,
though he never questioned the legality of her government.
His sympathy with the weak, together with his contempt for

---

[1] Simplicities Defence, 25, 27, in Force, Tracts, IV.   [2] Winthrop, II. 175.

magistrates who could trace their authority to nothing more than a civil or social contract, brought him into collision with the various plantations about Narragansett bay. When, therefore, he established a settlement at Shawomet or Warwick, on the western shore of the bay, powers of government were not at first assumed. Its only original and express bond of union was an agreement to settle disputes by means of arbitration.

The difficulties which beset Gorton and his associates in the founding of their plantation admirably illustrate the extreme individualism of the settlers about Narragansett bay, and the delicate relations under which they stood both toward one another and toward the neighboring colonies. After a brief residence in Massachusetts, and when the reaction there against the Hutchinson-Wheelwright faction was gaining irresistible headway, Gorton had sought refuge at Plymouth. But there he took up the cause of one Ellen Aldridge, who he thought was being persecuted for some slight offence committed in church.[1] For his conduct in connection with this Gorton was bound over to appear before the next general court. During the customary informal hearing which occurred there, one of the assistants, who of course was also a judge, at the request of the governor began to state the case against Gorton. Thereupon Gorton bade him come down from the judges' seat, and appealed to the people to stand for their liberties and not act as parties and judges in the same case. For this justifiable, though passionate, protest against the vicious judicial procedure of the time he was sentenced to banishment, and amid the severities of winter removed to Pocasset.

[1] Winslow, Hypocrisie Unmasked, 66–68, states that the court had ordered her out of the plantation because of offensive speeches and conduct. The Records (I. 100) state that she was required to appear, but absented herself and was conveyed away by the help of Gorton and his wife, "whereby the Court was deluded." It was therefore ordered that, if found, she should be corrected as the bench thought fit, and be sent from constable to constable to the place whence she came. Gorton states that, though a respectable woman, the court desired to expel her as a vagabond, because she smiled in the congregation; and that to escape the shame of this she fled into the woods, remaining there several days and part of the nights, so as not to be seen in the town.

During his residence of about eighteen months at Plymouth Gorton had apparently been attaching to himself friends who were prepared to share his opinions and his wanderings. In the course of a sojourn of about the same period of time on Aquedneck he added to their number. After the two plantations on the island had been united, Gorton and his friend Wickes violated all the proprieties before the court at Newport, and for what occurred on this occasion Gorton was whipped.[1] Years after he wrote that he respected the government of Plymouth, for he understood that they acted under commission from England, but those on Aquedneck had set up for themselves, and " I thought myself as fit and able to govern myself and family and perform the office of neighborhood as any that then was upon Rhode Island." To Gorton's experience at Providence and his subsequent removal to Shawomet reference has already been made.

In January, 1643, Gorton and his associates extinguished, as they thought, the Indian claim to the tract called Shawomet, on which they now proposed to settle. It was located on the west side of Narragansett bay, between Gaspee point and Warwick neck, and comprised the larger part of what were the later towns of Warwick and Coventry. A deed for the land was procured from Miantonomi, the Narragansett sachem, acting on behalf of the tribe whose rights of possession extended over this region. The deed was witnessed by Pumham, the local or subordinate chief.[2] Gorton was now clearly outside any English colony the jurisdiction of which seemed at all likely to be enforced. But he was not to remain unmolested.

William Arnold and three associates of Pawtuxet, who in 1642 had put themselves under the protection of Massachusetts in order to escape from the molestation of Gorton,[3] were active enemies of the Shawomet settlers. Arnold and his friends had bought land from Sacononoco,[4] the chief of

<hr />

[1] Winslow, *op. cit.* 52 ; Brayton, 55 ; Gorton, Letter to Morton, 8 ; Arnold, I. 170 ; Palfrey, II. 120 n.

[2] Winthrop, II. 144.   Colls. R. I. Hist. Soc. II. 254.

[3] Mass. Col. Recs. II. 26.   [4] Arnold, History of Rhode Island, I. 177.

Pawtuxet, without the consent of Miantonomi, and were
thus directly interested in proving, if possible, the independence of the local chiefs.   Benedict Arnold, acting as interpreter, soon brought Pumham and Sacononoco to Boston.[1]
Pumham declared that he had been forced by Miantonomi,
under the influence of Gorton, to sign the deed for Shawomet, and the two chiefs asked to be received under the
protection of Massachusetts.   Miantonomi was now summoned to Boston, but naturally could not prove to the
satisfaction of the magistrates that the two chiefs were
his subjects.   Others, including Benedict Arnold, affirmed
that they were not such.   The relations which existed,
especially since the decline of the Narragansett tribe had
begun, were in reality loose and hard to define, while the
interests of the Pawtuxet men led them to actively support
the claims of the local chiefs.

At this juncture, as usual, Gorton by his assertiveness
played into the hands of his foes.   He and twelve of his
associates, says Winthrop, " sent a writing to our court of
four sheets of paper, full of reproaches against our magistrates, elders and churches, of familistical and absurd
opinions, and therein they justified their purchase of the
sachems' land, and professed to maintain it to the death."
Passions already ran so high, that the possibility even of an
armed conflict was suggested in words.

Not unnaturally the general court, at the session of May,
1643,[2] ordered Humphrey Atherton and Edward Tomlins
to accompany William Arnold on a visit to Warwick, " to
understand how things were," and to bring back an Indian
named Will, if possible.   On the same day the magistrates,
together with the deputies of the towns along the southern
border, were appointed a committee to treat with Pumham
and Sacononoco concerning their submission to Massachusetts,
" and to receive them under our jurisdiction, if they see
cause, and to warne any to desist which shall disturb them."
About the close of June both these chiefs signed a form of
submission to the government of Massachusetts, and its
protection was extended over them.   They at the same

[1] Winthrop, II. 144 *et seq.*   [2] Mass. Col. Recs. II. 35, 38, 40.

time professed their willingness to receive religious instruction. Land-jobbing, missionary labors, and defence against
Indians and heretics, in a region far south of the limits
of Massachusetts, thus went conveniently hand in hand.
Gorton, in consequence, found himself within the grasp of a
stronger power than any he had before encountered.

Later in the year Gorton and his associates were summoned to appear before the general court at Boston. They
refused to go and denied the jurisdiction claimed, and this
denial was accompanied by more defiant, or, as Winthrop
calls them, more " blasphemous," messages. Massachusetts,
having received from the Commissioners of the United
Colonies permission to deal with her new claim as she
saw fit,[1] sent a commission — Captain Cook, Lieutenant
Atherton, and Captain Edward Johnson — to Shawomet,
accompanied by forty soldiers, to bring the offenders to Boston, where they might be tried for religious error and for
their alleged violation of the rights of Massachusetts citizens. The commissioners and soldiers, on their approach to
Shawomet, were warned away, but replied by threatening
an attack if they were not admitted to a conference. By
the interposition of some Providence men a truce was concluded and the Gortonists offered to submit to arbitration.
A messenger was sent to Boston for further instructions,
but came back with word from the magistrates and elders
that arbitration would not be allowed, because the Gortonists were not a state, but were under the jurisdiction of
Massachusetts, because of their blasphemous writings and
because the persons from Providence to whom they wished
to submit the case for judgment were not recognized as
belonging to any government. Upon the reception of this
message the siege of the house in which the Gortonists
were was begun. Gorton in his *Defence* gives a very full
account of this, and charges the Massachusetts men with
bloodthirsty cruelty, but these are denied seriatim by
Winslow.

The capture was effected without bloodshed and the
prisoners were taken to Boston. There they were tried on

[1] Plymouth Recs. IX. 12 ; Winthrop, II. 165.

charges of heresy and sedition.   On the first Sabbath which
they spent in Boston, Gorton, at his own request, was allowed
to speak in church after Cotton had concluded his sermon.
He then argued that all the ministers, ordinances, and sacraments of Massachusetts were human inventions intended
for display.   In his examination Gorton claimed that Shawomet was outside the jurisdiction of Massachusetts, but he
did not show his Indian deed.   It was answered that, if so,
it lay either within Plymouth or Connecticut, and they had
yielded their rights in the controversy to Massachusetts.
The religious and political doctrines of Gorton's letters were
gone over, but he could not be brought to deny the authority
of legal government backed by charter from England.   His
views, however, were confused and contradictory.   The
elders made a special effort to controvert and reclaim all the
accused, but without success.   The magistrates then voted
that Gorton should be executed, but the deputies were opposed
to this.   Gorton and six other were finally sentenced to
imprisonment with hard labor.   They were dispersed among
the different towns of the colony, and were forbidden to
depart therefrom or to utter their doctrines, except to an
elder or one licensed by the magistrates.   Each prisoner was
also to wear iron shackles on one leg.   But the following
year — 1644 — it was voted to set the prisoners at liberty and
to banish them from the colony.[1]   The reason for this was, that
their heresies were found to be spreading.   Massachusetts
was thus forced to confess its failure in this matter.   The
Gortonists took refuge at Aquedneck, where their sufferings
since their expulsion gained for them a welcome.   They at
once renewed intercourse with the Narragansetts and convinced them that in the wars in old England the Gortonogas
had conquered the Wattaconogas, or Massachusetts party.
Miantonomi had also been put to death, partly because of
his connection with Gorton.   The Narragansetts were thus
induced to put themselves by solemn declaration[2] under the

[1] Winthrop, II. 179, 188.
[2] Copy in Gorton's Defence, 90, signed by Pessicus and Canonicus, and
dated April 19, 1645.   It included the whole Narragansett country and its
people.   They were called subjects.

protection of the crown. Soon after Gorton and Holden
left for England to carry the submission of the Narragansetts. In 1646 they returned, bringing an order [1] from the
Commissioners of Plantations requiring Massachusetts to
allow Gorton and his friends to land and pass through its
territory to Warwick and settle there. Massachusetts had
however taken possession of the land in question, and in
1645 granted it to about twenty families from Braintree.
But on the ground that Warwick lay within its limits
John Brown, one of the magistrates of Plymouth, had interfered and stopped the settlers from Braintree, when they
were going to take possession. The magistrates of Plymouth did not sanction Brown's act,[2] neither did they renounce the claim which they had made to Warwick. It was
with difficulty that Holden, in 1646, and Gorton, in 1648,
obtained permission to pass through Massachusetts. Massachusetts meantime had sent Winslow to England as her representative, furnished with protests. Winslow appeared before
the commissioners, and presented the case of Massachusetts.
But, though sympathy with the political and ecclesiastical
system of Massachusetts was expressed, no attempt was
made to settle the question of jurisdiction over Shawomet.
It was left to be determined on the place, when the boundaries could be ascertained. The question was not settled
till it became involved with that of the boundary of Providence Plantations as a whole. The Gortonists meantime
held possession of Warwick, and the English government
prohibited molestation of them by any of the neighboring
colonies.

Had it not been for outside pressure, these four communities might have remained separate for an indefinite time.
The region about Narragansett bay, as occupied by them,
possessed no geographical unity, and causes proceeding from
that source tended to keep them apart. The bay was the
natural boundary between Connecticut and Plymouth, and,
had it not been for the specifications of its charter, Massachusetts might very properly have extended its bounds
to the northern extremity of the bay. Thus the tendency

[1] Winthrop, II. 332, 342.   [2] *Ibid.* 308.

was for Providence to be absorbed by Massachusetts, Warwick by Connecticut, and Aquedneck by Plymouth. They all were menaced by stronger and somewhat ambitious neighbors. As they clung to their respective shores, the danger that they would lose independent existence increased.

The spirit of individualism was so strong that it operated, in connection with geographical tendencies, to keep the plantations apart. The inhabitants of them all, under one form or another, were in revolt against authority. Government from a remote centre seemed to them oppressive, and they demanded that positive restraint in all forms should be reduced to a minimum. The influence of the church and clergy was lacking or seriously weakened in all these communities. Individual choice, caprice, or indifference were given unusually free play. The tendency was to divide into smaller groups, rather than to combine into larger ones. When the elders and magistrates of Massachusetts heard of the disputes which went on in their assemblies, of their failure to organize churches, and of the ideas of individual liberty which were held, they called it anarchy, and considered the Narragansett plantations fit only for subjection and discipline.

Events growing out of these conditions gradually made it evident to the plantations themselves that union of some kind was necessary to the preservation of their distinct existence. These events were: the encroachments of Massachusetts as evidenced by the surrender of the Pawtuxet men to her, and the submission made to her by Pumham; the imminence of an Indian war in 1643, in which event the Narragansett country would be most exposed of all to attack; the refusal of the United Colonies, though on the eve of this Indian war, to receive Rhode Island as a member of their confederacy; the claims advanced by Plymouth in 1644, under the Bradford patent, to jurisdiction over Aquedneck.[1] The attitude of opposition on the part of the neighboring colonies was strengthened by the fact that nearly all the settlers in the Narragansett towns were exiles from their own borders.

[1] Hypocrisie Unmasked, 83; Instructions to John Brown, Arnold, I. 159.

The first step which the plantations took toward union, and at the same time toward the rescue of themselves and their principles from destruction, was the despatch of Roger Williams, in 1643, to England to procure a charter. In March, 1644, the patent was granted, and with it Williams returned to the colony the following September. The charter was issued by the Earl of Warwick, the governor-in-chief and lord high admiral of the plantations, together with the Commissioners of Plantations, both of whom derived their authority from an ordinance of the Lords and Commons. Of this board Viscount Say and Sele, the younger Vane, and Samuel Vassall were members, all of whom, together with Warwick, had been interested in the colonization of New England. But among the eighteen members Vane and Cromwell were the two who had most sympathy with the ideas of Williams and the experiment in religious freedom, the faint beginnings of which it was his desire to cherish. The majority of the board was much more inclined to approve the polity of Massachusetts.

While Williams was negotiating for the charter, influences were brought to bear by Thomas Welde and Hugh Peters to thwart his plan. They secured the signatures of nine of the eighteen commissioners to a document, the purpose of which was to add to the territory of Massachusetts all the land [1] about Narragansett bay, including the Island of Aquedneck. But as the ordinance creating the Commissioners of Plantations required, for such transactions, the assent of a majority of the board, the so-called Narragansett patent was never legally issued. In 1645, however, it was sent over to Massachusetts, though that colony never clearly made it the basis of a claim to jurisdiction.

The patent [2] which was procured by Williams designated the settlements collectively as Providence Plantations in the Narragansett bay in New England, and purported to incor-

---

[1] New England Genealogical Reg. XI. 41 ; R. I. Recs. I. 133, 458 ; Mass. Recs. III. 49 ; Arnold, I. 118 ; Palfrey, II. 122 n. ; R. I. Hist. Coll. II. 250 ; Proc. Mass. Hist. Soc., June, 1862 ; Richman, I. 180. The so-called patent bore the date, December 10, 1643.

[2] Col. Recs. I. 143.

porate them under that name. In the most general terms it declared that these were bounded by Massachusetts on the north, Plymouth on the east, and the Narragansett country and Pequot or Pawcatuck river on the west.[1] It also referred expressly to the towns of Providence, Portsmouth, and Newport. It gave the plantations the authority to rule themselves and future settlers within their limits by such form of civil government as by the consent of the majority they should find most suitable to their condition. The separation of church from state was implicitly recognized in the patent by the exclusive use of the term " civil government." The only restriction laid upon the plantations was the one of such general conformity to English law as their condition and government would admit. The commissioners also reserved the right, which was theirs from the outset, to adjust the relations between this and the other colonies in such way as they should consider to be for the advantage of the realm and dominions.

This is noteworthy as the earliest attempt to incorporate a colony on the place, but it afforded no immediate guaranties against the kingship in England, though it did give some protection against other colonies as long as the government which issued it maintained itself. But it imposed no government or governing body on the Narragansett settlements, and left it wholly to them to decide whether or not they would unite and organize a government under the charter. This all was in keeping with the character and methods of Williams, as well as with those of most of the patentees concerned. Three years passed after the charter reached America before the tendencies toward union became so strong as to lead to the organization of government under it.

In May, 1647, a court of election, attended by the majority of the freemen of the colony, was held at Portsmouth.[2] This body included members from Warwick, as well as from the other towns, and it was voted that Warwick should have the same privileges as Providence. By Providence,[3] and

---

[1] Pubs. of Narr. Club, VI, Letter of Williams to Major John Mason. R. I. Recs. I. 458.

[2] Col. Recs. I. 147 et seq.   [3] Staples, Annals of Providence, 61.

perhaps by the other towns, representatives were chosen to
attend the court, but in addition to these the freemen attended numerously in their own right; [1] it was both a primary
and a representative assembly. So far as Rhode Island was
concerned, it is probable that the towns, rather than the
joint or colony government, were represented. Scarcely any
evidence of that government appears in the proceedings of
the assembly. By one of its acts [2] Portsmouth and Newport
were empowered to pass and enforce local orders either
jointly or apart. But it seems that, after a vote in Newport
favorable to continued joint action, Portsmouth voted unanimously to act apart. Thus the joint government on Rhode
Island disappeared, except so far as it was revived by the
Coddington episode. The colony then which was organized
in 1647 was formed by the union of a people which had previously for a decade been organized as towns. Providence
instructed its delegates to the Portsmouth assembly, reserving to itself full power to elect and control its own officers,
to transact all its town business, to try all cases save those
which should be reserved for the colony courts, and to keep [3]
its officers and their powers distinct from those of the colony.
Utterances of this character, when compared with any which
proceeded from towns in the other colonies, illustrate the
peculiarity of the Rhode Island system.

By the colonists in court of election at Portsmouth the
charter was accepted. This was done by means of an express
"engagement," [4] which was embodied in the preamble to the
code of laws. "Wee whose names are here underwritten, doe
engage ourselves to the uttmost of our estates and strength
to maintayne the authority and to enjoy the Libertie granted
to us by our Charter, in the extent of itt according to the
Letter." While acknowledging the source whence their
patent had come, yet, since it gave them a free hand, they expressly formed a social compact : "We do joyntlie agree to
incorporate ourselves, and soe to remaine a Body Politicke by

---

[1] Staples, Annals of Providence, 64. One of the orders of the general
court provided that the inhabitants of Portsmouth and Newport might choose
the officers of the Island, but that that should not be a precedent for the future.
Col. Recs. I. 150.   [2] *Ibid*. 206 ; Arnold, I. 214.
    [3] Col. Recs. I. 43.   [4] *Ibid*. 147, 156. Arnold, I. 202.

the authoritie thereof, and therefore do declare to own ourselves and one another to be members of the same Body, and
to have right to the Freedome and priviledges thereof, etc."
By virtue of the same authority they declared themselves a
democracy, "that is to say, a Government held by ye free
and voluntarie consent of all, or the greater parte of the
free Inhabitants."

Though Roger Williams was the agent who procured the
charter, Rhode Island seems to have taken the lead in the
organization of government under it.   This appears in part
from the fact that, after the above engagement and declaration had been adopted, a code of laws, selected from those of
England so far as they were known or thought to be adapted
to the conditions of the place, was accepted, and this code
seems to have been prepared and submitted by the islanders.[1]
Providence expressed in advance its assent to "that model
that hath lately been shown unto us by our worthy friends
of the Island."   To these "Lawes" was prefixed a reaffirma-
tion of the clause in Magna Carta which prohibited arbitrary
arrests and punishments, and a declaration that in this case
the law of the land (*lex terrae*) was the law ratified and confirmed by the general assembly of the colony.   That alone
was declared to be law in the colony which was made such
by assemblies called and held according to the charter.   This
meant the exclusion of English law when unconfirmed by the
general assembly, and a claim that the colony courts should
have the exclusive right to administer justice.   Only legally
constituted officers — meaning those of the colony — could
execute the laws.   The principle that public officials should
be supported by salaries and fined when they refused to
serve was also affirmed.   After reciting the more familiar
provisions of the English criminal law and those for the
probate of wills, the code concluded with provisions concerning the organization and powers of the courts of the colony,
the powers of judicial officers, and a few clauses about the
jury and pleading.

[1] Col. Recs. I. 42, 147, 157 ; Staples, 62. We may see here the influence of
Coddington and a few others on the Island who had been magistrates in
Massachusetts.

No act was passed creating a general court, but the assembly which was called together to organize the government of the colony was assumed to be that body. In the legislation of May, 1648, it appears as a representative body, and continues to be such thereafter. It consisted of six deputies chosen from each town, and was frequently called the "representative committee," as well as a "general court of commissioners."[1] In it the governor and assistants appear to have had no seats, and it was distinct from the May assembly or court of election, in which these and the other officials of the colony were elected. Two general courts were thus in existence : the general court of election, which was attended by outgoing magistrates and freemen, and the general court of commissioners, which was representative. They met in different towns in succession. Though, as in the other corporate colonies, authority proceeded wholly from the freemen through election, the executive and legislature were kept distinct.[2] Under such an arrangement there could be no question of a negative voice, and the political power of the executive would be seriously limited. The term "freeman" approximated also much more closely to inhabitant than it did in the other[3] colonies.

The prominence of the towns in this colony, as well as the prevailing jealousy of delegated power, is reflected in the method of legislation prescribed by the general court of 1647. It was a crude combination of initiative and referen-

[1] Col. Recs. I. 209, 228, 229 ; October, 1650. "It is ordered that a committee of six men of each Towne shall be chosen out of each Towne to meet foure dayes before the next Generall Courte, and to have the full power of the Generall Assemblie. . . ." The body here referred to met under the name of "Generall Assembly," October 26, and under the authority of this order passed laws. Among those was one "that the representative committee for the Colonie shall always consist of six discreet, able men, and chosen out of each Towne for the transacting of the affaires of the Commonwealth." The Records contain entries of their sessions, usually under the name of "general court of commissioners," till the issue of the royal charter.

[2] The meaning of this statement is, that the president and assistants had officially no status in the general court. The president was sometimes chosen moderator, assistants were not infrequently chosen as members of the general court ; but these were positions wholly distinct from that which they officially held.

[3] There is a list of the freemen, as they were in 1655, in Col. Recs. I. 299.

dum. Bills might originate in the towns, as well as in the general court. If in the former, and all the four towns should approve, the bill should be submitted to a "Committee[1] for the General Courte," consisting of six members chosen from each town. In this provision possibly appears the first sign of the general court in representative form. However, by this body of twenty-four the bill or bills were to be ordered to stand till the next general assembly, or court of election. It then might make the bills permanent law or reject them. When legislation was initiated in the general court, it should be submitted to the towns, discussed and voted on by them, and their votes returned to the general court. If the majority, apparently of the popular vote taken by towns, was favorable to the legislation, it should stand as law till confirmed or repealed by the next general assembly. At first no time limit was set within which the towns must act ; but in 1650 and 1658 it was enacted that they must send in their votes to the general recorder within ten days after the bills had been read to them. In 1660 the time limit was extended to three months.[2] This experiment continued in operation until the issue of the royal charter. Then the towns began to assume the subordinate position of administrative units which they had held from the first in the other corporate colonies, and the particularistic conditions of the early time to an extent disappeared.

In the code[3] to which reference has been made, the number and titles of officers of the colony were specified. They were the president, four assistants, a general recorder, general treasurer, and general sergeant. Later an attorney-general and solicitor-general were added. Of the board of four assistants one should be a resident in each town. In the code it was also declared that these officials should be annually chosen in the general assembly, by which was meant the court of election. For president, recorder, treasurer, and sergeant each town should present a nominee, and he who received the majority of votes should be declared elected. For the office of assistant each town should present two names, and the one who received the majority of

[1] Col. Recs. I. 149.   [2] *Ibid.* 229, 401, 429.   [3] *Ibid.* 191.

votes should be elected. Voting should be by ballot. By another clause it was provided that the military officers [1] should be chosen in each town by the majority of the inhabitants thereof. By these enactments the universality of tenure by election was secured. The principle thus guarantied was stated in the preamble of an order of 1647 [2] requiring officials whose terms had expired to surrender the public records in their possession. "And now forasmuch as the choice of all the officers that are to be employed in this Colonie, like the Colonies about us, (occurs) once a year, whereby it may be easily collected that he that hath an office or charge this yeare may have none another."

In the records the functions of officials to which reference is chiefly made are judicial. The president, whose title was later changed to governor, together with the assistants, constituted the court [3] of trials, the highest regular tribunal of the colony. It met in two sessions annually, one of which was held just after the court of election and the other in October. Its jurisdiction appears to have been substantially the same as that of the court of assistants in other colonies. That the board also performed the ordinary administrative functions is also certain, though little positive evidence of the fact appears in the records. The president was empowered by writ to the general sergeant to notify the colony of the approach of a general assembly. There is also express evidence that he called special sessions of the general court. Once in 1658 and twice the following year a "general council" met. [4] It consisted of the president, the assistants, and certain local officers, in one case wardens of Providence and Warwick. There is no record of the creation of such a body, or of its meeting subsequent to the three times mentioned. The business it then did was executive, such as a board of governor and assistants might regularly have done. [5]

---

[1] Col. Recs. I. 153.
[2] Ibid. 205.
[3] Ibid. 194, 195.
[4] Ibid. 404; Arnold, I. 270.

[5] It ordered the attorney-general to present the offences of one Anthony Parrant; to order the arrest and trial of Pumham and other Indians alleged to be guilty of riot, and of still other Indians who were charged with robbery at Pawtuxet. It also provided for publishing the proclamation of Richard Cromwell as Lord Protector.

The reasonable inference would seem to be that we have in
these entries a fragment of the records of the magistrates as
an executive board.   Whether or not that be true, one
should not infer from the absence of such records that
Providence Plantations had no executive.   The fact rather
would be that they kept no records of administrative action,
or, if they did keep them, they have been lost.   The same is
true to a considerable extent of the other corporate colonies,
and we are left in the same position with reference to them
all as that we should have occupied in the case of Massachusetts if Governor Winthrop had not written his *Journal.*

As in the other corporate colonies, the assembly of Providence Plantations kept resorting to committees for the performance of executive duties, like those which might have
fallen to a board of assistants.   In 1655 a committee was
appointed to treat with the Narragansett sachems, because
the latter contrary to agreement had deprived the inhabitants of Rhode Island of the use of grass on [1] Conanicut.
The same year a committee was appointed to consider how
to prevent the sale of ammunition to the Indians.   Treaties
with the natives were usually negotiated by such committees.[2]
Committees were frequently chosen to frame letters to be
sent to England or to the other colonies.[3]   In 1657 a committee was appointed to take the bonds of William Harris
and his son to perform the orders of the court concerning
the charge of high treason which had been preferred against
him.[4]   In 1660 a committee was instructed to maturely consider the purchase of Narragansett territory by men from
Massachusetts and to report thereon ; a little later another
was selected to treat with the purchasers.[5]   In 1661 a committee was appointed to raise money in the towns to send to
John Clarke, the agent in England, and in 1663 another committee was engaged on the same subject.[6]   Not infrequently
also committees were chosen to audit the accounts of officials;[7] occasionally also to consider petitions before the

[1] Col. Recs. I. 319.
[2] *Ibid.* 320, 328.
[3] *Ibid.* 321, 420–421, 433, 438, 448, 468, 496.
[4] *Ibid.* 365.
[5] *Ibid.* 429, 435.
[6] Col. Recs. I. 448, 505.
[7] *Ibid,* 331, 339, 340, 355, 358, 442.

assembly and formulate a course of action upon them.[1]   Committees also continued to be a prominent feature in Rhode Island government after 1664.

Unity in the colony, so far as it had been attained, was soon interrupted.   William Coddington, as the leading representative of the aristocratic tendencies[2] which existed at Newport, had for some time been planning the separation of the island from the mainland settlements.   Not only in 1644, but in 1648, the year after the union of the Narragansett towns had been effected, he had proposed an alliance of the island with the United Colonies[3] of New England.   But the commissioners refused to agree to the proposal, unless the island came in as a part either of Plymouth or of Massachusetts.   After the second refusal Coddington resolved to carry his demand to England, and, if possible, to secure a commission as proprietary governor of the island.   This plan was promptly executed.[4]   With the assistance, it has been conjectured, of Hugh Peters, Coddington, in April, 1651, procured a life commission to govern Rhode Island and Conanicut.   It empowered him to administer the law, to raise forces for defence, and upon nominations by the freeholders of the towns to appoint not more than six councillors and tender the engagement both to them and to the electors. In order to procure this commission Coddington represented himself as the discoverer and purchaser of the two islands involved, a statement in which he was as much in error as he was in his estimate of the reception with which his move was likely to meet from his fellow-colonists.

It is true that the colony government had resulted from a union of the people of the four towns, established under a charter which was merely permissive.   It was a federation which had originated in the consent of the parties who formed it.   It had existed but a few years, and was beset by many perils.   It was of course possible that the union might be broken and the parts fall asunder.   But, if they did so,

---

[1] Col. Recs. 473.   [2] Richman, II. 4.   [3] Plymouth Recs. IX. 23, 110.
[4] 4 Mass. Hist. Coll. VI. 321 ; VII. 281 ; Colonial Papers, 1579–1660 ; Turner, William Coddington in Colonial Affairs, R. I. Hist. Tracts, No. 4 ; Richman, II. 10 *et seq.*

it was not at all likely that the people would willingly submit to a proprietary system in any form. Their spirit and tendencies were as strongly opposed to a government of that type as it is possible to conceive. Of the truth of this Coddington received a vivid impression as soon as he returned to Rhode Island.

The immediate effect of Coddington's act was to separate the colony again into two parts. Two commissioners' courts met, one for Providence and Warwick and the other for Newport and Portsmouth, the former holding the larger number of sessions.[1] This situation continued from November, 1651, until May, 1654. Massachusetts and Plymouth now revived before the Commissioners of the United Colonies the question of again asserting their claims[2] to Narragansett territory, a subject which had been allowed to sleep since Williams had procured his charter. The legality of sessions held by commissioners from Providence and Warwick alone was quite open to attack, and the colony seemed to be in imminent peril of dissolution.

But the proposal to accept Coddington as governor of Rhode Island on a life tenure found few supporters. The mainland towns were, of course, a unit in opposition to it. Williams was sent to England as their agent to procure a confirmation of the charter. John Clarke was also sent as the agent of the opposition in the island towns to procure the recall of Coddington's commission. On the island meetings were held by the opponents of Coddington, and an attempt was made to break up a court which he was holding. So hard beset was Coddington that he even intrigued with the Dutch to procure soldiers to aid him in subduing the opposition on Rhode Island.[3] So strong did that opposition become that Coddington found it expedient to retire to Boston, where, in the spring of 1652, he signed a paper surrendering the Indian deed of Rhode Island to the purchasers, and admitting that he had no more share in the purchase than did the rest of his associates.[4] Before the

---

[1] R. I. Col. Recs. I. 233–273.   [2] Plymouth Recs. IX. 170, 218.

[3] N. Y. Col. Docs. I. 497 ; 4 Mass. Hist. Coll. VII. 283.

[4] Turner, in R. I. Hist. Tracts, No. 4, p. 23.

close of the same year the agents, assisted by Sir Henry Vane, had successfully overcome such influence as the friends of Coddington were able to exert in England, and had procured a recall of the commission. Early in 1653 efforts toward the reuniting of the colony began on the part of the mainland towns. Providence and Warwick empowered commissioners[1] to meet with representatives from the island, for the purpose of reëstablishing the government of the colony. But for a long time no response came. During the interval the war between England and the Netherlands broke out, and the settlements on the island issued commissions to Captain Underhill, William Dyer, and Edward Hull to prey on the Dutch. A court of admiralty was established for the trial of prizes.[2] Privateers from Rhode Island operated in Long Island Sound. At this the mainland towns were much disturbed, because they feared it would involve them in an offensive war with the Dutch. The town of Warwick forbade its inhabitants to join the French or Dutch, and disfranchised John Warner because he, as the result of a quarrel with the town, invited Massachusetts to assume jurisdiction.[3]

In May, 1654, the four towns united once more in a general court of election.[4] But the appointment by this body of a committee to prepare " some course concerning our dissenting friends " would indicate that all were not reconciled. Of this committee Williams, who had now returned from England, was a member. In the following August the union was fully restored. They agreed to resume government under the charter,[5] with the existing body of laws, and to allow the acts done by the towns separately during the interval to retain their validity in the localities for which they were intended. On September 12th a court of election was held at Warwick by which officers were chosen to hold till the next spring. Williams was chosen president at this time and also at the succeeding spring election. Now Williams appears more distinctly than formerly as a leader of

[1] R. I. Col. Recs. I. 268.
[2] Ibid. 266, 270, 271.
[3] Ms. Recs. of Warwick.
[4] R. I. Col. Recs. I. 273.
[5] Ibid. 276 et seq.

the colony. The Protectorate in England was fully acknowledged, and an engagement of obedience to it was ordered
to be administered to the inhabitants by the town officers ; [1]
a letter of warning against internal dissensions was received
from Oliver Protector, under the influence of which an
order was issued that those found to be ringleaders of faction should be sent to England for trial before the Protector and Council. In 1656 Coddington made full submission
before the general assembly to the "authoritie of his High-
ness in this Colonie as it is now united."[2] He at that time
took his seat as commissioner from Newport. A committee
of investigation reported favorably on his conduct, and it
was recommended that a letter be sent to the agent in England giving reasons for receiving his submission, and asking
that the charges against him, which were pending before the
Council of State, be dismissed.[3] Coddington also resigned
his Indian deeds and other records into the keeping of the
settlers of Rhode Island. Thus his great plan was totally
abandoned, and the peril which had seemed to threaten
the union of the Narragansett towns from that quarter
disappeared.

Boundary disputes furnished another perennial cause of
disturbance to the Narragansett settlements. To all colonies
which had no charters or other guaranties from the crown the
question of boundary was a vital one. Unless boundaries
could be determined and maintained by peaceful agreement
with neighbors, separate existence was seriously imperilled.
Because of its location and of the friendly feeling which for
the most part existed between it and Massachusetts, Connecticut experienced little difficulty of this kind. The
most serious menace to her territorial integrity came from
the Dutch and later from New York. But New Haven,
because she had no charter, or bounds which had been recognized by mutual agreement, was absorbed by Connecticut.
The question between the two was largely a territorial one.
The Narragansett settlements seemed for a time to be exposed to even greater peril from this cause than did New

[1] R. I. Col. Recs. I. 305, 316, 318.   [2] *Ibid.* 327.
[3] *Ibid.* 328, 332 ; Arnold, I. 259.

Haven.   As Connecticut had enclosed New Haven, so they were surrounded by Plymouth, Massachusetts, and Connecticut.   The bounds of none of those colonies had been definitely settled, and they all were eager to secure territory on the shores of Narragansett bay.   In consequence of the submission of Arnold and his friends to Massachusetts, that colony appointed justices of the peace for their territory, and sixteen years passed before her claim to control over them was abandoned.   What occurred in this instance might also occur in others.   Boundary disputes occupy a larger place in the history of Rhode Island than in that of any other colony.

The efforts to settle the eastern boundary of Connecticut and the southern boundary of Massachusetts occasioned the most serious struggle, and this involved the question of the right to the Narragansett country.   This tribe with its dependents occupied all of the territory of the modern state of Rhode Island west of Narragansett bay.   The boundary of the region on the southwest was the Pawcatuck river.   To the westward, but originally extending a short distance to the east of the Pawcatuck, lay the Pequot country.   To this region both Connecticut and Massachusetts, after the Pequot war, laid claim by right of conquest.   Connecticut, after she had bought out Fenwick, claimed also by patent and purchase, and began to settle the region.

During the conflict with the Pequot tribe, the Narragansetts aided the English.   Roger Williams, as early as 1634 and 1635, established friendly relations with the chiefs of the Narragansetts and, as we have seen, made from them his purchases.   Both before and after the Pequot war Massachusetts frequently negotiated with the Narragansett sachems, but never gained their friendship.   The degree of success which she had with them was largely due to the mediation and aid of Williams.   When, soon after the Pequot war, the feud between the Mohegans and the Narragansetts developed, in which Uncas and Miantonomi were leaders, the English of the United Colonies adopted decisively the cause of the Mohegans.   Williams, Gorton, and their associates of the Narragansett settlements always sympathized with Miantonomi. The animosity which Massachusetts showed toward Gorton and that which she felt toward the Narragansett chief had a related origin. With her crusade against them both was involved a desire to secure influence among the Narragansett Indians and also territory within the region which they inhabited.

Through the settlement of Warwick the Narragansett colonists were the first to secure a foothold within the country west of the bay. From their settlement Massachusetts was not able to dislodge them. Soon after 1640 Richard Smith, who removed from Taunton in Plymouth colony, bought a tract from the Indians at Wickford, some distance south of Shawomet. There he built a house and took up his permanent residence. With him Williams was from the first somewhat closely associated, and later he too built a trading house in the same region. These houses were near the old Pequot path, which skirted the shore from the vicinity of Providence round to the former home of the Pequots.

Early in 1657 a company, consisting of Samuel Wilbore and three associates from Newport, and John Hull, the mintmaster from Boston, bought a track just north of Point Judith, which was known as the Pettiquamscott Purchase. In October, 1658, the general court of Massachusetts, in the prosecution of its plan to occupy a part of the Pequot country, declared a small settlement which had been made just west of the Pawcatuck to be a plantation with the name of Southertown (now Stonington), and annexed it to Suffolk county. Special commissioners and a constable were appointed to administer it.[1] These events seemed to threaten the peace of the Narragansett towns. Therefore, in November, 1658, the assembly passed an act forbidding any one to introduce a foreign jurisdiction, or to put his lands under the government of any other colony, under pain of confiscation.[2]

But this did not check the encroachments of Massachusetts parties within the Narragansett country. In 1659 the Atherton company was formed, consisting of Humphrey

[1] Mass. Recs. IV². 353.   [2] R. I. Col. Recs. I. 401.

Atherton, John Winthrop, Jr., Edward Hutchinson, Jr., Richard Smith, and others, largely Massachusetts men. This company bought a large tract north of the Pettiquamscott Purchase, and adjoining Richard Smith's estate. Rhode Island protested against this before the Commissioners of the United Colonies, but without result. In 1660, as security for the payment of a heavy fine which had been imposed by the Commissioners of the United Colonies because of outrages which had been committed by certain of the Niantics, the chiefs mortgaged to the Atherton company all of the unsold land in the Narragansett country.[1] If the company was not reimbursed in two years for their outlay, the land was to be fully conveyed to it. The actual transfer was made in 1662.

Meantime the Narragansett settlements bought from the Indians, under the name of the Westerly Purchase, land a part of which lay in Southertown, and began to settle it. In October, 1661,[2] three of the settlers in Westerly were arrested by the order of Massachusetts, and two of them were taken to Boston. There they were fined and imprisoned till the fine should be paid, and were then required to give bonds of £100 each to keep the peace. In the course of its correspondence over this affair the Massachusetts government reasserted the claim under its alleged charter from the commissioners of parliament to " all that tract of land from Pequot River to Plymouth line." She warned all the Rhode Island settlers to withdraw, or they would be arrested. But Rhode Island replied with a similar demand upon Massachusetts settlers in the region and denied that the Pequot country extended east of the Pawcatuck. She also insisted that the Atherton purchasers should submit to her jurisdiction. When we remember that Connecticut was also claiming the entire region which was thus in dispute, it will be seen that the situation was becoming complex. The claims of Massachusetts and Connecticut were also supported by the Commissioners of the United Colonies against any steps

---

[1] R. I. Col. Recs. I. 464, 465.
[2] Col. Recs. I. 456, 461 ; Arnold, I. 277 ; Potter, in Colls. R. I. Hist. Soc. III. 241 *et seq.*

which Rhode Island could take.   The danger that the Narragansett settlements would lose all west of the bay thus became imminent.

The situation was to an extent cleared by the issue of the Connecticut charter.   By fixing the eastern boundary of that colony at Narragansett bay, Massachusetts was excluded, and she soon retired from the race.   The Atherton company, on being offered the choice of submitting to the Narragansett settlements or to Connecticut, of course without hesitation chose the latter.   Connecticut named the plantation of the Atherton patentees Wickford, and appointed magistrates for it, the first in the list of whom was Richard Smith.

But the provision of the Connecticut charter relating to the boundary made it especially imperative that the Narragansett settlements should secure a guaranty of equal strength.   Their agent, John Clarke, was instructed to offer a resignation of the existing charter[1] and to procure a grant from the crown.   Attention was called to the joy with which the colonists about Narragansett bay had welcomed the Restoration and to their speedy acknowledgment of submission to the king.   By agreement between Winthrop and Clarke in England,[2] a clause was introduced into the Rhode Island charter specifying that the Pawcatuck river should be the boundary between the two colonies, any provision in the earlier patent of Connecticut to the contrary notwithstanding.   The western boundary of Rhode Island was completed by a line drawn due north from the source of that river to Massachusetts.   On the east the boundary should be the shore of Narragansett bay and Seekonk river, to Pawtucket falls, and thence a line extending due north to the Massachusetts bounds.   All adjacent islands, including Block island, were made a part of the colony.

Except in minute details, the provisions of the charter relating to government were the same as those of the Connecticut patent.   In deference to the opinions of the colonists, and to the reasons for their establishing a distinct colony, as set forth in Clarke's petitions, the following notable clause

[1] Col. Recs. I. 485.   [2] *Ibid.* 518.

guarantying religious freedom was introduced : "Noe person within the sayd colonye, at any tyme hereafter, shall bee
anywise molested, punished, disquieted, or called in question for any differences in opinione in matters of religion,
and (he) doe not actually disturb the civill peace of our sayd
colony; but that all and everye person and persons may,
from tyme to tyme, . . . freelye and fullye have and enjoy
his and theire own judgments and consciences in matters
of religious concernments; . . . they behaving themselves
peaceablie and quietlie, and not useing libertie to lycentious-
nesse and profanenesse, nor to the civill injurye or outward
disturbance of others ; any lawe, statute, or clause therein
contayned, or to be contayned, usage or custome of this
realme, to the contrary hereof, in anywise, notwithstanding."[1]

The charter was received by a general assembly at Newport in March, 1664, and put into force.   Such laws as were
inconsistent with it were repealed.   Among them were the
laws requiring that measures should be submitted by the
general court to the towns for approval.

[1] R. I. Col. Recs. II. 5.

CHAPTER IX

THE NORTHWARD EXPANSION OF MASSACHUSETTS

IN an earlier chapter the history of the enterprises of Gorges and Mason as proprietors in New England has been traced. Reference was made to their connection with the New England council, to the various patents which were issued to them by that body, and to the efforts they made to establish permanent colonies. The Laconia company, their largest and most promising undertaking, proved a failure. The death of John Mason completed for the time the ruin of their hopes on the Piscataqua. Though Gorges survived and procured a royal charter for his province of Maine, his energy and resources were not equal to the tasks of colonizing and governing it. The struggle between king and parliament in England soon diverted his attention ; he entered the royal service, while his interests in New England were allowed to slumber. His peace was later made with parliament, but, being already an old man, he did not survive beyond the spring of the year 1647.

The failure of Mason and Gorges to establish and maintain an effective control over their provinces, and the death of the former before he had secured through a royal charter the necessary rights of government, left a number of small and scattered settlements on that coast destitute of a superior tribunal to which their differences could be referred for adjustment. Upon the Piscataqua were Strawberry Bank, — which was soon to be known as Portsmouth, — Dover, and Exeter. Beyond the Piscataqua lay a number of petty outposts, of which the most important were Saco and a settlement on the neck where now the city of Portland is situated. The interests and relations which existed on the Piscataqua first demand attention.

Above Mason's settlement at Strawberry Bank, which was Anglican and proprietary in character, developed the settlement at Hilton's Point. This in course of time became Dover. The date of its origin and the location of the grant from the New England council upon which it developed are still to an extent matters of controversy.[1] This is due in part to uncertainty as to the stream or body of water which constitutes the upper course of the Piscataqua river, in part also to the obscurity which attaches to descriptions of boundary and location in all ancient deeds. Tradition, moreover, has it that Edward Hilton, with a few associates, began a settlement on Hilton's Point or Dover neck as early as 1623. Nearly all of the authorities accept this as true, though no trace appears of the existence or progress of the settlement between that date and 1628 or 1630. In March, 1630, the same Edward Hilton, a communicant of the English Church and by trade a fishmonger, procured an indenture from the New England council for land on Dover neck, and gave as a reason for the grant the fact that he and his associates, at their own expense, had already built houses and planted corn there, and intended to do more.[2] The words describing the location of the grant are, " all that part of the River Piscataquack called or known by the name Wecanacohunt or Hilton's Point, with the south side of the said River up to the fall of the River, and three miles into the Maine Land by all the breadth aforesaid."

About the location of Hilton's Point there can be no doubt. It lies at the upper extremity of the main course of the Piscataqua river, between it and Back river, Oyster river, and Little bay, which in turn expands into Great bay. The latter is fed by Lamprey river and Exeter or Squamscot river. But both Little bay and Great bay are tidal inlets, which at ebb are left exposed as mud flats. The main body of

---

[1] Jenness, Notes on the first Planting of New Hampshire ; Quint, Historical Memoranda of Dover, edited by Scales; Thompson, Landmarks of Ancient Dover ; Charles Deane on Thompson's Patent, Proceedings of Mass. Hist. Soc. 1875 ; N. H. Prov. Papers, I. 118, 157.

[2] N. E. Historical and Genealogical Register, XXIV. 264 ; Jenness, Notes, Appendix.

water by which the Piscataqua in its lower course is steadily fed flows down the Salmon Falls river and over Quampegan falls. That river flows more nearly in the same direction with the Piscataqua proper than do any of the other streams mentioned, and it has been traditionally accepted as the upper part of " the river " Piscataqua, and the boundary between Maine and New Hampshire.[1] If this description be true, the grant to Hilton lay wholly north of Little bay, and did not overlap the territory, the possession of which was confirmed to the Laconia company in 1631. We are told that Hilton sold " this land " to some merchants of Bristol, who had it in their possession for about two years ; but whether all the Hilton grant was then disposed of, or only a part of it, we are not informed.[2]

The grant and confirmation of Pescataway to the Laconia company was issued, as we have seen, in November 1631, and was therefore later than the Hilton grant.[3] It comprised the land on both sides of the main course of the Piscataqua, extending on the south bank to the upper part of Great bay, and on the north and east bank to a distance of thirty miles inland. The breadth of the northern strip was three miles.[4] The southern half of the grant comprised a large part of the present towns of Rye, Newington, and Greenland. If the Hilton grant was located wholly inland and north of Little bay, it and the Pescataway grant would at no point have overlapped. But the time soon came when the terms of the Hilton patent received a different interpretation. A short time after the issue of the Pescataway grant Captain Thomas Wiggin, a Puritan, became interested in the settlement at Hilton's Point. Hubbard states[5] that he was the representative of certain adventurers from Shrewsbury in England. He also became, at a later time, a defender of

[1] Jenness, Notes, 50.

[2] Declaration of John Allen, Nicholas Shapleigh, and Thomas Lake, Farmer's Belknap, 435 ; N. H. Prov. Papers, I. 157.

[3] In 1652 the general court of Massachusetts ordered that the northern bounds of Dover should extend westward four miles from the first falls of Newichwannock river.

[4] Jenness, Docs. relating to New Hampshire, 10.

[5] Hubbard, History of New England, 217 ; Tuttle, John Mason, 69.

the claim of Massachusetts to the entire region. At the time
when Wiggin first appears, Captain Walter Neale was on the
Piscataqua as the manager of the Laconia enterprise.   He and
Wiggin are reported to have nearly come to blows over their
claims to the land on the south bank of the river immediately
opposite Dover neck.   Because of the threatened encounter,
this tract has always gone by the name of Bloody Point.

Not long after this event Wiggin went to England and
induced Lord Say and Sele, Lord Brook, Sir Richard Saltonstall, and others, all Puritans, to form an association and
buy out the Bristol merchants,[1] or at least to secure an interest in their grant. The governors and magistrates of
Massachusetts are said to have favored this step, because they
feared " some ill neighborhood " from the Bristol men.   The
purchase was made, and in October, 1633, Wiggin returned
as manager for the Puritan proprietors, bringing with him
a " godly minister " named William Leveridge.

A conflict soon began between the Anglican and Puritan
elements in the little settlement of Dover.   Between the years
1637 and 1640 Wiggin seems to have lost control.   George
Burdet, an Anglican clergyman of loose morals, was for a time
the leader [2] of the opponents of Wiggin, and was elected as
his successor in the magistracy.   Then Captain John Underhill, also of unsavory reputation in Massachusetts, and recently disfranchised there because of his adherence to the
Antinomian faction, came to Dover.   He was twice chosen
" governor," and was instrumental in gathering a Baptist
congregation, which chose Hanserd Knollys as its minister.

In 1640 forty-one inhabitants of the place signed a combination or plantation covenant.[3]   In this they stated that, for
the purpose of escaping the mischiefs and inconveniences
from which they had suffered because of their lack of
powers of government, they united as a body politic.   As
a result of this they hoped more comfortably to enjoy the
benefits of his Majesty's laws, together with those orders

[1] Farmer's Belknap, 435 ; N. H. Prov. Papers, I. 157.

[2] Belknap, History of New Hampshire, I. 40 et seq. ; N. H. Prov. Papers,
I. 119.

[3] Ibid. 126 ; Jenness, Docs. 37.

which they themselves should adopt by majority vote, provided they were executed in the name of the king and were
not inconsistent with the laws of England.   They engaged
to be true to this agreement until the king should otherwise
command.   Among the signers the name of Underhill appears,
but not that of Wiggin.   Francis Champernowne, a scion of
the famous west of England family, was also one of the signers, as were two Waldrons, a family which was long to hold
a prominent place in the town.   Thomas Larkham,[1] whose
name also appears in the list, was a minister who succeeded
Burdet as the head of the Anglican party.   Under his lead
the quarrel became violent between the Anglican and Puritan
parties in the little settlement.   Underhill supported the
latter.   They were unable to unite in one church or to live
peaceably as two.   Knollys undertook to excommunicate
Larkham, and Larkham assaulted Knollys.   An attempt was
made to arrest Underhill, whereupon he and his supporters
paraded the streets with a Bible on a halberd as an ensign.
Larkham then sent for Francis Williams, who was the leading
magistrate at Strawberry Bank.   He came and, sitting as
judge, found Underhill and his associates guilty of riot.
Some were heavily fined, while Underhill and others were
ordered to depart from the plantation.

While these dissensions were continuing at Dover, the
town of Exeter was founded at the falls of the Squamscot
or Exeter river, some distance above Great bay.   This was
the work of Rev. John Wheelwright, the Antinomian leader,
and his followers.[2]   In 1638 they extinguished the Indian
title to the territory between the Merrimac river and the
settlements on the Piscataqua.   A church was founded, and
in June, 1639, a civil compact was signed at Exeter, and
rights of government were assumed under it.   The obligation of allegiance to England was frankly acknowledged,
though "according to the libertys of our English Colony of
the Massachusetts."   The wording of the compact was later
somewhat changed to suit those who desired a less pronounced acknowledgment of English supremacy; but this
did not give perfect satisfaction.

[1] Winthrop, II. 32.   [2] Bell, History of Exeter, 8; N. H. Prov. Papers, I. 131.

In March, 1636, the general court of Massachusetts ordered that a bound house should be built and a plantation settled north of the Merrimac river.[1] This resulted in the settlement of Hampton, which in 1639 was made a town, with the usual officials and the right to send a deputy to the general court. As Hampton was located north of the three-mile limit beyond the Merrimac and was within the territory which Exeter had bought from the Indians, that town in 1638 protested. But the general court of Massachusetts replied that it considered this protest "as against good neighborhood, religion, and common honesty." The reason which it gave for so regarding the act revealed the theory concerning its northern bounds which Massachusetts had already adopted. It claimed Winicowett or Hampton "as within our patent or as *vacuum domicilium*," and therefore had built the bound house north of the three-mile limit. Of this act and the claim from which it proceeded Wheelwright and his associates were aware, and for that reason their protest seemed to the general court of Massachusetts to indicate bad faith. The people of Exeter were also informed by the court that the Indians had a natural right to only such land as they could improve, and that the rest of the country lay open to those who could and would improve it.

When the royal charter was granted to the Massachusetts company, with the specification that it should possess all the lands lying within three English miles to the north of the Merrimac river, "or to the norward of any and every part thereof," it was supposed that, through its entire course, the Merrimac flowed in an easterly direction. The northern boundary of the colony would then follow the course of the river, to its source, though three miles to the northward of it, and thence extend in a straight line to the South sea. But before settlement had progressed far it was found that the source of the Merrimac was at a point much farther north than was supposed. While the controversy with Exeter was in progress[2] an investigation was begun, and it

[1] Mass. Recs. I. 167, 206, 259 ; Winthrop, I. 349.
[2] Mass. Recs. I. 237, 261 ; Winthrop, I. 365.

resulted in the discovery that some parts of the river lay north of 43½°, or about a degree and a half north of the lower course of the river. Later surveys, made in 1652 and 1654, established the fact that the Merrimac took its rise in Lake Winnepiseogee, and that a line drawn due east from that point and three miles north of it, would reach the ocean in the latitude[1] of Upper Clapboard island in Casco bay. This line was then declared by the general court to be, according to the patent, the northern boundary of the colony from the source of the Merrimac eastward. This assertion, however, is manifestly contradicted by all we know of the views and policy, both of the New England council and of the crown, at the time of the issue of the charter to Massachusetts. It was clearly an afterthought, and gave to the clause of the charter in question a meaning which was not contemplated at the time of its issue. It ignored all the acquired rights of Mason and Gorges, and involved what was more clearly an usurpation than was any later act of the crown which affected New England. In fact, it is doubtful if this can be paralleled by any event of a similar character in the history of the American colonies during the seventeenth century.

But even this act of usurpation by Massachusetts carried with it an appearance of justification, and one, too, which was especially calculated to recommend it to the conscience of the Puritan and to his spiritual pride. The interests of the faith among the northern settlements needed support. Owing to the failure of their plans, both Mason and Gorges had left abortive proprietary provinces ; the local settlements were there, but either no executive or legislature existed to bind them together, or one that was inadequate for the purpose. They were left in isolation, rent and divided by controversies, and in danger of falling into anarchy. That this was the condition of the towns on the Piscataqua has already been shown, and it will appear that similar perils confronted the Maine settlements. The intervention of Massachusetts and the extension over them of its system of county and town

[1] Mass. Recs. III. 274, 278, 288, 329, 361 ; Tuttle, Captain John Mason, 94. The latitude was about 43° 40′.

government furnished a reasonable guaranty of good order among them until the right of the proprietors or the crown could again be asserted.

The settlements on the Piscataqua were the first to be annexed by Massachusetts, and the immediate occasion for this was furnished by the events which have already been described. Mason was dead, the Laconia company had been dissolved; the settlements were small, remote, and the residents of Dover were at odds among themselves. They had no adequate institutions or powers of government. In 1633 the magistrates of Massachusetts had been requested to try cases which had arisen on the Piscataqua, but they had then declined to assume jurisdiction. Early in 1641[1] Simon Bradstreet, with two of the ministers, Peters and Dalton, were sent by Massachusetts to Dover to mediate between the factions of Knollys and Larkham. Knollys, being found guilty of immoral conduct in the settlement, was forced to depart. Underhill also soon removed to Stamford in New Haven colony. Quiet was thus restored. Agreements were then reached with Edward Hilton and with Williams of the lower plantation, in consequence of which they made no opposition to the step which was now to be taken. The patentees of Dover who were[2] resident in England, seem also to have surrendered their rights, with certain reservations of land, to Massachusetts.

On June 14, 1641, George Willis and others, on behalf of Lords Say, Brook, and the other grantees of the Hilton patent,[3] made a full submission to Massachusetts, and agreed to be governed by its laws. But in this paper reference is for the first time made to a second grant, over which Willis and his associates seem to have had control, and for which also they made submission. This is called the Squamscot[4] patent and was located on the south bank of the Piscataqua, extending as far inland as Squamscot or Exeter falls, and having a breadth of three miles. It therefore included all, or nearly all, of that part of the Pescataway Confirmation

---

[1] Mass. Recs. I. 332; Winthrop, II. 34; Jenness, Notes, 48.

[2] Mass. Recs. I. 332.

[3] N. H. Prov. Papers, I. 155, 169.

[4] *Ibid.* 221; 3 Mass. Archives, 452; Jenness, Notes.

which lay south of the river ; in other words, it comprised
much of the territory which had belonged to the Laconia
company.   Later documents show that some families from
Dover had settled on Bloody Point, but they were only
squatters, being able to urge no claim save that originating
in purchase from the Indians and in possession.[1]

Among the extant records of the New England council
appears no reference to a Squamscot patent.   These records,
however, are not complete, and for that reason it cannot be
absolutely affirmed that such a grant was not issued.   So
many references to it appear in the proceedings of the time,
that it is manifestly rash to affirm that it was an invention
of Massachusetts.   The rights which existed under it, whatever they were, seem to have belonged to Lords Say and
Brook and their associates.   They were the parties who made
the submission to Massachusetts in 1641, reserving to themselves one-third of the land in the Dover patent and the
whole of the Squamscot patent ; simply putting it under
the jurisdiction of Massachusetts.   The political effect of
the extension of the claim was important, for it brought a
part of the former territory of the Laconia company, including Strawberry Bank, more directly under Puritan control.
In 1656, by order of the general court of Massachusetts,[2] a
division of the land within the Squamscot patent was made
between Wiggin, the town of Dover, and the survivors of
the Shrewsbury and Bristol men who had been its earlier
patentees.   Wiggin, with Lake, one of his associates, then
surrendered to Dover all the land, except sixteen acres, which
they claimed within its limits.

Though Exeter had not yet made submission, the act of
October 9, 1641, by which Massachusetts annexed Dover,[3]
referred to the Piscataqua as being within its bounds and the
inhabitants on that river as under its government.   The authority of Massachusetts courts was extended over them, and
a commission was appointed to hold courts there with the
jurisdiction of a county court, and with power to temporarily
appoint local magistrates.   Two deputies should be sent

[1] N. H. Prov. Papers, I. 175, 176; Jenness, Notes, 61 et seq.
[2] Ibid. 221–224.   [3] Ibid. 158–161.

from the whole river to the general court at Boston, though the next year it was provided that each town should send one deputy. Exemption was granted from all except local charges. It was also agreed that for no cases of debt involving less than £100 should parties be compelled to plead before courts outside of Norfolk county. In September, 1642, the requirement that representatives to the general court should be church members was suspended for these settlements.[1]

Early in 1643 the inhabitants of Exeter petitioned Massachusetts, but the document has not been preserved. The reply of Massachusetts was in substance that, since Exeter lay within their patent, "the Court took it ill they should Capitulate with them." Soon after, in May, 1643, Exeter again petitioned, asking that their bounds toward Hampton and toward Wiggin's farm down the river might be settled, and that local justices might be appointed. In the following September Exeter was formally received as a part of the county of Norfolk. It now became subject to the conditions of annexation which applied to Dover, though it was not granted the right to send a deputy[2] to the general court. Mr. Wheelwright then removed to Wells, which lay within the jurisdiction of Gorges. But later, having acknowledged his fault and gone through the form of submission, he was pardoned by Massachusetts and allowed to return within her bounds, where he became minister first of the church at Hampton and afterwards of that at Salisbury.[3]

While Massachusetts, through orders and commissions, carried on during the next twenty years the general business of the settlements on the Piscataqua, her influence was of course exerted for the extension and strengthening of Puritanism in that region. The control of the Puritan party in Dover was fully established at the time of annexation. Hampton and Exeter were Puritan from the beginning, though at the outset the strength of the adherents of Wheelwright made it undesirable to grant Exeter representation

[1] N. H. Prov. Papers, I. 161, 184, 187.

[2] *Ibid.* 168, 170, 171 ; Bell, History of Exeter, 44.

[3] N. H. Prov. Papers, I. 174 ; Winthrop, II. 195 ; Farmer's Belknap, 32, 33 n.

in the general court.   The inhabitants of Strawberry Bank were mainly Anglicans, and in that locality centred the interests of the Mason family.   Though from the outset the two upper settlements were treated as towns, more than a decade passed before Strawberry Bank received that honor. In 1643, because the commissioners who had been appointed to lay out the bounds between Dover and Strawberry Bank had not considered the latter to be a town and had not been accurate in their surveys, the general court ordered a reconsideration of the case.[1]   The land in dispute was Bloody Point, and its inhabitants, who had removed thither from Dover, asked that they might not be separated from that town. After hearing the arguments of both sides, the court adjudged the land to belong to Dover.

In 1651 the inhabitants of Strawberry Bank petitioned to be made a town and to have two courts annually, presided over by resident magistrates.   Some of the people were also reported to be planning withdrawal from Massachusetts control.   In response to this demand their bounds were extended toward Hampton, and three resident magistrates were appointed, with the authority to hold a court.   In 1653 they petitioned for the privilege of voting for magistrates of the colony, that their militia officers might be confirmed, and additional jurisdiction given to their local magistrates. The petition concerning the militia officers was granted, but as to the other points, the petitioners were told to be content with what they had received at the time of annexation. Another petition for extension of bounds failed to meet with a favorable[2] response.   The settlement, however, was permitted to call itself Portsmouth, and was referred to as a town.   But these references make it evident that discontent was felt in Portsmouth during the period of Massachusetts rule, and that perhaps the majority of its inhabitants were ready to welcome the Restoration.

In 1651[3] Joseph Mason, who had been sent over by Anne Mason, the widow of the late proprietor, to take charge of her affairs, appeared on the Piscataqua.   He had power of attor-

[1] N. H. Prov. Papers, I. 172–175.   [2] Ibid. 205, 207.
[3] Jenness, N. H. Docs. 78 ; Tuttle, John Mason, 92.

ney to hold and dispose of goods and lands.   One Richard
Leader,[1] who had been superintendent of the iron works at
Lynn, had occupied some of Mason's lands on the Newichwannock and had built a saw-mill there.   Joseph Mason
brought suit for trespass against him, and the case came before
the general court of Massachusetts.   It was as a step preparatory to the trial of this case that the location of the boundary line between the source of the Merrimac river and the
ocean was determined.   The court decided that Mason had
territorial rights at Newichwannock, and that land proportioned to his disbursements be laid off there for his heirs.
Joseph Mason then complained that encroachments had
been made on the rights of the family by settlers at Strawberry Bank and elsewhere, and he desired justice against
them;[2] but there is no record that Massachusetts noticed
this petition.   Mason then posted notices at Portsmouth,
Dover, and Exeter protesting against the conduct of Massachusetts toward those settlements, and forbidding grass or
timber to be cut in that region without license from him.
But he received no effective support from any quarter, and
was able to accomplish nothing until after the Restoration.
In 1655 Anne Mason died, leaving Robert Tufton Mason as
her executor and sole heir of the estate.   In 1659, as soon
as Richard Cromwell resigned the office of Protector, Mason,
with Edward Godfrey and Ferdinando Gorges, began petitioning parliament for relief.

Controversies also existed among the settlements to the
north of the Piscataqua, which gave even more direct occasion for the interference of Massachusetts than did any that
led to the establishment of her control south of that river.   In
a previous chapter reference has been made to the multiplication of grants along that coast and also to the beginning of
proprietary government within the region that for a short time
was known as New Somersetshire, but which under the royal
charter of 1639 became the province of Maine.   Members of
the Gorges family were sent over in succession as governors,

---

[1] Emanuel Downing gives most information concerning him in letters to
John Winthrop, Jr., 4 Mass. Hist. Colls. VI. 61, 76.

[2] Jenness, N. H. Docs. 38, 40; Tuttle, John Mason, 95.

and commissioners were selected to assist them.   Cours
were held at Saco, and at Agamenticus or York.   The latter
settlement, under the name of Gorgeana, with a city charter and territory enough to make it a proper residence for a
bishop, was intended to be the capital of the province.[1]   But
while Sir Ferdinando, already an old man and with impaired
fortune, was still busy with his plans, the civil disturbances
began in Scotland and England.   While they were in progress he died.   His relatives had already withdrawn from
the province.   Richard Vines, succeeded in 1645 by Henry
Josselyn, continued to administer government in Gorges's
interest at Saco, while at York Edward Godfrey lived and
acted as senior councillor, as mayor, and from 1649 as an elective governor under a " combination " which was made when
the inhabitants found it no longer possible to secure aid or
guidance from the family of the proprietor.   In this way [2] two
districts or germinal counties appear within the province, the
Kennebunk river being the boundary between them.   Though
not distinctly named, the westernmost of the two was often
called York, while to the easternmost the term Somerset was
sometimes applied.

The grantees within the region whose relations affected
most closely the events which follow, were Robert Trelawny
and George Cleeve.   The former was a merchant of ancient
and distinguished family, who lived near Plymouth in England.[3]   In 1631 he, with Moses Goodyear, also of Plymouth,
received from the New England council a grant of Richmond's island, and a tract on the adjoining mainland, being
a part of Cape Elizabeth.   According to the terms of the
patent this was to extend inland as far as did a grant of
fifteen hundred acres which had recently been made to
Thomas Cammock.[4]   Cammock's grant lay on the west side
of the Spurwink river at Black Point, adjoining that of
Trelawny.   Trelawny's grant, according to the wording of
his patent, lay between Cammock's land and " the bay and

[1] Baxter, Gorges and Maine, I. 173-187 ; Hazard, Hist. Colls. I. 470 *et seq.*
[2] Williamson, History of Maine, I. 285.
[3] Documentary History of Maine, III., The Trelawny Papers.
[4] *Ibid.* 4, 10.

river of Casco." This phrase could only have meant that part of Casco bay which is adjacent to Cape Elizabeth.

John Winter was sent over with servants as Trelawny's agent. A trading and fishing station of some importance was established on Richmond's island, and land was cultivated to an extent. The correspondence between the agent and his employer in England, which has been preserved,[1] affords a detailed picture of the fishing operations, which were the main concern of the settlers; and also of a small trade in skins with the natives and the raising of swine and Indian corn for food. Several vessels were employed in bringing supplies from Europe to the plantation and in carrying its commodities to the English markets. Some of these ships were of considerable size for the time, and details of their arrivals and departures and cargoes have been preserved. A bark for use in the fishery was built in the settlement. About fifty persons were employed on the plantation and in the fishery, all with a very few exceptions being men without families. It was a typical fishing station and plantation, of which there were many examples along the coast of northern New England.

While Winter was agent he claimed both banks of the Spurwink river through a part of its course, and this caused a dispute with Cammock. In 1636, during a visit of Winter to England, Trelawny's patent was enlarged by a grant from Gorges of a strip of land containing two thousand acres and extending inland from the sea, just west of Cammock's grant, as far as Casco river.[2] By the latter term was meant the tide-water inlet which forms the northwestern extension of the present Portland harbor.

About the time when Trelawny obtained his first patent, George Cleeve and Richard Tucker settled on the mainland near Richmond's island,[3] but had no valid title. As Winter was a harsh man and one who was not slow to assert the claims of his principal, he and Cleeve soon fell out. Cleeve also possessed a large amount of the resource which is so necessary to the squatter on the border of the wilderness.

---

[1] Documentary History of Maine, III. 22 *et seq.*   [2] *Ibid.* 131.

[3] Baxter, George Cleeve, in Pubs. of Gorges Society, 26 *et seq.*

Considering his interests imperilled by the grant to Trelawny of the two thousand acre strip, he soon visited England, where he was able to say a good word for the Puritans of Massachusetts before Archbishop Laud, and to obtain from Gorges a grant of the neck on which the city of Portland is now situated and the land extending northward of that to the Presumpscot river.[1] Tucker was also his partner in this grant. Cleeve moreover procured from Sir Ferdinando what purported to be a joint commission for Governor Winthrop of Massachusetts, himself, and others, to govern that part of New Somersetshire which lay between Cape Elizabeth and Sagadahoc.[2] But the Massachusetts authorities were not certain as to its validity, and concluded not to intermeddle. This, however, with other acts of his, showed that Cleeve was anxious to secure Puritan support for his ambitious schemes.

When Winter learned that Cleeve and Tucker had obtained their grant and also that charges against him, and against Vines, Godfrey, and Purchase, because of support they had given him, had been preferred before the Star Chamber, the feud was greatly intensified. Winter now claimed that the land which had been granted to Cleeve lay within the original grant to Trelawny and Goodyear, though it was always understood to extend back only a short distance from the coast. Later, changing the form of his claim, he urged that by Casco river, which was the designation of the eastern boundary of the original grant to Trelawny, as well as that of the northern boundary of his two thousand acre grant, was meant the Presumpscot river. Thus on the one count or the other, or the two combined, Winter hoped to prove the invalidity of Cleeve's patent. Though the interpretation which he put upon the language of his own patents respecting bounds was clearly false, he supported it with great vigor. It was opposed with equal activity by Cleeve, and therefore events soon occurred which called loudly for the interposition of some superior power.[3] The case under

[1] Baxter, George Cleeve, in Pubs. of Gorges Society, 217, 224.
[2] Winthrop, I. 276.
[3] Trelawny Papers, 225 et seq., 260 ; Baxter, George Cleeve, 91 et seq.

different forms was twice heard before the court of Governor Thomas Gorges at Saco, and in both instances was won by Cleeve. Winter then tried to have the jury which decided against him in one of the suits attainted, and also proposed to appeal to the proprietor himself. Arbitration, however, was first resorted to, and again the decision was favorable to Cleeve. Though this checked further proceedings, the Trelawny interest continued to threaten Cleeve with ejectment from Machigonne neck — where he had developed a prosperous Indian trade—and from his other possessions.

But the outbreak of civil troubles in England soon landed the royalist Trelawny in prison, where, about two years later, he died. It also completed for the time the ruin of Gorges's plans. Cleeve, who till now had sheltered himself under Gorges's authority, at once revisited England and induced Alexander Rigby, a parliamentarian, to buy the Lygonia or Plough patent. This included the territory between Cape Porpoise and Sagadahoc, and extended forty miles into the mainland. It thus included Saco, all the territory held by Cammock, Trelawny, and Cleeve, and much in addition. Cleeve secured from Rigby confirmation of his own [1] grant, and received appointment as governor of Lygonia. He also preferred charges before parliament against Vines and Godfrey, and asked that a commission, headed by Governor Winthrop, be appointed to inquire into them. Armed with this authority, or rather with these evidences of personal and party support, Cleeve returned to New England late in 1643. Winter died the following year, and his son-in-law, Robert Jordan, who officiated for a time as an Episcopal clergyman, appears as the equally persistent and far more skilful defender of the Trelawny claims.

Cleeve, as soon as possible after his return,[2] began appointing officers for his province and called a court to meet at Casco. He sent Tucker abroad to procure the signatures of all who approved his course. He sought to discredit the claims of the Gorges party. Concerning his doings Vines, who, after the departure of Thomas Gorges represented the interests of the proprietor, informed Governor Winthrop.

---

[1] Baxter, *op. cit.* 246.   [2] *Ibid.* 130, 233 *et seq.*

Cleeve, whose assumed Puritan leanings had already brought him into connection with Massachusetts, now sent Tucker to procure the intervention of that colony. But Vines had Tucker arrested while on his way, and bound him over for trial at Saco. His release, however, was followed by the despatch of the appeal to Boston, and later by a proposal that Lygonia should be admitted to the New England Confederacy.[1] Massachusetts was not disposed to act hastily upon either of these propositions, while the fact that the inhabitants of Lygonia could hardly be considered as living "in a church way" was likely to prove an insuperable obstacle to their union with the Confederacy. While Massachusetts delayed action the royal cause suffered irretrievable defeat in England, and with it the immediate prospects of the Gorges family in America vanished. It was this which caused the withdrawal of Vines to Barbadoes.

Henry Josselyn, the successor of Vines, now went with a body of armed men to Casco and demanded a view of the documents[2] on which Cleeve based his claim. Their demand was granted, but they of course were not thereby convinced, and presented in writing a protest and a demand that Cleeve and his associates should submit to the government of Maine. This was rejected, and both parties agreed to submit their case to the judgment of Massachusetts. The trial was held in June, 1646,[3] before the court of assistants, with a jury, at Boston. Cleeve and Tucker appeared in defence of the Rigby claim, Josselyn and Robinson in the interest of Gorges. Cleeve produced the assignment of the Lygonia patent to Rigby, signed by a part of the patentees, but he was unable to prove that the territory which he claimed was within its limits. Josselyn, on behalf of the defendant, was able to produce only a copy of Gorges's patent, and that was held to be not pleadable in law. For these reasons the jury could not find a verdict, and the assistants dismissed the case with the advice that peace be maintained until the controversy could be settled under authority from England.

Rigby now obtained from the Commissioners of Plantations in England a confirmation of the Lygonia patent.

[1] Winthrop, II. 187.   [2] Baxter, 265, 274.   [3] Winthrop, II. 314.

This settled the question for the present, and confined the possessions of Gorges to the small district between the Kennebunk and Piscataqua rivers, with the settlement at Kittery, Gorgeana, and Wells, and a hamlet on the Isles of Shoals. It was within this district, after Gorges's death, that the settlers formed a combination and elected Edward Godfrey governor, with a council from the towns. Meantime Cleeve, acting with the support of a commission of Massachusetts men which had been appointed by parliament,[1] had established government within the Lygonia grant. A general assembly was called, and a circuit court met at Casco, Black Point, and Saco in turn. Josselyn and Jordan coöperated with Cleeve in this, and with the help of the latter as a magistrate Jordan was placed in possession of all the property of the Trelawny heir in the province. At this stage of affairs Governor Winthrop died, and his death was followed, in 1650, by the death of Alexander Rigby. The first-mentioned event removed the source of hesitancy among the magistrates of Massachusetts to the annexation of the Maine settlements; the death of Rigby greatly weakened the influence of Cleeve and revived the hopes of his enemies that they might yet overthrow him.

Godfrey and the settlers between the Kennebunk and Piscataqua rivers now, in 1651, petitioned parliament for the recognition of their government, and Cleeve carried the document to England. Massachusetts at once took action. Bradstreet, Dennison, and Hathorne were sent[2] by the general court to urge upon those towns the claim of Massachusetts and to treat for submission. Godfrey refused to admit the claim which Massachusetts was urging in reference to her northern boundary, and insisted with truth that Gorges's royal charter was as valid as their own. He also called attention to services which he had rendered to Massachusetts when she was threatened with a *quo warranto* in England. Having petitioned parliament, he and his associates refused to submit.

In 1652, nothing having been heard from parliament,

[1] Baxter, 151.

[2] Mass. Col. Recs. IV[1]. 70; Williamson, History of Maine, I. 337 *et seq.*

another commission, with Bradstreet at its head and Wiggin and Pendleton of the Piscataqua settlements among its members,[1] was sent first to Kittery and then to Agamenticus. The people were called together. After considerable debate at both places, and persistent objections from Godfrey, submission was voted by large majorities of the inhabitants. Godfrey then for the time abandoned opposition and took the oath with the rest, though later he returned to England, where, both before and after the Restoration, he appeared as a determined opponent of the pretensions of Massachusetts.[2] Kittery and Agamenticus — the latter under the name of York — were now made towns, and provision was made for holding yearly in each town two sessions of a county court. A new county, named Yorkshire, was organized. All of its inhabitants who took the freeman's oath were nominally admitted to full political rights. In 1653 Wells,[3] Cape Porpoise, and Saco followed the example of these towns, and thus an important part of the Lygonia patent fell under the control of Massachusetts.

Cleeve, after his return from England, with the inhabitants of Casco, held out against Massachusetts until 1658. The plea which he urged was the validity of the Lygonia patent and of its assignment to Rigby,[4] and the fact that legal government was in existence under it. This of course involved a denial of the boundary claim now urged by Massachusetts, and there is evidence that in the protests from the settlers east of Saco this was as strongly enforced as it had been by the residents farther west. As a large proportion of the inhabitants of this region were Episcopalians, or sympathizers with that form of worship, Cleeve received additional assurance of support. He presented a petition from the settlers about Casco bay before the general court[5] at Boston, but received in reply only another assertion of its claim and of its determination to maintain it. Massa-

[1] Mass. Col. Recs. IV[1]. 109, 122 et seq. ; Williamson, I. 342.

[2] Colls. Maine Hist. Soc. IX. 326.

[3] Mass. Col. Recs. IV[1]. 158, 160–161.

[4] Baxter, op. cit. 161 ; Letter of Cleeve to the magistrates and deputies of Massachusetts.

[5] Mass. Col. Recs. IV[1]. 250.

chusetts also declared that she was not infringing the liberties of the planters, but was extending to them the same benefits which her own people enjoyed.

Meantime Edward Rigby, son of Sir Alexander, was urging his claims before the authorities in England against counter representations from Massachusetts; but at that time no decision could be reached. In May, 1657, the general court wrote to Josselyn and Jordan, calling their attention to alleged disturbances in Saco and Wells[1] and asking them to meet the commissioners at York and assist in establishing a firm government in "those parts beyond Saco to the utmost bounds of our pattent." The summons was disregarded, as was a later one from the commissioners to appear at the general court in Boston. But after some further correspondence, owing to the increase of disorder in the eastern settlements and the lack of sufficient authority there to repress it, in May, 1658,[2] Samuel Symonds and Thomas Wiggin were joined with the magistrates of Yorkshire and ordered to proceed thither and take "the residue of the inhabitants residing within our line" under the jurisdiction of Massachusetts. This was effected at the house of Robert Jordan at Spurwink. The inhabitants of Black Point, Blue Point, Spurwink, and Casco then signed a form of submission and took the oath. They were guarantied the same liberties as those which were enjoyed by the towns that had previously submitted. They were themselves organized as two towns, Scarborough and Falmouth, with the Spurwink river as the boundary between them. This finally was the form to which the settlements within the patents of Cammock, Trelawny, and Cleeve had come. The towns were given local courts and representation in the general court at Boston. They were also incorporated within Yorkshire, but owing to the size and remoteness of that county, with the consent of the inhabitants, Josselyn, Jordan, Cleeve, and two other residents were appointed for one year to try cases in the two towns which did not involve more than £50. Each of these appointees also pos-

[1] Mass. Col. Recs. IV[1]. 305, 318; Baxter, 298.
[2] Mass. Col. Recs. IV[1]. 338, 357.

sessed the authority of a local justice in his town, together
with the other powers of a magistrate.   The five in joint
session could appoint militia officers below the rank of captain and transact the probate business usually done in county
courts.   Provision was also made for sessions of the county
court at Saco and Scarborough, as well as at York.   This
court should consist of the five magistrates already mentioned,
and four associates chosen annually by the freemen.

The towns of Maine, as well as those on the Piscataqua,
were not taxed for the general purposes of the colony; they
were required to meet only the expenses of their local government.   This, however, was done under the forms of the
Massachusetts system.   This circumstance made it less needful than it otherwise would have been for these remote
towns to be represented in the general court.   Moreover,
no law at that time required deputies to reside in the towns
which they represented.[1]   In 1659 Edward Rishworth of
York represented Scarborough and Falmouth.   In 1660
Henry Josselyn of Scarborough was deputy.   The towns
were unrepresented from that date until 1663, when Cleeve
of Falmouth was chosen for two successive years.   No more
deputies were chosen until 1669, when Richard Collicot, a
resident of Boston, represented Falmouth.   From 1670 until
the organization of government under the charter of 1691
no more representatives were sent to the general court from
Scarborough or Falmouth.[2]

[1] Mass. Col. Laws, 1889, pp. 47, 49, 145.
[2] Willis, History of Portland, I. 147.

CHAPTER X

INTERCOLONIAL RELATIONS. THE NEW ENGLAND CONFEDERACY

THE process of growth which has been described in the preceding chapters gave rise to a group of colonies in New England which were similarly organized and whose inhabitants had kindred objects in view. But the boundaries between them were not definitely settled, while the expansion of trade and colonization sometimes brought them into conflict. In location, character, and institutions they were in the seventeenth century very distinct from the English colonies to the south, and they had few dealings with them. They had foreigners as neighbors on the north and west, while the presence of the Indians in their midst kept alive the feeling that at any time they might find coöperation in defence a necessity. There was no umpire or sovereign in Europe to whom they would willingly have submitted their controversies, and none whose sympathy could have been enlisted in the furtherance of their most cherished projects.

In 1634 an encounter took place between one Hocking,[1] from Cocheco, or Dover, on the Piscataqua, and some agents of Plymouth who were in charge of its trading post on the Kennebec river. The Plymouth people had a clear right there by patent, but Hocking forced his way past their trading house and anchored above them for the purpose of intercepting the Indian traders as they came down the river. In a collision which resulted from this, Hocking and one of the Plymouth men were slain. Though Massachusetts had not yet begun seriously to interfere in the affairs of the eastern settlements, this event seemed to her magistrates to be not only a cause of common reproach but likely to fur-

[1] Bradford, 316 ; Winthrop, I. 155 *et seq.*

nish the king with an excuse for sending over a general
governor. Therefore they interfered and detained John
Alden, who had been present at the Plymouth trading post
when the shooting occurred. The Plymouth magistrates,
surprised at this, sent Captain Standish to Boston to give correct information concerning the affair and to secure Alden's
release. This, however, was only conditionally granted. A
conference was also called, and parties from Plymouth and
Dover were asked to attend at Boston for the purpose of
discussing the affair and arranging a settlement. But no
representatives from Dover appeared. Winthrop, with two
ministers, conferred with Bradford, Winslow, and Ralph
Smith, the acting pastor at Plymouth. They, acting in a
purely private capacity, exonerated Plymouth from any
charge of criminal conduct, though Bradford and his associates admitted that their men had shown too great haste.
When, soon after, Winslow was sent to England, he took
letters from Governor Dudley and from Winthrop explaining the event and soliciting a mild judgment concerning it.

In 1635 a controversy arose between settlers from Plymouth who had been resident about two years on the Connecticut river and the emigrants who were then beginning
to arrive in the same region from Massachusetts. Those
from Plymouth, ignoring the protests of the Dutch, had
bought a tract from the Indians in what later became the
town of Windsor. There they built a trading post. But
the Massachusetts men, coming in this instance from the
towns of Dorchester and Newtown, coolly denominated the
region the "Lord's waste," and settled upon it, as they
thought, "without just offense to any man." But a part of
the tract of which they took possession was the same which
the Plymouth people had bought. The latter protested
through Jonathan Brewster, who was the agent in charge of
the interests of Plymouth on the Connecticut. The colony
also supported their contention. But the settlers from
Massachusetts, in addition to the argument already cited,
urged that their claim was justified by the strength of the
movement with which they were connected. The Plymouth
enterprise they called weak and temporary, and before this

appeal to the right of the strongest Plymouth was forced to give way. The Plymouth settlers thought at one time of appealing to the Warwick patentees, but their opponents would not agree to this. Therefore, after securing from the Dorchester men a formal acknowledgment of their right to the tract which they had bought from the Indians, the Plymouth people ceded to them all of the land which they claimed, except one-sixteenth. Upon the part of the land which was reserved stood the Plymouth trading house. With the settlers from Newtown, who occupied Hartford, an agreement on fairer terms was reached. " Thus," says Bradford, " was ye controversie ended, but the unkindness not so soone forgotten." [1]

In addition to frontier disputes concerning rights to land and trade such as those just cited, boundary controversies developed on a larger and more important scale. For a number of years after the grant of the Bradford patent to Plymouth uncertainty existed concerning the boundary between that colony and Massachusetts.[2] It originated in a dispute between the two border towns, Scituate and Hingham, over their right to the meadow which lay between them. Through those meadows ran the Cohassett river or brook, which was loosely designated in the Bradford patent as the northern boundary of Plymouth colony. Massachusetts had not determined where her line, three miles south of Massachusetts bay and the Charles river, would run, and was strongly inclined to claim everything drained by the southern tributaries of that river. As the controversy developed, Massachusetts claimed all of the town of Scituate and more, while Plymouth sought to balance this by claiming Hingham. Finally, the two colonies appointed commissioners, and in 1640, after much argument, the boundary throughout its eastern extent was fixed at the " bound brook " in the Cohassett meadows and at Accord [3] pond.

A similar dispute arose between Massachusetts and the colony of the River Towns on the Connecticut respecting the possession of Agawam or Springfield. Though this settlement lay north of the Massachusetts boundary, it was

[1] Bradford, 338 *et seq.*   [2] *Ibid.* 367 *et seq.*   [3] Plym. Recs. IX. 1.

much nearer to the Connecticut towns than to Boston, and
was connected with them by the river and by the natural
course of trade. A wilderness fifty miles in breadth separated it from the nearest town in eastern Massachusetts.
For this reason, in 1639, the local executive and judicial
powers of an assistant were bestowed by the inhabitants on
William Pynchon, their magistrate, and because of the few-
ness of the settlers the number required for the jury was fixed
at six instead of twelve.[1] Though towns were later founded
north of Springfield in the Connecticut valley, it continued
for more than a century to be the administrative and military centre of that region, and therefore held a position
somewhat more independent than was the case with most
New England towns. For a brief period after it was
founded the Connecticut towns insisted that they were
entitled to jurisdiction over it.[2] This both the magistrates
of Boston and the inhabitants of Springfield itself refused to
admit. But the trade of Springfield went down the river,
and it was considered bound to join with the Connecticut
towns in maintaining the fort at Saybrook. In this way
intercolonial relations of a somewhat delicate nature arose,
which might call for adjustment by some joint tribunal.

In addition to disputes over trade and boundaries which
might arise between the colonies themselves, their relations
with the Dutch and French easily occasioned controversies
over similar points, and these might involve issues of a far
wider and deeper importance. Along the course of the
Connecticut the territorial claim of the Dutch extended far
to the east of localities which by 1640 the English had
settled. During the next decade the English, in obedience
to a natural impulse, pushed on until their remotest outpost,
Greenwich, lay within thirty miles of Manhattan. This was
in accordance with the policy urged in 1642 upon the governor of Connecticut by Sir William Boswell, the representative of England at The Hague. " Doe not forbeare to put
forward their plantations," said he, " and crowd on, crowd-

---

[1] 5 Mass. Hist. Coll. I. 487. Pynchon had not at this time been chosen an
assistant by the general court.

[2] Winthrop, I. 343.

ing the Dutch out of those places where they have occupied,
but without hostility or any act of [1] violence." This fitly
describes the westward advance of the English from the
time when their traders passed beyond Narragansett bay
until the power of the Duke of York was established on the
Hudson itself. The tendency revealed itself as clearly on
Long Island as it did on the mainland. Three-fourths of
that region was settled by Englishmen, and most of the towns
which they founded there were exact reproductions of the
New England model; the larger part of them were also
independent of the Dutch. But until this process of westward expansion was more than half completed, the Dutch
retained a post at Hartford on the Connecticut, while it was
never possible to end the interminable boundary disputes by
an agreement which the English would observe. A similar
overlapping of claims existed on the north, but the English
and French were not yet in such proximity as to occasion
the difficulties which arose between the two rivals along the
western border. The relations, however, with both the
French and Dutch called for deliberation and action.

The Indians also confronted the English in nearly every relation of life. A visitation of disease, in which the Puritans
could see with special clearness the hand of providence, had
nearly destroyed the Massachusetts tribe a few years before
the arrival of the English. But when the English had
extended their settlements back from the coast a distance of
twenty miles or more, they came in contact with the Penacooks, Nipmucks, Wampanoags, Narragansetts, and had to
compete with them for the possession of the country. Those
who settled along the southern shore and on Long Island
sound found themselves in the presence of a relatively large
Indian population. The remote settlements in the Connecticut valley were surrounded by the Pequots, the Mohegans,
and the various tribes which occupied the highlands east
and west of the valley. In 1637 a war with the Pequots
called for the first armed coöperation of the colonies. It
was possible that Indian alliances and enmities might at
any time occasion war. Their alliances and enmities also

[1] Conn. Recs. I. 565.

extended beyond the borders, and were involved with the rivalries between the French, Dutch, and English. The sale of arms, ammunition, or liquor to the savages by colonists who belonged to any one of the three European nationalities might cause difficulties for the other two. The same result might follow from Indian trade of a more legitimate character. Internal policy, so far as it related to the savages, suggested also in other ways the advantages of joint management. This was especially true of efforts to convert and civilize the Indians. For these reasons the problems arising .from Indian relations occupied a prominent place among the causes which were contributory to the union of the New England colonies.

The sense of a common mission, which was so strong among the New England Puritans, naturally promoted joint action. They had a common civil and ecclesiastical system to uphold and extend. With this a system of schools, with its centre in Harvard College, was closely connected. Synods, whose members came from all the New England colonies, were called to regulate ecclesiastical polity and to give common expression to the principles of the faith. The strengthening of the churches and the maintenance of their purity through an educated ministry were regarded as objects of the highest importance. The restraint of error and schism suggested only the negative side of the same problem. These were objects of the most general attention, and could hardly fail to occupy a prominent place among the purposes of those who sought a closer union of the Puritan colonies. It was indeed in connection with the Synod of 1637, when the magistrates and ministers of Connecticut were at Newtown, that the adoption of articles of confederation was first seriously[1] broached. Notice was given to the magistrates of Plymouth, but too late for them to come or to send delegates. Hence the matter was for that time dropped.

In the history of Puritan New England nothing is more evident than the leadership of Massachusetts. This of course is to be explained in part by her superiority to the other colonies in population and resources. But apart from

[1] Winthrop, I. 283.

that, a decision, a power of initiative, a certain rigor, not to say ruthlessness, appear in her conduct, which does not show itself so distinctly in other colonies of the group. The oligarchy which governed Massachusetts was ready, whenever opportunity offered, to annex all weak or disturbed communities which were adjacent to its boundaries, and to assume protectorates with undefined possibilities over neighboring Indians. The dealings of Massachusetts with the Narragansett towns and with the settlements on the Piscataqua and in Maine furnish conspicuous examples of this spirit. This conduct shows that in the relations with the neighboring colonies Massachusetts utilized to the full the advantages which came from her royal charter. It gave steadiness to the policy which she adopted for the advancement of the Puritan faith and for the repression of dissent. She could adopt measures, both administrative and judicial, to which the colonies that had no charters would hesitate to resort. The foes of the Puritan system, both in New and Old England, showed a correct appreciation of the facts when they directed against Massachusetts their heaviest assaults. It was therefore certain that any confederation which might be formed would be a union among unequals, and its character would depend very largely upon Massachusetts.

In 1638, while the boundary dispute between Massachusetts and Plymouth was still unsettled, and the controversy over the towns in the Connecticut valley was in progress, Massachusetts proposed that two or more commissioners from each of the colonies interested should meet,[1] with power to agree upon articles of union. Connecticut objected to the bestowment of power on these commissioners, and desired that the general courts should have the final decision. Connecticut also submitted certain propositions of her own. These the magistrates at Boston began to discuss and amend, one of their objects being to give "some preëminence" to Massachusetts. To the proposed amendments Connecticut objected. The conference failed of its immediate purpose, though it occasioned much discussion respecting claims to

[1] Winthrop, I. 342.

Springfield and to the Pequot country, and concerning the
claims of Connecticut democracy as compared with Massachusetts aristocracy. Winthrop was of opinion that the
motive for it all was "their shyness of coming under our
government."

In 1642, perhaps because she feared an Indian war, Connecticut proposed that a confederacy should be established.
Plymouth was now willing to join. The proposals were
read before the general court of Massachusetts and referred
to a committee for consideration after the court rose. By
this body some changes were made and articles added, and
the whole was sent back to Connecticut, "to be considered
upon against the Spring." [1]

In May, 1643, commissioners from the four colonies which
were interested met at Boston.[2] All except those from Plymouth had authority to sign the articles. After two or three
meetings the terms were settled. It was resolved that the
settlements in Maine should be excluded, "because they ran
a different course from us both in their ministry and civil
administration." We do not know whether or not the admission of the Narragansett settlements was discussed, but
it is certain that when, in 1644, and again in 1648, those on
Rhode Island applied for admission, it was refused unless
they would consent to annexation by Massachusetts or
Plymouth.[3]

In the preamble to the Articles of Confederation the
reasons for the formation of the union were stated. They
were, that the parties to it had come to America with the
common purpose of extending the Christian religion and
enjoying its liberties in purity; that by the providence of
God in the process of settlement they had been scattered
further along sea-coasts and rivers than was at first intended,
so that they could not conveniently live under one government and jurisdiction; that they were surrounded by people
of foreign nationality, and were exposed to attack by the
Indians; and finally that, because of distractions in England,

[1] Mass. Recs. II. 31; Winthrop, II. 96, 102.
[2] Plymouth Recs. IX.; Winthrop, II. 119 *et seq.*
[3] Plymouth Recs. IX. 23, 110.

they could not appeal to her for help.   For these reasons they entered into a " consociation."

The name which was selected for the confederation was the United Colonies of New England.   Though in the language of the articles it was an union between plantations which were under the government of the colonies concerned, it would be absurd to draw the inference that it was a confederation of towns.   The nature of the union was stated in the articles to be " a firm and perpetual league of friendship and amity, for offence and defence, mutual advice and succor upon all just occasions, both for preserving and propagating the truths of the Gospel, and for their own mutual safety and welfare."   The territorial and governmental integrity of each of the confederating colonies was guarantied.   No other colony should be admitted, nor should any two of the confederated colonies join in one, without the consent of the Union.

The only governmental machinery created by the Articles of Union was a board of eight commissioners, two from each colony and chosen annually by their respective general courts. This body was little else than a joint committee of the general courts.   At each of its meetings it chose a president, who had only the powers of a moderator.   One regular meeting was held annually in September, and others on extraordinary occasions.   Meetings should be held in succession in each of the contracting colonies, though two sessions in each cycle must be held in Boston.   All the commissioners must be " in church fellowship."

The most important powers which were intrusted to the commissioners were those relating to defence.   The language of the articles implied that they should have full power to decide upon offensive, as well as defensive, war, also on peace, leagues, aids, charges, and numbers of men for war, and division of all the gains of war.   If in the case of attack on any of the colonies the danger should be slight, the nearest colony might give aid alone.   If the attack should be serious, on the appeal of three of the magistrates of the imperilled colony the entire force of the Confederacy should be called out.   At such times Massachusetts should equip one hundred men and the other colonies forty-five men each.

With the consent of the commissioners this proportion might be changed. No charge should be laid on the confederates for a defensive war, unless it was levied by order of the commissioners, and after they had decided the war to be just. The expenses of war should be borne by the colonies in proportion to the number of their male inhabitants between the ages of sixteen and sixty. The assessment and collection of revenue was left under the control of the respective colonies. The booty and other gains of war should be distributed in proportion to the burden sustained.

In addition to their war powers, the commissioners were authorized to take measures for the prevention of quarrels between the colonies; to see that escaped servants, prisoners, and fugitives from justice, fleeing from one colony to another, should be returned; that the administration of justice should be speedy and sure; that Indian affairs should be justly regulated, and that migration from one colony to another should be unhindered.

If unanimity could not be reached by the commissioners as the result of their discussion of any subject, the vote of six should be decisive. If so many as six votes could not be obtained, the question might be referred to the general courts. If they all approved, the proposal should become a law of the confederation. Room was left for the amendment of the articles by the provision that, if any article was found by one of the colonies to have an injurious effect, it should be considered by the commissioners of the other jurisdictions, "that both peace and the present confederation may be entirely preserved without violation."

The signers of the articles were Winthrop and Dudley of Massachusetts, Fenwick and Hopkins of Connecticut, Eaton and Greyson of New Haven, Winslow and Collier of Plymouth. They were chosen commissioners for the first year, and Winthrop was their first president. Bradford, Prince, Endicott, Bradstreet, John Winthrop, Jr., and Leete were afterwards prominent among the members. The articles provided for a very crude and simple form of union. The powers bestowed upon it were very limited, and the contrivance devised for executing the powers was of the

simplest description. The commissioners could not execute their own orders or provide the revenue necessary
thereto. It was possible that their projects might at any
time be checked by the opposition of two members. Their
orders must therefore take the form of advice, and were in
many, if not most, cases couched in that form. Still by
periodical meetings many common interests were advanced
and a steadiness was given to New England policy which
might otherwise have been unattainable.

Though members of the confederation were equally represented on the board of commissioners, they shared un-
equally in burdens and rewards. Massachusetts was the
leading colony in population, wealth, and influence. The
question of her precedence therefore naturally arose. At
the third meeting [1] of the commissioners she claimed as her
right the first place in the subscription of acts and orders.
The other colonies denied that any such privilege had been
proposed or granted, but to prevent further trouble they
agreed that the commissioners of Massachusetts should
continue to subscribe the acts first after the president, as
had thus far been the practice. This concession was repeated in 1648, but in neither case was it based on the claim
of right. All of the extraordinary sessions — five in number
— which were held by the commissioners during the continuance of the union were called at the instance of Massachusetts. In nearly all cases the occasion of the call was
the supposed necessity for measures of immediate defence.
In 1647, 1649, and twice in 1653, extraordinary sessions were
called for this reason. In each case the fear of conflict
with the Indians of southern New England, or with them
as the allies of the Dutch, furnished the occasion for the
sessions.

Annual sessions were regularly held until 1664, the year
of the royal commission and of the submission of New Haven
to government under the newly granted charter of Connecticut. As the confederation was wholly extra-legal and
its formation was one of the acts of the New England
colonies which might irritate the king, the Restoration

[1] Plymouth Recs. IX. 16, 109.

necessarily terminated the more active period of its life. In England in the person of the king an umpire now existed who was ready to decide intercolonial controversies. The disappearance of New Haven, thus reducing the number of confederated colonies to three, was followed by an order that the commissioners would henceforth meet triennially. The changes in the Articles of Confederation which were necessitated by the disappearance of New Haven as a separate colony were not adopted until 1670.[1] A few unimportant meetings were held between that time and the opening of Philip's war. During the period of that conflict the commissioners held several meetings.[2] After that their activity practically ceased, and the recall of the charter of Massachusetts in 1684 put an end forever to their existence.

The right to interpret the Articles of Confederation rested by implication, and in the first instance, with the commissioners, but finally with the general courts of the colonies themselves. If such questions became involved with political issues a single colony might decide the case for the confederation. This was done by Massachusetts in one notable instance. From this fact it appears — and the inference is justified by the entire history of the Confederacy — that the power of the commissioners was only advisory. Against the resolve of one colony, or in any case against that of two colonies, they were powerless to act. The function which they performed was that of a joint advisory board for the colonies, with certain designated spheres of action and subject to annual renewal.

To certain questions which Massachusetts submitted in 1648,[1] involving interpretation of the articles, the commissioners replied that, though they should issue orders on all matters within their powers, as treaties, sending messengers, designation of men, provisions and charges for common enterprises, censuring offenders, and the like, yet the execution of these measures belonged to the jurisdiction where the com-

---

[1] Plymouth Recs. X. 319, 324, 334, 345, 346.
[2] Ibid. 358 et seq. ; Conn. Recs. III. Appendix.
[3] Plymouth Recs. IX. 119, 126.

missioners sat or the colony where the offenders might be found.   If the colony in question, however, should refuse or delay action in such case, it would be guilty of breach of covenant.   The same would be true if it should change its religion.   But what remedy could be applied in such cases the commissioners confessed themselves unable to state. Several of the questions which were then raised were referred to the general courts for final decision.

The most important controversy that ever occurred respecting the nature of the union was occasioned in 1653 by rumors that the Dutch were plotting with the Indians for a massacre of the English in [1] the Connecticut settlements.   Color was given to these reports by the fact that war was then in progress between the parent states in Europe.   However, special inquiries by agents of the commissioners among the Indians and in New Netherland revealed no evidence of plots or intended hostilities.[2]   Still New Haven and the River Towns seemed very much alarmed and insisted on immediate war with the Dutch.   Two extraordinary sessions were held by the commissioners, and the general court of Massachusetts, after consultation with the clergy, took decisive action. The clergy, after hearing the charges which could be urged against the Dutch, reported that they did not consider these a sufficient cause for war, and recommended that clearer evidence be procured before resort was had to arms. The deputies of the general court of Massachusetts expressed the same view, and urged that messengers should be sent to the Dutch to demand satisfaction and security for the future.   When, however, at a later meeting the colonies on the Connecticut became more urgent for war, the general court of Massachusetts propounded the question, whether the commissioners had authority under the articles to commit the colonies to an offensive war.   The language of the sixth article, though far from precise, seemed to imply that they had the power.   But a committee of magistrates, to which the question was referred, reported that the commissioners were judges of defensive, but not of offensive war, and that

[1] Plymouth Recs. X. 56 et seq.
[2] Ibid. 27–52 ; Brodhead, History of New York, I. 550 et seq.

they could begin an offensive war only under express authority from the colonies involved. It could not have been the
intention of colonies which were so jealous of their independence to divest themselves of power in such weighty
matters.[1] It would be a " bondage hardly to bee borne by
the most Subjective people ; and cannot bee conceived soe
free a people as the Colonies should submite unto." With
this the deputies in the Massachusetts general court con-
curred, and insisted that any other conclusion was inconsistent not only with the right of self-government enjoyed
by each colony, but with the higher rights of conscience.[2]

The regular meeting of the commissioners at Boston, in
September, 1653, was mainly occupied with the controversy
over this subject. The commissioners from the smaller
colonies came resolved to insist on the literal interpretation
of the sixth article. But the general court of Massachusetts,
which was again in session, reaffirmed its position, that " the
Commissioners have not power to determine the Justice of
an offensive war so as to oblige the severall Colonies to acte
accordingly."[3] As execution must ultimately devolve on
the general courts, Massachusetts was confident that they
would agree in authoritatively interpreting the acts in harmony with her view. But the six commissioners remained
firm, and declared that Massachusetts desired to break up
the league. This, of course, Massachusetts denied, and
claimed that she was reserving only what was necessary to
her independence. Bradstreet and Hathorne, her two commissioners, then proposed that the board should proceed to
the regular business of the session. But soon after, a petition came from New Haven submitting the question whether,
since England and the Dutch were at war in Europe and
affairs were so unsettled in the colonies, war should not be

[1] Plym. Recs. X. 75.

[2] That this was not wholly a new doctrine in Massachusetts is shown by
objections which its general court made in 1645 to action on the part of the
commissioners which was likely to commit the colonies to a war with the
Narragansett Indians. The general court then objected to the despatch of
troops by order of the commissioners without express authority from the
colonies. Plymouth Recs. IX. 36. See Art. 7 of Body of Liberties.

[3] *Ibid.* X. 79.

declared.   The six commissioners voted unanimously in favor of this proposition, and Hathorne finally gave his vote with the majority.

Massachusetts appealed to Plymouth on the point at issue, but received a reply unfavorable to her view.   But still the Bay colony held out, and the session closed without any conclusion being reached.   Before the commissioners met again peace had been concluded in Europe, and the imagined peril had passed away.   By thus opposing action, the impulse to which originated in panic, Massachusetts rendered a valuable service to all New England, and to the Dutch as well.

The following year Massachusetts coolly announced that she abandoned the interpretation on which she had so strongly insisted.   She now acknowledged that the colonies were bound to execute the resolves of the commissioners according to the literal sense of the articles.   This the commissioners accepted, provided the general court of Massachusetts at its meeting would certify to the other general courts its consent and agree to act accordingly.[1] We have no evidence to show whether or not this was done. Among the changes, however, which were made in the articles in 1667 and 1670 was the introduction of a clause providing that neither the colonies nor the confederation should be involved " in any war " without the consent of the several general courts.[2]

Additional light will be thrown on the nature of this confederacy by reference to the influence actually exerted by the commissioners upon the questions which grew out of relations with the Dutch, French, and Indians.   Relations with the Dutch enlisted the interests of all the New England colonies, and, because they were generally sure of the united support of the English, the commissioners were able to act toward them with more than their usual decision and effect. In 1646 the commissioners began corresponding with Director Kieft concerning alleged injuries inflicted on the English by the Dutch at Good Hope, the destruction by them of the settlement planted by the New Haven people on the Delaware river, and the sale by Dutch traders of arms and

[1] Plymouth Recs. IX. 114.   [2] *Ibid.* 328, 338, 343, 350.

ammunition to the Indians at Fort Orange, on Long Island, at Narragansett bay, and elsewhere. The seizure in New Haven harbor by order of the government at Manhattan of the Dutch ship of a trader named Westerhouse, who was about to sail for Virginia without paying the required duties, also attracted much attention. Its significance arose from the fact that this was an assertion by the Dutch of jurisdiction in New Haven harbor. Relations between the Dutch and English on Long Island demanded some attention, as did the duties and fees collected at Manhattan from those who were engaged in trade with New Netherland. Behind the whole lay the question of boundary.[1]

During the administration of William Kieft at Manhattan the claims and counter claims of the two parties were asserted, but no progress was made toward an adjustment.[2] By the time Peter Stuyvesant was well installed in office the points at issue had increased in number, while the westward advance of the English made the establishment of some boundary line a necessity to the Dutch. Stuyvesant took up the question in a statesmanlike way and with an earnest desire for settlement. In 1650 he came to Hartford to meet the commissioners, while in session there, and to treat with them.[3] The Dutch had complaints to offer of a nature much more serious than those of the English, for they concerned the very existence of New Netherland itself. The discoveries of the Dutch had extended as far east as Narragansett bay and as far south as Delaware bay. They had taught the Plymouth settlers the value of trade about the Narragansett coast. They were the explorers of the lower course of the Connecticut river and of Long Island sound. They were the first to establish a temporary settle-

CHAP.
X.

---

[1] For a statement of English complaints made by the commissioners, see Plymouth Col. Recs. IX. 181. A statement still more full, made in 1653, appears in Plymouth Col. Recs. X. 13 *et seq.* For a statement of Dutch grievances, see *Ibid.* 65 *et seq.* The laws of New Netherland respecting trade will be found in Laws and Ordinances of New Netherland, 4, 15, 18, 66, 72, 92, 126, 175. Special complaints of the English concerning "recognitions" appear in Plymouth Col. Recs. IX. 108, 113.

[2] Plymouth Col. Recs. IX. 61, 76.   [3] *Ibid.* 171 *et seq.*

ment on Delaware bay, which was later followed by the permanent occupation of that region. Of their prior occupation of the valley of the Hudson and of Delaware bay and the Connecticut river there could be little doubt. In the Delaware region they had not yet been seriously disturbed by the English. But their claims in the Connecticut valley and along the sound were wholly ignored. Since English colonies had been founded both north and south of the Dutch settlements, and since all the territory which the Dutch occupied had repeatedly been included in grants from the English crown, prior occupation in their case was likely to avail little more than original discovery, unless it was supported by vigorous colonization. At that point the Dutch failed, and an important landmark in the history of their withdrawal before the advance of the English on the north is the boundary treaty which was concluded between Stuyvesant and the Commissioners of the United Colonies at Hartford, in 1650.

The first letter which Stuyvesant sent to the commissioners after his arrival at Hartford contained the words "New Netherland" as a part of its caption. He was informed by the English that that expression must be dropped, or the negotiation could not proceed. The word "Connecticut" was then substituted by the Dutch governor. After some further correspondence Stuyvesant suggested that two persons be appointed by each party and fully empowered to settle minor differences, to agree upon a provisional boundary subject to final determination in Europe, to agree upon the treatment of fugitives and, so far as possible, upon conditions of peaceful intercourse between the people of the two nationalities in America. This proposal was accepted by the. English. They appointed Simon Bradstreet and Thomas Prince; Stuyvesant appointed Thomas Willett and George Baxter, both English residents of New Netherland. They drew up the following agreement,[1] which was accepted by both parties. Reference to its terms will show how inconclusive it was.

The question of reparation for the wrongs which the

[1] Plymouth Col. Recs. IX. 188.

English alleged that they had suffered while Kieft was
director, was deferred until they could be investigated and
passed upon by the States General and the West India company. The controversy between the Dutch and English on
the Delaware was disposed of in the same way. Stuyvesant
explained that in seizing Westerhouse's ship he had not
intended to lay claim to New Haven, but was executing an
order to seize any Dutch ship found trading in the English
colonies without a license. New Haven accepted this explanation. In regard to the boundary, it was agreed that the
provisional line should run across Long Island from the west
side of Oyster bay directly south to the sea. From the sound
into the mainland the line should run from the west side of
Greenwich bay twenty miles due north. Northward of that
point its course should be determined by agreement between
the Dutch and the colony of New Haven, provided the line
ran through no point within ten miles of Hudson river.
The Dutch should not build any house within six miles of
the boundary. For the present Greenwich should be regarded as lying within Dutch territory. The Dutch should
retain the land they possessed at Good Hope, but all the
rest of the Connecticut valley should belong to the English.
It was agreed that this boundary should be maintained and
respected until the states of England and Holland should
approve or modify the agreement. In due time it was ratified by the States General, but the English government
never gave it the slightest notice. Had it done so, it would
have recognized the validity of the territorial claims of the
Dutch, a step which it consistently refused to take. When,
a decade later, the advance of English colonization had
gained increased momentum, it swept across this paper
barrier and English control was extended almost to Manhattan itself.

When the Confederacy was formed Massachusetts was
deeply involved in a controversy growing out of a recent
privateering expedition from Boston against certain French
settlements near the mouth of the Penobscot river and eastward of that point. This expedition was occasioned by the
appeals of Charles de la Tour, who occupied a post on the

St. John river, for aid[1] against his rival D'Aunay Charnisay, who held possession of Port Royal, and who in 1635 captured the trading post which had been established by Plymouth near the mouth of the Penobscot.   When, in 1632, by the treaty of St. Germains, Canada and Acadia, after the exploits of the Kirks and the Canada company, were restored by England to France, Claude Razilly had been made governor.   He brought over D'Aunay, who in the name of the governor took possession of the settlements in Acadia.   In 1635 Razilly died and left to D'Aunay his authority in these parts, the latter taking up his residence at Port Royal.   The territorial claims of the French extended indefinitely toward the west and southwest.   The two easternmost trading posts of Plymouth were regarded as clearly within their bounds.   The one at Machias had been seized in 1632, and now D'Aunay took possession of the other.   A vessel was sent under the authority of Plymouth to recover it, but the attempt did not succeed, while an application by the Plymouth colonists to Massachusetts for aid in the enterprise proved unavailing.

The interests of the family of La Tour in Acadia dated from the first French occupation of that region, and had been strengthened by grants from Sir William Alexander during the period of his proprietorship.   As soon as D'Aunay appeared Charles de la Tour went to Paris, got his grants confirmed, and secured from the company of New France the title of lieutenant general at Fort Lomeron and commander at Cape Sable.   Later he secured from the same source a grant of land on the St. John river, where he built the fort to which reference has already been made. La Tour was intensely jealous of D'Aunay, and as soon as the latter assumed office as the successor of Razilly a bitter rivalry began.   D'Aunay derived his authority immediately from the crown, while La Tour exhibited a letter from the company of New France and a commission from the vice-admiral of France.   Whether or not those documents were genuine it was difficult to tell.   After the rivalry between

---

[1] Winthrop, I. 246, II. 128 *et seq.*; Bradford, 431; Plymouth Col. Recs. IX. 24, 56; Parkman, Feudal Chiefs in Acadia.

the two had developed into an open conflict and La Tour had been once captured and imprisoned, he came to Boston and appealed for help, June, 1643.

At intervals during the two previous years Massachusetts had had dealings with La Tour. In 1641, through a Protestant emissary, he had asked for help and also for freedom of trade with the English. The former request was refused, but the latter was granted. In 1642 Catholic emissaries were sent to Boston and trade with La Tour was actually begun. The merchants of Boston found the trade to the eastern parts especially profitable and attractive. The Massachusetts people, however, were at this time informed by D'Aunay that he had an order from the French government for the arrest of La Tour. France was a friendly power. The authorities at Boston were therefore aware of the delicate and uncertain relations in which they were tempted to interfere. But the chances of profit from a filibustering expedition to the eastern parts operated as a strong attraction on the minds of the merchants. Though Winthrop was governor, yet with the approval of such magistrates and deputies as could be consulted at Boston, and without calling a session of the general court, permission was given La Tour to hire vessels for his purpose in Massachusetts. They promised also not to hinder such persons as would volunteer for the expedition. La Tour secured four vessels and about seventy men. Captain Edward Gibbons[1] and Thomas Hawkins were deeply interested in the enterprise, and the latter was the English commander of the expedition. He took with him a letter from the magistrates stating that the men who had been allowed to go were instructed not to " do or attempt anything against the rules of justice or good neighborhood." This letter he delivered to D'Aunay at Port Royal, and from the reply which he received, was convinced of the rightfulness of D'Aunay's claim, and refused to attack him. But some of his men joined La Tour in an attack, which resulted in the killing of three of D'Aunay's men and the burning of a mill. A pinnace loaded with furs belonging to D'Aunay was also

[1] Hazard. Hist. Colls. I. 499.

captured, and the plunder divided between La Tour, the shipowners, and the men.   The expedition then returned, having given D'Aunay sufficient cause for complaint, without seriously crippling him.

D'Aunay at once went to France, and secured there a grant of authority which beyond question put him legally in the right as against his rival.   The next summer, 1644, La Tour again appeared in Boston with an appeal for aid, and now stated that his adversary had prevailed against him in France.   At this time the Plymouth partners who had been interested in trade on the Penobscot made over their claims against D'Aunay for the destruction of their settlement to John Winthrop, Jr., Gibbons, and Hawkins.   They were empowered by force of arms or otherwise to recover possession.   This would indicate that another expedition was planning.   About the same time Warnerton of Piscataqua, with about twenty men, at the solicitation of La Tour, attacked D'Aunay's settlement on the Penobscot. Warnerton was killed, but his men destroyed the house and cattle and took the guard prisoners.   Thus D'Aunay was furnished with an additional cause of complaint.

But months before events had reached this point of development a storm of protest against the conduct of the Boston merchants in this affair, and the apparent indifference of the magistrates toward ,their proceedings, had arisen in the colony.   It first manifested itself when the nature of Hawkins's expedition in 1643 became known.   The feeling was strongest in Salem and vicinity, and it certainly proceeded in part from the jealousy with which Boston was regarded by the people of that section.   Saltonstall, Bradstreet, Symonds, and four of the ministers sent a remonstrance[1] to the governor and magistrates concerned, insisting that La Tour had not made out his case and that the course which was being pursued would bring down upon the colony the anger of France.   The fact that La Tour was a papist alarmed many, for an alliance with such was regarded as a league with idolaters.   At a meeting[2] of magistrates and a part of the deputies, which was called to discuss the arguments

---

[1] Hutchinson Papers, I. 129.   [2] Winthrop, II. 132.

raised by the opposition, the larger part of the time seems to have been spent in the consideration of the question, whether it was lawful for Christians to aid idolaters or to hold communion with them. Those who supported the negative ransacked the histories of the kings of Judah and Israel — Jehoshaphat, Josiah, Amaziah, and others — for precedents, while their opponents resorted to the good Samaritan argument drawn from the New Testament. Finally, coming to genuine historic precedents, the magistrates urged that European states frequently allowed aid to be hired among their subjects to be used against countries with which their governments were at peace. This was true, and precedents were cited from the relations between England and Holland and Spain to prove it. Emphasis was also laid on the unfriendly attitude of D'Aunay as a justification of the policy of Massachusetts.

Before La Tour made his second application for assistance Endicott had succeeded Winthrop in the governorship. Now, while trade relations were kept up with La Tour, a message was sent to D'Aunay stating that, if he could prove that he had suffered wrong, justice should be done him. Further decisive action was postponed till the general court should meet, and the substance of the letter which had been sent to D'Aunay was laid before the commissioners of the United Colonies[1] at their second meeting. The opinion which they expressed on this specific question was that, unless D'Aunay should abandon his offensive conduct, war with him might be risked in defence of La Tour, though it should be undertaken with the advice of the Confederacy. But at the same meeting, though in another connection, the commissioners adopted the rule, "that no Jurisdiction within this Confederation shall permitt any voluntaries to go forth in a warlike way against any people whatsoever, without order & direction from the Commissioners of the several Jurisdictions." When the event occurred, the machinery of the league was scarcely in operation, and such rule as the above did not exist.

During the interval before the next meeting of the com-

[1] Plym. Recs. IX. 24.

missioners, in response to satisfactory proof from D'Aunay that he was the legal representative of the French government, Massachusetts abandoned her defence of La Tour. A vessel from Massachusetts was however captured while carrying supplies to La Tour's fort. The fort was besieged by D'Aunay and captured, and all the men found in it were put to death. La Tour himself escaped. An agreement of peace was concluded between Massachusetts and D'Aunay. This was approved by the commissioners at their meeting in 1645.[1] Several opinions were also expressed by them at that time which by implication condemned the course pursued by the magistrates of Massachusetts in attempting to pass on the merits of the quarrel between the two French rivals. The following year, through negotiations with the envoys sent by D'Aunay to Boston, an agreement was[2] signed concerning the damages which he claimed, and the end of this troublesome affair was reached. It however helped to intensify the struggle between the deputies and magistrates in Massachusetts, which was in progress at that time.

The commissioners exercised supervision over relations between the Indians and the colonies in general. Indian relations occupied their attention more continuously than did any other subject. The tribes of northern New England, of Plymouth, of Massachusetts itself, gave little trouble. The attention of the commissioners was occupied almost wholly by the Narragansetts and their dependants, by the Mohegans and the remnant of the Pequots. These all were resident within the territory over which Connecticut was extending her authority, or which was adjacent thereto. The colonies continued to deal separately with the smaller or more peaceful bodies of Indians within their own limits. The principles of their policy in reference to trade and intercourse in general were occasionally approved or confirmed by the commissioners, but their time was not seriously occupied with this.

The commissioners interested themselves chiefly in keeping the peace among the Indian tribes of southern New

[1] Plymouth Recs. IX. 59.   [2] Winthrop, II. 334.

England, or between them and the English.　Collisions also between these tribes and the less warlike natives of Long Island were, so far as possible, prevented.　When the Confederacy was established, the feud between the Mohegans and the Narragansetts was at its height.　Uncas and Miantonomi were the leaders of the two hostile tribes.　The former was under the protection of the United Colonies, while the latter had the sympathy of the exiles in the Narragansett settlements.　Some of the aversion with which Massachusetts regarded Gorton was transferred to the sachem from whom Warwick was bought and who had befriended Williams.　The first question which came before the commissioners was one growing out of hostilities between these chiefs and their followers.　When Miantonomi hazarded a battle and was captured, the English unhesitatingly supported the Mohegan chief, and under their order the Narragansett sachem was put to death.

For ten years after this event the English were never free from the dread of an Indian war.　The Narragansetts and their dependants were enraged at the death of their chief and threatened revenge.　They declared that the Mohegans had agreed to accept a ransom for Miantonomi, and that it had been paid before his death.　But the statements of Uncas that this was false were accepted as satisfactory by the English.　The commissioners in the first interview with the hostile chiefs, in 1644, were able only to secure from the Narragansetts a promise not to attack Uncas before the end of the next planting season.　Occasional outrages, however, could not be prevented.　In 1645, under the threat of an expedition into their country and through the mediation of Williams, the Narragansetts were induced to meet the commissioners at Hartford.　There a treaty [1] was arranged, according to which the Narragansetts, because they had broken the agreement of 1638, promised to restore all they had taken from Uncas and pay the English two thousand fathom of white wampum.　Resort was no longer to be had to war until the questions in dispute had been submitted to the English.　Neither were the Narragansetts or Niantics

[1] Plymouth Recs. IX. 45 *et seq.*

to dispose of any land without the consent of the commissioners. Hostages were given by the Indians for the due observance of the treaty.

During the next five years the commissioners strove to secure the execution [1] of this treaty, but with very imperfect results. Only a part of the wampum was delivered, and that after persistent coaxing and threats. Occasionally the Indians were restless, while the fears of the English were kept alive by the tales and incitements of Uncas. Finally, after hope that the tribute would be paid had nearly vanished, the anxieties of the colonists culminated in the panic of 1653 over rumors of the conspiracy between the Dutch and Indians for the destruction of the English.

Considerable attention was also paid by the commissioners to the settlement of the remnant of the Pequots in Connecticut, and to the collection of tribute from them.[2] In this work the services of Uncas as chief Indian agent and governor were in constant requisition. In this connection the labors of the commissioners had chiefly to do with the after results of the conflict with the Pequots. Their work forms in a way the connecting link between that conflict and the much larger struggle, at a later time, with the Narragansetts and the other allies of Philip. But though their activity was extended and touched the natives at many points, it by no means comprised the whole of Indian relations in New England. As that subject is of importance sufficient to deserve special treatment, the Indian policy of the commissioners in some of its other features will be reserved for reference under the general subject of Indian relations.

Apart from the question of the war with the Dutch and Indians in 1653, the most serious controversy which arose during the existence of the confederacy was that between Massachusetts and the River Towns, over the attempt of the latter to levy a tribute on the trade of Springfield which went up and down the Connecticut river. The purpose of the River Towns in this policy was to maintain the fort at Saybrook, and fulfil their contract with George Fenwick

---

[1] Plymouth Recs. IX. 74, 85, 117, 143, 168.
[2] *Ibid.* IX. 97, 99; X. 142, 168, 199, 285, etc.

for its purchase. This provided, among other things, that
he should receive for ten years the duties collected from all
vessels which passed in and out of the river.[1] While Springfield was claimed by the River Towns, but after they had
ceased to exercise jurisdiction there, they ordered in 1645
the collection of two pence per bushel on corn, and twenty
shillings per hogshead on beaver, together with levies on
biscuit, horses, and cows, which should be sent down the
river from Springfield. Clearances were to be issued at
Hartford, Windsor, and Wethersfield, and officers at the fort
were ordered to stop vessels which did not produce a certificate that they had been duly cleared. The payment of
this duty was refused by the traders of Springfield, on the
ground that they belonged to the jurisdiction of Massachusetts. The penalty of confiscation, which the order provided for such cases, was not immediately enforced by the
River Towns, but was postponed until the opinion of the
commissioners of the United Colonies could be obtained.

In 1647, though the fort at Saybrook had been destroyed
by fire, the question was presented in due form before the
commissioners.[2] The Massachusetts commissioners brought
a declaration from her general court, to the effect that one
colony had no authority to force the inhabitants of another
colony to purchase a fort or lands outside its jurisdiction. It was also considered unfair to demand custom on
Springfield trade, and not on that of the Dutch. Massachusetts also claimed that the port of Saybrook afforded no
protection to Springfield, that the insistence on the imposition had long hindered the formation of the confederacy, and
that it tended to oppress the inhabitants at a time when their
resources were spent in building. The statement closed
with the suggestion that, if Hartford insisted on its claim,
reprisals on the part of Massachusetts might be expected.

The commissioners from Connecticut could of course
show no legal right for what they were doing, and simply
attempted to justify it on the ground of equity. They
claimed that the fort was useful to Springfield, and that on
river traffic in Europe similar levies were imposed and for a

[1] Conn. Col. Recs. I. 119, 266, 272, 568. [2] Plymouth Recs. IX. 90 *et seq.*

like purpose.   In their contention they had the support of
the commissioners from Plymouth and New Haven, with
whom the decision of the board rested.   It was therefore decided that for the ensuing year the toll should be
collected.   It was also held by the commissioners that the
levy of the tax for the defence of the mouth of the river or
for dredging it, was not an infringement of the liberty of
traders along its banks, even though they lived in another
jurisdiction.   The rate of duty, however, should not be increased without the consent of the colonies, and it should be
continued only so long as the fort was maintained and right
of passage thereby secured.

When the question came up again, in 1648,[1] Massachusetts
suggested some changes in the articles, which indicated, either
that she desired an increase in her representation on the
board, or that she was ready to free herself in part from even
the weak restraints which the confederation seemed to impose
upon her.   Since there were more poor laborers and artisans
in Massachusetts than in the other colonies, she considered
the rule unfair that burdens should be distributed among
members of the Confederacy strictly in proportion to numbers.
She suggested that it would be sufficient if the commissioners
met triennially.   She was suspicious that the commissioners
might appoint some officers to execute their orders, and thus
take that work from the officials of the colonies.   " Forasmuch," its delegates concluded, " as orders by way of advice
are in some cases introductions to orders of power, where the
advice is not followed, it is to be propounded if it were not
seasonable to be declared that in such Caces, if any of the
colonies shall not thinke fitt to Folow such advice, the same
not to be accounted any offence or breach of any article of
the Confederation or to give power or occasion to the commissioners to prosede to any act of authority in such Cace."
To these propositions the commissioners from the other
colonies naturally refused to consent.

After urging some rather theoretical arguments in support
of their contention the commissioners from Massachusetts demanded that the River Towns should produce the patent by

[1] Plymouth Recs. IX. 119 *et seq.*

which they claimed Saybrook, and the order of their court
levying the impost.[1] The former was produced, but the
latter they had not brought with them to the meeting. Then
the delegates from New Haven interposed and asked that
the matter be postponed until the next year, and in the meantime that Massachusetts should have her southern boundary
ascertained, so that it might be positively known to which
jurisdiction Springfield belonged. With this the discussion
of the subject at that meeting closed.

In 1642 Massachusetts, at her own expense, had surveyed[2]
a line from Wrentham to Windsor, which lay twelve miles
or more south of what was later ascertained to be the correct
boundary. To this, at the meeting of the commissioners in
1649, she referred Connecticut,[3] and continued to maintain
for seventy years that it was her southern boundary. But
the rival colony refused to be satisfied with this decision.
Massachusetts had also in the meantime laid countervailing[4]
duties on goods of Plymouth, Connecticut, and New Haven,
which were imported or exported through Boston harbor.
To this Connecticut replied by confirming its previous order
levying the toll on the river trade of Springfield and sent a
copy of the same to the commissioners. The commissioners
from the colonies immediately affected[5] protested against
the conduct of Massachusetts as an injury to those who had
no share in the dispute, and a violation of the spirit of the
articles. In 1650 Massachusetts, on condition that Connecticut would no longer levy toll at Saybrook, repealed the
duty. Though no act of repeal appears, the disappearance
of reference to the controversy from the records shows that
at least the order was no longer enforced against Springfield.

The labors of the commissioners in the interest of schools,
of the church, and of missionary work among the Indians
were continuous during the entire period of the existence of
the confederacy. At their second meeting, in the year 1644,
they recommended[6] to the general courts that those who

[1] Plymouth Recs. IX. 125, 133, 134.

[2] Larned, History of Windham County, Connecticut, I. 13. This was
known as "Woodward's and Saffery's line."

[3] Plymouth Recs. IX. 151 *et seq.*

[4] Mass. Recs. II. 269; Plym. Recs. IX. 157.

[5] *Ibid.* 157.

[6] *Ibid.* 20.

refused voluntarily to contribute the due proportion toward church expenses should be rated by authority and compelled to pay. At the same meeting a communication was received from Rev. Thomas Shepard of Cambridge soliciting support for Harvard College, "that school of the prophets that now is." He urged the commissioners to recommend that families which felt themselves able so to do, should give one quarter of a bushel of corn per annum, or its equivalent, and that ministers be urged to stir up the hearts of the people once a year on this subject. This was approved and the suggestion recommended to the general courts as worthy of their consideration. In response to this Massachusetts and Connecticut took the desired action.[1] The disposal of these gifts was left to the president, and he administered the trust subject to advice[2] on the part of the commissioners. Occasionally the college applied to the commissioners for aid in repairing or enlarging buildings, seeking funds raised by the Society for the Propagation of the Gospel in New England as well as contributions from residents of the colonies[3] themselves.

In 1644 a letter was received[4] from the governor of Massachusetts on the spread of error among the churches and the way in which it might be checked and the truth fully established. The meeting that year being at Hartford, the elders who were present were asked whether some confession of doctrine and discipline should not be prepared and published for the strengthening of the weak and stopping the mouths of adversaries. The ministers agreed that this was the proper course, and said that they would acquaint the rest of their brethren with it, and endeavor to satisfy the desires of the commissioners in this as soon as possible. Thus the project for the synod of 1646 originated.

At the meeting in New Haven, in 1646, the spread of error was again considered[5] with apparent reference to the Narragansett settlements, and it was observed how "licentious liberty" was granted in some parts of New England,

---

[1] Mass. Recs. II. 86 ; Conn. Recs. I. 112.   [4] *Ibid*. 28.

[2] Plymouth Recs. IX. 94 *et seq*.   [5] *Ibid*. 81.

[3] *Ibid*. 216.

" whereby many, casting off the rule of the Word, profess and practice what is good in their own eyes." A reference to the recent efforts of the Presbyterians in Massachusetts may be seen in the statement that petitions against " the good and straight waies of Christ " had been presented in some of the colonies. Though the delegates from Plymouth desired to consider the matter further, the commissioners advised the several general courts to keep " a due watch " at the doors of God's house, that none be admitted as members but such as had an effectual calling and had entered by an express covenant; that baptism should be administered only to such members and to their immediate seed, and that all errors which undermined or slighted the Scripture, the Sabbath, and other ordinances, or which favored unwarrantable revelations or inventions of men, or any carnal liberty " under the deceitful color of liberty of conscience," might be suppressed. This was one of the earliest declarations against the rising notion of the halfway covenant, and we may suppose that it contained the sentiments, if not the words, of John Davenport.

At the same meeting the commissioners from Massachusetts were urged to consult with the general court and elders there in order to devise a way by which ministerial graduates of Harvard College, especially those who had been helped through their course by contributions, might be induced not to remove into other colonies or countries, but to enter on the service of the churches of New England. Another most interesting and characteristic resolution of this meeting provided that all the colonies should be urged to interest themselves in making a collection of special providences, for the purpose of showing in how special a manner God had dealt with New England. This proposal was reported in 1656.[1]

When the Quakers began to appear in 1656, Massachusetts called loudly and repeatedly on the commissioners to support an united policy of exclusion against them and to uphold the orthodox ministry.[2] To these appeals a ready response was given. Strong resolutions on the justice of the claim

---

[1] Plymouth Recs. X. 176.   [2] Ibid. 155, 180, 212.

of the ministry both to financial and moral support were adopted. In 1656 the commissioners urged the general courts to prohibit Quakers entering the colonies, and to expel those who had come in. In 1658 they then went to the full length with Massachusetts in recommending that convicted Quakers should be banished under pain of death, and, if they afterwards returned, they should publicly renounce Quakerism or be executed.

The activity of the colonies in missionary work among the Indians occupied much of the attention of the commissioners after 1649. In that year, partly through the efforts of Edward Winslow, who had then returned finally to England, and in accordance with a plan which was proposed by the Commissioners of Plantations, the Society for the Propagation of the Gospel in New England was created, by an ordinance of the Council of State.[1] Its officers were a president, treasurer, and fourteen assistants, and it was empowered to hold land in England or Wales not exceeding £2000 per annum, and any goods and sums of money whatever. A general collection should be made through England and Wales for the foundation of the charity, and the Commissioners of the United Colonies, or such as they should appoint, were designated to receive and expend the funds in such a way as would best promote the extension of the Gospel among the natives and the education of their children.

By this act some recognition was given to the colonial union, as was also done by the express continuance of this relation when, after the Restoration, the society was again chartered with Robert Boyle as its president.

During the entire existence of the Confederacy, an active correspondence was maintained between the commissioners and the officers of the society. Besides Winslow, William Steele, the president of the society while it existed under an ordinance of the Council of State, and Robert Boyle, who was the first president after it had been chartered by the crown, were their chief correspondents in England. In New England John Eliot, the Mayhews, Pearson, Thomas Stanton and others, as missionaries, interpreters, Indian

[1] Hazard, Hist. Colls. I. 527, 635; Palfrey, II. 198.

workers or patrons of the enterprise, labored to an extent un- CHAP.
der the advice and direction of the commissioners. The com- X.
missioners from England ordered supplies of clothing, tools,
and other articles for the praying Indians. These were
purchased by the society from its fund or from funds available through contributions in New England. They were
sent over to the commissioners and distributed through their
agents. Edward Rawson, the secretary of Massachusetts,
acted, for a considerable time after 1651, in this capacity.[1]
Hezekiah Usher began in 1657 to act as foreign exchange
banker for the commissioners, and drew bills of exchange for
their convenience in transactions with the society.[2] He
seems also to have kept some of their[3] funds. An account of expenditures in this service was kept by the commissioners and annually submitted to the society in England.
It contained the salaries of the missionaries and schoolmasters, of the Indian helpers and interpreters, the fees of
agents and others who were appointed to administer justice
among the Indians or to care for their health, the expenditures for clothes, books, and other supplies for the Indians, the
payments for printing catechisms and other text-books, and
finally for Eliot's Indian Bible.[4] Payments were also made in
this account for the board and other charges of Indian youths
who were being educated in private families or at Harvard
College. The permanence and success of the work of course
depended largely on the number and ultimate usefulness of
the young men. With a tone of discouragement the commissioners were forced repeatedly to note the high mortality
which prevailed among them, and how few survived the
period of training. But the joint efforts of the society in
England and of the commissioners in New England continued until Philip's war caused its collapse and ruin.

[1] Plymouth Recs. IX. 195, 205.   [3] Ibid. 356.
[2] Ibid. X. 195, etc.   [4] Ibid. 205, 218, 240, 256, 314.

CHAPTER XI

THE LAND SYSTEM IN THE CORPORATE COLONIES OF NEW ENGLAND

PART
II.

THE form of group settlement which we have seen developing in Plymouth was reproduced throughout New England, and wherever New Englanders settled. The joint action of the settlers in locating dwellings and home lots, in laying out village streets, in subdividing the adjacent arable land, in subjecting the meadow and the forest for a time to common management, resulted in the founding of the town of Plymouth. The agrarian policy of the settlers constituted the most characteristic element in the town organization. The church fellowship, originating in this case at an earlier date, formed another bond of union within the group. It was the coexisting agrarian and ecclesiastical bonds which united the inhabitants into a group and made the creation of a town government both natural and a necessity.

That which occurred at Plymouth happened also at Salem, in each of the settlements about Massachusetts bay, in the towns of Plymouth colony, as one after another they came into existence, among the settlements of northern New England, in the towns which were founded on the shores of Narragansett bay and along the course of the Connecticut river. On Long Island, too, and wherever in New Jersey New Englanders found their abode, the same form of settlement was reproduced. Throughout this entire section the study of local settlement and of town government is the study of a single model and of the somewhat minute variations to which as an original type it was subjected. Local settlements in the section referred to conform as strictly to a single type as do the colonies themselves. A high degree of uniformity distinguishes the colony governments of New

424

England, but it is no greater than that which appears among CHAP.
the towns.   XI.

It would seem that the explanation of this is to be found
in the fact that settlement throughout New England, and in
the outlying districts which were colonized by New Englanders, was effected by groups.   Each group was moved by
an impulse which at the outset was shared by all or nearly
all its members.   Incongruous elements might later creep in,
but as a rule they were carefully excluded.   The migrations
and removals which resulted in the colonization of New England were effected by congregations, by neighborhoods, by
families.   Some of these groups religious or political conflicts
had united, while the same struggles had separated them from
former associates.   Others, acting under a common social
impulse, sought better farming lands or locations more favorable for trade.   The familiar history of the settlement of the
oldest towns in each of the New England colonies furnishes
detailed illustrations of this fact.   The extension of settlement from the original centres and the reproduction of towns,
whether by the division of old ones or by the formation of
new and remote villages, simply multiply illustrations of the
same process.

The groups which formed the population of the New England towns were democratically organized.   This does not
mean that they were without class distinctions, or that they
were destitute of leaders or of families which possessed strong
aristocratic instincts.   But it does mean that a considerable
degree of social and political equality existed within them,
and that it was the conscious policy of each group to
maintain such equality.   The towns of the seventeenth and
eighteenth centuries were in the main simple farming communities, where many small freeholders and almost no large
ones, existed.   In local concerns they were governed by non-
representative democratic assemblies, and by officials who
were elected in these assemblies.   The very plan upon which
the town was founded and in accordance with which it was
governed discouraged the growth of large properties and the
development of social inequality.   Its object was to perpetuate the unity and the simplicity of the town as they were at

the beginning. Families were able to accumulate large wealth only in port towns and by means of trade.

Though there were aristocratic elements in the New England town and its society, the monarchical element was totally lacking. The town has been likened to the manor, and the analogy to an extent is justified. The European manor was peopled by what may roughly be called a peasant democracy, settled in villages and hamlets. In England in the seventeenth century these early organizations for general local purposes had grown together into the parish. From such groups in many instances came the early American colonist. The characteristics of these groups were to a degree perpetuated in the New World. Experiences, suggestions, customary modes of action derived from the manor, the village, the hamlet, the parish, probably influenced the course of action of the first settlers, though no written evidence of the process appears. The town was an adaptation of well-known English forms of local settlement to new, or at least modified, conditions at the beginning. In a similar sense were all the features of colonial government — the executive, legislative, judicial, military, ecclesiastical systems — imitations and adaptations of English, or more general European, practice. But in no case were they slavish imitations of a model, while the emphasis will doubtless be incorrectly laid if any one of the entire list were selected as *par excellence* an example of either imitation or adaptation.

The manor, especially in its later and customary form, was a democratic group with a monarchical head. The New England town was a democratic group without a monarchical head. In English-American colonization the proprietor, both socially and politically, was the representative and embodiment of the monarchical idea. Monarchy, as an institution, secured its foothold in American soil, in one form or another, through the proprietorship. Wherever the genuine proprietary régime existed, emigration and settlement were largely directed from a single centre, because the proprietor sought income from the land of his province, he advertised its advantages, planned its settlement, sold its lands, exacted a quitrent from its grantees, in short, developed a provincial land system, the nature of which will be the subject of future inquiry. In a real, though not in the fullest sense, emigration to the proprietary provinces was assisted emigration, the encouraging and directing influence of the proprietor being felt through it all. That emigration to New England and the progress of settlement within that section were wholly unassisted or left without direction, it would be a mistake to claim. Salem was founded under a proprietary system, though it soon escaped from control of that kind. A plantation or two, like that of Cradock at Medford, was granted, on which tenants may possibly have lived. Productions like White's *Planters Plea*, and events like the removal of the Leyden congregation, the Agreement at Cambridge, and the consequent action of the Massachusetts company, and many events connected with the settlement of other colonies and of towns as well, show that Puritan emigration was not without intelligent control.

But the method and the purposes of that control differed from those which appear in connection with the settlement of the proprietary provinces. Moved by the pressure of religious disabilities at home and by the fear of greater sufferings which were believed still to be in store, the Puritans removed spontaneously and in large numbers to the New World. They did this under a common impulse, and as the result of agreements and widespread understandings. Occasionally an entire congregation removed. The departure of ministers or prominent laymen induced parts of congregations and large numbers of families and individuals to go. This was accomplished without special aid from broadsides, pamphlets, or sermons setting forth the advantages of the new country, without the offer of head rights or concessions of land in other forms. The fact that a prospect was opened for escape from episcopal domination, for the establishment of their favorite ecclesiastical polity under the protection of a government of their own, was tacitly accepted as a sufficient guaranty of the rest. It was instinctively believed that comfort and prosperity would follow in the wake of this much desired liberty.

This view of the problem resulted in the development by

the Puritan colonies of a land system which differed characteristically from that of the proprietary provinces. The Puritan colonies as such did not seek profit from their land, but granted it freely to actual settlers and in such amounts as suited their immediate and prospective needs. No distinct land office was established by any New England colony. Land was not sold by the colony; neither, except in the case of certain islands[1] and very rarely of some other tract, was it leased. Rent[2] formed no appreciable part of the colony revenue. Many grants of land to individuals were made by the colony, usually as a form of reward for valued public service. But such grants were the exception rather than the rule. By far the greater part of the land in the New England colonies was granted to towns, that is, to groups or communities of settlers by whom it was allotted to individuals. The grants to towns were made in large tracts, six miles square[3] or more, the grant often being described in the most general terms, without even a specification of its bounds. Under the pressure of immediate need the earliest settlers about Massachusetts bay located themselves where the best chances seemed to offer, without formal grants, and the bounds of their towns were afterwards fixed by the general court, or were determined by the establishment of new towns. The sickness which prevailed at Salem during the winter of 1629–1630, and that which followed among Winthrop's colonists at Charlestown during the next summer and autumn, forced the settlers to divide. This resulted in the settlement of Boston, Roxbury, Dorchester, Watertown, Newtown, Medford, and Saugus. These towns were named

[1] One of the rare instances was the lease by Plymouth colony in 1679 of a tract of land at Pocasset to Captain Benjamin Church. Church was to pay fifty shillings for the use of this land for one year. Plymouth Recs. VI. 14.

[2] In the Body of Liberties of Massachusetts, and in the Connecticut Code of 1650, it was declared that the lands of these colonies should be free from all fines and licenses upon alienation, from heriots, wardships, liveries, primer seizins, year, day and waste, escheats or forfeitures on the death of parents or ancestors. Colony law, however, generally provided for the escheat of land when no heir for it could be found. Mass. Col. Laws, Ed. of 1889, p. 35; Conn. Col. Recs. I. 536, 525; New Haven Recs. II. 589.

[3] Egleston, Land System of the New England Colonies, J. H. U. Studies, IV. 577.

by order of the assistants, while six years later their powers were recognized by the general court,[1] and the authority of the court over them was fully asserted. Even before this general township act was passed, the general court had declared that none but itself had power to dispose of land or to give and confirm property rights.[2] Towns, therefore, in allotting lands, acted legally as agents of the Massachusetts company.

Massachusetts, after the first few years had passed, carefully superintended the founding of towns, and did not scruple to interfere in their affairs when occasion seemed to demand it. The magistrates and general court sought in this matter, as in all others, to follow a system, having regard not only to local interests, but to the welfare of the colony as a whole. It was customary for the general courts to appoint committees, consisting in most though not in all cases of residents, to superintend the laying out of plantations. The founding of Ipswich, first as a plantation and afterward as a town, was undertaken with express reference to the need which was felt, during the years 1633 to 1635, that the northern part of Massachusetts should be settled, so as to keep it out of the hands of the French.[3] In 1635 Newbury, in the same region, was also made a plantation. The court ordered land to be set apart there for the keeping of sheep and cattle which had recently come over in "the Dutch shipps," and also granted permission for the building of a mill and weir. In 1638 a committee was appointed by the general court to assist in the settlement of Hampton and in the allotment of land there, and it was ordered that nothing should be done without their allowance.[4]

The establishment of a plantation at Marblehead was ordered and regulated by the general court, and none were allowed to inhabit there without its leave, or without the permission of two of the magistrates.[5] The process of lay-

---

[1] Mass. Col. Recs. I. 172; Chamberlain, 2 Proceedings of Mass. Hist. Soc. VII. 235.

[2] Mass. Col. Recs. I. 117.   [4] *Ibid.* 236.

[3] Winthrop, I. 118; Mass. Col. Recs. I. 103, 136, 149.   [5] *Ibid.* 147.

ing out Lancaster — then called Nashaway — under the
authority of the general court, began in 1644. In 1645,
upon the petition of the interested parties, a committee of
residents was designated to lay out lots there to all the
planters in proportion to their estates and charges, to locate
their houses, and to see that all grantees took the oath of
fidelity. But delays[1] in the settlement followed, and not
until 1653 were town rights fully bestowed, and then under
very comprehensive regulations as to the laying out of lands.
When, in 1655, Groton was made a plantation, the general
court made the grant, designated Mr. Danforth of Cambridge and those whom he should associate with him[2] to lay
it out, and appointed those who for two years should serve
as its selectmen. Controversies having arisen in Sudbury
concerning both common and allotted lands, a committee
which was appointed by the general court reported in 1656
in such a way as to indicate that the management of town
lands might be subject to review to almost any extent.[3]
This report was accepted by the inhabitants of Sudbury and
ratified by the general court, as embodying a satisfactory
adjustment of the dispute.

In 1660, in response to a petition of certain inhabitants of
Ipswich, the general court granted them a tract, six miles
square, near Quaboag ponds, on condition that within three
years twenty families should be settled there, and that they
should have a minister. These[4] conditions were not fulfilled. In 1667 there were only six or seven families on the
place. The general court then declared that the original
grant was void, and that the Ipswich men, with the exception
of those who had become actual settlers, had lost their rights.
But in response to a petition and in order to promote the
settlement of the place, the court now appointed a committee,
with Captain John Pynchon at its head, to admit inhabitants,
grant lands, and manage local affairs until the plantation had
become sufficiently strong to be made a town. If the inhabitants of Ipswich who had professed a desire to settle there
would give security that they would make the removal

[1] Mass. Col. Recs. II. 75, 76, 136, 212 ; IV[1]. 139, 296.
[2] *Ibid.* IV[1]. 235.   [3] *Ibid.* 274.   [4] *Ibid.* 421 ; IV[2]. 342, 568.

within one year, their rights should be secured. The experiment now proved a success. In 1673 the plantation was made a town with the name of Brookfield, and a post was thereby planted in the Nipmuck country, midway between the settlements along the streams and tide-waters of the east, and those which were already developing in the Connecticut valley.

The attempt of the magistrates to divert the inhabitants of Newtown, Watertown, and Dorchester from removal in 1635 to the valley of the Connecticut agitated the whole colony. Though in the end the removal could not be prevented, it was to an extent controlled by the general court. When in 1641 the question arose whether Springfield lay within the jurisdiction of Massachusetts or Connecticut, the general court at Boston[1] specially commissioned William Pynchon to administer justice in Springfield, trying and adjudging minor causes there according to Massachusetts law, and granting appeals to the court of assistants. Commissions were issued to Pynchon, to Henry Smith, and afterward to a board of three members whose jurisdiction should extend over Springfield, Northampton, and Hadley. The last mentioned board was continued in existence until Hampshire county was established.[2] These commissions, however, were judicial in character, and did not extend to the entire management of town affairs. But Northfield, the remote frontier town, was laid out by commissioners of the general court, was twice resettled under such jurisdiction, and continued under it far into the eighteenth century.[3] In 1679 a general order was passed that localities which had been abandoned during the late war should not be resettled, or new plantations formed, except under the direction of committees appointed by the governor and council or by the court of the county where the settlement was to be located.

The outline which has now been given of the way in which the Massachusetts general court, by means of committees, superintended the settlement of the colony, will show

---

[1] Mass. Col. Recs. I. 321 ; II. 41, 109.
[2] *Ibid.* IV[1]. 49, 67, 115, 214, 379; IV[2]. 52.
[3] *Ibid.* IV[2]. 528, 542; V. 213 ; Temple and Sheldon, History of Northfield.

how easy it was for her to extend such control outside the bounds which were set by the royal charter. A mode of procedure which would prove effective on the Connecticut, might also be used on the Piscataqua, among the Narragansett settlements, or in the Pequot country. As we have seen, attempts were made with greater or less success to use them in all those regions. Inhabitants of Roxbury were granted a remote plantation, which, when the lines were correctly run, developed into Woodstock, Connecticut. Dedham, as well as other towns in the eastern part of the colony, was interested in the same way in settlements along the Connecticut valley. To the forming of plantations and the reproduction of towns there need be no limit. From the existing hive swarms might be sent off in any direction, and might establish a new hive at any point. The process was already begun by which the continent was to be peopled; by which much of Europe had been peopled centuries before. It is clear that circumstances of climate and soil were more favorable to the extension of settlement in the northern than in the southern colonies. But the process of settlement itself was more effective and vital in New England than was that which obtained under the proprietary régime in the south.

The legislation of Massachusetts affected the towns not only at the time of their organization, but continuously and in reference to their most important internal affairs. As in this connection we are immediately concerned with the land system, only a passing reference will be made to the utilization of the towns by the colony as local units for the election of deputies, for the assessment of rates, for the organization and training of the militia, for the maintenance of the peace, the care of the poor, the building and repair of roads and bridges, the registry of deeds, and of births, deaths, and marriages, and for all purposes of government. The towns also were the ecclesiastical centres within the colony, and upon them devolved the obligation of maintaining the common schools. In regard to all these things colony legislation to an extent prescribed and directed their action. In the matter of land, fences, and town herds — the subjects now under consideration — the towns were not left to themselves.

Not only were the boundaries of all the towns fixed by order of the general court, and boundary disputes settled by it, but by an act of 1647 [1] they were required to perambulate their bounds once every three years. This should be done in May by officers of the selectmen's appointment, and by them the heaps of stones and the trenches by which the bounds were marked should be renewed. From early times the law required the maintenance of fences about fields and meadows, and imposed upon him who was faulty in this respect the damage which might be inflicted by cattle.[2] The obligation to fence enclosed commons was imposed on all who shared in their use, and that in proportion to their shares. The same principle also applied to the decision of questions relating to the management of common fields. The voices of those who held the largest shares should carry the greatest weight.

The act of 1643 on the subject of common fields gave to town officers the decision of disputes among commoners. It read as follows : " Whereas it is found by experience that there hath bene much trouble and difference in severall townes about the manner of planting, sowing, and feeding of common corne fields, & that upon serious consideration wee finde no generall order can provide for the best improvement of every such common ffield, by reason that some consists onely of plowing ground, some haveing a great part fit only for planting, some of meadowe & feeding ground; also so that such an order as may bee very wholesome and good for one field may be exceeding priudiciall & inconvenient for another, — it is therefore ordered, that, where the commoners cannot agree about the manner of improvement of their field, either concerning the kind of graine that shall be sowen or set therein, or concerning the time or manner of feeding the herbage thereof, that three such persons in the severall townes that are deputed to order the prudential affaires thereof, shall order the same, or in case where no such are, then the maior part of the freemen, who are hereby enioyned with what convenient speed they may

---

[1] Mass. Recs. II. 210.
[2] *Ibid.* I. 106 ; II. 15, 39, 49, 195.

to determine any such difference as may arise upon any information given them by the said commoners."

In the early years of the colony many special orders were passed concerning the care of herds of cattle and swine, but soon the regulation of details in this matter had to be left to the towns. The appointment of fence-viewers and maintenance of pounds were required by law.[1]

Upon the policy which was followed in the admission of residents into the towns depended not only the moral and religious character of the people, but also the number of paupers, or of those who were likely to become such, who solicited admission to the colony or transference from town to town. In 1637, while Massachusetts was in the heat of the Antinomian excitement, she passed for religious reasons a rigid law of settlement.[2] It forbade any town, under penalty of heavy fine, to entertain a stranger for a longer period than three weeks, or to allot him any land without the consent of one of the council[3] or two of the other magistrates. In the following year this act was made permanent. The towns very generally passed a similar order, though in their case it was intended more as a protection against the settlement of paupers than was the original colony act.

The land systems of Plymouth, Connecticut, and New Haven differed in no important particular from that of Massachusetts. The control which was exercised by those colonies over their towns was quite as complete as that which has just been described. In the case of Plymouth it was somewhat more complete. The general court granted land very freely to individuals, both in the town of Plymouth and outside, and continued to do so for[4] some time after distinct town governments came into existence. The colony did not hesitate, through committees, to regulate in great detail the distribution of land within towns when controversy[5] had arisen. A peculiarly close connection existed

---

[1] Colonial Laws of Mass., Ed. of 1887, 18, 19.

[2] Mass. Col. Recs. I. 196, 228.

[3] This apparently refers to the standing council.

[4] Plymouth Col. Recs. III. 142, 164 ; IV. 3, 4, 8, 18, 108, etc.

[5] See especially the cases of Sandwich and Yarmouth. Plymouth Col. Recs. I. 88, 117, 147 ; II. 121, 128.

between the colony government and the town of Plymouth, so that occasionally, subsequent to 1640, records of grants by town meetings appear also in the colony records. Somewhat the same confusion appears in the early records of New Haven town and colony, showing that in the early years the two were not kept so distinct as was the case in the other colonies.

The system followed by those colonies in the establishment of plantations, the recognition of them as towns, the fixing and maintenance of their bounds, the regulation of the granting of lands, of common fields, fences, herds, the punishment of trespass, the admission of inhabitants and freeholders, the requirement that fence-viewers and pound-keepers should be appointed, that records of land titles should be kept, is substantially the same as that which has been already described, and the details need not be repeated. Orders were issued and committees were appointed by the general courts for the regulation [1] of those matters as freely as in Massachusetts. The extension of settlement by the multiplication of towns finds as remarkable illustration in the history of Connecticut and New Haven as it does in that of Massachusetts. Stamford, in Connecticut, and Hadley, in Massachusetts, were offshoots of Wethersfield; Newark, in New Jersey, was an offshoot of Branford, while New Haven attempted to reproduce itself on the Delaware.

In the Narragansett settlements the towns were always much more independent of colony action than they were elsewhere. In the records of the colony during the seventeenth century very few references to town affairs occur. The colony was occasionally forced to attempt the settlement of disputes among the towns, especially those which almost perpetually agitated Providence. Between the first calling of a general assembly in 1647 and the close of our period, there was little occasion for the establishment of new

---

[1] See especially Plymouth Col. Recs. XI. (Laws); Conn. Recs. I. 36, 58, 100, 133, 185, 210, 214, 221, 351, 381, and the provisions in the Code of 1650, 512 *et seq.;* New Haven Recs. II. 77, 156, 178, 221, 232, 261, 298, 490, 579 *et seq.*, the Code of 1656. A dispute over the building of a fence in Milford came before the general court, *ibid.* 179, 214.

towns. The colony laws make no important reference either
to that, or to the regulation of town lands[1] and herds.
Neither do references to such regulation by the colony appear
in the extant records of the original towns. The necessary
inference must be that in the management of their lands, as
in everything else, the towns of Rhode Island pursued a more
independent course than did those in the other New England colonies. A comparison, however, of their internal history with that of the towns in the adjacent colonies will
show that in all essential particulars they conformed to the
New England model. The original Narragansett towns
were themselves offshoots of Salem, Boston, and other pre-
existing towns, and their founders remained true to the
polity with which they were familiar.

In our discussion thus far of the form of settlement in
New England, and of the relations between the colony and
the town, we have attempted to show that in those colonies
there was no *land system* apart from the towns. The colony,
in other words, did not attempt a territorial policy apart
from that which was implied in the making of grants to
towns, and in the exercise of necessary control over them
as centres of local government. Such grants as the colony
made to individuals were mere incidents of its administration in general. They may be regarded in some instances
as a form of pension, and in others as a rudimentary form
of salary for public officials. The management of land
throughout those colonies was left to the towns. It was
partly for that purpose that they were created as centres
of local government. Notwithstanding the supervision
which was exercised over them, they enjoyed an authority
which was adequate to the purpose. Therefore, in order to
discover what the land system in New England really was,
it will be necessary to examine in outline the territorial
arrangements which existed within the towns themselves.

In nearly all cases the settlements which were made prior

---

[1] In 1684 the assembly passed an act confirming the grants of land which
had been made by the island towns, and declaring that the undivided lands
were the possession of the freemen of said towns and of their successors.
R. I. Col. Recs. III. 153.

to 1660 were located on arms of the sea or on the banks of streams within the tide-water area. The land which was subject of grant, when cleared, consisted of upland, meadow, salt marsh, and fresh marsh or swamp. In many cases the upland which was first utilized was an Indian corn-field or clearing. As the clearings were extended into the primeval forest, the area of upland and meadow which was made available for use was increased. The continuity of upland and meadow was frequently interrupted by rocky hills and ridges, or by marsh. The meadow was usually located adjacent to streams and on the rocks or points which formed the varied contour of the coast. The different varieties of land[1] were distributed in the most heterogeneous fashion, thus making the problem of division and allotment a complicated one. To the variety in the surface of the country of which the colonists took possession is largely due the ever changing characteristics of local topography. The colonists, though working on a simple and consistent plan, were obliged to adjust it to the face of the country. From this process resulted the infinite variety in the extension, directions, and relations of village streets and commons, in the location of fields and meadows, and of the outlying forest and waste, in the direction, extent, and number of highways, lanes, and bridges which were needed to connect the different parts of each settlement, or to unite adjacent towns and plantations with one another. To these unyielding natural conditions is to be added such variety as was due to human choice and judgment. The influence of this it is impossible with any accuracy to estimate. But to the two sets of causes, acting in conjunction, is due the fact that, though the plan of settlement in its general outlines was uniform, in the result there was infinite variety of detail. It was not possible that the topography of any two villages or towns should be the same.

The settlers made use of the upland for home lots and planting fields. The meadow was generally utilized for

[1] Interesting reference to the localities in the town of Groton, Massachusetts, and especially to the meadows, appear in the Early Records of Groton, edited by Dr. Samuel A. Green, 141, 142.

hay and pasturage. From the marshes and swamps hay and thatch were also procured. In the remote uncleared or only partially cleared tracts, swine, sheep, and young cattle were pastured. Oxen, horses, and milch cows were pastured upon land nearer the village. That part of the cattle which were daily driven to and from their pasture occupied the chief attention of the town herdsman. In the autumn, after the hay and other crops had been gathered, the cattle were admitted to the meadows and upland fields. Having thus indicated in a general way what was the physical substratum of the town and the use which the settlers made of their land, it is necessary to describe the plan according to which the towns were laid out.

Several of the towns which were first planted about Massachusetts bay, those which later formed the colony of Rhode Island, as well as many others in Connecticut and on Long Island, were established by the spontaneous act of their settlers and upon land which they had occupied in most cases after the extinguishment of Indian claims. All other towns—and they soon became by far the larger number—were organized under definite grants from the general courts of their colonies. The issue of the grants, however, was occasioned by petitions from would-be settlers. In either case the first settlers constituted a reasonably definite group. As a quasi-corporation they received the land of the town and proceeded to dispose of it.

The settlement of a town normally began with the laying out of the village plot and the assignment of home lots. This to an extent determined the location of highways, of the village common, and of some of the outlying fields. On or near the common the church was built, and in not a few cases the site that was chosen for this building went far toward determining the entire lay-out of the town. The idea of a home lot was a plot of ground for a dwelling-house and outbuildings, for a dooryard and garden, and usually also an enclosure for feeding cattle and raising corn.[1] In Salem at the beginning the home lots appear to have con-

[1] Adams, Village Communities of Cape Anne and Salem, 31, J. H. U. Studies, I.

tained two acres each.   Somewhat later they were reduced
to one acre.   At Winter Harbor, an outlying settlement in
the town of Salem, they contained one-half acre each.
Fishermen's lots at Marblehead were not above two acres
each.[1]   In the Charlestown records homesteads are referred
to as containing "half an acre by estimation."[2]   In the
Boston *Book of Possessions* they are referred to as "a house
and lot," "a house and garden," and usually contained half
an acre.[3]   In the Roxbury land records home lots varying
in size from two to five acres — some even larger[4] — are referred to.   Some of the home lots in Cambridge (Newtown)
were as small as a quarter of an acre.   Those which were
located in the town were usually less than an acre in extent.[5]
At Hingham they approximated five acres.   At Newbury
the smallest home lots were four acres each.   In Springfield
we are told that no man, except William Pynchon, should
have as many as ten acres for his house lot.   At Northampton the house lots varied from four acres upward.   At
Hartford some contained two acres and others only half an
acre each.   In Providence they contained five acres.[6]

The assignment of the first home lots was accompanied or
immediately followed by the earliest allotments of arable
land and meadow.   This process steadily progressed with
the increase of population in the towns and with the clearing of the forests.   By means of it the settlers secured
planting land, and the process advanced through various
stages until the available land of the towns was approximately or entirely occupied.   When the process was
completed the township had been entirely laid out, and
settlement within it had assumed a relatively permanent
form.   This was accomplished in part by the granting of
lots to individuals and in part by the laying out of common
fields.   The common fields too, in their turn were later

[1] Upham, Salem Recs., Colls. of Essex Inst. IX. 9, 11, 27, 33.

[2] Reports of Boston Rec. Com. III. 8 *et seq.*

[3] *Ibid.* II. Part 2.   [4] *Ibid.* VI.   [5] Proprietors' Recs. of Cambridge.

[6] Ms. Recs. of Hingham ; Currier, History of Newbury, 36 ; Burt, First
Century of the History of Springfield, I. 158 ; Trumbull, History of Northamp-
ton, I. 20 ; Porter, Hartford and West Hartford, 18 ; Dorr. The Planting of
Providence, 17 ; R. I. Tract, No. 15.

subdivided among their proprietors. As the result of this process a system of individual ownership gradually took the place of a system of joint ownership and management ; a settled and cultivated township came to exist where previously there had been only an unappropriated forest and waste. The order of this process differed in the case of each town, but its general characteristics, as they appear in the records of the older towns, may be briefly indicated.

At Salem a standing order was first issued that a ten-acre lot should be granted with each house lot. But in 1636 this was repealed, and it was resolved that the size of such lots should be fixed at the discretion of the town. Lots and farms of various extent were then granted, some of them reaching the area in a single tract of three hundred acres. In April, 1637, it was ordered that if any lots of land were so located that they had little or no marsh or meadow, " the Layers out allott such proportions of marsh and meadow ground . . . in such places next adjoining as may be most fitt and equall for each." Near the close of the same year it was agreed, " that the marsh and meadow Lands that have formerly layed in common to this Towne should be appropriated to the Inhabitants of Salem, proportioned out to them according to the heads of their families. To those who have had the greatest number an acre thereof and to those that have least not above half an acre." [1] Under the authority of this order a large number of small lots were granted. In 1638 fifteen lots, varying in size from three to eight acres, were granted at Marblehead. The records, during the early years, abound in grants to individuals.

But this did not preclude the existence within the town of many common fields, each of which, under authority of the town, had its associated proprietors. These had common fences and were cultivated under a joint system. We are told that in Salem in 1640 there were no less than ten such fields,[2] and that their fences were under the supervision of fence-viewers, who were chosen in town meeting. Of the fields the most important were the " north field " and

---

[1] Salem Recs. 45, 61, 101–104, 74.
[2] Adams, *op. cit.* 37.

the "south field,"[1] the former containing 490 acres and the latter 600. The proprietors of the latter continued as a distinct organization until after the Revolution, while the "north field" was divided soon after 1742, and became a part of the estate of its proprietors considered as individuals.

The "town neck" was also a common, as was the old "planters' meadow" and various other tracts of the same sort within the limits of the town. The "town neck" was used for baiting cattle. A large tract, originally embracing about four thousand acres, and extending southward toward the modern Swampscott and Peabody, was long reserved under the name of the "cow pastures" or "cattle range." There the town herds were kept. Salem, like all other towns, for a time retained adjacent islands as common.

Newtown,[2] or Cambridge, in 1635 was a compact settlement on the north bank of the Charles river, from which it was separated by a narrow marsh. The arable land of the town lay chiefly toward the north, the northeast, and the northwest. The village consisted of a market-place and house lots, the latter being distributed on three streets which extended back from the river and on two streets which ran nearly parallel to the river. Their intersections formed the village blocks or squares. A curved street extended around the village on its landward side, and outside of that lay the defences of the town. Somewhat remote from the village in the east lay marshes, while on the west, adjacent to the Menotomy river, lay the "great swamp." Toward the marshes of the east lay "small lot hill," while at the opposite extreme "west field" adjoined the great swamp. Nearer to the village lay the "cow common," "pine swamp field," the "ox pasture," the "planting field," the "little neck," Roads and paths led out from the little village to each of the subdivisions of the town area. They were known as the "highway to the common pales," "highway to the great swamp," and by other similar names.

In the records of Cambridge the orders may be read which resulted in the division of these tracts. In February, 1634,

---

[1] Adams, *op. cit.* 37; Felt, Annals of Salem, I. 184.
[2] Recs. of the Town of Cambridge, Map; Proprietors' Recs. of Cambridge.

the planting ground in "the neck" was divided.   In the following August a considerable number of lots in the "west field" were granted to individuals.   Later, other lots in the field were granted, as well as lots in the "pine swamp."   In April, 1635, it was ordered that all the undivided meadow ground belonging to the town should be divided, and allotments followed accordingly.   In February, 1636, an order was issued that the ground "lyeinge between Charles Towne path and the Comon Pales foremerly aponted to be measured as also Remaynder by watertowne" should be divided.[1] Thus in quick succession were the more available tracts divided, and the complaint of the inhabitants that their supply of land was inadequate soon led to the migration which gave rise to Hartford on the Connecticut.

At Hingham planting ground was assigned at about the same time with the house lots, and the first grants were near "bare cove."   "It is likewise agreed upon, that they whose names are hereafter mentioned are to have their Planting ground near Pleasant Hill, in a manner and form as followeth: that is to say — Thomas Lincoln sen'. is to have four acres for planting ground next the poynt, which lyeth against the open bay as we come from Weymouth, and is to have it for four acres, be it more or less."   The other grants follow in the same form.   Planting ground was also laid out toward the west, on the way toward "turkey hill."   The first meadow lots were "in a sartayne marsh called the Home Meadow, next to the Cove."   John Otis, the ancestor of the Otis family, was the first in a list of six grantees of this meadow.   Another tract, known as "broad cove meadow," was laid out in thirteen lots, and among the grantees appear the names of the pastor, Rev. Peter Hobart, or Hubbard, and two of his family.   In June, 1636, the "great lots" adjacent to Weymouth river and abutting on the home lots, were granted.   There were eighteen of them, and they included from fourteen to twenty-four acres each.   In the following year more grants were made in the Weymouth meadow.   A variety of entries show that the "great lots" of grass and arable land varied in size from ten to thirty-five

[1] Cambridge Town Recs. 7–16.

acres.   At the same time thirty-nine shares, each containing
from half an acre to three acres of meadow, and from three
and one-half to twenty acres of upland, were allotted at
"Nantascus." Twenty lots were also assigned in "crooked
meadow," "beyond the Playne," this being fresh or upland
meadow.[1] In 1670 occurred extensive divisions of meadow
and upland at Cohasset, lying between the Plymouth line
and Accord pond.   Four "divisions" or ranges of lots,
each containing seventy-eight or eighty-three lots, were surveyed and assigned in that region.   By this policy the common land of the town was steadily reduced in quantity, but
was by no means eliminated.

The town of Dedham, near the falls of the Charles river,
early ordered that every twelve-acre lot of upland should
have four acres of swamp added to it, besides what might
be granted in later divisions of swamp land.   Eight-acre
lots should have a proportional addition of swamp.   It was
also the policy of the town to give to each grantee as many
acres of meadow as he had of upland.[2] Owing to its inland
location Dedham had no "neck," but it had several "plains,"[3]
meadows, and swamps.   These constituted at the outset its
common lands, and from them grants to individuals and
successive allotments were made.   In 1652, 1656, and 1659
three important divisions of common land were made.[4] One
was the Five-Hundred-Acre Dividend; the second was of
about the same size, while the third included two thousand
acres which had previously been granted to the Indians of
Natick.   Each of these divisions, like all others which
occurred, were made among those who had houses and lands
in the town, and in proportion to their estates.

[1] Ms. Recs. of Hingham, 1635–1700.

[2] Dedham Town Recs. III. 4, 5, 30.

[3] Like nearly all towns Dedham had its "great plain."   But in addition
to that there were the "smooth plain," the "island plain," the "low plain,"
the "middle plain," the "south plain," the "swamp plain," "wigwam
plain."   It also had its "planting field," "purchased lands," "broad
meadow," "fowl meadow," "baldpate meadow," "great meadow," "south
meadow," "rock meadow," "rosemary meadow," "great island," "turkey
island," "purgatory swamp."

[4] *Ibid.* III. 142, 211 ; IV. 9.

As Ipswich was laid out on the bank of a stream which runs in an easterly direction, it had its "north field" and "south field," besides the other customary localities.   Its early records abound in grants to individuals.   A range of grants of six acres each was made near the upper end of "labour in vayne Creek."   Another range of six-acre lots for planting was laid out "on this side Muddy River."   The following April three men were chosen by the commoners, and confirmed by the selectmen, for surveying the fences on the north side of the river.   Similar action repeatedly follows, not only in the annals of this town but in those of many others.   When, in 1664, Ipswich divided "plumb island," "hog island," and "castle neck" among the commoners, their shares were determined by the amount which each paid in a single country rate.[1]   In "plumb island" Newbury also had an interest, and we find in its records reference to a first and second division of this insular territory.

Old Newbury comprised a large area, even for one of the original New England towns, and it was settled successively at two different centres.   In 1635[2] house lots, planting lots, and meadow lots were laid out on Parker river, a stream which finds its way to the ocean a short distance south of the mouth of the Merrimac.   On or near the common or green which was there reserved, a meeting-house was built. A town government was fully organized, with its centre at this place.   Although several families removed from this settlement to found Hampton, north of the Merrimac, and others helped to found Salisbury and Rowley, yet those who remained soon found that the supply of arable land near Parker river was inadequate.   Therefore, in 1642, the majority of the townsmen decided to remove the centre of the town to the plains, three or four miles nearer the Merrimac river.   The plan was vigorously opposed by a minority, and an appeal was taken to the general court.   That body sustained the majority who favored removal, and the plan

---

[1] Ms. Recs. of Ipswich. A part of the first volume has been privately printed under the title of Ancient Records of Ipswich, 1634–1650.

[2] Currier, History of Newbury, 36 *et seq.* ; Ms. Recs. of Newbury.

was consummated without a division of the town. A considerable number of house lots and planting lots which had been granted on Parker river, were then resigned in exchange for others near the Merrimac. The former again became common land, or were regranted to the settlers who remained on Parker river. With the building of a meeting-house in the new settlement, on "a knowle of upland by Abraham Tappans barne," the decision of the majority was confirmed beyond the possibility of reversal. But the "Old Green" still remains, and the outlines of the settlement which was first made on Parker river have never been obliterated.

Among the towns of the Connecticut valley, the records of Springfield are unusually explicit concerning the early assignment of lots.[1] The home lots were laid out in rectangles adjacent to the river. The wet meadow and the wood lots lay back of them, extending to the high ground on the east. The planting grounds lay in the west side of the Connecticut, near the lower course of the Agawam river. "We intend," declared the first settlers on May 14, 1636, "that our town shall be composed of fourty families, or if we think meet after to alter our purpose yet not to exceede the number of fifty familys, rich and poore." After requiring that every inhabitant should receive "a convenient proportion" for a house lot, they agree that each householder should receive a share of the cow pasture at the north end of the town, of the "hasokey Marish" adjacent to their lots, and of the woodland. Every one also should receive a share of the meadow opposite on the Agawam side of the river, as near as might be to his house lot. "The long[2] meddowe called Masacksic lyinge in the way to Dorchester" (Windsor) should also be distributed among all the settlers, unless better accommodation for the cattle or a part of them could be found elsewhere. The meadow and the pasture which lay on the Agawam side of the river, but about four miles to the north, should be laid out in four to six lots, and assigned to persons who would be likely to improve it as tillage and

---

[1] Burt, The First Century of the History of Springfield, I. 156, et seq. 171, 200. See also Burt's Map.

[2] This was the lowland in the present town of Longmeadow.

pasture. Under this arrangement it was expected that some of the town herd would find pasture.

In the distribution of planting ground and meadow the settlers of Springfield followed the rule which was adopted by most towns, namely, that they would "regard chiefly persons who are most apt to use such ground : and in all meddowe and pasture to regard chiefly Cattell and estate, because estate is like to be imp'ved in cattell, and such ground is aptest for their use." The minimum grant of mowing ground for those who had no cattle should be three acres. Two acres should be added for each cow, steer, or yearling, and four acres for each horse. Special grants of meadow at the north end were made to William Pynchon, John Burr, and Henry Smith, in recognition of their services in founding the plantation.

Hartford was located adjacent to the west bank of the Connecticut river, and on both the north and south banks of a small tributary called Little river. The two parts of the town were therefore called "sides," the "north side," and the "south side," a usage which was in harmony with common European practice. The town also included a tract of land on the east bank of the Connecticut river, which was known as the "east side." The settlers on the "north side" and the "south side" respectively had their separate meetings, called "side meetings," in which they to an extent regulated the fences, the use of the common lands, the impounding of stray cattle and swine, and on one occasion voted a grant of land. Selectmen, constables, collectors, fence-viewers, pound-keepers, chimney viewers, haywards, surveyors were chosen in town meeting respectively for the "north side" and the "south side," the members usually being equally divided between the two sections.[1] The "east side" had a similar organization, and this later was wholly separated from Hartford and became a distinct town.

Hartford was settled and its fields were subdivided according to the general plan which was followed in the parent towns of eastern Massachusetts. Among its early orders

[1] Hartford Town Votes in Colls. of Conn. Hist. Soc. VI. 34, 43, 74, 111, 139, and many other references in the index.

appear certain of the regulations of Newtown, which were
also widely reproduced by the other towns of the Puritan
colonies.   Their object was to insure the speedy settlement
of lots and to keep under the control of the town the admission or the rejection of settlers.   They were to the effect that
no new inhabitant should be admitted or allowed to build a
house in the town without the town's approval; and that
lots should be improved and settled within six months or a
year from the time of their grant.   Abandoned [1] lots and the
lots of those who were removing out of town should return
to the town for its further disposition.

Northampton and Hadley in Massachusetts were founded
mainly by people from Hartford, Wethersfield, and Springfield, and they a second time reproduced the form of settlement which had developed in the towns near Boston.   The
sites which were chosen for Northampton and Hadley lay
among the broad meadows of the Connecticut, and were near
two sharp bends in that river.   The site of Northampton was
also adjacent to Mill river, a stream which enters the Connecticut at that point from a northwesterly direction.   Though
the town was laid out on both banks of Mill river, the parts
were so unequal that the "sides" do not appear as they did
in Hartford.   Its original lots were [2] located in somewhat
irregular fashion on two streets, which extended northward
from Mill river toward the rising ground that was selected
for the site of the meeting-house.   As later settlers appeared
home lots were assigned to them on three or four streets adjacent to the meeting-house, and on the south side of the
Mill river.   To the owner of each house lot were granted
upland and meadow in tracts varying in extent from eight
to fifty acres.   The meadow lots were small, and several in
different locations were granted to each individual.   The
rule adopted for the assignment of meadow was that twenty
acres should be bestowed for every £100 of estate.   Each head
of a family was entitled to fifteen acres, and for each son three

[1] Town Recs. of Cambridge, 4 ; Town Votes of Hartford, 1, 2 ; Town Votes
and Land Recs. of Wethersfield, two vols. Ms.   Also the records of many
other towns.

[2] Trumbull, History of Northampton, I. 17.   See especially Trumbull's Map.

acres should be added. The meadows where these grants
were allotted were extensive, and they fell naturally into no
less than twelve divisions, each of which had its peculiar name,
like " old rainbow," " young rainbow," " venturer's field,"
and the like. Each of these divisions was separately laid
out, and when divided gave rise to a distinct allotment.
On the highlands back of the town lay the undivided forest
and waste, used by all for wood, timber, and pasturage.

The location of Hadley on the level expanse of meadow
adjacent to the east bank of the Connecticut made possible a
very regular and simple [1] arrangement. The original house
lots, which were less than fifty in number, were laid out on
the opposite sides of a single street. The street extended
north and south across a neck of land, and like the street of
Wethersfield, whence the settlers had mainly come, it was
twenty rods in width. From the street extended westward
three " highways to the meadow," and eastward three " highways to the woods." The house lots, when of full size, were
thirty rods in width and eighty rods in length, and extended
back on one side of the street toward the river, and on the
other side toward the woods. At the north end of the street
lay the " little meadow," at the south end, the " south
meadow." Beyond the " little meadow " was the " forty-
acre meadow," while the land between the house lots and the
river was known as the " great meadow." South of the village also lay " fort meadow " and " Hockanum meadow."
The farms of the early settlers consisted of the successive
allotments which were made of the adjacent meadows. The
" forty-acre meadow " went to the inhabitants of the northern
part of the town, while the " fort meadow " was assigned to
those who dwelt at the southern end of the street. The
" great meadow " was divided into four parts, and was among
the first land of the town to be allotted.

. The original grant to Hadley lay in part on the west side
of the river, its grantors being known as the " west side proprietors," while the others were known as the " east side
proprietors." In the history of this town the " side " assumed unusual proportions. Allotments of land were made

[1] Judd, History of Hadley, 31.

among the "west side proprietors," in the same way as among
the dwellers on "the street." In 1668 the "west siders" began a separate existence as the town of Hatfield.

Among the towns of New Haven colony the requirements of space forbid special reference to any except New Haven itself. It was distinguished by the regular and elaborate character of its plan.[1] The village itself was laid out in the form of a square, one-half mile in length on each side. It was cut into nine smaller squares by two parallel streets running east and west and two running north and south. Of these smaller, but equal, squares, the central one was reserved as a market-place. The others were subdivided into house lots. The land adjacent to them, where the farms in parts were allotted, were known as the "suburbs," while the squares were known as "quarters." The "quarters" were long distinguished by the names of prominent inhabitants who lived in them, as Mr. Eaton's quarter, Mr. Newman's quarter, Mr. Davenport's quarter. The west-centre was allotted to colonists from Yorkshire, while the Herefordshire men occupied that on the southwest. So far as possible, the farms or out-lands of each quarter were located adjacent to the house lots. In order the better to effect this, land on the north side of the town plot, which was chiefly known as the "cow pasture," the "ox pasture," and "Beaver pond meadows," was retained as unfenced common. Besides this tract and the market-place, — now New Haven Green, — three other tracts were reserved for the benefit of the town at large. These were a tract on the "west creek," another on the "east creek," and a third still farther east, called "oyster-shell field." The first two of these reservations were granted in small lots to individuals who were not proprietors, while the third was leased from year to year to those who desired to cultivate more land than they owned.

A necessary consequence of the method of allotting land which has just been described was, that the estate of each individual would consist of a number of small tracts located in different parts of the town plot. The terriers or lists of

[1] Atwater, History of the Colony of New Haven ; Levermore, The Republic of New Haven.

holdings, which occupy much space in the proprietors'
records of all the towns, show this to have been the case.
One or two typical instances will suffice for illustration.[1]   In
Newtown, as recorded May 1, 1635, John White possessed the
following estate : In "cowyard row" two small tracts of
about three roods each, one containing his dwelling-house,
with outhouses and gardens ; three tracts, one of two acres
and a half and the other two of one acre and a rood each,
located in "old field"; about one acre on "long marsh hill"
together with another piece of about three acres and a rood
in "long marsh"; about thirteen and one-half acres in the
"neck of land" ; eleven acres in the "great marsh," and
about one acre in the "ox marsh."   Some estates were much
larger than this, others were smaller.   This estate, like others,
might be enlarged and the number of small tracts composing
it might be increased by later allotments.

The estate of Elder Edward Howe, of Watertown,[2] consisted of a homestead of forty acres, fourteen lots of upland,
varying in size from three acres to two hundred acres, and
four lots of meadow, the largest of which contained twenty-
five acres.   Three of the lots of upland are expressly
described as ploughland.

In Wethersfield, Connecticut, Thomas Parke, in 1647,
possessed two home lots, one abutting on "bell lane" and
the other on "the way" ; four pieces of land in the "great
meadow," containing from two to five acres each; a lot of
one hundred acres east of the Connecticut river ; a lot of
eleven acres in the "west field," another of twenty-two
acres in the "west swamp"; a lot of twenty-four acres in
the "south field" ; two lots, one of eight acres and another
of nine acres in the "dry swamp" ; a piece of three acres
between "beaver brook" and the "new fence" ; a piece of
eight acres in the "wet swamp," and one of two acres in
"beaver meadow."[3]

[1] Proprietors' Recs. of Cambridge, 4.

[2] Watertown Recs., Lands, Grants, and Possessions, 17.

[3] Ms. Land Recs. of Wethersfield.   Lists of estates like the one from
which this entry is taken were sometimes called "terriers."   This term was
applied to them in Guilford, Connecticut.

The early lists of estates in all New England towns
reveal a situation like that indicated by these examples.
But before the towns had long been settled, a tendency
toward consolidation of estates appears. Many exchanges
of land were effected which had this as their object. Purchases and sales often had a similar effect. So did inter-
marriages and inheritance. The result of this process,
operating through generations, has been to substitute for the
early system of parcelled estates the consolidated farms of the
present day.

Common fences and herds were characteristic accompani-
ments of the system of common fields and joint cultivation
which were the basis of the town economy. They appear
in all towns, and the devising and enforcement of regulations concerning them occupied much of the attention of
officers and town meetings. As a rule, instead of fencing
off by itself the allotment of each individual in a field or
meadow, the entire field was surrounded by a common fence,
and this was furnished with gates and approached by paths
or highways. All grants of land were made subject to the
right of the community to open highways through them.
The earliest highways in many instances originated in paths
to the common field, to the pastures and marshes, which lay
within the limits of the town.[1] Of the common fences, each
shareholder was bound to build and keep in repair the part
which was adjacent to his lot or lots. Like the forts, which
occasioned the officials of all the colonies so much trouble,
the fences were continually exposed to decay. Every spring
they had to be viewed and repaired, and orders for enforcing this duty were annually issued by the town authorities.
On March 20, 1637, the town meeting of Salem ordered that
all fences should be sufficiently repaired by the close of the
month. They should be made of posts and rails, or in such
other form and of such height as the surveyors of fences
approved. The penalty for neglect was a fine.[2]

A typical order for the joint fencing of a field appears in

[1] A notable entry descriptive of the highways of a town appears in Early
Recs. of Groton, 32. See also Early Recs. of Lancaster, 60.
[2] Salem Recs. 40.

the records of Cambridge, under date of May 19, 1648.[1] "It was ordered by the townsmen that that part of the fence which belongs to the ould ox pasture on the south side of the High Way, Both against Charlestown feilde, & the High Way, should be measured, and proportioned to the severall proprietors, Beginning at Th. Danforths lott, and so ending at John Betts according to there number of ac^{rs} therein & they whoe have more then there proportion of fence against the High Way to have soe much according to ther proportion deducted of ther end fence agst Charleston & they whoe have not there proportion of the fence agst the High Way according to ther number of ac^{rs} to make soe much agst Charleston feilde. . . ."

Among the general orders of the town of Dorchester,[2] which were passed in October, 1633, was one that the fields already enclosed should be kept sufficiently fenced, and if, upon warning, any failed so to do, the officers who were appointed for the purpose should have the fence built, and its cost should be levied by distress, if necessary, from the goods of the delinquent. In 1650 the town of Rowley[3] ordered that the fences of all the common fields within the town should be divided according to the proportion of land and meadow which belonged to each shareholder, and the fences should be marked with numbers accordingly. The entries for each field, distributed by rail-lengths, then follow in the records. On January 13, 1637–8, by the settlers of Newbury it was agreed that, where many planting lots were laid together, if the major part of their grantees agreed to fence them in, it should bind the rest to do the like, "both for manner and time." It was also voted that a general fence should be made from the end of the town to "Egypt river"; also from the east end of the town on the way to "Jeffrey's neck" from the fence of John Perkins to the end of "a creek in the marsh near the land of Wry Foster." The fence should be built at the charge of all who had land within the said compass, and the labor spent upon it should be proportional to their respective shares.

[1] Town Recs. of Cambridge, 75.
[2] Boston Rec. Comm. Fourth Report, 3. See also p. 36.
[3] Town Recs. of Rowley, I. 61.

This is a regulation which appears in all towns,[1] and repeats itself almost as often as a common fence is mentioned. In many orders the height of the fence is specified, also the fact that it should be built of posts and rails, the exact spot at which each shareholder should begin and end his work, and the location of the gates.

In 1648 the town of Ipswich ordered that the fence surrounding the common field on the north side of the river should be repaired, and that the two men who were hired by the town to do it should be paid out of forfeits levied upon the shareholders, and, if these should fall short, they should be paid by the commoners proportionally. At a meeting of the seven men — the selectmen — which was held in February, 1649, it was ordered that all commoners who had shares in the field on the south side of the river — the field in which "Heartbreak Hill" was situated — should meet at the house of Symon Tomson to consult and settle all [2] differences respecting the field and its fences.

The records of Hartford abound in orders [3] for the fencing of various fields and meadows, and in full statements of the duties of fence-viewers and pound-keepers. In accordance with general practice Wethersfield, in February, 1648,[4] assessed the inhabitants of "the plaine" toward making "the great fence." The assessment was in proportion to the improvable land which each one held. The charge was 2s. 4d. per acre, and it ranged from 18s. to £6 per man. In January, 1660, it was voted that the meadow fence be divided by lot, and where men's lots fell they should fence their proportions. All who had lands adjacent to the fence should be allowed a rod or two where they might make a gate through which to pass to their land. Gates were important, both from the standpoint of fences and of highways, and orders frequently appear for building them and keeping them in repair.

Comprehensive orders, both respecting fences and gates,

[1] Very comprehensive orders on this subject appear in the Town Recs. of Rowley, I. 61, 146.

[2] Ancient Recs. of Ipswich.

[3] Town Votes, 24, 26, 43, 44, 205. See also the index.

[4] Ms. Recs. of Wethersfield.

were passed by the towns of New Haven colony. Guilford ordered that "all fence in the quarters of upland out lots, whether out-fence or division fence, shall be as well maintained as made by the acre proportionally — so many rods for every acre."[1]   At Milford the building of common fence on both sides of Mill river was apportioned according to the land which had been granted.   When the fence had been built, each man should maintain the share which he himself had made.   Gates in the common field about the town were to be built at the public[2] charge.

In Warwick, Rhode Island, the "front fence" which separated the homesteads from the large common that lay west of the village marked a most[3] important line of division.   Orders for its repair continually recur, and it was maintained both summer and winter.   The fence at Conemecock point — which was set apart as a pasture for calves and lambs — and that of the "common on this side Coesset" were objects of frequent attention.   A rate was sometimes levied for the building of a common fence.

The town herd and herdsmen figure in the local annals of all parts of New England.   They had their origin in the system of common fields.   From early spring until after the harvest had ended in the fall, the fields were[4] regularly closed, and grazing in them was not permitted.   When the crops had been removed, cattle were admitted to the fields under the charge of herdsmen.   Milch cows, working oxen, and horses were pastured in tracts reserved for the purpose not far from the village.   As a rule, these were daily driven to and fro.   Young cattle and dry cows were turned into the remote pastures of the town in the spring and were kept there under the charge of herdsmen until the close of the season.   Swine[5] were kept as far away from the cultivated

[1] Ms. Recs. of Guilford.

[2] Ms. Recs. of Milford.   Similar orders appear in the Recs. of New Haven. See also especially the Early Recs. of Lancaster, Mass. 53.

[3] Ms. Recs. of Warwick.

[4] One of the many typical entries on this subject appears in the Dedham Town Recs. III. 124.

[5] An elaborate order on the keeping of swine is in Salem Recs. 100. Wethersfield required that they should be kept two miles away, and Guilford

tracts as possible, and were generally required to be yoked
or ringed. The records abound with orders for keeping
them away from the enclosures, and with threats of fines for
injuries which they had done or might do. The pound-
keeper found his occupation in seizing stray hogs quite as
much as stray cattle.

A resolution of the selectmen of Watertown[1] in 1669
illustrates not only the necessity which was felt for town
herds and herdsmen, but also all important phases of the
subject. Complaints had been made that the inhabitants
had not been able to agree upon an orderly way of herding
their cattle. Many employed private keepers for them.
Others drove their cattle to pasture themselves. Still
others turned them loose, knowing, however, that[2] they
would trespass upon the lands of their neighbors across the
line in Cambridge. Some who lived near the feeding
place were unwilling to herd or pay a herdsman. Others
were willing to contribute toward a herdsman for a part,
but not the whole, of a season. To remedy this condition
of things, the selectmen resolved that three herds should
be kept in the town. The first should be the "mill herd,"
which should include all the cattle from the house of William Bond, and should be driven by the mill to the house of
Richard Cutting, and so over "beaver brook" at the bridge;
and the limits of their range should be the river on the south
and "prospect hill" on the north. The range of the second
herd should be from the south side of "prospect hill" to
the south side of "the great pond." The third should be
the "pond herd," and its range should extend from the
south side of "the greate pond" to Cambridge bounds.[3]
All the inhabitants of the town were required to put their
cattle in one or another of these herds; if any continued to

one mile, unless they were yoked. See also Dorchester Recs. 25, 33, 37. In
the Recs. of Groton, 28, the necessity of keeping fences in repair and employing a swineherd is enforced on the ground that otherwise it would be difficult
to "preserve love and peace in the town." See also p. 49.

[1] Watertown Recs. I. 94.

[2] See Dorchester Town Recs. 22, 38, 45, 47, for evidence that this evil also
existed there.

[3] A similar entry relating to three herds appears in Groton Recs. 50.

employ private herdsmen, they should be fined the same as if they allowed their cattle to go without a keeper. Provision was finally made for calling meetings of those who were included in the respective herds, and in those meetings the majority were authorized to agree with a herdsman, and all should be bound by the contract they made. In towns where there was but one herd, or in which but one agreement was reached with herdsmen, their employment was usually one of the duties of the selectmen. Herdsmen were annually appointed, and commonly served from April till November. Upon stinted commons only a limited number of cattle could be driven, while of those which were unstinted the use was unrestricted.

In the assignment of town lots and the drafting of regulations for the use of the common lands a rigid numerical equality was occasionally maintained; each individual received just as many acres and just as much accommodation as any other, no more and no less. But in most instances an effort is discernible to make the grants proportional to what might be called the investment of the individual settler in the enterprise of founding the town. This assumed two forms, that of the expense or cost to which he was subjected and that of the ability which he contributed to the undertaking. The expense was incurred first, in the removal of colonists from Europe or from other towns in New England to the new place of settlement. In the case of companies like those which settled Dorchester in Massachusetts, the River Towns of Connecticut, the oldest towns of New Haven colony, this was considerable. In the case of the early towns of Connecticut and New Haven, and those especially on Narragansett bay, the cost, small though it was, of extinguishing the claims of the Indians had to be borne by the towns rather than the colony. The surveying and laying out of a town also involved some expense. In some cases a "great house," or common house was built at the general expense and temporarily occupied. It thus appears that the founding of a plantation required in some form or other a joint stock, from which advances could be made. Those who met these expenses were proprietors and received their dividends in the form of lands.

The other element, of which account was taken, was the ability of the colonist to advance the interests of the plantation, when once it was founded. This depended in part on his wealth, but also on the number of heads in his family, and on the ability of the settler to use his resources for the advantage of all who were concerned. Express references to considerations of this kind appear in the orders for the allotment of lands in not a few of the towns. Sometimes it was roughly estimated by heads, as in the order of the Salem town meeting of December 25, 1637. This provided that, of the marsh and meadow which was about to be divided, one acre should go to those who had the largest families, half an acre to those who had the smallest, and three-quarters of an acre to those the members of whose families fell between the two extremes. Dedham made its allotments proportional to the number of persons in every family and also to its estate. Lancaster made the lots in its first division equal, but afterward they were proportional to estates.[1] Springfield early adopted the rule, in dividing planting ground, "to regard chiefly persons who are most apt to use such ground"; and in dividing meadow and pasture, "to regard chiefly cattell and estate, because estate is like to be improved in cattell, and such ground [2] is aptest for their use."

The original contribution to the founding of the town by a natural transition developed into the town rate. That also furnished a rough index, year by year, of the ability of each settler to serve the interests of the town. It was levied on the same varieties of property as the country rate, and the two were pretty strictly proportional. Therefore we frequently find divisions of common land made proportional to the amount which was paid by each commoner in a single country rate. In 1664 two islands, together with "castle neck," were divided among the commoners of Ipswich, the shares being proportioned to the amount which each paid toward a tax of this kind.

[1] Salem Recs. 61 ; Dedham Recs. III. 142 ; Nourse, Early Records of Lancaster, 29, 39, 42.

[2] Burt, First Century of Springfield, I. 158.

The colonists possessed the elements to which reference has just been made in varying proportion. Some had made no original investment; the investments of others were large. Some had large families, others small ones, others none at all. Some had considerable wealth in the form of cattle or in other forms. One man was a miller, another a blacksmith, another a carpenter. Other men had capacity to serve the town as selectmen, clerk, constable, captain of the watch. Above all there was the minister, whose services were always deemed worthy of the highest consideration. Some were merely inhabitants, and had no voice either as proprietors or in town meeting. Some had served out their indentures as servants, and in consequence of a small grant from their former masters or from the town had found a place among the class of cottagers. On the outskirts of the settlement, in the tracts which had early lain common as pasture, provision was usually made for families of this class.

Within the town tracts, with all their variety of soil and elevation, form and contour, provision had to be made for an equal variety of human conditions and needs. This was the problem that faced the administrative bodies which were intrusted with the duty of dividing town commons, and it involved, if accurately solved, a somewhat complicated process of averaging. It was a problem which could not be solved by simply counting heads and striving to make a mathematically equal division of lands. There was in these communities a demand for equality, though it was held in check by the aristocratic spirit of the leading families. Sylvester Judd, the historian of Hadley, writing from a wide knowledge of the original records, expressed the truth when he said, " In making allotments, no uniform rule was adopted ; lands were variously distributed in different towns, and even in the same town."[1]

In 1647 the town of Milford, in New Haven colony, ordered that those who were " deducted " in their house lots should be considered in the quarter divisions. Two parties were to have one acre each added to their division in the quarter, because their house lots were small. These acts

[1] Judd, Hadley, 30.

were the result of a " fundamentall Agreement " of the previous year, that all lands, whether upland, meadow, or home
lots, should be made equal ; if the quality was inferior, it
should be made up in quantity. Remote lots should be
made larger in size than the others, or be exempted from
taxes.[1] Provision was made in Hartford for small lots for
poor men. In New Haven non-commoners were freely admitted to quotas of upland and meadow in the quarters.
The fundamental agreement of the settlers of Guilford contained a provision against the engrossing of lots. The division of " nut plain " and " the rocks " by the same town in
1646 was made for the express purpose of providing accommodation for those who, as yet, had had no allotments, or
whose grants were altogether inconvenient. In 1652 Warwick, in Rhode Island, laid out its meadow near the town,
for the inhabitants who, as yet, had not been provided for.[2]

The poorer inhabitants of Boston and those who had no
cattle received allotments at Muddy River, now Brookline.[3]
In 1657 the town of Dedham, in response to a petition of
certain parties who considered themselves aggrieved by a
recent division of land and stinting of commons, granted
them additional rights of common for twenty-five cows and
a proportional increase of their dividends of land.

In the proprietary records of Newbury, Massachusetts, we
find that in December, 1679, it was voted that, if ever town
commons be divided, every freeholder .shall have a like
share. But several dissented. from this vote, and their dissents were recorded. In January, 1684, the question of
dividing commons again came up, but the town could not
agree upon the quantity which should go to each man.
Two years later it was voted that every freeholder should
receive five acres in the common nearest the town. Henry
Short, who had been among the previous dissentients, demanded more than the specified share. Fifteen entered

[1] Ms. Recs. of Milford. An order as clear as this, but less comprehensive,
was passed in 1644.

[2] Hartford, Votes, 46 ; Levermore, Republic of New Haven, 83 ; Steiner,
History of Guilford, 50 ; Ms. Recs. of Warwick.

[3] Second Report of Boston Rec. Comm. Pt. I. 6. Recs. of Muddy River
and Brookline, 13.

their dissents against the vote for an equal division, but the measure was carried by a majority of five. By the same majority it was decided that twenty acres of upland in the "upper commons" should be laid out to every freeholder. But before the year was ended this majority vanished, and it was resolved, in the division of six thousand acres of the "upper commons" and eleven hundred acres of the "lower commons," that only one-half should be divided equally among all, while the other half should be shared by the freeholders who, during the past two years, had paid rates, and in proportion to what each man had paid in the minister's rate of 1685.[1] Such references as this show how the tendencies toward equality and inequality within the towns were balanced.

"In many towns in Massachusetts and Connecticut," says Judd,[2] " some tracts were distributed equally to all the proprietors. Home lots were sometimes nearly equal. In a few towns the least share was half as much as the greatest, or the poorest man received half as much land as the richest. In others the smallest share was only one-third, one-fourth, one-sixth, or one-tenth as much as the largest. In some the inequality was much greater, a few individuals receiving very large allotments on account of large estates and disbursements." Probably in many cases individuals were thus distinguished because of their wealth. But in many other instances it was due to what was considered the value of their public services. The towns, like the colonies, bestowed gratuities in the form of special grants of land. The minister was almost always so distinguished. Governors or magistrates who were inhabitants of a town were almost sure to receive such recognition. In addition such individuals were often permitted to select their land where they chose, or to draw the first share in an allotment. The history of New Haven, and of the other towns of that colony, furnish notable examples of this custom.

But it is evident that town officials in making allotments were in the main controlled by a spirit of fairness and equity. They approached the problem in the same spirit as

[1] Ms. Recs. of Newbury.   [2] History of Hadley, 30.

that with which they levied taxes or, in most cases, administered justice. The system which they followed precluded the development of very large estates, while it insured to nearly every inhabitant a house lot and garden. The existence of large areas of common land greatly facilitated the access of all to the gifts of nature. Town records also abound in references to grants, the purpose of which was to equalize inequalities which had resulted from earlier allotments. Individual allotments were frequently eked out and inconveniences of location were removed in this way. If parties suffered from real grievances of this nature, a petition was almost sure to bring relief. As we have seen, the system of allotments resulted in giving each commoner a share of every variety of land which existed in the town. It was in these ways that the corporate instinct, or, stating it more broadly, the instinct of fellowship and neighborhood, worked itself out in the agrarian system of New England.

The question of the policy by which the New Englanders were guided in the distribution of lands is closely connected with the development of boards of commoners or proprietors. In the discussion of the land system of the towns on its administrative side this is a subject of prime importance. The land of the towns, their herds and fences, were subject to joint management. But the question arises, To what extent did this originate with the town meetings or how far did it proceed from distinct boards of proprietors?

By the commoners or proprietors is meant the original grantees or purchasers of the land of the town and their legal heirs, assigns, or successors, with such as from time to time they chose to add to their number. The original lists would closely agree with those of the early grantees of town lots. In every case they formed a *de facto* land company, as truly as did the companies which received the grants of the New England colonies. They were proprietors in the true sense of the term, and their functions might closely approximate, though on a much smaller scale, to those of Baltimore, Penn, or the Carolina grantees.

In a few towns, like Middleborough,[1] in Massachusetts, to which additions were made by purchases, we hear of distinct boards of proprietors for special tracts. The settlers upon a plain or other tract which was more or less remote from the original village in a town, were often designated as proprietors of that tract. Such a settlement might become a separate town, but, if it did not, its proprietors tended to become a part, or always were a part, of the general body of proprietors of the town.

When the original grant was made by the general court, the town and the proprietors or commoners were approximately the same. The town meeting was at the same time a meeting of proprietors, or might easily become such. In the early history of towns a very important part of the business of the town meetings consisted in making grants of land. When this business was in progress, the town meeting was acting as a board of proprietors. The selectmen, or special committees, acted as agents of the town in the surveying and allotting of land. But for a long time after the settlement of the colonies no records were kept, except those of the town meeting and selectmen. Allotments of land and regulations connected therewith were entered indiscriminately with other forms of town business. From a study of the early records alone, one would with difficulty discover that there was a body of proprietors distinct from the town.

In the town of Plymouth it was always a principle, which was reiterated in 1657, "that all lands or parcells of lands that shalbee granted to any within this township . . . shalbee granted in towne meeting. . . ."[2] Almost every page of the extant records of Salem bears evidence to the fact that the same rule was followed there, or that the power was temporarily intrusted to selectmen, committees, or layers out. The earliest printed record which we have of the

---

[1] Among the town books of Middleborough are Proprietors' Records of the Suipatuet Purchase, of the South Purchase, of the Twenty-six Men Purchase, of the Twelve Men Purchase, and of the Sixteen Shilling Purchase. The entries in those books are for the most part subsequent to 1690.

[2] Plymouth Town Recs. I. 35.

annual choice of layers out, is that of November 16, 1635.[1]
In Boston the selectmen, under authority from the town,
made allotments. In the early years the formula by which
their powers were commonly expressed was, to "looke into
and sett order for all the allotments within us, and for all
Comers in unto us, as also for all other the occasions and
businesses of this Towne, excepting matters of election for
the Generall Courte."[2] At times also special commissioners
were appointed, as on the 18th of December, 1634, to divide
and allot certain tracts of the town lands ; but these bodies
were usually composed mainly of town officers and colony
magistrates. Special committees of this character, if not
also the selectmen, were frequently called "allotters." In
Boston, as in many other towns, the power to prohibit the
sale of lots to newcomers whom they did not approve was
also exercised by the town itself or was bestowed on the
allotters. In Duxbury, Hingham, Roxbury, Braintree, Dorchester, Muddy River, Watertown, Woburn, Lynn, Ipswich,
Newbury, and Rowley [3] the town meeting and its immediate
appointees made or withheld all grants of land. The same
rule obtained in the early towns of the Connecticut valley.[4]

Among the earliest town votes of Hartford are these : that
the townsmen, that is, the selectmen, should not grant more
than an acre or two of land to any inhabitant without the
consent of the town, and that to satisfy a pressing necessity;
that they should receive no inhabitant into the town without
the approval of the body; that within a year after the grant
of a house lot a house must be built upon it, and that abandoned lots and the lots of those who were removing out of
town should return to the town for further disposition.[5]
The records of Wethersfield show that nearly all business
relating to land was done in town meeting. In the towns
of New Haven colony the same rule obtained, though pro-

---

[1] Town Recs. of Salem, Colls. Essex Inst. IX. 10.

[2] Reports of Boston Rec. Comm. II. Pt. I. 3, 5, 9, 22.

[3] See the records of these respective towns.

[4] Judd, History of Hadley ; Trumbull, History of Northampton, I. 13–23.

[5] Hartford Town Votes, Colls. of Conn. Hist. Soc. VI. 1, 2 ; Porter, Hartford and West Hartford, 13 ; Town Votes and Land Recs. of Wethersfield,
two vols. Ms.

prietors of special tracts frequently appear.[1] In Rhode
Island, on the other hand, boards of proprietors of common
lands appear at an early date in the towns of Providence
and Warwick, though in Portsmouth the town lands were
directly controlled by the town meeting.[2]

But in all towns, even from the outset, there were certain
grantees of land who were not admitted to the body of proprietors. They might become freemen of the town and thus
have a voice in town meeting, or even be freemen of the
colony, and yet not find admission within the circle of the
proprietors. The idea of freemanship was political in its
nature, that of proprietorship was territorial. Individuals
were admitted to the position of freemen by vote of the town,
and only persons whom the town fellowship found acceptable
attained to this privilege. They were also required to take
a resident's oath. Boston for a time restricted its admissions to those who became members of the local congregation. This practice, however, was not generally followed,
though all towns insisted as strongly on moral qualifications
as did Plymouth and Connecticut in their requirements for
the colonial franchise. For this reason, especially in Massachusetts, the conditions of the town franchise differed from
those of the colony, and were themselves never precisely
defined. Those who were admitted to that franchise constituted the town meeting, and when they acted in that capacity they elected officers and transacted all town business.

In every town there were also certain cottagers who, in
the language of the Hartford records, " were granted lotts
to have onely at the towne's courtesie, with liberty to fetch
woode and keepe swine or cowes on the Common." [3] These
were not even freemen, and their admission to the town was
safeguarded in such way as, if possible, to prevent their
adding to the number of the town poor. They were simply
inhabitants. The freemen and the proprietors were inhabit-

[1] Ms. Town Recs. of New Haven, Milford, Branford, and Guilford. See
Levermore, 81 *et seq.*

[2] Recs. of Portsmouth ; Recs. of Providence, I. and II. ; Ms. Recs. of Warwick, I.

[3] Hartford Town Votes, 19 ; Adams, Village Communities of Cape Anne
and Salem, 65 ; Levermore, New Haven, 83.

ants, but they were something more. When it is stated in the records that a general meeting of the inhabitants of the town was held, the meaning is that a folkmoot had met, from which no males who were residents of the town were excluded. But the business in that meeting had been transacted by the freemen.

The nucleus of the body of freemen consisted of the proprietors. That body was perpetuated by gifts, sales, and inheritance of property. In later times the personnel of such boards consisted of the heirs and assigns, or successors, of their earlier members. They were kept together by their joint ownership of the common or unallotted land of the town. Admissions to the group usually ceased at an early date, leaving it a relatively small body and very likely to be dominated by narrow and selfish traditions. Around the nucleus of proprietors developed a fringe of freemen who were not proprietors. The nucleus and the fringe together made up the active part of the town meeting. For a long time the fringe was small and unimportant; the proprietors constituted a large majority and could easily control the town. Under these conditions, allotments of land could be easily and safely made, as well as other forms of business done, in town meeting. The proprietors and those who were simply freemen were not vividly conscious of their difference, and the records of their doings were freely intermingled.

But, as time passed, the distinction between the proprietors and those who were simply freemen became more evident. This was due to the increase in the number of the latter, and to the diminution of the supply of unoccupied lands. As the supply from which allotments could be made grew less, land became an increased object of desire, both to those who controlled it and to those who were seeking to possess it. In towns where the proprietors constituted a safe majority, they were able to maintain their control without serious difficulty. But in towns where the number of non-commoners came to equal that of the proprietors, struggles over the management of the town lands were very likely to occur. In the town meetings the non-commoners sought to carry through resolutions for division of the common lands

on the basis of equal shares for all.   These were opposed by
the proprietors, the latter in most cases being supported by the
traditional sentiment of their towns and by the general court.

As we have seen, the earliest controversy of this kind
developed in Providence ; but toward the close of the seventeenth century, as the country filled up, collisions began to
occur in some of the Massachusetts towns.   As early as 1667,
disputes over the use and the division of common lands of
Woburn reached such proportions that they came under the
notice of the general court.   A committee was appointed
which heard the questions in dispute.   Its report upon the
principles of settlement was accepted by the court, and presumably put into effect.[1]   In this case there was apparently
a question at issue between those who were entitled to a
larger and those who could only claim a smaller share in the
common land.

An order which was passed in Ipswich, in March, 1660,
shows how the increase of population might arouse the fears
of existing proprietors.   The order declares, that it had
been found by experience that the common lands were over-
burdened by the multiplying of dwelling-houses contrary to
the interest and meaning of the first inhabitants in granting
house lots and other lands.[2]   To check this evil, it was
ordered that no house, thereafter erected, should carry with
it a right to common land, nor should the persons inhabiting
houses use lands for timber, wood, or pasture, on pretence of
title from such houses, without express leave of the town.
Divisions of land were confined to commoners, but from
time to time additions were made to that body.

In Haverhill, in 1699, the commoners began to deny applications for free grants of land and would only agree to sell
it.[3]   There the question arose, to whom does ungranted
land belong ?   Growing opposition appeared among the
commoners to the non-commoners voting in the disposal
of land.   A committee was appointed to ascertain who the
commoners, or proprietors, were, and it was ordered that
no land should be granted till this point was settled.   The

---

[1] Mass. Recs. IV². 355.   [2] Felt, History of Ipswich, 16.
[3] Chase, History of Haverhill, 75 *et seq.*

proprietors held that they were the heirs and assigns of the

original purchasers.   The original purchasers had come into possession of the entire town tract, and were its sole proprietors.   Later grants by them or their heirs did not carry with them a share in the undivided lands.   The non-commoners, or legal voters, took the ground that the land of the town had been granted to the inhabitants collectively and that to them all undivided land belonged.   On these lines the conflict was waged in this town till far into the eighteenth century, the non-commoners usually holding the balance of power.   In other towns, as Northampton, similar struggles occurred, in some cases extending over long periods of years.   They brought into requisition town records, and made it necessary that proprietary records should be kept with greater care than had been customary in the seventeenth century.   These local agrarian disputes, analogous as they were to many famous conflicts in ancient and mediæval towns, are an interesting feature of New England social history.   But they belong to the eighteenth, rather than to the seventeenth, century, and they form a subject which still awaits the attention of an investigator.[1]

[1] See the interesting suggestions in Egleston, Land System of New England, J. H. U. Studies, IV.

CHAPTER XII

THE FINANCIAL SYSTEM OF THE CORPORATE COLONIES

THE industrial and commercial basis on which the system of self-government in the corporate colonies ultimately rested, revealed itself most distinctly in their finances. That is the point where, in all systems, economic and political institutions come most closely in contact. The estates of the colonists consisted mainly of land, of the inexpensive buildings which stood upon it and of the cattle and farming utensils which were required to stock it. In the settlements which were located on the coast were to be found small warehouses, wharves, merchant vessels, and stocks of imported goods. A few small iron mines were worked here and there. The beaver trade was, or might be, a source of income to many individuals; in some of the colonies it was such, though in New England it never reached great proportions. Trade with the Indians and the sale of liquor were forms of business which especially called for control by a system of licenses. These references suggest the chief sources of income, from which, together with judicial fines, public revenue in all the colonies was derived.

It is necessary at this point to briefly outline the system of taxation and expenditure, together with its chief administrative features, which developed in the early New England colonies. In their finances, as in all other departments of their activity, the colonies of this group resemble one another in all essential particulars. They differ only in comparatively unimportant details. The main outline of their system was the same as that of the provinces, but the divergences between the two groups — the provinces and the corporate colonies — were greater and more numerous than those which appear among the corporate colonies themselves.

In all the colonies, provincial as well as corporate, the supply of coin was far smaller than was needed, even for their limited exchanges. The permanent excess among them of imports over exports tended constantly to draw away to Europe, or elsewhere, the supplies of coin which came through trade or were brought by pirates. Massachusetts sought to supply its need by the establishment of a mint, and its coins circulated widely among the neighboring colonies. The proprietor of Maryland caused small coins to be privately stamped in England for use in his province. On a minute scale a few other experiments of this kind were tried. But, taken all together, they did not prevent a general resort to barter.

The reversion of the colonists toward primitive conditions of life was evidenced, perhaps, more clearly by this fact than by any other. It was reflected in the financial systems of all of them. It necessitated the payment of taxes — especially direct taxes — in kind. In the tax laws of the period, if they were drawn with any care, the rates at which various commodities or products common to the region would be received in payment of public dues had to be prescribed. These commodities were chiefly the cereals and other farm products, skins, cattle, and wampum ; in the southern provinces tobacco and rice. In New England corn was the representative commodity ; elsewhere it was tobacco. The requirement that taxes should be paid in commodities made it necessary that collectors and treasurers should keep a magazine,[1] where the products could be stored until they were marketed for the government or transferred in payment of its debts. When cattle were receivable, a stock-yard had to be maintained. The commodities in particular were liable to deterioration while in transit, and to losses of this kind the government was continually exposed. In this way, as well as in others, the system of barter added to the financial difficulties of the colonies. In 1655, in order to spur the constables to greater prompt-

[1] In Connecticut we hear of a proposition in 1667 to hire "a chamber for the keeping of the Country Rate in the respective towns from the time of the gathering of it till it is payd." Conn. Recs. II. 64.

ness, they were ordered by the general court of Massachusetts "to impresse boates or carts for the better & more
speedy sending in the rates according to the times appointed
by lawe."[1] In order to avoid "the charge and trouble of
transportation of the rates," the general court ordered, in
November, 1675, that if bills for wages and other government debts were sent from the localities to the colony
treasurer, he should return certificates which would enable
the debtors to secure their pay from the commodities collected as rates in those same localities.[2]

The levy of direct taxes by the corporate colonies was a
remarkable extension of the right of trading corporations in
England to levy assessments on their stockholders. This
practice, however, if literally followed by the Massachusetts
company after its removal into the colony, would have restricted the obligation to pay taxes to freemen. But no
limitation of this kind was ever observed. From the outset
non-freemen were taxed equally with freemen in all the
New England colonies. The principle which they aimed
to follow in their systems of taxation was set forth in the
Massachusetts order of 1634 : "It is further ordered, that
in all rates & publique charges, the townes shall have
respect to levy every man according to his estate, &
with consideration of all other his abilityes, whatsoever,
& not according to the number of his persons."[3] In 1638
the court declared that every inhabitant was liable to contribute to all charges, both in church and commonwealth,
and this declaration was specially made in view of the
fact that many non-freemen had refused to share in certain voluntary contributions.

New England was the home of the " rate." The country
rate, the county rate, the town rate, these were the designations of the chief forms of direct taxation in all that group of
colonies. It was the country rate — the tax that is of chief
importance in this connection — which developed out of the
assessments on stockholders. It was defined by the general
court of Massachusetts in 1639 as " such rates as are assessed
by order of the publique Court for the countryes occations &

[1] Mass. Recs. IV[1]. 247.   [2] Ibid. V. 66.   [3] Ibid. I. 120, 240.

no[1] other." In Plymouth the rates were levied on the inhabitants of each town "according to goods, lands, improved faculties, and personall[2] abillities." By improved land was then meant meadow, ploughed and hoed land. In 1658 the law specified in greater detail that rates should be levied, though in varying proportions, on all appropriated lands, whether improved, meadow, or dormant ; upon cotton goods, stock employed in trading, boats and other vessels, mills, and other visible estate. The equivalent of this description, though usually in briefer terms, can be found in the records of all the other corporate[3] colonies. In 1668 and 1669 Massachusetts carefully provided for the levy and collection of the rate even upon imported goods at the ports. Entry of such goods before officers specially appointed for the purpose was required. These acts were passed in response to complaints of inequality of taxation.[4]

The rate, whether it was a colony or a local levy, was a general property tax. It was levied on the entire estate, so far as it could be ascertained, of those who were liable to the tax. Occasionally slight[5] exceptions were made, but the rule was as just stated. An order which was issued by the general court of Massachusetts in 1651 indicates that, then as now, merchants were able to conceal their property, and therefore the weight of the tax fell unfairly on the farmer.[6] For this reason the court ordered that all merchants, shopkeepers, and factors should be assessed " by the rule of common estimation, according to the will and doome of the assessors in such cases appointed." Regard should be had to the stock and estate of the parties, in whose hands soever it might be, " that such great estates as come yeerely into the countrie may beare their proportion in publicke chardges." In the loans relating to rates the estimated values of domestic cattle were often stated in detail, but no effort was made to do the same in reference to other forms of property.

---

[1] Mass. Recs. I. 277.   [2] Plymouth Col. Recs. XI. 42, 142, 211.
[3] Mass. Recs. I. 120 ; II. 213 ; Conn. Recs. I. 548 ; New Haven Recs. I. 494 ; II. 581 ; R. I. Recs. II. 510.
[4] Mass. Recs. IV[2]. 363, 418.   [5] *Ibid.* II. 174.
[6] *Ibid.* IV[1]. 37 ; Douglas, Columbia Studies in History, etc. I. 274.

With the country rate was regularly combined a poll tax, and sometimes also a form of income tax. In the Massachusetts law of 1646, by which rates were more carefully defined than in any previous act, this statement was made: "That a due proportion may be had in all publicke rates, it is ordered that every male within this jurisdiction, servant or other, of ye age of 16 years & upward, shall pay yearly into ye common treasury ye summe of 20d. . . ." Though provision was later made for exemptions, this enactment accompanied all subsequent levies of country rates in Massachusetts. In 1647 the rate of the poll tax was increased to 2s. 6d. This was maintained until 1653, when the former rate was restored.[1] The same combination of the poll tax with the property tax appears in Connecticut and New Haven,[2] but not in Plymouth or in Rhode Island.

The levy on incomes was introduced in Massachusetts by the act of 1646. This was intended to reach artisans who could afford to contribute more toward the public charge than could mere day laborers. According to the law of 1646 artificers who received 18d. per day in the summertime should pay 3s. 4d. annually in excess of their poll tax, while smiths, butchers, bakers, cooks, victuallers, and the like, if they were not disabled by sickness or infirmity from exercising their callings, should pay in proportion to their incomes.[3] The express intention of the law was to tax the incomes of this class proportionably to the levy which was imposed on the estates of other men. This feature of the Massachusetts system was favored by Connecticut and New Haven, and was incorporated in their codes, the one of 1650 and the other of 1656.[4] No trace of it appears in Plymouth or Rhode Island. How long the tax was continued in Massachusetts it is impossible to tell.

The country rate as originally levied was a lump sum, which was distributed by the general court in the form of quotas among the towns. In September, 1630, the magistrates

[1] Mass. Recs. II. 173, 213; IV¹. 155, Douglas, op. cit. 277.

[2] Conn. Recs. I. 548; New Haven Recs. I. 494; II. 581; Howard, Local Const. History of the United States, 342.

[3] Mass. Recs. II. 173, 213.   [4] Conn. Recs. I. 549; New Haven Recs. II. 582.

at Boston ordered that £50 should be collected for the support of the two captains, Patrick and Underhill, and each town was assigned its proportionate quota. In September, 1634, the general court ordered a similar levy for general public purposes, and it was distributed in the same way.[1] This was originally the form of enactment in all corporate colonies. It devolved upon the towns the task of assessment and collection. It appears to have continued as the form of levy in Plymouth as long as that colony had a separate existence. It was[2] adapted to the relatively independent position of the towns in Rhode Island, and to the unusually loose administrative methods which obtained there. In that colony the rate seems to have continued in this crude form until about 1695.[3] From a single reference in the records it may be inferred that the assembly, sometimes at least, ventured a " guess " that a penny or a farthing in the pound, as the case might be, would yield the needed sum.[4]

In Massachusetts, however, beginning in 1646, definite provision was made that the country rate should be a tax of one penny in the pound on all visible estate in the colony. Though the towns still continue to be units of levy, the quota system disappears. A common levy was made throughout the colony. The same form of rating was introduced in Connecticut as early as 1650, and by or before 1656 it went into force in the colony[5] of New Haven. By this process the country rate came to mean in any colony, at any given time, a definite amount of revenue. Given a certain list of taxables and a certain valuation of their estates, the amount of revenue which would result, provided it was all collected, would be a fixed sum. It was this sum which the New England legislators had in mind when they voted " a rate." The sum was as truly a fixed one as was that which the English government had in view when in the later middle age it levied a tenth and fifteenth. When a

[1] Mass. Recs. I. 77, 129.

[2] Plymouth Recs. IV. 77, 91 ; R. I. Recs. I. 384, 395, 416. Also a number of rates which follow in this and the next volume for the payment of the charges of John Clarke as agent.

[3] R. I. Recs. III. 275, 300 ; Arnold, I. 534.   [4] R. I. Recs. II. 510.

[5] Mass. Recs. II. 173. See the Codes of Connecticut and New Haven.

smaller sum was required, a fraction of a rate, for example a half-rate, was levied. Sometimes one or more farthings in the pound, instead of the full penny, was levied. When a larger sum was required than that yielded by a single rate, a multiple of the rate was levied. During Philip's war as many as nine or ten rates were levied by Massachusetts at once. In 1680 four rates were levied, two to be paid in money and two in corn. In 1681 two and one-half rates were levied ; in 1683, two rates ; in 1684, two rates in money and one in country pay.[1] In Connecticut at the same period the appropriation increased in a similar manner. In 1675 a rate of 12d. in the pound, in 1676 one of 18d., and in 1677 another of 8d. were levied.[2]

It is a curious fact that every increase in the number of rates which were levied was accompanied by a corresponding reduplication of the poll tax, which always formed a part of the general levy. It might be doubled or trebled ; in such a crisis as that of Philip's war it might be increased tenfold. Under such circumstances it became very burdensome, and not unnaturally called forth protests from those who suffered from its imposition.[3]

The administrative process which was necessitated by the imposition of the country rate was the preparation of the list of taxables, with the estates which they possessed at their estimated value, the correction of these lists, the issue of warrants in accordance with them, and the collection of the tax.

The earliest comprehensive act concerning the mode of levying rates in Massachusetts was that of 1646, reënacted in 1647, 1651, and 1657. The treasurer should issue a warrant to the constable and selectmen of every town, requiring the constable to call together the inhabitants of the town. When assembled they should choose one of their freemen, who as a commissioner with the selectmen should make a list of all males in the town who were sixteen years old and upwards and an estimation of their real and personal estates. In the first week in September of every year the

---

[1] Mass. Recs. IV[2]. 415, 464 ; V. 45, 76, 81, 88, 139, 296, 324, 417, 454.
[2] Conn. Recs. III. 493.   [3] Douglas, *op. cit.* 278.

commissioners of the several towns in each shire should meet at the shire town, bringing with them the above lists, and there they should be examined and perfected. Then the lists should be sent to the colony treasurer, and the treasurer should issue warrants to the constables of the several towns to collect the sums[1] specified. In 1665 an act was passed providing that merchant strangers, who had been attempting to escape taxation by bringing in goods and selling them and leaving the colony between the making up of the tax list of one year and that of the succeeding year, should be assessed by the selectmen of the towns where they were, and according to the value of cargoes they should bring; if they refused to declare these, they should be taxed according to a single rate at any time of the year when they should be present, " by will and doom."

Substantially the same system of assessment existed in the other colonies of the group. In Plymouth each town was required to choose two or three men, who should make a list of the ratable estates of the town. When it had been prepared, the town was called together to hear the list read. After the necessary corrections had been made, as the county had not developed in this colony, the list was submitted directly to the general court in June of each year. By it the treasurer was ordered to issue warrants ordering the constables to collect.[2] In Connecticut the town lists had first to be examined and equalized by the commissioners of all the towns in the respective counties, and then they were submitted to the general court. In the colony of New Haven either townsmen, or men specially appointed for the purpose, could prepare the list in each town. The lists must be submitted to the May court by the deputies from the respective towns. Each plantation should collect its country rate and pay it to the colony treasurer, as directed by the general court.[3] In Connecticut, at least, towns sometimes neglected to submit their lists, and had to be threatened with fines.

---

[1] Laws, ed. of 1887, p. 25.

[2] Plymouth Recs. XI. 166, 219, 241. A typical order of the general court for the levy of a rate is that of June 7, 1665. *Ibid.* IV. 91.

[3] Conn. Recs. I. 549 ; II. 48 ; New Haven Recs. II. 581, 582.

Until 1673 no express regulations seem to have been made by Rhode Island concerning the subject. In the briefest possible terms the towns were ordered to raise their quotas. In the last-mentioned year, apparently forced in part by the repeated failure of their efforts to raise a fund with which to pay John Clarke for his services as agent in England, a rambling, ill-drawn act [1] was passed on the subject of the collection of rates. This act left it to each individual, under an order from his town, to report his ratable estate. If it should be found by the general assembly that parties — possibly whole towns — had not rated themselves or had not reported the fact, it might appoint men " to guess at their estates, and rate them as they should have done themselves." That all the colonies found difficulty in securing the payment of rates, is shown by their repeated orders on the subject. The right to collect by distraint was generally given to constables. But personal influence or indifference often rendered all efforts ineffective. As might have been expected, Rhode Island had more difficulties in this respect than the other colonies, and her administrative system continued to be too weak to overcome them.

In two of the New England colonies, Massachusetts and Connecticut, counties developed during the seventeenth century. When the revenue which was yielded by the county court in the form of fines and costs failed to meet the necessary expenses, the justices of the court were empowered to levy a rate. The county rate was similar in every respect to the country rate, and the method of assessing and collecting the two was the same.[2] In Massachusetts an elected county treasurer received the revenues, whether in the form of fines, dues, or tax. When a rate was levied, the treasurer issued the warrants under an order from the county court. He was bound annually to account to the court for his use of the funds. With the levy of the country rate the counties had no concern, except as areas for equalization.

[1] R. I. Recs. II. 510.
[2] Mass. Recs. IV[1]. 184, 259. In Connecticut, under an order of 1671, the county treasurers were appointed by the county courts. Conn. Recs. II. 163.

The direct taxes were not the only source of colony revenue. In all of them a system of indirect taxation existed as well. They all, with the exception of Rhode Island, resorted to export and import duties and to the excise. For a brief period about 1645 a tonnage duty was levied by Massachusetts.[1] In 1667 and 1679 that colony again levied a tonnage duty, making it payable in the former case in powder and in the latter case in money at the rate of 1s. per ton on vessels which traded to and from its ports, but which were not owned in the colony. This was a form of duty which was ultimately resorted to by all the colonies, and the revenue from it was in very many, if not most, cases used for the maintenance of fortifications. In 1632 Massachusetts imposed a duty of 12d. per pound on beaver that was bought from the Indians; but three years later the act was repealed. Like the beaver trade itself, this form of tax played no great part in the commercial or fiscal systems of the New England colonies.

In 1636 an import duty of one-sixth their value was laid on fruits, spices, sugar, wines, liquors, and tobacco, and for those who intended to retail these commodities the rate was doubled.[2] Commodities in transit and wine which was bought for use by the churches in the communion service, were not subject to this duty. This was the beginning of the system of customs revenue in New England.

With the Puritans the tendency toward police regulations for the repression of drunkenness was strong, though it by no means went as far as to discourage the liquor traffic as a whole. This neutral attitude led naturally to the introduction of the excise on the retailing of liquors. In 1644 the first act on the subject was passed by Massachusetts. The next year it was revised, and a customs duty on wine imported for sale was combined with the excise. The duty was an ad valorem rate of one twenty-fourth, while the excise was an additional one-twentieth. In 1648 specific duties, varying with the place of origin of the product, were substituted for the uniform ad valorem rates. In 1668 cider, mumm, ale, and beer were added to the list of excisable liquors, these all being domestic

[1] Mass. Recs. II. 107, 131.   [2] *Ibid.* I. 186.

products.[1] This combination of duties remained as a part of the fiscal system of Massachusetts throughout the colonial period. In 1668 the list of imported commodities which were made subject to duty was greatly increased, so as to include not merely wines and liquors, money, plate, bullion, salt, but provisions and merchandise in general. The rate was two per cent ad valorem. During Philip's war the rates of duty on wine and brandy were doubled.[2]

Plymouth levied export duties on a number of its domestic products — on boards and plank, barrel and hogshead staves and heading; on tar, oysters, and iron. This policy was continued from 1662 to the period of the absorption of the colony in the Dominion of New England.[3] At about the time when both Massachusetts and New Netherland were resorting to the excise on the retail of liquors,[4] Plymouth also imposed it, adding tobacco and oil to the list. The immediate object sought was to secure means for defraying the charges of the magistrates' table, but the older officials of this colony may well have remembered the prominent place which was occupied by the excise in the fiscal system of the Netherlands.

Interest attaches to the experiment of Plymouth with a government monopoly in the mackerel fishery at Cape Cod, and also to the enforcement of its royalty over drift whales. In 1646, when the excise was first enacted, a license fee was imposed on fishing at the Cape. In 1661 the rate for non-residents was fixed at 6d. per quintal. In 1670 inhabitants of the colony were required to pay 6d. per barrel for mackerel brought to shore there, and strangers, 1s. 6d. per barrel. A water bailiff was specially appointed to collect the impost and enforce the act. In 1677 the colony leased its privileges in this fishery for seven years at £30 per year. In 1684 the treasurer was ordered to lease the fishery for another period of years;[5] and it was leased, though the contract was broken

---

[1] Mass. Recs. II. 82, 106, 246 ; IV². 365 ; Colonial Laws, 1887, 69.
[2] Ibid. V. 138.
[3] Brigham, Laws of New Plymouth ; Plymouth Recs. XI. 132, 134.
[4] Ibid. II. 101, 103, 105 ; XI. 51.
[5] Ibid. XI. 131, 228, 231 ; V. 244 ; VI. 132, 218.

by the lessor before the period had elapsed. For a time the trade to the Kennebec river seems also to have been leased by the colony, but the revenue from that source was temporary and very slight.

On the subject of drift whales there was repeated legislation. In 1652 a declaration was made that, " whereas the publicke charges of the colonie are encreased and whereas by God's providence many whales and other fishes are cast on shore in many ports of this Jurisdiction, out of which the court sees reason to require some part of the Oyle made of them," it was ordered that one barrel of merchantable oil from every whale thus cast or brought on shore should be delivered to the colony treasurer by the town where the whale was found. Four years later the town was required to deliver the oil at its own cost at the Boston market. Later still it was proposed to allow the towns to lease this business, but this plan was not executed.[1]

In Connecticut and New Haven the import duty and the excise on liquors were combined in much the same way as in Massachusetts. But in neither of these colonies, during the period under review, was the tariff list extended to include imported commodities in general. With the exception of an import duty on tobacco, which was imposed by Connecticut in 1662, wines and liquors were the only imports on which duties were levied.[2]

In the accessible records of Rhode Island no reference to a customs duty appears until 1700, when a rate of five per cent was imposed upon goods which were imported for sale by persons who were not inhabitants. No provision was made in the act for a custom house, but the duty was made payable to the clerk of the town where the importer or pedler appeared with his goods for sale. He must also submit a true inventory of his goods under oath to the assistant, justice, or warden of the said town. The penalty of

---

[1] Plymouth Recs. XI. 61, 66, 114, 132, 138, 207.

[2] Conn. Recs. I. 332, 380, 383, 396 ; New Haven Recs. II. 145, 591. The duty on tobacco was imposed in order to check its importation from the southern colonies, while really in transit for Europe. The act had as its ostensible purpose coöperation with England in the enforcement of the acts of trade.

violating the act was forfeiture, the same to be enforced by the town sergeant, and return thereof should be made to the recorder of the colony. No provision whatever was made for a custom house for the colony. It is safe to say that nowhere, even among the laws of Rhode Island, were the powers of the town extended farther beyond their customary sphere than in this instance.[1] We are told that many orders were issued for the levy of an excise in Rhode Island, but of these only the act of 1669[2] appears to have survived.

By the first act imposing a customs duty in Massachusetts provision was made for a collector, though the title was not conferred in the law. He was to be appointed by the governor and council, and was empowered to have deputies. He was put under oath.[3] He should survey all vessels in the harbors of the colony, and search all warehouses and places where goods subject to the duty might be stored. Forfeiture of the goods was made the penalty for smuggling. The sums collected by the customs officers must be paid over to the treasurer of the colony, and with the last-named officer rested the authority to levy by distress, if payment was unduly delayed or was refused. The act of 1636 provided that the collector should receive as his reward one-third of what he collected. After 1648, however, the collection, first of customs on wines and later of those on all other liquors, together with the excise, the fur trade, and the sale of ammunition to the Indians, was farmed out for periods of three or five years. At first the sum of £120 per year was paid by the farmer for the privilege, but the sum was gradually increased[4] until, in 1668, £600 per year was offered. Under this system the farmers were the collectors, and they were concerned with the excise as well as with the customs.

According to the law of 1645 the invoices of imported liquors had to be sworn to before the governor or deputy

---

[1] R. I. Recs. III. 422.   [2] Ibid. II. 252.

[3] The oath of Bendall, the first customer, is in Mass. Recs. II. 284. See IV¹. 10, 193.

[4] Mass. Recs. IV¹. III. 112, 327 ; IV². 315, 366, 398, 495. Richard Way, who took the contract at the last-mentioned sum, three years later, had to plead for an abatement in order to prevent a total loss of his profit.

governor, while by the law of 1648 stricter regulations were made concerning the duties of the collector. These were slightly modified both ten and twenty years later, the chief officer, in imitation of English usage, being known as the customer, and his deputies as searchers and waiters. Constables and other officers were required to assist them in the work of search and seizure.[1]

In Connecticut, by the act of 1659, customs officers were designated for nine settlements along the River and Sound, and the fees which they were to receive for their services were specified.[2] As time passed offices of this class were limited to the two or three leading ports on the Sound.

In all the colonies, with the possible exception of Rhode Island, defence was the principal object of expenditure. This involved the payment of wages of soldiers and officers, payment for their supplies, for such stockades or forts as might be built by the colony, pensions and other forms of support for wounded soldiers and their families and for the families of those who had been slain. The support of the militia captains appears among the earliest objects of appropriation in Massachusetts. In September, 1634, the treasurer was ordered to furnish such money as the commissioners of defence should require. A year later Ludlow was expending money on Castle island for which he was ordered to account to the treasurer and Mr. Nowell. For these purposes personal service was also impressed, and that on a considerable scale, in 1635. Many instances occur of the advance of money to towns to be used by them in building breastworks or other defences. It was in 1637, to meet the debts incurred on the Pequot expedition, and as the result of other measures of defence, that a rate of £1000 — the largest at that time levied — was imposed.

Each of the successive expeditions against the Indians of course occasioned votes of supplies by all the colonies concerned. The expedition of 1645 and the preparations[3] for that of 1664 against the Dutch, occasioned such appropriations. Toward the former expedition Plymouth appropriated £70.

---

[1] Mass. Col. Laws, 1887, 68.   [2] Conn. Recs. I. 332.
[3] Mass. Recs. I. 129, 138, 158, 165, 209; II. 124; IV². 121, 123.

Of this nearly one-half was to be paid by the towns directly to their soldiers, and the remainder was to be expended through the office of the colony treasurer.[1] The earliest rates which were levied by the river towns were intended to meet the cost of the expedition against the Pequots. The building and repair of the fort at Saybrook was another important object of expenditure.[2] Charges for the maintenance of the fort and of the castle in Boston harbor appear at frequent intervals in the records.[3] The most detailed among the early acts for the levy of rates in Rhode Island was that of 1667 for the improvement of the defences of Newport, and to repair the arms of its inhabitants and secure a new supply.[4] A part of the cost of supplying arms was in all the colonies imposed on the towns, but a colony magazine was also in most cases maintained. Cannon were purchased by the colony.

It was in connection with Philip's war that expenditures for military purposes attained by far their largest development. This has been indicated in what has already been said concerning rates. In March, 1676, Plymouth levied by quotas on the towns what was for her the unprecedented sum of £1000. This was to be expended in clothing and provisions for the soldiers. Shortly after this the sum of £121, 10s., which had been contributed by "Christians in Ireland" for the relief of those who had been impoverished by the war, became available, and was distributed among the towns. Rehoboth and Dartmouth received the largest share. In June, 1677, a committee was appointed by the general court to hear claims against the colony on account of the war and to report,[5] so that the debts of the colony might be known. According to accounts which were submitted to the Commissioners of the United Colonies, Plymouth, through its towns and through the office of the colony treasurer combined, had expended £11,743 upon the war. Massachusetts reported an expenditure of £46,292.[6]

---

[1] Plymouth Recs. II. 91.   [2] Conn. Recs. I. 11, 12, 95, 139, 161, 235.

[3] Mass. Recs. I. 231 ; II. 255, 260 ; III. 5 ; IV[1]. 281 ; V. 204, 222.

[4] R. I. Recs. II. 196.   [5] Plymouth Recs. V. 191, 222, 234 ; VI. 118.

[6] Recs. of the United Col. in Conn. Recs. III. 492, 493, 502.

Three rates, which were levied by Connecticut during the years 1675 to 1677, yielded a total of £23,185.

The extent to which Plymouth, during and after the struggle, devoted its resources to the support of those who had suffered injury or loss in consequence of it, is remarkable. On that occasion a pension system was developed on a larger scale than appears elsewhere during the entire colonial period. Plymouth, as early as 1636, had enacted that, if any one should return from military service maimed, he should be maintained by the colony for life.[1] During Philip's war she made many grants to wounded soldiers and to the widows and families of those who were slain. In October, 1675, £60 were granted to Theophilus Witherell, who had been wounded in the war and made a cripple for life. By the same court £10 from the profits of the fishery at Cape Cod were granted to the widow and children of John Knowles, who was a recent victim. Two other widows received grants at the same time.[2] Many other similar instances might be cited. A special grant of land was made to Captain Gorham for his services.

The Massachusetts court, in October, 1678, granted to Richard Russ, who had been wounded in the war, the sum which the curing[3] of his wounds had cost him. Several other cases of such grants are recorded, but they are not relatively so numerous as in Plymouth. Rewards for public service in Massachusetts, whether rendered in peace or war, not infrequently took the form of exemption from rates, or the grant of special gratuities. This leads directly to the consideration of another object of expenditure, the reward or salaries of public officials.

A generation or more passed after the founding of the New England colonies before what can be called a salary system began to develop. Gratuitous service, or service without definite expectation of reward, was long rendered by many of the early magistrates of those colonies. In New England, as among the other colonies, fees formed an im-

---

[1] Plymouth Recs. XI. 182.
[2] *Ibid.* V. 177, 241, 271 ; VI. 18, 32, 40, 52, 65, 88, 93, 109, 130, 188.
[3] Mass. Recs. V. 206, 264, 280, 282, 283, 298.

portant part of official reward, especially for all who were in any way connected with judicial business. As a class, the clergy were the first to receive salaries. Magistrates and clergymen were also regularly exempted from the payment of rates. Special services, whether in war or in civil life, were not infrequently followed in Massachusetts by exemption from rates. In 1636 Nowell, the secretary, was permanently exempted from their payment. After the Pequot war Stoughton was exempted for one year. In 1639 the property of Cradock was exempted, because of the expense which he had borne in the building of a bridge. In 1653 the estate of Governor Dudley was exempted from a rate. In 1668 the people of Marblehead, because of a poor fishing season and of the charge which the town had incurred in building a battery, were exempted from a single rate. Certain inhabitants of towns which suffered severely in Philip's war were temporarily exempted ; for example, residents in Medfield and Hatfield. The town of Lancaster was exempted by order of 1682 for two years. Its share in two rates was allowed to Sherborn as an aid toward the building of a meeting-house for the town and a house for the minister. In response to a petition the selectmen of Boston, in February, 1684, were empowered to abate the rates of such as had suffered by the recent fire. In 1685 John Fiske of Wenham, because he had been disabled by wounds in the late Indian war, was permanently exempted from country rates.[1]

Reward for public services also took the form of special grants. This was the germ from which the system of salaries developed. At the May court in 1632 Winthrop, who had been granted no salary, stated that he had received gratuities from individuals and from several towns ; but he did so with trembling, because of God's law and of his own infirmity.[2] He declared that he would take no more, except from assistants or from particular friends. In July of the following year, it was voted to give him £150 toward his

---

[1] Mass. Recs. I. 182, 215, 257 ; IV[1]. 174 ; IV[2]. 377 ; V. 182, 188, 341, 345, 433, 471.

[2] Winthrop, Journal, I. 92 ; Mass. Recs. I. 106.

charges for the year, and that he be repaid the sum — between £200 and £300 — which he had advanced for the payment of officers' wages and to meet other public charges. In September, 1634, through a committee which was appointed to audit his accounts, Winthrop reported that, during the four years of his official service, he had expended £1200 in excess of what would have been necessary if he had remained in private station. In return he had received an allowance of £150 and gratuities to the amount of £100 more.[1] He, however, made no demand for a salary. In 1636 a stipend was fixed on the marshal which, with his fees, would amount to £40 per year. In 1637 £100 was allowed as the governor's salary, "the same allowance to be given to the succeeding governor as a settled stipend." In 1638 it was enacted that each town should bear the charges of its magistrates and deputies during the sessions of the general court, and the daily rate of their wages was fixed. The next year it was ordered that the cost of their diet and lodging should be paid out of the revenue from the fines. Thus a practice was established in reference to these items of expenditure which was widely followed by the colonies. In 1644 the governor was receiving a salary of £100. In 1645 the deputy governor was receiving an allowance of £50. From time to time gratuities were added to these sums.[2] When agents were sent to England, their expenses were paid and they received special remuneration. This was the practice in all the colonies.

In 1653 something which might be called a salary system was established by law, as a means, however, of reducing rather than increasing expenditure.[3] This provided that magistrates who had been in office ten years should be allowed £30 per annum, and from this should pay all their expenses while in attendance on courts. Magistrates who had served less than ten years should receive £20 per annum ; persons who hereafter should be appointed to the

[1] Mass. Recs. I. 130.
[2] Ibid. I. 182, 215, 228 ; II. 53, 116, 136, 165, 194, 271 ; IV[1]. 4, 35, 46, 65, 66, 68, 74 ; IV[2]. 75, 88, 113.
[3] Ibid. IV[1]. 154.

magistracy should receive £15 a year. The governor should be paid "from year to year," £120, and this was for himself and his "attendants." The salary of the secretary was fixed at £45. In 1651 the allowance of the secretary was fixed at £40. In addition he was entitled to fees for transcribing documents for the towns and individuals.[1] In 1659 his salary was increased to £60 per year. That of the surveyor general had been fixed, as two years before, at £5 per annum. The charges of the county courts,[2] including judges, juries, and officers, must be met from the actions arising in those courts. The wages of jurymen were prescribed in this act. Towns should continue to pay the wages of their deputies to the general court, but towns of not more than thirty freemen might send deputies or not, as they chose. In 1654 the salary of the clerk of the deputies was declared to be £16 per annum, he bearing the expense of his diet and lodging.[3] We know that the Commissioners of the United Colonies received wages for their services. The inference is that officers like the treasurer, who were not mentioned in this act, were supported by fees, receiving, it may be, an occasional gratuity in addition. The rates of fees were, in all cases and in all the corporate colonies, determined by the general court or by officials whose responsibility to the court was clear and definite. Under the corporate system the question of fees, which caused so much dissension between the executives and assemblies in the provinces, could not arise.

It thus appears that salaries in colonial Massachusetts were very moderate, and in the gross they amounted to only a small sum. They were, however, supplemented by some fees and by gratuities. But of greater importance than the gratuities in money were the grants of land which were repeatedly made to leading magistrates and their favorites, especially to Winthrop, Endicott, Bradstreet, Symonds, and Rawson; so also to a less extent to others. Land was the form of wealth in which the colony could most easily dis-

---

[1] Mass. Recs. IV[1]. 63, 391.

[2] Ibid. 185. The rates of salary had not been greatly changed when Randolph was in Massachusetts in 1678. Toppan, Randolph, III. 11.

[3] Mass. Recs. IV[1]. 206.

charge its obligations. Its bestowment did not increase taxation or lessen revenue. Symonds and Leverett were also buried at the public expense.

In the early records of Plymouth colony entries appear to the effect that wages of officials should be paid in commodities, at certain rates, but the amount of wages and the officers to whom they were paid are not specified. While in session, the magistrates were boarded and lodged at the public expense. To the contracts which were made with private parties relating to this, several references appear.[1] As in the other colonies, gratuities were bestowed as rewards for unusually prolonged or faithful service. In 1651 and 1652 a gratuity of £20 was granted to Mr. Collier, who had long been an assistant and did much public business. In 1659, because of his advancing age and his continued occupation with business, he was allowed a servant at the public expense.[2] In 1660 £10 was granted to John Alden, whose estate was small, but who for many years had devoted himself to the service of the colony.[3] Among the propositions which were considered in 1665 was one to the effect that the governors should thereafter be allowed £50 or £60 per annum, and that the assistants — five in number — should receive £20 yearly and bear their own charges.[4] The plan was not adopted. In 1673, however, the sum of £50 was granted to Governor Josiah Winslow, as " his sallery or gratuity . . . for this present year."[5] The form of this grant shows very clearly how gratuities developed into salaries. When the gratuity became the subject of regular annual grant, it was a salary. Not until about 1690 do we have proof that a salary system existed in Plymouth. In.that year allowances were made to the governor, the deputy governor, the secretary, to each of the assistants, to the chief marshal[6] and the under marshal. The deputies, in Plymouth as elsewhere, had long received daily wages.

Reference to the other New England colonies will involve mainly a repetition of what has been stated concerning Mas-

[1] Plymouth Recs. III. 120 ; V. 38, 124 ; VI. 93.
[2] *Ibid.* II. 169 ; III. 14, 51, 74, 166.
[3] *Ibid.* III. 195.
[4] *Ibid.* IV. 102.
[5] *Ibid.* V. 124.
[6] *Ibid.* VI. 245.

sachusetts and Plymouth. In all of them the advance was through gratuities to salaries, and the sums involved were very small. The governor was the officer who first received a salary. Grants were also made after 1660 in Connecticut to the secretary, the treasurer, the deputy governor, the marshal. The records of New Haven refer only to definite annual grants to the governor and deputy governor. About 1670 £150 was the customary salary of the governor of Connecticut. The governor of New Haven never received more than £50 per year. The backwardness of Rhode Island in such matters is illustrated by a vote of the assembly in 1698. "This Assembly having considered the great charge and expense that our Honored Governor is daily at on the Collony's concerns, have enacted . . . that there shall be added to the Governor's sallary the sum of twenty pounds per annum, so that the whole sum shall be thirty pounds, to be paid out of the Generall Treasury [1] upon demand."

The salary and other expenses of agents who were sent to England were burdens which all the colonies had occasionally to bear. In a few cases such outlays were met by private contribution, but the agency came generally to be regarded as a public function, the cost of which must be met from the treasury of the colony.[2] The object of such expenditure being remote, the colonists often met it with less willingness than they did other costs of government. But the expenditures of Governor Winthrop in procuring the charter of 1662 were met by a special rate for three years of a penny in the pound. We are told, however, that many were unwilling to pay Mr. Whiting for his services on behalf of Connecticut in 1686.[3] Rhode Island failed to pay all the expenses of Roger Williams, while a bill of John Clarke for services as agent in procuring the Rhode Island charter of 1663 remained unpaid when he died in 1676. Proof is lacking that it was ever paid. Repeated efforts were made by the levy of rates and the appointment of committees to secure the payment of this debt, but the independence of the towns,

[1] R. I. Recs. III. 345.
[2] Mass. Recs. II. 162, 218 ; III. 79 ; IV[1]. 65.
[3] Conn. Recs. II. 231 ; III. 237.

combined with general indifference, proved stronger than the sense of public obligation.[1]

In the Puritan colonies the support of the ministry, the building and repair of churches and the support of schools, were regular objects of public expenditure. The discussion of their ecclesiastical systems has made this evident. This, with the building and repair of roads and bridges, building and repair of jails, the care of the poor and the support of local officials and courts, rested mainly on the localities. Laws making such expenditures obligatory abound. But on occasion supplementary grants were made from the colony treasury. By Massachusetts, in 1640, the ferry between Boston and Charlestown was granted to Harvard College. The original grant of money by the general court for the founding of the college was £400, one-half of which was to be paid when the work was finished. The payment of this grant, however, fell greatly into arrears. Later, grants were made for the support of the president, and for other expenses of the college, a few of them being in the form of land. But the College was chiefly supported by contributions from the four distinctively Puritan colonies and from England. In 1655 a project was broached for the establishment by similar means of a college at New Haven; but it came[2] to nothing.

Under the act of 1642 the towns of Massachusetts began their expenditures for elementary and grammar schools, the same policy being followed in the other three colonies. Special efforts were made for the founding of a colony grammar school at New Haven, the general court conditionally appropriating £100 for the purpose. But this scheme did not prosper. Massachusetts occasionally made grants of land for the endowment of grammar schools, and Connecticut,[3] in 1672, set apart six hundred acres of land

[1] R. I. Recs. II. 77–80, 131, 181, 514; III. 22; Arnold, I. 313.

[2] Mass. Recs. I. 183, 304; IV[1]. 30, 91, 178, 186, 312, and many later entries stating the grants of salary to the president; Quincy, History of Harvard College, I. 22, 27, 31; Clews, Educational Legislation and Administration of the Colonial Governments.

[3] New Haven Recs. II. Index under Education and Schools; Conn. Recs. I. 554; II. Index, Schools.

in each to be used for this purpose. In 1671 the general
court of Plymouth voted to devote the revenue which arose
from fishing at the Cape to the support of a free grammar school at the town of Plymouth. With this fund a
school was soon started. In 1678 a grant of £10 was
made toward the support of a school at Rehoboth. Grants
came regularly to be made out of the fund from the fishery,
both to the schools in these towns and to one in Duxbury.[1]
The support of both the grammar and the elementary schools
continued to be mainly a local charge. Towns which failed
to maintain them, as required by law, were liable to fine.
Of activity on the part of the colony government in Rhode
Island in support of education, we hear nothing.

For the purposes of the present discussion it is not necessary to refer at greater length to local revenues or expenditures. The chief objects of colonial expenditure have been
sufficiently reviewed. In addition service was rendered to
the colony by messengers who were sent to the Indians or
to other colonies, by persons who furnished entertainment
or means of conveyance for officials or agents of the colony
when in the public service, by those who assisted in emergencies like that of the hue and cry, by laborers on public
works of all kinds. An instance of a large extraordinary
payment is that which was imposed on the River Towns by
the purchase of Saybrook. In Massachusetts a clergyman
or magistrate was occasionally paid a sum for answering
some heretical publication or producing a specially valued
book. The services of the clergy as advisers, or of others in
preparing codes of laws, also called for special recognition.

Payments from the colony treasury had therefore to be
made each year in small sums to a considerable number of
individuals, who, taken together, had performed a large
variety of miscellaneous services for the public. The general courts, however, were not in the habit of passing annually a single itemized appropriation act, as came to be the
custom in some of the provinces. Scattered through the
court records, particularly of Massachusetts, appear special
orders for the payment of sums to a designated individual

[1] Plymouth Recs. V. 107, 259; VI. 19, 31, 81, 102; XI. Index, Schools.

and for a specific service. These orders were often framed in response to petitions. John Ruddock petitions for payment for the services[1] of himself and horse on a journey on behalf of the colony to Connecticut, and payment is ordered. Specific sums are granted[2] for meals and lodgings of magistrates, deputies, or governor's men, as the case might be. Payments are ordered in similar form for arms and ammunition. Salaries and wages, not only of officials but of those who are engaged on building or repairing a prison, a fort, or other public structure, are usually stated in precise form. The general assembly of Rhode Island, in May, 1664, for example, ordered four payments, each for a distinct and specific service. More than twenty such payments were ordered during the session of October 26, 1670.[3] Entries of this kind are not so common in the records of the other corporate colonies, but such fragments of treasurers' accounts as have been preserved indicate that payments were made in the same specific form.[4]

In many, if not most, cases the objects for which rates were to be expended were not definitely stated in the orders for their levy. The purpose of the regular annual rate was very often stated to be the payment of the debts of the colony. When a rate was levied for a specific purpose, as the outfit of a military expedition, the fact was usually stated in the order.

In the corporate colonies the official who had immediate charge of the revenue from all sources and of its expenditure was the treasurer. As there was no private or territorial revenue, distinct from that which went into the public chest, the office of receiver general does not appear. In the case of the Massachusetts company the office of treasurer existed in England. He was there annually elected by the general court of the company. He continued to be so elected after the removal into Massachusetts, and the same was the practice in all the other corporate colonies. William Pynchon was the first treasurer of the colony of Massachusetts of whom we have record, though we do not know when he was

---

[1] Mass. Recs. IV[1]. 191.
[2] Ibid. II. 116, 117.
[3] R. I. Recs. II. 51, 365.
[4] See especially the Records of Plymouth.

elected.[1] In September, 1634, William Coddington took the oath of office as treasurer. He was succeeded in 1636 by Richard Dummer, and in 1637 by Richard Bellingham. Bellingham was the next year chosen an assistant, but whether he was continued in the office of treasurer, the record does not state.[2] Both Richard Russell and James Russell held the two offices at the same time.[3] But no record of another election of treasurer appears until 1640, when William Tyng was chosen. He was annually reëlected until 1645,[4] when Richard Russell was chosen in his place. He was annually reëlected till his death in 1676, — probably the longest tenure of the same office in the history of Massachusetts as a corporation. In 1677 Captain John Hull was chosen treasurer, holding the office until 1680, when James Russell, the son of the former treasurer, was elected as his successor and continued in the office until the dissolution of the corporation.[5] In Plymouth Miles Standish held the office from 1644 to 1656. He was then succeeded by John Alden, who served for three years. After that Constant Southworth was annually reëlected until 1678, the year of his death.

In the other colonies of New England the office of treasurer was among the earliest which were created.[6] In all cases he was chosen in the court of election. His duties were to issue warrants for the collection of taxes, to receive and keep the public revenue, from whatever source it came; and to pay it out under order from the general court or from magistrates to whom such authority might be delegated. According to the terms of Massachusetts law no disbursement could be made except under the authority of some law, order, or settled custom of the general court or assistants. The same was true in all the corporate colonies. In their case there could never be any doubt that both the exclusive power to appropriate revenue and to direct its expenditure

---

[1] Mass. Recs. I. 136. In 2 Mass. Hist. Colls. VIII. 228, are the accounts of Pynchon as treasurer, rendered in 1636. They are for 1632–1633 and part of 1634.

[2] Mass. Recs. I. 129, 175, 195.   [4] *Ibid.* I. 288, 333 ; II. 97.

[3] *Ibid.* IV². 417 ; V. 27, 77, 265.   [5] *Ibid.* V. 131, 265.

[6] Plymouth Recs. I. 48 ; XI. 7 ; Conn. Recs. I. 12 ; New Haven Recs. I. 51 ; R. I. Recs. I. 148, 197 ; Mass. Col. Laws, 1887, p. 196.

belonged to the general court.   The treasurer was not under a divided control, as was often the case in the provinces, but was the servant of the general court.

In all the corporate colonies the control of the legislature over the finances, and especially over expenditures, was maintained through a system of audit.   This they inherited from the trading corporations in England.   In Massachusetts the treasurer was by law obliged to account yearly, at the time of the court of election, to the general court or to such persons as it should designate.   As early as 1644, and probably earlier, the same system was in operation in Plymouth.   By order of 1638 the treasurer of Connecticut was forbidden to pay any bills which had not been " alowed " by the proper committees.   By a law of 1647 the treasurer of the Providence Plantations was required to account to the general assembly.[1]

The references, year by year, in the legislative journals to the appointment of committees of audit show that the obligation was maintained.   By the Massachusetts court of election in 1640 Nathaniel Johnson and Captain Robert Sedgwick were appointed to join with the new treasurer, Mr. Tyng, in examining the accounts of the former treasurers.   The accounts of Tyng[2] were examined in 1644 and accepted. Thus, in general, the custom continued through the century. Its continuance can be traced in a similar manner in the other corporate colonies.   The oath, as administered to the treasurer of Plymouth in 1659, provided for the annual audit. In 1658 the town of Scituate in Plymouth colony petitioned the court that the accounts of the treasurer might be sent to the several towns.   It was therefore ordered that town auditors might meet with the others for the purpose of examining his accounts, and report thereon to their towns.[3] It is probable that this practice was continued after that date.   In Rhode Island we hear of separate audits of accounts of the recorder, or secretary, and of the sergeant or sheriff.

But there is abundant evidence that the same faults which

---

[1] Mass. Col. Laws, 1887, p. 151: Conn. Recs. I. 26 ; Brigham, Laws of New Plymouth, 77 ; R. I. Recs. I. 197.
[2] Mass. Recs. I. 288 ; II. 73, 79.   [3] Plymouth Recs. XI. 142, 211.

characterized the system of colonial administration as a whole, appeared in the audit of accounts. Long delays frequently occurred, sometimes the work was loosely done or not done at all. It was the same way with the collection of revenue, and delays in the audit were often caused by delays in collecting. In 1645 Massachusetts created the office of auditor general, with a salary of £30 per annum, and he was given very full powers with the purpose that he should cause exact accounts of the colony's finances to be kept and rendered.[1] Entries appear from time to time respecting his employment, alone or with the treasurer and others, in the examination of accounts. Committees of audit, however, were still appointed by the general court. In May, 1654, we find that, though a committee had been appointed the year before, the task of auditing the accounts had not been completed, because the constables of several towns had not yet collected all the rates. The audit was therefore postponed until the next session of court. The August session passed without reference to the matter, but in the October session a committee was appointed to examine the treasurer's accounts immediately after adjournment, so that the report might be published for the satisfaction of the colony. In November of the next year an order was passed that constables should clear their accounts with the treasurer annually by May 1st. The office of auditor general was apparently[2] found not to be so useful as it was expected to be, and in 1657 it was abolished. Thenceforward its duties were performed by the treasurer in conjunction with annual committees of audit.[3]

The assembly of Rhode Island in May, 1670, after struggling with protracted delays in the payment of rates, and consequent inability to pay the debts of the colony, passed[4] an act and appointed a committee for the general audit of accounts. The powers and procedure of the committee were

---

[1] Mass. Recs. II. 141, 148, 162, 226.

[2] *Ibid.* IV[1]. 186, 202, 247.

[3] References to the appointment of such committees abound in Vols. IV[2]. and V. of the Records.

[4] R. I. Recs. II. 303, 358.

set forth with unusual fulness. They were ordered to extend their inquiries at least as far back as 1664, and to include the rates which were levied to defray the cost of the charter. All who had claims against the colony were instructed to apply to them. If the account of any town was found defective, the auditors should order the collection of its deficit. At first the committee, which consisted of four persons chosen, according to Rhode Island principles, equally from the four towns, was prohibited from acting except with the unanimous consent of its members and in the presence of all. The member from Providence stayed away or otherwise hindered proceedings until, in October, the assembly was forced to drop the requirement for unanimity of consent. Later entries indicate that some progress was made by the committee, but we do not know whether or not its work was ever completed.

CHAPTER XIII

THE SYSTEM OF DEFENCE IN THE NEW ENGLAND COLONIES

PART
II. In the treatment of this subject, as of the others which have passed in review, the experience of Massachusetts will be brought chiefly into requisition, while that of the other New England colonies will be cited so far as to show that the measures adopted for defence were substantially the same in them all. The Narragansett plantations took a less prominent part in the expeditions and wars of the seventeenth century than did the neighboring colonies; but that in the beginning is to be attributed to the fact that they were excluded from the New England Confederacy and were forced by their situation to cultivate friendship with the Indians. At a later time the addition of a Quaker element to their population, together with the growth of commercial interests, increased the disinclination to war.

The charter of Massachusetts, in language very similar to that used in all the other royal charters, empowered the governor and company "for their speciall defence and safety, to incounter, expulse, repell, and resist by force of armes, as well by sea as by lande, . . . all such person or persons as shall at any tyme hereafter attempt or enterprise the destruction, invasion, detriment or annoyance to the said plantation or inhabitants." The exercise of this power gave rise to the militia system of Massachusetts and to its provisions for coast and frontier defence. In consequence of the removal of the governor and company into the colony, the power was exercised by them directly and not through the medium of appointees acting at a great distance from the centre of authority. As the other New England colonies, until they

496

received royal charters, assumed the power, and used it in
much the same way as did Massachusetts, the result was the development of a military system which in its main features was common to them all.

The Puritan belonged to the militant type of humanity, and considered the defence of his inheritance, by force of arms if necessary, as nothing less than a religious duty. " For," said the general court of Massachusetts in the preamble to the militia law of 1643,[1] " as piety cannot bee maintained without church ordinances & officers, nor justice without lawes & magistracy, no more can our safety & peace be preserved without millitary orders & officers." " Although," says worthy Edward Johnson, " the chiefest work of these select bands of Christ was to mind their spiritual warfare yet they knew right well the Temple was surrounded with walls and bulworks, and the people of God in re-edifying the same did prepare to resist their enemies with weapons of war, even while they continued building."[2] The Massachusetts company, before its governing body was removed from England, bought cannon, with military equipment for approximately one hundred men, sent them, together with a master gunner, to Salem, and ordered Endicott to have all planters and servants instructed in the use of arms, and to designate certain days[3] for trainings.

But it should be borne in mind that in the American colonies the subordination of the military to the civil power was quite as much a cardinal principle as it was in England. Winthrop states that when, during the Antinomian excitement, certain gentlemen and others of Boston desired incorporation as an artillery company, the magistrates reflected on the example of the Pretorian band among the Romans and the Templars in Europe. They thought "how dangerous it might be to erect a standing authority of military men, which might easily in time overthrow the civil power," and resolved to "stop it betimes."[4]   The anxiety was

---

[1] Mass. Col. Recs. II. 42.

[2] Johnson, Wonder-working Providence of Sion's Savior in New England, Poole's Ed. 190.

[3] Mass. Col. Recs. I. 26–37 g, 392.   [4] Winthrop, I. 305.

unnecessary, for the industrial forces in colonial society so greatly outweighed the military as to effectually remove the peril that was feared.   A few who had received training in European armies came to the colonies with the first settlers, but their successors and the great body of their contemporaries never gained any military experience save that which came from Indian fighting or from an occasional muster. Officers and privates alike were civilians ; they were husbandmen, artisans or small traders, withdrawn from their homes and business for a brief scout, march, or campaign. In the colonies there was no opportunity for the development of the professional soldier.   Indian warfare was not favorable to that.   Time for training and service must be taken, at considerable cost, from occupations which, if they were to yield even a modest livelihood, demanded strenuous application and effort.   Families were large, resources were small. Population was sparsely distributed.   The home was often located in places where danger lurked, and where the presence of the grown men of the household was imperatively needed for protection.   Fields must be planted and harvests gathered at the proper time, or the community would immediately suffer want.   Under these conditions it was impossible for the colonists to do more than organize a militia system, which in a more or less crude way would meet the need for defence.   Military law, like all other law, emanated directly or indirectly from the general court.   The committees and administrative boards which controlled the equipment of soldiers and directed their movements consisted in most cases of the same men who guided the affairs of the colony in civil relations.   The officers were in many cases elected by the men — their neighbors — whom they commanded, and in all cases they derived their authority from an elective body.   Under these conditions training was imperfect and discipline a result of voluntary consent almost as much as of positive law.   These conditions, combined with the limited resources both of the soldier and of the colonial treasury from which his wages were paid, and with the fact that the commissariat played a very subordinate part in the outfit of a force, explain why it was that the military arrangements of the colonies were crude, and their soldiery was unfit for long periods of active service.

In all the colonies, as in England, the militia system was based on the principle of the assize of arms.   This implied the general obligation of all adult male inhabitants to possess arms, and, with certain exceptions, to coöperate in the work of defence.   In this duty, as in the payment of taxes, the distinction between freemen and non-freemen to an extent disappeared.   The possession of arms also implied the possession of ammunition, and the authorities paid quite as much attention to the latter as to the former.   In Massachusetts the arms and ammunition which had been purchased by the company in England were doubtless distributed, and all were required to furnish themselves with a proper equipment.   The court of assistants, in March, 1631,[1] ordered that within the next two weeks every town should see that all men, servants included, should be furnished with good and sufficient arms, such as were approved by the captain or other officers.   Magistrates and ministers alone were excepted.   Those who had no arms, and who were able to purchase them, should do so.   Others should be supplied by the town, and return to it the sum expended as soon as they were able.   A year later it was ordered that any single man who had not furnished himself with arms might be put out to service, and this became a permanent part of the legislation of the colony.[2]   In 1634 more weapons were brought from England, and they were distributed among the towns, in order that they might have them ready at all times as a town stock.   It was then provided that any one who was delinquent in the matter of furnishing himself with arms should be fined ten shillings.[3]   Supplies of ammunition were at various times procured from England or the continent. In 1653 a stock of arms, as well as ammunition, was procured through the Commissioners of the United Colonies, and it was distributed among the four Puritan commonwealths.[4]   In

---

[1] Mass. Recs. I. 84.

[2] *Ibid.* 93, II. 222 ; Col. Laws, Ed. of 1889, 177 ; Col. Laws, Ed. of 1887, 109.

[3] Mass. Recs. I. 125.   [4] Conn. Recs. I. 239, 244.

1667 [1] Massachusetts began to increase its supply of powder by a tonnage duty. The manufacture of powder was also encouraged, and occasionally its exportation without special license was forbidden. Periodical inspections were ordered.

Clauses intended to insure the possession of arms and ammunition by all who were subject to military service appear in all the important enactments concerning military affairs. Fines were the penalty for delinquency, whether of towns or individuals. According to the usage of the times, the infantry of Massachusetts consisted of pikemen and musketeers. The law,[2] as enacted in 1649 and thereafter, provided that each of the former should be armed with a pike, corselet, head-piece, sword, and knapsack. The musketeer should carry a " good fixed musket," not under bastard musket bore, not less than three feet, nine inches, nor more than four feet three inches in length, a priming wire, scourer, and mould, a sword, rest, bandoleers, one pound of powder, twenty bullets, and two fathoms of match. The law also required that two-thirds of each company should be musketeers.

The law in Plymouth concerning the size of the musket, when used for military purposes, was much the same as that of Massachusetts.[3] Provisions concerning the equipment in general were substantially the same as those of Massachusetts. In March, 1638, just before the expedition against the Pequots, the purchase of fifty corselets for the towns along the Connecticut river [4] was ordered. All were commanded to keep in readiness powder and bullets,—and match if the piece was a matchlock. In the Connecticut Code of 1650,[5] and in the New Haven Code of 1656, appear explicit provisions relating to equipment which might well have been suggested, not merely by the existing law of those colonies, but by that of Massachusetts and by earlier practice in England.

---

[1] Mass. Recs. IV². 331.   [2] Col. Laws, Ed. of 1889, 177.

[3] Recs. XI. 104. Provisions concerning equipment in general, which were substantially the same as those in the Laws of Massachusetts, are in Brigham, Laws of New Plymouth, 31, 44, 45. References to the pike appear in Plymouth Col. Recs. XI. 127, 181, 183.

[4] Conn. Col. Recs. I. 14, 15.   [5] Ibid. 542 ; New Haven Recs. II. 602.

Following European traditions, the law of Massachusetts in the early time required that two-thirds of each trained band should be musketeers and one-third pikemen.[1] Whether or not this proportion was maintained among the infantry of the other colonies we are not informed. The staff of the half-pike which was carried was not far from ten feet long.[2] As a weapon it was found practically useless in Indian warfare; but, as New Englanders had no prolonged or very serious conflicts with the natives till Philip's war, the pike kept its place in the general equipment.[3] But that war banished it from Massachusetts, and probably from New England as a whole. By an order[4] of October, 1675, all pikemen from Massachusetts were commanded to furnish themselves with muskets and the ammunition required therewith. When, in the following year, Edward Randolph transmitted to the home government an account, among other things, of the militia system of Massachusetts, he stated that pikemen formed no part of it, for they were found to be useless in wars with the Indians.[5] With the pike we may suppose that the use of armor also disappeared.

Previous to the time of Philip's war, the musket which was in common use was the matchlock.[6] In this the powder was fired by a slow-burning match-cord, prepared by being soaked in saltpetre. So heavy was the gun that the soldier had to carry a "fourquette," or forked stick, on which to rest the weapon when he fired it. Around his left side, hanging under his right arm, was his bandoleer. This was a belt two inches wide, to which were attached twelve small cylindrical boxes, each holding one charge of powder. From the belt likewise hung a priming wire, a bullet bag,

---

[1] Col. Laws, Ed. of 1889, 177.   [2] Conn. Recs. I. 74.

[3] In the comprehensive militia law of 1643 Massachusetts repealed a previous order that every man should be supplied with a musket, and encouraged the use of pikes. Recs. II. 43.

[4] Mass. Recs. V. 47.

[5] Pubs. of Prince Society, Hutchinson Papers, II. 220 ; Judd, however, states (History of Hadley, 229) that Boston had some pikemen in 1686.

[6] Elton, The Compleat Body of the Art Military ; Judd, History of Hadley, 224 ; Roberts, History of the Ancient and Honorable Artillery Company of Massachusetts, I. ; Bodge, The Soldiers of King Philip's War, 478.

and a case containing several yards of match. The musketeer also carried a short sword. The "postures of the
musket," or movements to prepare, aim, and fire this weapon,
were no less than fifty-seven. The matchlock was thus not
only most clumsy, but very crude, being apt to fail at the
critical moment, while the heavy equipment necessitated by
it proved a serious obstacle to the mobility of the troops.

But from the earliest days of the colonies flint-locks or
firelocks, carbines, and pistols had been to an extent in use.
As the century advanced[1] they became more common.
Therefore, with the opening of Philip's war the matchlock
disappeared almost as quickly as did the pike. In November, 1675, Massachusetts ordered that every town should
provide six flints for every listed[2] soldier of the town. The
previous month it enacted that every trooper should provide
himself with a carbine.[3] In November, Connecticut ordered
a "stock of flints"[4] to be sent to New London for the
expedition against the Narragansetts. In February, 1676,
the Massachusetts committee of war estimated that two
thousand flints were necessary for an expedition of five
hundred men.[5] By order of July, 1677, Plymouth banished
the matchlock, and ordered that all should supply themselves with firelock muskets.[6] Thus by the close of the
war the matchlock, as well as the pike, had been practically
discarded, and by a law of 1693 it was provided that Massachusetts infantry should be furnished with firelock muskets
and the troopers with carbines and pistols.

The men who were procured for service, armed and furnished with ammunition in the way indicated, were first
organized into trained bands, in imitation of the trained
bands of London and of the English counties.[7] In Massachusetts, soon after Winthrop's arrival, two veterans, Underhill and Patrick, were employed for a year to train the
companies,[8] their wages for the first half year being specified.

---

[1] Judd, *op. cit.* 228.   [3] *Ibid.* 47.   [5] Judd, 229.
[2] Mass. Recs. V. 63.   [4] Conn. Recs. II. 383.   [6] Plymouth Recs. XI. 245.
[7] For the efficiency and training of these, see Firth, Cromwell's Army,
5–11.
[8] Mass. Recs. I. 75.

As towns were formed, the number of trained bands was increased, each town being required to form one.

These became the militia companies of the colony. In 1652 the general court ordered that the number of men in a company should not be less than sixty-four, nor more than two hundred.[1] When the number of soldiers exceeded the maximum, the company was divided; in cases when it was less than the minimum, the soldiers of one or more towns were joined to form a company. As the companies were organized, the duty of training them devolved immediately on locally elected military officers, — captains, lieutenants, sergeants, ensigns.

One of the most important officers connected with the militia company, and one who appears in all the colonies, with the possible exception of Rhode Island, was the clerk of the band. His powers appear with the greatest clearness in the laws of Massachusetts and Connecticut.[2] He kept the list of the company, and hence of all residents of the town who were liable to military service. He, therefore, it was who, in Massachusetts and Connecticut, was chiefly active in taking the assize of arms, though in some of the colonies the captain, or other strictly military officer, seems to have borne a more prominent part in it than he did. According to Massachusetts law, the view of the arms and ammunition of the company was taken in the towns twice every year. Once yearly the arms of all other inhabitants were surveyed. On training days the clerk attended, called the lists of those who should be present, and noted the names of absentees. The arms of the company must then be submitted to the inspection of the captain. All fines which were imposed for failure to attend trainings, or to keep the required weapons, or to keep them in proper condition, were collected by the clerk of the band. To this end he was given the right to levy by distress. The fund thus collected he might, with the advice of the chief officers, expend for ensigns, drums, or other supplies needed by the company.

[1] Mass. Recs. IV[1]. 86.
[2] Mass. Recs. II. 118 ; Mass. Laws, Ed. of 1889. 178 ; Conn. Col. Recs. I. 542 ; New Haven Col. Recs. II. 602 ; Brigham, Laws of New Plymouth, 145.

The oath of the clerk of the military company in Plymouth required him to keep a list of the men, to attend all their trainings, to note all violations of the laws of the company, to collect all fines and duly to account for the same.[1] In Connecticut his duties were expressed in much the same terms, with the addition that he should take the assize of arms twice every year.[2] According to New Haven law the clerk of the band acted in conjunction with the other officers of the company in taking the assize of arms, and it was his particular duty to present the names of the delinquents before the plantation court or the proper officer for punishment.[3]

The first act providing for troopers, or cavalry, in Massachusetts was passed in 1648.[4] This authorized the listing within each regiment of such as would willingly serve on horseback ; they were to be organized as troops, each to contain not less than thirty nor, until 1663, more than seventy[5] men. Each trooper must be furnished with a horse, bridle and saddle, a sword belt, a case of pistols with holsters, or a carbine in a belt, one pound of powder, and twenty bullets. The cost of furnishing a horse, with its equipment, was such as to exclude all but the well-to-do from this branch of the service. In 1663 it was enacted that none should be listed as troopers except those whose parents, or who themselves, possessed a taxable estate of the value of £100. As special inducements to encourage the enlistment of troopers, they were granted exemption from training in all foot companies and from constable's watches, freedom from rates for person and horse, free commonage for their horses, a wage of five shillings yearly, liberty to choose lieutenants and other inferior officers, free ferriage to and from their places of training or service, the exemption of their horses from being impressed for any other service. The officers of the troop were the same as those of an infantry company, with the addition of a cornet and quartermaster. The importance of this arm of the service steadily increased during the century, troops being formed in many of the towns. During Philip's

---

[1] Plymouth Col. Recs. III. 50, XI. 181.　　[2] Conn. Col. Recs. I. 542.
[3] New Haven Recs. II. 602.　　[4] Mass. Recs. II. 243.　　[5] *Ibid.* IV[2]. 97.

war many of them were converted into dragoons, or mounted infantry, and did good service in winter as well as summer.

The first troop of horse in Plymouth was organized in 1658.[1] It consisted of thirty-three men, who were drawn in small quotas from all the towns of the colony. They were exempted from watch and ward and from service on foot. Their horses were no longer to be counted among taxable property. Later, authority was given to increase the number through volunteers to forty-eight, commissioned officers excepted. When, in 1675, these troopers were required to procure carbines and serve as dragoons, they declined to do so. Therefore the general court ordered that they should be disbanded and return to their foot companies, to serve there subject to the usual regulations for infantry. The jurisdiction of New Haven had, after 1657, one small troop of horse, raised chiefly in the towns of New Haven and Milford. It seems to have been disbanded when the separate existence of that colony came to an end.[2] Among the River Towns troopers appear in 1658, and then first presented the officers they had chosen to the general court for confirmation.[3]

Not until 1667, when England was at war with the Dutch, did the assembly of Rhode Island recommend[4] to the towns the taking of steps preliminary to the formation of a troop of horse. Before the end of that year such a troop was organized on the Island, and officers were appointed by the governor and council. In 1682, on petition of certain persons of the towns of Providence and Warwick, permission was given for the organization of a troop there, its number not to exceed thirty-six.

The raw material of New England soldiery was subjected to not infrequent trainings. The attention of the magistrates and lawmakers was directed quite as much to this subject as to the necessity of procuring a sufficient quantity of arms and ammunition. At first it was ordered in Massachusetts that captains should train their companies every

[1] Plymouth Recs. XI. 107, 183, 240.

[2] New Haven Recs. II. 173, 218, 302, 489, 550.

[3] Conn. Recs. I. 309, 381.

[4] R. I. Recs. II. 190, 214, 218 ; III. 117.

Saturday.[1] The next year, 1632, it was provided that trainings should be held once a month.[2] But experience soon convinced the court that this number imposed too heavy a burden, and accordingly trainings were omitted during July and August.[3] In 1637 the number was reduced[4] to eight per year, and later to six days, where it remained till 1679. Then the number of general compulsory trainings was reduced to four, though the officers of the companies were given authority to train their men two additional days in the year if they so wished.[5]

With a few exceptions, all males of military age, — sixteen to sixty years, — whether freemen, free residents, or servants, were compelled to train. According to the Massachusetts law of 1647[6] the exempted classes included all members of the general court, officers, fellows and students of Harvard College, elders and deacons, schoolmasters, physicians and surgeons, the treasurer and surveyor general, public notaries, masters of vessels of above twenty tons burden, fishermen who were employed at all fishing seasons, millers, constant herdsmen, and all others who, from bodily infirmity or other just cause, should be excused by any county court or the court of assistants. According to a law of 1642[7] all who were exempt from trainings, save magistrates, clergymen, physicians, scholars, and surgeons, should appear fully armed before the military officers twice a year to be trained. In 1652 it was enacted[8] that all Scotchmen, negroes, and Indians, inhabiting with or servants to the English, should attend trainings ; but this law was subsequently repealed. Farmers who lived at too great a distance from the training grounds of their companies were excused from attendance a part of the time,[9] but provision was made that, where as many as twelve could be brought together, an officer should be specially detailed to drill them. For a time after 1645 the law required that youths from ten to sixteen years of age should be trained.[10]

---

[1] Mass. Recs. I. 85.
[2] Ibid. 102.
[3] Ibid. 124.
[4] Ibid. 210 ; Laws, Ed. of 1887, 108.
[5] Recs. V. 212.
[6] Laws, Ed. of 1889, 177 ; Recs. II. 221.
[7] Recs. II. 31.
[8] Ibid. IV¹. 86, 257.
[9] Law of 1652, Recs. IV¹. 87.
[10] Ibid. II. 99.

In 1675, as Philip's war was beginning, it was ordered that only such masters of vessels as traded in foreign countries should be exempt from trainings.[1]

When the militia was regimented, regimental trainings of both horse and foot, under command of the sergeant-major, were provided for. At first these occurred yearly;[2] but in 1648 this requirement, because it was "found by experience burdensome to the country," was repealed. Thenceforth the regiments were trained in turn, no one of them being required to meet for the purpose oftener than once in three years.[3] Absences from trainings, as well as other minor military offences, were punished by fine, the usual amount being five shillings.[4] Disorders and contempt of authority while on duty were punishable with the stocks, pillory, and other customary military punishments, or by a fine of not more than twenty shillings.[5] The determination of the kind and degree of the penalty was apparently left to the military officers in charge; they were perhaps being guided by articles of war. As an alternative course, the offender might be delivered to a constable who would carry him before a magistrate, by whom he might, if the case required, be bound over to the next court of assistants. The disorders on training-days to which the laws refer were drunkenness and firing at random or at marks after dismissal, when the soldiers should have been in quarters.[6] These offences were forbidden and threatened with the usual penalties.

In Plymouth the inhabitants of every town who were able to bear arms were required to train at least six times every year.[7] In the Plymouth *Records* several interesting orders or rules of discipline have been preserved, and those enacted in 1643 for the company of Plymouth, Duxbury, and Marshfield, of which Miles Standish was then captain, are worthy of special mention.[8] Those were also extended to Sandwich, Barnstable, and Yarmouth. They provided that

---

[1] Mass. Recs. V. 33.

[2] *Ibid.* II. 43.

[3] *Ibid.* 256; Laws, Ed. of 1889, 176.

[4] Laws, Ed. of 1887, 109; Recs. V. 212.

[5] Laws, Ed. of 1889, 177; Recs. II. 223; IV². 97.

[6] Recs. IV². 97.

[7] Plymouth Recs. XI. 36, 104, 180.

[8] *Ibid.* II. 61.

the exercise at each training should begin and end with prayer, and once a year at the election of its officers a sermon should be preached before the company. None should be received into the company but freemen of honest and good report — not servants, — and they must be approved by the officers and the majority of the company. They must also take the oath of fidelity, if they had not previously taken it. During the time of exercise, talking, jeering, quarrelling, fighting, and other misdemeanors should be forbidden and punished. All minor offences should be punished by the officers of the company, but no attempt appears to have been made to expressly limit their discretion, save in the amount of fines imposed on those who appeared without arms or with defective arms. Every time a soldier appeared without a musket or a sword, a rest, or bandoleers, he was, in the case of each weapon, to be fined six shillings. Six months were allowed him in which to procure the weapon he lacked, and if at the end of that time he failed to do so, his name should be struck off the list. Each member must pay six shillings per quarter for the use of the company. "That all postures of pike and muskett, motions, ranks and files, etc., messengers, skirmishes, sieges, batteries, watches, sentinells, etc.," say the orders, "bee always performed according to true military discipline!"

Trainings in Connecticut and New Haven were held during six days in the year, and present[1] no features to indicate any essential difference from the practice in Massachusetts. Among the few rules of discipline which have come down from that time, one issued by the council of Connecticut in 1676[2] will be found interesting, not only in comparison with that of an earlier date just cited from the records of Plymouth, but as a statement of the strict moral code which the Puritan ever desired to see enforced among soldiers when on the march or in camp. During the later provincial wars many a diarist was forced to note with sorrow how far both discipline and morals among the soldiers fell short of the ideal which is clearly set forth in these articles.

Though in the records of some of the towns of Rhode

[1] Conn. Recs. I. 97, 266, 542; New Haven Recs. II. 603.   [2] *Ibid.* II. 392.

Island abundant references to trainings and to the organization of militia companies appear, slight mention of the subject appears in the records of the colony.   In the early legislation of 1647, however, provision was made, not only that the inhabitants of the several towns should choose their military officers, but that the companies should be trained[1] eight times annually.   The limits of military age, the requirements as to arms and taking of the assize, the functions of the clerk of the band, were in all essential respects the same as in the other New England colonies.   As was natural, the town council shared prominently in these functions among the Narragansett plantations, while in the other colonies little mention is made of them in this connection. Though it is certain that a colonial militia system existed from and after 1647, yet the first clear evidence afforded by the records that officers of the town companies were commissioned by authority from the general assembly appears in 1667.[2]   One captain at that time refused for a time to accept his commission because the word " chosen " did not appear in it.

Through the constable's watches in the towns the provisions for local defence shaded off into ordinary police functions, to the performance of which all adult males, with certain special exceptions, were liable.   But in Massachusetts, at least in times of peril, military watches were set. These were first provided for in 1640, and were placed first under the charge of the militia officers of the respective towns, but later under the local committees of militia.[3] These continued from half an hour after sunset to a half hour after sunrise.   It was their duty to arrest all suspicious persons, and in case they were resisted, to discharge their muskets and raise an alarm.

In all the New England colonies provision was made for

[1] R. I. Recs. I. 153, 218, 381; II. 52.

[2] *Ibid.* II. 190, 211, 215.

[3] Mass. Col. Recs. I. 293 ; II. 120, 121. For military watches in Plymouth, see Recs. III. 24 ; IV. 144, V. 186 ; XI. 43. In Connecticut, see Recs. II. 361. In New Haven, Recs. II. 603. Very little, if any, reference to the institution appears in the early Recs. of R. I., but there is no doubt that it existed.

giving a general, as well as local, alarm.[1] The former was
given by discharging a musket three times, and, in the night,
beating a drum continuously, firing a beacon, or discharging
a piece of ordnance. It was taken up and spread as rapidly
as possible from town to town. The local alarm was given
by firing a musket once. On the approach of vessels suspected to be hostile a special alarm was given from the
castle in Boston harbor. When a general alarm was given,
every trained soldier must repair to his colors, on penalty
for failure of a fine of £5. It is said that on the night
of Sept. 23, 1675, during Philip's war, as the result of giving a false alarm at Mendon, a town thirty miles southwest of Boston, and its spread from town to town, within an
hour twelve hundred militiamen were brought under arms.[2]
But, though the alarm was resorted to in emergencies, it
played no regular part in the preparation for expeditions.

The years 1634 and 1636, while Massachusetts still possessed only an infantry force, witnessed the organization of
trained bands into regiments. In December, 1636, an act
was passed which definitely accomplished this result.[3] One
of these included the companies of Boston, Roxbury, Dorchester, Weymouth, and Hingham, with John Winthrop as
colonel and Thomas Dudley as lieutenant-colonel. The
second regiment included the companies of Charlestown,
Newtown, Watertown, Concord, and Dedham, and of this
John Haynes was colonel and Roger Harlakenden lieutenant-
colonel. The third regiment consisted of the companies
of Saugus, Salem, Ipswich, and Newbury, with John Endicott
as colonel and John Winthrop, Jr., as lieutenant-colonel.
The governor for the time being was general. For each
regiment a muster-master was appointed. It was also provided that for the future colonels and lieutenant-colonels
should be chosen by the members of their regiments and
presented to the general court for confirmation. When the

[1] References to giving the alarm in Plymouth appear in Recs. XI. 26, 106.
In Connecticut, in Recs. I. 94 ; II. 45. In New Haven, Recs. I. 78. In Rhode
Island, Recs. I. 154.
[2] Mass. Recs. II. 24, 28, 64 ; Drake, Old Indian Chronicle, 158.
[3] Mass. Col. Recs. I. 186.

counties of Massachusetts were formed, these earliest organizations became known respectively as the regiments of Suffolk, Middlesex, and Essex counties. As settlement extended and other counties were formed, new regiments were added.

At the opening of Philip's war the regiments of Suffolk and Middlesex [1] each contained one company of horse and fifteen companies of foot. The Essex regiment consisted of one mounted company and thirteen companies of foot. The regiments of other counties were smaller. In Massachusetts there were seventy-three organized companies, and an independent cavalry company, called the "three county troop," made up in Suffolk, Middlesex, and Essex. In 1680, because of the increase in their numbers, the organizations of these three counties were in each case divided into two regiments. [2] Expeditions were regularly organized by drafting or impressing quotas from the companies and regiments. Occasionally, as in Philip's war, volunteer companies were also formed. A famous body of this kind, consisting of strangers, adventurers, apprentices, men who were released from prison that they might win freedom by fighting the Indians, served at that time under Captain Samuel Mosely. [3]

By an act of September, 1643, [4] a council, of which the governor should always be one, was given authority in cases of danger to call out the entire force of the colony and distribute it at its pleasure, yet the command of the forces in action should be intrusted to a sergeant-major general. Instead, also, of colonels and lieutenant-colonels each regiment should be commanded by a sergeant-major. He was the chief military officer [5] of the shire, and was required to hold annually a regimental training. Twice [6] a year he conferred with the chief officers of the trained bands in his regiment respecting points of discipline and training in which the companies were concerned. At these meetings, with the consent of the officers mentioned, he was empowered to impose fines

---

[1] Bodge, *op. cit.* 45.   [2] Mass. Col. Recs. V. 294.
[3] Bodge, 59 *et seq.*   [4] Mass. Recs. II. 42.   [5] *Ibid.* 118.
[6] In 1653 this part of the law was repealed, and majors were allowed to call such meetings at their discretion. Recs. IV[1]. 155.

for defective arms, ammunition, appearance, watches, and other offences. The regulation of the militia of the smaller towns and the duty of uniting them into companies of at least sixty-four men each, devolved on the sergeant-majors.[1] During most of the colonial[2] period it was their duty to raise the force of their shires, and, in case of alarm, to send any part of it to the assistance of the place imperilled, and to give constant and speedy intelligence respecting the situation to the governor, council, and major-general. During Philip's war majors occasionally raised, equipped, and conducted expeditions.[3] In deciding upon military operations the commanders always took the advice of councils of war. The office of shire lieutenant was also created in 1643. Though it continued in existence for only a short time, we may suppose that it was suggested by the lord-lieutenancy of the English shire. The duty of its incumbent was to levy the force of the shire in sudden emergencies and to retain control of it till orders came from the governor and council, or the sergeant-major took command. Provision was also made that the higher officers, as well as the lower, should meet together from time to time to discuss military affairs, and take such action to promote efficiency as might be needed.

The office of sergeant-major general was successively held by such men as Dudley, Endicott, Atherton, Leverett, and Denison. Its powers and duties, as shown by the commissions,[4] were those of a commander in active service or in preparation for such. But he was hampered to an indefinite extent by the necessity of consulting a council of war composed of his subordinate officers, and of receiving directions from the civilians who formed the council of the colony and even from the general court itself. It should be remembered that, though his commission was for a short period of time, the incumbent was usually reappointed as long as he was able or willing to serve. The men who were appointed to the position also came as near being trained soldiers as any among the colonists. The duties of the sergeant-major gen-

---

[1] Recs. IV[1]. 86.

[2] For a short period this was the duty of the lieutenant of the shire.

[3] Recs. V. 57, 72, 122.   [4] *Ibid.* II. 76.

eral were to see that inferior officers did their duty, in time
of special danger to appoint military watches, raise troops by levy from regiments, and use them till directions came from the council or general court, to command in the expeditions which might follow, with authority to impress all supplies and aids to transportation which he might need. In the council of war which he must consult he had the casting vote, and in the actual conduct of battles he was to be left unhindered. Until the general court should prescribe rules, he, with the coöperation of his council of war, was empowered to prepare orders for the maintenance of discipline, and to execute them even to the extent of inflicting the death penalty. Many special duties [1] were also imposed on the sergeant-major general, both in time of peace and of war, while it was customary for him to be sergeant-major of one of the regiments.

In the Massachusetts system the germ of the modern staff appears chiefly in the office originally designated as that of surveyor of ordnance, or later as general surveyor of arms. Early in 1631 Jost Willust was chosen by the general court to be surveyor of ordnance, and was allowed £10 per year.[2] But in 1632 he returned to Europe, and the office does not reappear under its former designation. In 1634 [3] a reference appears to the overseer of the arms, but from the records one would infer that, until 1642, the business of the office was mainly transacted through committees.[4] In 1642, owing to fear of an Indian attack and the desire that the colony might be well supplied with powder, John Johnson was appointed surveyor-general of the arms.[5] From that time until the downfall of the colony government the many references to the office indicate its importance. Captain Edward Johnson [6] of Woburn was one of its incumbents, while in 1660 it was for a time put into commission.[7] The surveyor-general of arms was a custodian of the colony's supply [8] of ordnance, arms, and ammunition. Under author-

---

[1] Recs. II. 42, 118; IV[1]. 149; IV[2]. 296, 297; V. 58, 124.

[2] *Ibid.* I. 83, 97.   [4] *Ibid.* 120, 125, etc.   [6] *Ibid.* IV[1]. 391.

[3] *Ibid.* 125.   [5] *Ibid.* II. 26.   [7] *Ibid.* 422.

[8] *Ibid.* II. 26, 31, 51, 73, 82, 84, 140.

ity from the general court he delivered powder to the towns, and received back from them any excessive supplies which might have been issued. He could also sell ammunition. He was empowered to recover arms belonging to the colony from individuals or towns that had them in their possession, to either preserve them pending an order of the general court, or to sell them at a fair price and procure others in their place. Purchases of ammunition were usually made through the surveyor-general, though in coöperation with the treasurer.[1] Orders of the general court that he should loan munitions to individuals are common. When, in 1643, arms and stores were brought from Castle island, an invoice of the whole was given to the surveyor-general, and the arms were delivered into his custody.[2] Though orders for the delivery of ordnance to towns for use in forts, and the return of the same, were issued through the surveyor-general, it was not the policy of the general court to permit him to sell this without special authority.[3] The towns were ordered[4] by the legislature to make returns to the surveyor-general of the amount of powder they had in stock. In May, 1656, it was ordered that the surveyor-general should annually lay before the council an account of the common stock of powder, that the general court might be guided by this information in supplying the colony's need.[5] Committees were frequently appointed to examine the accounts of the office.[6]

In a fully developed military system a commissary-general would have occupied a position relative to supplies of food and necessities for camp life and transportation analogous to that borne by the surveyor-general to munitions of war. But Massachusetts had no permanently organized commissariat, and this characteristic she shared with all the other colonies.[7] Their troops, being militia, were disbanded

---

[1] Mass. Recs. 124, 239, 282; IV[1]. 147, 423; V. 218.   [2] Ibid. II. 36.

[3] Ibid. IV[1]. 5.   [4] Ibid. II. 282; IV[1]. 440.   [5] Ibid. IV[1]. 258.

[6] The office of surveyor-general will be found to have been a prominent one in the proprietary and royal provinces, but his duties there related to land and not at all, as in Massachusetts, to military supplies.

[7] The term commissary-general appears in the Plymouth Records under the

as soon as an expedition or brief campaign was ended. Only
a few men were kept under arms for garrison purposes.
Hence the need of provisions disappeared almost as quickly
as it arose. They had no uniforms. Of tents they made
little, if any, use, and their companies were followed by
small baggage trains, or none at all. With their arms,
blankets, and small supplies of food, cooked or uncooked,
they forced their way through the forests as best they could.
When an expedition or campaign became necessary, the general court appointed one or more commissaries for the time
being, though the word "commissary" does not appear in the
records till 1645. Richard Collicott was appointed to collect provisions for the expedition against the Pequots.[1] In
1645 Edward Tyng and Frank Norton were appointed commissaries for the force of two hundred men who were sent
to the aid of Uncas,[2] and a schedule of the provisions needed
for the expedition has been preserved. It included bread,
salted beef, fish, pease, oatmeal, flour, butter, oil, vinegar,
sugar, rum, and beer. Jacob Greene of Charlestown was
appointed commissary of the force which was raised to
march against the Dutch in 1664.[3] Commissaries were
more or less active during Philip's war, though there is
evidence that supplies did not always pass through their
hands.[4] Chaplains and surgeons were appointed to accompany the expeditions.

In none of the New England colonies except Massachusetts, in the period now under consideration, were the forces
distinctly regimented. Plymouth, in 1658,[5] permitted the
companies of any two or four of its towns to train together
if they chose. The highest military officer in that colony
was a major, and a copy of his instructions and the names
of the council with whom he should act in 1658 has been
preserved.[6] Similar statements apply of course to New
Haven, and to Rhode Island as well. Counties were organized in Connecticut, in 1666; but not until the peace of the

date 1649, but it was used loosely as one of the designations of Miles Standish
in his capacity of commander of the colony levy. Plymouth Recs. II. 146.

[1] Mass. Recs. I. 195.   [3] *Ibid.* IV[2]. 123.   [5] Recs. III. 138.
[2] *Ibid.* II. 124.   [4] *Ibid.* V. 44, 74, 90, 92.   [6] *Ibid.* 152.

colony seemed to be imperilled through the reoccupation
of New York by the Dutch, does the organization of the
militia by counties come clearly into view. A major was
then appointed for each county, and his command in each
case was a regiment in all except name. This continued to
be the situation throughout Philip's war.[1] Prior to the
French wars the title of general does not appear in any of
the New England colonies except Massachusetts. The same
is true of the office of surveyor-general of arms. All the
colonies had commissaries in some form or other. Though
Connecticut had during Philip's war an official with that
title, the treasurer, being a resident of Hartford county, was
often ordered to procure and deliver food as well as ammunition.[2] He thus performed the functions both of a surveyor-
general and of a commissary.

The description of the system of defence in colonial New
England would be left incomplete if some reference were
not made to forts and garrison houses. The forts of the
early time were located chiefly at the port towns, — Boston,
Salem, Portsmouth, Plymouth, Newport, New London, Saybrook, New Haven. The fact that, especially in Massachusetts, the general court sometimes ordered that great guns
should be delivered or lent to certain towns, would indicate
that the towns in question had small redoubts. Dorchester
and Charlestown had each a fort from early times, but they
formed a part of the system of defence of Boston harbor.
The towns of the interior, unless with here and there an exception, possessed no defences except stockades and garrison
houses. When Massachusetts, in 1667, under fear of Dutch
attack, and Connecticut, in 1675, at the opening of Philip's
war, ordered every town to provide itself with defences
where women and children and others who sought protection might take refuge, blockhouses or garrison houses
were meant.[3] The limited supply of artillery which the
colonists possessed, they kept almost wholly in the coast
towns.

[1] Conn. Recs. II. 34, 206–207.
[2] For a typical order, see Recs. II. 453, 506 ; also 384, 464.
[3] Mass. Recs. IV². 332 ; Conn. Rec. II. 268.

Salem had Darby Fort, so called, located at Naugus Head, where Marblehead was later built,[1] and a fort on Winter island. The former was built not far from 1630, while the latter, begun as early as 1643, was in the usual process of construction, decay, and repair during the remainder of the century. When, in 1673, the arrival of a hostile Dutch fleet was feared, the "great artillery," we are told, was got ready for use, and all else was done as the juncture required.

The defences of Boston were the most important of any in New England, and consisted of the North Battery, situated at Merry's Point, at the north end of the great cove of the town ; the Sconce, or South Battery, which was at the south end of the same cove and was an outwork of the earliest of Boston's defences, that on Fort Hill. Fort Hill was one of the three eminences of the peninsula on which Boston was built. During the years between 1632 and 1636, by the labor of the people of the towns near the bay and the contributions of the remote towns to the north, the fort on this hill was built.[2] It was the earliest fortification in Boston, and the famous Lyon Gardiner, who built the fort at Saybrook, was the engineer in charge during a part of the time of its construction.

In 1634 a plan was formed to build a "moving fort," or floating battery, forty feet long and twenty feet wide.[3] It was to be built by the contributions of the promoters — who had recently arrived from England — and of others, who, it was thought by the court, had not borne their share in the expense of founding the colony. A considerable subscription was taken, but the structure was never built.

In 1672, when an attack from the Dutch was expected, a " barricado," or wall, probably of stone and earth faced with wood, was built. It faced the water, and extended from one side of the great cove or basin in front of Boston to the other, being twenty-two hundred feet in length, fifteen

---

[1] Colls. of Essex Institute, XXXIII. ; Salem Neck and Winter island. Felt, Annals of Salem, I, 192.

[2] Mass. Recs. I. 110, 125 ; Boston Record Commissioners, Second Report, 8 ; *Ibid.* Eleventh Report, 67.

[3] Mass. Recs. I. 113.

feet in height, and twenty feet in breadth at the top. At
intervals there were openings for the entrance of vessels.
The undertaking, being too expensive for the town to bear,
was prosecuted at the expense of private citizens, they receiving from the town certain valuable grants of land in
return.[1]

But the chief feature in the Boston system of defences
was the fort on Castle island, which commanded the channel by which vessels approached the town. The records
throughout the entire colonial period abound with references to this fortification; and its history, if worked out
in detail, would illustrate the progress of military engineer-
ing in the colonies for a century and a half. The defensive
works on that island were begun during the years 1634
to 1636, when the colonists were apprehensive of forcible
interference by the home government. A committee of
military men was appointed by the general court to locate
and lay out the works.[2] At first it was ordered that a
platform should be built on the north-east side of the
island and a blockhouse on the top of the adjacent hill.
An earthwork was actually constructed, men and carts
being impressed for the purpose. This, however, soon
decayed, and the remoter towns of the colony were unwilling to bear the expense of repairing and maintaining
it. Accordingly the general court, in March, 1638, appointed a committee to bring the ammunition from Castle
island and dispose of it. But at the instance of private
parties it was resolved to complete and maintain the works
by private subscription, the general court giving aid. The
court voted £100 per annum for maintaining the fort, and
a year later granted £250 in addition. But this impulse
soon died out, and in May, 1643, it again ordered that all

---

[1] Boston Record Commissioners, Fifth Report, 11 ; Shurtleff, Topographi-
cal and Historical Description of Boston, 115–119. The modern Atlantic
Avenue was built on the line of the "barricado," and Fort Hill was demol-
ished to furnish earth for the purpose.

[2] Mass. Recs. I. 123, 124, 136, 139, 158, 166 ; Memoirs of Roger Clap, in
Young's Chronicles of Massachusetts, 357 *et seq.* ; Winthrop, I. 163 ; Johnson, Wonder-working Providence.

arms, ammunition, and ordnance be brought from Castle island.[1]

But the arrival, a month later, of La Tour with a ship of one hundred and forty tons clearly revealed the defenceless condition of the town,[2] for in consequence of the recent order of the court no one remained on the island to challenge his right to enter. The result was that Boston and four other adjacent towns offered to repair and support the castle at their own expense. This[3] proposal was accepted, the court offering to contribute £100 when the work was finished, and to appropriate £100 annually for its maintenance. The castle was then rebuilt. The garrison now consisted for a time of a captain, a gunner, twenty men from the first of March till the first of October, and ten men during the rest of the year. But this number was not maintained, the court stating in 1648 that "the Castle hath seldom or never been supplied with the full number, . . . and many times with unmeete and unserviceable men." Therefore the garrison was reduced to ten men from April to October, and six men during the other months.[4] The towns failed to bear their part of the burden, and the court during the succeeding years repeatedly complains of the neglected state of the castle ; the pay of the garrison was in arrears, and the batteries seem never to have been kept in repair. It required danger from a foreign enemy — the expected arrival of De Ruyter, in 1665 — to bring about the repair of the works and the establishment there of a garrison of sixty-four men. The castle, which was still of wood and earth, was burned in 1673. Then, by the combined efforts of the adjacent towns and the general court, it was rebuilt of brick and with larger dimensions than before.[5] In this condition it was when Philip's war began, and Edward Randolph reported that it was in relatively good repair, mounting thirty-eight guns, but was without a permanent garrison.

---

[1] Mass. Recs. I. 220, 228, 231 ; II. 36.   [3] Mass. Recs. II. 56.
[2] Winthrop, II. 129.   [4] *Ibid.* 63, 107, 255.
[5] Mass. Recs. III. 50, 110, 137 ; IV[1]. 89, 110, 149, 154, 183, 202, 204, 206, 260 ; IV[2]. 35, 42, 276, 281, 285, 551, 566, 576 ; V. 15, 29, 33 ; Hutchinson, Papers, II. 221.

It has seemed wise to dwell thus at length on the castle in Boston harbor, because such extended references to it have been preserved, and also for the reason that its history is typical of all other forts in the colonies. They were built or repaired only to fall quickly into decay. The ordnance with which they were furnished was small and ineffective. The expense of repairs and the garrison exceeded the feeble resources of the colonial exchequers and could with great difficulty be met. Hence coast defence, though the weak garrisons were intended to be reënforced in time of danger by the local militia, was perhaps the least satisfactory feature of the entire system. Fortunately the ocean, during the seventeenth century and much of the eighteenth, proved of itself a sufficient protection, and the colonist was left free to contend as he could with the enemies who came upon him from the forest. Against them the garrison house and the stockade were his only defence.

Dwelling-houses, when built with thick walls perforated with loopholes, and, when the house had two stories, the upper, if possible, projecting over the lower story, were used as garrisons. Flankers at the corners were considered very useful as outlooks. Sometimes houses were specially built for the purpose ; often common dwelling-houses were used in this way in an emergency. When in danger of attack, as many as possible of the inhabitants of a settlement took refuge in the garrisons, and there with firearms and by means of sorties defended themselves as best they could. The number of garrison houses rapidly increased during Philip's war, and their number was fully maintained during the French and Indian wars which were to follow. A report of a committee [1] which had been appointed by the council of Massachusetts early in 1676 shows that the following garrison houses were then standing in Essex county: there were twelve in Andover, three at Bedford, three at Rowley village, four at Topsfield, several remote fortified houses at Newbury. At Rowley there were sufficient garrisons to shelter all the inhabitants. At Beverly there were three garrisons, at Cape Ann there were two ; but at Marblehead there were none, and the inhabitants

---

[1] Mass. Archives, Vol. 68. The report was dated March 29, 1676.

considered them unnecessary.   At Lynn there were several
garrisons, and the residents had been assigned to them.
This report may probably be taken as fairly indicative of the
distribution of garrison houses in the other exposed towns of
the New England colonies.

But exclusive reliance on garrison houses involved the
abandonment, in case of attack, of all the other buildings in
the village, with domestic animals and crops, to destruction.
For this reason the imitation of the Indian stockade recommended itself to many as a superior form of defence.   Newbury, we are told, had a general defensive work.   So had
Ipswich and Salem, while garrison houses had been erected
to protect those who lived on the outlying farms.   When,
early in 1676, Major Savage was commander in the Connecticut valley, the council advised that the inhabitants be
concentrated in two defensible towns, as Hadley and Springfield, and that all the rest be abandoned.   But the inhabitants of the towns which were likely to be left to pillage
would not listen to the proposal, and it never passed beyond
the stage of discussion.   Hadley, Northampton, and Hatfield
had built stockades, and found them a sufficient protection.

The building of a stockade about twelve miles in length
from the head of navigation on the Charles river to the
Merrimac river was proposed, but was voted down by the
towns concerned as too expensive.   The opinion generally
expressed in town meetings was that the accustomed system
of watching and scouting was the only feasible one.   The
conservatism of the farmers was shown in their adherence to
the comparatively inexpensive methods of defence to which
they had been accustomed and which they had found sufficient in peaceful times.

The varied activities which have now been outlined were
regulated by acts and orders of the general court, and controlled by the governor and assistants or by special councils
and committees which were appointed by the general court.
Committees were frequently created by the court, consisting,
it might be, wholly of civilians, or wholly of military officers,
or sometimes of a combination of the two, whose duty it was
to share in the task of military administration.   Among the

duties intrusted to such committees were the inspection of ordnance, arms, and military supplies ; hearing complaints of soldiers ; overseeing the location, building, repairing, equipment, and garrisoning of fortifications, appointing their quotas of troops among towns, drawing up commissions for military officers, putting the country in a posture of defence, equipping and sending out expeditions, treating with commissioners from other colonies respecting joint military operations.

But regularly in the New England colonies the control of military administration was vested either in the governor and assistants, or in a council of war which consisted of the magistrates with the addition of certain military officers. In 1635 Massachusetts created a special council of war,[1] consisting of eleven members, two of whom were the governor and deputy governor and nearly all the rest were assistants. Large powers were given to this body. It could execute all military laws, appoint and remove military officers, command and discipline the entire militia, even make offensive or defensive war. But this council owed its existence to a panic, and powers dangerous in extent were bestowed upon it. It therefore was short-lived. The following year its powers were transferred[2] to the standing council, which was given authority to commission military officers. The origin and the ineffective career of this body have already been described. Its establishment did not for any long time, or to any great degree, remove the control of military administration from the hands of the governor and assistants. Though only fragmentary records have been preserved, yet enough exist to furnish evidence of their prominent concern with all phases of the work.

In 1645 the general court declared[3] that, when it was not in session, the assistants or council of the commonwealth had authority to impress and send forth soldiers, to " presse all manner of victualls, vessells, carriages & all other necessaries & to send warrants to the Treasurer to pay for them." In March, 1653, the council ordered arms, flints, and other supplies to be sold to the colonists, forbade the export of

[1] Mass. Recs. I. 138.   [2] Ibid. 183.   [3] Ibid. II. 125.

provisions, and ordered the constables to collect supplies of food. These things were done because of danger that the colonies might become involved in war with the Dutch.

In April, 1653, this body fully discussed the question, whether or not the colonies should go to war with the Dutch and Indians. In May the troops were ordered to be in readiness, and in October, 1654, all the necessary orders were issued by the council for the levy of troops. In July, 1669, because the wheat crop had been ruined, it ordered the training of the Essex regiment to be omitted for that year. When, in August, 1673, news came that the Dutch had re-occupied New York, the council issued ten or more orders for placing Massachusetts in a condition to meet the expected crisis.[1] Throughout Philip's war the activity of the council was incessant ; commissioning officers, corresponding with the neighboring colonies and with officers and agents of all sorts who were in active service, receiving and answering petitions, preparing for expeditions, sending them out, watching or directing their movements, ordering their recall and the dismissal of troops. The administrative history of the war as a whole can be studied only by beginning with the activities of the councils of the various colonies involved.

In October, 1643, a council of war was created in Plymouth colony, consisting of the governor and four other members, all of whom, except Standish, were assistants.[2] This was a part of the preparation then made for a joint expedition against the Narragansett Indians. It was not dissolved at the end of that effort, but was continued as a part of the colony government as long as Plymouth enjoyed separate existence.[3] It was given authority to commission officers from the major down, to issue warrants for impressing men and provisions, to hear and punish all offences committed during service, to instruct officers. Among its duties for the expedition then immediately in hand were the appointment of a treasurer to keep the account of

[1] The above facts are derived from fragments of the council records in Mass. Arch. Vol. 67 ; Military Affairs, I.

[2] Plym. Recs. II. 64; XI. 102, 178.

[3] *Ibid.* IV. 142 *et seq. ;* V. 64, 76 ; VI. 109, 237–239.

receipts and payments, to value and keep a record of all arms used, and to keep a list of the soldiers.

As Philip's war approached, its work again became more important. In June, 1671, eight men were associated with the magistrates to constitute the council of war, the new members being put under a special oath. Throughout the war the activities of this body were similar to those of the Massachusetts council.[1]

In Connecticut a distinct council of war was first created in November, 1673.[2] The occasion of its appointment was the recovery of New York by the Dutch. The body, as then organized, consisted of the governor, deputy governor, assistants, and in addition to them five prominent military officers of the colony. It could be called together by the governor, deputy governor, or secretary, and could then commission officers, issue laws of war, impress men and all necessary supplies, and do all else for the expedition that was being planned which otherwise the general court might do. This was a temporary act and expired in a few months. But in July, 1675, in anticipation of the struggle with Philip, the council of war[3] was revived. Its composition was practically the same as before, and its powers and discretion were made as large as was possible under the charter. It was to continue in session during intermissions of the general court. Under orders from the general court and subject to its approval, this body administered the affairs of Connecticut which related to Philip's war. As late as October, 1677, an order appears continuing its existence, but some time later it was allowed to disappear, and was not revived till the beginning of the wars with the French in 1690.[4] In New Haven no similar body appears. In Rhode Island we hear only of special councils of war in the towns, and that in 1676. The same year special commissioners were appointed to order the watches on the island.[5]

The efficiency of the militia system depended to a con-

[1] See references in Plymouth Recs. V.   [2] Conn. Recs. II. 219.

[3] *Ibid.* 261, 270, 271, 275, 327. See Journal of this body from July 14, 1675, to October 9, 1677, *ibid.* 335–509.

[4] *Ibid.* IV. 18.   [5] R. I. Recs. II. 532, 539.

siderable extent on the method of filling military offices and the permanence of their tenure. In the corporate colonies military offices, like all others, were filled by election or through appointment by the general court. In Massachusetts, during its earliest [1] years, officers were appointed by the general court. But when, in 1636, the militia was organized into regiments, a change was made. It was then provided [2] that each regiment should choose fit persons to be its colonel and lieutenant-colonel, and through their deputies present their names before the general court for approval. In the companies nominations should be made in the same way for the offices of captains and lieutenants, and their names should be presented before the standing council for approval. In 1647 a law was passed requiring nominations for company officers to be submitted to the county courts for approval. It would appear, however, that in practice the general court passed on nominations for company, as well as regimental, officers.[3] By a law of 1637 it was provided that residents who had taken the oath, as well as freemen, should vote for company officers, but only freemen should be chosen.[4] According to the law of 1643 sergeant-majors were elected by the freemen of their respective shires, but, in 1645, non-freemen who had taken the oath were also permitted [5] to vote for them. The sergeant-major general was annually chosen, together with the magistrates and other leading officials, in the court of election.

In 1668 the method of electing lower officers was abandoned.[6] By an act of that year all commissioned officers, except the sergeant-major general, became appointive by the general court. To the council, or board of assistants, was given the power to appoint in cases of emergency. Non-commissioned officers were appointed by the commissioned officers of their companies, or in cases where there were none,

---

[1] Mass. Recs. I. 90, 120.

[2] *Ibid.* I. 187 ; II. 191 ; Laws, Ed. of 1889, p. 176 ; Laws, Ed. of 1887, p. 107. For an example of a contested election in a militia company, see the Hingham case, Winthrop, II. 271.

[3] *Ibid.* Mass. Recs. I. 190 ; II. 133 ; IV[1]. 58, 88, 173 ; IV[2]. 62.

[4] *Ibid.* I. 188.   [5] *Ibid.* II. 49, 117.   [6] *Ibid.* IV[2]. 368.

by the major of the regiment. In 1675, however, the law was again changed,[1] giving the town committees of militia the right to present to the general court two or three names of persons proper to fill vacancies among local military officers.

Since no record appears of successive nominations and confirmations, it is probable that, prior to 1668, military officers were chosen for an indefinite term. After that time it is clear that their appointments were permanent. The incumbent of the office of major-general, when satisfactory, was reëlected year after year. This was notably true in the cases of John Leverett and Daniel Denison. In the case of military officials, as well as others, the elective system, thus modified, insured a considerable permanence of tenure.

The other New England colonies chose their militia officers in much the same way as did Massachusetts. An order[2] of the Plymouth general court of September, 1642, provided that the towns should have power to nominate to the court for its approval two or three persons as candidates for military offices above the rank of sergeants. These officers, when duly approved, might appoint under officers, with the consent of their companies. When vacancies occurred, the same procedure should be repeated. In 1683 it was enacted that, in cases where towns and militia companies neglected to choose officers, the council of war should appoint them.[3] In 1690, when the expedition against Quebec was fitting out, we find the council of war approving the action of towns in electing officers, and interposing to settle a dispute over such a matter in Taunton. This proves that in that colony the general court and commissioned officers never assumed the power of appointment, as was the case in Massachusetts. Everything indicates that in Plymouth, as in the Bay colony, militia officers were elected for indefinite terms.

[1] Recs. V. 30.   [2] Plymouth Recs. XI. 39, 50.   [3] *Ibid.* VI. 109.

CHAPTER XIV

INDIAN RELATIONS, PHILIP'S WAR

THE European colonists who settled on the American coast were confronted by a savage people, who were already occupiers of the soil and were alien to the whites in almost every respect. No clear precedents then existed or could exist for the guidance of the colonists in their relations with the natives. A system of relations between the two races had to be worked out upon the spot, and under the changing conditions which time and place presented. The development of an Indian policy was one of the most important problems of colonization, and it was so understood at the time, though historians have treated the subject, except on its picturesque side, in the most desultory manner. It is not necessary to look exclusively to the Orient, or to the history of colonization in recent times, in order to learn how Europeans have conducted themselves in the presence of inferior races. In this work we are concerned with the beginnings of an Indian policy among the English colonists on the North American continent. In this, as in other respects, the New England of that time naturally lends itself to separate treatment.

The natives of that section belonged wholly to the Algonkin branch of the American race. The most important tribes there located were the Narragansetts and their dependants, the Pequots of Connecticut, the Wampanoags of Plymouth and the adjacent country to the west, the Massachusetts about Massachusetts bay, the Nipmucks who lay west of the Massachusetts, the Penacooks of New Hampshire, and the Abenakis of Maine. Fortunately for the English the Massachusetts tribe was almost entirely destroyed by pestilence a few years before colonization began. The colonists about Massachusetts bay for that reason found the country in which they first settled almost unoccupied, and were practically secure against Indian attack. The plague had also extended into the region occupied by the Plymouth colonists, and had so weakened the natives as to facilitate colonization for the Pilgrims. Owing to conditions of climate and soil, the Indian population in central Massachusetts and northern New England was sparse. The natives of New Hampshire and Maine were chiefly hunters. The more prominent settlements and largest Indian population lay between Narragansett bay and the lower course of the Housatonic river. That region was the home of the Narragansetts and Pequots. Connected with the Narragansetts, possibly as fragments[1] of one great people, were the Nihantics, or Niantics, of eastern Connecticut and western Rhode Island, and a number of groups or clans which dwelt on the banks of the Connecticut river. The Pequots lay west of the main body of the Narragansetts, and occupied the territory extending along the Sound as far as the Niantic river and northward to a breadth of about twenty miles. The Mohegans of Connecticut were a clan of the Pequots, and occupied the northern part of their territory, the west bank of the Thames near the present city of Norwich. The entire Pequot people, not so very long before the arrival of the English, is supposed to have been driven eastward from the banks of the Hudson river, where they had originally lived as a part of the Mohegan people of that region. In the relations between the natives of southern New England and the whites centres the chief interest of the Indian history of that section during the seventeenth century. After 1689, when the French began to influence the Indians of New England, the centre of conflict and of interest moved northward to Maine, New Hampshire, northern and western Massachusetts.

The intercourse of the colonists with the Indians began with exploration, with the procurement of small supplies of corn and game from them, and with the so-called purchase of their lands. In New England the colonists were never so dependent as those at Jamestown upon the Indians for

[1] De Forest, History of the Indians of Connecticut, 60.

supplies of food, or for instruction in the raising of maize.
Trade relations never assumed the extent and importance
which they had where furs were the staple commodity. But
the first important fact to notice is the system of regulation
which was provided by law, and was intended to cover all
forms of intercourse between the English and the natives.
That it was executed in all its parts or without interruption
would be far too much to claim. The frequent reënactment
of some of the laws proves the difficulty which was found in
enforcing them. But the passage of the laws indicates the
purpose of the colonies, and corresponds in a fair degree
with their achievement. The acts themselves stand out as
a branch of colonial legislation distinct from the laws concerning whites, and from any laws or legal traditions which
the colonists brought with them from England.

In all the New England colonies the purchase of land from
the Indians by individuals or private parties, without license
from the government of the colony or from local authority,
was discouraged or absolutely forbidden. In Plymouth a
stringent act of this character was passed,[1] and it was more
than once reënacted at a later time. It prohibited the purchase or lease of land, herbage, wood, or timber. In 1633
Massachusetts began legislating on the same subject, but
limited her enactments to the purchase of land.[2] The laws
of New Haven and Connecticut on the subject differed[3]
slightly from those of the other colonies. They expressly
provided for purchases, under authority from the general
court, for the benefit of the whole colony. Connecticut did
not pass her act until 1663. In 1651 Rhode Island forbade
any one to purchase lands from the Indians without permission, unless it were to remove them from plantations which
were already settled.[4] But in 1658, because of the purchase
of Conanicut and Dutch islands in the bay by Coddington
and Benedict Arnold, such acts without the license of the

[1] Plymouth Recs. XI. 41. For instances of the purchase by the colony of
Indian rights on behalf of individuals and towns, see Plymouth Recs. IV. 20,
45, 82, 97, 109, 167.

[2] Mass. Col. Laws, Ed. of 1889, p. 161.

[3] New Haven Recs. I. 27, 200 ; Conn. Recs. I. 402.

[4] R. I. Recs. I. 236, 403.

court were prohibited for the future.   The objects of these
regulations were to prevent misunderstandings, disputes,
and fraud in connection with the extinguishment of the
Indian title to land, and also to prevent the undue dispersion of settlers.   The New England colonies followed very
consistently the principle that the Indian right of occupancy
should be extinguished, and since it was done very largely
with the knowledge and consent of the general courts, the land
frauds which were later committed in some of the other colonies do not appear among them.   The natives sold freely
and for the customary array of trinkets; they were also
irritated and finally driven to resistance by the steady advance
of English settlement, but complaints of deception by purchasers or surveyors play little part among the protests of
Indians in New England.

Trade with the natives, and especially traffic in arms, ammunition, and intoxicating spirits was also carefully regulated
by law.   In 1639 Plymouth forbade any individual to trade
with them under penalty of the forfeiture of twenty to one,[1]
and this continued to be the law of the colony throughout
its separate existence.   In 1656 the sale of boats or their
rigging to the Indians was prohibited.   In 1677 individuals
from outside the colony were forbidden to trade with the
natives, because they were driving away the means of payment which the Indians possessed, and were selling them
arms and ammunition.   During the later history of the
colony, the sale of horses to them was expressly forbidden.[2]

The legislation of Massachusetts on this subject was to the
same general effect as that of Plymouth,[3] and in addition provision was made during a large part of the period for farming out the peltry trade.   In 1636[4] the standing council was
empowered to farm out this trade for three years at an
annual rent to be paid to the treasurer; after the contract
had been concluded no one except the farmers should trade
with the Indians in any of the specified commodities.   In
1641 the trade was farmed to Lieutenant Simon Willard, of

[1] Plymouth Recs. XI. 33, 184.   [3] Laws, Ed. of 1889, 161 ; Col. Recs. I., etc.
[2] *Ibid.* 65, 222, 229, 246.   [4] Mass. Recs. I. 179, 208.

Concord, and others.[1] In 1644 the Commissioners of the
United Colonies[2] proposed that for ten years the trade of
each of the four colonies be managed in joint stock, and made
several recommendations on the subject. Among these was
one, that the profits, after the first year, should be so divided
as the Commissioners of the United Colonies and the committees of the respective colonies having this trade in charge
should think best. The general court of Massachusetts,
from which colony it is almost certain that the proposition
came, at once adopted the plan, and ordered that subscriptions to the joint stock should be received. But in the
records of the general court no further reference to the
subject under this form appears. We learn, however, from
the same records that, in 1658 and 1668,[3] the trade in furs
was being farmed out. At the former date certain centres
where this trade was carried on are mentioned, — on the
Merrimac, at Springfield and Norwottock, at Concord, Cambridge, Sudbury, Nashua, and Groton. One or more individuals were designated to have charge of the business at each
of the centres. In 1668 a committee of the general court
leased this trade, as well as other privileges, for three years
to Richard Way. Connecticut[4] voted, in 1644, to adopt the
recommendations of the commissioners in reference to the
fur trade, if the other jurisdictions did so. But neither
Plymouth nor New Haven established the joint stock, and
therefore no further action was taken by Connecticut. In
Rhode Island the usual regulations existed concerning the
sale of arms and liquor to the Indians, but trade in other
commodities does not seem to have been restricted. Massachusetts, Connecticut, and Rhode Island had orders prohibiting the Dutch and French trading with the natives.

Indians were not allowed to bear arms without special
permission, and in some of the colonies smiths were forbidden to repair their weapons.[5] Connecticut, being more
exposed than any other New England colony, passed several

[1] Mass. Recs. I. 322.

[2] Plymouth Recs. IX. 22 ; Mass. Recs. II. 83, 86, 110.

[3] *Ibid.* IV[1]. 354 ; IV[2]. 364, 398.   [4] Conn. Recs. I. 113.

[5] Plymouth Recs. XI. 43, 242 ; Conn. Recs. I. 74 ; R. I. Recs. I. 155.

acts prohibiting settlers from allowing Indians to enter their
houses or fields, and particularly to touch or use their arms.
In the last enactment of the series an exception was made
of magistrates and traders.[1] Indians were not permitted to
bring arms into the towns. Their services were very generally employed in killing wolves, and for this they were
rewarded by bounties.

Plymouth and Massachusetts carefully provided by law
for the keeping of bounds between the land of the Indians —
especially that which they planted — and that of the English. Both colonies ordered that the corn lands of the
Indians should be fenced, and that certain assistance might
be rendered by the English in this work.[2] Connecticut
sought the same object by a general order, forbidding any
one to take away the corn or other estate of an Indian without his consent. For damages done by the Indians, they
were held responsible before the courts of the colonies. This
was expressly provided for by Plymouth, Connecticut, and
Massachusetts. In Rhode Island, as elsewhere, drunkenness
among the Indians and the disturbance and injuries which
resulted therefrom, were frequent subjects of legislation.

The colonists also kept a watchful eye over the feuds
between the Indian tribes or clans, and were alert to discover signs of approaching attacks on the English. The help
of friendly Indians was utilized for this purpose. The
experience[3] of the Plymouth settlers with Corbitant, the
Narragansett, and with the Indians of Wessagussett, furnish
early instances in point. The doings and fate of Weston's
colony, of Thomas Morton at Merrymount, of Oldham and
Stone in the Narragansett region and on the Connecticut,
and of many of the fishermen and settlers in the eastern
parts, revealed the necessity of regulating intercourse with
the Indians so far as possible. In the laws to which reference has already been made, the New England colonies were

[1] Conn. Recs. I. 52, 73, 106, 294, 351, 529.

[2] Plymouth Recs. XI. 143, 213, 219, 220; Mass. Laws, Ed. of 1889, 162;
Conn. Recs. I. 355.

[3] Bradford, Ed. of 1899, 125, 135; Young, Chronicles of the Pilgrims,
219, 323, 327.

developing the policy foreshadowed in the royal proclamation of 1622. Some of these events were among the occasions of Endicott's expedition to Block island and of the
conflict with the Pequot tribe. When that struggle approached, a conference was held[1] at Boston with Miantonomi, the Narragansett sachem, and others of the same people,
and they agreed to keep the peace and to coöperate with the
English against the Pequots. The Indians agreed, among
other things, not to protect Pequots, but to deliver up those
among them who had murdered Englishmen, and that during
the war no Narragansett would come near the plantations of
the colonists, unless he was accompanied by some English-
man or by an Indian who was known to the whites. The
services of Roger Williams as virtually an agent of the English in negotiations, especially with the Narragansetts, at
this time and during a long subsequent period, are well
known. To the admission of Pumham and Sacononoco
under the protection of Massachusetts as a consequence of
the sale of some of their land by Miantonomi to Samuel
Gorton and his associates, reference has already been made.
While this was an incident in the history of the dealings
of Massachusetts with Gorton, it also clearly illustrates the
trend of Indian relations. It strengthened the growing
prejudice of Massachusetts against the Narragansett sachem.

Consequences of importance in the development of relations with the Indians naturally followed the conflict with
the Pequots. It was at that time that Uncas, the Mohegan,
broke away from his own tribe and became an ally of the
English. That relation, with an increasing element of dependence, he maintained toward Connecticut until his death
nearly fifty years later. Upon it, as the doings of the Commissioners of the United Colonies have shown, hinged much
in the relations between all the four colonies and the Narragansett tribe until about 1660. Uncas, in his intense rivalry
with Miantonomi, and in his conflicts with the Narragansetts
and Niantics after the death of Miantonomi, could always
count on the moral support of the English. By means of
that, as a skilful diplomatist, he maintained himself against

[1] Winthrop, I. 236.

foes who were much stronger than himself. But as the numbers of the English increased and their settlements came to encompass his own, his condition of alliance was changed into that of a dependant living under English protection. He came, in other words, to be protected as Pumham and his associate had been by Massachusetts. At Hartford, in October, 1638, a tripartite agreement was reached between the English, the Narragansetts, and the Mohegans, that perpetual peace should be maintained.[1] By the provision that, in case a quarrel should arise between the two Indian parties to the agreement, the aggrieved party should appeal to the English, and their decision should be held binding, the English assumed the position of arbitrators. The English also reserved the right, if their decisions were rejected or violated, to enforce obedience to them by arms. That position, both as distinct and united colonies, they maintained, so far as possible, until the opening of Philip's war.

The agreement of 1638, at Hartford, also provided that the Mohegans and Narragansetts should destroy the Pequots who had shed English blood, and that the two hundred that remained should be divided between Miantonomi, Ninigret, and Uncas. The first named received eighty, the second twenty, the third one hundred. For these captives the chiefs were to pay an annual tribute of a fathom of wampum for every man, half a fathom for every youth, and a hand for every male child. The Pequots were not to live in their ancient country or to be called by their former name, but to become Narragansetts and Mohegans. The Pequot country should be considered the possession of Connecticut. By this arrangement Uncas secured temporary possession of the northern part of the Pequot country, and nearly doubled the number of his tribesmen. But the English also, by a right of preëmption which they claim to have gained in 1640,[2] and by the influence which they maintained over the Mohegans, made use of them in order to strengthen their hold upon the Pequot country. Uncas they also utilized as their agent for keeping the Pequots quiet and collecting

---

[1] R. I. Hist. Colls. III. 177 ; De Forest, Indians of Connecticut, 160.
[2] De Forest, *op. cit.* 183, 495.

from them the tribute which was due the English. The
Pequots, on the other hand, tried to get free from his control, appealed to the English, and finally asked to be taken
directly under their government. Uncas craftily made use
of the influence which he had with the English to outwit or
destroy his enemies and to maintain his control over the
Pequots. The tribute fell permanently into arrears, and
the difficulties met with in its collection helped to keep the
affairs of the Connecticut Indians constantly before the
Commissioners of the United Colonies and the government
of Connecticut itself. In 1650 complaints on the part of
the Indians drew from the commissioners the statement that
the payment of the tribute would be demanded for only ten
years longer. Its collection actually ceased in 1663, when
the last sum was accepted in lieu of all arrears.

But in 1655, eight years before the tribute disappeared,
two bodies of Pequots, because of their complaints against
Uncas and the other Indians under whose control they had
been left, were placed directly under the government of the
English. They were settled chiefly at Paucatuck and New
London. Herman Garret, a Niantic, and Cassasinamon, a
Pequot, who had been their leaders in protest against the
rule of Uncas and the Niantics, were now made their governors.[1] Each of the governors received a commission from
the United Colonies. Special regulations were also issued
for the government of these Indians, which prohibited the
ordinary crimes, as well as plotting against the English and
making war without their permission. Submission to the
Indian governors who had been placed over them was also
required. The governors were annually appointed, and each
had one or two Indian assistants. In 1661 two Englishmen
were appointed under the title of overseers to assist the
governors, and officials under this title continued thereafter
to be annually reappointed. They were to advise them in
their administration and see that the Indians were not
deprived of any rights by their English neighbors. They
might hear and decide all but capital cases among the
Indians, and hear appeals from the decisions of the governors.

[1] Conn. Rec. II. 39; De Forest, *op. cit.* 226, 245 *et seq.*, 261.

Both the governors and overseers were ordered to promote the civilizing of the Indians, and the former were to encourage them to listen to Christian teachers and to seize all spirituous liquors which were brought among them.

The only step which remained to be taken in order that a protectorate in all its features might be established over these Pequot communities, was the settling of them on reservations. This, in the case of Cassasinamon's people, was done in 1667.[1] About two thousand acres were then reserved for them in that part of the town of New London which later was set off as Groton and still later as Ledyard. The other body was settled,[2] in 1683, in what is now the town of North Stonington. Already, in 1659,[3] the Golden Hill reservation had been set off for the Poquanock Indians on land which now lies within the limits of the city of Bridgeport, but which then lay on the boundary between Fairfield and Stratford. To this reservation an addition was made,[4] in 1680, for the benefit of the Indians of Milford, whose lands had in part been bought by the settlers of Stratford. Permission was also given these Indians to hunt and fish within the bounds of Stratford, Milford, and Derby. While the system of reservations was thus developing, the government of Connecticut was continually issuing orders respecting the bounds of Indian lands, the relations between Indian groups and tribes, their encouragement, protection, or restraint in various ways.

In Massachusetts the course of events which led to Indian reservations and to the beginning of a protectorate was somewhat different. Owing to the destruction by pestilence of the Massachusetts tribe, the Boston government was not led into this policy by pressure and by courses so purely secular as those which prevailed in Connecticut. The decisive impulse in the Bay colony came from the efforts of Rev. John Eliot and his associates to convert the Indians to Christianity, and by that means to civilize them. Before this work was undertaken in earnest the general court expressed its sympathy by ordering that the county

[1] Conn. Recs. II. 78; Plym. Recs. X. 332.   [3] Ibid. I. 336.
[2] Conn. Recs. III. 8, 117, 125.   [4] Ibid. III. 55, 68, 81, 444.

courts should exert themselves for the civilizing of the
Indians [1] within their jurisdictions, and should have them
instructed in the true worship of God.   Early in 1644 five
chiefs with their dependants, who afterward settled at
Natick, voluntarily submitted to the government of Massachusetts and put themselves under its protection. [2] In 1645
the clergy were called upon to suggest a comprehensive plan
for civilizing the natives.   The following year they were
ordered annually to choose two ministers who, with the aid
of an interpreter and others who might join in the work,
should preach the gospel among the Indians.   Indian pow-
wows and the worship of false gods were at the same time
forbidden.

At the very time when these last orders were being passed,
Eliot began preaching in the Indian tongue at Nonantum,
near Watertown.   At once the initial step was taken toward
the establishment of the first Indian reservation.   A committee, including the surveyor-general, was appointed by the
general court to purchase land, with the advice of certain of
the ministers, "for the encouragement of the Indians to live
in an orderly way amongst us." [3]   The elders were ordered
by the court to annually choose two ministers to work among
the natives.   A gratuity was voted to Mr. Eliot.   In May,
1647, the magistrates were ordered to establish a court for
hearing small causes once every quarter at the place or
places where the Indians usually assembled for worship,
while once a month the Indians might hold a court themselves.   The synod, also, which met in 1646, gave the work
its approval and encouragement.   Somewhat earlier than
this Thomas Mayhew, a merchant, and his son of the same
name, who was a clergyman, had begun a similar work on
Martha's Vineyard. [4]   The work of Eliot extended until it
resulted in the collection of settlements of Christian or pray-

---

[1] Mass. Recs. II. 84, 134, 177, 178.

[2] Gookin, History of the Christian Indians, in Arch. Am. II. 498.

[3] Mass. Recs. II. 166, 178, 188, 189.

[4] In 1641 the Mayhews, who lived in Watertown, bought Martha's Vineyard, Nantucket, and the Elizabeth islands from the agent of the Earl of
Stirling, and in consequence of that they were brought under the jurisdiction
of Massachusetts.   Hutchinson, Hist. of Mass., Ed. of 1795, I. 151.

ing Indians at Natick, Marlborough, Stoughton, Littleton, Grafton, Hopkinton, Chelmsford, and a number of places in the Nipmuck country near the northeastern border[1] of Connecticut.   In 1652 it was enacted by the general court that allotments of land might be made to those Indians who adopted civilized customs, and that they should be protected in their rights to planting grounds and fishing places.   A plantation was surveyed for them at Natick, and on the request of Mr. Eliot the court authorized the formation of other Indian towns, with the land which was necessary thereto, provided former grants were not injured and that they should not dispose of the land without the previous consent of the court.[2]   At first Humphrey Atherton, and afterward Daniel Gookin,[3] was appointed to hold courts among the Christian Indians.   The latter became a lay superintendent over them, showing much intelligence and zeal in their care until after the crisis of Philip's war.   In 1665 there were six towns of praying Indians within Massachusetts, each of which was located on a reservation, and had resident agents to govern and instruct them in civility and religion, and to decide controversies among them.   Of curious, rather than practical, interest is the fact that, out of the theories in vogue at the time concerning the origin of the Indians, Eliot and the Puritans generally selected that which identified them with the ten lost tribes of Israel. Viewed from this standpoint, there was a peculiar fitness in the selection by Eliot for the government of the plantation at Natick of the arrangement into tens, hundreds, and thousands which appeared among the Hebrews during their wilderness journeyings.   In August, 1651, through elections by the Indians held under Eliot's superintendence, the native officials were chosen.   But the scheme proved a failure and was soon abandoned.[4]   It is also interesting to note that the

[1] Gookin, Hist. Colls. of the Indians of New England, 1 Mass. Hist. Colls. I. 180 ; Gookin, History of the Christian Indians, Arch. Am. II. 435.

[2] Mass. Recs. III. 281 ; IV[1]. 192.

[3] *Ibid.* IV[2]. 34, 199.

[4] Eliot, Christian Commonwealth, Preface ; Letter of Eliot, in Whitefield's Light Appearing, etc.   For the internal history of the Indian missions as viewed by the clergy, see the famous tracts reprinted in 3 Mass. Hist. Colls. IV.

barbarities of Philip's war materially weakened the belief
of New Englanders in any theory of Indian origin save this,
that they were the offspring of the devil and were themselves devils incarnate.

The Colony of Plymouth followed the same line of policy
in general as did Massachusetts. In 1674 Richard Bourne
of Sandwich, who had been prominently concerned in missionary work among the natives of that colony, wrote[1] to
Captain Gookin that there were at that time about seven
groups or communities of praying Indians in Plymouth.
These were located in Sandwich, Eastham, Harwich, Yarmouth, Barnstable, Marshfield, Middleborough, and Wareham.
Land was reserved for the Indians in all or nearly all of
these places, the reservation at Sandwich being about ten
miles in length and five in breadth. It was reserved "for
them and theirs forever under hand and seal." The governor and magistrates, wrote Bourne, were "always very
careful to preserve lands for them, so far as is in their power
to do it." It was at Mashpee that at a later time the remnant of the Indians of Plymouth colony were gathered.[2] In
1675[3] Thomas Hinkley was appointed to hold courts among
the praying Indians of the colony, and in coöperation with
the heads of those communities to issue orders respecting
their government. The courts which he held had authority
to hear and punish all except capital crimes, and to settle all
civil controversies subject to the right of appeal on the part
of the Indians to the court of assistants. This was as far as
the system of control over the natives in Plymouth colony
was carried prior to Philip's war.

In Connecticut,[4] after the founding of the Society for
Propagating the Gospel in New England, some missionary
work was undertaken ; in that colony, however, it did not
originate the system of protection, but slightly furthered it
without seriously modifying its character. The Reverends
Abraham Pierson, of Brandford, and Thomas Fitch, of Nor-

[1] Gookin, 1 Mass. Hist. Colls. I. 196.
[2] Love, Samson Occum and the Christian Indians of New England, 17.
[3] Plymouth Recs. XI. 239.
[4] De Forest, *op. cit.* 272 *et seq.;* Gookin, 1 Mass. Hist. Colls. I. 207.

wich, were the leaders in this work.   The efforts of Pierson resulted in little, and were cut short by his removal, soon after 1660, with a part of his congregation, to Newark in New Jersey.   Mr. Fitch labored among the Mohegans after about 1671 with some success, and was partly supported by funds of the society.   In order to encourage the converts to settle in a fixed community, he gave them about three hundred acres of land, which should continue to be theirs as long as they remained true to their professions of Christianity. No other community of praying Indians appears to have been formed in Connecticut, and at the beginning of Philip's war this is said to have contained only forty members.   In Rhode Island neither communities of praying Indians nor Indian reservations appear.   It is estimated that at the opening of Philip's war the Christian Indians of New England numbered more than four thousand, and to all of them the system of reservations was fully applied.

After the death, in 1660, of Massasoit, the aged sachem of the Pokanoket or Wampanoag Indians, the relations between them and the English rapidly changed from those of friendly alliance to those of dependence and increasing jealousy. This became clearly apparent after the death of Alexander and the accession of his brother, Philip, to the dignity of chief sachem, in 1662.   As Mount Hope peninsula, the chief possession which then remained to the tribe, lay within what was supposed to be the territory of Plymouth colony, the dealings of Philip were principally with the magistrates of that jurisdiction.   However just might have been the intentions of the English, their steady encroachment upon the lands of the Indians — all of which they had long claimed as their own — could have no other result than to provoke the savage to hate, intrigue, and war.   Philip, and the Narragansett chiefs as well, were clear sighted enough to perceive that they must fight or presently acknowledge themselves as really subjects of the English.   The negotiations of Philip with Plymouth furnish an added illustration of the growth of the protectorate till it merged itself in sovereign control.

As soon as his brother, Alexander, had died, Philip was summoned to Plymouth and there found it necessary to sign

an instrument by which he acknowledged himself a subject
of the king of England and promised to observe the treaties
which his predecessors had concluded with the English.
Mutual pledges of friendship were exchanged, and the English promised to aid the Indians thereafter with advice, or
in such ways as might be possible. In 1667, while the
Dutch war was in progress in Europe, Philip was reported
to have expressed his readiness to join with the French or
the Dutch against the English, and so not only to recover
lands which had been sold to the whites, but to make spoil
of their goods. For this a party of horse was sent into his
country, and he was called before the court of Plymouth.
Though he declared the report to be a fabrication of Ninigret, the sachem of Niantic, he was ordered to contribute
£40 toward the expense of the expedition which had
been sent to summon him, and was told that he must
come thereafter when sent for by letter or messenger. Four
years later, in 1671, renewed alarms caused another meeting with Philip at Taunton, where, in the presence of Massachusetts men, he promised to surrender to the government
of Plymouth all his English arms, to be kept by them as
long as they saw cause. Several of the guns, however, he
kept back, while he was reported to have spread false reports about Plymouth. For these reasons the arms were
cónfiscated, and the council of war which Plymouth now
called into activity summoned Philip to another interview
and also sought the assistance of Rhode Island and Massachusetts. At the instance of Philip, Massachusetts caused
the appointment of a joint commission, in which Connecticut, but not Rhode Island, was represented. They conferred
with Philip at length, and secured from him another acknowledgment of subjugation to the king of England. This
was accompanied by an agreement to pay a yearly tribute
to the English, to make the governor of Plymouth the arbi-
trator of any difference between him and the English, and
not to make war or part with lands without the approval of
said governor.[1]

[1] Plymouth Recs. IV. 25, 26, 151, 164–166 ; V. 63–80. See also the Plymouth Narrative of the Beginnings of the War, Plymouth Recs. X. 362 ; Hub-

Had these promises been kept, the protection of the English over the Wampanoags would have been complete.
Their subjection would have surely followed.   But the murder of Sausamon and the later doings of Philip showed that he
preferred war to the peaceful acceptance of these conditions.

The encounters with the Pequot tribe and the alarms
which were later occasioned by the Narragansetts and Niantics were preliminary skirmishes.   They occasioned in each
case a single expedition.   The decisive conflict between the
colonists and the natives of southern New England came in
the years 1675 and 1676, when Philip of Pokanoket attacked
the settlements of Plymouth and Massachusetts, and the
Nipmuck and Narragansett tribes came to his assistance.
That was a genuine Indian war, with its accompanying
barbarities and sufferings on both sides, — the first and last
experience of the kind which southern New England was
forced to undergo.   In the end it broke the hold of the
natives on the Narragansett country and on central Massachusetts, and thus gave to the English reasonably free and
peaceful possession of their own territory before the more
prolonged conflict with the Indians and French of the north
began.   Like the war between the Dutch and the tribes of
southern New Netherland in 1642, the conflict of the French
with the Iroquois in the seventeenth century, and that of the
English of North Carolina with the Tuscarora tribe at a later
time, it was a conflict of Europeans with natives who were
unassisted by civilized leaders.   None of the later Indian
wars until just before the Revolution were of this character.
   When this struggle occurred, the frontier of eastern New
England south of the Merrimac river was an irregular line
extending through the towns of Chelmsford, Groton, Lancaster, Marlborough, Mendon, and thence southward a
short distance west of Narragansett bay.   This frontier lay
chiefly in the modern Worcester county, and along its
course lay many of the communities of praying Indians.

bard, Narrative of the Troubles with the Indians ; Increase Mather, Relation
of the Troubles in New England by reason of the Indians ; Palfrey, III.
142–153.

At no point was it much more than thirty miles distant from the eastern coast. To the north of Massachusetts the frontier line quickly approached the coast, and in Maine [1] followed its course very closely. Between the frontier to which reference has been made and the Connecticut river lay a stretch of country fifty miles wide in which no white settlement existed save Quaboag, or Brookfield, which was situated near the middle of the region. Along the course of the Connecticut itself were a few towns, lying between Springfield and Northfield, and including among their number Northampton, Hadley, Hatfield, and Deerfield. These towns, instead of being a part or extension of the frontier of eastern New England, can be more properly regarded as the northern frontier of Connecticut. This they distinctly became in the later wars with the French and the Indians of the north. In Philip's war the Connecticut settlements were menaced directly from the east as well as from the north.

Altogether in New England at this time there were 110 towns and plantations, of which Massachusetts contained 64. The white population is estimated to have numbered 80,000, which according to the usual basis of calculation would have included 16,000 males of military age. The Indians of this region numbered about 10,500. Among the tribes the Narragansetts of western Rhode Island and eastern Connecticut were the strongest, numbering perhaps 4000. The Nipmucks of central Massachusetts came next, with a possible 2400. The Massachusetts and Pawtucket tribes, living about Massachusetts bay and extending northwest to the territory of the Abenakis in Maine, were about equal in strength to the Nipmucks. The Wampanoags and Pokanokets of Plymouth and eastern Rhode Island numbered less than 1000.[2] All of these tribes, though unconnected in government, spoke dialects of the same language, and were of related origin.

[1] Palfrey, History of New England, III. 168, 215.
[2] H. M. Dexter, in Introduction to Church's Entertaining Passages, II. De Forest, Indians of Connecticut, Chap. II., gives conservative estimates of numbers, rightly criticising Trumbull's figures as too large.

When the struggle began, the New England Confederacy was still in existence. Since the Restoration the commissioners had rarely met, but nothing had occurred to necessitate the express dissolution of the union. On the other hand, the need of joint action on the part of the Puritan colonies was as great as ever. In the past, as we have seen, the commissioners had concerned themselves most seriously with Indian affairs and with the outfit of such expeditions as it had been necessary to send into the Indian country. Naturally their activity was now revived and a few important meetings were held.

But the commissioners did not take a prominent share in events until it became necessary to fit out the joint expedition which marched against the Narragansetts in December, 1675. The general orders for that expedition they issued, as well as those for one or two later operations. With the disbursements occasioned by the war and the accounting connected therewith, they also concerned themselves. To an extent, by affording a medium of consultation, the commissioners facilitated joint action at this crisis. But the task of securing coöperation rested essentially with the councils of war in the respective colonies. Though the Narragansett plantations were in part the seat of war, they took no share in its general operations. Those were planned and executed wholly by the colonies which were members of the Confederation. The isolation of Rhode Island, even in this great crisis, was as complete as at any time in its previous history. The way in fact to its coöperation with the rest of New England in the work of defence was not opened until the Confederation had wholly ceased to exist, and defence had become a matter of imperial, as well as colonial, interest.

When viewed from the standpoint of administration, the chief interest of Philip's war is found in the light which it throws on the problem of securing the joint action against a common enemy of three or more colonies, each containing a considerable number of towns, scattered through a large area of mostly unsettled and uncleared country. Boston was the chief centre whence the movements of the English were controlled. Plymouth, though it took the initiative, and later contributed the general of the Narragansett expedition, was a centre of far less importance than Boston, even among the settlements of the eastern coast. The council of war at Hartford directed or greatly influenced all the operations in the Connecticut valley, and a part of those in central Massachusetts and in the Narragansett country. The two subordinate centres in the west were Springfield and New London. The administrative problem of the war was not only to fit out and direct the successive expeditions which were organized by the individual colonies, but to maintain harmonious relations within the group.

As was to be expected, the war took the colonies by surprise. They had made no special preparation for it, and were forced to rely on militia organizations as they had been developed in time of peace. Means of communication were exceedingly poor. Officials, whether at home or in the field, must rely on Indian runners or scouts, some on horseback and others on foot, to convey information. If possible, no section should be left without adequate protection. Only gradually was the extent of defection among the Indians revealed. So secret and hidden were their movements, that their central encampments were not always known, while the presence of their armed bands was usually revealed by an ambuscade or the surprise of a village and the massacre of its inhabitants. The people of New England were shocked and terrorized by a long series of events of this kind, each of which was followed by renewed efforts, on the part of the councils of war and other officials concerned, to discover and exterminate the enemy who had wrought the destruction. Much correspondence passed, men were drafted from one or more of the near-by regiments ; they were furnished with provisions and ammunition enough for a few days, or, at most, a few weeks, and were sent upon a raid in pursuit of the enemy. The most important of these raids were undertaken by the colonies jointly. At the same time more stringent regulations for scouting were usually issued, and special scouting parties might be organized. The watches in the frontier towns were kept alert. The system of spreading alarms was perfected. Garrison houses and stockades were made as strong as possible. Where possible, cattle and movable crops were brought within protected enclosures ; but much movable property must needs be left to destruction, and many houses also, except in the few stockaded villages.

War, when carried on under these conditions, resolves itself into a series of raids, each of short duration, each extending over a limited territory and participated in, as the case might be, by a score or by a few hundreds of men. In the most of these raids the Indians took the initiative, and the blows which they inflicted elicited counter-strokes from the English. The Indian went more lightly armed and with a smaller supply of food than did the colonist ; but the colonist quite successfully imitated him in both these respects. He also made use of horses more than the Indian, in that region, was able to do. War such as this furnished no opportunity for strategy, though it did require skill and promptness in a multitude of details and minor operations. Its encounters were skirmishes and *mêlées* rather than battles. In tactics and equipment its requirements differed most widely from European warfare. It was such a variety of warfare as frontier conditions necessitated. It involved the only method of fighting to which the colonists of that generation were accustomed or for which their conditions in any way prepared them. Its processes and results, therefore, should be judged not wholly by European standards, but by those standards which are applicable to the frontier.

The war passed through several phases, and before its course was run nearly all parts of New England had felt its devastating effects. At the beginning it was a local struggle, confined to Mount Hope peninsula and the adjacent towns. The combatants on one side were the Wampanoags and a few neighboring Indians who were the immediate allies or dependants of Philip, and on the other side the few companies of foot and horse which were first sent to the scene of action by Plymouth and the authorities [1] at Boston.

---

[1] Hubbard, Narrative of the Troubles with the Indians ; Church, Entertaining Passages relating to Philip's War ; Bodge, Soldiers of King Philip's War, 46, 85, 95.

It was the attacks made by the Indians upon the town of
Swansey, between June 20 and 24, 1675, which roused Plymouth and Boston to action. Plymouth sent out two companies of foot under Major Cudworth and Captain Fuller;
Massachusetts, in response to the appeal of Plymouth, sent
a company of one hundred foot soldiers, drafted from the
militia of Boston and the surrounding towns, and a troop of
fifty horsemen from the three counties, Suffolk, Middlesex,
and Essex. These were under the command respectively
of Captain Daniel Henchman and Captain Thomas Prentice.
Henchman's company was also furnished with horses.[1]
They were accompanied by Moseley with about one hundred
volunteers, among whom are said to have been several youths
who were too young to be enrolled in the militia. A few
days later Captain Thomas Savage followed, with Paige's
troop of about forty horsemen, and additional men sufficient
to bring the Massachusetts contingent to the total of four
hundred.[2] Among them were a few friendly Indians. Of
the Massachusetts troops Savage was appointed commander.
But since the war was now being waged in Plymouth colony, Major Cudworth, the senior officer from Plymouth,
according to the custom of the United Colonies, became
commander-in-chief of the joint levies.

The troops from Massachusetts were followed by several
carts laden with supplies of food and ammunition. Two
vessels — a sloop and a brigantine — were also loaded with
supplies and despatched round by sea to the scene of the
conflict.[3] The Massachusetts troops were accompanied by
two commissaries and a surgeon, while Constant Southworth is credited with the dignified title of commissary-general of the Plymouth force.[4] When the general court of
Massachusetts met in July, it voted three country rates to
defray the expense of this expedition and to supply the
further needs of the treasury.[5]

[1] Bodge, *op. cit.* 95.

[2] Of these, three hundred were foot and about eighty were horse.

[3] Bodge, 91.

[4] Church, *op. cit.* 5, 7. The Plymouth Records, V. 175, show that in October,
1675, Thomas Huckens was chosen commissary-general of the Plymouth
forces.   [5] Mass. Col. Recs. V. 45.

By the joint efforts of the troops on this expedition protection for a time was brought to the terrified people who
had crowded into the three garrison houses of Swansey and
Rehoboth. Moseley's volunteers raided the peninsula of
Mount Hope for a distance beyond Swansey bridge, and so
frightened Philip and his Indians as to compel them to remove to the eastern shore of Narragansett bay, to the region
then known as Pocasset, but which is now a part of the
town of Tiverton, Rhode Island. There Philip and his men
took refuge in a swamp which proved inaccessible to the
English. While the Plymouth men were left to skirmish
with various parties of Indians and to watch Philip's retreat,
the entire Massachusetts force for a period of ten days —
July 5th to July 15th — was withdrawn into the Narragansett country. This move was made under direct orders from
the council at Boston, and was in the nature of an armed
demonstration for the purpose of extorting from the Narragansetts a treaty of peace.

An estimate of the wisdom of this measure can be found
from the following considerations. It seems quite probable
that, if the Massachusetts troops had continued to act vigorously with those of Plymouth at Pocasset, Philip's men
would have been trapped then and there, and the war would
not have extended beyond that locality. But in that case the
power of the Narragansetts, as well as that of the tribes of
central Massachusetts, would have remained unbroken, and
the English would have found them a constant source of
peril when at a later time the struggle with the French
began. At the time when Massachusetts took the step in
question, it was by no means certain that the Narragansetts
were inclined to break peace with the English. It is true
that many of the women and children of Philip's tribe had
taken refuge among them. Individual tribesmen here and
there were ready to take up against the English, and actually
did so a few weeks later. Such events, however, were always
an incident resulting from the loose control which the councils
of sachems held over their young warriors, and did not
necessitate hostile action on the part of the tribe as a whole.

Unless the English were consciously prepared to precipi-

tate a conflict with all the nations of southern New England
and to decide the race question in that section once for all,
prudence would seem to have demanded that nothing should
be done to offend the Narragansetts. Yet at the very
beginning of the struggle the entire Massachusetts force
was sent into the Narragansett country to make an armed
demonstration in support of a so-called embassy of peace.
The English, indeed, said that they "should go to make
peace with a sword in their hands." The sachems and
young men would not meet them, and the pretended treaty
at Pettiquamscutt was concluded with a few irresponsible
old men. It was even more worthless than Indian treaties
usually were. So little confidence did the Massachusetts
authorities themselves have in the binding force of the
agreement upon the tribe as a whole, that soon after Canonchet was called to Boston, and there, in order to escape
arrest, was forced to promise to fight against the Indians.
This promise served only to increase his irritation and to
make it certain that Narragansett warriors would not be
hindered by their fellow tribesmen from actively helping the
enemies of the English.

But other more immediate consequences of Massachusetts
policy at once became apparent. While her force was in
the Narragansett country, the towns of Middleborough and
Dartmouth in Plymouth colony were visited by the enemy,
and many houses with their inhabitants were destroyed.
When the Massachusetts men returned, a brief effort was
made to penetrate the recesses of the swamp at Pocasset.
It was believed that the force which had taken refuge
there was small and must have nearly exhausted its provisions; and therefore, if they were watched for a few days,
they would be starved into surrender. For this reason all
the Massachusetts men, except about one hundred under
Henchman, were recalled, and Henchman, with the Plymouth
force, was left to watch Philip. The crafty savage took
advantage of this to transport his men across Taunton river
and to escape up the valley of the Blackstone into central
Massachusetts. Captain Henchman pursued him, men from
Rehoboth and Providence, together with a company of Mohe-

gan Indians from Connecticut, coöperating.   But whether, as
some said, it was due to Henchman's tardiness or not, Philip
and his small force effected their escape.   This insured the
extension of the war to central Massachusetts.

Already, in June, the suspicions of Massachusetts concerning the fidelity of the Nipmucks had been aroused and
an embassy had been sent among them.   Though favorable
replies had been made by a part of them, evidence continued
to accumulate that their leaders were preparing for war.[1]   The
reports of Ephraim Curtis, of Sudbury, who, with an escort,
was twice sent among them, confirmed the rumors which had
been previously circulated.   About the middle of July a party
of Nipmucks attacked the town of Mendon.   Still the Massachusetts authorities, not fully conscious of the extent of the
disaffection, sent Captains Hutchinson and Wheeler, with a
mounted force of twenty men and Curtis as a guide, to secure
information, if possible, concerning the doings of Narragansetts in the region of Quaboag, to ascertain whether or not the
Nipmucks intended to keep their promises, and to secure the
surrender by them of those who were guilty of the recent outrage at Mendon.[2]   After reaching Brookfield, or Quaboag,
they arranged a place of meeting at Wenimeset, a point about
three miles north of Brookfield Church, whither the Qua-
boags had retired to form an alliance with the Nepnets and
Nashaways.   Philip had arrived in the region by this time,
and his agents had preceded him by some days or weeks.

But, on arriving at the appointed place, the English were
fired on by those with whom they were expecting to treat.
Eight were killed outright, and both Wheeler and Hutchinson were wounded, the latter mortally.   The survivors fled
back to the village of Brookfield.   There, with a large party
of the inhabitants, they took refuge in a garrison house.   In
this, with great heroism and good fortune, they succeeded in
defending themselves against the persistent attacks of a large

---

[1] Temple, History of North Brookfield, 76 *et seq.*; Bodge, 102 *et seq.*

[2] Temple, 79.   Wheeler's True Narrative, etc., is reprinted in this volume
and also in N. H. Hist. Colls. II.   On the location of the meeting place, see
New England Hist. and Gen. Register, October, 1884; Proc. of Mass. Hist.
Soc., 1893, 280; Bodge, 111.

body of Indians for three days. Then they were relieved by
Major Simon Willard, with a force of forty-seven troopers
from Lancaster. Willard was about starting westward with
orders from the council of Massachusetts, when news came
to him from Marlborough of the straits to which Brookfield
was reduced. His forced march of thirty miles for its relief,
with the brave defence of its garrison, rank among the notable
events of the war. This occurred in the early days of August,
and in consequence of it Brookfield was abandoned for a time.

These events opened the second and more important stage
of the war, which continued during the late summer and
autumn of 1675. The uprising of the Nipmuck people broadened the scene of conflict till it covered all of central Massachusetts, extended throughout the Connecticut valley, and
drew the authorities at Hartford into active coöperation with
the other colonies. In discussing the measures which were
then adopted, the operations in the valley of the Connecticut
first demand attention. Because of the location of the towns
in that region, Connecticut was more directly interested in
them than were the settlements of eastern Massachusetts.
Major John Pynchon was then the leading resident of
Springfield, and had charge of preparations for defence
among the valley towns themselves. In this capacity he
served as an intermediary between the upper towns and the
magistrates both at Hartford and Boston. At Hartford the
standing council of war, which met very frequently except
during the winter months, naturally directed its attention
first to the defence of Stonington and New London, the
towns that were adjacent to the Narragansett country. But,
as Governor Andros of New York was seeking to establish
his jurisdiction over western Connecticut, Captain Bull was
also instructed to protect its rights at Saybrook. As soon as
intelligence was received of the conclusion of the treaty with
the Narragansett Indians, to which reference has already
been made, the disbanding of the troops at Saybrook, with
the exception of about twenty men, was ordered.[1] Bull was
commanded at the beginning of August to limit himself to
the defence of Saybrook.

[1] Conn. Recs. II. 337, 344.

But the intelligence, a few days later, of the attack on Quaboag, which came in a letter from Major Pynchon, and was accompanied by a request for relief at Springfield, aroused the council to activity. Forty men were raised in the three River Towns and sent to Springfield, where they were to join in the defence of the upper valley towns, or march to Quaboag, if there was need of that service. Major Pynchon was requested to furnish the company suitably with provisions. Immediately orders were issued that one hundred dragoons should be impressed in Hartford county, sixty in New Haven county, and seventy in Fairfield county, and held ready to march on an hour's warning. All persons who by law were required to be supplied with arms and ammunition were commanded to meet on the next Monday morning, an hour after sunrise, at the meeting-houses in the respective plantations and await such directions as should be given them by their officers. Several bands of Pequot and Mohegan Indians were also set in motion, and a chief named Joshua, a son of Uncas the Mohegan, was sent with about thirty men to Springfield, to be employed there as circumstances might dictate.

Eighty Indians were sent in company with a body of troops from Norwich directly toward Quaboag. Great care was taken to preserve the good-will of the Indian allies. Meantime Captain Henchman's pursuit of Philip had brought him into the region south of Brookfield. Captain Moseley was sent again from Boston[1] with sixty men and supplies. In Massachusetts the first draft of soldiers had just been made from the Essex regiment, and the news of the disaster at Brookfield caused a company from Salem under Captain Lathrop, and one from Watertown under Captain Beers, to be sent out. They, with Moseley, the men under Watts from Connecticut, and the Springfield men, ranged the country west and north of Brookfield in all directions, going as far west as Hadley, but without discovering the enemy. The Springfield men then returned home, taking the Connecticut force thus far with them. Lathrop and Beers, under orders so to do, marched for extended service into the

[1] Conn. Recs. II. 348.

Connecticut valley. There is evidence that already the plan [1] of Philip to retire toward the Mohawk country for the purpose of securing aid was suspected, and decisive steps were taken, with the aid of Governor Andros of New York, to insure the continued fidelity of the Mohawks to the English.

On August 24th, in consequence of an attempt on the part of Lathrop to disarm the Pocumtucks, who lived near Deerfield, and of whose treachery the English were well assured, the first conflict in the Connecticut valley occurred, near Sugar Loaf Hill.[2] This made it clear that the valley Indians were committed to war. Hadley had by this time been selected as the English headquarters, whence Pynchon, as major of the Hampshire county regiment, and his officers, with those from eastern Massachusetts and from Connecticut, directed operations. A small guard was left in Northfield and another at Deerfield, but these might at any time be recalled, if there was prospect of quiet along the frontier.

At the close of August, influenced by reports from the north, the dragoons and other available forces from Connecticut, constituting what was familiarly known as the "army," was sent northward under the command of Major Robert Treat, of Milford. During the remainder of the war he was intrusted with the chief command among Connecticut men. His control over his troops, however, was limited, as was the rule in those times, by the necessity of consulting his officers as a council of war. He was also ordered to take counsel and coöperate with the Massachusetts officers. Treat was commanded to march through Westfield to Northampton, and thence to pass farther northward, if necessary. James Steele was appointed commissary for the expedition, and one or more officers with that function appear, thenceforward, as a feature of the Connecticut establishment.

The uncertainty of military operations and the limited resources of each colony for defence is well illustrated by

[1] Conn. Recs. II. 350, 377.

[2] Rev. Benjamin Stoddard's letter in Mather, Relation of the Troubles in New England, 73 *et seq.*; Judd, History of Hadley, 141 ; Bodge, 129 ; Sheldon, History of Deerfield, I. 90.

what occurred two days after Treat was ordered to begin his march.   Because of the appearance of certain Indians skulking near Hartford, he was summarily ordered to return and search for the enemy on both sides of the Connecticut river as far south as Wethersfield.   But on September 1, the very day on which the order for the return of the soldiers was issued, occurred an attack on Deerfield, in which the inhabitants were saved by taking refuge in three stockaded houses.   The consequence of this was that, on September 2, Major Treat was commanded to return northward, with the forces from New Haven and Fairfield counties and certain picked men from the towns of Hartford county.[1] This was followed by an order for the strict maintenance of the night watch in the towns of the colony, and that work should be carried on in the fields in companies, with arms at hand ready for use.   Special patrols also were ordered to keep the roads in each town clear for travellers.

On the day when Treat received his command to march northward Northfield was attacked and eight persons, caught outside the stockade, were killed.   Captain Beers was already on the march from Hadley to bring off the inhabitants from Northfield, when, not being aware of the attack two days before on that place, he fell into an ambush near the town, and, with twenty-one of his men, was slain.[2]   As soon as the fugitives reached Hadley, Captain Treat was sent to Northfield and brought away all its inhabitants.   Thus the second frontier town was abandoned.

The lesson drawn by the council of war at Hadley from the fate of Beers and his men was, that operations in the field should be given up and attention paid solely to garrisoning the towns.   This Major Treat reported[3] at Hartford, and the council there resolved that all its men, except those who were needed for that purpose, should be recalled.   They were especially desirous that Westfield should be garrisoned, because the Indians, if they passed that point, might easily approach the towns of the lower

---

[1] Conn. Recs. II. 359, 360.

[2] Temple and Sheldon, History of Northfield, 73 et seq.

[3] Conn. Recs. II. 364.

valley by the way of the Farmington river. But this policy of inaction was not satisfactory, and, at the instance of the Connecticut council, the Commissioners of the United Colonies voted, on September 16, that one thousand men, inclusive of' those already in service, should be organized, and that the contingents from Massachusetts and Connecticut should operate among the valley towns of Massachusetts. Of the total number in service, according to the proportion specified in the Articles, Massachusetts should contribute 527, Connecticut 315, and Plymouth 158. It was ordered by the commissioners, in concurrence with the council of Massachusetts, that for the present Major Pynchon should command the troops in service in the west, and Connecticut was asked to designate the second in command. Major Treat was duly appointed to the place. The commissioners confessed that they did not know how many soldiers were then in service in that region or what was the strength of the natives; therefore the duty of deciding upon numbers and operations must be left to officers who were serving in the locality. " And considering," they wrote, "the great trust and dependence that is upon Major Pynchon for the constant management of the public affairs in those parts, we do not expect that he should be personally present in every expedition against the enemy, further than himself and his council of officers should see a necessity of." [1] The council of Massachusetts wrote to Pynchon personally to the same general effect, and Connecticut fell in with the arrangement. Thus the system under which affairs in the west were already being conducted received formal confirmation.

But it did not avail to prevent one of the most serious disasters of the war, the slaughter of Captain Lathrop and more than sixty men [2] at Bloody Brook, a short distance south of Deerfield. This occurred on September 18, while Lathrop was convoying teams loaded with wheat, which was being carried to headquarters. The fatal result was largely due to the failure of the commander to throw out scouts in advance, while only the opportune arrival of Moseley and Treat, with

[1] Conn. Recs. II. 367, 368.

[2] The various estimates, with his own revision, are given by Sheldon, I. 106.

vigorous fighting on their part, forced the enemy to retire. This event caused the abandonment of Deerfield and a still further contraction of the frontier. The effect of these disasters now began to be felt throughout the entire colony. Men began to avoid impressment and to desert after they had been impressed. So great was the danger of scouting that many were loath to undertake it. A feeling of terror pervaded all the exposed settlements.

Still it was the plan of the commissioners that a large expedition should be sent out to clear the valley of Indians, and that soldiers in garrison should be utilized in part for the purpose. To this the instinct of residents in the threatened localities — among them Pynchon — was opposed. But in obedience to orders, on October 4, Pynchon took all the garrison from Springfield to Hadley to join the force which was preparing to march from that point. The next day Springfield was attacked by Indians of the neighborhood, with allies, and more than thirty houses were destroyed. Treat attempted to relieve the place, but was unable to effect a crossing from the west bank of the river. Pynchon and Appleton moved rapidly down from Hadley, but arrived too late to be of service.[1] The inhabitants, as usual, were saved by taking refuge in garrison houses. Pynchon, who had long been pleading his unfitness for command, and who now saw a large part of his property destroyed and his family distressed, was allowed to retire, and Appleton was appointed in his place. He assumed command on the twelfth of October.[2]

The Connecticut towns now seemed more than ever exposed to attack. Indians were discovered at Glastonbury, and Rev. Thomas Fitch of Norwich found that Philip, with a large body of Narragansetts, was about to invade Connecticut. It was rumored that a general uprising of the Indians of Connecticut was imminent. Governor Andros wrote that five or six thousand Indians were planning a descent on western Connecticut. To meet this peril, on October 7, two days after the attack on Springfield, Treat was ordered

[1] Morris, Springfield; Sheldon, I. 115.
[2] Appleton's commission is printed by Sheldon, I. 118.

to return to Hartford with sixty men. Massachusetts was
urged to send more men into the valley, as a condition of
beginning active operations with a strong force in the field.
An order was issued by the council of war at Hartford that
local officials should prepare fortified places into which the
women and children might be brought on any alarm. Hartford, Windsor, and Wethersfield should gather their maize
into secure places, and all should coöperate in this work,
" this being a time for all private interests to be laid aside
to preserve the public good." A few days later flankers
were ordered to be built near the houses on the outskirts of
Hartford, and in such position that the spaces between them
could be commanded and the town thus protected. Orders
were also issued for watches and for improvement in the defence of the other towns; and, on November 22, because of
the negligence of some, the town committees were instructed,
if the defects were not remedied, to hire the work done, and
levy by distraint on the property of the delinquents to meet
the expense.[1]

The correspondence [2] of Major Appleton at this juncture —
October and November, 1675 — reveals with great clearness
the difficulties which he had to meet. In the first place, he,
like Pynchon, was convinced that it would not do to leave
the towns unprotected in order that troops might be procured for scouting or for large expeditions. The fate of
Springfield filled some of its inhabitants with a desire to
abandon the place, though sixty houses in all, on both
sides of the river, were still standing. If the policy of
neglecting garrisons was persisted in, a clamor for the
abandonment of towns might become general. Therefore
Appleton urged the council of Massachusetts to revise this
part of its orders. On the other hand, Connecticut claimed
that it was not intended that her troops should be kept
simply to garrison Massachusetts towns, but that, as a part
of a confederate army, they should vigorously pursue the

---

[1] Conn. Recs. II. 372, 375, 382.

[2] The letters to and from him in manuscript are in Mass. Arch., Vol. 67.
The most important of them have been printed by Jewett in his Memorial of
the Appleton Family.

enemy. They considered it the duty of each colony to garrison its own towns.

In reply to Appleton the council of Massachusetts stated
that its order about garrisons originated in the fact that five
hundred men had been raised at the expense of the colony
as a whole, and that they were needed at many points.
Hence it was thought that the towns might provide their
own garrisons. But this order was subject to the exigencies
of the conflict, and might be modified in the interest of the
general welfare. Thus the council yielded to the representations of the officers who were acquainted with local conditions
and an order was at once issued permitting the garrisoning
of Springfield.

Throughout the period of his command Major Appleton
and the men associated with him continued active scouting and raiding throughout the valley. But garrisons were
not neglected, as was shown by the fact that the attacks
on Hatfield and Northampton, both of which occurred in
October, were successfully repelled by the aid of garrisons
and stockades. Aid was at the same time given by the
scouting bands outside. In this way the various methods of
defence were brought into successful coöperation. When
the time came for closing the campaign, the Massachusetts
council ordered Appleton to leave sufficient garrisons in the
valley towns and return home with the rest of his troops.
The garrisons should be put under the command of the chief
officers in their respective towns. A council of war should
be left in charge for the winter of the affairs of the upper
valley. It should consist of the chief officers of Hadley,
Hatfield, and Northampton, together with some of the principal inhabitants, and should report its doings for confirmation
to the council at Boston. These orders were duly obeyed
by the commander, twenty-six men being left at Northampton and thirty each at Hadley and Hatfield.

The other question which for a time perplexed Appleton,
was that of the relations which should exist between him
and the commander of the Connecticut troops. The sudden
recall of Treat, just as Appleton took command and was
organizing a force for a considerable move against the

enemy, was irritating. Appleton now summoned Lieutenant
Seely to appear. Seely had been left at the head of the
Connecticut men who remained behind in Massachusetts.
He appeared, but without his men, stating that by his commission he was ordered to obey the instructions of his chief
commander and the orders which he should receive from
Connecticut authority. His chief commander he understood
to be Treat. Of this Appleton naturally complained to the
Massachusetts government, and also wrote letters of protest
to Hartford. He fell back upon the principles followed by
the Commissioners of the United Colonies, that the chief
command over any force should rest with the officer of
highest rank who was a resident of the colony in which the
troops were serving. In this contention the council at
Boston supported him, holding that Treat should not have
departed without the consent of Appleton, and that if Connecticut continued to withhold her troops, Massachusetts
would consider it a breach of the Articles of Confederation.
Sharp letters were exchanged between Appleton and the
authorities at Hartford, in which the course of each party
was defended. Connecticut accused Massachusetts of long
delays, and Appleton of trying to act separately. This
Appleton denied.[1]

As soon, however, as the rumors of peril to Connecticut
disappeared, Major Treat was sent back and performed
much good service among the upper towns of the valley
before the close of the campaign. On November 12,
Appleton issued a proclamation, addressed not only to the
three towns which he afterwards garrisoned, but to Westfield and Springfield, where some Connecticut men were
stationed, forbidding soldiers to withdraw from the colony
without orders from the Commissioners of the United Colonies, or from the joint council of war, or without the consent
of the commander-in-chief. Conduct in violation of this
proclamation would be considered a breach of the Articles.
In this form Appleton asserted his claim to the end, though
his reference to the Articles of Confederation could have
practically amounted to no more than an appeal to the spirit

[1] Appleton Memorial; Conn. Recs. II. 380, 381.

of coöperation. The question was not reopened during the later stages of the conflict.

While the Connecticut valley was the scene of chief interest, the government at Boston was occupied also with measures for the protection of the frontier from Marlborough northward, and with the beginnings of the struggle among the eastern settlements. Minor expeditions were sent out in many directions, the energies of the colony being all the while fully tested. The war had now developed so far as to involve the final decision of the rivalry between the white man and the Indian in southern New England. The pressure which from the outset the English had put upon the Narragansetts implied this as a final result. The English were now so fully aroused as to be ready for the final struggle, even with this tribe. And in the end it proved fortunate for civilization that it came at once, for it removed the peril which must have threatened the English if the Narragansetts had retained their strength unimpaired until the outbreak of the French wars fifteen years later.

When it was found that Canonchet had not surrendered the hostile Indians as he had promised to do, that the Narragansetts were systematically harboring foes of the English, and that members of the tribe had been concerned in minor outrages, action was resolved on.

When, on November 2, the commissioners met again at Boston,[1] it was resolved to raise a thousand more men, and, if the Narragansetts did not perform their covenants, to proceed against them as enemies. It was also voted that Governor Josiah Winslow of Plymouth should command this force, and that the second in command should be appointed by the general court of Connecticut, and should exercise his powers while the force might be in that colony. The troops from Connecticut should rendezvous at Norwich, Stonington, and New London, and those from the other two colonies at Rehoboth, Providence, and Warwick. No effort was made to secure the coöperation of Rhode Island. It was urged that strong and active men should be selected for the service, and that they should take food in their knap-

---

[1] Plymouth Recs. X. 362–365, 456–459 ; Mass. Recs. V. 69.

sacks for a week's march.   Each colony should furnish its
own soldiers with provisions and ammunition.   They should
be ready to start from the places of rendezvous by the tenth
of December.   The expedition was to be preceded by a
solemn fast.

Appropriate orders for the execution of this design were
issued by the general court of Massachusetts and by the
councils of war of Plymouth and Connecticut.[1]   The executive records of the last-named colony reveal all the important
steps which were taken.   Robert Treat, with the title of
major, was appointed commander of the Connecticut troops,
and ordered to act as such until they should reach the
place of rendezvous for the entire expedition.   Contingents
were levied from the towns within each county by the resident assistants under orders from the council of war.   The
weekly wages of officers and men were specified by the
council.   The assistance of friendly Indians was also invoked.   A commissary, Stephen Barrett, was appointed
for the "army," and was empowered to grant tickets for the
quartering of men and horses, and also by his warrants,
under authority from the major or other officers, to impress
whatever might be needed by the soldiers.   Three hundred
bushels of wheat were ordered to be procured from the
counties and taken to New London to be ground and baked.
The colony treasurer was intrusted with this duty in Hartford county, and designated committees were ordered to
perform the same task in the other counties.   The export of
provisions from New London county during the space of
two months was forbidden, except under license from the
council of war.   In Connecticut, after the troops had
marched, a special guard was called out for the protection of
Norwich, while in Plymouth daily trainings in each town of
the men who were left behind were ordered.

The expedition consisted of six companies and one troop
— 540 men — from Massachusetts, under Major Samuel Appleton; two companies — 158 men — from Plymouth under
Major Bradford and Captain Gorham; and five companies

[1] Mass. Col. Recs. V. 69; Plymouth Recs. V. 182; Conn. Recs. II. 384
et seq.

— 315 men with 150 Mohegan Indians — from Connecticut.[1] Governor Josiah Winslow of Plymouth was commander of the expedition. The place appointed for the rendezvous of the forces was the garrison house of Jerry Bull at Pettiquamscutt, a short distance west of Narragansett bay. But shortly before the arrival of the troops Bull's garrison was entirely destroyed by the Indians. Therefore no shelter was left for the soldiers, and they were forced to lie out of doors in the snow during the night of December eighteenth. In the morning they advanced toward the Indian position, which they reached about one o'clock on the same day. The Indian fort was built upon a tract of upland four or five acres in extent and entirely surrounded by swamp. It was situated in what is now the town of North Kingston, and, as the army marched, was about sixteen miles northwest from Pettiquamscutt. The location, which was well-nigh inaccessible, except over the snow and ice of winter, was such as the Indians had chosen for their permanent camps in central Massachusetts. The enclosure was much like that in which the Pequots had taken refuge forty years before. It was surrounded by palisades, within which was an embankment of earth, while outside of both was an abattis of trees. At the corners and exposed parts were rude flankers, or blockhouses. Near one corner of the fort the structure was still incomplete, and, though galled by a destructive fire from a neighboring blockhouse, it was at this point that the English made their attack. Within the stronghold about 3500 Indians are supposed to have gathered. The attacking force numbered not far from 1000 men, with an Indian contingent from Connecticut. A part of the Indians were supplied with firearms, and for these they had a limited amount of ammunition. The English were all armed in this fashion and were well supplied with ammunition.

The assault upon the Indian position was begun as soon as the English troops arrived. They did not wait even to form, but rushed upon the enemy as they found him, seeking to force their way past the blockhouse and through the open space in the defences of the enclosure. The Massa-

[1] Bodge, 184.

chusetts men led and the Connecticut men followed, and the Plymouth men were probably brought into the action last of all. The fighting was entirely done by the foot-soldiers, the troopers being held in reserve. At first, and until their ammunition began to give out, the fire of the Indians was very galling. Several of the officers were slain as they led the assault, and the loss was heavy among the privates. But the English persisted, fell upon their stomachs till the fury of the Indian fire had somewhat spent itself, and then pushed their way past the blockhouse and stormed the palisaded enclosure itself. Though the natives made an obstinate resistance, the English gradually overmastered them, inflicting terrible slaughter. But, as in the Pequot fight, fire was at last applied to the wigwams inside the palisade, and its terror and destruction made the triumph of the English complete. This step was taken contrary to the advice of Captain Church, who was present, he thinking that they should be preserved as a shelter for the troops during the winter, or at least for some weeks to come, and that the stores of grain which the Indians had accumulated should be seized by the English for food. But the Indian citadel was totally destroyed, and those who were unable to escape to remoter parts of the swamp perished miserably amid the flames or at the hands of the English.

The English loss was about 70 men killed and 150[1] wounded. Connecticut lost 40 men, who were killed on the spot or afterward died of their wounds. The Indian loss it would be impossible to estimate, but it was numbered by hundreds.

After a toilsome night march through the snow, which was necessitated by the lack of shelter or any conveniences for the wounded at the scene of conflict, the English reached Richard Smith's plantation at Wickford. Several of the wounded died before morning; others expired later. The force was compelled by the severity of winter to remain at Wickford for some weeks. The fortunate arrival of a vessel laden with provisions from Massachusetts saved the men from hunger; though they were again brought to low

[1] Bodge, 190.

rations before the time came for leaving the camp. After a time the Connecticut men were withdrawn to Stonington, while many of the wounded were taken for better nursing to Rhode Island.

By the "swamp fight" the first severe blow was inflicted upon the Narragansett nation. By that event, however, its power was only shattered, not destroyed. The immediate effect of the battle was to transform the Narragansetts into the active allies of the Nipmucks, and to make them leaders in the devastation of many towns along the Massachusetts frontier and in the colonies of Plymouth and Rhode Island. War to the knife was now definitely begun between the English and the Narragansetts, and the sufferings attendant upon it must be endured until the strength of the Indian was exhausted, and his land was left free for settlement by the whites. During this process the tide of war flowed back to its starting-point, and the struggle became fiercer than it had been at any previous time.

The Commissioners of the United Colonies at once called for one thousand more men,[1] and the colonies concerned were urged to send money to Boston and have provisions and other supplies collected and distributed from that point. Vessels could be utilized for that purpose.

In response to this call Plymouth ordered out 122 men. In Connecticut active steps were taken to supply fresh levies. The hardships of their recent experience had caused some of the Connecticut men to return home without leave. While the authorities reproved them severely for this conduct, they were inclined to lenient treatment of the offenders in view of their inexperience, and of possible difficulties which severe measures might cause in the raising of future levies.[2] Supplies were again collected at New London, while the council of war urged that the Connecticut men might henceforth be permitted to remain near their own borders and not be required to march to remote points. "The truth is," they wrote to the commissioners, "our souldyers have beene so much drawne off from our borders already whenas the enemy

[1] Plymouth Recs. V. 184; Conn. Recs. II. 391.
[2] Conn. Recs. II. 394 et seq.

was above, . . . & againe for this engagement very neare to us . . . when he seems to be seated even at our doores, within 15 miles of our townes & in our Colony. Now for us to march 40 or 50 miles with all our accomodations, in a desolate country, to engage him in conjunction with the other forces, doth seeme intollerable & too disgusting to all our souldyery to be drove upon them." They thought that, especially as the war had not begun within Connecticut, Massachusetts was as much bound to seek the convenience of its western neighbor as Connecticut was to march to the relief of the eastern settlements. But no disposition was shown to stand out against what seemed best to the commissioners and to the colonies generally. A Connecticut force of about five hundred men was soon ready to march, and the embargo was raised sufficiently to allow Captain Belcher, the commissary of Massachusetts, and others to export from Connecticut a quantity of provisions for the Massachusetts troops.

When, on January 23, Major Treat was ready again to march eastward from New London, he wrote [1] to the council at Hartford, " The trouble and difficultys, with such commanders, to prepare for my service is almost too hard & heavie for me; and if you had appointed me a victualler of your army, I hope I might have done something at it." He apparently had at this time only a steward, Benjamin Curtis of Stratford. Major Treat's excuse for the brevity of his letter was, that he had neither clerk, commissary, or others who seemed immediately helpful to him in preparing for the march.

The midwinter raid into the Nipmuck country in which these preparations resulted, began on January 28, and continued about five days. The united force of fourteen hundred men, including some Indians from Connecticut, started from Smith's garrison in the Narragansett country and dispersed after they had seen the Indians retire into the wilderness beyond Brookfield. Notwithstanding the efforts which were made to collect provisions, not enough could be brought together and transported to supply the soldiers for

[1] Conn. Recs. 401, 402.

a longer time. Indeed, their privations during the short time occupied by the raid were such that it was popularly known as the "hungry march." No appreciable injury was inflicted on the Indians by this laborious and costly effort.

Philip was now on the Hudson, hoping to enlist the aid of the Mohawks. The Narragansetts, led by Canonchet, who was now the soul of the Indian revolt, were everywhere active. On February 10 Lancaster was destroyed. This exploit was followed, during the spring and early summer of 1676, by attacks on nearly a score of towns in eastern Massachusetts, Rhode Island, and Plymouth. Prominent among the places which suffered were Sudbury, Groton, Marlborough, Medfield, Chelmsford, Andover, Wrentham, Bridgewater, Scituate, Rehoboth, Providence, and Warwick. In the Connecticut valley, Northampton, Hadley, and Hatfield were attacked, while a decisive victory was won by the English at Turner's Falls. At Sudbury Captain Wadsworth, of Milton, who was marching to the relief of the place, fell into an ambush, and he and nearly all his command of seventy men were slain. From their retreats or strongholds, several of which lay between Mount Wachusett — north of Worcester — and the region of Northfield,[1] the Indians spread terror throughout the English settlements. Under its influence many became averse to leaving their houses for service of any kind. To meet this evil the general court of Massachusetts, in May, ordered that very heavy fines should be imposed on all who sought to avoid military service.[2]

From the beginning of March until about the 7th of April, Major Thomas Savage was again in command of the Massachusetts troops. At this time he was pursuing the enemy through the region between Mount Wachusett and the Connecticut river, and was attempting, though with little success, to protect the border settlements. At the last named date Savage was recalled, leaving Captain William Turner to garrison certain of the towns. It was during this interval, on April 20, that the disaster occurred at Sudbury.

[1] Indian encampments were situated near Mount Wachusett, in Brookfield, in Athol, and in Northfield.
[2] Mass. Col. Recs. V. 78 *et seq.*

That, however, was more than offset by the exploit of a body of Connecticut volunteers under captains Denison and Avery. They surprised and captured Canonchet near Patuxet river, and he was at once executed. Thus the Indians lost their ablest chief and leading spirit. About a month later — on May 19 — Captain Turner won his notable success at the "Falls," inflicting heavy loss on the Indians. This, however, was to an extent offset by the death of Turner himself and the loss of many of his command during their march back to Hatfield.

As the peril increased, the efforts of the colony governments were redoubled. In May Massachusetts defined its inner frontier as a line passing through Medfield, Sudbury, Concord, Chelmsford, Andover, Haverhill, and Exeter. A committee of militia was appointed and instructed to organize a system of scouts for the protection of these towns and of the country which lay to the east of them. To this end the soldiers from the frontier towns who were abroad on general service were ordered home, and joined with others of their townsmen in squads which, under suitable officers, should patrol the frontier and be ready to give immediate aid to any neighboring town that should be attacked.[1] Trade with the natives was absolutely prohibited. So great was the terror which now prevailed along the frontier, that many were ready to flee thence to places of safety. But the general court passed an act strictly forbidding any who could render military service, or serve on the watch, thus withdrawing under penalty of £20.

Quaboag was maintained as an outpost and a garrison was kept there. By this court also a general draft from the county regiments was ordered and from their troops, as well as from the "three county troop." The commissioners, of whom there now were three, were ordered to contract for provisions for five hundred men during one month. Friendly Indians were also employed. A part at least of these soldiers were sent into the Connecticut valley. Captain Moseley again offered to raise volunteers, with a body of fifty or sixty Indians,

---

[1] Garrisons were specially ordered to be maintained at Sudbury and Concord. *Ibid.* 93.

if he might be reasonably free from the control of the regular commander, might have the privilege of acting to an extent on his own initiative, and if his men might have the captives and plunder which they took. On the advice of the military committee, Moseley's proposals were accepted, and subscriptions were ordered for supplies for the expedition. So reduced, in fact, were the resources of the colony, that the court at its previous session had declared its readiness to pledge the public domain of the colony as security for loans. As we have seen in another connection, garrison houses were multiplied in all the towns, and a plan even was broached to build a stockade from the Charles river to the Merrimac.

The colony of Plymouth was also the seat of active war, and had problems to face of the same nature in general as those of Massachusetts. On February 29, 1676, the Plymouth council of war ordered that the inhabitants should abide in their towns, and not depart therefrom without the permission of the government, on penalty of the forfeiture of all their personal estate.[1] At the same time a special council of three was appointed for each town within the jurisdiction, and empowered, with the commissioned officers of the colony, to order the watches and garrisons in their respective towns and to care in all respects for their defence. An armed watch should be on duty perpetually in each town, and any who neglected to serve thereon were threatened with heavy fine. Youths under sixteen years of age were summoned to perform this duty. Special assessments were authorized both on the towns and on the colony to meet expenses. People were repeatedly ordered to take refuge within garrison houses or other protected enclosures ; but in many instances it was found impossible to secure obedience to the order.

Plymouth was greatly hampered by the refusal of men to serve under arms. When, in April, the attack on Rehoboth occasioned the issue of an order for the levy of a force for an expedition, it was found that many of the soldiers who had been drafted, especially in Scituate and Sandwich, had

[1] Plymouth Recs. V. 185 *et seq.*

refused to serve. They would not go even to the relief of
Rehoboth, much less on more distant service. A few only
of the soldiers from the southern towns of the colony went
as far as Middleborough and then returned home. Sandwich had been delinquent before, and we may attribute that
in part to the strength of the Quaker element there. But
generally the cause of inertia was fear of leaving their
homes, lest during their absence these too might be destroyed. As it was, the efforts of the government were
temporarily frustrated, and all that could be done was to
continue watch and ward in the localities. In June the
general court took up the case, and ordered that 150 English [1] and 50 Indians should be sent out, while power was
given to the deputy governor and two assistants, in the
absence of others, to levy and despatch troops. Persons
who refused to obey the draft, or to procure substitutes,
should be fined £5, or be compelled to run the gantlet, or
suffer both punishments. The commissioned officers and
town councils were also ordered to institute a system of
scouts, and men who should refuse, when levied, to perform
this service, should forfeit five shillings per day. But, notwithstanding its abundant legislation, Plymouth was not able
to assist in the offensive operations which Massachusetts and
Connecticut were undertaking against the enemy.

At that time the Connecticut valley and the region surrounding Mount Wachusett were the chief points of attack.
In May a Massachusetts force under Captain Henchman was
ordered to advance [2] through the Wachusett country on
their way to Hadley in the Connecticut valley. The authorities at Boston also asked Connecticut to send a force of
English and Indians to the upper towns in the valley, that a
joint movement might be directed against the natives about
Deerfield and Northfield.[3] As soon as sufficient preparations could be made, Major John Talcott marched from Norwich for Wachusett, with the intention of going thence by
the way of Brookfield to Hadley and the other valley towns.
He arrived at Brookfield on June 7, and passed thence by a

[1] Plymouth Recs. 197 et seq.   [2] Mass. Recs. V. 97.
[3] Conn. Recs. II. 444–455.

forced march the next day to Hadley. Finding that the Massachusetts force had not yet arrived there, he quartered his soldiers and awaited further orders from the council at Hartford. During his march his force had killed and captured fifty-two of the enemy. From Northampton, on the night of the 8th, Talcott wrote to the council for more bread, for a barrel of powder and three hundred pounds of bullets. The bread which they had with them, though kept dry, was already "full of blue mould," and that which might in the future be sent he thought should be well dried. Orders were at once issued by the council to the commissioners to provide the supplies for which Talcott wrote. Captain Henchman, the Massachusetts commander, was detained at Marlborough [1] by the presence of the enemy in that region. About the middle of June, however, Henchman, with his force, arrived in the valley, and together the two commanders marched some distance up the river above Hadley. [2] But finding no important trace of the enemy, their commands were soon after withdrawn from the valley.

Talcott, after recruiting at Hartford, was ordered to march out again, the council leaving it wholly to him, when on the march, to decide as to the details of his operations and the directions in which he should proceed. Since the service had been hard and little plunder had been gained, a coat was given to every Indian who had shared in the expedition. It was decided that the raid on this occasion should be directed eastward, [3] and it proved to be one of the most successful in the whole war. Talcott and his men, with their Indians, crossed the Narragansett country, taking 171 prisoners at the first onset ; then, advancing through Warwick neck, they increased the number captured and slain to 238. The Connecticut men then traversed the entire western shore of Narragansett bay, clearing the country of Indians as they passed, and, had their Indian allies been willing, would have sought out Philip himself, who, they heard, had returned to

[1] Conn. Recs. II. 454.

[2] See Bodge, 57, 270, though in the latter reference the author seems to have dated the event a month too early.

[3] Conn. Recs. II. 458.

Mount Hope. Raids of this nature, which were repeated by the Massachusetts troops a little farther north and east, revealed the fact that the power of the Indians was at last broken.

The cause which, in this case as in many others, ultimately decided the fate of the savages, was the exhaustion of their food supply. The store of corn which had been laid by the previous year was now consumed. They had been driven from many of their hunting and fishing grounds as well as from their corn-fields, and were now unable to return. The journal of Mrs. Rowlandson shows that through the spring of 1676 they had been compelled to subsist largely on groundnuts. They could plant nothing for their support during the coming fall and winter. Under these conditions, their captives became a burden, and they were ready to restore or exchange them. The efforts of Philip to secure the aid of the Mohawks had failed, and, with the collapse of the power of the Narragansetts, he found himself unable longer to hold out. Parties of Indians came in from all directions and surrendered themselves. The rest became fugitives.

The pursuit of Philip and his death, August 12, at the hands of one of Captain Church's Indians, was only the dramatic close of a struggle which was already decided. Though the conflict will always continue to bear his name, it is not probable that, after the first encounter, he ever exerted influence over it other than that of a diplomatist. His immediate followers were always few in number. When he fled into the Nipmuck country, he is believed to have been accompanied by no more than fifty warriors. One writer of high authority says : " We have no proof that Philip was ever in a single action in the colony (Massachusetts), or that he was the leader of more than a small clan. He never held rank as commander-in-chief of the allied forces." [1] He never persuaded a single tribe in Rhode Island, Connecticut, or New Hampshire to join him,[2] though Indians from two of

[1] Sheldon, History of Deerfield, I. 81. Judd, Temple, Bodge, and the later authorities generally agree in this view. It is confirmed by the narrative of Mrs. Rowlandson.

[2] Judd, History of Hadley, 135.

those colonies aided the general cause which he was engaged in.

Nearly a month before Philip's death, the succession of fasts, which had been continued since the outbreak of the war, was broken by thanksgivings.[1] These were testimonies to the general feeling that the successful close of the war was already assured. The vigorous efforts, which were continued during the last weeks of the struggle by all the colonies concerned, were inspired by the confidence which this knowledge awakened. " Thus did God," wrote Increase Mather, " break the head of that Leviathan and gave it to be meat to the people inhabiting the wilderness."[2]

Among the settlements of New Hampshire and Maine, still dependencies of Massachusetts on the northeast, conflicts with the Indians had begun almost as early as September, 1675.[3] Some of the frontiersmen of that region were charged with cruelty toward the natives and gross breaches of faith toward them. Squando, a sachem of the Saco Indians, had been specially offended in this way. This chief, together with Modockawando, the sagamore of the Tarratines on the Penobscot, and his ally, Mugg, were the leaders in organizing attacks on the English from Piscataqua to Pemaquid. Wannalanset, however, chief of the Penacook tribe and successor of the famous Passaconaway, followed the opposite policy. Not only did the Penacooks avoid conflicts with the English, but they refused as far as possible to entertain any of the enemies of the English: But the Abenakis generally, from the borders of Maine eastward, broke out into the fiercest hostilities against the English, using for the purpose the arms and ammunition which they were already obtaining from French traders. So remote and weak were the English settlements in that region, that the savages massacred and burned without serious opposition. During the fall of 1675 most of the settlements south of Falmouth had been visited. Berwick, Saco, and Scarborough had suffered severely.

---

[1] Conn. Recs. II. 467, 469.

[2] Mather, Relation of the Troubles in New England, 197.

[3] Hubbard, Narrative, Part II.; Hough, Pemaquid Papers; Williamson, History of Maine, I. 515–553; Bodge, 296–341.

Major Richard Waldron of Dover was placed by Massachusetts in charge of the defences of the region.   Under his orders the inhabitants, as far as possible, were brought within the protection of the garrison houses and stockades at Wells and other points.   Small bodies of soldiers rendered what aid they could, by marches along the coast and into the interior.   But it was all to little purpose, for the Indians, from their lurking-places in the woods, struck down individuals and families and destroyed settlements on all sides. Those who were not slain were hurried away into captivity. The bewildered troops and settlers knew not where to strike or in what direction to turn.   When the tide began to turn against the Narragansetts and their allies in the south, they fled in considerable numbers to the north and added to the bitterness of the conflict.

By an agreement which was reached with some of the hostile sachems at Dover in July, 1676, they were to cease from hostilities and were not to entertain any of the enemies of the English; if any of said enemies should appear among them, they should aid in forcing their surrender.   Early in the following September captains Sill and Hathorne, with two companies, were commissioned by Massachusetts to go to the east and "kill and destroy" all hostile Indians, wherever found.   When they arrived at Dover, they found four hundred Indians assembled at Captain Waldron's house. Among them was Wannalanset and many of his Penacook tribe, as well as many others who had probably come in to testify their fidelity to the treaty of the previous July and to accept terms of amnesty.[1]   But among the number were some hostile Indians and some who had recently been concerned, either in southern New England or elsewhere, in outrages on the English.   Their presence was detected. Whether by stratagem or not, two hundred Indians out of the total of four hundred were seized by Major Waldron and the Massachusetts men and sent by sea to Boston.   The rest were allowed to go free.   Of those who were sent to Boston, a few were executed, but many were sold into slavery.   The natives charged Waldron with gross treach-

---

[1] Bodge, 305.

ery in this affair, and cherished the memory of it till, at the opening of the French wars, they were able to make him atone with his life.

The war now flamed up anew. Hathorne and his men made a fruitless expedition to the eastward. The settlements east of Falmouth were almost or quite abandoned. No cessation, save that which was caused by the severities of winter, came in the dreary list of hostilities until the summer of 1678. Then a treaty was concluded at Casco with the hostile chiefs who still survived. It provided that the prisoners held by the Indians should be surrendered and that the settlers should be permitted to return to their homes; but, by each family a peck of corn should be annually paid to the Indians as a recognition of their claim to the soil. With this event the long and bloody Indian war came to an end.

In all the colonies the outbreak of the war, as well as its results, greatly strengthened the control which the colonists exercised over the Indians. Existing laws concerning intercourse and trade with them, especially in arms and ammunition, were at once made more stringent and were more vigorously executed. In 1682 Plymouth passed a very comprehensive [1] law, which provided that for every town in the colony where Indians lived an able and discreet man should be appointed by the court of assistants to have the oversight of them. He, with the assistance of the tithing-men, should exercise the judicial powers which were formerly bestowed on the overseer of the praying Indians. They should also appoint constables, while a system of frank-pledge was to be put in operation among the Indians themselves, and once a year they were to be assembled and listen to the reading of the criminal laws of the colony. They were also to be subject to taxation, and were prohibited removing from one place to another in the colony without written permits from their overseers. Indians from other colonies were not to be allowed to hunt within the jurisdiction unless they obtained permits from the overseer of the towns where they desired to seek for game.

[1] Plymouth Recs. XI. 252.

In Massachusetts, as elsewhere, at the beginning of the war praying Indians and other friendly natives were called into the service on the side of the English. Some [1] of the former were sent into the Mount Hope country, and were employed later as scouts when Philip was retiring toward the northwest. These are said to have been faithful and to have rendered good service. But some of their brethren among the reservations escaped to Philip and soon appeared among those who were burning towns and massacring their inhabitants. This at once provoked a clamor throughout Massachusetts against all the Christian Indians, and a passionate denial of their fidelity. The outcry was accompanied by the demand that the Indians should be removed from the reservations and placed under guard in some locality whence it would be impossible for them to escape to the enemy. This seemed to involve the ruin of the enterprise which Eliot had started, and the removal of a body of men who could render most valuable service in the defence of the frontier. But nothing that Gookin or other friends of the praying Indians could say weighed at all against the popular frenzy. The officers and soldiers supported the clamor, Captain Moseley and his men being very active against the praying Indians.

The first step was taken on August 30, 1675, by the issue of an order from the council that all natives who desired to show themselves faithful to the English should be confined within six of the Indian towns, and not go thence except in the company of Englishmen. About a month later the proposal to remove them all to points nearer Boston and some to an island in the harbor were discussed. Before the close of October the Indians of Natick were removed to Deer island and Long island in Boston harbor, and thither soon after were brought all the rest of the praying Indians who had not been driven into the woods by the attacks and threats of the whites. There they were kept, poorly fed and housed, during the rest of the war. Some proposed to remove them entirely from the colony, or even to destroy them. Their defenders found themselves for the time the object of popular hate. But as the war approached

[1] Gookin, History of the Christian Indians.

its later stages, this feeling wore off. Some of the Christian Indians were employed as messengers and scouts and even participated in the encounters which followed Sudbury fight.

At the close of the war the Indians were removed from the islands and found their way back to the principal reservations. In May, 1677,[1] an order was passed by the general court that all the Indians who were permitted to live within the settled parts of the colony, whether christianized or not, should be confined to four towns, — Natick, Stoughton, Grafton, and Chelmsford. The Indians about Piscataqua should be settled near Dover. In these places they should be subject to inspection, should be governed by such as the court or council should appoint, and a census of them should be taken once a year. Indian servants or slaves should remain in the families with which they were already connected. The privilege of Indians to carry guns in the woods was restricted, and they were to entertain no Indians from outside the colony without permission. Large Indian claims in the Nipmuck country were soon after bought for the colony,[2] William Stoughton and Joseph Dudley receiving each a grant of one thousand acres as a reward for their services in the transaction. One of these purchases resulted in a considerable addition to the reservations in Natick and Grafton.

Some important steps were taken by Connecticut for the final disposition of Indian prisoners and of the "surrenderers," or those who had made submission. The general court, in October, 1676, enacted[3] that Indians who should surrender themselves before the following January, unless they were proved to have murdered Englishmen, should not be sold as slaves. But they should be put to service among the English for ten years, and after that time they should remain as sojourners in their respective towns, working for themselves and observing English laws and customs. Those who were under sixteen years of age should serve till they were twenty-six. The terms of service for older people might be shortened by the council, if it saw cause.

[1] Mass. Recs. V. 136. [2] *Ibid.* 328, 342.
[3] Conn. Recs. II. 297.

By means of a committee, named in the act, the Indians
were to be distributed among the counties and later among
the towns in each county.

The natives who surrendered themselves either came in
with the Mohegan chief Uncas, or passed temporarily[1]
under his control; but he was early informed that, as the
war chiefly concerned the English, they would dispose of
the captives. To this he assented, but at the same time
persisted quietly in retaining and exercising such influence
over the Indians as was possible. As the services of Rev.
James Fitch of Norwich had been valuable during the war
as a chaplain and in securing the fidelity of the Indian
allies, so use was made of his knowledge and influence in
the somewhat delicate task of settling relations with the
natives at the close of the war. A meeting was called by
the council of war, to be held at Norwich in December,
1676, at which it was proposed, through commissioners appointed for the purpose, to make known to the Indians,
both allies and captives, the will of the general court concerning them.[2] The commissioners were instructed to
associate Mr. Fitch with themselves in this task. They
were ordered to select a fit place of residence, or reservation, for the adult captives and those who had families, and
to appoint English rulers and teachers for them, and require
the submission of the Indians to the counsel and directions
which these should give, as well as to the orders which from
time to time should be issued concerning them by the
council or the general court. Indian constables were to
be appointed, who should serve warrants, publish orders,
collect tribute, and perform other duties among their fellow-
tribesmen. A yearly tribute of five shillings per head was
imposed on the adult Indians as an acknowledgment of subjection to the government of Connecticut.

All young and single persons, as pledges of the fidelity of
the whole body of the Indian wards, were to be put out as
apprentices for ten years among English families. At the
end of that time, if both children and parents were faithful,
the children should be returned to their parents, but if not,

[1] Conn. Recs. II. 472.   [2] Ibid. 481, 498.

they should be sold into slavery. The general committee
should deliver those who were designated for apprentice-
ship to the persons in each county who were empowered
to dispose of them in suitable families. Uncas was later
paid for the corn which he contributed to the "surrenderers"
before they were removed from his care. But such were
the wily arts of Uncas that Mr. Fitch had little confidence
in the honesty of his intentions and warned the general
court concerning him.[1]

[1] Conn. Recs. II. 591.